D1506740

GENERAL WADSWORTH

GENERAL
WADSWORTH

The Life and Times of Brevet
Major General James S. Wadsworth

WAYNE MAHOOD

DA CAPO PRESS
A Member of the Perseus Books Group

Designed by Lisa Kreinbrink
Set in 11-point AGaramond by Perseus Publishing Services

Cataloging-in-Publication data for this book is available from the Library
of Congress.

First Da Capo Press edition 2003
ISBN 0-306-81238-X

Published by Da Capo Press
A Member of the Perseus Books Group
http://www.dacapopress.com

Da Capo Press books are available at special discounts for bulk purchases
in the U.S. by corporations, institutions, and other organizations. For
more information, please contact the Special Markets Department at the
Perseus Books Group, 11 Cambridge Center, Cambridge, MA 02142, or
call (617) 252-5298.

1 2 3 4 5 6 7 8 9—05 04 03

To Alex, Christopher, and Jake,
who represent the future

CONTENTS

FOREWORD

The life and death of one man may define the temper of his time with greater clarity than a volume of social commentary. What Professor Wayne Mahood has given us in his meticulously researched biography of General James S. Wadsworth of Geneseo, New York, is not only an absorbing account of a remarkable life of contrast and contradiction, but a vivid reminder that our Civil War was, indeed, fought on moral grounds; that the impetus to put all to the hazard in that uncompromising fratricidal conflict derived from a deep-rooted, long-standing division of opinion on the fundamental requirements of humanity—rather than, as has occasionally been advanced, disparate economic interests. The values and sensitivities that are urged upon us in our own day have not sprung full-blown from the foreheads of contemporary observers of the American experience. The seeds of such awareness were well planted before Sumter was fired upon. From her beginning America produced men and women who were convinced that a harvest of universal freedom and equal justice, with all its complications, both known and unknown, was a safer bet for their country than one infested with the residue of slavery. They were not the majority, but they would become one. In today's world, who but the demented would consider the call for "abolition" not only wrongheaded but dangerous? Yet "abolitionist" was a distinct pejorative in Wadsworth's time, certainly in the South, but only to a lesser degree in the North.

The constitutional compromises deemed essential to the formation of a union of states included noninterference with the "peculiar institution." For a time the country was content to let the matter rest; as if men of conscience and character could let it rest, men like Wadsworth, whose innate hatred of it would, in a testing time, overcome the inertia of national acceptance. The testing time arrived. And only armed conflict along the fault line of that compromise could settle the matter.

But why would the country's "last gentleman," as Wadsworth was once described—this respected, silver-haired squire in his sixth decade with a happy family, a bountiful estate, and admiring friends and neighbors grateful for his multiple contributions to community life—plunge headlong into a conflagration that would bring him to ground in the blood-soaked thicket of the Wilderness? With an ancestor's saber strapped to his belt, he was answering the call of country, yes, but also of conscience. For he quickly became a resolute abolitionist and wore that badge so defiantly, against the advice of cautious friends and seasoned advisers that he lost the otherwise winnable New York gubernatorial election of 1862. Nor was his campaign enhanced by his refusal to leave his post in Washington, where his energies were devoted not only to its defenses but also to the rescue of "contraband" from the Federal marshal whose job it was to return them to their "rightful" owners.

Wadsworth's penchant for ignoring rules that did not accord with his preference may have resulted years earlier in his expulsion from Harvard. It certainly explained his blithe indifference to the Fugitive Slave Law and attendant regulations. He left no diary, and, with the exception of a few poignant letters, kept all but his public thoughts to himself. We must rely on his actions to explain his motivation. Nevertheless, as Professor Mahood conveys with insight and every scrap of documentation available, this once young and seemingly directionless scion of privilege was somehow transformed into a flint-hard, risk-taking buccaneer, a man of daring action, first in business, agriculture, land management, and politics, and finally in war.

Descended from a family line of frontiersmen handy with axe, plough, horse, and harness, he could, with cheerful dispatch, drive oxen, corduroy a mud road, ford a stream, and supervise all the constructions of an encampment. He did this and more to the astonishment, admiration, and occasional amusement of his troops, whose welfare, next to victory, was his first concern. His innumerable kindnesses to them, freed slaves, indigent refugees, Virginia farmers, and Southern citizenry overtaken by events augured a healing leadership role in the years to come. His ideas for preparing a class of persons inured to servitude for the opportunities and obligations of citizenship might have altered the course of postwar events. This was not to be. James S. Wadsworth would not be allowed to bring his considerable experience and insights to bear on his country's future. The best he could do, like the president he served, was to die for it; but only after living for it as described with insightful care in this illuminating work.

Hon. James W. Symington

PREFACE

James S. Wadsworth:
A Complex of Contradictions

"A true American," nineteenth-century historian-diplomat John Lothrop Motley labelled James Samuel Wadsworth. Motley, who had first seen Wadsworth as a callow Harvard freshman, was now assessing a wealthy landowner on a yearlong tour of Europe with an entourage that would do justice to a Mideastern potentate. Sidney George Fisher, a Philadelphia lawyer and acquaintance, regarded Wadsworth as an inexplicably restless spirit. Wadsworth's hometown of Geneseo, New York, which celebrated his safe return from a perilous sea voyage with flares that lit the night, regarded him as a vigorous and courageous man. Soldiers who served under Wadsworth regarded him almost reverentially. By contrast, one-time political ally John Van Buren came to ridicule Wadsworth, and popular Major General George B. McClellan condemned him as a meddling abolitionist who helped prolong a brutal Civil War. Lewis F. Allen, a New York state legislator and president of the New York State Agricultural Society, who did the background for the Century Association's memorial to Wadsworth, probably had as good a perspective as anyone, and he was not awed by Wadsworth's wealth or position.[1]

So, how does a biographer capture on paper another's life, specifically James Samuel Wadsworth, the Squire of Geneseo and Brevet Major General of Volunteers? Little can be learned from his sketchy correspondence, the earliest and possibly most revealing of which appears to have been culled, if not censored in some cases. His correspondents at that time offer tantalizing glimpses, but too often their letters fail to offer details or insight according to custom or discretion. Later those writing to or about him offer somewhat more, but they tend to extol, even pander. His beautiful and admired wife left virtually no record of her intimate knowledge of him. Nor did James Samuel's daughters, as far as can be determined. His sons, particularly the middle son, Craig, offer little more.

Worse, too much of what we have is anecdotal. His acquaintances could readily identify or talk about one of the richest men in New York State, but each saw only a part of him.

The task is much like piecing together a jigsaw puzzle without the completed picture to serve as a guide. Worse, there are pieces missing. How does one discern the subtle colors and shapes that are so necessary to form the larger picture? To say the least the task is daunting.[2]

Yet, there is no lack of materials upon which to draw. Artifacts and family records are available to researchers. Additionally, there are any number of books and articles about the family, including a useful nineteenth-century genealogy of the Wadsworth family after its arrival in the United States in the 1600s. Even an older, well-researched and written biography exists.[3]

The incomplete picture that emerges is that of a complex man whose personality tends to be revealed through the beholder's eyes. Indeed, James Samuel Wadsworth was a bundle of contradictions. For example, barely a decade after he was tossed out of Harvard (to his father's chagrin) he was in the company of former president John Quincy Adams, Massachusetts governor Edward Everett, U.S. Supreme Court associate justice Joseph Story, and, ironically, Harvard president Josiah Quincy II.

Mostly we know him from his behavior. He was a man of action much like his Uncle Bill. For example, an admirer recalled an incident in the early 1840s when rains had washed away the underpinnings of a railroad near Syracuse, New York. Wadsworth "walked through mud & water directing and encouraging the laborious repair." When the admirer, a youth at the time, asked his father who the hero was, the father replied, "My Son, that is the *first gentleman* in America."[4] Wadsworth disliked details, preferring the grand gesture. Yet he could be reflective when he allowed himself time to pause.

When nominated by the newly formed Republican Party to run for governor of New York State in 1862, he recalled his general reluctance to undertake the duties of public office, though he harbored no doubts about his ability to discharge them. In the immediate instance, however, he informed the nominating committee, which included influential newspaperman Horace Greeley, that he hesitated based on the "serious & rather increasing" implications of the nomination. He questioned whether his beliefs were acceptable to New Yorkers:

> At the outbreak of this rebellion I was barely a Republican, that is, only opposed to the extension of slavery. I have slowly come to the conclusion that the time has arrived to strike it down for ever [*sic*]. This is the rebellion of an aristocracy, base, selfish & degraded, but still a distinctly formed aristocracy. We cannot put down the rebellion & save the aristocracy & we ought not do, if we could.[5]

He reminded the committee members that such thinking had compelled him to offer his services to the Union; to serve as an unpaid aide to Major General Irvin

McDowell at First Bull Run and to occupy his then current position as military governor of Washington, D.C.

Yet Wadsworth himself represented aristocracy, managing to blot out his youthful indiscretions and dissolute ways, thereby preserving the family name much as his father had. Moreover, increasingly he would lay the same burden on his children. He actively engaged in commercial interests, speculated beyond even his means at times, and was a soft touch for almost any cause or friend.

Unfortunately, often it is necessary to hazard guesses about Wadsworth's feelings based on his actions and the reactions of others, so care has to be taken to avoid reading too much into these reactions, especially postwar recollections. Many of them, influenced by the manner of his death, accorded him almost mythical qualities. Nor did proximity necessarily result in greater accuracy. Those who shared his political beliefs saw a man of principle. Necessarily, his opponents, especially former allies, viewed him differently. Few, however, challenged the courage or the passion of his convictions. Many who served under him on his "Home Farm" and in the Civil War tended to respect and even adore him. By contrast, one close observer during that fratricidal conflict was openly contemptuous of Wadsworth, and some more recent critics have even characterized his military actions as those of a reckless bumbler. Whatever one's opinion, it is virtually impossible not to be impressed by the élan that characterized the Squire of Geneseo's fifty-six years.

ACKNOWLEDGMENTS

I dentifying and thanking those who helped me is almost as daunting as the
writing itself. Clearly, I am grateful to George G. Otott, whose extraordinarily
diligent reading of the draft and suggestions for ridding it of excessive detail and
making it more entertaining can never be repaid; Robert K. Krick, Chief Historian, and Donald Pfanz, of the Fredericksburg and Spotsylvania Military Park,
whose critical reading and acute comments on the Wilderness battle proved particularly useful; D. Scott Hartwig, Supervisory Park Historian at Gettysburg, who
took time from his many duties to offer an equally critical reading and insightful
suggestions regarding Wadsworth's activities in the battle of Gettysburg; David W.
Parish, Geneseo Village and Town Historian, and Charles "Dutch" Van Ry, local
historian, both of whose invaluable expertise on the Genesee Valley and tight
reading helped me avoid errors, while encouraging me to go on; and Benedict R.
Maryniak, whose sharing of his encyclopedic knowledge of the Civil War and his
extensive file on General Wadsworth cannot be adequately compensated.

It is impossible to thank properly the Symington brothers, Stuart Symington, Jr. and James Wadsworth Symington, whose mother was a direct descendant of James Samuel Wadsworth. Their thorough and thoughtful editing of the
manuscript demonstrated not only their lawyer's skills but their obvious affection for the Wadsworth family.

I'm also indebted to their cousin, the late Alice Wadsworth Strong, who provided access, materials, and anecdotes unavailable elsewhere; her husband, Trow-
bridge, who went out of his way to accommodate me, even serving coffee and
providing lighting for photographs; her son, Corrin, whose love of the general's
valley was demonstrated in his *Genesee Country* magazine; and Alice's cousin,
Harry Wadsworth, who opened up his house to me to examine and photograph
valuable artifacts. Thanks are due also to the late Judge Robert Houston, who interrupted his work to help me obtain and interpret court records and who constantly encouraged me; Donald Tiffany, who oriented me to the battlefield at
Gettysburg and the positioning of Wadsworth's division; Dr. Martin Fausold,
whose challenges to my interpretations were a constant goad; Patricia Schaap, Livingston County Historian, whose endless supply of materials and patience served
me throughout the research; David Minor, Eagle Bytes Historical Research, whose

continuing research led to many valuable materials, particularly about early New York State history; Craig Senfield, an archivist in his own right, who brought to my attention materials easily overlooked; Scott Price, who discovered me and whose encouragement, writing (which he shared), and citation of sources served me well; Frank K. Lorenz, Editor, College Publications and Archivist, Hamilton College, who once more came to my aid to try to verify James Samuel Wadsworth's attendance at Hamilton College; David Oliver, a true Civil Warrior whose work as intern at the Livingston County Museum uncovered useful material and access to invaluable photographs; Andy Kmiec, my young friend who supplied me with information about Pennsylvanians who served under Wadsworth; Michael Musick and Todd Butler of the National Archives, who provided materials and guided me through the intricacies of research there; the late Francis A. O'Brien, lawyer-writer and fraternity brother, who personally escorted me and instructed me about the labyrinthian procedures at the Archives; Dean North of Aberdeen, South Dakota, who interrupted his research to provide materials on Fort Wadsworth; John Carson, my fellow Civil War Round Tabler, who found a useful anecdote about Reynolds Battery at Gettysburg; Theodore Caplan, who opened his house and file of his ancestor Captain Henry Wiley; Dr. Frances Bock, whose fortuitous acquaintance during the aftermath of a hurricane resulted in more details from an ancestor about the death of Wadsworth; Michael Albanese, collector and friend, who obtained photos for me; and Ronald Pretzer, Coordinator, Photographic Services, College Relations and Development, SUNY–Geneseo, who, for the umpteenth time, somehow temporarily escaped his myriad duties to create or reproduce photographs with an unmatched competence.

Every researcher is indebted to "those little unnamed ladies" who located and made available the bedrock materials. I am no exception and can name at least the most helpful ones, first and foremost the SUNY–Geneseo librarians and staff: Judith Bushnell, who never failed to come to my aid; Anita Whitehead and Sonja Landes; retired reference librarian Bill Lane, who explained the unexplainable (how the Wadsworth Family Papers are filed and where); Harriet Sleggs, head of Interlibrary Loan, who flawlessly handled too many requests to be recalled, and Mina Orman, who called immediately when a source had arrived; Nick Pasternostro, at the time Fraser Librarian, whose diligent use of the Internet to contact others made possible an interpretation of money exchange; Dr. David G. Martin, Professor, School of Management Science, SUNY–Geneseo, who walked me through the intricacies of historical indexes; Virginia H. Smith, Reference Librarian, Massachusetts Historical Society, who helped me understand nineteenth-century Boston; Mark Lloyd, Director of the University of Pennsylvania Archives, who took valuable time to answer esoteric questions; Steven S. Bell, Wharton School Library, University of Pennsylvania, who ran down sources on Philadelphia's Wharton family; and Brian McCarthy, Harvard University Archivist, whose diligent search and quick response to my request for information about Wadsworth's attendance at Harvard was vital.

Special thanks are due others who, in fairness, must be identified. Publisher Ted Savas started this book in the publication stream; Bob Pigeon, Editor,

Perseus Books, pushed it along; Kay Mariea, Project Director, Perseus Books, skillfully directed it thereafter; and eagle-eyed John C. Thomas, copy editor, Perseus Books, applied a fine touch to the manuscript. George Skoch, whose maps help orient the reader, was the model of patience when asked to make corrections at the last minute. Brian Bennett, Director of Design and College Publications, SUNY–Geneseo, and an accomplished Civil War historian, supplied me with sources, readily loaned materials, thoughtfully read the copyedited manuscript, and made valuable suggestions. Robert ("Bob") Marcotte, *Rochester Democrat & Chronicle* columnist and author of a popular Civil War book, interrupted his busy life to read and react to the copyedited manuscript in the insightful way that only he could.

Finally, I thank Bobbi, who once more put up with an "absent" husband.

To those I've failed to name, apologies and grateful thanks.

Chapter 1

"INTO THE VALLEY OF THE SHADOW OF DEATH"

The unscheduled battle, which had begun eighteen hours earlier, had started abruptly in a dense, second-growth forest where a year earlier the Union was almost fatally defeated; where Army of the Potomac commander Major General Joseph Hooker allegedly had lost his nerve. The ghostly remains of that earlier battle littered the area—a silent reminder, perhaps an omen, of what the soldiers', indeed, the Union's, fate might be again. Barely three miles west of Fredericksburg, Virginia, lay this dense forest of "scrubby, stubborn oaks, and low-limbed, disordered, haggard pines." The stunted trees were "so close together," recalled Morris Schaff in his highly readable reminiscences, that their lower limbs intermingled into "thick underbrush," which entangled with "bright-green, bamboo-like vine." Yet, preciously holding on to life, as if to give hope to the weary soldiers, "a swamp honeysuckle, and now and then a wild rose will greet you joyously." Poking through the thick underbrush also were "tall huckleberry bushes, from whose depending limbs hang racemes of modest, white, bell-shaped flowers." Even more incongruously, fragrant dogwoods, like "shrouded figures," thrust through the "billowing smoke." The usual denizens, the rabbits and quail, had disappeared before the crack and boom of capricious intruders who seemed bent on destroying not only themselves, but everything before them. Dim paths connected scattered clearings where cattle had roamed in search of the few blades of grass that protruded out of the sandy Virginia soil.[1]

It was pure, unmitigated hell. The insufferable heat, the heavy cloud of smoke that enveloped combatants, and the cries of the wounded seemed unbearable. It was impossible to make out anything in that aptly named Virginia "Wilderness," where confusion reigned. Brigades, even divisions, became intermixed. Commanders relied on subordinates whose talents they knew more by reputation than by direct experience. Subcommanders relied on the men who had to do the fighting, men who had marched in dust and mud and had shouldered their deadly weapons for three years. In turn, Commander of the Army Ulysses S. Grant had to rely on reports of the progress of the battle while trying to figure another way to thrust his command between Robert E. Lee's Army of Northern Virginia and Richmond.[2]

No one actually chose this setting for battle. Yet here a battle raged with troops just as intertwined as the bright-green vines through which the soldiers tried to make their way. The denseness of this scrub forest had constrained the usual battle formations of divisions and brigades into battalions and columns of four. Gaps existed between regiments. Lines that started in one direction soon found themselves headed in another, separated from one another. Regiments lost sight of each other and faced enemy fire from the flanks as well as the front. A column would simply disappear into the thick underbrush. Maintaining any semblance of order was impossible.[3]

The battle that began the day before, May 5, 1864, had resulted in Lieutenant General Richard S. Ewell's Corps controlling the Confederate left (the Union right) on the Orange Turnpike. Now, May 6, the focus had shifted to the Union left, near the intersection of the Orange Plank and Brock Roads. In command, if anyone there could be said to command, was Major General Winfield Scott Hancock. He had earned his sobriquet "the Superb" at the battle of Williamsburg in 1862 and is credited with coolly realigning the Union troops at Gettysburg on July 1 the following year.

However, this time there was no Cemetery Hill or Ridge to which the Union could retreat and regroup. Worse, Hancock and his subordinates, Major General David B. Birney, Brigadier General John Gibbon, and Brigadier General Gershom Mott, now commanded not only their own but also unfamiliar troops. Hancock's corps held the center and left (south) portion of the Plank Road. By noon, the struggle had brought the usual crash of bodies, wild yells, and steady roar of musketry. The Federal advance, which had earlier threatened to cut Lee's army in half while driving the Confederates back a mile, had been met and repulsed by Lieutenant General James Longstreet's men, who had raced to join and reinforce Major General Ambrose Powell Hill's III Corps. At first the Federals seemed to sustain their advance, scattering Brigadier General John Gregg's Texas Brigade after its legendary charge, but Brigadier General Henry Benning's Georgians plunged into the contest followed by Brigadier General McIver Law's Brigade of Alabamians. The latter tossed Hancock's corps into greater confusion and threatened a repeat of Chancellorsville, fought almost a year to the day earlier.[4]

Once more the white-haired, but still trim, man saw his duty. Though wearing only one star, he had commanded a division at Chancellorsville and Gettysburg, and now found himself issuing orders to Brigadier General Alexander Webb and Colonel Sumner Carruth of the II and IX Corps, respectively. He had already been fighting almost nine hours and had two horses shot from under him, but he found that he would have to call up some hidden reserve to inspire his men once more. He was exhausted, which he had admitted to his aide, Captain Robert Monteith, and had contemplated turning over command to one of his brigade commanders. His fatigue was certainly not surprising, for by this time virtually everyone there in that Wilderness seemed sapped of all energy.[5]

But he was not just an ordinary soldier. He was James Samuel Wadsworth, a 56-year-old millionaire from Geneseo, New York, described by one close observer as "rather tall, an eminently handsome man of commanding presence, but showing gentle breeding." He had already proven his mettle, even recklessness, at Gettysburg, his willingness to make sacrifices for the cause he espoused, and his ability to inspire his men. Yet he too could be inspired by others. In this instance it was by Hancock, who earlier in the day had given him command of the II Corps brigade of Webb and the IX Corps brigade of Carruth, in addition to his own division command, and charge of the sector north of the Orange Plank Road. It was daunting, for Hancock had just been apprised of Longstreet's flank attack. The flankers were converging on the Plank Road to Wadsworth's left in support of the frontal assault on Wadsworth's command by the Confederate divisions of Major Generals Charles Field and Richard H. Anderson. Beyond the smoke from a fire that raced through the woods Wadsworth heard the Rebel yell and a rapid succession of sharp volleys. He prepared to mount another attack and directed a protesting Webb to the left to find four regiments to stop the throng of fleeing Union troops. Meanwhile he tried to organize the mixed brigades for a concentrated assault against the combined forces of Field and Anderson on the north side of the Orange Plank Road.[6]

The Federals broke slowly at first, then rapidly, but the dry leaf fire spread and momentarily checked the Confederate advance. Unhindered was the 12th Virginia of Brigadier General William Mahone's Brigade, which found its way down an unfinished railroad and through the thicket, quickly crossed the Plank Road, and struck the left of Wadsworth's amorphous command. Wadsworth seized upon the 37th Massachusetts Volunteers of the VI Corps and ordered its commander to throw the regiment across the path of Field's Confederates, who, with their artillery raking the Union line, were advancing along the Plank Road. Wadsworth then directed Colonel Oliver Edwards to have his 37th Massachusetts assail Field's charging troops, which he did, thereby garnering Wadsworth's praise, "You have made a splendid charge." After repositioning his main line, Wadsworth then allowed the 37th to fall back.[7]

But as the Federals withdrew and began repositioning themselves, the sounds of another Confederate counterattack foretold further peril. The problem was that, despite the noonday sun, the dense, almost impenetrable forest rendered enemy movements virtually unobservable until contact was made. The usual commands and maneuvers to which the troops had responded so readily in the past failed. Hancock admitted that he learned what was transpiring only from reports of subordinates. It was thus left to individual commanders to determine how to proceed. His exhaustion momentarily forgotten, Wadsworth reacted to the threat from Field's and Anderson's inspired thrusts. He ordered the 20th Massachusetts to make a suicidal attack to stem the tide and to allow the Federal troops to reposition themselves. But he could not let them go alone to certain death; he must lead them. Urging his third horse of the day forward, Wadsworth charged the Confederates.[8]

This act was vintage Wadsworth, the reincarnation of his uncle William, "General Bill," who had suffered a broken arm and lasting wounds at the battle of Queenston Heights in the War of 1812. Virtually everyone saw General Bill's nephew as a man of action; a practical man is how it was usually expressed, though he could be eloquent when the occasion demanded it. Brevet Major General James Samuel Wadsworth, for all his gentle breeding and wealth, could still play the western New York frontiersman. After all, before he reached his teens he had accompanied his uncle on the tough cattle drives from Geneseo over 300 miles to Baltimore and to New York City. He knew how to break horses and to control the bulls that he had bought to enhance the herd of cattle he raised on the alluvial flats of his Genesee River farm.

Still, it jars the senses to think of him leading a charge against Southerners whose style he had admired as a college student—to his father's dismay. In fact, "Tom," as Wadsworth was known to some of his Harvard companions, had enjoyed their fellowship and horsemanship on his frequent trips from Cambridge to Boston. What his father viewed as intemperance, young Wadsworth regarded as fashionable, though such behavior would not serve him well with the Harvard faculty.

Even more incongruous was Wadsworth's absence from responsibilities that would have proved daunting to men years younger: the care of a wife, a son in boarding school, a sister-in-law and her two sons, a large personal estate, and a larger land business involving approximately 70,000 acres in New York, Michigan, and Ohio. Burdened with these responsibilities, this landed gentleman, nearing senior citizenship, had every reason to stay at home and to profit from the burgeoning opportunities the Civil War offered eager entrepreneurs. Yet here he was risking life and limb for the Union, just as two of his three sons, following his example, had already done.

What kind of man was this James Samuel Wadsworth, this citizen-soldier, this aristocrat, who was driving himself and those serving under him to certain death?

★   ★   ★

It is easy enough to trace the lineage of this tall, prematurely white-haired man, to list public offices he held, to describe his relations with a variety of politicians, to detail his landholdings and business dealings, and to record his short, but meteoric, military career. However, to know the private man is another matter. He enjoyed the privileges that came with wealth, the bulk of which were derived from his father's tireless and focused efforts. Though almost universally described as personable, he could be brusque. Like his father, he was strong willed. Indeed, his strongly held opinions may well have cost him the governorship of the largest state in the Union at a particularly critical time in America's history.[9]

It is more difficult to understand exactly why this millionaire took up the cause of abolition. What would lead a man to leave a wife admired for beauty, a truly aristocratic lifestyle based on dozens of servants, a 15,000-acre estate with blooded cattle and thoroughbred horses, and a thriving business? Why would he give up all this to become surrounded by sworn enemies in an impenetrable, marshy tract of land known as the Wilderness?[10]

To assess and characterize Wadsworth's military worth is even more difficult. Was he an inspired leader? Did his "habit to command" overcome his lack of military training? Or was he simply reckless, a nervous bumbler who preferred action to reflective preparation? Was his ride into the face of the enemy on this May day the inevitable result of his hastiness, the precipitousness against which his father had repeatedly warned him? Was Wadsworth, like a hero of Greek tragedies, riding headlong to meet his preordained fate?[11]

Chapter 2

"AQUILA NON CAPTAT MUSCAS"

The blood that ran through the veins of this intrepid warrior can be traced back approximately seven generations—to William Wadsworth, a "Puritan of some standing." He arrived at Boston Harbor with a family of four aboard the ship *Lion,* which landed Sunday evening, September 16, 1632. After briefly settling near Cambridge, Massachusetts, William and other followers of the Reverend Thomas Hooker moved to the Connecticut Valley town of Hartford, then little more than a trading post. These Congregationalists promptly framed a government under the Fundamental Orders, whereby authority rested upon the free consent of the "admitted inhabitants." This contrasted with what they regarded as the overly strict membership requirements of the Massachusetts Bay Colony. William thus founded the Connecticut–New York branch of the Wadsworths.[1]

The spirit that motivated William may well reflect the character of the Wadsworths, whose name literally means "Woods Court." However, the ancestral motto *Aquila non captat muscas* is more meaningful. It is translated as "the eagle does not catch flies," or in the words of the family genealogist Horace Wadsworth, writing in 1883, "our great progenitors stooped not to small things." Whether or not this was a hindsight attempt to enhance the family reputation, James Samuel Wadsworth, the future general, clearly would live up to this motto.[2]

Of the ten children sired by William Wadsworth (four by his first wife, remembered only as Sarah, and six by his second wife, Elizabeth Stone of Hartford), the best known is Joseph. Commonly referred to as "Captain Joseph," he was born approximately sixteen years after William's arrival in the colonies and is credited with secreting the Connecticut charter in the "Charter Oak" to protect it from Sir Edmund Andros. Following British orders, Andros, newly appointed governor of all the New England colonies but Connecticut and Rhode Island, had attempted to impose "Dominion" over Connecticut (as he had over Rhode Island) and seize Connecticut's charter. The generally accepted version of what happened at a meeting on the evening of October 31, 1687, was that during discussion by the Connecticut Assembly of how to stop Governor Andros, "the lights were instantly extinguished, and one Capt. Wadsworth, of Hartford, in the most silent and secret manner, carried off the charter and secreted it in a large hollow tree fronting the house of the Hon. Samuel Wyllys." The captain was rewarded by being elected the Hartford representative to the Connecticut General Assembly and, twenty-eight years later, by a sum of money.[3]

Apparently, Joseph's love of freedom also led to excesses, including threatening a Hartford sheriff and a New York colonial governor with bodily harm, which resulted in formal reprimands by the Assembly and an appearance before the Court of Assistants.[4]

It is not hard to imagine the ardent Captain Joseph, who lived to age 80, as a forebear of James Samuel Wadsworth, who would lead that charge of the 20th Massachusetts Infantry at the Wilderness. However, it was the captain's half-brother, the "Hon. John" of Farmington, an assemblyman and witness to Joseph's Charter Oak heroism, from whom James Samuel descended. John Wadsworth had nine children, one of whom was Colonel James Wadsworth, who was born in Durham, Connecticut, in 1677, and who sired Squire James Wadsworth. In turn, Squire James claimed three children, the best known of whom was the first General James Wadsworth, the great-uncle of James Samuel.

This James, born in 1730, graduated from Yale eighteen years later in the top third of his class. He earned his reputation by raising a company to invade Canada in 1758 during the French and Indian War and by serving as a major general from Connecticut in the Revolutionary War. Reminiscent of Captain Joseph, his great-grandfather's brother, this James Wadsworth also managed to counter public opinion, though he was neither fined nor hauled into court. For example, at the 1788 Connecticut convention to ratify the newly written Constitution, General James argued forcefully against it, claiming that the rights of the states would be trampled by a despotic central government. Though he was soundly voted down, his reputation apparently did not suffer, for he held other offices and was remembered for his "large, erect, military figure." Oral tradition attributes to this ancestor ownership of the saber that James Samuel brandished during the Civil War and that his Uncle Bill had worn during the War of 1812.[5]

However, hands down, the Wadsworth ancestor who had the most profound effect on the Geneseo Wadsworths was Colonel Jeremiah Wadsworth of Farmington, Connecticut, of the same generation as and a cousin of the first General James Wadsworth.

Jeremiah, born in 1743, was the son of Reverend Daniel Wadsworth, a 1726 Yale graduate, who died prematurely at 43 when Jeremiah was only 4 years old, leaving what has been described as a handsome estate to his wife, two sons, and four unmarried daughters. But Jeremiah's circuitous route to fame and fortune came by way of Mathew Talcott, his mother's brother, who advised Jeremiah to take to the sea to restore his failing health. His health restored, young Wadsworth followed the sea for approximately fifteen years, rising to captain, but in 1775, at age 32, his life changed abruptly when Connecticut joined the Revolutionary cause. Jeremiah became a commissary for the newly raised Connecticut troops, which led to additional duties and, three years later, to a call by the Continental Congress to assume similar duties for the Revolutionary army.

As the first commissary general of the United States, Wadsworth's primary responsibility was to act as commissary for Count de Rochambeau and the French army. Eventually Jeremiah would travel to France with his only son Daniel to present his accounting personally.[6]

Not surprisingly, Jeremiah, who reputedly was an intimate and occasional postwar host of General George Washington, carried on his public duties after the peace treaty, becoming a delegate to the Connecticut Constitutional Convention. But his interests took him in another direction, which would greatly affect western New York. This direction involved the contract for sale of 6 million acres of land situated in western New York by the state of Massachusetts to two entrepreneurs, Oliver Phelps and Nathaniel Gorham. The complicated deal, known as the Phelps–Gorham purchase, would directly link Jeremiah Wadsworth and his younger cousins, William and James, aged 29 and 22, respectively, two men whose traits were synergically combined in the subject of the present narrative, James Samuel Wadsworth.[7]

This link between the cousins may well have been initiated by the death of William's and James's father, John Noyes Wadsworth, the younger brother of the first General James. Little is known about John Noyes, who was born in 1732 in Durham (New Haven County), Connecticut, to Squire James Wadsworth and Abigail Penfield of Guilford. A deed recorded April 3, 1730, shows that Squire James bought from Abraham Blackly two acres on the "west side of the swamp" in Durham, about twenty miles northeast of New Haven. John, who served as a justice of the peace in Durham from the 1760s until about the time of his death at age 55 in 1787, left to his wife, Esther Parsons Wadsworth, and their three sons, John Noyes (born 1758), William (1761), and James (1768), what was then regarded as a fairly substantial sum of money, though his family was not considered wealthy.[8]

The fateful connection between the Wadsworth cousins might have been initiated by a visit from John Noyes's youngest son, James, to Colonel Jeremiah's house in 1789. The accepted version is that Jeremiah viewed the young man, who had graduated from Yale College two years earlier (the only one of the three Wadsworth brothers to attend college), as having "ambition," "clear mind," and "tenacious will." In a speculative mood, Jeremiah needed someone with these qualities to improve and sell the western New York lands included in the Phelps–Gorham purchase, which he intended to acquire. He decided to enlist cousin James instead of his only son Daniel. (Purportedly Daniel was temperamentally and physically unfit for the challenge of settling this frontier and managing the property in which Jeremiah had "made a considerable investment.") According to their agreement, James would emigrate to western New York, buy part of the land at an advantageous price, and serve as Jeremiah's agent for the sale of the rest. Apparently a condition of the agreement was that James's older brother William would accompany him.[9]

Before examining the results of this arrangement between the Wadsworths, it is useful to review briefly the Phelps and Gorham purchase to understand the environment that so greatly influenced James Samuel Wadsworth. With the end of the Revolutionary War and the declining threat of Indian attacks as a result of the 1779 expedition by General John Sullivan against the Loyalists and Indians in western Pennsylvania and New York, the vast lands in this western frontier of New York had become particularly attractive for settlement and, thus, for speculation. Oliver Phelps, deputy commissary of the Continental Army, quickly saw the potential and formed a syndicate with Nathaniel Gorham, member of the Massachusetts war board and the Continental Congress, to acquire these lands. However, first the speculators had to resolve the issue of ownership of this almost unimaginably large tract.[10]

The tract ran from Seneca Lake, bordering on Geneva, New York, west to present-day Buffalo (over one hundred linear miles), and extended from the Pennsylvania border to Lake Ontario. It had been claimed by both Massachusetts and New York as a result of grants by English kings to the Plymouth and Massachusetts Bay Colonies and to the Duke of York, respectively. However, to complicate matters further, the new Federal government also recognized prior claims by the Iroquois, whose ancestors had long before formed settlements on the disputed land. To resolve the matter and to avoid placing it before the U.S. District Court, Massachusetts and New York agreed to send representatives to a convention in Hartford, Connecticut. The December 1786 resolution of the issue was that New York would cede to Massachusetts the preemptive (or first) right to sell the land, subject to valid sales, that is, titles, granted by the Iroquois who occupied the land, but New York would exercise sovereignty, or government, over the area.[11]

Two years later Phelps and Gorham contracted to purchase the tract from the state of Massachusetts for the unheard of sum of $1 million in specie. A bargain was struck, but ultimately there would have to be a settlement with the Iroquois. Within the land in the western portion, approximately two and a half million acres west of the Genesee River, lay eleven Iroquois reservations. For more than a half century, demand for this huge parcel would cause conflict between competing speculators and the Senecas, one of the six members of the Iroquois Nation that occupied these reservations, and would involve even presidential intercession. The conflict would provide visibility, occasional livelihood, and wealth for James Wadsworth and his son James Samuel.[12]

Tracing the precise investments by the Wadsworths in this vast acreage is very difficult, but apparently Jeremiah made the initial purchases on April 9, 1790. He bought nearly 7,000 acres in the county of Ontario (now Livingston) from Phelps and Gorham in two separate transactions. The first was for "one twelfth" of Township No. 9, 7th Range, known as the "Big Tree Township." The township was bordered by Conesus Lake on the east and the Genesee River on the west, and ran about four miles north and south of the present village of Geneseo, some 25–30 miles south of Rochester. The second purchase was of 5,000 acres in Township 11, Range 6, northeast of the present Avon. Both sales by Nathaniel Gorham and Oliver Phelps were witnessed by young James Wadsworth.[13]

The claim that Jeremiah made a considerable investment is no exaggeration—his purchases soon totaled almost 50 square miles, 32,000 acres—and he

LIVINGSTON COUNTY, N.Y.

Livingston County, New York (map by Author)

was entrusting this investment to two inexperienced cousins more than twenty years his junior.

James and William apparently used their inheritances from their father to make their own initial purchases. That is, a William Wadsworth of Farmington in South Hartford County is recorded as having bought 11,520 acres (18 square miles) in Township 11, Range 5 (approximately where Honeoye Falls, New York, is today) on July 9, 1790. The purchaser appears to have been James's brother William, but whether it was for himself, for himself and James, or for Jeremiah cannot be determined. We do know that on July 1, 1795, William did invest, paying $100 for 345 acres. Their older brother, "Major John," retained the family home in Connecticut as his inheritance.[14]

By most accounts James was the businessman, William the practical pioneer; they were a perfect complement to implement cousin Jeremiah's planned investments. Their relationship to western New York was forged in the spring of 1790 when they set out from their Durham, Connecticut, home with a small band of other pioneers, provisions to sustain them in their first season, necessary agricultural implements, and oxen to pull their load. The pioneers' journey, the paths of which diverged at times, took them from Long Island Sound, up the Hudson River, then to the Mohawk River, and eventually to their destination, the banks of the Genesee River, more than 350 miles. William began the trek with a team of oxen pulling a cart, two or three hired men, and Jenny, an African-American, who allegedly was the family's favorite slave. The hardy older brother and his small band had to cut and move logs from the narrow sleigh path on their way to Cayuga Lake, which they crossed by means of two canoes lashed together. From the Hudson River, James navigated the water route from Schenectady to Canandaigua outlet, three days ahead of his brother and his entourage. The final path was virtually hacked out by these adventurers.[15]

Averaging barely twelve miles per day, from Canandaigua they followed an Indian trail, then the route of General Sullivan's army to the foot of Conesus Lake, about eight miles east of Big Tree (now Geneseo). James, traveling by horse, arrived first and backtracked the following day to locate his brother's party, which had gotten lost. Reunited, the brothers followed James's trail to their destination, arriving at Big Tree on June 10, 1790. They found only Lemuel Jennings tending cattle for Oliver Phelps and, later, the Jones brothers, Horatio and John H., occupying an Indian cabin and shanty they had built a year earlier. A house—at best a dirty, uncomfortable hovel—was soon erected using timber obtained from the plentiful oaks that covered the land. However, almost immediately the Wadsworth brothers faced another threat, the ague, a fever that would visit the Genesee Valley periodically with devastating effects and that caused the premature departure of their hired men and James before winter.[16]

The ague (or "Genesee fever"), a malarial-like condition brought on by the clouds of mosquitoes that infested the area, struck both James and William their first summer. Various accounts credit Jenny, who accompanied William to Geneseo, with nursing the seriously ill brothers back to health. Local legend also claims that William's survival that first winter, 1790–1791, was due to her ministrations. Additionally Jenny is credited with learning various Native American remedies and preparing delicacies, including corn and wheat bread.[17]

The division of labor that characterized the Wadsworth brothers' lives thereafter found William actively managing their home farm—planting food crops and raising herds from the cattle they had purchased on the long trek from Durham and that would prove their most sustaining source of income. William's energy, hardiness, and adventurousness assured not only their survival, but the success of the immediate operation. Familiarly called "General Bill" for his later role as a militiaman—and often visible astride his black charger—William would become known far and wide for his vigor. More importantly, his pioneer spirit and skills allowed James to be the entrepreneur, traveling far and wide on behalf of their investments and those of Colonel Jeremiah. However, it is inaccurate to claim that James was unsuited for life along the Genesee River, despite his tendency toward hypochondria. He may have been temperamentally less inclined toward frontier life than his older brother, but the physical exertion required for traveling hundreds of miles, largely by horseback, stopping at rustic taverns where guests were not only the two-legged variety, eating whenever and wherever, and negotiating business transactions, was not for the weak of spirit or body. Also he had been admitted to practice law by Ontario County judge Oliver Phelps in 1791, which added more responsibilities, though it facilitated his business dealings.[18]

Indeed, James was perfect for the entrepreneurial role, though even he admitted that he might be overzealous. His February 20, 1793, letter from New York City to cousin Jeremiah illustrates the spirit with which James served as his cousin's agent. He hoped that Jeremiah (always addressed as "Sir"):

> will not consider me too officious if I should express a wish that you would take Township No. Six at half a dollar per acre. If the present holders will give a years or even nine months credit, there is not a doubt, there is a moral certainty, that it will command a dollar pr. acre the ensuing summer. A number of West Indian gentlemen are now in town, who would not hesitate to give it. . . .

Two months later James had minutely inspected the Wadsworth lands to price them appropriately and heartily wished that he had the power to exhibit this land along the Genesee River to Connecticut residents. "I'm sure the banks of the Connecticut River would be deserted for those of the Genesee." However, he claimed to "forbear giving you my sentiment . . . because I am considered as an enthusiast." Illustrative of his enthusiasm, a year earlier, James had become a speculator in his own right. With an advance from Jeremiah, and giving a mortgage for the balance of the purchase price, he bought an estimated 27,000-acre parcel in Big Tree Township, which Jeremiah owned. Before long, the management of his own holdings would begin to occupy much of his time.[19]

James was not alone in his enthusiasm. In the 1780s public lands, sold by the Federal government to repay Revolutionary War debts, were being avidly bought on credit with the intent to resell before payment became due. The outstanding example of this practice was the Phelps–Gorham syndicate. However, by 1796, the land bubble had burst and sales lagged behind due dates for payment, soon leading Phelps and Gorham to bankruptcy. Their land then reverted to Massachusetts, which sold it to Robert Morris, financier of the Continental Congress, on terms similar to those granted Phelps and Gorham. Foreign investors, particularly the Holland Land Company, the principals of which had been influenced by Morris on a trip to London in 1792, also had become interested in buying up these lands, pushing prices up.[20]

James, on his frequent travels to New York City, Philadelphia, and Hartford (despite the hardship of riding much of the way on horseback), became convinced that it was necessary to expand the sales field to England. He entreated Jeremiah to authorize a trip there. While he did not expect to make a fortune from sales in England, he argued that if he exercised good judgment, a handsome profit could be made. He had met with several "other English Gentlemen, who are of the opinion that if I set out on a moderate scale, offer no lands but what I have explained . . . then there is a moral certainty of a swap." (James was prone to "moral certainty" in business and family matters, a trait he passed down to his eldest son, James Samuel.) Moreover, on the flats away from the river there were some clear areas within the hardwood stands (called white oak openings) that were conducive to settlement. But he clearly deferred to Jeremiah's judgment and was making plans to visit the latter in Hartford to discuss details in person. Brother Bill had things under control at home, for in January 1795 he had driven three teams of oxen from New York City and had escorted six families to work the flats.[21]

Surprisingly, in July 1795, James reported to cousin Jeremiah much greater demand than expected for farmland at 20–24 shillings ($2.40–$3.84) per acre, because the Six Nations of the Iroquois had relinquished all their titles to land in the eastern part of the Phelps–Gorham tract the previous fall. He was equally upbeat at the end of the year when he wrote confidentially to Jeremiah that Robert Morris wanted to rid himself of a mortgage on the Genesee lands. These reports likely were manifestations not only of his usual enthusiasm but also of his campaign to go to London, which apparently was successful, for Jeremiah's patronage had obtained for James many social invitations. James also had made contacts on his own, including with a Mr. Murray and some other Englishmen who were interested in purchasing large land tracts in America. Because, as foreigners, they were unable to own land, James would act as agent. That is, James would buy land from Morris and other sellers for foreigners in his name and derive a commission.

This was facilitated by a bill introduced in the U.S. Congress by Aaron Burr, who was beginning to incur large debts from overspeculation. If passed, aliens could buy land in the United States through American agents, like James. This would pave the way for James, Charles Williamson, resident agent for English speculator Sir William Pultney, and Thomas Morris, Robert's son, to manage the Holland Land Company's possessions in America. If all his projections were realized, James considered settling in New York City, where prospects for sale appeared better. But at age 27, he had not made up his mind. Geneseo was a certainty; New York was less so. That would be decided later. Now he was off to England.[22]

Soon after arriving at Plymouth, England, in February 1796, James was busy making contacts with English investors interested in land in Maine. However, in June he reported that the scarcity of money in the United States, which had induced him to travel to England, prevailed there too. The financial situation would worsen a year later, due to the French Revolution and the British

Privy Council's order to the Bank of England to stop paying in specie. Meanwhile, the ever-curious James visited British farms and factories, obtaining information that would prove useful to him later.[23]

A potentially more profitable experience for James was a trip to the Netherlands. There he met with officers of the Holland Land Company, a combination of Dutch banks, which had bought almost half the original Phelps–Gorham purchase from Thomas Morris. Depending on the status of Iroquois titles to this land west of the Genesee River, James might become an agent for the Dutch combine. For now he had to content himself with "promissories" (written promises to pay when asked or on a specified date) for the sale of an undetermined amount of Genesee land at $2 per acre.[24]

James impressed the Dutch businessmen with his more conservative approach to land sales that encouraged settlement, but the Dutch failed to employ him then as a retail seller in Geneseo. Apparently they believed his private interests would lead him to devote too little time to sales on behalf of the Holland Land Company. There was also concern over unspecified charges of dishonesty levelled against James by Thomas Morris, his one-time partner.[25]

By late 1798 James was glad to be back in the United States, and in early January 1799, he anticipated a return to Geneseo. This was a change of heart, which he felt would surprise his friends. However, he remained in New York City and planned a visit to Philadelphia. On February 22, he was still in New York, responding to Jeremiah's advice about eschewing politics, and, indeed, resolving to confine himself to business, though he remained current on the political situation the rest of his life. From this decision to avoid politics James deviated only once.

In June Wadsworth, having returned to Geneseo, again made the tortuous trek to New York City to relax, which included a side trip to attend graduation at his alma mater, Yale. However, aboard a stagecoach bound for Albany, New York's capital, he wrote to apprise his cousin Jeremiah that Robert Morris was surrendering his property to creditors and that the Phelps and Gorham syndicate was extinguishing its rights to one of the townships in which Jeremiah had an interest. From Albany he rode horseback to Hartford, where he met with Jeremiah, whose health was failing, to discuss in detail these matters and his desire to buy from Jeremiah the "Big Tree Farm" for himself and William. Geneseo was to be his home, the place where he would settle down.[26]

Apparently during this visit remarks by Jeremiah questioning the management of his land sales hurt James's feelings and led him to write a long, highly defensive letter after his return to Geneseo. James was prone to be peevish when criticized, a trait he passed down to his son James Samuel. His feelings were easily hurt, and he became incensed when his integrity or honor was questioned.[27]

Such was the case involving duels with Oliver Kane in February and March of 1801. Unfortunately—and deliberately, it would seem—James offered few details in letters to cousin Jeremiah. The first "affair of honor" resulted from an insult he and his acquaintances considered so violent that he had no other choice. Apparently during a game of cards with Kane, one of five merchant brothers, a quarrel erupted. That led to a challenge and a sunrise exchange of shots between James and Oliver on a bluff behind brother Charles Kane's store near Schenectady. James got the better of it, nicking Kane. Though James hoped never to be engaged in another duel, it did not turn out that way. Three weeks later he and Oliver Kane dueled again, but James claimed he had "nothing to reproach myself with—under similar circumstances I should pursue the same steps again." This time James was wounded slightly.[28]

It is possible that James also was still affected by the loss of his mother, Esther Parsons Wadsworth, who died on October 6, 1799, at age 67, and was buried in what would become the Wadsworth plot in Temple Hill Cemetery, Geneseo.[29] However, brother William was the first to reveal the depth of their feelings about the loss of their "tender mother" and fell into a deep depression. Instead, James, hoping to distract himself from his mother's death, traveled to New York City on business, but he quickly returned home. That did no good. In a letter to cousin Jeremiah he confessed that returning home depressed him also. He acknowledged that it would have been better to have gone to Jeremiah's home in Hartford, where he could find relief in society and in what became an abiding passion, books.[30]

Throwing himself into business, James was on the road almost daily, traveling west on horseback to Buffalo Creek on Holland Land Company business, then to New York City by coach, up to Middletown, New York (approximately forty miles), and by horse to the nearby Catskills, a peripatetic pattern James Samuel would emulate. After the Catskills stop he rode horseback roughly one hundred miles more to Utica, where, quite unexpectedly, he met Oliver Phelps. This encounter reminded him of Robert Morris, who "would have been in prison and at the mercy of creditors of whom he has added insult to injustice had it not been for my exertions." That is, Morris had failed to give good title to some land that he was obligated to convey to James, forcing the latter to use money he planned to give to his brother to clear the title. But, there was a positive result from Morris's troubles. James's desire to make Geneseo his home was reinforced. To that end he reserved for himself 600 acres in Big Tree Flats and 8,000 acres of upland, which he considered less than his due, but more than he had ever expected.[31]

Though he would be back on the road traveling to New York City, Hartford, Washington, and Baltimore, James always returned to his beloved upland overlooking the Genesee River flats. Sealing his determination, in 1804 James and William began construction of what would become a commodious house. There, it is said, General Bill lived, and James squired.[32]

Of typical New England design, the initial structure had a square front door facing east on the 18'-by-12' oak-framed house, with mortar and stone filling the spaces between the studs and 3" oak plank siding set on end. The original hall, running east to west, was 12' wide.[33] Additions would come, and in time it became the largest home in the Genesee Valley, suitable to entertain in the style for

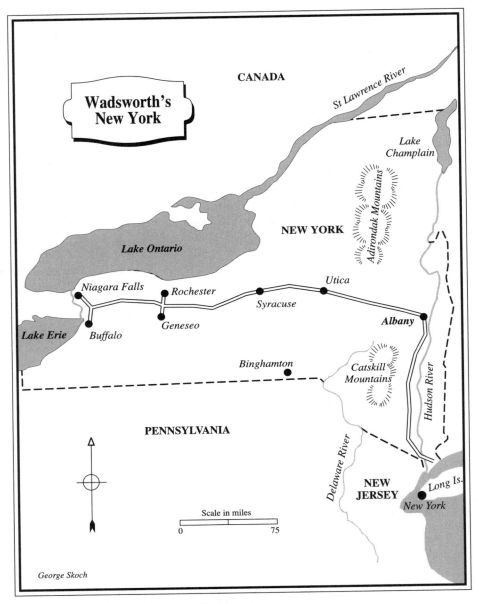

Wadsworth's New York (by George Skoch)

which the Wadsworths came to be known. Visitors waxed poetic about the house, which James called the Mansion House (now the Homestead), and the lush land below. Characteristic is the description written in 1841, shortly before James's death, by William L. Stone, editor of the *New York Commercial Advertiser*.[34]

His [James's] mansion, the abode of refinement and elegant hospitality, is finely situated at the southern extremity of the principal street of the village, embosomed in groves of ornamental trees, thickly sprinkled, among which are the elm, locust, and willow, and looking out upon a princely domain of his own, including a broad sweep of flats. . . . Adjacent to the mansion is a large garden, rich with every description of fruit which the climate will allow, and adorned with flowers of every variety and class of beauty.

When the "upright part of the . . . building" was erected, it "made an imposing appearance in a region of log houses, where a framed house of any size was a rarity."[35]

Even earlier, by February 1801, the Wadsworth name had spread to Russia, where James was honored by foreign membership in the Imperial Moscow Society of Agricultural Husbandry under the authority of Alexander the Second. This may have resulted from James's unusual interest in agricultural science, for he was constantly seeking new ways to improve farming techniques and animal husbandry. It could be argued that the honor was equally—or more—due brother William. William superintended not only the hard-working men who worked the farm, but also the animals that constituted the heart of their enterprise. For example, in early June 1801 Bill drove a herd of cattle to Baltimore (over 240 miles), averaging twenty miles a day, and returned five weeks later driving twenty head of oxen. Three years later the brothers would sell wheat in Albany, approximately the same distance away as Baltimore, to take advantage of the higher prices being offered there. However, while James would take care of the business end—buying and selling land and developing the tenancy agreements—he also claimed that his farming chores left him virtually no time to himself.[36]

Yet both found time for the militia reviews over which General Bill exercised authority and from which James, the observer, could derive justifiable sibling pride.[37]

With the new home started and farming going relatively well, James was able to demonstrate his inveterate eclecticism: railing against fanatic Methodists, exclaiming over good crops despite a drought, challenging Colonel Charles Williamson's plan to import Marylanders with their slaves to the Genesee Valley, extolling brother Bill's election as gaol superintendent, and decrying politics.

Droughtlike conditions in the early 1800s, a cold winter in 1805, which exhausted their hay stores, and poor markets led James in 1806 to claim the brothers were "literally pennyless" and unable to make payments on debts coming due. The situation was so dire that an embarrassed James had to ask his oldest brother John back in Durham to make a $200 payment to a creditor. Still, somehow James managed to make payments totaling $1,000 to that same creditor during August and September 1807, but admitted to the creditor he was mortified when he made payments of only $750 in February 1808. The Wadsworths were feeling the double-barreled effects of overvaluation of property and the embargo placed on export of goods to Europe by President Jefferson. However,

James would scramble to repay their debts, which exceeded $62,000 (close to $1 million in today's currency) by 1812.

Eventually the brothers would acquire more than 70,000 acres, making them the largest single landholders in western New York, possibly the state. However, their liability for taxes became a particular incentive to the system of land tenancy they developed (which was unique in America at that time), whereby the tenants paid the taxes as well as cleared and improved the land. The principle was that the brothers' capital should not flow from the region where it was accumulated. Reinvestment in and improvement of the land was the key. Wadsworth leases even forbade tenants from selling hay, instead requiring them to feed it to livestock and thereby to return it to the land. The result was that farm yields remained nearly the same from the 1800s to 1945.[38]

By 1814 every tenant had to plant a number of apple trees and replace any that died, build proper fences, erect a house with pine or cedar shingles, and even rid the land of noxious weeds. Further, tenants were to deliver to the nearest storehouse or mill a proportionate amount of the crops being raised to pay all taxes and assessments. A side benefit of the latter was the greater likelihood that the assessors would be more careful about taxing their friends and neighbors rather than rich landlords, including the Wadsworths. Also the tenants would take more interest in politics and government. Early on tenants were offered annual leases and two years free of rent, in return for, say, a specified amount of grain per hundred acres, the typical size of the leased parcels. In the 1840s, life leases replaced the annual leases and the sizes of the parcels increased. Dairying and hemp (used to make rope) and wheat raising, particularly the latter, were typical uses of the land by tenants. Though known for their fairness, following Jeremiah's advice that "laying a man under a great obligation was a sure way of making an enemy," neither James nor brother Bill was averse to foreclosing on unpaid mortgages. Even then fairness was the rule. For example, when James had to repossess land from a delinquent buyer, he refused the unsuccessful buyer's offer to pay the interest, because it was not his or his brother's policy to do so.[39]

James, now in his thirties, began entertaining thoughts of marrying and settling down. Only the faintest hint of what inspired this is revealed in his wide correspondence. In fact, there are virtually no letters to or from his future wife, as if the two simply chanced upon each other and married, though this would be totally out of character for James. In an 1801 letter to his cousin Jeremiah he was convinced that he would "become a desperate old Bachelor," though apparently it was not for lack of opportunity, for he had met a "pretty girl" in New York City just before writing the letter. But beauty was not enough: "I cannot and will not make a bow till I meet with what I call a fine woman. She must neither be un-educated or over-educated." Yet, he was vacillating. Observing his married friends, he concluded that remaining single had advantages and determined to remain so until his judgment and heart were equally involved. Even then, he feared that when he would finally make "his bow, it will be an awkward one."[40]

It may have been awkward, but bow he did, on October 1, 1804, and there are no known recriminating letters to explain his change of status—and heart—at the relatively advanced age of 36.

Not surprising for the Wadsworths, whereby the males clearly dominated, little is known about James's wife, Naomi Wolcott, nine years his junior. However, it is generally agreed that the Wadsworths married well. Naomi was the daughter of Samuel Wolcott, a cousin of the second U.S. treasury secretary, Oliver Wolcott, and Jerusha (II) Wolcott of East Windsor, Connecticut.[41]

Yet James's life, like his lifelong bachelor brother William's, was in many respects unchanged by marriage. Farm and business occupied most of his time. Still, he was determined to carry on the Wadsworth name. Typical genealogical charts of the Wadsworth family carefully detail the male descent, but refer to the females only as their wives. Genealogists were blameless, according to a late-1880s letter from Mrs. M. C. Wadsworth of Canfield, Ohio, who argued that leadership, a Wadsworth characteristic, extended even to "woman repression."[42] But, of course, it would be far from the truth to claim that the Wadsworth women played no role in child-rearing. James Jeremiah ("Jerry") Wadsworth, great-great-grandson of James and a U.S. delegate to the United Nations, readily acknowledged that the influence of the women in his family may have been greater than the men's.[43] It remains that James's influence on his son James Samuel was especially powerful.

In addition to leadership, male dominance, restlessness, and enthusiasm for various causes, the Wadsworths, including James Samuel, could be irreverent. For example, Thurlow Weed, a power in New York politics with whom both James and James Samuel had an on-and-off relationship, recalled a chance encounter between the two and Oliver Kane, with whom James had twice dueled some thirty years earlier. James Samuel, who exchanged greetings with Kane while his father seemed to take no notice, is supposed to have asked his father if he did not know Kane. The elder Wadsworth laconically replied, "I met him once." When Weed later asked whether James Samuel was unaware of the Wadsworth–Kane duels, the latter laughed and readily admitted he knew about them; he was simply needling his father.[44]

However, above all, the Wadsworths' vast landholdings (including, in time, James Samuel's) positioned them to greatly influence state and national matters at a time when western New York was becoming settled and increasingly prosperous.

Chapter 3

"WHAT WILL YOUR AMBITION LEAD YOU TO DO?"

Despite debts, when James Wadsworth married in 1804 he could consider himself comfortably affluent. The little settlement at Big Tree was rapidly developing into a village called Geneseo. Twenty-five miles to the south lay the hamlet of Arkport, bordering on the Canisteo River, on which goods and animals could begin their river journey south down the Chemung and Susquehanna Rivers to Baltimore. More important was the settlement to the north. Near Lake Ontario at the mouth of the Genesee River, in time it would bear the name Rochester after one of three partners who had just bought a hundred-acre tract there. Though it would not attain a population of 3,000 nor have a bank for another two decades, Rochester seemed ideally situated for a commercial center. In fact, annual shipments up the Genesee River to Lake Ontario soon would total $30,000. And there was talk of a cross-state canal.[1]

With his natural energy and business acumen, James aspired to an even brighter future, one that included a son who could carry on his name and fortune. Moreover, because he married late, his family was both an abiding concern and an object of special affection. Always signing his family letters "Papa" or "Your Affectionate Father," he nonetheless imposed a strict code of honor and a passion for life and causes on his five children, especially his eldest son, James Samuel, and youngest daughter, Elizabeth, the latter born when James was 47. His prominence dominated every aspect of their lives, directly or indirectly.[2]

In order, the five children of the union between James and Naomi Wolcott Wadsworth were Harriet, born in 1805; James Samuel, October 30, 1807; William Wolcott, 1810; Cornelia, 1812; and Elizabeth, three years later. It is understandable that James Samuel, the first son, would become the primary object of James's familial exhortations. It would be a heavy burden for a boy whose high spirits more resembled those of his uncle, General Bill, great-uncle General James, and Captain Joseph of Charter Oak fame than the business-directed temperament of his father.

Though his father was an inveterate correspondent, there is virtually no record of James Samuel's early life other than occasional allusions, including (according to legend) helping his uncle drive cattle to New York City when he was 12. Nor is there any evidence of an inclination toward military service, despite the military reviews conducted by his uniformed uncle who suffered scars and ailments due to his heroism at the battle of Queenston in the War of 1812, where he nearly lost his life.[3]

The first, rather vague records are James's admonitions to his son to remember the consequences of having kept "bad company" at Hamilton College, near Utica, in 1823, which may have occasioned his dismissal when he was not yet 16.[4] However, these admonitions were not issued until 1826, when 18-year-old James Samuel was admitted to Harvard (not his father's alma mater, Yale!) as a "Temporary Student" in the class of 1828.[5]

We do know that, despite his father's wealth and accompanying privileges, James Samuel grew up on what was still largely frontier. It was plagued in having only a few roads, which were largely dirt paths atop the clay soil that turned to sticky mush in rains, the omnipresent mosquitoes (and accompanying ague), and rattlesnakes. Survivors were hardy souls.

It appears that James Samuel may have been tutored by Reverend Abram Foreman, a scholarly but eccentric 1815 Union College graduate and the first pastor of the Presbyterian Church in Geneseo. James Samuel may also have received some schooling at the Brick Academy on Center Street. Whatever the case, he must have met entrance requirements at Harvard—and earlier at the fledgling Hamilton College. The latter required the entrant to be at least 14, demonstrate "an ability to read, construe and parse Virgil's *Aeneid,* Cicero's *Select Orations* and the Greek Testament," and possess knowledge of English grammar and basic arithmetic.[6]

For a time there were frequent letters from the father to the son at Harvard reminding the latter how impatient his parents were to hear from him, but just as frequently James admonished his firstborn to be cautious about the company he was keeping. He was referring to James Samuel's riding into Boston with high-spirited "Southern blades," for he was convinced that "bad scholars & dissipated young men generally ride the most." One of his son's contemporaries recalled riding hell-bent-for-election from Cambridge to Boston and back, which always drew a crowd of spectators.[7]

James Samuel also was reminded by his parents that he was free from duties at home on the condition that he improve in his studies, and they hoped for a positive report from one of his tutors, Harvard Professor of Belles Lettres George Ticknor.[8]

While concerned about his elder son's educational advancement, James was no less concerned about his emotional growth, but Harvard may not have been the right environment at this time. Despite its famous alumni, it was still probably better known as a finishing school. The median age of entering students was barely 16. Necessarily, the college served in loco parentis, but, inconsistently, offered classes only in the morning, leaving students free afternoons and evenings.[9] Boston, to which James Samuel, almost 20, was often riding, offered a particular attraction, for according to Oliver Wendell Holmes, a contemporary, "nothing but vinegar-faced old maids and drawing room sentimentalists" lived in Cambridge.[10]

Further, Harvard was in turmoil when the Wadsworth scion attended it. The president, John Thornton Kirkland, was about to submit a forced resignation, the century-old curriculum was considered too rigid, and faculty were warring with an increasing number of students described as "loafing around Boston, smoking, drinking, and whoring." This mix, which included an irksome dress code for entering students, would prove to be the younger Wadsworth's undoing.[11] However, his first academic year, 1826–1827, was generally without incident, though he was "Consigned to Prof. Willard for illegal dress" on October 30, 1826, and four months later he was threatened with expulsion for a similar infraction.[12]

Still, this was not enough to portend any major problem in his second school year, but clashes between him and the college, and, more importantly, between him and his equally strong-willed father, now almost 60, were inevitable. On the other hand, more temperamentally suited contemporaries survived the turmoil and became prominent in various fields in later life. They included Cornelius C. Felton, Oliver Wendell Holmes, Benjamin Curtis, Charles Sumner, Charles Francis Adams, and John Lothrop Motley.

The father's anxiety caused sleeplessness and the need to repeatedly counsel his son, which led to a lengthy—and revealing—description of the person who was to inherit the expanding Wadsworth estate and, more importantly, name. Professing his love, old James chided his son for exercising bad judgment: spending money excessively, keeping wild company, and neglecting his studies. Then, going for the jugular, old James challenged James Samuel: If he couldn't act properly "among complete gentlemen & scholars[,] *what will your ambition lead you to do?*" Then he laid on the oldest parental guilt trip: He was "*sacrificing his own happiness*" for his son's future. He begged his son to study diligently and patiently to meet the difficulties that would make him a man.[13]

Not surprisingly, James Samuel's friends and siblings viewed him very differently. His sister Cornelia, barely five years younger, acted toward him almost like a dutiful child, reporting on her progress at school, promising to behave, and wishing his company. Elizabeth, eight years younger, adored her older brother. However, his brother William could be much more objective, even critical. For example, he protested vigorously when James Samuel applied his own and William's credit toward the extravagant purchase of a bull. This incident reveals not only the nature of their relationship, but James Samuel's propensity to spend money and to keep one foot on the "Home Farm" regardless of where he was and in whatever else he was engaged.[14]

While James Samuel's companions and correspondents admired him, the reasons may have depended on the particular relationship. Cornelius Felton, soon to become Professor of Greek at Harvard, appreciated the younger Wadsworth for successfully recommending him to become one of the two first tutors (instructors) at Temple Hill Academy in Geneseo. A pet project of old James, it had opened in 1827 as Livingston County's first high school and James wanted it to succeed. Felton, whose friendship James Samuel had gained at Harvard, also predicted that James Samuel would distinguish himself intellectually.[15]

Felton may have been hoping that James Samuel would help the fledgling academy to drive out what Felton considered the bigotry and ignorance that blighted the Genesee Valley.[16]

This episode is important for a number of reasons. First, it illustrates the confidence others placed in James Samuel. Second, it reveals the father's unacknowledged, but incipient, reliance on the son, who had been asked to suggest the first tutors for the new academy. It also illustrates a passion for education that the father, now approaching his eighth decade, wanted his son to possess. However eclectic James's interests and philanthropy, next to his family nothing was as important to him as education. "Uneducated man always has been and always will be a puppet in the hands of designing demagogues," he had proclaimed to his older son.[17]

However, Felton was not unaware of young Wadsworth's busy social life and inattention to his studies. James Samuel, called "Tom" (for tomcat?) by many friends, apparently had a lively time, as his father correctly gauged, especially with the attractive and enticing Boston and Concord maidens. Letters to James Samuel most often mention the long, on-and-off-again relationship with a "Sally," possibly Sarah Sullivan, reportedly "the belle of Boston." The seriousness of this relationship is uncertain, though letters from friends referring to it continue for some time. Apparently "Sally" was serious enough to leave Boston to visit Geneseo. She preceded him in the summer of 1828 so as "to be all ready and armed & equipped with songs, sighs & sheep's eyes" when James Samuel arrived, according to his friend C. Jones Richards. However, there were other adventures. One was with a widow. Two female correspondents simply used initials, while another was embarrassed enough later on to request the return of her letters.[18]

It is a mystery why so many letters referring to James Samuel's romances, some of which occurred barely two years before he was married, remain in the Wadsworth Family Papers, while there are very few letters between him and his eventual wife, Mary Craig Wharton Wadsworth, and none that could be called "love letters." Nor is there any indication of just when or how the relationship with Miss Wharton was begun and maintained before their marriage.

Also at this time the older Wadsworth son was chided for being not only a profligate, but a soft touch. This profligacy, which would become more pronounced later, was evident, for example, in his taste for clothing.[19] The only image we have of him as a young man is a painting in which he is wearing a black frock coat, matching ascot, white vest, and light-colored pants, typical of the period. On the other hand, the long, curled dark hair and beard covering the side of his face and chin give him the appearance of a fop, rather than a tall, well-proportioned, vigorous man, as he was usually described.

The Wadsworth scion was regularly hit for loans while at Harvard. George Turner's indebtedness to him would gnaw at Turner for the next twelve years. At other times young Wadsworth was himself the borrower, despite the rather healthy account his father set up for him, which resulted in yet more of his father's criticism.[20]

Clearly, the father's fears for his son were not groundless, which the parents' letters increasingly revealed. Naomi, who acknowledged that typically she corresponded only upon instructions from her absent husband, advised more obliquely. In a letter to her younger son, William Wolcott, who was attending a Harvard prep school near Boston, she asked whether his brother was "keeping his good resolution of being the third in his class." While James Samuel may well have made such a resolution, likely it was more to pacify his parents than out of any genuine intent. At least the father was not persuaded and planned a visit to Cambridge as soon as convenient.[21]

Before he could do so, however, a bombshell struck. A letter from Harvard President Kirkland so "unnerved" James that he found himself "quite unable to write," which his virtually illegible handwriting verified. Copied for James Samuel and enclosed with his letter was Kirkland's:[22]

Oct. 2, 1827
Dear Sir:
   The faculty of the University request me to inform you that the conduct of your son in College does not correspond to your & their expectations. During the last Term he was admonished for repeated absences at exercises & public worship. He returned this Term on the 19th of Sept. & since then he has attended almost no exercises. The Faculty think it their duty to advise you to remove him from Cambridge as he is by no means answering the purposes of his connection with this Institution.
   With much consideration & earnest wishes for the improvement of your Son,

I am, Dear Sir,
Your Ob't Ser't

Old James was devastated. His son had virtually nothing to show for his attendance at Harvard. On the only scale showing his class rank, there was a grade of "9" in mathematics (presumably out of 10).[23]

Though "unnerved," on October 17 James made it clear that his son had only two courses of action: "Instantly go to Doctor Kirkland while the affliction you have brought on those who love you tenderly is in your mind & fully confess all your faults & promise a thorough reform & commitment in your conduct. Quit your follies & become what you ought to be. The other course will spread your disgust from Boston to New York & Geneseo."[24]

Despite his wife's advice to "set out immediately to Cambridge," James, who was attending a meeting of the inspectors of the Seneca Reservations near Buffalo, felt that no good would come from a visit. There was nothing more to be said, which was apparent from the absence of his usual closing. He ended the letter simply and uncharacteristically, "J. W." However, on the twenty-second, all too aware of his son's temperament and the unlikelihood of his apologizing to President Kirkland, he laid it on thick. First, he enclosed "a sketch of the life of a just and good man." Then he asked his son whether he derived sufficient plea-sure from his dissipation and wildness to "compensate for the pain[,] anxiety & distress which you are inflicting upon your parents." Alternately begging and chiding, the father could not find words to express his astonishment at his son's behavior. Only boys, not men, acted without motives. What motivated his son? What kind of man would he be if he did not change?

The irony was inescapable. The old man had tackled the frontier when roughly his dissolute son's age. By hard work, persistence, and love of learning he had built a fortune—and reputation. His elder son, the person to whom he looked to become the conservator of the Wadsworth estate and name, was not only a failure, but an acute embarrassment. His life's work and the Wadsworth inheritance, which was becoming increasingly important to James, were in seri-ous jeopardy. Not uncommonly, he had pinned his hopes and dreams on his firstborn. In his heart he knew the boy had the ability and the physical constitu-tion to carry on, but he was throwing it all away by his incorrigible ways.

The errant son spent the winter of 1827–1828 in Geneseo, where "business by days and books by night protect[ed]" him from his Harvard friends.[25] How-ever, he maintained important Harvard contacts, including Cornelius Felton; Thomas Giles, son of ex-U.S. senator and Virginia governor William Branch Giles; Nathaniel Parker Willis, who would later found and edit the *American Monthly*; and John Lothrop Motley, historian and diplomat. In turn, Motley's friends included Harvard Professor Ticknor, Daniel Webster, Richard Henry Dana, author of *Two Years Before the Mast,* and Edward Everett, later Massachu-setts governor, Harvard president, and principal speaker at the dedication of the National Cemetery at Gettysburg in November 1863.[26] However, acquaintances exercising even greater influence on Wadsworth lay in the future. For now he was simply the expelled, spoiled heir to a veritable fortune.

So James Samuel was home, momentarily chastened. Yet he enjoyed his val-ley home, which offered open spaces upon which to ride, the chance to work with Uncle Bill, and a steady stream of interesting guests taking advantage of his father's hospitality.

It is important, too, to recall that this was an exciting, though difficult, time in his father's life, which would spill over onto his older son. While eschewing politics, James was being drawn into a brewing political stew. It began with the at-tempted publication of an exposé of the Masonic Order by William Morgan of Batavia, New York, a Mason himself. A shadowy character better known as "Cap-tain," Morgan was murdered near the Niagara River, north of Buffalo, in the fall of 1826. The "Morgan Affair" erupted into the Anti-Masonic movement that spread from New York State into the national arena before it died down. Because the whole affair has been detailed elsewhere and becomes complicated with the telling, it will be dealt with only briefly here. The gist is that in 1827 and 1828 public meetings were called throughout the state to nominate Anti-Masonic can-didates for state and national offices, leading to pressure on James to run for U.S. senator from New York. He preemptively refused, based on his vow to avoid poli-tics. Nonetheless, the Wadsworths came in for criticism for using their wealth and influence in the Anti-Masonic movement, and in 1829 James faced a dilemma: How to support public education without engaging in politics. He reluctantly agreed to be the Anti-Masonic candidate for the University of the State of New York Board of Regents, the state's educational policy-making body.[27]

While James was unsuccessful in his only bid for public office, it presaged James Samuel's ultimately fatal involvement in politics. In fact, he was being drawn into politics through his father's land speculation already. In a reprise of the earlier episodes, the bankruptcies of and subsequent defaults in payment by Oliver Phelps and Nathaniel Gorham and then Robert Morris necessitated resales to the Holland Land Company, from which the notorious Ogden Land Company had bought preemptive rights in 1810 for 50¢ an acre. The land in question this time was the ten reservations that the Senecas occupied as a result of an earlier treaty. Any sales of their land by the Ogden Land Company required approval by the Seneca chiefs, who, again, were supposed to be protected by the U.S. government through its representatives.[28]

James Wadsworth was appointed a Federal representative to inspect contracts being made, though he stood to profit from land sales, either as purchaser himself or agent for the Ogden Land Company. This conflict of interest appears to have been ignored by the government. Unfortunately, James, an indefatigable worker, found himself confined to his office on Main Street, suffering more headaches than usual. So, having decided that his firstborn son needed to take on more responsibility, James had James Samuel accompany his business partner, William Spencer, to Buffalo to participate in the negotiations for the Reservation lands. However, James recognized that the son would need additional skills, those available to a lawyer.[29]

Thus, April 1828 found James Samuel in Boston, reading law under Senator Daniel Webster. An apparent change of attitude had occurred. James Samuel had written Cornelius Felton that he could be enthusiastic about law, studying Latin to further his legal knowledge and enjoying the bustle in Webster's office.[30] While James Samuel's unsystematic legal education was intended to help him manage his family's increasingly complex business affairs, actual practice of law was not yet out of the question.

Despite his new-found enthusiasm for the law, the apprentice was back home in Geneseo three months later after a departure so abrupt that Webster learned about it only when young Wadsworth did not respond to Webster's dinner invitation. Whether or not his departure was due to rumors about his romances, he was once more in exile, where he maintained his desultory correspondence with friends. They had trouble keeping up with him and wondered whether he was "in a certain house on Chestnut Street, Boston . . . at Geneseo or shooting the wild deer at Angelica," southeast of Geneseo. His inveterate restlessness was already established.[31]

Though his mother believed James Samuel was attending to business, the son's behavior was still suspect in his father's eyes. So much so that the elder Wadsworth claimed that he considered turning to his second son, especially if

William's character proved more principled and his health improved. Nonetheless, increasingly James was calling on his elder son to act as his surrogate. Also James Samuel was filling in for his ailing Uncle Bill around the home farm.[32]

By January 1829, James Samuel had resumed his law studies, this time at Yale, where again he would try the father's patience because of his spending habits. Problematic too, James had no correspondent in New Haven to monitor his older son, unlike at Harvard. However assiduously young Wadsworth pursued his law studies and the ladies, he returned home frequently. One reason may be the vague, lingering fevers his mother and his sister Cornelia were experiencing, which frequently forced them to bed. The specific cause of these illnesses, which also afflicted James Samuel's older sister, Harriet, is unknown, but tuberculosis ran in the family at that time.[33]

James Samuel too may have been suffering from an equally vague illness, which his mother described as "those distressing attacks of sickness with which you used to be afflicted." Because there are only two more, equally vague references to "alarming" maladies visiting James Samuel, the cause of and effects on his behavior are left to conjecture.[34]

Back in New Haven, James Samuel received a letter from John P. Murray of New York City—an ironic one, given James Samuel's less than exemplary behavior. Murray praised young Wadsworth for writing about his son, whose study habits were not good, and for offering the kind of advice that Murray's son would accept only from someone like Wadsworth, a few years older. While his parents would have trouble viewing James Samuel as a levelheaded leader, increasingly others would, which may have reinforced the qualities his parents desired, but were unable to drill into him.[35]

The timing of Murray's letter could not have been more puzzling. Scarcely two months later, in a long, steaming letter (the second of two such letters), the elder Wadsworth went from begging to advising to admonishing and finally to threatening banishment. As far as he was concerned, his 22-year-old son had less than one chance in ten of his health or well-being ever being reclaimed.[36]

Following his father's injunction, the younger Wadsworth remained at Yale until May, when he headed to Albany for study in the law firm of McKeon and Deniston, to which his father accompanied him. Still, the son found time to correspond with Boston acquaintances about law, politics, and women, though not necessarily in that order. He also pursued business contacts for his father, which included dealings with Henry Seymour, the Erie Canal Commissioner (with whose son, Horatio Seymour, James Samuel would experience a conflict-filled relationship the rest of their lives), and John Young, a Geneseoan, who was serving in the New York State Assembly.[37]

Despite conducting business for his father, James Samuel demonstrated an ambivalence toward it, which apparently would continue throughout his life. For example, years later it was said that, while his "judgment was always clear and sound . . . he disliked the details of business and the petty cares of an office."[38] Yet, his judgment was respected by many associates, and his father and his increasingly lame uncle would necessarily come to rely on him. It remains one of the many ironies and inconsistencies of James Samuel Wadsworth's life and character, one that would carry through into his military service.

While the Wadsworth scion apparently was applying himself to the law, in the fall and winter of 1830 his attention was drawn to letters from home that were taking on a rather ominous tone. His mother was ill. In January 1831, Naomi's poor health prompted a request from James for James Samuel to escort his youngest sister, Elizabeth, home from a Philadelphia boarding school.[39] Yet, ever the businessman, James wanted his son to stop in Harrisburg to do some business. His son, aware of his father's occasional overstatement, was not wont to move quite as fast as his father expected, and was initially reassured by a letter from his brother William.[40]

This time his father's alarm was not overstated. On March 1, 1831, Naomi Wolcott Wadsworth died. Then James's fears turned toward his three daughters, particularly Cornelia, whose "nervous system is [so] greatly affected [that] we were obliged to keep her room dark." Unfortunately, the elder Wadsworth's intuition once again proved reliable in Cornelia's case. The last ten days in March she experienced the same symptoms as her mother, and on the 28th, not yet 19 years of age, she succumbed. James's handwriting clearly revealed how poorly he was faring over the loss of two loved ones in a month.[41]

Even "Jimmy is broken up," the grieving husband and father wrote his cousin Daniel Wadsworth, Jeremiah's son. James Samuel had good reason: He had lost his mother and a sister, and his father, already prone to hypochondria, was seriously depressed.

This was clearly a turning point in James Samuel's life. These were, as his father wrote in a slightly different context four months later, "[the] trials that sometimes *fixes* [sic] a man's character for many years."[42]

Chapter 4

"NEVER FORGET WHAT IS DUE TO YOURSELF & FAMILY"

James Samuel Comes of Age

While James could claim that his son "Jimmy" was broken up, the son left no record of his feelings about the loss of his mother and younger sister, though later he would exhibit a "morbid curiosity" about cholera. (Whether he attributed the deaths of his mother and sister to this cause can only be speculation.) Nor was there any evidence of an immediate change in his behavior. His father would continue to exhort, while his friends would follow his love life and sporadic study of law.[1]

The rest of that year, 1831, James Samuel bounced between Albany, Geneseo, and Philadelphia. One reason for the Philadelphia trips was to check on his younger sister Elizabeth, who had returned to a boarding school.[2] However, James Samuel may have had other reasons, for his correspondents mention unnamed young ladies there, as well as in Boston and New Haven. Yet, writing his brother from Albany in August, he made it clear that he intended to "bear down to prepare for that *severe* ordeal," the bar exam, and wanted his father to call upon the appropriate persons for the necessary certificates attesting to his study and character. Still, he allowed himself to be distracted: escaping an unusual Albany heat wave, checking on notes given for 500 head of Wadsworth cattle that had been driven to Albany by a family farmhand, and responding to John Church's invitation to be an attendant at his wedding in Angelica, near the Pennsylvania border, where the two frequently hunted.[3]

In the meantime James Samuel's anxious father reminded him to build his character, to maintain his friendships (not to appear curt, a tendency that occasionally would be noted by others), and to respect himself, which would lead to respect from his friends. James also reminded his son to develop contacts that would lead to opportunities for further investments in land. But uppermost, James Samuel must intensely apply himself to studying for the bar.[4]

Despite exhorting his older son to study, at the same time the elder Wadsworth was diverting his elder son's attention and—perhaps not so subtly—drawing him into management of the family farm and into land speculation, roles that would serve him well later. He also had James Samuel accompany him to Philadelphia, ostensibly to check on Elizabeth at her boarding school, but also to attend the Free Trade Convention in Philadelphia and the National Anti-Masonic Convention in Baltimore. However, characteristic of the differences between father and son, the former divided his time in Philadelphia between the Atheneum and the Franklin Library. The latter called on young ladies, and, when cajoled, took his sister Elizabeth to the "confectionary" for ice cream and cakes.

For one who claimed to refrain from politics, the elder Wadsworth showed an unusual interest in the subject and may well have planted the seeds for his son's later political activities. Likely James's intent was to make business contacts, much as he had done when serving his cousin Jeremiah almost forty years earlier. Whatever the reason, father and son attended the Anti-Masonic Party Convention. It was James Samuel's formal introduction to national politics and contacts that would prove important then and later. Attendees, with whom James Samuel would become identified as a friend or enemy, included future New York State governor William Seward; Francis Granger, son of and himself a future U.S. Postmaster General; and future U.S. president Millard Fillmore. More immediately important was the Free Trade Convention in Philadelphia, which drew what James Samuel regarded as a large number of talented Southerners. He was impressed by the harmony that the Northerners and Southerners enjoyed regarding the constitutionality of the tariff. Ironically, a meeting thirty years later with some of those same Southerners would be much less harmonious, in no small part because of James Samuel's politics.[5]

After the Free Trade Convention the two Wadsworths toured Maryland, visiting large landowners for three weeks before returning to Geneseo. It appears that this particular excursion had two purposes: first, to offer James Samuel another view of large-scale farming and, second, to combat the son's haste to take the bar exam, for which James felt his son was unprepared. He did not want his son to be admitted to the bar because of his own influence, so he advised James Samuel to study hard and to take frequent practice examinations.[6]

Yet the elder Wadsworth was dragging his son away from his studies with increasing complaints of various afflictions and the need for assistance in traveling. Likely this was also a not-so-subtle attempt to monitor James Samuel, whom he reminded "never [to] forget what is due to yourself & family."[7]

Returning by way of Washington, James introduced his son to Secretary of State Edward Livingston, an old friend who had grown up in the Albany area, and renewed their acquaintance with former Michigan Territorial Governor Lewis Cass, for whom the son claimed great respect. Unfortunately, the pair were disappointed that most of the persons to whom James had sent letters of introduction were out of town, though they "passed a day" with 96-year-old Charles Carroll of Carrollton, signer of the Declaration of Independence and former U.S. senator, and enjoyed a tour of his 14,000-acre estate, 4,000 of which were cultivated by slaves. The younger Wadsworth's views of slavery apparently were forming, for he found that "under a selfish and ignorant overseer . . . they [the slaves] do not all do as much work as half a dozen good Yankees," though "they appear to be treated very kindly and live quite comfortably." His recommendations three decades later to what would become the Freedmen's Bureau regarding the treatment of ex-slaves appear to be born out of this visit.[8]

Back in Albany, James Samuel prepared for the January 1832 bar examination, completely ignoring his father's admonition to wait until October when it would be given again. At least that is the excuse he gave his lonely, adoring younger sister, Elizabeth, when she pleaded with him to visit her in Philadelphia or New York at Thanksgiving. Meanwhile, he inquired of his brother about the two bulls he had directed his uncle to buy in Ohio, which were to sire the cattle he would sell for a profit, and about the sale of some real estate in Buffalo the two owned, which had increased in value. James Samuel was becoming involved, as his father hoped and prayed, and was developing skills that would prove particularly valuable when, during the Civil War, he would manage thousands of men and millions of dollars worth of matériel.[9]

Old James, still not satisfied, continued to admonish and counsel his 24-year-old son. For example, he recommended against some paintings his son wanted to buy to replace paintings in the Mansion House, but assured him that he could hang a number of the family's valuable paintings in a great house of his own in a few years. Then backing down on his earlier ultimatum, he advanced his law-student son $50, drawn on the latter's account with Tibbits in New York City. This is the first allusion to his older son's settling down and having a home of his own.[10]

Whether or not James Samuel actually was shaping up, shortly he would have good reason to do so. In December 1831, his old friend Charles A. Terry, then in Philadelphia, mentioned meeting and walking with the beautiful daughter of one of the city's finest families, the Whartons. This is the first reference to Mary Craig Wharton, the "peerless girl" who would play such a large part in James Samuel's life. Shortly thereafter, writing from Europe, Nathaniel Parker Willis asked whether James Samuel would bring "his bride" to visit him.[11]

Vague references in the elder Wadsworth's February 7, 1832, letter and instructions advising his older son to go slowly and prudently reinforce the notion that James Samuel was, in fact, considering marriage. On the other hand, he apparently fooled his sister Elizabeth, who surmised that he was arranging to live with someone she referred to familiarly as "Isabele."[12]

James Samuel, who had been admitted to the bar at the January 1832 term, was, in fact, entering a new phase of his life. Horatio Seymour and John A. Dix, two others admitted with him, were also, which over the next three decades would result in political alliances and rivalries with him. As always, there was little evidence of any change in James Samuel's behavior on his return to Geneseo. Siblings William and Elizabeth found his correspondence just as irregular as before.[13]

Nonetheless, subtle changes in the new lawyer's behavior were occurring. For example, hereafter there would be few or no letters from his Harvard and

New Haven friends, though it is not clear whether this was an inevitable or forced change in relationships. Instead, his correspondence from then until 1861 increasingly reflects his business and political interests.[14]

One family matter was the delicate health of James Samuel's older sister, Harriet, wife of Martin Brimmer, Boston businessman and financial advisor to James. Then—more alarmingly—it was James Samuel's own health. He had suffered an "attack of paralisis [sic]," according to a March 9 letter from David Piffard in Geneseo to James, then in New York. Because the son's most recent letter to his father had not mentioned any illness, the old man wanted a report. Apparently, the undefined but extended illness was being kept secret from the father. Charles Terry, writing from Philadelphia, privately suspected the nature of the illness, vaguely referring to James Samuel's "peculiar idiosyncrasy." Two weeks later William Farmer, his father's former clerk and agent for the land company, was similarly vague in his letter to James Samuel, but hoped for a complete restoration of his health.[15]

His father's next two letters had an even more ominous tone. At first James advised, then he instructed, James Samuel not to publish or write or send anything unless reviewed by his friends so long as his health was failing. James had sent for his younger son, William, to help at home, so James Samuel, who was careless about his health, could remain in Philadelphia and recuperate completely. The old man even recommended traveling by rail rather than coach when he could. This episode will probably always be a mystery, for there are no more references to it and there are no clues given as to exactly what was ailing James Samuel.[16]

Health worries began to dominate the Wadsworths' correspondence. The Wadsworths tended to be relatively long-lived, but James Samuel's mother had died at 54 and his sister Cornelia at 18. Moreover, his 71-year-old Uncle Bill, suffering from war wounds and gout, was failing and would die on March 8, 1833; his younger brother had seriously hurt himself at Harvard; his older sister's health was precarious; his father was complaining about his health; and he himself was suffering from some vague malady.[17]

Sick or not, James Samuel had to assume greater responsibilities, including acting as his father's agent in a variety of transactions, including purchasing Seneca Reservation land and investing in a canal from Rochester to Olean in Cattaraugus County, which would facilitate more efficient transportation of the Wadsworth's produce and stock.[18]

An added reason was that James was directing his attention toward much-delayed philanthropic activities, principally education. An example was his creation of a trust to print and distribute a series of lectures to each common school in New York State, for which James Samuel and his brother would serve as trustees.[19]

Notwithstanding health problems, James Samuel was also becoming occupied by marriage plans, to which there were only tantalizing allusions in his correspondents' letters to him. Mary Craig Wharton, the amiable, beautiful daughter of Philadelphia merchant John Wharton, was a real catch. Not surprisingly, the Wadsworth patriarch hoped and prayed that his son's choice of partner was a good one.[20]

The old man remained skeptical about his older son, whose vanity contributed to extravagant expenses. Reluctantly James mailed a $100 check to James Samuel in Washington, to which he had been sent to meet the U.S. surveyor general, to consult with Lewis Cass, and to examine maps of land in Ohio and Michigan in the Land Office. The 66-year-old James also feared that his son was becoming a pet of Martin Van Buren (then U.S. vice president and presidential candidate), who James claimed lacked principle and demanded the same of his followers. The older Wadsworth was especially concerned about his son's burgeoning alliance with Van Buren's son, "Major" or "Prince" John Van Buren. Instead, he wanted James Samuel to pay attention to Daniel Webster and John Calhoun, whom the father considered great men. From them he could learn more about national affairs, for the Wadsworths' financial future was in the hands of politicians.[21]

Despite increasing business and wedding concerns, the Wadsworths continued to entertain a steady flow of visitors, including those from across the sea who came to observe the Wadsworths' acclaimed estate and farming practices. One visitor was 28-year-old Charles Augustus Murray, lawyer-son of the fifth Earl of Dunmore. The handsome, adventurous Murray found the Wadsworth estate impressive, but he was more attracted to Elizabeth Wadsworth. Though nine years younger, Elizabeth, whose beauty and vivacity were coming to notice, apparently stole his heart. He asked James for permission to marry her. But, according to the oft-told story, the old man said no; he needed her to serve as nursemaid and hostess of the large manse. This would not end the matter for her—or for her more understanding older brother, however.[22]

Finally James Samuel's courtship came to a successful conclusion on Sunday evening, May 11, 1834, in Philadelphia, when he married Mary Craig Wharton, seven years his junior and universally described as beautiful. The service was conducted by the Right Reverend Bishop William White, presiding bishop of the Episcopal Church in the United States.[23]

The new couple honeymooned in England and on the Continent, carrying letters of introduction to influential Englishmen. Before he left, young Wadsworth, then in Philadelphia, hit on his father, who was fit to be tied, for more money. James had given what he regarded as a considerable sum to his elder son when he left Geneseo. Now he was being called on for $10,000 (over $150,000 today) to cover James Samuel's overdraft on his New York City bank account. James reminded his son that these were not good times. Debts owed the Wadsworths were not being paid. Yet his son was going on an extended European honeymoon while owing $5,000 for property in Columbus, Ohio, with $2,500 plus interest due in one year.[24]

Even on the honeymoon politics interceded. In early March 1835, fellow Geneseoan John Young wrote to James Samuel in London about the national scene, including Martin Van Buren's prospects for the presidency. Then, with a sense of real urgency, Young asked when James Samuel and his bride would be home. Young felt that James Samuel's political prospects demanded that he return home as soon as possible, for his name was not being "mentioned as often as formerly." A month later the younger Van Buren wrote that his father needed James Samuel's support for his presidential bid.[25]

Apparently James Samuel had left the impression that he and his bride would be back in the United States in May. First they had to finish their itinerary, which included a brief trip to Switzerland and Italy, where they saw diplomat and Harvard friend John Lothrop Motley. Back in London on May 20, James Samuel was admitted to the "Committee of the Travellers" Club for the month of June. However, their actual return date may have been dictated at least in part by some medical problem experienced by Mary Craig Wadsworth. Likely, it was pregnancy, for Charles Frederick, the first of their six children, would be born later that year, on October 6, 1835.[26]

Before returning, however, the Wadsworths visited the villa of Lord Hertford in Regent's Park, London, and obtained a copy of the architectural plans of the villa that were used to design their own house. Shortly after their return to Geneseo, they selected a site overlooking the valley at the north end of the village's main street, less than a mile from James Samuel's ancestral home, and began construction.

The structure, called Hartford House, was a two-story, Palladian country-style building with two wings. It was heated by seven fireplaces, four of which were in the main section. Large plaster crown moldings and high ceilings, which would accommodate a 10-foot-high canopy bed, accentuated the size of the structure and reflected the owner's expansive nature. Wealthy Philadelphia socialite and sometime lawyer Sidney George Fisher, who visited in 1836 while the house was under construction, described it as "large and handsome, covered with light grey stucco with a low front, 150 feet long, situated in a park of about 400 acres and commanding an extensive view of the magnificent flats." It was too grand for Fisher's tastes, but there was no denying that Hartford House was—and remains—impressive.[27]

During construction the Wadsworths apparently divided their time between Geneseo and Philadelphia, but James Samuel was fully occupied with business and completion of the house. True to form, he spared no expense. Furnishings included marble mantels and vases, a case of pedestals, and various other items, costing approximately £1,466, or $6,700 (greater than $100,000 today). Wash stands, oil and lead paints, linseed oil, and glass plate totaled another $7,800. Turkish carpets and rugs covered the floors, while evergreens, horse chestnuts, and ornamentals graced the grounds.[28]

It appeared that James Samuel, with a wife, son Charles, and new house, a mansion by most standards, was about to settle down—to the extent that he could.

Chapter 5

"ONE OF THOSE RESTLESS SPIRITS"

Despite his father's repeated warnings about his vanity, hasty judgments, bad companions, and prodigality, James Samuel was ready to make his mark. In many ways his character was still unformed, but Sidney George Fisher, who attended to some of Wadsworth's business in Philadelphia and had visited Geneseo, certainly captures the young man's peripatetic dimension in a journal entry:

> *January 8, 1838* Wadsworth came in & sat for an hour or two. . . . He is a fellow of a great deal of character & ability, and one of those restless spirits who cannot live without excitement. He is always flying from one end of the country to the other, speculating in land, shooting & pursuing all sorts of adventures which life in the backwoods affords. He has just returned from bear hunting in Potter County [Pennsylvania], where he camped out in the forest for several weeks. He married our great beauty Mary Wharton, certainly the handsomest woman I ever saw, & with such a wife, a child, and a large landed estate one would suppose he might be contented to remain at home for a month or two at a time, which however he is never known to do.[1]

Though Fisher tended to be waspish (except when describing Mary Craig Wharton Wadsworth, whom he clearly admired), his rather critical (jealous?) description of James Samuel fit. For example, in a period of six months the older Wadsworth son had signed notes for 8,000 acres on a St. Lawrence River island at an astronomical price of $1,000 per acre, tried to negotiate a $20,000, seven-year loan at 7 percent annually, and paid $7,500 for 24,053 acres in seven northwestern Ohio counties bordering on Indiana and Michigan. In the process he had overextended himself and had unsuccessfully pressed his case with New York City and Philadelphia bankers.[2]

A pattern, if one can ever say Wadsworth had one, was emerging. From outward appearances he and his brother reprised their father's and uncle's roles: James Samuel assumed their father's entrepreneurial role while bachelor brother William worked the farm as his namesake had. To an extent this was accurate, with one major difference—James Samuel was, as Fisher noted, more restless

Holland Land Purchase and Indian reservations
(courtesy of Genesee County Historical Society)

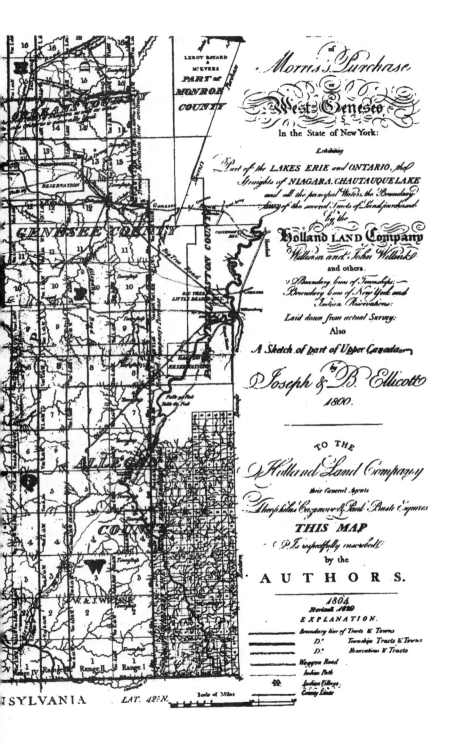

than the father, more high spirited and more erratic. Yet, increasingly, as the father was forced to pull back, the elder son was drawn into the family businesses. Still, the old man would never totally let go of management during his lifetime.

Another pattern was also emerging. In the late fall of 1836, even during his speculation forays, James Samuel, Mary Craig, and infant Charles traveled down to Philadelphia for the winter (late October to early April). Both attended social events, but James Samuel tended to focus on business, primarily trying to obtain loans for his land speculation. While the elder Wadsworth had engaged in similar pursuits virtually his entire adult life, there was a difference. The elder Wadsworth had carefully developed many contacts in the United States as well as in Europe. By contrast, his elder son, consistent with his father's worst fears, lacked the same kinds of contacts. In time he would have that base, building on that of his father, which increasingly involved James Samuel in the game of politics that his father claimed to avoid, but could play well.

Unfortunately, others had the same speculative fever, which resulted in the so-called Panic of 1837. Inflation, fueled by the issuance of paper money and pressure on state banks, forced up both land prices and interest rates. In turn, this led to widespread financial distress and an economic depression that would last almost six years. James Samuel's hope lay with what a business associate called a "free banking system," whereby individuals created a joint stock bank through the purchase of shares and loaned money to the shareholders. James Samuel even approached Nicholas Biddle, former director of the Bank of the United States and Philadelphia's most powerful banker, but was "unsuccessful."[3]

Even though the young speculator was unsuccessful, this suggests the kind of connections he had as a wealthy man married to a woman from a prominent Philadelphia family. This episode also suggests that James Samuel was playing both sides of the street. He was seeking money from the conservative Biddle, while allying himself politically with President Martin Van Buren, who seemed to prefer a more liberal banking system.

James Samuel and his business associates, needing to borrow money to buy lands in Michigan that had risen in value 500 percent, were counting on Van Buren, whom they had supported and who was now in the White House. (Not surprisingly, Wadsworth had disregarded his father's warnings about Van Buren's lack of principles.) However, Van Buren was up to his ears with the recession, abolitionist petitions to Congress, increasing tension with England, and his own reelection. Wadsworth and associates were on their own unless they could create their own bank, from which they could borrow.[4]

Meanwhile, the elder Wadsworth son was pressed on other sides. His 69-year-old father was expecting him to take on even greater responsibilities, but he could not resist telling his son exactly how he ought to attend to business, even to the grinding and bagging of oats and barley in a particular way.[5]

One of these responsibilities was serving as agent for the unscrupulous Ogden Land Company, an activity that reflects unfavorably on both of the Wadsworths. While the whole controversy goes back to the complicated Phelps–Gorham purchase in the latter 1700s, this particular episode, universally condemned as "one of the most flagrant land swindles in New York history," is referred to as the Treaty of Buffalo Creek of 1838. It stemmed from concentrated efforts by settlers and speculators to obtain more land in a strip west of Batavia from the Pennsylvania border to the Niagara River, beginning in 1827 and resulting in close to one hundred separate treaties with the Iroquois. More than 50,000 acres of reservation land, obtained from the Senecas in 1826, were advertised for public sale in 1827. Another 47,000 acres became available the following year. James Wadsworth's office in Geneseo was one of the places accepting bids. Presumably this included the sale of lands by the Senecas. However, beginning in 1837 the Ogden Land Company began negotiations for the remaining reservations. It was at this point that the younger Wadsworth became directly involved. On December 14, 1837, Thomas Ludlow Ogden, successor to David A. Ogden, conferred power of attorney on James Samuel and instructed him to attend (with Joseph Fellows, an Ogden associate) a forthcoming Council to negotiate the purchase of commercially desirable Seneca lands near Buffalo.[6]

How the Wadsworth scion viewed his role is uncertain, but James had clearly revealed his attitude almost two decades earlier. He had then written Thomas Ogden that he was satisfied for the present with the purchases of one-half of the Tonawanda and Buffalo reservations.[7] Moreover, he warned that to negotiate for more would give too much notice to the speculators' plans. He believed the Quakers, whom he regarded as having too much influence over the Senecas, had already created enough problems not only for purchasers, but for the Senecas. If he had any say, he would "civilize" the Senecas in the manner of his English ancestors, not of the Quakers, who had "left the Indians in a worse State than they found them." There is some truth to this, for by 1838 only 5,000 Senecas remained in New York, and they were destitute. The combination of land speculation, encroaching white settlers, declining game, and poverty was forcing the Senecas to sign over their rights to the land. Red Jacket, the famed and aging Seneca orator, fearing the effects, had appealed to the Quakers for protection earlier.[8]

Such was the situation in which James Samuel Wadsworth became heavily involved. From 1834 to 1838 the Federal government had invited committees of Senecas to visit and to migrate to land purchased from the Menominee Indians near Green Bay, Wisconsin. Protests against the Ogdens (and what appeared to be government complicity) by the Quakers aroused the concern of *New York Evening Post* editor William Cullen Bryant and Washington Irving of the *Knickerbocker.* Bryant and Irving contacted Senators Daniel Webster, John Calhoun, and Henry Clay, among others, which led to the appointment of U.S. Commissioner Ransom Gillet to oversee the Treaty of Buffalo Creek negotiations.[9]

Attorney Wadsworth's role remains rather vague and while he was pursuing other projects at the same time, he was active in the negotiations, including securing the services of the venerable Horatio Jones to assist as interpreter. In response, Jones assured his employer that he had induced not only a majority, but three-quarters of the old (Revolutionary War) chiefs to sign. This would assure ratification of the Treaty by the U.S. Senate, which had to approve any deal. However, word that alcohol and outright bribery had induced the chiefs to agree to the Treaty led to more protracted negotiations involving the Senecas, the Federal government, and the state of Massachusetts, which appointed its adjutant general, H. A. S. Dearborn, to attend a July 10, 1838, meeting. This caused a flurry of letters between Wadsworth, Thomas Ogden, Joseph Fellows, and the Ogden Land Company trustees about how to proceed.[10]

Wadsworth, who visited Buffalo a second time because of the delays, believed Jones had misrepresented the number of chiefs who had signed the Treaty. James Samuel also questioned the expenses incurred by the Ogdens in paying what amounted to bribes to various parties to the negotiations, including Commissioner Gillet, Adjutant General Dearborn, and others.

What appeared to be the final crisis in the negotiations was word that Secretary of War Joel R. Poinsett intended to visit the Cattaraugus Reservation in early August of 1839. Ogden wanted Wadsworth to go to Buffalo as soon as he could to carefully watch and to give "the proper spirit" to the emigration of the Senecas. In preparation Ogden wanted to meet with James Samuel in Geneseo, where they both could profit from the elder Wadsworth's suggestions. Before then, as the younger Wadsworth had advised, the two Wadsworths should confer with Commissioner Gillet and Fellows in Geneva.[11]

From Buffalo in late August James Samuel informed one of the Ogden negotiators that on behalf of the land company he had authorized the payment of up to $8,000 to signers of the Treaty. Whether this makes Wadsworth an accessory to the bribery for which Ogden and Fellows are castigated by historians and a subsequent state investigation is unclear. He claimed he was simply holding the negotiators to "strict accountability," spreading a total of between $500 and $3,000 to each of the chiefs. But he acknowledged that the negotiators themselves were diverting funds intended for the chiefs. One person diverting funds was interpreter Horatio Jones, whom Wadsworth had personally recommended.[12]

In short, agent Wadsworth wanted the proprietors of the Ogden Land Company to know their money was being misappropriated by some of the company's negotiators, Commissioner Gillet, and others. However, apparently he saw nothing wrong with bribing the chiefs to sell their reservation lands.

Ogden then asked James Samuel to meet with Secretary Poinsett in Washington to explain what appeared to be the bribery of Commissioner Gillet. Wadsworth dined with Poinsett and President Van Buren at the latter's invitation and discussed the Treaty negotiations, despite Van Buren's claim that he did not want to do so, which could taint the proceedings. Ultimately, a commission was appointed to oversee the negotiations, concerning which attorney-agent Wadsworth advised Thomas Ogden to avoid discussion that might raise other concerns about the validity of the Treaty. However, he suggested submitting to the commission empowered to review the Treaty three points of information: (1) explanation of the allegations of fraud in procuring signatures, (2) reasons for failure to achieve unanimity among the Seneca chiefs, and (3) difficulties in achieving the removal of the Senecas within the stipulated time frame.[13]

On December 10, 1839, Wadsworth, on his way to Buffalo for two to three weeks, offered further advice, namely, to withhold unwarranted payments to individuals whom the Ogdens had contracted to negotiate for them. The payments nearly doubled the land purchase price.

He could not escape his responsibilities even in Philadelphia, where he was spending the summer of 1840. There he was hounded for $5,000 by an Ogden negotiator who had not specified how the money was to be spent. Even so, he assured Ogden that the total payments by the company to obtain the Seneca's sale of the lands (to negotiators and chiefs and for the actual property) were not expected to exceed $60,000 to $70,000. This left a balance of $155,000, which Ogden should advise him about spending. Then, in October James Samuel was castigated by the Indian missionary Asher Wright. Wright claimed that unnamed negotiators for the Ogdens were alleging that Wadsworth had paid "hush money" to members of Wright's presbytery so the latter would not reveal the Ogdens' underhanded dealings. Wadsworth was asked to testify that no money had been paid to members of the presbytery and to provide particulars. Apparently Wadsworth satisfied Wright, for there is no more correspondence about this matter.[14]

Whatever James Samuel's role, it remains that his involvement in the whole sorry episode with the Ogden Land Company does little to contribute to his image as a statesman.

Yet, throughout his life his varied associations make it difficult to draw a simple characterization of him. For example, in June 1837 the 29-year-old attended an Agricultural Society meeting near Boston. Luminaries included former U.S. President John Quincy Adams and his son, Charles Francis Adams, Supreme Court Associate Justice Joseph Story, Massachusetts Governor Edward Everett, and Josiah Quincy III, president of Harvard (from which Wadsworth had been expelled less than a decade earlier). Later that year, along with future New York State Governor John Young and Geneseo banker Allen Ayrault, Wadsworth was a county delegate to a Friends of Internal Improvements Convention. Improved roads and a canal were among the projects discussed.[15]

The restless Wadsworth also welcomed a second child, Cornelia, born in 1839 and named for his sister who had died so young. He continued to engage in an expensive social life (which included spending almost $600 for a shipment of Madeira wine) and juggled more land transactions. Not even a "churchyard cough" (or "death rattle") at one point seemed to limit his activities, which included managing his and his father's farms (though his brother was largely responsible for the latter), avoiding a duel with a sometime business associate, W. S. Church, and becoming entangled in politics that would set the course for the rest of his life.[16]

The extent of his political activities at the time was revealed in a letter from *Atlantic Monthly* founder-editor Nathaniel Parker Willis. Willis was incredulous over his friend's latest political involvement: "What the devil has a thorough-paced aristocrat like you to do with democracy . . . I can no more fancy *you* 'writing loco-foco resolutions' than I can fancy your divine wife incident to the ills of common clay." It seems James Samuel, who had invited Willis to visit, had mentioned his involvement with the radical urban wing of Jacksonian Democrats, which was promptly dubbed "loco-focos" after the newly introduced, self-igniting, friction matches. At a rancorous October 1834 Tammany Hall meeting in New York City the radicals countered the regular Democrats' platform by advocating the abolition of monopolies and special privileges, hard money, direct popular vote, direct taxes, and free trade. When the regulars attempted to adjourn the meeting by dowsing the gas lights, the radicals lit candles with the new matches and nominated their own ticket.[17]

James Samuel had also written President Van Buren about a meeting of young Democrats in Livingston County and had received a reply expressing the president's belief that James Samuel was a man of high principles, not simply an office-seeker. Barely two months later Henry P. Gilpin, a Pennsylvanian who shortly would become Van Buren's attorney general, enthusiastically responded to Wadsworth's declaration that he soon would be a candidate for office. In what would seem a particularly ironic assertion, Gilpin stated that if a truly democratic Union was to succeed, those, like Wadsworth, who were influential must put an end to "the power of associated wealth."[18]

While the younger Wadsworth's incipient political leanings may have seemed incongruous, he was, in fact, adhering to his father's belief (and actions) that wealth and ability to lead should be directed toward the preservation of a democratic society. Whatever the motivation, James Samuel, "more genial and more ardent than the father," increasingly was forming a political conviction that would come to consume him.[19] For example, in late November 1839, from home he wrote his Allegany County friend "Capt. Church," with whom a runaway slave was living, that the slave's story had "excited our sympathy." But, for legal and political reasons, he advised Church not to employ the runaway. Then, while in Washington, the Wadsworth scion interceded with the executor of the estate of the runaway's former owner and concluded that the only solution was for some of Wadsworth's friends to purchase the runaway.

While it would be another twenty years before James Samuel Wadsworth would call himself an abolitionist, he was already showing some signs.[20]

Still, he found time for other things, including a family trip with Mary Craig, Cornelia, and his two sons, Charles Frederick and Craig Wharton, in late May 1841, to attend Harvard commencement and a soiree at President Josiah Quincy's. First, however, he conferred with Dr. Charles Meigs about Mary Craig's wound and pain in the heart, which may have been caused by swallowing a needle. Like his father, James Samuel looked to advances in medicine, but he was told that the needle could be extracted only by an incision, not by a magnet, as he had hoped. Also on July 1 that year, along with his brother and William A. Mills, founder of the village of Mount Morris, he helped form the Livingston County Agricultural Society, of which he became one of the vice presidents. Not surprisingly, the fair was held in Geneseo, with an overflow of exhibits in the adjacent courthouse.[21]

Barely six months later, James Samuel vaulted to the presidency of the New York State Agricultural Society, having been elected unanimously at the annual meeting on January 19, 1842, though he had not been present. The Society's secretary, Luther Tucker, editor of Rochester's *Genesee Farmer*, hoped he would accept the office and bring to it the influence his eminence offered. (Without taking anything away from James Samuel, the election to the Society's presidency was more due the father and may well have been an oblique way of honoring him.) No doubt Tucker was anticipating that the Wadsworths could help the Society match the $700 it received from state funds by encouraging private subscriptions. He was not disappointed, for James Samuel, who agreed to serve, raised $2,000, almost three times the required amount, some of which funded essays on topics such as varieties of wheat and diseases injurious to the wheat crop.[22]

At one of the monthly meetings of the Society's executive committee during Wadsworth's tenure, an annual state fair was instituted to meet in Albany on September 27–29, 1842. At that fair the new president, his brother, and sister managed to walk off with prize money for their stock and flowers, the latter in competition with Elwanger and Barry, Rochester's preeminent nursery. One of his duties as president of the state society was to attend not only the monthly meetings of the executive committee in Albany, but also the national meeting in Washington on May 1, 1842, as one of three western New York delegates. Less than two years later he was made an honorary member of the Philadelphia Society for Promoting Agriculture. This honor would bring greater out-of-state recognition, though it distracted him from far more important matters.[23]

Meanwhile, old James's failing health led him to propose to his two sons on November 19, 1841, that they take charge of his office, whereby one or the other would pass an hour a day there. This would prove irksome for the older son, who disliked being cooped up in an office for even an hour a day. (They would even learn to use their father's large 11"-by-17" leather-bound Letterbooks and would create their own in which their clerks would inscribe copies of correspondence.) The old man reserved the right to execute deeds and to sell their old farms. Edward R. Hammatt, James Samuel's Whig political ally and later his Home Farm manager, was responsible for selling land in and out of the village, subject to the brothers' approval.[24]

The sons, who were to "consult [with James] in important sales," were authorized to draw from the balance in their father's Rochester bank account when it was necessary to remit funds to New York or to other business concerns. However, James reminded them that they were only acting as his agents and should confer with him when they disagreed, which he fully expected. James Samuel and William were expected to benefit from conducting their father's office business. James's need to have a finger in the pie was vintage Wadsworth, notwithstanding that he was 73 years old, his health was failing, and he was even more prickly than usual. This agency relationship represented the last will and testament for the business to which James had devoted over a half century and that now would devolve primarily on his elder son.

In the final three years of his life the old man was going to indulge himself, increasingly requiring James Samuel to manage his vast estate (extending over thirty linear miles) and the philanthropies he was establishing. Nevertheless, he continued to offer fatherly advice to his elder son. For example, while in Philadelphia in late November 1843, the son was reminded that, as a trustee of the newly created Atheneum Library in Geneseo, he should familiarize himself with modern books and libraries generally, and obtain a list of recent purchases of Philadelphia's Franklin Library and a copy of its loan policy. He could render important service by devoting even a few hours to the elder's fledgling Atheneum. His father also suggested that he should "get up a Lecture on the decomposition of the atmosphere and of water & perform some of the manipulations" himself, if he were to be a "modern scientific farmer." Finally, James Samuel was advised to find suitable schools for his two older children, for a good education was indispensable to a bright future.[25]

The demands on the elder son were inversely proportional to the health of his increasingly crotchety father. For example, James wanted James Samuel to bring him a "vapor bath" and to consult a homeopathic physician (in whom, however, the old man had only limited confidence). Yet, in his last letter to James Samuel, the final point was a request to find out about tar and other paints for fences on the flats, particularly the "best kind of cheap paint."[26]

James Samuel tried to comply with his father's demands, conduct his own business, and, now, oversee that of his brother William, which would nominally be in the care of clerk William Cushing. Brother William intended "to pass a year or two in Europe."[27] Conduct of his brother's business would consume even more of James Samuel's time before the decade was out.

Because of William's absence, the elder son's peripatetic nature, and the characteristic Wadsworth male dominance, the burdens of serving as nursemaid to and hostess for the old man fell to Elizabeth. However, she needed her adored brother's help. At one point she wanted him to attend to an urgent request from William, the tourist, for $1,000 without their father learning about it. Shortly thereafter, in a note with a desperate tone to it, she asked James Samuel, then in Philadelphia, to talk to and, if possible, escort a Dr. Post to Geneseo. Their irritable father was relying on inexperienced doctors who were experimenting on him. Yet, as much as she wanted her brother home, she feared the effect of his return on their father, who was railing against James Samuel's perceived neglect of him.[28]

Despite the ministrations of his devoted Elizabeth and various doctors, James Wadsworth died on June 7, 1844, at age 76, having outlived his two brothers, his wife, and two daughters. He left a burdensome legacy to his sons, primarily to James Samuel—carrying on the magnificent ancestral estate, the extensive Wadsworth businesses, and the family name while caring for his younger sister. Typically, there were few immediate signs that the elder son felt the burden. Only later would he hand down the same advice to his children as his father had and in a similar tone.

Chapter 6

"INTELLIGENT ENTERPRIZE & INDUSTRY"

James S. Wadsworth, whose passionate nature and inattention to business had so worried his father, was now being called on, much like his sire, to play the role of public-spirited citizen. The Wadsworth wealth, so consciously and laboriously earned by the father, now thrust his elder son into positions of authority and influence, just as his father had anticipated. James Samuel seemed to revel in his newly acquired status.

Even before his father's will was admitted to probate on September 9, 1844, the nature of the legacy began to sink in. As a trustee with his brother, now back from Europe, and brother-in-law Martin Brimmer, James Samuel was administering the estate his father had spent over fifty years building. Put briefly, Elizabeth would receive use of the family's Mansion House during her life, its library, engravings, pictures, furniture, horses and carriages, the 150 acres on which the house was located, the original Big Tree Farm, and a quarter of all her father's personal property in trust. James Samuel and William were each granted half of all the remaining real estate in the Towns of Geneseo and Avon, a quarter each of all their father's personal property and real estate located elsewhere, and all the horses, cattle, and sheep not located at the Mansion House. The final quarter of James's personal property and real estate located outside Geneseo and Avon was to be in trust for his minor grandson, Martin Brimmer, Jr.[1]

With his usual zest, James Samuel divided his time for the next half dozen years between familial, financial, and political affairs, though not equally. Initially, he plunged into his duties as trustee even before the will was probated, but he was advised by fellow trustee and brother-in-law Brimmer, a businessman and former Boston mayor, to take out letters of administration and to let Brimmer help more. No doubt aware of James Samuel's impetuosity and prodigality, Brimmer also warned his brother-in-law not to take on more responsibility than necessary, nor exceed his authority nor make decisions that would embarrass himself or the family.[2]

Even while reading and responding to highly flattering memorials to his father, the newly designated head of the family was playing the political game with élan. Likely as a result of his father's efforts on behalf of education, he was appointed by the State Legislature to the New York State Board of Regents, the educational policy-making body of the state, just a month before his father's death. In fact, the flurry of political activity in which he was becoming engaged would mark a major transition in his life.[3]

The contrast between the father's and son's attitudes toward politics could not have been greater. The elder son exercised none of the father's customary caution toward what the old man labeled the "vile business" of politics. Rather, the Wadsworth scion was jumping in with both feet, though it is more accurate to say he was constantly being drawn in because of his wealth and contacts. During the past three years he had helped defray the Democratic Party's campaign expenses and had advised and interceded on behalf of congressional candidate John Van Buren, but he had declined an offer to run for secretary of state of New York. The offer, suggesting the ensuing opportunity for higher office, may have been a ploy, based on James Samuel's claimed lack of political ambition and inveterate restlessness.[4]

With the New York Democratic Party in disarray, a number of state and local officials counted on James Samuel's partisanship, energy, and money to help assure its success. They also warned him against supporting Martin Van Buren for a second term, because of opposition from within and without the party.[5]

Despite the warning, Wadsworth supported Van Buren, including (at Van Buren's urging) pledging $500 to sustain the failing Democrat political organ, the Albany *Atlas,* and writing letters to other would-be subscribers. However, the Democratic Party rejected Van Buren and nominated former Tennessee governor and dark-horse candidate James K. Polk for the presidency. This prompted Wadsworth to explode in a letter to Van Buren. Wadsworth wrote that he was "prostrated" and outraged by the selfish South, which had "filled the Executive Chair 44 years" and had extended slavery at every turn. Nonetheless, he swallowed his anger long enough to support Polk's election and to lay bets on it. His wagers paid off. Then, according to local lore, he used his winnings to install log pipes to bring water from a spring outside Geneseo to the reservoir on Main Street that he had constructed for village use.[6]

With characteristic restlessness James Samuel turned from politics long enough to check on land in Wisconsin, where he was flooded by letters from his sister Elizabeth. In her correspondence she revealed not only her strong affection for him, but also the extent to which he dominated her life. This was despite the fact that she regularly entertained visitors, including would-be suitors, and was proving surprisingly (because of Wadsworth male dominance over business affairs) capable of managing the large estate she had inherited.[7]

Beginning in 1846, politics, including a flood of requests for money, came to dominate James Samuel Wadsworth's correspondence, if not his life. The Democrats were at a crossroads. James Samuel, the younger Van Buren, and others were embarked on a radical course, one that Wadsworth (but not Van Buren) would take to its inevitable conclusion—abolitionism, support of the Republican Party, the election of Abraham Lincoln, and the Civil War.[8]

Because of Wadsworth's political antipathy toward the South, which he believed had extended slavery at every opportunity, it is important to examine his participation in events that would alter history, beginning with the quarrels among New York's Democrats. The conservative wing of the state Democratic Party, led by former New York governor William Marcy (then Polk's secretary of war), likened Wadsworth and the other radicals to "Barnburners" (imitators of the fabled Dutch farmer who burned his own barn to rid it of rats). The radicals countered by calling Marcy and his followers "Hunkers," from the Dutch word *hunkerer* (one hunkering or hankering for office). While slavery was the central issue dividing the state Democrats, the immediate dispute was over the Hunker-dominated legislature's canal policy in the mid-1840s, one feature of which was to stop payment for canal construction. Wadsworth, in common with many western New Yorkers, viewed construction of the Genesee Valley Canal, begun less than a decade earlier, as necessary for economic survival.[9]

By 1847, there were no fewer than five divisions in the state election that year, including the Barnburners and Hunkers, the Anti-renters and Nativist Americans dividing the Whigs, and the Abolitionists. The 40-year-old Wadsworth was regarded as an influence in party councils, but he was not averse to helping fellow Geneseoan John Young, a Whig, in his successful gubernatorial race.[10]

The extent to which James Samuel was committed was illustrated by the bitter, five-day contest in Syracuse between the two major factions of the Democratic Party in late September 1847. The Barnburners, also called "Soft Shells," included Wadsworth, John Van Buren, William Cullen Bryant, Samuel Tilden, and David Dudley Field. The first fight with the Hunkers ("Hard Shells") was over the seating of delegates at the Democratic Convention to nominate state and Federal candidates for the 1848 elections. This led to a verbal duel between Wadsworth and an individual identified only as "a Hunker." The latter's remarks reportedly ignited Wadsworth, who leaped onto a table from which he shouted that the Hunkers were assassins. Their unwillingness to support incumbent governor Silas Wright, a respected Barnburner, had led to his untimely death. Wadsworth's outburst brought cheers, hisses, and calls for order. More importantly, Wadsworth's ardor impressed editor Bryant and lawyer Field, who became his allies during the even more acrid 1860 presidential campaign.[11]

The issue that permanently divided the party and resulted in a pitched battle arose over the party platform, specifically the Barnburners' resolution to support the Wilmot Proviso. The proviso, introduced by David Wilmot, a Pennsylvania congressman, as an amendment to a bill funding negotiations with Mexico, would have barred slavery in the territory acquired from Mexico after the Mexican War. After a riotous, around-the-clock debate, Wadsworth was heard shouting above the din, "Why this cowardice and recreancy? Are the gentlemen afraid to meet this question?" This led to the Hunkers' departure to prevent a roll call vote and the Barnburners' call for a state convention to be held in Herkimer on October 26, signaling a permanent rupture in the party. Wadsworth, despite encouragement to do so, did not attend, contributing $500 instead. Nor did he accept John Van Buren's offer to nominate him for lieutenant governor. However, he was now viewed as openly anti-slavery.[12]

While politics dominated, they did not occupy all of Squire Wadsworth's time—or money. Less than a year earlier he had been elected a trustee of the newly chartered University of Rochester, which was touted as western New York's university and which needed $140,000 to get off the ground. A strong supporter of education like his father, James Samuel pledged $1,000 then. But, ever the businessman, he later indicated he would enlarge his pledge if the university authorities located the school on a piece of land in which he had invested.[13] About the same time he was elected to a committee to explore the possibility of constructing a plank road from Hornellsville (about twenty-five miles south of Geneseo) through Geneseo to Rochester. And in April 1847, along with other Geneseoans, he donated 1,000 bushels of corn at more than 50¢ a bushel to a committee formed to receive contributions for the relief of the Irish famine.[14]

Strangely, the April 25, 1847, death of his 54-year-old brother-in-law, Martin Brimmer, did not result in any reported reaction by Wadsworth. At least there is no correspondence to reveal Wadsworth's feelings. This is particularly surprising, given their personal relationship and the former Boston mayor's faithful correspondence with James Samuel over the years. Moreover, Brimmer, who had helped conduct much of the Wadsworth family business for over two decades, was co-executor of James Wadsworth's estate. Finally, now James Samuel was the primary executor of his father's will and of the trust set up for Brimmer's son, a minor.[15]

James Samuel's behavior then, as always, is difficult to explain. Perhaps failure to record any reaction to Brimmer's death was the result of politics interceding; perhaps he let politics intercede. Correspondents, particularly "Prince" John Van Buren, outgoing New York state comptroller, were urging him to take an even larger role in state politics, beyond the money he was pledging and letters he was writing, despite his repeated refusals to run for office.[16]

Meanwhile, the reluctant candidate's attention was drawn to an urgent letter, dated December 3, 1847, from Reuben Walworth, a Saratoga Springs congressman. According to Walworth, William Wadsworth's mind "was very excited in relation to property." It was imperative that James Samuel persuade William to "go into some retreat for the insane & put himself under the care of those who understand the subject." Walworth advised that it would be injurious to commit William, who already believed his brother wished to restrain him improperly, but something had to be done immediately. William's wife, Emmeline, dared not do it, but maybe their sister Elizabeth could. Whoever did it, something had to be done about William to prevent further calamity, an apparent reference to mismanagement of his funds.[17]

Reminiscent of his father, who could appear insensitive, James Samuel did not let William's situation prevent him from taking a late February trip to Washington, where he enjoyed an animated discussion with Senator Henry Clay about farming and cattle. Nor did he forego attending the National Democratic Convention in Baltimore in May. Split over the issue of slavery, New York's Democrats had sent two sets of delegates to Baltimore, where the convention refused to seat the Barn-burners. Thus, they held their own convention in Utica in June, which drew considerable attention to Wadsworth, one of the speakers. Maryland politician-journalist and future cabinet member Francis P. Blair, who had read James Samuel's speech, wrote him, praising his efforts to purify the party and champion the cause of democracy. According to Blair, Wadsworth's simple, forceful, even elegant message would strongly impress readers. Curiously, Blair did not regard Wadsworth as an abolitionist, a "Negro lover." Rather, Blair believed the New Yorker had correctly focused on the need to extend the country's prosperity.[18]

Perhaps emboldened by the attention he was getting, Wadsworth called for a July 4 meeting of Livingston County residents who opposed the extension of slavery. He was also being pressured by the Barnburners, who had joined dissident New England Whigs, at a Buffalo convention of Whigs and others calling themselves Free Soilers. There he supported Martin Van Buren's election over the Whig candidate, Mexican War hero Zachary Taylor, and Democratic candidate Lewis Cass. Despite the efforts of Wadsworth and others who had been warned, the outcome was foreordained—another four years in the White House for what Wadsworth regarded as a united South.[19]

James Samuel's growing influence led to his appointment by New York governor Hamilton Fish to serve as one of eight unpaid commissioners to plan a state agricultural college and experimental farm. The outcome was the agricultural college at Ovid, the state's first public college, which would become the foundation for the agricultural school at Cornell University in Ithaca. Also in 1849, along with other prominent Livingston and Erie County businessmen and public officials, he became involved in routing the New York and Erie Railroad, discussions of which piqued his interest in iron manufacturing. [20]

✯   ✯   ✯

Now, at midcentury, the 41-year-old Wadsworth comfortably wore the mantle of Squire, with an estate that rivaled any in New York and a large, extended family. His family now included his attractive, socially prominent wife, Mary Craig, and their six children: Charles Frederick, born in 1835, Cornelia (1839), Craig Wharton (1841), Nancy Wharton (1843), James Wolcott (1846), and Elizabeth (1848). Additionally he was helping manage the finances of his brother William.[21]

Still, Wadsworth found time to entertain, much as his father had. In late October 1848, Philadelphian Sidney George Fisher came ostensibly to see James

Samuel, but no doubt also to see Mary Craig Wadsworth and Wadsworth's sister, Elizabeth, whom he admired. Fisher found Wadsworth's estate located in "a beautiful, rich & well-cultivated country," which featured diverse trees, fertile soil, fat cattle and sheep, luxuriant wheat, and prosperous homes and residents. The peripatetic Squire, who reflected the area's "intelligent enterprize & industry," met Fisher six miles from Geneseo. The Squire was on his way to make a stump speech, but he promised to return the next day.

Returning to the valley after twelve years, Fisher was impressed by changes in Hartford House. Protected by empty lots and approachable by a public road some 400–500 yards in front, the house, with its large rooms, costly furniture, and complement of good servants, reflected the owner's good taste. Even the view from the huge house's back porch, overlooking the flats, was labeled "superb" by Fisher.[22] In short, James Samuel seemed to have all that any man could want.

However, luxuriating was not the restless Wadsworth's style. In late November of 1850, James Samuel accompanied his sister Elizabeth and chambermaid Mary Greene to England. He was giving Elizabeth away to Charles Murray, almost twenty years after old James had peremptorily quashed any such union. A spectacular wedding ensued, appropriate to the standing of the bride and groom, but the return trip was a nightmare for Wadsworth and for his family anxiously awaiting his return.[23]

Wadsworth's ship *Atlantic* left Liverpool on December 28 in a gale that worsened by 6:30 P.M. on January 6, when, in midocean, the main shaft of the starboard engine broke and overlapped the other shaft, causing its engine to stall. After the crew set the icy sails and lashed the wheel, James Samuel and others aboard waited for the wind to abate or change direction, both of which occurred three days later. The ship, now 180 miles south and 70 miles west off course, headed toward Halifax, Nova Scotia. Then it was hit by a southwester that forced it to return to England. On January 22, three weeks after setting sail, the *Atlantic* dropped anchor in Cork Harbor, Ireland, within 230 miles of where it started. A relieved James Samuel boarded the ship *Cambria* at Liverpool on February 4, and finally arrived in New York City approximately two weeks later.[24]

James Samuel's anxious sister and her new husband rejoiced at learning of his safe arrival. However, nothing could compare with the reception Wadsworth experienced when he arrived in Geneseo on Saturday, March 1. His return was celebrated by discharges of cannon that shook the village and surrounding country, the ringing of bells, and bonfires that lit Geneseo's streets as bright as day. The event was culminated by his narration of the ordeal at the American Hotel on Main Street. Equally enthusiastic neighbors in Mount Morris also fired cannon. The only noticeable effect on Wadsworth of his harrowing experience was his suddenly white hair.[25]

During his absence there were two reminders of his political influence. The first came from Azariah Flagg. He and General John Dix, both former secretaries of state in New York, wanted James Samuel to run for governor. Their appeal was that Wadsworth, a respected and prosperous citizen, could represent the liberal wing of the Democratic Party and through his office distribute patronage.

True to form, James Samuel demurred. The second apparently was a request by Henry Randall, ultimately the successful Democratic candidate for New York secretary of state, for advice and support. In the nearly illegible handwriting to which the Wadsworths seemed particularly prone, he belatedly and facetiously acknowledged that a favor might accrue if Randall were elected—and expressed his support.[26]

Business and family matters also greeted James Samuel's return. The Livingston County Bank's charter was due to run out and by law could not be renewed. Further, its capital had already proved inadequate for Wadsworth and other Geneseo businessmen. His efforts to sell stock subscriptions for a new bank were so successful that on April 21, 1850, when the Genesee Valley Bank was created, he was promptly named president and member of the board of directors. About this time he also became one of fifteen incorporators of the University of Buffalo and one of eight shareholders in the Marine Bank of Buffalo. From the latter he hoped to obtain a return on his investment in the construction of a plank road running east from Buffalo, in which he had plunged $5,000.[27]

James Samuel's generosity and influence also provided comfort to the local Roman Catholics, toward whom Geneseoans apparently were inhospitable. Without a place for their services, Mass and the sacraments were administered by visiting priests in the Concert Hall on Main Street or in private homes. Even the county courthouse was used until Geneseo banker Allen Ayrault, "a prominent 'Know-Nothing,'" challenged the use of a public building for worship. According to local legend, while riding down Main Street, Wadsworth, an Episcopalian, spotted the Catholics huddled in the rain at a fence corner, worshipping. He asked his coach driver what was happening. After receiving the answer, the Squire of Geneseo is reported to have said, "It is a shame. Certainly they could do no harm to the building [the courthouse]."[28] Thereupon he informed the visiting priest that he would deed the congregation a lot for payment of $1 and loan them $500 to begin construction on their own church. The deed was given to Bishop John Timon of the Buffalo diocese on August 19, 1851.[29] Thus, Squire Wadsworth is largely responsible for the existence of St. Mary's Church, which today sits across the street from the driveway entrance to his Hartford House.

While ironic, it reveals the character of the Wadsworths. James Samuel's father had raised and donated money to—and his uncle had superintended construction of—the first Presbyterian church in Geneseo in 1816, in which James Samuel's mother, Naomi, became a member two years later. But neither his father nor his uncle was a member and, again according to local legend, they refused to attend services there after a minister objected to their behavior—and they became Episcopalians. The Wadsworths were public-spirited, but also willful.

Then, once more, James Samuel's attention was directed to his family. The first, a seemingly minor matter, to which he appeared to give little notice—for this was Mary Craig's domain—was the conduct of his 16-year-old son Charles. Apparently Mary Craig had written her sister-in-law Elizabeth Wadsworth Murray that the errant son was smoking cigars and playing billiards in the village. No doubt old James would have viewed this as the sins of the father visiting the son and would have wondered whether 10-year-old Craig ("Tick"), who was attending the local academy, would be similarly tempted.

A far greater concern of James Samuel's was the health of his brother William, which had deteriorated to the point that William's wife, Emmeline, and his sister Elizabeth were preparing for the worst. Then soon thereafter Elizabeth's health became the family's main concern. Doctors in Egypt, where the Murrays resided, had determined that there was nothing more they could do for "Lizzie," who had recently delivered Charles James Murray. (The middle name reflected Elizabeth's veneration for her adored older brother.) James Samuel was asked by Elizabeth's husband, Charles, to prepare Mary Craig for the bad news, which came on December 5, 1851. The beautiful, ill-starred, but irrepressible Elizabeth had died.[30]

Then, a little more than seven months later, brother William, not yet 42, also was dead.[31] Like his father, William had delayed marriage until he was 36. Three children resulted from his marriage to Emmeline Austin: William Austin Wadsworth, born in 1847, Livingston, born two years later, and Herbert in 1851. The exact cause of William's death is not recorded, but generally it—and the aberrant behavior about which James Samuel had been informed by Reuben Walworth previously—is attributed to a fall on the ice on his Street Farm six years earlier.[32]

So, Squire James Samuel Wadsworth, at age 45, was the sole survivor of settler James Wadsworth's family, which, counting Uncle Bill, had once numbered eight. Elizabeth's death compounded James Samuel's responsibilities as the sole trustee of his father's will, which now included Elizabeth's "Mansion House," its contents, and surrounding land, which would normally devolve on Elizabeth's husband and infant son. However, because state law still forbade aliens to hold land, James Samuel, showing what Charles Murray regarded as "great kindness & liberality," purchased the farm from the latter for $37,000.[33]

Again, as with earlier deaths in his family, the record is barren of any reaction by James Samuel, except for his notation on Elizabeth's October letter to Mary Craig: "From Cairo last letter from my dear sister . . ."[34] This is one of those points in his life where he was particularly enigmatic. He could help his grieving brother-in-law financially, but there is no evidence that he offered emotional help—or sought any.

Chapter 7

"MY OBLIGATIONS TO MY COUNTRY . . . ARE MANIFEST"

In eight short years, James Samuel's role had shifted from eldest son to sole survivor of the family that James Wadsworth had labored to make comfortable and worthy of the name. And ineluctably the new Squire was drawn back to politics. His fiery speech after leaping on the table at the Barnburners' convention in 1847, which had so impressed newsman William Cullen Bryant and stormy lawyer David Dudley Field, was only a portent of what was to come.

For a time the compromise between the two New York Democratic factions brokered by John Van Buren after the 1848 election held, though the radical "Free Soilers" (formerly the Barnburners) sought the upper hand. The Whigs were in retreat, never to hold power again, while the Democrats had abandoned the Jeffersonian-Jacksonian tradition. In fact, the only thing that united the diverse factions was opposition to The Compromise of 1850.

This momentous legislation had resulted from a series of five resolutions the senatorial triumvirate of Henry Clay, Daniel Webster, and John Calhoun (all of whom would be dead within two years) had offered the nation as a relief from secession threats. The resolutions, labeled collectively The Compromise of 1850, included admission of California as a free state, popular sovereignty (the right to permit or deny slavery) for the territories of New Mexico and Utah, Federal enforcement of the return of fugitive slaves, and abolition of the slave trade in the District of Columbia. Lewis Cass and Stephen Douglas supported the compromise. New York's senator and former governor William H. Seward, supporter of the Wilmot Proviso, which would have barred slavery in the land acquired after the Mexican War, reflected New York's—and Wadsworth's—opposition to any constitutional protection of slavery.[1]

Wanting to influence the direction of the 1852 Democratic National Convention that would take place in Baltimore, Horatio Seymour, formerly a "Hard Shell" Democrat, or Hunker, and now a prospective gubernatorial candidate, was hard at work in New York State. New York, which continued to be a key player in national politics, would hold its convention in Syracuse in September. Seymour had written James Samuel in May that it was imperative that the New York Democrats show a united front if they were to achieve a victory in the 1852 election.

He urged Wadsworth to attend the state convention with Buffalo's Dean Richmond, a future state Democratic Party chairman, because a counsel of "cool & dispassionate men" would be needed. Seymour, with whom Wadsworth had been linked (often in conflict) since their admission to the bar twenty years earlier, was employing the persuasive, conciliatory manner for which he was known. Clearly, this was an attempt to restrain Wadsworth's impetuousness and draw him into the fold. At this point Wadsworth was viewed as a viable candidate for governor, whether due to his earlier speeches or the machinations of those who liked his style and money. Former governor William Marcy, Seymour's mentor, also was counting on Wadsworth's support of Seymour and played on Wadsworth's principles. Marcy wrote that he was satisfied Wadsworth would not allow his name to be placed in nomination for governor and hoped Wadsworth would line up delegates for Seymour. Less than three weeks later Marcy was up in arms over attempts by opponents to subvert Seymour's gubernatorial candidacy and urged Wadsworth to attend the convention.[2]

Three days after the convention Marcy again wrote Wadsworth, who had not attended. Marcy feared Wadsworth would not be pleased by the party's nomination of Seymour, who would be elected governor, nor with the election of Franklin Pierce as president. His apprehensions were not groundless. In fact, the internecine warfare among the convention delegates over the issue of slavery would end in the permanent defection of Wadsworth and a number of influential members from the Democratic Party.

However, momentarily Wadsworth was distracted from politics.

Among the distractions were construction of a railroad line from Avon, north of Geneseo, to Mount Morris, southwest across the flats, capitalization of a county livestock association, additions to his house, and a European trip. The rail construction, in 1852, came about because an attempt the previous year to raise $200,000 for a company through subscriptions (of which $20,000 was expected to come from Wadsworth and other Geneseo investors) had failed. This time the group was successful. Upon the formation of that new company in the summer of 1852, Wadsworth, already director of the Genesee Valley Bank and various other organizations, was duly elected a director of the Genesee Valley Railroad Company. (However, after completing construction to Mount Morris, the new railroad failed and the rights to the line were sold to what became the Erie Railroad.)[3]

An anecdote related to the need for such a rail line also characterizes the hardy and impetuous temperament of Wadsworth. A stage line ran south from the city of Rochester through Geneseo. Because of notoriously bad roads and frequent stops, the trip took about twelve hours. One time Wadsworth and a fellow traveler mounted the stage in downtown Rochester and rode to what locals still call Methodist Hill, some seven to eight miles south. There Wadsworth "got out, said he could walk to Geneseo [something like twenty-two miles] and get there before the stage." True to his word, he and his traveling companion beat the stage by an hour and a half.[4]

Other Wadsworth characteristics were again revealed about the same time: his spending habits, restlessness, and republicanism. In 1853, the Squire of Geneseo used the proceeds from the sale of wheat, which was selling at a record price, to add a third story to his Hartford House and to finance an extended tour of Europe during the construction. The first stop for Wadsworth, his wife Mary Craig, 15-year-old Cornelia, 11-year-old Nancy, 9-year-old James Wolcott, and a chambermaid was Paris. There they met their oldest son Charles, who had returned to his study at École des Mines (the School of Mines) after a visit to his diplomat Uncle Charles Murray in Egypt. In Paris the Squire showed his true colors. According to Cornelia, her father had contracted smallpox from Charles and was forced into what must have been excruciating idleness for weeks at a Paris hotel where he rented an entire wing. Upon his recovery and before resuming the trip, he bought a large secondhand carriage, a "berline." First, however, the coat of arms on it had to be "painted out and [his] republican spirit appeased!"[5]

After his recovery Wadsworth and his entourage spent the following summer, of 1855, at Vevey, Switzerland, where Wadsworth passed time with his Harvard friend and historian John Lothrop Motley. The diplomat found Wadsworth an "agreeable and genial man of the world," though the restless Wadsworth found the need to interrupt the trip to return to Geneseo for an unspecified length of time.[6]

Once home for good, he was beset by problems. Requiring immediate attention was a gnatlike insect, the "midge," which had infested the wheat crop in western New York beginning in 1854. By 1858, according to Wadsworth's report to the New York State Agricultural Society, the midge had reduced yields by "one-half to thirds" and had almost halved the price of lands sold there. Following his father's practice, Wadsworth required his tenants to make whatever payments they could to square the books at the end of the year rather than to carry a debt or to migrate west. Of course, this also reduced Wadsworth's income, no small matter to a man with his obligations and propensity to subsidize others and various causes.[7]

★   ★   ★

Also pressing upon Wadsworth was the slavery-states' rights issue that balkanized New York and national politics into regular Democrats, Free-Soil Democrats, Whigs, Know-Nothings, and Abolitionists. The immediate cause was the passage of the Kansas-Nebraska Act in 1854, which called for "popular sovereignty," permitting new states to be admitted with or without slavery and, by implication, repealing the Missouri Compromise.[8]

Exactly where the restless James S. Wadsworth, with his catholicity of interests, stood on these issues can only be extrapolated from letters to him and from his subsequent actions. Clearly, the republicanism he inherited from his father caused him to oppose the extension of slavery. From his testimony later it does not appear that he was ready yet to call for the abolition of slavery, fearing a violent backlash. Though straddling fences, increasingly he seemed to be aligning himself with the fledgling Republican Party, which at its first meeting in 1854 in Ripon, Wisconsin, united Whigs and Democrats who opposed the extension of slavery.

Typical of the times, in 1856 there were three separate conventions in New York, representing the various views on slavery: the "Democratic-Republicans," the "Old-Line Whigs," which held an August convention mainly to prove the party was not defunct, and the "Republicans." New York's Democratic–Republican Convention, called by Wadsworth and others to challenge the national Democratic Party's pro-slavery stance, was held in Syracuse on July 24, 1856.

Wadsworth was elected convention chairman, which not only indicated his increasing prominence but offered him an opportunity to make his views public. On assuming the chair he asked the assembled delegates to exercise caution in their deliberations to avoid permanently separating political associates. Yet, he promptly recalled the names of party leaders who eight years earlier in that same city, in heated debates, had stood for the popular will, which opposed the extension of slavery. And he alluded to the fact they had bolted out of the convention rather than become seduced "by the allurements of office and the flatteries of power." Apparently his voice was heard. The delegates endorsed the Republican Party's nomination of "Pathfinder" John Charles Fremont and William Lewis Dayton, thereby openly repudiating Democratic presidential candidate James Buchanan. Then, having aligned themselves with the Republican Party, which had been wooing them, Wadsworth and other "Democratic-Republicans" held a second convention in Syracuse on September 17 to nominate a state Republican ticket.[9]

Wadsworth's prominence was evident on the first ballot, when he received seventy-two votes for governor, only twenty fewer than for the eventual nominee, John A. King. The votes for Wadsworth were considered to reflect "a radical sentiment concerning slavery." Whether out of spite or honest avoidance of office, he refused to accept the nomination for lieutenant governor. Political historian D. S. Alexander, who claims that the unsuccessful candidate "had an itching for public life" and had actually made a "stubborn play for governor," suggests that Wadsworth's egotism led him to decline. However, Wadsworth declared to a correspondent that "the zeal of some of my friends placed me in the unfavorable position of appearing to seek what I affected not to desire." It is not clear whether he truly did not want the burden of office, especially a secondary one, or as editor-politician Thurlow Weed claimed, he "would have been over-whelmingly defeated, had he received the nomination" for governor or lieutenant governor.[10]

This did not end Wadsworth's involvement, for he was named presidential elector at large by Livingston County Republicans, whose surprising strength "resulted in an overwhelming victory for its nominees" for local offices. However, this was only a warm-up for the battle over U.S. Senate candidates in 1858. According to the ubiquitous and self-serving Weed, the prominent "aspirants" were Wadsworth, former Utica mayor Ward Hunt, and prominent lawyer David Dudley Field, all of whom were moving toward a more extreme anti-slavery position than many former Jacksonian Democrats were willing to take.[11] The claim by Weed that the Geneseoan was an aspirant apparently was based on the support he had received for the gubernatorial nomination. Whatever the case, the senatorial candidate of former Democrats who opposed slavery, now nominal Republicans, was not Wadsworth, but Preston King, whose credentials made him acceptable to a larger number of delegates.

Nonetheless, Wadsworth, now splitting his time between Geneseo, Philadelphia, and his New York City home on Fifth Avenue, was being drawn into the conflict like a moth to the flame. On August 14, 1858, Joseph Blunt of New York wrote to him that "Your letter to [the unnamed] Troy editor has placed us in a dilemma & I now write to ask you if there are no circumstances which may occur that might not induce you to accept the [1860 gubernatorial] nomination."[12]

Apparently Wadsworth's anti-slavery views appealed to Blunt, who was moved by national events impinging on the state. Of immediate concern was the U.S. Supreme Court's 1857 decision in the *Dred Scott* case, which denied the rights of citizenship to slaves who, by the Missouri Compromise of 1820, had lived in Louisiana territory north of the line 36 degrees, 30 minutes north latitude, which had been declared free territory. The result was that Congress was rendered powerless to regulate slavery in the territories. Blunt believed the Court must be reined in. A Republican president, put into office by New York's heavy electoral vote, might be able to do so. And then the hook—Wadsworth could well lead New York into the national presidential election two years hence.[13]

Predictably, the Squire again refused the proffered gubernatorial nomination. He explained to a Livingston County Republican that in the interests of party unity the incumbent, Edmund Morgan, deserved renomination. To another supporter he stressed the fact that in 1856 he had been put "in the unfavorable position of appearing to" want the office, but he would "not allow this to occur again." More candidly, he confessed to the supporter that "my want of habits of mental application render me unfit for the place." He did accept election to New York City's Century Association upon the nomination of Frederic S. Cozzens, though Wadsworth was an infrequent attendee. Founded by William Cullen Bryant in 1846 and limited to one hundred authors and artists and their supporters to promote interest in literature and the arts, it was one of the oldest and most prestigious social clubs in the United States.[14]

Refusal to run for office did not mean that Wadsworth was inactive politically. In the summer of 1860 the presidential candidacy of New York's William Seward was being pressed on the Republican Convention in Chicago. Significant opposition came from fellow New Yorkers Wadsworth, newspapermen Horace Greeley and William Cullen Bryant, and the man for whom Wadsworth bowed out of the 1856 gubernatorial nomination, David Dudley Field. Greeley and Field were active on the convention floor, while absentees Wadsworth and Bryant attacked Seward with "pungent letters" to delegates.[15]

After the Republicans nominated Abraham Lincoln and running mate Hannibal Hamlin, Wadsworth agreed to be a presidential elector again and took an active part in the campaign locally.[16]

Sereno French, a Lima, New York, native and later a correspondent for the *Chicago Evening Journal,* vividly recalled Wadsworth's presence and message at a rally in Lima. Not generally regarded as an orator, Wadsworth did not mount the stage until dark, after "several eminent speakers [had] exhausted the time." "As for me," Wadsworth concluded in his brief talk, "I am prepared for the emergency— my obligations to my country and to posterity are manifest as the sun at noon-day." Then, reminiscent of his ancestors, he told his listeners: "I cannot avoid them and continue to respect myself even—nor shall I try to do so. Duty is with me— results with God."[17] In short, he was obligated to do whatever was necessary to preserve the Union. The first task, he felt, was to help elect Republicans to office.

After Lincoln's election Wadsworth's name was bandied about for a seat in the presidential cabinet, to which the New York Republicans believed they were entitled. Supporters included anti-slavery journalist H. B. Stanton, who wrote Ohio senator Salmon P. Chase claiming that Wadsworth "is one of the most reliable [and popular] men in the State." Wadsworth's actions certainly placed him with the radicals, yet he would later claim that "At the beginning of the war, I was hardly a Republican. I thought slavery should be restricted to the ground where it stood, but was opposed to interfering with it there. I dreaded insurrections, massacres, and violence."[18]

Whether Wadsworth's beliefs were still evolving, he was inaccurate in his later recall, or he believed he was misunderstood cannot be determined. Certainly, his actions over the previous fifteen years gave the impression that he was rabidly anti-slavery, or one of the "Black Republicans," as the most radical came to be known. At any rate, he became the "principal spokesman" for a small group of New York Republicans who feared that Secretary of State William H. Seward would gain political control over the Lincoln administration. As Charles A. Dana recollected, Secretary of the Treasury Salmon Chase set up an appointment with President Lincoln for Wadsworth. A pained Lincoln heard him out, assured Wadsworth that "one side shall not gobble up everything," and demanded a list of candidates from which he would make his selection for Federal offices. Unable to remain in Washington, Wadsworth left a list with T. B. Carroll, a member of the group Wadsworth represented, to deliver to President Lincoln the next day. Unfortunately, Dana offers only this tantalizing glimpse, so we are left to speculate about the early relationship between the president and the Squire of Geneseo.[19]

Even before Lincoln took office New Yorkers struggled over how to prevent wholesale secession by the South, for which Lincoln's minority election had provided the rationale. Though six states had already seceded, Horatio Seymour and other "Douglas Democrats" sought to restore harmony, which led to their inconclusive January 1861 session in Albany. However, it proved a prelude to a much larger Peace Conference. At noon on February 4, 1861, some 132 delegates from twenty-one states began assembling at Willard's Dancing Hall on the corner of 14th Street and Pennsylvania Avenue in Washington. They were responding to the Virginia General Assembly's invitation "to adjust the present unhappy controversies." James Samuel Wadsworth was appointed a delegate by Governor Morgan, whose 1860 reelection Wadsworth had supported.[20]

The issue, of course, was whether war could be averted. The attendees immediately focused on a resolution by Kentucky senator John Crittenden. He proposed a thirteenth amendment to the Constitution recognizing slavery in the territory south of 36 degrees, 30 minutes north latitude (now Oklahoma, Texas, New Mexico, and Arizona). Most attendees were inactive from February 6 to February 15, while a committee of representatives, one per state, met to hear resolutions before issuing any report. Not so, James Samuel Wadsworth, who, on February 7, rounded up like-minded commissioners, including Ohioan Salmon P. Chase. The latter chaired at least three inconclusive gatherings to discuss the progress of the committee's deliberations. Though the committee's report on February 15 was less acceptable to Southerners than Crittenden's resolution, radicals feared that it would, nonetheless, prove acceptable to the majority. Immediately, firebrands Chase, David Dudley Field, New York's very vocal chairman, and Wadsworth, fearing that "Union savers and Democrats" would unite with Southerners to vote down the Republicans, appealed for recruits from Michigan, Minnesota, Wisconsin, and Kansas. Among their supporters was Michigan's Zachariah Chandler, who was prepared to fight. "Without a little bloodletting," Chandler exclaimed, "this nation would not be worth a rush."[21]

Speeches following the report were alternately heated and conciliatory, including those by New York's commissioners. Field was clearly the most vocal. On the other hand, Wadsworth, for whom no speeches were recorded, was active behind the scenes. For example, he moved a negative vote by the New York delegation on various sections of the conference report. Clearly viewed as a radical, he affixed his name to the final report, which condemned the Crittenden Compromise and which the House of Representatives voted not to receive.[22]

★   ★   ★

The 53-year-old Wadsworth had irreversibly committed himself. He was now an avowed radical. His father's worst fears would be realized. His passion for the cause, even his vanity, would compel him to acts that would lead to the inevitable. Yet there is an ironic twist. His beloved uncle, after whom he modeled himself no little, had brought the family slave Jenny to the Genesee Valley. Now, seven decades later, his nephew was challenging the whole institution of slavery and putting his reputation, his wealth, and, ultimately, his life on the line.

Hindsight reveals it was inevitable that conflicting principles, short tempers, and itchy fingers would trigger a conflagration. It was, as Seward labeled it, an "irrepressible conflict." It was from the start in 1787, just as it was in 1820, 1850, and 1854. The recently concluded and ineffective Peace Conference clearly illustrated the deep divisions that characterized the nation.

Yet it is curious why James Samuel Wadsworth, who represented "American gentility," which historian Martin L. Fausold defined as the "aristocratic concepts of integrity, education, leisure, class, family . . . and public service," had become so enmeshed in politics. Possibly Wadsworth was constitutionally unfit to play exclusively the role of landed gentry. His manners reflected New York's frontier: "simple, cordial and unaffected"; his style a "direct, straight-forward manliness." Add to that the restlessness that Philadelphian Sidney George Fisher observed, the ambition and vanity old James warned against, and the patriotism that had energized his forebears. This was a combustible mix.[23]

☆   ☆   ☆

Little is known about his activities immediately after the Peace Conference.[24] Meanwhile, the inevitable separation that Wadsworth feared occurred. In short order eleven states had seceded, the Confederate States of America was established (with its capital later situated in Richmond), and former U.S. senator and secretary of war Jefferson Davis was elected its president.

Squire Wadsworth was at his New York City "home" when he learned of the April 12th firing on Fort Sumter in the Charleston, South Carolina, harbor and its surrender two days later. The vacillation and protracted dispute over the Union's control of the fort had been decided when President Lincoln provisioned Fort Sumter over the objections of South Carolinians. Unable to persuade the Union to evacuate the fort, the Carolinians believed they were forced to take matters into their own hands. Instant Southern heroes were Brigadier General Pierre Gustave Toutant Beauregard, whose guns were turned on his former West Point instructor, Major Robert Anderson, and Edmund Ruffin. Ruffin, the 67-year-old slavery zealot, had ceremoniously pulled the lanyard on one of the columbiads, smoothbore bronze cannons firing fifty-pound shots.

Then Wadsworth and others learned that on April 19 angry Marylanders had fired on the 6th Massachusetts Volunteers when the regiment attempted to pass through Baltimore on its way to Washington. The next day there was a noisy, speech-filled War Committee rally in Union Square, New York City, which led to the creation of a Committee of Safety and subsequently to the organization of the Union Defense Committee with an office at 30 Pine Street. An agitated Wadsworth was elected to the committee, which included John Jacob Astor II, former governor Hamilton Fish, and Edwards Pierrepont, a prominent New York City lawyer and later U.S. attorney general.[25]

Secessionists' destruction of railroad tracks and bridges, which blocked the 7th New York's access to Washington, was the proximate cause of a far-reaching decision by Wadsworth. His father's admonitions to restrain himself were ignored; he had decided he must now back up his words with action.

With the resolution that characterized him, Wadsworth threw himself into the task of procuring a vessel to transport the 7th New York with provisions to Annapolis per the regimental colonel's plan. After inspecting the boats and examining the owners for the Union Defense Committee on Sunday evening, April 21, Wadsworth offered a $17,000 personal draft to charter a side-wheel ferry boat, the *Kill van Kull*. Though he would be reimbursed by the committee in the amount of $15,588, he had demonstrated his commitment. Over the next three days Wadsworth personally supervised the stocking of the chartered ferry and the hundred laborers who were to lay and repair rails between Annapolis and Washington. Finally, on Thursday, April 25, the *Kill van Kull,* accompanied from Pier 2 on the North River by the armed convoy *Monticello,* headed for Annapolis. Meanwhile Wadsworth entrained with editor-politician Thurlow Weed and Union Defense Committee secretary William Evarts to Philadelphia, where he learned the extent of the capital's demoralization and confusion—and was appalled. Only the soldiers' and laborers' enjoyment of the "tea, coffee, cheese, biscuits, hard bread, hams, etc., etc.," which he provided, offered Wadsworth any satisfaction. He communicated his frustration with the Federal government's incompetence to Union Defense Committee vice chairman Simeon Draper by mail and in person when he returned to New York City on May 1.[26]

In truth, Washington was in a mess. Although Unionists outnumbered Southern sympathizers two to one, it was hard to tell friend from foe. This was particularly true among the capital's well-born, largely Southerners, who had occupied many select posts under the Democratic-controlled Congress and presidency for so many years. Worse, it extended down even to clerkships. "Abolitionists were frowned upon, and New England civilization was sneered at as being made up of 'weak-minded men and strong-willed women.'" After Fort Sumter, Washingtonians' fears were multiplied.[27]

On May 6, Wadsworth tried to explain an earlier telegraph to Governor Morgan in which he expressed the alarm of members of the Union Defense Committee from accounts of Washington by General John A. Dix. While he was not convinced the situation was dire, he admitted "that there is some ground to fear an attack on Washington while troops were defending Baltimore." Thus, he recommended another route to Washington, but he was decidedly against sending any more three-months men.[28] (Early on the states called out militia to serve for three months, which proved unworkable to sustain the war. A three-year enlistment would become the norm.)

Additionally there was confusion resulting from the raising of troops by both the Federal and state governments. On May 20, Wadsworth had a hurried interview with President Lincoln. The president's intentions were unclear except that he would not interfere with the regiments already raised by Governor Morgan. Nor did an interview with General Winfield Scott clarify matters as to the disposition of New York troops. Wadsworth was to dine with Scott that same day. Wadsworth telegraphed Governor Morgan to ask whether Wadsworth should bring any matters to Scott's attention. Three days later Wadsworth, still in Washington, vented his spleen: "the Government is weak, miserably weak at the head. The President gets into at least one serious scrape *per diem* by hasty, inconsiderate action. While I was there he accepted X_____'s regiment and regretted it an hour later." Were he governor, Wadsworth noted, he would require loyalty oaths in terms of morals and patriotism.[29]

Whether or not this letter, his providing transportation for the 7th New York, or his political influence was determinative, on May 16, 1861, Wadsworth was appointed Major General of Volunteers by Governor Morgan. Union Defense Committee chairman John Dix had been appointed major general on May 8. The two represented New York's quota, according to Secretary of War

Cameron's requisition. Then, a day later, in a communiqué to Scott, Morgan gave Wadsworth command of a division consisting of two brigades of eight regiments of New York volunteers, with twenty-one additional regiments to be divided between him and Dix, who also was given command of a division.[30]

While expressing some reservations, Wadsworth appeared to want the position and responsibility, which he spelled out in a May 5 letter to Governor Morgan:[31]

> As against a graduate of West Point or an officer of the regular army of fair reputation . . . I can on no account allow my name to be presented as a candidate. As against men who have no advantage over me but a more recent connexion with the Militia, and a fresher knowledge of military technicalities, I do not think it would be presumptious [sic] in me to offer my name.

Then he assured Morgan that he would accept whatever decision the governor made.

Believing the matter settled, on May 22, Governor Morgan ordered Wadsworth to immediately occupy quarters at the State Arsenal vacated by Dix the previous day and to assume the job Dix had been performing, namely, forwarding the state's volunteer regiments "to the Seat of hostilities." However, the governor admitted that on his visit to Washington he had obtained no assurances by Lincoln or Cameron that Wadsworth's appointment had been accepted. This only made Morgan "more serious about the recognition of [Wadsworth]."[32]

Though Wadsworth accepted congratulations on his appointment, his status was still in doubt toward the end of the month, inducing Governor Morgan to write Secretary Cameron again. Taking nothing away from the individuals appointed, Cameron wrote Morgan on June 3 that by General Orders 15 the president "has reserved to himself the appointments" of volunteer officers. Furthermore, New York had not mustered the requisite number of men to permit the two appointments. The problem was resolved by the approval of Dix's appointment and Wadsworth's resignation "without regret or hesitation." He formally resigned on June 23, 1861, but thanked Governor Morgan for the governor's confidence in him.[33]

Whether Wadsworth resigned simply as a thoughtful gesture or recognized that he was not ready for such responsibilities cannot be determined. No doubt he believed that he was "better than a worse man" and that he had demonstrated the necessary administrative competence when he expedited the 7th New York's trip to Washington. Moreover, as eulogist William J. Hoppin later would claim:

> he was now considerably past the military age; . . . his private affairs were numerous and engrossing; . . . he was able to give wise counsel and large pecuniary aid which the most exacting patriotism might be supposed to require. He had . . . a home made attractive by every thing which wealth and taste and the love of friends could supply. His children were just coming into the active duties of life. . . . [34]

Wadsworth's obligations to his country were manifest—at least to him.

Chapter 8

"HIS RESOLUTION TO TAKE MILITARY SERVICE"

Likely the Squire of Geneseo, convinced that his obligations to his country were manifest, chafed at the confusion and inactivity in the nation's capital before he decided it was time to do something. So, it is not surprising that he requested military service and sought the intervention of Treasury Secretary Salmon P. Chase, with whom he had served at the Peace Conference earlier in the year. His request was granted on June 29, when he became Major James S. Wadsworth, New York State Militia, volunteer aide to newly brigadiered Irvin McDowell. The dogmatic and censorious McDowell, a 42-year-old West Pointer and prodigious eater, was selected because he had served on Army Commander Winfield Scott's staff and had studied French military operations firsthand. Recognizing his lack of command experience, on May 27 McDowell had reluctantly agreed to head the Department of Northeastern Virginia. Just as reluctantly, Union Army commander Major General Winfield Scott made the appointment. This was not a good omen for the first real test of the Union's strategy, matériel, or will.[1]

The sighting of Confederate pickets from the capital in late May of 1861 had exacerbated Washingtonians' fears about Confederate movements in the lower Shenandoah Valley. Also Major General Joseph E. Johnston's Army of the Shenandoah occupied Harpers Ferry only forty miles to the west, the "gateway" to the Shenandoah Valley.[2]

Washingtonians wanted action, and McDowell's movement into Virginia led to cheers of "On to Richmond," as if it would be a lark. However, first McDowell had to dislodge Brigadier General Pierre G. T. Beauregard's army from Manassas near the Bull Run, barely twenty-five miles from the Union capital. A muddy stream originating in the Bull Run Mountains west of Manassas Junction, Bull Run meandered southeasterly across the Manassas plains past Sudley Springs and Lincoln Mills before draining into the Occoquan River. Though nondescript, the muddy stream would soon acquire a lasting place in American history as the site of the First Battle of Bull Run (First Manassas to Southerners). Beauregard, a West Point classmate of McDowell and a Creole from a distinguished Louisiana family, had already made his mark by capturing Fort Sumter and would have another opportunity to build a reputation. His Bull Run line defended Manassas Junction, a strategic rail junction necessary for transporting supplies from Richmond and "teeming with livestock and cereal subsistence."[3]

McDowell's move against Beauregard was, in fact, an alternate plan. On June 3 General Scott had ordered McDowell to support Major General Robert Patterson's move against Johnston's troops at Harpers Ferry. But Johnston evacuated Harpers Ferry first. Thus, on June 15, McDowell, assuming a force of 25,000 Confederates at Manassas, asked Scott for 30,000 men with 10,000 reserves, a force sufficiently large to form three columns. The troops would cross Bull Run at a number of fordable places (where the stream banks were less steep), turn Beauregard's position, seize or threaten communications, and force him out.[4]

The real fighting war was about to begin, but both sides were relying on raw troops, especially the Union, which counted on men whose average length of service was barely sixty days. In fact, a depressed McDowell subsequently was heard to say: "This is not an army. It will take a long time to make an army." Further, he did not believe that "there was one [man] in the whole country, at least I knew there was no one there, who had ever handled 30,000 troops [in combat]." Worse, the government inefficiency that Wadsworth had decried three months earlier when trying to get the 7th New York to Washington continued to prevail. In fact, it took eight days for McDowell to obtain the troops he was counting on, and the absence of standard blue dress resulted in "brilliantly uniformed," even gaudy, militia- or state-issued uniforms, a variety that would never be seen again.[5]

Many of the Federal officers, though in regulation blue, were scarcely better prepared than the men they commanded. Among the poorly trained officers was Ohioan Robert C. Schenck, a congressman and diplomat. The five Union division commanders—Brigadier General Daniel Tyler, Colonel David Hunter, Colonel Samuel Heintzelman, Brigadier General Theodore Runyon, and Colonel Dixon S. Miles, the latter two in reserve—were generally superannuated regulars like their infirm commander Winfield Scott, or totally incompetent, or both. The 56-year-old, paunchy, bug-eyed Heintzelman, with combat command experience, was the best of the lot. On the other hand, the 62-year-old Tyler, an ordnance and artillery authority in the old army after his graduation from West Point and for close to twenty-five years a successful businessman, best illustrates the type of officer McDowell had to rely on. He was more used to giving than taking orders, which would be demonstrated shortly. At best, Hunter, barely four years younger, could claim only useful political connections. A division commander with what would become an even more checkered career was Colonel Dixon Miles. Miles would be the scapegoat for the loss of Harpers Ferry in the South Mountain campaign in mid-September 1862, and would, in the process, lose his life. Even before that battle he was under a cloud from Colonel Israel Richardson's charges that Miles was drunk at Bull Run.[6]

By comparison, Beauregard's forces, smaller and less equipped, may have been commanded by superior officers, for the Confederacy was not as shackled by the seniority system as the Union army. Confederate officers included himself and Johnston, as well as Brigadiers Thomas Jackson, James Longstreet, Kirby Smith, Richard Ewell, Theophilus Holmes, Barnard E. Bee, and D. R. Jones. Others were Colonels Jubal Early, Nathan Evans, Arnold (Jones) Elzey, and Thomas Jordan.[7]

Further stacking the deck, Beauregard daily received information from a network of high-placed politicians and War Department clerks with Southern sympathies, not to mention outright spies, like the notorious Rose O'Neale Greenhow. (The spy network had been organized by former Federal quartermaster Captain Thomas Jordan. "I was almost as well informed of the strength of the hostile army as its commander," Beauregard wrote later.) While McDowell planned to drive out the Confederates, Beauregard dabbled with grandiose plans to retake Alexandria—even Washington, but ultimately settled on defending the Bull Run line.[8]

By mid-July Beauregard felt prepared for any offensive McDowell would make, and McDowell believed he had no choice but to mount an offensive. He began it on July 16, realizing "that the consequences of that battle would establish the prestige in the contest, on the one side or the other."[9]

So it was that James Samuel Wadsworth, now volunteer aide-de-camp, faced a real test of his beliefs and courage. The Federal troops, carrying three days' rations, tramped toward Centreville, some six to seven miles east of Manassas Junction and twenty miles west of their staging site at the Potomac, where they had left their belongings. Two days later, on July 18, they arrived at their destination. The outcome of this first real test of strength for the two armies would depend on whether the Federals could ford the well-defended stream, climb the steep, tree-lined banks, and flank Beauregard before General Johnston arrived from the Shenandoah Valley. Of the three obstacles, the latter was most critical. In fact, as Wadsworth later testified, minus Johnston, "there would have been no battle at all then; that we would have walked over the field."[10]

The picnic air created by swarms of curious civilians from Washington on the sidelines, the raw troops, the inept or aged commanders, and the Confederate fire at short range negated McDowell's demonstration against the Confederate right in a sharp engagement at Blackburn's Ford. After a two-day pause to reassess, on July 21, General McDowell attacked and turned the Confederate left. He was almost successful, but delays and hard fighting by the Confederates enabled Johnston's force to reinforce Beauregard and turn the tide.[11]

The seesaw battle raged around the Robinson House and Henry Hill on a plateau until about 3:30 P.M., when the Federals found themselves flanked on the right. The result was total disarray and then panic as the Federals attempted to retreat across the narrow Cub Run bridge. It was every man for himself as the bluecoats ran wildly back toward Centreville and eventually back to their original staging site along the Potomac. The Battle of Bull Run was over, and cries of "On to Richmond" quickly faded, as would the unfortunate McDowell.[12]

Losses, while light compared to later battles, were not inconsiderable. Union totals were 19 officers and 462 enlisted men killed, 64 officers and 947 enlisted

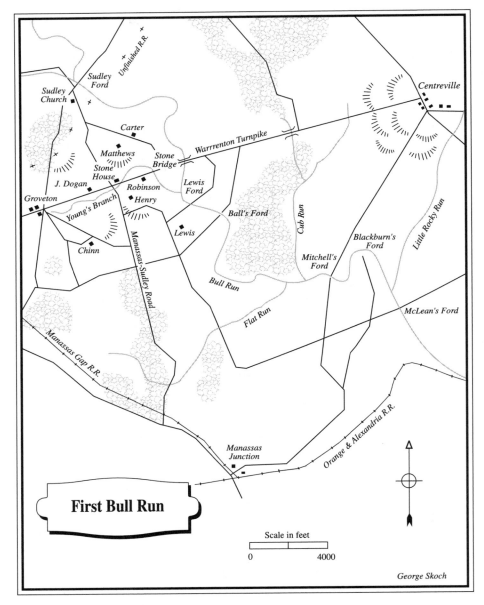

First Bull Run (by George Skoch)

men wounded, 40 officers and 1,176 enlisted men missing, and 25 artillery pieces lost. Confederate losses were comparable: 25 officers (including Brigadier General Barnard E. Bee and Colonel F. S. Bartow) and 362 enlisted men killed, 63 officers and 1,519 men wounded, but only 1 officer and 12 men missing. For first-time combatants the psychological effects were greater. A survivor from the 2nd Wisconsin recalled: "The first lesson taught us . . . that while the sound of big guns was more terrific, the real danger in battle was the whistling minnie [minié ball named for its French inventor] which reached one without note or warning."[13]

The lesson for most Northerners, however, was that instead of a one-battle war, their army had suffered a humiliating defeat.

✶ ✶ ✶

Wadsworth could not have chosen a more significant place to begin his military experience, though it could well have ended ingloriously there, as it did for some others. As an aide-de-camp, he was in a role that not only could be personally dangerous, but was highly unusual for a 53-year-old, let alone a man of wealth and influence. Aides were typically young, educated officers of demonstrated ability to deliver (often under fire) a commander's orders "twenty-four hours, day and night, if their service was required," energy to flit from sector to sector, and trustworthiness to represent the commander. However energetic, and admittedly he was, Wadsworth was not a 20-year-old, like his son, Craig, who too would become a McDowell aide. Nor was he used to carrying out others' orders. Lastly was the issue of whether a man who enjoyed his prominence could be considered expendable. McDowell knew that Wadsworth held the confidence of Treasury Secretary Chase, so one has to wonder whether the old, untested, businessman-politician was thrust upon McDowell to monitor him. Why, for instance, was Wadsworth not given some safe assignment like his compatriot John Dix, albeit ten years older, whose service was largely restricted to administrative duties in New York City? On the other hand, in his postbattle report McDowell noted that the newly minted major "does me the honor to be on my staff."[14]

Whatever the rationale for his duties, Major James Samuel Wadsworth, the unpaid volunteer, was fortunate. First, he came through unscathed. Also, as a volunteer without portfolio, he escaped the ignominy attached to so many others, including McDowell and Colonel William Tecumseh Sherman. More importantly, he had observed battle firsthand. In fact, he is reported to have been all over the battlefield, personally directing movements to carry out McDowell's orders while flying from point to point, belying his age. In the process he gained the respect not only of McDowell's adjutant, Captain James B. Fry, and other combatants, but also of McDowell, who was impressed by Wadsworth's courage when his horse was "shot from under him in the hottest of the fight."[15]

✶ ✶ ✶

Major Wadsworth's enthusiasm quickly became the subject of comment by men he would come to command. Members of the 14th Brooklyn (14th New York Militia) of Hunter's division admired his dash and courage. "Just as we were going into the battle General Wadsworth—that gray-haired old veteran whom the soldiers all loved—rode up. He held a revolver in one hand and with the other he caught the edge of the colors and said, 'Follow me, boys.' [Color Sergeant Frank] Head replied: 'General, I'll follow you anywhere.'" (Unfortunately, Sergeant Head did, which led to his death.) Wadsworth also got to know and to gain the respect of the 2nd Wisconsin, an outfit soon to become part of the famous Iron Brigade.[16]

However, the cessation of the firing did not spell the end to Wadsworth's duties. Rather, he assumed responsibility for the wounded Union soldiers and remained on the field to succor them, thereby risking capture. Throughout the night Wadsworth stayed on the field, sleeping where and when he could. At one point he linked up with his son-in-law, Captain Montgomery Ritchie (daughter Cornelia's husband), an aide to Colonel Dixon Miles, who commanded the 5th Division in reserve at Centreville. Taking advantage of the heavy rain the following day, July 22, Wadsworth searched Fairfax Court House "to see that the stragglers and weary and worn-out soldiers were not left behind," while Ritchie rode off to Washington to obtain a flag of truce to perform their humanitarian duties. After Ritchie's return the two remained until late in the day, becoming the last to leave the field.[17]

One soldier later recalled that, however helpful the late Squire of Geneseo was or intended to be, the results were not uniformly positive. Private Elisha Reed of the 2nd Wisconsin and a comrade

> were pretty well played out . . . [and] fell in with one Maj. [James S.] Wadsworth. He advised that we go into a hospital and not attempt to go any farther. We could not walk and there was no possible chance to ride and he advised us by all means to stop. Trusting to his superior knowledge and judgment of military affairs, we stopped and went into a small building containing about a dozen sick and wounded men, little dreaming what might be the final result.[18]

The "final result" was their capture by a Confederate cavalry unit the following day.

Back in Washington, Wadsworth was praised by his New York friends on the Union Defense Committee for "the spirited conduct and gallant bearing shown by one of their number at the recent conflict in Virginia." The committee dwelled on the fact that having "declined the Commission of Major General tendered to him by the Executive of this State, which did not confer an active Command in the Field, *Mr. Wadsworth* volunteered his Services on the Staff of the Commanding General immediately before the battle." The committee took particular pride in one of their own who not only put his money and reputation, but now his neck, on the line as a newly appointed brigadier general. On August 9, 1861, Wadsworth had been notified by acting War Secretary Thomas Scott of his appointment as a brigadier by President Lincoln in the wake of First Bull Run.[19]

First, however, the new brigadier took a leave of absence to check on business at home. He also petitioned the U.S. Senate for an armory in Geneseo and the governor for authority to raise a Livingston County regiment. The request for an armory was denied, but approval of the second request resulted in recruitment of seven companies ("the Wadsworth Guards"). Along with three companies from Troy, New York, in March 1862, they became the 104th New York Volunteers, to whom Wadsworth later personally presented its blue silk regimental colors.[20]

General Wadsworth's command was being formed in August during his leave. It was the 2nd Brigade (the 12th, 21st, 23rd, and 35th New York regiments, with the 80th New York, or 20th State Militia, added in November) of McDowell's newly constituted division of the Department (or Army) of the Potomac. All had been mustered originally for two years of state service. However, they were not formally brigaded until October 3, when a third brigade, commanded by Brigadier General Rufus King, was added. The Department of the Potomac, consisting of the Departments of Washington, Northeastern Virginia, and the Shenandoah (and as of September 19 the Department of West Virginia), was responsible for Union forces in Delaware, Maryland, the District of Columbia, and Virginia from the Potomac River to north of the James River.[21]

General Wadsworth's appointment virtually coincided with the appointment of Major General George B. McClellan, whom Wadsworth would get to know all too well, to command the new Department of the Potomac. The administration wanted McClellan to bring order out of the demoralized troops who had suffered defeat at Bull Run. So it turned to someone who had the stuff that McDowell lacked and who could succeed the increasingly infirm General Scott. It was a tall order that would result in a number of changes in the organization of the army and defenses of Washington—and to head-spinning changes to Brigadier General Wadsworth's commands.

McClellan, in his inestimable style, brought a martial air to Washington and then outlined for Secretary of War Simon Cameron his plans to defend the capital. In six steps General McClellan clarified how he intended to remedy deficiencies, beginning with serviceable weapons and ending with a total reorganization of the army command structure. The key to that reorganization was control by McClellan of the "fitness" of appointments, meaning that general officers should be West Pointers. This view was shared by Major General Henry W. Halleck, a fellow West Pointer, who would become general-in-chief. Halleck openly lambasted "*mere* politicians" who were being appointed to "conduct armies where thousands of human lives, millions of money and the safety of the Government itself are involved." These "military charlatans . . . have neither judgment, sense nor courage." On the face of it, Wadsworth certainly had to be suspect.[22]

Throughout that fall, winter, and early spring of 1861–1862, Wadsworth's responsibilities were threefold: to drill his brigade to combat readiness, to maintain picket lines, and to forage for food for his soldiers and horses. Foraging was no small matter; the Union army's daily food requirement was 400 tons. In fact, "more than half the supplies forwarded to a field army daily consisted of forage, and the train animals consumed much of this quantity. While a soldier required three pounds of provisions daily, an animal required twenty-six pounds of forage, and the forage generally exceeded subsistence stores for the men as much in bulk as in weight."[23]

By mid-August of 1862 Wadsworth was getting to know his command on Upton's Hill, across the Potomac from Washington. It formed a defensive line arcing around Washington and extending from Alexandria to the Chain Bridge, approximately seven miles north of Washington. Squarely in front of Wadsworth's brigade lay Beauregard's Confederate force at Munson's Hill. The nature of this threat to Washington is evident from the topography. Four hills, running generally north to south, looked across the Potomac to the capital: Hall's, Upton's, Munson's, and Mason's. Upton's Hill, where Wadsworth was located, was slightly in advance of and elevated over Munson's. However, from the top of Munson's, where the Confederate flag was posted, the dome of the capitol building was in full view—and vice versa, which unnerved Washingtonians. On the western rim of Upton's Hill was Fort Upton, merely an earthwork with an abatis (trees felled and pointed toward the enemy) and a moat in front. Just behind the fort was Charles Upton's mansion, where Wadsworth was headquartered.[24]

General Wadsworth posted pickets near Ball's Crossroads, where "general slight skirmishes . . . [and] firing between Pickets" became constant, despite his efforts to stop the unnecessary practice. While the main task was for the soldiers to build earthworks, the immediate fear at the end of September was the threat of an attack on Washington. Demonstrations by the Confederates on September 29, announced by the firing of cannon, seemed to portend the worst. But shortly the Rebel forces were found to have drawn back to Fairfax, leaving Quaker guns (wooden pieces devised to look like real guns) at Munson's Hill. Wadsworth immediately ordered out two companies of the 35th New York, which encountered only a small cavalry detachment, confirming the Confederate withdrawal.[25]

Of more immediate importance to Wadsworth was the arrival at his headquarters on October 31, 1861, of Lieutenant John Kress, a young man whose army experience would greatly affect both him and Wadsworth. On October 29 the patriotic Kress, not quite 22 and fifth in his class, had resigned from West Point as 1st Captain of Cadets, less than a year from graduation. "I have hourly need of his services," Wadsworth wrote Governor Morgan on September 10. "I have had no end of difficulties in getting a staff. All the applicants are even greener than the Genl." Wadsworth also wanted a second lieutenancy for his son, Craig W., from the governor, so Craig could join his staff as well. They could be appointed to any of the regiments in his command. Kress's posting was officially to the 25th New York, but he was assigned immediately as an aide to untried Brigadier General James S. Wadsworth. Like any aide, his duties would run the gamut, the most important of which now were instruction, drill, and discipline of the still-green soldiers.[26]

From the outset the new brigade commander had his hands full. The 12th New York was of particular concern, for it was "in a deplorable condition, almost entirely disorganized." He was "desperate to save it." A regular army colonel, a New Yorker, was available to command it, if the general could get the present commander, Ezra Walrath, to resign. In fact, he wanted all the field officers to resign, and had already asked for Walrath's resignation. Walrath "must resign. There is no alternative." However, Walrath was "very poor," so Wadsworth asked the governor to offer Walrath a pension for a short time. The general was already talking with individuals in Onondaga County to persuade Walrath should he hesitate. Barely two weeks later, Walrath complied, but he saw subsequent service with the 115th New York, serving until the end of the war, during which time he rose from captain to lieutenant colonel.[27]

As was obvious from these letters, Wadsworth was taking charge, but he was momentarily distracted by Governor Morgan's "kind and flattering note" dated September 25. Apparently it referred to efforts to persuade Wadsworth to run for governor to succeed him. Though Wadsworth remonstrated that he did not look forward to passing two years of his life in Albany if elected, he would be "content" to discharge matters as well as Morgan. But he did find one area of disagreement with the governor: General McClellan. Wadsworth warned that Morgan's eyes "will be opened yet. We shall not differ long as to this genl." Wadsworth's disdain for McClellan's generalship would become more obvious in a short time.[28]

Typically, Wadsworth was an active commander. For example, Tuesday, October 15, he was ordered by McDowell "to advance a regiment to Mill's X [Cross] Roads." Before he was able to do so, however, Wadsworth had learned of the Confederate withdrawal. Wadsworth then made "a reconnaissance with 50 Infrty & some [undecipherable] Cav'y to Fairfax Ct H. where I found the enemy in force. The Enemy's Pickets or Skirmishers fired upon us but without effect & I without loss." Though General McDowell considered it proper for Wadsworth to order out a party to observe the Confederates, "I only felt uneasy to learn that the General [Wadsworth] had gone himself." Wadsworth had to be where the action was, despite the danger, even folly, in doing so. In fact, Wadsworth followed up this episode with an even more daring one, when he marched the bulk of his brigade out in the vicinity of Vienna, loaded thirty wagons of cut corn "in full view of the rebel post," and returned with his "valuable prize without molestation."[29]

Evidence that McDowell's gentle warning fell on deaf ears appears in a Baltimore newspaper article that General Beauregard enclosed in correspondence to General Johnston:

> . . . Yesterday [November 8] General Wadsworth, accompanied by two privates of the Twenty-third New York Regiment, went to Brush's house, three miles from Falls Church, on the road leading to Fairfax Court-House, for the purpose of finding forage. While at the house [eating a hearty lunch] a squad of Confederate cavalry was seen rapidly approaching. The general quickly mounted his horse and succeeded in making his escape, but the privates were taken prisoner.[30]

Colonel Gates of the Ulster Guard recalled that it was General Wadsworth's restlessness that caused him to obtain permission to forage, but Gates believed that Beauregard was mistaken about Wadsworth's involvement in this episode.[31]

The brigade commander also disclaimed any involvement. Rather, he notified General McDowell that the capture of the Union contingent, to which Beauregard was alluding, was, instead: "a captain, lieutenants, and 35 privates of the Thirtieth [*sic*] and five teams loaded with corn," *and* was not his fault. "This [forage] party was sent out contrary to my advice and without my knowledge." Wadsworth had good reason to be upset, for in addition to the total of thirty prisoners captured by the 2nd Mississippi Cavalry, the Union lost wagons loaded with forage, horses, muskets, and cartridge boxes.[32]

Still, two days later Wadsworth was out on the picket line again after Lieutenant Colonel Fitzhugh Lee's 1st Virginia Cavalry had driven in, surrounded, and hemmed in Union pickets of the 14th Brooklyn. The pickets, fighting desperately, managed to chase off the Confederates, after which an impressed Wadsworth regrouped and directed them to occupy the same line and to prepare for another possible attack. Thus, Wadsworth was reintroduced to a regiment that he would come to know well.[33]

Other than these relatively minor incidents, there was little activity of military significance in and around Washington for the new commander. In fact, it can be fairly said that the soldiers had already begun to occupy their winter quarters, affording time for them and their "prematurely white . . . tall, well proportioned, and firmly knit" commander to become acquainted. They would find his manners, like most observers had, "simple, cordial, and unaffected," in sharp contrast to many politician soldiers. Wadsworth clearly came to identify with some of the regiments that he would command, including the 2nd and 6th Wisconsin, Westerners who had reluctantly turned in their gray uniforms for Federal blue.[34]

Wadsworth also got to see his two older sons, 26-year-old Charles Frederick, who, on August 21, had enlisted at Buffalo for three years in the 116th New York Volunteers, and Craig Wharton, a 20-year-old who found his father "all bone and muscle now." Given their father's actions, it is not surprising that all three sons would see service, including his youngest, "Jimmy," who would receive a commission in 1865 when he was not quite 19. In fact, Wadsworth was quoted by General Erasmus Keyes as saying in the blunt fashion the New Yorker so readily adopted: "If my father were alive now, and would not devote his mind, body, and estate to the cause, I could not respect him."[35]

Officers, of course, would get to know Wadsworth and to enjoy his hospitality. For example, the 94th New York's Colonel Adrian Root, a Buffalonian, was invited to dine with Wadsworth on Thanksgiving Day. Root was suitably impressed: "The dinner was prepared under the auspices of the famous Sanderson of the New York Hotel, who you recollect managed the Prince of Wales' tour through Canada . . . [and was now] Commissary of Sustenance to Wadsworth's Brigade." (James M. Sanderson would become Wadsworth's aide-de-camp the following July and eventually the commissary of I Corps.) Other invitees to the sumptuous meal at Wadsworth's headquarters were the "French Admiral of the American stations, the French Minister, the Archbishop of Halifax, etc., etc., and then a grand scene ensued, of introductions, etc., etc." Root noted how ironic it was to pass the evening so "delightfully, considering that we are engaged in a bloody civil war!!!"36

Yet the picture of Wadsworth's military lifestyle more commonly drawn was of Wadsworth occupying the house of Charles H. Upton, a loyal Unionist. The house had been pillaged by Confederates and showed the effects: charcoal-inscribed graffiti on the walls, broken stools, and unhinged doors serving as tables for Wadsworth to dine on "camp fare."37

The brigade commander had quickly established a reputation for attending to the welfare of the enlisted men. One of the more memorable stories involved the Ulster Guard, the 80th New York (or 20th New York Militia, as it preferred to be called), in early November 1861. The weary soldiers had marched fifteen miles from Washington via the Chain Bridge to reach a point that lay only eight miles away by a more direct route. Worse, according to their commander, Colonel Theodore Gates, they arrived "too late to cook coffee or to make any arrangements for a comfortable night's rest." Unexpected relief came when lanterns appeared and the "kind, cheery voice [of Wadsworth] called out, 'Twentieth, where are you?'" After supplying the troops with fuel for fires and copious amounts of hot coffee the General "personally superintended" the Guard's arrangements. In fact, "There was no matter too trivial for his ready personal attention, if it concerned the health or comfort of his men," Gates recounted. "The guard-house, the kitchens, the sinks [latrines], the stables: all were frequently subjected to his inspection and required to be in the cleanest and best possible condition." He was even known to inspect and supervise construction of stoves and chimneys in the soldier's huts at all hours, good weather or foul.38

Civilians also praised the general. "While in command at this post," wrote Charles Upton, "he exhibited so much wisdom, and tempered the firmness of his command with so much kindness and forbearance that he won the confidence and respect of the [distrustful] citizens of Fairfax." This included caring for the families whose providers were away fighting for the Confederacy. Upton was no sycophant, readily acknowledging that "Gen. Wadsworth entertains some opinions with regard to public policy not in accordance with my own views."39

To avoid offending Unionists here in Virginia, Wadsworth was careful to issue vouchers that recipients could redeem to compensate for property taken by Union soldiers. However, later he would have to pay these vouchers out of his own pocket when he was informed he had violated Paragraph 1007 of the Revised Regulations. Not surprisingly, this would not be the only incident where the impatient general would violate regulations or empty his own pockets on behalf of his men.40

About this time the general was introduced to John Gibbon, former commander of Battery B of the historic 4th U.S. Artillery. Gibbon had been ordered transferred from Camp Floyd, Utah Territory, to assume command of McDowell's division artillery. An 1847 West Point classmate of Union general Ambrose Burnside and Confederate generals A. P. Hill and Henry Heth and a former academy artillery instructor, Gibbon soon "became quite well acquainted with the brave old man." His observations virtually echo those of anyone who came to know Wadsworth: "He chafed very much under what he considered unnecessary delay in the movement of the army."[41]

On the other hand, Gibbon, who "never doubted [Wadsworth's] honesty or sincerity[,] . . . always suspected that his opinions on military matters reflected those of his political associates with many of whom he was intimate." In fact, Wadsworth visited Washington regularly. Gibbon's suspicions were confirmed by a matter of particular personal importance. General McDowell had recommended Gibbon for promotion to brigadier general of volunteers, but Gibbon, a North Carolinian, was not confirmed by the Senate. "Not knowing what steps to take in the matter or whether I ought properly, to take any," Gibbon later recalled, "I went in my perplexity to my good friend Gen. Wadsworth and told him that as there was no North Carolina senator present to second my nomination, I learned it had hung fire! He at once sat down and wrote a note to, I think, Senator Wilson of Massachusetts and in a few days the nomination was confirmed." Gibbon had correctly assessed Wadsworth's political clout, but to Wadsworth's credit, he recognized the merits of recommending Gibbon, a future corps commander.[42]

Though Wadsworth was learning the ways of the military and proving capable of command, he found himself uncharacteristically inactive and relegated, as Gibbon noted, to discussing "with anybody" ways to move the war forward. Shortly, he would work to change the situation.

Chapter 9

"ABILITY AND INTENTION TO DO RIGHT"

Wadsworth the Military Governor

Though now commanding approximately 3,500 officers and men, supplying them and the animals with food, and performing minor administrative tasks, the restless Wadsworth chafed from idleness. He wrote Henry J. Raymond, a political ally, former congressman, and *New York Times* co-founder, to "free his mind" about affairs on the Potomac. Wadsworth believed there was something mysterious about the conduct of the war by Army of the Potomac commander McClellan, who was deluding the public about any advance against the Confederacy. Raymond responded that Wadsworth's "mood is very widely shared" and confided to the general that he feared recognition of the Confederacy by France and England if "we have not struck a blow." A ray of hope was news about Edwin Stanton, legal advisor to Secretary of War Cameron, that Raymond could not share by letter, but it would provide Wadsworth "less provocation to profanity and despair."[1]

The news Raymond could not share with his political ally Wadsworth was twofold. First, President Lincoln also was very frustrated about the conduct of the war. In mid-January a despondent Lincoln had asked Quartermaster General Montgomery Meigs, "What shall I do? The people are impatient; [Secretary of the Treasury] Chase has no money; . . . the General of the Army [McClellan] has typhoid fever. The bottom is out of the tub. What shall I do?" Second, Lincoln was coming to the conclusion that he needed a different war secretary.[2]

Paradoxically, the restless Wadsworth was at once too far from—and too close to—the action. The West was where the fighting was being done. The early February capture of Forts Henry and Donelson on the Kentucky–Tennessee border brought the first real satisfaction to the North, thirsting as it was for some sign of success. Previously unheralded Brigadier General Ulysses S. Grant had forced the Confederates out of Kentucky and a good part of Tennessee. At the same time, Brigadier General John Pope was preparing a force to drive down the Mississippi and thereby to split the Confederacy.

On the other hand, Wadsworth was too close to the domestic battles in which he could play only a minor part. Indicative of the political situation, radical Republicans, including Ohio senator Benjamin Wade and Representative Thaddeus Stevens of Pennsylvania, had in December convened a Joint Committee on the Conduct of the War. They used the Union defeat at Ball's Bluff on October 21, 1861, to press the administration for more military action and to emancipate the slaves. One immediate result was the January 14 replacement of Secretary of War Simon Cameron by Ohio native Edwin M. Stanton, the reassuring but unannounced news that Henry Raymond could not divulge when he wrote General Wadsworth.

While the blustery Stanton, former U.S. attorney general under President James Buchanan, had no military experience, he was thought to have administrative skills. And he clearly was unsympathetic to the Southern cause, a failing with which the corrupt Cameron had been charged. Though unflatteringly described as "a long-haired, fat, oily, politician-looking man," "a physical coward," "arbitrary . . . and chronically dishonest in his human relationships," Stanton offered Lincoln an administrator who was financially honest, "energetic almost to the point of frenzy and as industrious as a hive of bees."[3]

The combination of radical Republicans, Stanton's appointment, and victories in the West focused the spotlight on army commander Major General George B. McClellan and the resplendent West Pointers so apparent in the capital. Stanton's feelings about McClellan and his idle Army of the Potomac were well known. To *New York Tribune* newsman Charles A. Dana, Stanton had vowed to clear the "rats" out of his office and focus on the army. "This army has got to fight or run away; and while men are striving nobly in the West, the champagne and oysters on the Potomac must be stopped."[4]

The inactivity of the Army of the Potomac was even more intolerable to Wadsworth, whose troops smarted from smallpox vaccinations and were demoralized by "rain, rain, rain." Camps in and near Washington had become "one sea of mud six inches deep." Rain seemed to fall every day well into mid-February.[5]

The break Wadsworth wanted (and likely sought) came on March 8, 1862, in the President's General War Order No. 2. It required General McClellan to reorganize the Army of the Potomac into four corps, preparatory to his planned incursion into peninsular Virginia. However, the removal of these four corps, numbering in excess of 100,000 men, from Washington would necessitate other means to protect the capital. Enter Brigadier General Wadsworth, who would become commander of the newly created military district of Washington and the troops therein. However, General War Order No. 3, issued the same day, made it clear that there could be no change in the Army of the Potomac's base of operations (that is, no more than 50,000 troops could be moved) until the Potomac River from Washington to Chesapeake Bay was secure (or Lincoln gave "express permission"). Further, this shift of operations by McClellan had to take place by March 18. Over this matter of security a conflict between Wadsworth and McClellan would simmer and finally erupt into a full-blown confrontation.[6]

Four days later, on March 12, Wadsworth was temporarily relieved from brigade duty and ordered to report in person to Stanton. As newly appointed military governor of Washington, Wadsworth would no longer be idle, though he claimed that his duties "were never clearly defined in my orders" and even appeared contradictory.

While responsible for these ill-defined duties (and troops), General Wadsworth would rely heavily on Provost Marshal William E. Doster, a 25-year-old Yale graduate, acquaintance of Charles Dana, and ultimate political insider. Major Doster's revelations about Wadsworth and his activities in the capital are as intriguing as they are indispensable. The two met when now Military Governor Wadsworth, bypassing Doster's superior, ordered the 4th Pennsylvania Cavalrymen to report to him at his headquarters on the corner of 19th and I Streets. Though cordial, Wadsworth kept Doster in the dark as they rode out with Wadsworth's aide, Lieutenant Kress, to inspect camps and troops north of the Potomac. The next day was similar, with Doster, who had served as officer of the day throughout the area, introducing Wadsworth to the troops. Riding back to the city Wadsworth stunned the young officer by asking him if he would be willing to succeed General Andrew Porter as Provost Marshal. Thus, for almost eight months Provost Marshal Doster would maintain order within Wadsworth's district while Wadsworth "devoted himself to the care of the defenses." (Begging explanation is Doster's claim that he commanded a mixed brigade of infantry, cavalry, and artillery—and "a corps of detectives.") Basically, he was to carry out Wadsworth's peacekeeping duties in the capital, which included receiving and exchanging prisoners and caring for escaped Blacks. However—and this offers a fascinating glimpse into the workings of Stanton—Doster claimed that though Wadsworth had appointed him, he reported daily, in person, to Secretary Stanton or his assistant, Peter Watson.[7]

Major Doster also offers the best physical description of the 54-year-old Wadsworth, who impressed him because, unlike officers who owed their ranks to intrigues, Wadsworth "won his star before wearing it." Years later the former provost marshal could recall first seeing Wadsworth in a plain, common, light-blue army overcoat. He was distinguished only by the "carved sabre of ancient pattern" of his ancestor, General James Wadsworth. The current General Wadsworth, Doster's superior, was approximately "six feet in height, of a spare but well-knit frame, with blue eyes, white hair, and side-whiskers, a thin aquiline nose, and an amiable, frank, and firm expression of countenance." More important than the physical appearance was the subordinate's feeling that Wadsworth was an unaffected, incorruptible man. The latter was illustrated soon after Doster assumed his duties. A "near relative" of Wadsworth, a commissary officer in one of the Carolina departments, visited Washington to obtain a transfer on the grounds that an honest man could not stand the swindling he was observing. General Wadsworth's curt reply was, "Then you are just the man to put a stop to it," and told his visitor to return to his duties.[8]

Necessarily, though he delegated many duties to Major Doster, Military Governor Wadsworth was responsible for the capital itself. Still little more than a set of public buildings amid "dingy brick houses and small shops" and "roaring" saloons, Washington was slowly showing the positive effects of Colonel Charles P. Stone's earlier efforts to put it on a wartime status. At the outset of the war, Washington was a city of badly divided loyalties. Worse, it was defended by an inept militia and only antiquated Fort Washington, looking toward Mount Vernon. Stone, inspector general for the District of Columbia, had been instructed to drill the capital militia, dismiss those of questionable loyalties, incorporate army regulars brought in from Kansas, Louisiana, and Georgia, and fortify positions across the Potomac in Virginia.[9]

Within a week of General Wadsworth's appointment, orders were issued transferring to him all buildings and public property in Washington, including military prisons, the occupants, among which were ex-slaves, and the city's military police. He was to locate his headquarters in the building vacated by the provost marshal and he was to enforce congressional laws, like the one requiring all Washington voters to take an "iron-clad oath" of loyalty to the Union.[10]

Supervising the Old Capitol Prison would prove to be one of the nastiest aspects of the job. At best the prison was little more than a filthy, cobwebbed, lice-infested hole, which had to be rehabilitated. Decayed walls had to be remortared, broken doors, partitions, and stairways repaired, and spaces between the buildings boarded up. Unsavory food, a limited number of "sinks" (toilets), and the distribution of privileges among the odd mix of military and political prisoners made for an almost unmanageable situation. Originally set aside for prisoners of war, it also held spies, blockade runners, and Federal military offenders. Also, a nagging problem for radical Republican Wadsworth was accommodating the former slaves occupying places in the jail until work could be found for them.[11]

While Colonel Stone's efforts to upgrade Washington's defenses offered some relief to the new military governor, it was offset by Secretary of State Seward's heavy-handed attempts to ensure internal security. Seward's policies had resulted in the imprisonment of hundreds of individuals. Some were guilty of disloyalty, like the notorious Rose O'Neale Greenhow and associates, who had supplied Beauregard with military information; others were suspected of it. Thus, Seward had not only created new enemies, but, by overloading the Old Capitol Prison, he had increased problems for General Wadsworth. "If [the prisoners] are guilty," Provost Marshal Doster recalled Wadsworth grumbling, "this imprisonment is too light,—if they are innocent, a day's confinement is too long."[12]

The problem of overcrowding at the jail was temporarily relieved by Secretary Stanton, to whom authority for internal security had been transferred from Seward. Prisoners against whom no charges had been brought were paroled, and, at Wadsworth's urging, two of Wadsworth's political allies, General Dix and Judge Edwards Pierrepont, were appointed to examine the cases of the remaining prisoners. Before this measure the Old Capitol Prison had almost 200 inmates, not counting prisoners of war. On the other hand, Wadsworth had to contend with Stanton's almost paranoid concern for Washington's safety, which clearly extended to the prison, where paid informers interacted with prisoners. The removal of Mrs. Rose O'Neale Greenhow and two others, whom on April 1 Wadsworth escorted beyond Union forces and released on their parole of honor not to return north of the Potomac River, only temporarily alleviated this particular problem. Scarcely three months later the vivacious and spirited Belle Boyd replaced Greenhow and caused Wadsworth another headache. Though female prisoners appeared to be relatively minor in the scheme of things, Wadsworth wanted nothing to do with them, especially those as notorious as Greenhow and Boyd, whose spy activities seemed to drive Stanton to throw tantrums.[13]

The overzealous Stanton even engaged Wadsworth in an affair that gave him desired action, but must have caused him some discomfort. In February, shortly before Wadsworth assumed his new position, Stanton's ire was raised by newspapermen he accused of reporting what he regarded as secret military operations. To stop the practice he sent a circular to police chiefs of major cities notifying them of his order to seize whole editions of newspapers and to arrest newspaper editors and publishers who published intelligence regarding military operations. Though he revoked the order almost immediately, two weeks later he became incensed by a *Washington Sunday Chronicle* item. Stanton then ordered Wadsworth to "immediately take military possession of the printing office in which publication is made, arrest the printers and publishers of the paper, take possession of all papers that can be found and destroy them, and hold the parties in custody that they may be dealt with according to the Rules and Articles of War." Reportedly Wadsworth "ransacked the office and arrested the employees, but released them after" the editor offered an exculpatory statement.[14]

However busy General Wadsworth was with these prickly civil matters, he soon became preoccupied with more strictly military affairs, specifically command of all the defenses "north and south of the Potomac in the vicinity of Washington." That vicinity embraced the District of Columbia, Alexandria, "the ground in front of and in the vicinity of the defensive works south of the Potomac from the Occoquan River to Difficult Creek, and the post of Fort Washington." His encompassing, but ill-defined, duties ranged from instructing Colonel Dixon S. Miles's Railway Brigade, which was protecting rail lines within the district, to supervising provisional brigades composed of new arrivals. The latter included, at least temporarily, the 104th New York (the "Wadsworth Guards"), whose recruitment he had encouraged. Further, Wadsworth not only retained command of his brigade (the 12th, 21st, 23rd, and 35th New York Volunteers), but by Special Orders 83 he was assigned troops stationed in Charles, George, and Montgomery Counties on the Maryland side of the Potomac.[15]

Difficult Creek not only identified one of the limits of his command, but could well describe the situation in which Wadsworth increasingly found himself. The first problem was obtaining an accurate count of men within his command because of constant turnover, including a number of three-month men. By Wadsworth's calculations, on April 2 he had between 19,200 and 19,400 "effectives," though this count and the condition of those troops came into question when the Army of the Potomac began its move to the Virginia Peninsula. For example, in late March he commanded seven artillery divisions, one of which had only three batteries (rather than the usual four to six); six cavalry regiments, four of which were dismounted and were sent to Colonel Dixon Miles; and twenty-three infantry regiments, of which two were only detachments and one was composed of the District of Columbia Volunteers.[16]

General Wadsworth's command also included "23 forts south of the Potomac, 14 forts and 3 batteries between the Potomac and Anacostia rivers, and 11 forts beyond the Anacostia." Except for Fort Washington, a virtually useless, old masonry fort, the forts had been constructed hastily under the supervision of Chief Engineer Colonel John G. Barnard and represented the second phase of protection for the capital. However, in January Barnard had informed Army of the Potomac adjutant general Seth Williams that without "more effective measures" the works and armament would "fall into ruin" and cited Fort Corcoran as being "in a shocking condition from neglect." Twenty-eight earthworks were ungarrisoned (that is, without artillerymen), the inefficient guards were failing to maintain them, 200 mounted guns lacked ammunition, and generally the half million dollars already spent would be wasted unless something was done immediately.[17]

Wadsworth, equally troubled by the condition of the forts, had written Army of the Potomac chief of artillery William F. Barry to the same effect. The situation was so bad that Barnard even recommended that no offensive operations be taken until the forts were preserved and garrisoned with regular army artillerymen. Steps were taken in late March and early April to garrison the forts, as Barnard had suggested, though the troops were still largely recruits.

However, the biggest difficulty Military Governor Wadsworth faced was Army of the Potomac commander George B. McClellan. General McClellan was vainglorious, contemptuous of politicians (especially Republicans), and possibly too successful in civilian and military life to this point. A 36-year-old professional soldier who had ranked second in the famous West Point class of 1846, McClellan had first garnered praise for service during the Mexican War. Afterward he had served as instructor at the Military Academy and had studied the European armies during the Crimean War before resigning to become chief engineer of the Illinois Central Railroad and later president of the Ohio and Mississippi Railroad.[18]

Not surprisingly, General McClellan had a distinct preference for West Pointers and resented civilian interference in military matters. He may have reserved his harshest criticism for the Squire of Geneseo, who seemed to him to symbolize Lincoln's disposition to award command to political allies.

Earlier, in a letter to then Secretary of War Cameron, McClellan wrote that he had "selected [officers to command positions] with distinct reference to their fitness for the important duties that may devolve upon them." Fitness meant West Pointers whose military training and, thus, loyalty he could count on. Wadsworth clearly did not meet either criterion: "I objected to [Stanton] the selection [of Wadsworth] for the reason that Gen. Wadsworth was not a soldier by training," explained McClellan. (The Young Napoleon was more blunt in a draft of his memoirs, writing: "Wadsworth was no doubt an excellent agriculturist & a brave man, but he was no general; he was a man of bad character & a pseudo-fanatic.") McClellan had urged the appointment of Brigadier General William Franklin as military governor, a post that he considered *"next in importance to"* command of the Army of the Potomac [italics added]. However, General McClellan recalled that Secretary Stanton bluntly informed him "that it was useless to discuss the matter [of Wadsworth's appointment], because it would in no event be changed."[19]

McClellan also claimed his distaste for Wadsworth stemmed from the impression Stanton gave him that Wadsworth was appointed to "conciliate the agricultural interests of New York." Compounding matters, McClellan was convinced that only three days after General Wadsworth met with him at Fairfax Court House the civilian general had become his "enemy." This was in direct contrast to what he regarded as Wadsworth's profession of "the greatest devotion and friendship" when he left the meeting. McClellan attributed the apparent change of heart to Stanton's having informed the military governor of McClellan's objections to his appointment. On the other hand, Provost Marshal Doster claimed that the antagonism between McClellan and Wadsworth began even earlier, when Wadsworth publicly criticized McClellan's timidity in the winter of 1861–1862. Wadsworth, who had checked on his pickets in front of Munson's Hill, had reported that there were only a handful of Confederates and a few wooden cannon. He concluded that a Union advance easily could overcome them.[20]

Contributing to the image of Wadsworth as a meddling politician is his January letter replying to Massachusetts senator Charles Sumner: "I tell you confidentially but advisedly that the army has lost confidence in its commander [McClellan]." McClellan's policy of allowing the Confederates to offer "us battle in sight of our Capital which we decline is a pusillanimous, cowardly one." Wadsworth believed the only "hope" was for Congress to take action to "save the country; but you must do it soon or [it will] be too late." (This was shortly before Stanton replaced Cameron.) The New Yorker claimed that he was acting only from the purest of motives, "the desperate condition of our affairs," especially "the feeling of the army." The restless, inactive general had even invited Sumner (and Senators William Fessenden and James Grimes) to dine with him to discuss the situation.[21]

General McClellan also objected to Wadsworth's beliefs about slavery. McClellan is reported to have written New York Democrats interested in nominating him for president, "Help me to dodge the nigger—we want nothing to do with him. I am fighting to preserve the integrity of the Union. . . . To gain that end we cannot afford to mix up the negro question." In short, he believed Wadsworth had priorities reversed.[22]

Wadsworth thus represented almost everything that McClellan disliked: a civilian general, a politician, an abolitionist, and, it could be added, a Lincoln confidant. At least Wadsworth was considered a confidant by the *New York Tribune*'s Washington correspondent Adams Sherman Hill, who claimed to cultivate his sources assiduously. Hill reported that General Wadsworth revealed to him more than one conversation with President Lincoln, which suggested the extent to which Wadsworth had the president's ear. A similar claim about the relationship between Wadsworth and Lincoln is made by Provost Marshal Doster.[23]

However the antagonisms originated, the stage was set for what historian T. Harry Williams labeled "one of the great controversies of the war." The situation was aggravated by the fact that the war had been going especially well for the Union in the West, while the Army of the Potomac's commander still had not been prodded into action after four months on the job. The extent of McClellan's activities was to convene a council of war at which he obtained a virtually foreordained eight-to-four vote by his generals to transport the Army of the Potomac by water to Urbana, about fifty miles northeast of Richmond. Conversely, President Lincoln, like Generals Wadsworth, McDowell, and Heintzelman, wanted an overland campaign, which would entail crossing rivers and railroads subject to Confederate attack. The president also wanted the capital made safe, which represented both a military and political imperative.

Grudgingly Lincoln had agreed to the Urbana plan, but on March 8, by General War Order 2 (the order making Wadsworth military governor), he announced two additional decisions that indicated his mistrust of McClellan. First, as noted, Lincoln ordered the twelve divisions of McClellan's army organized into four corps. Second, the president named four senior generals, all regarded as Republicans, to command those corps: McDowell (I), Major General Edwin Sumner (II), Brigadier General Samuel Heintzelman (III), and Brigadier General Erasmus Keyes (IV). Major General Nathaniel Banks was named V Corps commander five days later. McClellan, who wanted to surround himself with younger, more trusted men and had already communicated his need to make such appointments, had to have been insulted by these decisions. Then, to General McClellan's further discomfort and Lincoln's mortification, before military operations could begin, Major General Joseph Johnston's clearly outnumbered forces (half McClellan's estimate) withdrew from Manassas. Now McClellan could no longer flank Johnston (via the Urbana route), so he had to change plans. This led to a conference with Lincoln in which McClellan proposed another waterborne campaign, this time to begin farther south, at Fortress Monroe at the mouth of the James River. The president again expressed his concerns about McClellan's proposed advance by water, though he made it clear he wanted pursuit of the Confederates "at all events" and "at once." To satisfy Lincoln that his plan had the support of military men, General McClellan convened another council of war at army headquarters in Fairfax Court House on March 13.[24]

After the council McClellan reported agreement that a campaign against Richmond up the peninsula between the York and James Rivers could be conducted successfully. However, he listed a number of provisos: The Confederate ram *Merrimac* had to be "neutralized," sufficient transportation had to be provided, enemy batteries on the James must be silenced, and, of course, Washington was to be given "an entire feeling of security for its safety from menace." Secretary Stanton assented to McClellan's plan in a carefully worded reply that indicated Lincoln did not object to the campaign (not that he genuinely approved it). However, Stanton directed McClellan to "make it entirely certain that" Manassas Junction could not be reoccupied by the Confederates and that Washington was left "entirely secure." Conflicting interpretations of what force was necessary for that security became the rub.[25]

Three days after the council and Stanton's reluctant assent, General McClellan's interpretation was conveyed to the two civilian commanders who respectively would protect Manassas Junction and the capital, Generals Banks and Wadsworth. Wadsworth was to: garrison troops not needed to police Washington north of the Potomac and move others assigned to special duties south of the river; post "the main body of troops in the center of your front" and proportion other troops on the right and left flanks; maintain the forts and armaments (and rigidly inspect the troops); take care of the railways, canals, depots, bridges, and ferries; scour the neighboring country south of the eastern branch of the Potomac (which curved northward toward the Navy Yard Bridge); maintain good order; and forward and facilitate the movement of arriving troops to active commands after forming them into provisional brigades. Finally, as if to underscore the significance of his duties, General Wadsworth was to transmit monthly returns and submit consolidated reports "every Sunday morning."[26]

General McClellan was satisfied that if his instructions were followed, Washington would be secure, and thus began moving his army. Still, not until he was aboard ship did he fully reveal to Lincoln his plans, and only after departure did he provide his estimates of forces to protect the capital. However, the day after McClellan's departure his plans began to unravel. Military Governor Wadsworth, who "deem[ed] it my duty," directly challenged McClellan's estimate of approximately 77,000 men available for the safety of the capital. By Wadsworth's calculations there were only 19,022 "new and imperfectly disciplined men fit for duty."[27]

The problem was that the two generals were reflecting different perspectives. McClellan's count included approximately 11,000 men garrisoning forts around Washington and 11,400 "disposable troops" with Wadsworth, 7,780 men at Warrenton under Brigadier General John J. Abercrombie, Brigadier General Louis Blenker's 10,859 at Manassas, 35,467 in Banks's V Corps in the Shenandoah Valley, and 1,350 on the lower Potomac (one of Brigadier General Joseph Hooker's regiments, plus 500 cavalry). Though he didn't include them in his 77,000, McClellan also relied on 4,000 that General Dix would forward to Washington from New York City, and 3,500 from Pennsylvania and Maryland. Wadsworth was counting only troops under his immediate command in Washington.[28]

Reporting directly to Stanton, possibly at the secretary's urging, Wadsworth claimed 15,335 infantry, 4,294 artillerymen, and six mounted companies of cavalry (848 men), a total of 20,477 troops under his command, from which were deducted 1,455 sick, in arrest, or confinement. Moreover, he had no mounted light artillery and had orders to detail "four of his best regiments" to Brigadier Generals William French and Oliver O. Howard of the II Corps and to transfer another 4,000 to Manassas to relieve General Sumner's II Corps, which was to join McClellan. Thus, General Wadsworth believed he was left to rely on inadequate and unfit replacements. He did acknowledge that it was "very improbable that the enemy will assail us at this point," but he hoped that the Confederates did not realize how weak his forces were. Concluding that Washington was not secure, Lincoln then ordered Stanton to detain either General McDowell's or General Sumner's corps to "operate at, or in the direction of Ma[na]ssas junction, or otherwise as occasion may require."[29]

While correspondence between principals would fly, tempers flare, and recriminations occupy reams of testimony, it remains probable that Washington had sufficient troops for its defense. The problem was McClellan's cavalier way with Lincoln and his advisers, whom McClellan dismissed as incapable of understanding military matters. Unfortunately, McClellan, with whom Lincoln and Wadsworth were quite disenchanted, compounded the problem by playing loose with numbers. For example, he double-counted Abercrombie's 7,780, which was, in fact, part of Banks's Shenandoah Valley command, and Brigadier General Louis Blenker's troops, which were on their way to support Major General Fremont's newly created Mountain Department. That McClellan's calculations were hurriedly communicated while aboard the steamer *Commodore* awaiting departure from Washington ("that sink of iniquity," according to McClellan) was hardly an excuse. Rather, McClellan was assuming that Lincoln could not add and that Wadsworth would not undermine him.[30]

Wadsworth aggravated the situation in an April 4 report to Secretary Stanton. As ordered to do three days prior, he had dispatched the four regiments to Generals French and Howard, but he did "not find any regiments fit" to forward to Generals Sumner and Hooker, who were awaiting orders to embark. He had already telegraphed General Sumner to that effect, which the latter had, in turn, confirmed to Stanton. Wadsworth then asked what he was to do. Ironically and inconsistently, on April 2, Wadsworth indicated he did not want any more troops sent to him, though it is possible that he had so many "unfit" troops that he did not want to have to deal with more at the time.[31]

Further complicating the overall situation was the March 11 military reorganization by Lincoln. Eight military departments were created, with General McDowell commanding the Department of the Rappahannock, which included the District of Columbia. Like two other major departments, Banks's Department of Shenandoah and Major General John Fremont's Mountain Department, assignments and boundaries were at times amorphous, confusing, overlapping, and ultimately unmanageable. For example, General Wadsworth understood he was "under the immediate advice of" Secretary of War Stanton and Adjutant General Lorenzo Thomas and was to act "in many respects the functions of Departmental Comdr," although after April 4, once again he reported to his old commander General McDowell.[32]

A test of Wadsworth's command to defend the capital would come on April 19, because the nervous Stanton feared Major General Thomas ("Stonewall") Jackson's ubiquitous presence in the upper Shenandoah Valley. Wadsworth was directed to "assume a supposed [simulated] attack" by assembling troops within the city limits at the Long Bridge and the Aqueduct. When Wadsworth's request to postpone the maneuvers was denied, he reluctantly attempted the simulation. Confirming his appraisal of military conditions in Washington and exacerbating Stanton's almost paranoid apprehensions, Wadsworth was able to produce only the equivalent of four poorly armed or unarmed infantry regiments. For example, he reported that only two companies of the 102nd New York appeared at the Aqueduct with muskets, and, worse, they lacked ammunition. Four other companies, a total of 436 men, showed up with only 400 rounds—less than one round per man. The Massachusetts Artillery had six rifled guns, but no ammunition. Two regiments did not arrive at the Long Bridge until four hours after his orders were given. Only Colonel Mix's 1st New Jersey Cavalry was singled out for efficiency.[33]

Wittingly or not, the military governor had played to the administration's fears, and the response ultimately came from Lincoln. On the basis of the combined reports of Wadsworth and McDowell (and, no doubt, pressure from Republican radicals), the president detained McDowell's I Corps and so advised McClellan. Immediately McClellan, bogged down in front of Yorktown by Major General John B. Magruder's minuscule force, protested. Calling forth his customarily inaccurate figures (to make his case with the administration), General McClellan telegraphed Lincoln that he faced not only a "large force," but one that was being reinforced daily. He did not want Lincoln to force him to fight such opposition "with diminished numbers." Though Lincoln had withheld roughly one-third of the troops McClellan had anticipated for the campaign, the president did not buy McClellan's argument. Instead, he replied through Stanton that the forces under Wadsworth and Banks were "deemed by experienced military men inadequate to protect Winchester [being threatened by Jackson] and the railroad, and [were] much less than had been fixed by your corps commanders as necessary to secure Washington." McDowell's corps, not Sumner's, was detached because it was not due to join McClellan yet; Sumner's was ready to depart.[34]

The president's decision was particularly distasteful to McClellan for two reasons. First, it reduced his anticipated forces by roughly a third. Second, McDowell's corps was composed of particularly qualified officers who, before the war ended, would be corps commanders themselves, including Henry Slocum, John Newton, John Reynolds, George Meade, John Gibbon, and Edward Ord. (Fortunate for McClellan, and at his request, all but General Gibbon were transferred to the peninsula before the campaign was over.) On the other hand, McClellan made it clear that he wanted nothing to do with McDowell: "After all that I have heard of things which have occurred since I left Washington and before I would prefer that Genl McDowell should not again be assigned to duty with me."[35]

McClellan was convinced, if he needed any convincing, that there was a cabal in Washington that included Wadsworth and McDowell (Lincoln's private secretary John Hay would later call them Jacobins). In fact, Judge Edwards Pierrepont claimed that McClellan had written a letter to an unnamed friend, the contents of which found their way into an article in the April 15 *New York Commercial Advertiser,* which was scathingly critical of Stanton. According to Pierrepont's source,

Stanton's conduct toward McClellan stemmed from the desires of Stanton, Chase, McDowell, and Wadsworth to assure McClellan's defeat. Stanton would benefit because he could eliminate McClellan as a rival for the presidency. McDowell would succeed McClellan as commander of the Army of the Potomac and the political aspirations of Wadsworth, who disliked McClellan, would be improved. By contrast, Stanton, explaining his actions toward McClellan in a private letter to the pastor of his youth, omitted any mention of Wadsworth. Instead, he claimed to have relied on the advice of Major General Ethan Allen Hitchcock, Adjutant General Lorenzo Thomas, and an informal organization of officers. Among his informal advisors were the army's chief engineer, ordnance chief, quartermaster general, and commissary general.[36]

McClellan's formal response to Lincoln's withdrawal of McDowell's corps was to complain that he had insufficient troops (only 85,000 in his Army of the Potomac, of which barely 53,000 had so far joined him) as opposed to his wild overestimate of 100,000 troops under General Joseph Johnston. Moreover, he suffered from lack of transportation for matériel and men. Further, he reminded Stanton that at least 50,000 men had been removed from his command since he had made arrangements for the campaign.[37]

This infighting between General McClellan and the administration—and consequently Wadsworth—over numbers had been going on at least since the previous December. McClellan's personal intelligence service, headed by Chicago detective Allen Pinkerton, had been reporting wildly exaggerated numbers of Confederate troops near Washington. Because newspapers were critical of Pinkerton's intelligence operation, McClellan had imposed a gag order on officers in his command. Brigadier General Wadsworth, who had been doing his own counting and may well have been the inspiration for the gag order, was undeterred, based on the opinion of his immediate superior, General McDowell. Wadsworth countered Pinkerton's numbers, asserting that intelligence gained from his brigade's expeditions as far south as Fairfax, Virginia, revealed that General Johnston had no more than 50,000 men, close to the actual total. Further, he recalled that he had supplied this information to Generals McDowell and McClellan, who had treated him quite rudely, and finally to Secretary Stanton. Not surprisingly, Stanton was impressed by General Wadsworth's clarity and forcefulness, which could resemble the "moral certainty" of the general's father.[38]

Ultimately, the Peninsula campaign was a demoralizing failure for the Union, for which all the principals, including McClellan, Stanton, and Lincoln, have been blamed. An issue that would not die was whether McClellan had been ill-treated by the administration. Underlying that was the question of whether Washington would have been amply protected if McClellan's plans had been implemented. The issue was reexamined indirectly in the court of inquiry initiated by General McDowell later in the year to clear his name of charges of incompetence when commanding troops at Fredericksburg. One of those called to testify was Brigadier General James S. Wadsworth.

Though the object of the court of inquiry was to examine McDowell's conduct (which was questioned by McClellan's defenders, who were bent on getting even for the treatment of McClellan), the focus quickly became the defense of Washington in spring 1862—and necessarily, General Wadsworth's role. To McDowell's questions General Wadsworth testified that the forces he had been assigned were inadequate on any number of grounds, including the fact that two cavalry regiments were "without horses or arms except sabers." Reflective of the situation, Wadsworth asserted that he "was not furnished with an accurate list" when he assumed command and had to publish "an order [in the newspapers] for the commanders of all troops within my command to report to me." General Banks's corps was approximately eighty miles away, so it was clearly not intended for the protection of Washington. Finally, questioned about whether McClellan had ever specified the number of men he had left to defend Washington and their locations, Wadsworth claimed to "know nothing of it."[39] In short, Wadsworth concluded that Lincoln and Stanton had acted properly in retaining McDowell's corps.

The hearings had scarcely ended before Wadsworth found himself under attack for falsifying figures. One of his more articulate critics was Richard Frothingham, managing editor of the *Boston Post,* who has been praised for his exhaustive research "and painstaking accuracy." Editor Frothingham carefully marshaled documents with which he attacked Wadsworth and the administration. At least one of these documents, marked "Private," came from an officer within Wadsworth's command and suggests Frothingham was consciously building a case against Wadsworth. The main thrust of his argument was that Wadsworth had sufficient troops under his command, but he was incapable of making proper dispositions of them.[40]

Like McClellan, Frothingham believed there was a cabal "of petty interests and ambitions" in the capital who were guilty of "preventing the capture of Richmond, and sacrificing thousands of precious lives, to say nothing of treasure." Members of the cabal had not only withheld McDowell's troops, but had ordered the cessation of recruiting, had extracted incorrect meanings from McClellan's communications by "a torturing of the documents," and had relied on a political appointee, Wadsworth. Frothingham declared that Wadsworth, whose judgment about the "condition and character" of the troops became the crux of the matter, had "grossly deceived" Lincoln by "the utter untrustworthiness of [his] sworn testimony." The result was that officials who "ought to have seconded [McClellan] in every possible way" were, instead, caught up in their own "impertinent self-conceit."[41]

This was representative of the attacks on Wadsworth and radical Republicans by McClellan's supporters, who were still smarting over criticisms of McClellan's conduct of the war. Wadsworth was particularly incensed by an editorial in the April 20, 1863, *New York World,* the content and tone of which were similar to Frothingham's. Because he regarded the article as "impeaching my veracity," he felt compelled to respond in the *New York Times,* owned by his political ally Henry Raymond. In his defense, Wadsworth virtually repeated his testimony at the McDowell Court of Inquiry. He again noted that he had reviewed forces in his command on March 31, 1862, on April 2, and again at the end of April. However, his point here was not how many troops he had to defend Washington, but their rawness, the lack of arms, and the incompetence of their officers. That is, he stuck to the "condition and character" issue that Frothingham had challenged.[42]

The flurry of charges and countercharges soon abated, but the issue may never die. Over the years the extent to which the principals (McClellan, Lincoln, Stanton, and congressional radicals) have been blamed for the failed Peninsula campaign has depended on the critic's particular perspective. Criticisms of Brigadier General Wadsworth range from the overused characterization of him as simply a tool of the administration to the claim that Wadsworth was a member of a cabal bent on destroying McClellan's military career to further their anti-slavery interests.[43]

Contemporaneous accounts offer little help, because of the allegiances of those who rendered them. One of the more objective assessments is by then Brigadier General Oliver O. Howard, who was in Washington at the time. While he believed that McClellan had amply protected the capital, he recognized Lincoln's dilemma. Lincoln wanted McClellan to be successful, but he "did not dare to" shift Fremont, Banks, or Wadsworth from the capital without replacements. The real problem, according to Howard, was not "Mr. Lincoln's apprehensions," but Stanton's leadership, which, in turn, was dictated by his abolitionist sentiments and his political supporters. While not naming anyone, Howard appeared to be referring to political appointees Wadsworth, Fremont, and Banks.[44]

On the other hand, Provost Marshal Doster, who was even closer to the scene, countered that the number of troops left behind when McClellan departed "was far less than the number Wadsworth had counted on." Doster recalled that "the consolidated report showed only about 17,000, composed chiefly of fragmentary organizations." It was only later, after new regiments arrived, that Wadsworth would command as many as 36,000 men. It should not be assumed that Doster was a sycophant because he owed his appointment to Wadsworth. He could be critical of the military governor, once declaring: "I can but think that it was fortunate that his [Wadsworth's] capacity as defender of the capital was never tested." Also Doster never made any bones about the fact that there was mutual distrust between McClellan and Wadsworth. Nevertheless, Doster unhesitatingly supported Wadsworth's troop count.[45]

Certainly Wadsworth's views toward slavery and his expectations of the Lincoln administration were well known and seemed to justify McClellan's fears about appointing politicians to command, especially in the politically sensitive capital. Wadsworth's influence in New York State was long apparent to radical Secretary of the Treasury Salmon Chase. His influence also was apparent in the appointments of Dix and Pierrepont to the parole commission and of the provost marshal in which he bypassed Major Doster's superior. Moreover, Wadsworth's communications with influential senators, like Sumner, certainly must have helped undermine the Young Napoleon. Thus, if the military governor was next in command to the Army of the Potomac commander, as McClellan claimed, and Wadsworth's antipathy toward McClellan was as well known as Doster asserted, then Wadsworth was perfectly positioned to undercut McClellan.

However, even accepting the conspiracy theory, to what extent did Stanton use Wadsworth, or vice versa? And to what end? Put bluntly, was this a setup? Did Wadsworth purposely misrepresent the quality and quantity of the forces under his command at a critical moment in the campaign? And, if so, was it to resurrect the career of the more politically acceptable McDowell? Even more to the point, how would Wadsworth gain from McClellan's dismissal?[46]

Wadsworth cannot be dismissed simply as "an aging politician-general" as revisionist historian Thomas Rowland did in his recent examination of the failed Peninsula campaign. Wadsworth was not a Fremont, Sickles, Butler, or Banks. He had never held office; in fact, he had shown an aversion to do so. Rather, his willingness to champion the cause and his political prominence gave him influence. The real question is a two-part one: Was Wadsworth sufficiently anti-slavery—*and temperamentally suited*—to consciously undermine McClellan? The answers are probably, yes, he was sufficiently anti-slavery, but no, subterfuge was not his style. Though Wadsworth's letter to Senator Sumner supports the charge of political intrigue, War Secretary Stanton's private letter to his pastor, revealed only years later, fails entirely to mention Wadsworth in connection with the withholding of McDowell's troops.[47]

T. Harry Williams's reexamination of his claim about a Jacobin cabal in the third edition of *Lincoln and the Radicals* tended to downplay the conspiracy theory. Rather, Williams concluded that General McClellan "failed because he was a poor soldier as well as because he aroused political opposition." That opposition included Wadsworth, the ardent patriot who uncompromisingly sought to eradicate slavery by prosecuting the war vigorously. Provost Marshal Doster vividly recalled Wadsworth pacing his office floor alone late at night during the summer of 1862, "seeming to feel our defeats in a personal way." He would demonstrate that patriotism again after Gettysburg more bluntly. Whatever his faults, whatever his politics, Wadsworth's reports and subsequent comments about the quality and quantity of troops to defend Washington in early April were based on what he regarded as a correct assessment.[48]

The uncharacteristically public response by Wadsworth, who could be prickly when his integrity was attacked, ended the unhappy episode as far as he was concerned. He would now turn his attention to other matters.

Chapter 10

THE "COUNCIL OF MILITARY PUNDITS"

Wadsworth Skirmishes in the Capital

One of Military Governor Wadsworth's more pleasant activities was attending the presentation by his wife, Mary Craig, of the blue silk colors (with "Wadsworth Guards" prominently sewn on them) to the 104th New York Volunteers on April 12, 1862. At the ceremony the 104th's Captain Henry Wiley was introduced to Wadsworth as "Uncle John's son from Springwater." In the cordial manner that could characterize him, Wadsworth replied that, indeed, he knew Captain Wiley's father, John Wiley, the Methodist minister. Equally memorable to Wiley was Wadsworth's appearance: "He is much older looking than I thought, for his hair is whiter than fathers [*sic*], if anything." The irony is that Wiley's father was 68, while Wadsworth was 54.[1]

The general's duties, never fully spelled out, seemed endless. Beyond the necessity of receiving, drilling, disciplining, and positioning troops and maintaining the forts and armaments, Wadsworth now was to secure and maintain the canals, depots, railways, ferries, and the stores.[2]

Additionally, he was to assure good order within the limits of his command. An example of his interpretation of this responsibility was the arrest of the quartermaster of the 5th Pennsylvania for selling government pistols. Another example was his restriction of the sale of liquor where he felt it was "necessary to maintain the discipline of the Army." However, he did permit four boxes of liquor to pass through the commissary to officers of Brigadier General Christopher C. Augur's brigade. He also directed Provost Marshal Doster to release a private of Company F, 10th New Jersey Volunteers, from the guardhouse. The private was charged with shooting a prisoner who attempted to escape from Old Capitol Prison, but Wadsworth saw this as an opportunity to commend the private's behavior. "It appears," wrote Wadsworth to the provost marshal, "that [the private] . . . is rather deserving of praise than censure for his vigilance and promptness of action."[3]

Maintaining order also resulted in his putting a stop to the prisoners' practice of insulting sentinels and others outside the prison. Per Wadsworth's orders, any prisoner caught doing so was to be put "in irons and on bread and water." If the culprit could not be identified, Wadsworth intended to board up the windows. If that did not stop the practice, Wadsworth was prepared to "put all the inmates of the room in irons and on bread and water." Further, he was going to arrest any persons outside the prison who made any signals to the prisoners.[4]

The real test of Military Governor Wadsworth's interpretation of his extensive responsibilities—and the focus of more criticism—was his treatment of escaped slaves. The emancipated District of Columbia was becoming a magnet for slaves, or "contrabands" as they were called, escaping from Virginia and Maryland, which led to clashes between authorities and abolitionists. Wadsworth not only inherited a problem, but, because of his anti-slavery views, he compounded it. When civil authorities caught and jailed escaped slaves pursuant to the Fugitive Slave Law, the radical Wadsworth often attempted creative evasions of the law. The most notable—and humorous—example occurred after the arrest of Wadsworth's cook. It also offers an interesting insight into Wadsworth's behavior in Washington. According to Lieutenant Kress:

> One morning the general's orderly came to my quarters about four o'clock, and said General Wadsworth wished to see me at his residence, on arriving there, the general, lying in bed, (and I, standing in the hall), door open, directed me to take about 30 cavalrymen, mounted, and ride to the city jail and release therefrom every escaping slave, also his black woman cook, who, he had just learned, had been arrested by the police as a contraband, and she was needed to get breakfast for him and his family. I obtained the cavalry, went to jail and found quite a crowd of contrabands, released every one of them including the general's cook, despite protests by the jailor. The civil authorities were excessively indignant at the military outrage, but it was General Wadsworth's scrape, not mine, and it did not worry him a bit.[5]

Margaret Leech, author of *Reveille in Washington,* offers some details that Kress may have conveniently omitted. Kress and his squad grabbed the keys from the jailer and deputy, released the "mulatto cook," and locked up the jailer and deputy, as well as the Maryland owner's lawyers. But hot-tempered U.S. marshal Ward Lamon subsequently disarmed the two soldiers Kress had left, "recaptured the jail," released the lawyers, and locked up the soldiers instead. Leech neatly concluded that this absurd melodrama ended in a tie: "Lamon had his jail, but Wadsworth had [the cook] Alethia Lynch."[6]

Ignoring the pettiness of the two principals, Wadsworth and Lamon, Lieutenant Kress correctly assessed the situation. Wadsworth dismissed the incident as unimportant—simply "the liberation of a slave woman believed to have been improperly held under the forms of Law." Wadsworth knew he had no fears, which was amply confirmed by a later, more notorious, clash with Lamon. While the particulars of this incident are unknown, the affair stemmed from

Wadsworth's quartering, provisioning, and employing Blacks coming into the city, particularly the latter. That is, the abolitionist military governor was doing everything in his power to circumvent the Fugitive Slave Law, which authorized commissioners in Washington to obtain warrants for the return of fugitives to their Maryland or District of Columbia masters. This cut into a lucrative business for slave catchers and for Lamon, who lost fees prescribed under the law. It also led to protests of Wadsworth's actions by border-state slaveholders.[7]

Almost immediately Wadsworth received a letter from Senator Henry Wilson, who wrote:

> I have consulted several of the Senators in regard to the demand of Marshall [*sic*] Lamon and they all say you should pay no regard to his commands. If the president sends you the orders you will have to obey it, but I advise you to pay no regard to W. N. Lamon.[8]

Writing concurring comments on the letter were radical Senators Benjamin F. Wade, Charles Sumner, Daniel Clark, Justin M. Morrill, William Howard, Zachariah Chandler, and Daniel Wilmot.

Wadsworth also had the support of a character as shady as, if not more than, Lamon, one "Count" Adam Gurowski, who proclaimed in his diary that "General Wadsworth is the good genius of the poor and oppressed race. But for Wadsworth's noble soul and heart the Lamons and many other blood-hounds in Washington would have given three-fourths of the fugitives over to the whip of the slavers." At this point, Gurowski's star was still in the ascendancy in Washington; it would fall rapidly thereafter.[9]

With such support Wadsworth could safely challenge Lamon and follow his political and humanitarian bent. In fact, he would claim, quite disingenuously, that he was simply putting "a stop to the abduction without process of Law, of col'd persons within this Dist. which had long been practiced to the disgrace of the Capital." He even erroneously alleged that he had "succeeded in avoiding any collision with the Civil authorities."[10]

Despite Wadsworth's disclaimer, his actions did not go unnoticed. President Lincoln was confronted by a committee of a hundred Prince George's County, Maryland, slaveholders who complained to him about "the hindrances [to enforcement of the Fugitive Slave Law] alleged to have been thrown in [the] way by Gen. Wadsworth." They protested that Wadsworth was deliberately slow to execute the law, and in fact was "taking the evidence of the slaves" rather than the slaveholders. However, the May 20, 1862, *New York Tribune* reported Lincoln's confidence in General Wadsworth's good intentions. The intermittent warfare with Marshal Lamon would continue, but declined after July 17, when the second Confiscation Act (liberating slaves of secessionists) was passed.[11]

Unquestionably Wadsworth was playing fast and loose with the rules under the Fugitive Slave Law in pursuit of his abolitionism. And he had the support of those who mattered, including Lincoln and congressional radicals. Moreover, this may well have been one reason he was given the appointment, though there is nothing to indicate it. In fact, his actions complicated matters for a harassed Lincoln and his cabinet, especially Seward and Stanton, who had to defend Wadsworth's actions in the face of criticisms. Additionally, when the fugitives poured into Washington they presented real problems for the authorities. They had to be housed, fed, and cared for in overcrowded quarters where disease, including smallpox, spread rapidly. Additional prison guards were hired, and more military officers were employed to handle the influx of fugitives. Yet from the few reports and accounts available, General Wadsworth seemed unconcerned about the problems he was creating, willingly challenging any who reminded him of the law, and ignoring threats of his own arrest.

Paradoxically, Wadsworth was particularly solicitous of Southerners when the situation involved farming. He claimed that in that part of Virginia "within my Com'd I endeavored to prevent wrong & outrage [against civilians] by military authority as far as possible." Where fences had been destroyed by warring forces he "ordered that no farm stock should be allowed to roam at large, so as to allow of the cultivation of the Land." Detachments sent into the country near Fredericksburg were ordered "to scrupulously respect the persons and property of citizens." He investigated complaints promptly and "severely punished" officers who disregarded this order. For example, on one occasion he telegraphed Brigadier General Abram Duryee (also spelled Duryea) to the effect that he understood that members of the 12th Virginia (Union) were "committing depredations on the inhabitants" and directed Duryee to put a stop "to outrages of every description." Officers who failed to comply were to be mustered out.[12]

Much less pleasant was the necessity of arresting "a large no. of citizens, mostly in the state of Va as suspected spies, as persons likely to give aid to the Enemy, those who had been guilty of wrong & outrage upon their fellow citizens, who in violation of Law were carrying supplies beyond our military lines & committed other offenses which required the interposition of Military Authority."[13] Special pains were taken to adjudicate cases where wrong was done to individuals and the unnecessary government expense of feeding, sheltering, and guarding prisoners could be avoided.

While this became a greater problem later, partly of Wadsworth's own doing, the case of Patrick McCracken deserves mention here. The essence of the incident, which has taken on the character of legend with its retelling, is that the 32-year-old, Irish-born McCracken had been arrested as a spy not far from his Spotsylvania County home. Wadsworth interviewed McCracken and extracted from him that he and his younger brother, Michael, were farmers. Comfortable with McCracken's story, Wadsworth released him with McCracken's promise not to take sides against the Union. McCracken would later repay this courtesy.[14]

General Wadsworth's good deeds while military governor also illustrate his growing reputation as a caring officer. Typical is his intercession on behalf of two Union officers wounded at the battle of Fair Oaks, May 31–June 1, 1862, and hospitalized in Washington. Secretary of War Stanton had placed restrictions on medical leaves, thus requiring soldiers to remain in hospitals, including those in Washington. The two officers (one had lost his left arm and the other had a shattered arm in a splint) appealed to one of Wadsworth's staff for a furlough. Wadsworth called the two officers into his office, handed them money, and remarked: "Gentlemen, I am sorry to see you so situated. . . . Farewell, may God bless you." Once out of their sight, according to his staff officer, "tears started from his [Wadsworth's] eyes." Apparently General Wadsworth did not take seriously—or ignored—an earlier rebuke from McClellan for granting disability furloughs without permission from headquarters.[15]

Similar sensitivity was demonstrated by him and his unlikely partners, Generals Winfield Scott, George McClellan, and John Wool, when they obtained legislation to incorporate a "Soldiers' Home" in New York State, with the four of them as incorporators.[16]

✶   ✶   ✶

After the administration's March 23 reorganization of the Union forces in northern Virginia, General Wadsworth's responsibilities, however endless they seemed, remained largely administrative. That reorganization found McDowell commanding the Department of the Rappahannock, which, along with Banks's Shenandoah and Fremont's Mountain Departments, was to protect against any Confederate advances in the Shenandoah Valley. McDowell's constantly changing department initially comprised three divisions, Brigadier General William Franklin's 1st, Brigadier General George McCall's 2nd, and Brigadier General Rufus King's 3rd. Franklin's division left for the peninsula on April 10 and eventually was replaced by Brigadier General James Shields's division. A fourth division, commanded by Brigadier General Edward O. Ord, was added May 16. Brigades commanded by Brigadier General Abner Doubleday and Colonel John W. Geary would also become part of the ever-changing department, with Geary reporting to Wadsworth at one point.

The creation of these independent commands (McDowell, Banks, and Fremont) was the direct result of the ubiquitous Major General Thomas ("Stonewall") Jackson's presence in the valley at that time. His presence was intended to cause the Union to withhold troops from McClellan on the peninsula—and it did. Though Jackson himself was forced to withdraw southward up the valley, his withdrawal marked the beginning of his famous Shenandoah campaign, which so greatly influenced the administration's plans. And, necessarily, it increased Wadsworth's responsibilities, including the mind-boggling tasks of temporarily commanding, monitoring, and shifting forces within the department. He even found himself directing troops to escort the transport of beef cattle to Fredericksburg, where McDowell had been relocated preparatory to joining McClellan on the peninsula.

Momentarily, the administration's fears subsided, but caution prevailed and expeditions were sent out to ascertain the size and location of Confederate forces. For example, in early April Wadsworth joined McDowell, Brigadier General Daniel Woodbury, commander of the newly formed Engineer Brigade, and Lieutenant David Houston to examine defenses near Fredericksburg and to determine what forces were needed to prevent a Confederate blockade of the Potomac at Aquia. Their report—that only a small contingent of Confederates was in the vicinity—momentarily reassured the nervous Stanton.[17]

Then, in early May General Jackson reappeared in the Shenandoah Valley. He had been joined by the division of the equally eccentric Major General Richard Ewell, resulting in a combined strength of 17,000, and he intended to prevent General Banks from advancing up the valley. Until then, McDowell was still preparing to join McClellan and was shifting troops to occupy and defend Fredericksburg. For example, on May 1 he ordered Wadsworth to move Brigadier General George McCall's 2nd Division, I Corps, from its occupation of the Orange and Alexandria and Manassas Gap Railroads to Fredericksburg "by the most expeditious route." McCall was being readied to move to the peninsula. Additionally, until General Banks was ready to assume the duties, Wadsworth was "to make such dispositions as may be necessary" for the defense of these rail lines to Alexandria.[18]

On May 7, General Wadsworth was alerted by General McDowell that he had been directed by the War Department to prepare for a forward movement, though McDowell was not sure when the order to move would be given. McDowell also asked Wadsworth what was happening to Colonel Samuel S. Carroll's 4th Brigade (the 7th Indiana, 84th and 110th Pennsylvania, and 1st West Virginia) of Brigadier General James Shields's division. McDowell wanted to know "What can be done and when?" with the brigade. It was almost impossible for McDowell to keep track of the shifting forces in the department, and he was counting on the military governor to help him.[19]

Colonel John Geary, commanding the advance brigade (5th, 7th, 66th, and 29th Ohio, and his own 28th Pennsylvania), and soon to wear a star, was even more confused. He had just been transferred from Banks's Department of the Shenandoah and was now reporting to Stanton, McDowell, Wadsworth, *and* Banks. Attempts to clarify the situation were made on May 5 and 13, when Geary was directed by McDowell to report his troop strength and position to Wadsworth. In turn, Wadsworth, who was responsible for guarding the Manassas Gap Railroad from Alexandria to White Plains, would give Geary orders necessary to protect the railroad from Manassas Junction west. The crux of the matter was that Geary had to extend his lines and to keep Wadsworth informed, for Wadsworth was responsible for reinforcing Geary. Yet, two weeks later, Secretary Stanton was still trying to clarify the chain of command for Wadsworth. If nothing else, it shows the confusion resulting from the mid-March reorganization and General Wadsworth's added responsibilities.[20]

Ominously, on May 15 General Geary reported a surprise attack at Linden, Virginia, near Falmouth, by more than a third of Jackson's 2,600-man cavalry. He also telegraphed Wadsworth asking for reinforcements because his small command of 1,400 men scattered over fifty-five miles was in danger from Major General Ewell's 8,000-man force at Luray. McDowell, to whom Geary was also reporting, discounted Geary's fears, but instructed Wadsworth to send Geary some of his dismounted cavalry if, in his judgment, the situation merited it. Apparently

Wadsworth checked into the situation, but a noticeably uncomfortable Geary was convinced that he and General Shields near Warrenton faced a serious Confederate threat to Washington, not some scattered guerrillas.[21]

A concerned General McDowell ordered Wadsworth, now acting more like McDowell's adjutant than military governor or brigade commander, to shift the constantly changing troops in the Department of the Rappahannock to meet the Confederate threats. This included protecting General Duryee's forces by moving them from Catlett's Station to Bristoe, behind Broad Run, on May 19, sending troops from the Maryland side of the Potomac to Brigadier General Abner Doubleday on the 21st, and posting Doubleday's brigade opposite Fredericksburg two days later. Wadsworth himself was to hold his forces in readiness to move on short notice, for Banks had been attacked near Front Royal, had been forced to retire to Middletown, and wanted reinforcements as soon as possible.[22]

Now, on the eve of McDowell's departure to reinforce McClellan, the administration in Washington once again was fearful for the capital's safety. As intended, the combined Jackson–Ewell strikes in the Shenandoah Valley, which were designed to prevent the departure of General Shields from Banks's department to join McDowell, had diverted Stanton's attention from the Peninsula campaign. The fear was reflected by General Wadsworth, who, on May 23, reported to McDowell that Geary's thinly distributed troops had been "worsted" at Front Royal, eight miles from Strasburg, and that Banks was "seriously threatened."[23]

Then, as if Wadsworth did not have enough to be concerned about, that same day his middle son, 21-year-old Craig ("Tick"), was appointed Fremont's aide-de-camp by Lincoln, with the rank of captain. Captain Wadsworth was to report to McDowell for orders, so father and son would see each other momentarily. Yet the father had to perceive the appointment with mixed emotions: He could not deny his son's need to be involved, but he knew firsthand the dangerous duties that aides sometimes performed.[24]

The flurry of dispatches between Banks, McDowell, Fremont, McClellan, and Lincoln clearly indicated the extent to which the Confederate offensive–defensive strategy was working. In scarcely three weeks Jackson had thoroughly disrupted the Union plans by defeating part of Fremont's force at McDowell on May 8 and by striking Banks's army at Front Royal and Winchester on May 23 and 25. The latter action was particularly significant, for it drove Banks back across the Potomac. McClellan, with his insatiable appetite for more troops and still preparing his strike on Richmond, could not count on McDowell's men. They were now needed to counter Jackson's thrust up the valley, though Lincoln was not convinced of the threat at first. In fact, Lincoln was exasperated by the conflicting reports, including one that General Geary's scouts had found no sign of Jackson "this side of the Blue Ridge," and asked McDowell whether the scouts "had been *to* the Blue Ridge looking for" the enemy.[25]

McDowell was equally exasperated. He kept receiving and shifting more troops to match each perceived threat by Jackson. Thus he was forced to rely even more heavily on Military Governor Wadsworth, who, consequently, experienced similar changes on May 25, when the brigades of Generals Geary and

Duryee specifically were added to his command. Then the next day, he was ordered to assist Major General Ord's division to board the train at Alexandria bound for Manassas.[26]

However, General McDowell was inclined to downplay the threat, writing Wadsworth that he saw no point in shifting any forces to Banks, because, if an attack by Jackson was imminent, there would not be time to do so anyway. More importantly, McDowell revealed his understanding of what Jackson was doing in his comment to Wadsworth (though really aimed at Stanton): "If the enemy can succeed so readily in disconcerting all our plans by alarming us at one point, then at another, he will paralyze a large force with a small one." The frustrated McDowell begged Wadsworth to sustain him and "quiet the cry of danger to General Banks."[27]

McClellan, desperately wanting—and still expecting—McDowell's troops, reacted predictably. He reminded Lincoln of his March 16 instructions to Generals Wadsworth and Banks and his April 1 letter to the adjutant general. Wadsworth and Banks had been directed to entrench a strong force near Manassas, erect blockhouses at the railway bridges, employ cavalry "well to the front," post guards as far as the Rappahannock, and obtain information about the enemy. Above all, they were to "cover the line of the Potomac and Washington." Further he urged Lincoln to concentrate on Manassas and Front Royal, not Fredericksburg. More pointedly, in his memoirs McClellan blamed Banks and Wadsworth and, indirectly, Stanton, Lincoln, and McDowell for the panic they were experiencing. Had the "precious lot of fools" complied with his instructions "we should have been spared the shame of Banks' stampede." He could even imagine Lincoln calling him home from his campaign to take Richmond.[28]

On May 28, after Jackson had defeated Banks at Winchester and driven him back across the Potomac, there was another flurry of dispatches between Stanton and McDowell. The dispatches, which may well have been initiated by Wadsworth, focused on Wadsworth's command and the safety of Washington. The issue was whether the harassed McDowell had, as Stanton charged, taken troops from Wadsworth to meet Jackson's thrust toward Harpers Ferry. A chagrined McDowell, fearing he risked "censure for stripping Washington" of troops, felt compelled to ask Wadsworth for War Department permission to retain an unserviceable cavalry regiment.[29]

The wily Jackson had managed to traverse 245 miles, win four battles, and paralyze forces in and around Washington. On May 31, a nervous Stanton ordered a blockade of the Potomac between Harpers Ferry and Washington. To that end Major General Dix was to seize and to sink immediately all the ferry boats from Point of Rocks, southwest of Harpers Ferry, to Edwards Ferry. Wadsworth was to do the same on the remaining twenty-five miles of river from Edwards Ferry to Washington.[30]

At the same time, Wadsworth's hodgepodge command was consolidated into two brigades of mostly incomplete regiments under brigadiers Amiel W. Whipple, McDowell's topographical engineer at First Bull Run, and Samuel D. Sturgis, a classmate of McClellan at West Point. With the exception of the 101st

New York, Whipple's command consisted of heavy artillery batteries and regiments, while Sturgis oversaw newly arrived infantry regiments. The vast majority of the remaining troops were unbrigaded infantry, cavalry, and artillery outfits under Wadsworth's direction, but commanded by Provost Guard Doster. Though a simpler structure, it was scarcely more satisfactory administratively than before.[31]

Less than three weeks later, when Jackson's forces were recalled to the peninsula to defend Richmond and the immediate threat to Washington had subsided, Sturgis was appointed to command a Reserve Corps, but it was never fully organized, and he continued to report to Wadsworth. Whipple's brigade remained in the fortifications south of the Potomac, and Wadsworth directed the troops described vaguely as those "required or incident to his command," plus arriving troops until assigned to the Reserve Corps.[32]

For the next few months Wadsworth's attention was directed to an influx of prisoners, soldiers, spies, and secessionists, who were being rounded up and imprisoned in unprecedented numbers. He was running out of room for them, and they just kept coming. Yet General Wadsworth was partly responsible, for he was receiving reports of secessionists' activities harmful to Virginia Unionists. For example, in early June he had ordered Colonel James B. Swain of "Scott's Cavalry" to take thirty men to Leesburg to arrest "rebel authorities" trying to hold court and giving aid to the rebellion. Characteristically, Wadsworth instructed Swain to haul his own forage and provisions, so his cavalrymen would not have to subsist off the inhabitants. Then on June 21, Wadsworth ordered another expedition, this one conducted by Captain S. Pierre Remington of that same outfit. Remington was to seize up to one hundred horses and mules from the residences of "leading secessionists" in Fairfax and Loudon Counties, but he was directed to refrain from taking anything from those in "reduced circumstances." The military governor also was making arrests closer to home, rounding up Confederate officers who apparently had been paroled, but who remained in the capital.[33]

Wadsworth's actions in connection with arrests he made from mid-June to mid-October had more serious consequences. In fact, he was trying to force the administration's hand. Under color of arresting secessionists, he was also holding them "hostage," pending the release of an equal number of Unionists imprisoned in Richmond and Salisbury, North Carolina. Four times that summer he arrested and detained upward of thirty secessionists reported to be threatening Unionists. He based his actions on a July 29 article in the *New York Tribune* that listed prisoners at Salisbury, which, it was claimed, were held only because they were loyal Unionists.[34]

Apparently Wadsworth's battle with Confederate authorities (and the Federal government) had the intended effect. On October 7, William P. Wood, representing Secretary of War Stanton, and Sydney S. Baxter, on behalf of Confederate Secretary of War George W. Randolph, developed an understanding. Henceforth Wadsworth and his counterpart, General John Winder, superintendent of Richmond prisons, were: (1) to consider only persons in arms as prisoners of war; (2) to hold no more peaceful citizens hostage; and (3) to tolerate no marauding parties. It appears that Stanton, Randolph, and General Dix, who were responsible for prisoner exchanges, had had enough of the military governor's practices. Wadsworth may well have been harassing them with his listing of prisoners ("111 state prisoners" by his count in late August) and his arrests of equal numbers of secessionists. Though he had been holding hostages "at great inconvenience," he was unwilling to give in so long as Union prisoners, especially at Salisbury, were suffering. Also it may be that Wadsworth was smarting from an order by Lorenzo Thomas, the army's adjutant general, directing him to grant no more paroles from the Old Capitol Prison and to recall all prisoners he had released in the last ten days. What precipitated this order is unknown, but Wadsworth was prone to take matters in his own hands. An example was his treatment of fishermen, though he may have cleared the matter with Secretary Stanton. The military governor wanted to offer fishermen more latitude, regardless of loyalties, because they "will furnish a variety of food beneficial to the Army."[35]

In early July, Wadsworth, now commanding only 4,358 men, momentarily relaxed and entertained at his headquarters in ex-senator William Gwin's mansion at the corner of 19th and I Streets. His guests were reported to be "Stanton sympathizers" and correspondents eager to hear firsthand accounts by participants in the Peninsula campaign, including Brigadier General Joseph Hooker and the one-armed and newly promoted Major General Philip Kearny. Wadsworth also found time to write one of his daughters to express his dismay "at the great disaster before Richmond" and the "enormous" loss, including the 1,500 men who had been delivered to Washington the previous day, most of whom bore upper-body and arm wounds.[36]

On July 17, the 54-year-old brigadier requested and received a leave of absence and immediately headed for Willard's Hotel. His elder son, Captain Charles F. Wadsworth, accompanied him as an aide on a staff that was temporarily in flux, given what seemed to be uncertainty about Wadsworth's military future.[37] Apparently Wadsworth was back at his post in less than a month.

After General Wadsworth returned from his brief leave, he picked up pretty much where he had left off. However, he held out hope that his military duties would change. In June a new command structure had been initiated, with the appointment of Major General Henry Halleck as general-in-chief. Lincoln intended to rely heavily on Halleck, whose scholarly activities had earned him the unflattering nickname "Old Brains," because of successes in the West attributed to him.[38]

One reason Wadsworth expected a change was that Captain Craig Wadsworth was working behind the scenes for a field command on behalf of his father, and Wadsworth himself had made a formal request on June 23. But nothing happened immediately. However, shortly after Halleck took up his duties another Westerner was brought to Washington. On June 26, Major General John Pope, basking in the glow of successes in the West, was appointed commander of the newly created Army of Virginia.[39]

This move would consolidate all the Union forces spread across northern Virginia and the lower valley, including those under McDowell, Banks, and Fremont. Over the next several weeks, in a series of addresses to his new command,

Pope proclaimed his determination to succeed, but his statements came off as self-serving and bombastic. This inauspicious beginning compounded an already difficult situation. Meanwhile, McClellan was bogged down on the peninsula after losing ground to Lee during the Seven Days' Battle, and Washington's safety remained an issue. The latter may well have resulted in part from Pope's playing on the fears of the administration. Lincoln originally expected Pope to cover Washington, disrupt Confederate communications within the valley, and create a diversion for McClellan's proposed advance against Richmond by way of Petersburg. But McClellan's reverses against Lee caused Pope to adopt a more defensive posture centered at Culpeper.[40]

The only immediate impact on Military Governor Wadsworth from the arrivals of Generals Pope and Halleck was Secretary Stanton's authorization of Wadsworth to raise and organize infantry regiments from Washington, D.C. While there is no evidence that he did so, he took particular pride in Charles Frederick's intent to recruit a regiment in Buffalo, which would become the 116th New York Volunteers. Charles Frederick, who until then had served as his father's aide, wrote the latter on August 10 that he was doing so out of "a sense of duty" and hoped his father would "not be displeased." True to form, upon receiving the letter the general approved his son's "honorable reasons" for enlisting and intent to take "the modest position of Lieutenant." Actually the father was quite pleased with his son's decision and offered an "extra bounty of ten dollars" to be paid to Charles's recruits. His only words of advice to his son were "Study the 'Tactics' thoroughly and the Army Regulations, and make yourself master of all your duties."[41]

Meanwhile Wadsworth had his hands full following a series of moves and countermoves by Union and Confederate commanders. In mid-July General Pope had begun an offensive in northern Virginia along the line of the Orange and Alexandria Railroad headed toward Gordonsville and Charlottesville. In coordination and after some mixed signals, McClellan's Army of the Potomac was ordered to shift from the peninsula north to Alexandria and to Aquia Landing near Fredericksburg to assist Pope and to protect Washington. Lee, no longer fearing McClellan's threat to Richmond, countered Pope's advance by forwarding Jackson's and Ewell's divisions toward Gordonsville. General A. P. Hill's division was added subsequently when the size of Pope's army was discovered. A bloody battle between Banks's and the Jackson–Ewell–Hill commands at Cedar Mountain on August 9–11 resulted in little advantage to either side, but the near capture of forces under General Pope near Clark's Mountain a week later reinforced the administration's fears for the safety of the capital.[42]

To reduce the danger of attack by water, five days later Wadsworth was ordered to help enforce the blockade of the Potomac begun earlier. Ferry boats were to be burned, all traffic on the river interdicted, unauthorized vessels destroyed, and prisoners sent to Wadsworth. The arrival of prisoners caused a minor fracas when a woman was captured aboard the vessel *Reliance* and delivered to him. Lieutenant Commander Samuel Magaw, senior officer of the Potomac Flotilla, was promptly notified to avoid sending women to General Wadsworth via the provost marshal without "positive proof" of disloyalty.[43] Wadsworth had had enough of women prisoners.

This period was the lull before the storm. On August 26, Pope's 75,000-man Army of Virginia appeared poised for victory at Second Bull Run (Second Manassas) against Lee's Army of Northern Virginia in what Halleck was calling "the greatest battle of the century." But for three days Lincoln, lacking information because the Confederates had cut communication lines, nervously paced. Then on Sunday, September 1, the news began filtering in, and, according to Lincoln's secretary, John Hay, Lincoln feared "we are whipped again." Pope, after losing 16,054 killed, wounded, and missing, had withdrawn behind Centreville. There was nothing to do now but to order Pope back behind Washington's entrenchments. Lincoln's high hopes for Pope had been rudely dashed.[44]

Abruptly Wadsworth was drawn into the fray when the wounded began pouring into Washington, with reports of many more lying on the battlefield. He was given the necessary, but undoubtedly irritating, responsibility for what John Hay called "a vast army of Volunteer Nurses . . . probably utterly useless." Hay was right. An overwhelming number of volunteers who had descended on the capital in response to Stanton's August 30 call were useless. While most of the volunteers (small-town doctors, nurses, college faculty, and students) were well intentioned, Washington was not prepared for their number, for the makeshift transportation that had to be provided, or for their safety on the battlefield. To top it off, many, possibly to bolster their courage, had imbibed too heavily in spirits. The frustrated railroad genius General Herman Haupt disciplined the drunken nurses by providing them only one-way transportation; the long walk back would sober them up. Meanwhile, Wadsworth was forced to post guards at bridges and wharves to limit the number of volunteers coming into the city.[45]

Adding to the confusion, beginning September 2, a blue horde of "hatless, shoeless and ragged, stragglers" limped across the Long Bridge bringing with them wildly differing, but generally horrifying, stories. The post–Bull Run panic had begun, including the erroneous rumor that the Confederates were on the brink of overrunning the capital. Preparations were made for its fall, and Wadsworth ordered places serving liquor closed. Further, Assistant Adjutant General Edward Townsend ordered all public clerks and employees in Washington organized immediately into companies and placed under Wadsworth's direction. The second part of the order directing him to arm these clerks and to issue them ammunition must have sent chills down Wadsworth's spine.[46]

Towering panic alternated with abject despondency in Washington. In Lincoln's phraseology, the "tub was out of the bucket" again, and Military Governor Wadsworth got caught up in some minor conflicts over authority.

Events on and off the field seemed to accelerate the bickering and pettiness among the Union high command. For example, on August 29 General McClellan, then located at Alexandria, was irritated and possibly embarrassed by Wadsworth. (Whether this was intentional or not is uncertain.) Seth Williams, McClellan's assistant adjutant general, was stopped by guards at the Long Bridge on his return to headquarters because he did not know the countersign. Like any common soldier, Williams was "compelled to go to your [Wadsworth's] office for the countersign." The next night a lieutenant colonel on Williams's staff was treated just as rudely. The temporary resolution of this embarrassingly petty incident was for Wadsworth to notify McClellan if his countersign was different from McClellan's and to instruct his guards accordingly. An even sillier countersign controversy occurred shortly after this, but other, more pressing matters caused the commanders to refocus.[47]

On September 2, General McClellan was restored to command of the Army of the Potomac. McClellan had virtually predicted this scenario in a July 24 letter to his wife. He presumed to "hear something . . . from that council of military pundits who have been about in Washn—there is not a handful of brains among them all & a nice mess they will make of it." McClellan's wife, who urged him to resign, figured she knew to whom her husband was alluding: "probably Pope, McD[owell] & Wadsworth." Soldiers' reactions to General McClellan's return were almost immediate and electrifying.[48] Lincoln's cabinet greeted the decision with an equally galvanized, but contrary, reaction. The president countered dissenters with the assertion that the low morale of the soldiers and McClellan's administrative skills justified the decision.

For all the promise that McClellan's return offered, it also posed some problems. One was the need to clarify the duties of Generals McClellan and Wadsworth. Wadsworth was still military governor of the capital while McClellan was charged to defend it. The mutual dislike that characterized their relationship virtually from the moment of Wadsworth's appointment did not bode well for the kind of cooperation the circumstances demanded.

Nonetheless, the generally optimistic Wadsworth carried on with his duties, even assuring the president that reports of his anxiety over Washington's defenses and the danger to which the capital was exposed were exaggerated. This may have been a change from Sunday, September 7, when, according to Treasury Secretary Chase, Wadsworth was in Stanton's office and was "uneasy on account of [the] critical condition of affairs." By contrast, shortly thereafter, in the company of both Lincoln and Stanton, Wadsworth claimed that he not only believed that Washington was safe, but "that the man ought to be severely punished who intimated the possibility of its surrender."[49]

A continuing, and increasingly more urgent, demand on Wadsworth's time was the blockade of the Potomac, which had been instituted at the end of May and was being tested regularly by suspected Confederates. That same Sunday, September 7, when Chase claimed Wadsworth had been uneasy, the military governor was notified that Union gunboats and revenue cutters were unable to intercept a flatboat that was suspected of carrying mail and passengers in support of the Confederacy. In response, periodically throughout the next two months Wadsworth sent cavalry to monitor the Potomac between Port Tobacco, Maryland, and Upper Machodoc Creek, Virginia, which resulted in his having to accommodate yet more inmates.[50]

The problem was compounded by arrests made by Commodore Andrew A. Harwood's Potomac Flotilla, which was responsible for enforcing the blockade of the Potomac. On September 26, Harwood made it worse for Wadsworth when, in a very lengthy letter, he asked the latter for ideas to make the blockade even more effective. The flotilla simply could not do it alone. Wadsworth's land forces could put a stop to recruiting and the provisioning of Confederate recruiters in Maryland. Also Harwood wanted Wadsworth's men to screen boats landing at Alexandria, intercept price-inflated goods headed for Secessia, protect Unionists, and nab draft dodgers crossing over to Virginia.[51]

Apparently Wadsworth's reply failed to satisfy Harwood, who informed Navy Secretary Gideon Welles three days later that General Wadsworth claimed to be "embarrassed with the numbers" and was freeing those "who under other circumstances would have been treated with more rigor." Wadsworth had assured Harwood that he was "perfectly willing to detain any who may be designated as dangerous persons by the naval authorities," but he did not regard the smugglers caught by Harwood's forces as dangerous. Harwood agreed. Yet Harwood was not willing to dismiss these Maryland smugglers who were not only engaged in forbidden trafficking, but who were also recruiting and "carrying information to the rebels." If Wadsworth would not imprison them, at the very least he should take precautions to assure that those who were captured were not brought to Washington, where there were opportunities for "gathering intelligence and hatching new and more secure plans of operation." Harwood's suggestion to Navy Secretary Welles, which Welles promptly instituted, was to make it "a certainty" that these "contrabandists" were locked up for at least six months. Wadsworth's reaction is not recorded, but presumably, given his occasional displays of temerity, he acceded.[52]

After his restoration to command of all the forces in Virginia on September 2 (officially the 5th), General McClellan reorganized the forces in and around Washington and tightened discipline. Pope's Army of Virginia was consolidated into the Army of the Potomac and command changes were made in the wake of the Second Manassas debacle. General Wadsworth retained his command: the 2nd D.C. Volunteers; 10th New Jersey; Company D, 20th Pennsylvania; Company F, 27th Pennsylvania; 135th Pennsylvania; and the 11th New York Cavalry. Of more immediate importance were General Orders No. 3, which General Banks, commanding the Defenses of Washington, issued on September 15. Wadsworth was directed to cooperate with Brigadier General John Slough, who had been appointed military governor of Alexandria, across the Potomac from Washington. The gist of the orders was that Slough was to round up and establish a camp for convalescents, stragglers, and recruits who would be organized into squads according to their respective divisions or corps at Alexandria. Wadsworth was to shelter, feed, equip, and supply a daily list of these men, and arrest all officers and men without proper passes in the capital. Once these men were armed and equipped, he was to forward them to the army.[53]

Almost immediately orders to forward the estimated fifty officers and 3,500 men were countermanded. Instead, Wadsworth was instructed to wait until he heard from Major General Banks. The military situation had changed dramatically in the time between the two dispatches: The bloodiest one-day battle of the war had been fought along Antietam Creek near Sharpsburg, Maryland, on September 17. On that barbarous Wednesday the two opposing armies had suffered over 26,000 casualties (killed, wounded, and missing), almost evenly distributed between the two forces.[54]

After failing to bag General Pope and realizing the futility of attacking Washington, Lee had decided to take the war to the North to relieve pressure on Virginia and to obtain support from Marylanders. He began crossing the Potomac on September 4 and occupied Frederick, Maryland, on September 6. Lee then split his army five ways, sending three columns under the overall direction of Jackson to capture Harpers Ferry while he crossed South Mountain with the two remaining ones. Meanwhile, McClellan, groping for the elusive Lee and protecting Washington and Baltimore, cautiously moved northward. On September 13, he had advanced to Frederick, where he came into possession of a copy of Lee's orders specifying the objectives of his five columns. McClellan pushed ahead to South Mountain, but was held up there on September 14 by the stubborn rearguard action of Lee's forces. This also caused Lee to fall back to Sharpsburg, where he intended to reunite his forces. Upon hearing that Jackson had captured Harpers Ferry on the 15th, McClellan decided to attack Lee at Sharpsburg, which led to the fearful battle of Antietam on the 17th.

Shortly, Washington was inundated by a vast number of wounded soldiers and was "transformed into a hospital—the vast base hospital of the Army of the Potomac." Government buildings, confiscated homes of ex-senators, hotels, warehouses, schools, and fraternal lodges became instant hospitals. Once more it appeared that Wadsworth would have to seize churches as he had been directed to do in June, during the Peninsula campaign, when Trinity, the Ascension, E Street Baptist Church, and the Epiphany were converted to hospitals. He also housed the wounded in the northwest wing of the Patent Office. Now, however, congregations were offering their church buildings to accommodate the staggering number of wounded soldiers.[55]

About the same time Wadsworth suffered a left-handed rebuke from his former political ally, Major General John Dix, commander of the Department of Virginia at Fort Monroe. Dix had complained to General Halleck about Wadsworth's issuance of permits to "improper persons" to obtain supplies from the army quartermaster. Wadsworth's defense was that he was issuing permits to those he believed were supplying quinine and coal only to Union sympathizers in Norfolk. Apparently the matter was dropped after this minor exchange, though Dix must have remained skeptical about the integrity of a Virginian who was apprehended with 2,000 tons of coal.[56]

Actually, Wadsworth was sympathetic to Dix's concerns about trafficking by fraudulent suppliers, for they were not only supporting secession, but were draining the Federal treasury. Wadsworth had already complained about government spending: "Millions of money were to them [Lincoln, Stanton, and Meigs] as to ordinary men star distances; whether two or three hundred billions, what difference."[57] Old James Wadsworth would have been astounded at his profligate son's conversion, but the general was increasingly frustrated with the course of the war.

In fact, he poked his nose into policy once more about this time. According to "Count" Adam Gurowski, the influential but "shabby and spiteful" Pole with the "snarling manners," General Wadsworth had proposed "one of those bold movements by which campaigns are terminated by one blow." That is, Wadsworth allegedly wanted the administration to send him and General Heintzelman, with some 25,000 men, to Gordonsville, to "cut off the enemy from Richmond, and prevent him from rallying his forces." But Gurowski claimed Halleck opposed such a move because he anticipated an attack on Washington, which the goggle-eyed Count regarded simply as coming out of "McClellan's imagination."[58] Despite the unreliability of the narrator, it has a ring of authenticity, given Wadsworth's access to the administration and his impetuousness. For now, however, the military governor remained in Washington, awaiting further events.

Chapter 11

"A HERO
AND A STATESMAN"

Wadsworth the Gubernatorial Candidate

General Dix's rebuke coincided with events elsewhere, events that would lead Wadsworth onto a path he had studiously avoided until now. One who might have predicted this unexpected and uncharacteristic change of behavior was *New York Tribune* correspondent Adams Sherman Hill.

Diligently cultivating his sources, Hill had previously overheard Wadsworth characterize the political picture as "gloomy." Wadsworth's assessment was based on frequent and extended visits (up to six hours) with Lincoln and Stanton, which indicated to Wadsworth that "the President is not with us; has no anti-slavery instincts." The issue was pressing on Wadsworth, which made him popular with other anti-slavery advocates in New York and may have led to an August 22, 1862, letter from James C. Smith, a Canandaiguan and long-time political ally. Would Wadsworth accept the Republican gubernatorial nomination? Unionist governor Edmund Morgan, who had been swept into office only two years earlier with a 50,000-vote majority, had provoked too much opposition to be reelected. The field was open. In fact, as early as January 11, 1862, Wadsworth's name had been suggested by Governor Morgan, who felt Wadsworth "will be willing, and will be far more available than any one yet mentioned as my successor."[1]

Wadsworth's admittedly hasty reply must have surprised Smith, given Wadsworth's previous reluctance to being nominated. This time he claimed he did not have "sufficient reason for absolutely refusing" it. Then, more characteristically, he listed his reservations. While satisfied that he could "get on reasonably well with the ordinary duties of the office," he dreaded them. He longed to be at home and "rid of public cares." He also feared that he would "disappoint many of his supporters." Still another reason for Wadsworth's reluctance was his desire for field command. So far it had been denied by Stanton, who "wishes me to accept the nomination" and unite New York against slavery. Wadsworth's final reservation was based on his belief that he might well "be able to do more good here" in Washington than in "the exalted position referred to."[2]

This supports correspondent Hill's allusions to Wadsworth's extended visits with Lincoln and Stanton. With his headquarters close to the White House and having become the center of opposition to McClellan, Wadsworth's voice was increasingly being heard. Whether he thought of himself as a politician—and that is unlikely—he was perceived as such and was making his views known. To him slavery and military policy could not be separated: An aggressive military policy would result in the Confederacy's defeat and slavery's elimination.[3]

On September 13, when the Union's fortunes seemed so low after Pope's defeat at Second Bull Run, Wadsworth had second thoughts about running for governor of New York, and he expressed them to his political ally Smith. Though his duties in Washington were "unimportant," he had some influence there, which he did not want "to relinquish" to a pro-slavery replacement. On the other hand, a plan to appoint military governors in Union-occupied districts in the South offered the appealing prospect of a governorship there, where he could help put an end to the "infamy of slavery." However, if he were to be the gubernatorial nominee of the New York Republicans, he would demand a "strong, decided platform." If it were not, "I shall surely kick it over when I accept."[4]

Simultaneous with the posting of his letter to Smith, Wadsworth heard from a committee of Republicans, including David Dudley Field and Horace Greeley, with whom Wadsworth had supported Lincoln in 1860. They asked the same question as Smith had: Would Wadsworth accept the gubernatorial nomination? Wadsworth's virtually instant reply was almost identical to the one he had sent Smith. Yes, unless offered a field command, he would agree to run, for he had "no serious fear as to my ability to discharge the ordinary duties of the Governorship of New York." But he would not be able to campaign because his duties in Washington precluded it.[5]

Before he would accept the nomination, however, he reiterated his views about the platform. The party must take a stand "on the one great question which probably for the remainder of our lives will absorb all others of a political nature, Slavery." He had "slowly come to the conclusion that the time has arrived to strike it down for ever." This conclusion was based on the fact that this war

> is the rebellion of an aristocracy, base, selfish, & degraded, but still a distinctly formed aristocracy. We cannot put down the rebellion & save the aristocracy & we ought not do, if we could. We have paid for their slaves in our best blood and untold treasure. Let us take them & free them. All the fears I once had of a "St. Domingo Massacre," [Haitian independence] have passed away. The blacks will make the most quiet & peaceful peasantry on the face of the earth.

However, Wadsworth feared that he did not know the popular mood of New Yorkers, having been removed from the state for over a year, and wanted assurance that the state was prepared "to bear her share of the consequences of this great social and commercial change." If not, he was "not the man for you." His strong disposition would "sooner or later give you trouble." Thus, having spoken "with the frankness [their letter] merits," he left the nomination in the hands of the convention.[6]

Wadsworth's nomination would present New Yorkers with a clear choice. In mid-September the Democrats had nominated ex-governor Horatio Seymour, a well-known Peace Democrat who had narrowly lost the Democratic senatorial nomination the previous year. Seymour had laid the groundwork for the upcoming gubernatorial nomination by supporting General McClellan, and he was gathering strength through the declining popularity of Governor Morgan. Apparently he already had the support of lawyer and future presidential candidate Samuel Tilden, historian George Bancroft, and other prominent New Yorkers. However, he had to persuade Thurlow Weed, the indefatigable *Albany Journal* editor and backroom politician. Weed supported Major General John Dix, a War Democrat, who Weed thought might be able to carry out his plans to unite the Republican and Democratic Parties.[7]

Weed was long since convinced that he could not support Seymour. Nor could he support Wadsworth, "a gallant Union officer and a gentleman of unimpeachable character," let alone "a personal friend." Wadsworth had, according to Weed, "become an Abolitionist." In fact, Weed, who liked to play kingmaker, felt himself totally excluded by both sides, especially after the Republicans moved their campaign office from Weed's Albany to New York City. He blamed the move on Wadsworth and the Radicals. Undaunted, the editor-politician appealed to *New York Times* founder-editor Henry J. Raymond, who initially agreed to shift his support from Wadsworth to Dix. Weed's appeal was based on the belief that Dix was a symbol of "Union for the Union." He would prosecute the war without dragging in the slavery issue. The 42-year-old Raymond, a particularly skillful leader as speaker of New York's lower house previously and as lieutenant governor from 1855 to 1857, was important to Weed's cause, for he had been chosen to preside over the Republican–Union State Convention in Syracuse.[8]

Weed, with a distinct preference for being on the winning side—and unwilling to give up so easily—finally agreed to support Wadsworth's nomination on the basis that it was "not to be considered as a triumph over him."[9] That is, Wadsworth had to moderate his platform. But Weed's plans were thwarted by news out of the White House. At a small dinner party Treasury Secretary Chase had confidentially informed Wadsworth and Judge Edwards Pierrepont that Lincoln intended to issue an Emancipation Proclamation the next day, September 23. This seemed not only to assure Wadsworth that he need not modify his views, but it spelled the end of Dix's candidacy. Now New York's Republican Party could safely go ahead with the nomination of Wadsworth, which came on September 24, 1862. Though it is not clear whether there was more than one ballot or how Thurlow Weed voted, Wadsworth came out ahead 234 to 110. On behalf of the convention, Raymond, who made the issue either loyalty to the Lincoln administration or treason (voting for Seymour), emphasized that Wadsworth had been nominated by "men resolved to maintain the integrity of the Union without regard to their past party relations."[10]

This news was received warmly by the Syracusan Alfred Wilkinson, who described himself as a "juvenile admirer." It seems that twenty years earlier Wikinson's "admiration was excited by the labour & conduct" of a stranger "who walked through mud & water directing & encouraging the laborous [*sic*] repair" of the superstructure of a railroad that had been washed away. At the time Wilkinson had asked his father who the intrepid stranger was. The father replied, "My son, that is the first gentleman in America. James S. Wadsworth of Geneseo." Moreover, the elder Wilkinson often repeated this opinion "till the last hour of his life" [ironically, the very day Wadsworth was nominated]. The son was now acting as surrogate to congratulate Wadsworth, for his father had "longed for your nomination and advised and advocated it." In fact, "one of the last things" the elder Wilkinson had said was that "I wish I could think that there is enough integrity in our political leaders to nominate Wadsworth." Wadsworth's reaction to the letter is unrecorded, but it must have warmed his heart.11

Wadsworth's long, carefully drawn letter to Raymond accepting the nomination should have left no doubt about his intentions. If elected, he would "zealously labor to carry out [the party's] wishes." Wadsworth made it clear that the election hinged on the extent of popular support for the Lincoln administration and emancipation. Without the support of the freed slaves, Wadsworth believed the South would collapse. Ultimately a new economy would benefit "this great domain, from the Lakes to the Gulf, from the Atlantic to the Pacific, one country, governed by one idea—freedom."12

Raymond replied to the nominee almost by return mail. If the matter were left to him, he would "not alter a syllable of your reply." However, he did wish that Wadsworth "had put in a sentence about conducting the war with more vigor. . . . It is not a time for dodging great questions. No voters are to be had by that course now." He praised Wadsworth's stand on the "slavery issue" and contrasted it with Seymour's. The latter had made the campaign issue the failure of the Federal government. Raymond was optimistic that Wadsworth "shall carry the State by a rousing majority," for Seymour will look for peace propositions from Jefferson Davis.13

Curiously, Wadsworth's initial campaign speech was made on Friday evening, September 26, not only before Raymond had formally notified him of his nomination but in Washington, not in New York. Employing the usual disclaimers about having earned the honor, Wadsworth recalled that he had neither pursued nor held a public position. Thus, his support now was based "largely on trust." But he left no doubt where he stood. He recalled that he had been nominated by men who believed he "was in earnest [and who believed] that this rebellion can be crushed." These men were willing to devastate the country, if necessary, to assure that it was a refuge for the oppressed. While in his present capacity it would be improper for him "to enter at large into a discussion of the conduct of the war, or the policy of the Government." As far as he was concerned, military and civil policy were one. The aim was to eliminate "the base and selfish" aristocracy of the South, at whose feet could be laid the blame for the "blood of our sons." Wadsworth wound up his speech, which reportedly was greeted by "prolonged, enthusiastic cheering," with a warning. "The struggle" had advanced to the stage whereby there would be either "permanent dissolution" of the Union or "exorcism [of the] devil which has tormented and disgraced us from the hour of our national birth."[14]

Wadsworth's nomination and speech drew the expected reactions. The *Albany Atlas & Argus* saw a thinly veiled plot to force his abolitionist views on the Lincoln administration and the dismissal of General McClellan. A *New York Times* correspondent recalled an October 28 conversation with a Southern "gentleman" and a Confederate officer to the effect that Wadsworth and the Republicans were "unconsciously playing into our hands; recklessness and stupidity characterize every act." The *Richmond Examiner* was even more direct. Referring to the New York election, the editor claimed that "it is not to be denied that a Democratic victory . . . would be a subject of much gratification." The meddlesome Weed claimed that Wadsworth's abolitionism meant the Republican Party's defeat. Closer to home, the *Ontario Repository & Messenger,* Canandaigua's Democratic organ, proclaimed that Wadsworth had "fully justified his selection as the candidate of the rabid extremists." His talk, coupled with his criticisms of General McClellan, confirmed his radicalism. According to the paper, for more than a year the western New Yorker had been *"plotting the disgrace of the best General this war has developed."*[15]

In sharp contrast was a flattering letter to Wadsworth from Columbia College president Charles King. Despite pressing college business, King could not refrain from expressing his "admiration & thanks for the manly & high principled [gubernatorial acceptance] letter [which] was like a trumpet note." King's brother, Brigadier General Rufus King, was equally enthusiastic in a letter to his friend Charles Henry Webb in New York City: Wadsworth "would make a splendid head for the Empire State."[16]

Navy Secretary Gideon Welles was more privately supportive. Almost immediately after Wadsworth's nomination, Welles confided to his diary that despite the opposition of "the Weed and Seward class [of people] . . . the positive element selected Wadsworth . . . an earnest and sincere man." George Templeton Strong, a New Yorker and treasurer of the Sanitary Commission, was much less restrained than Welles in his diary:

> I hope Wadsworth and the so-called radicals may sweep the state and kick out our wretched sympathizers with Southern treason back into the holes that have sheltered them for the past year. . . . Seymour's election would be an encouragement to Jefferson Davis worth 100,000 men.

Still, Strong recognized that Seymour was a formidable candidate because of his wealth, his record as governor earlier, and the fact that "he represented the old up-state Democracy of Van Buren and Silas Wright."[17]

The bitterness that characterized the contest found public expression also. For example, Henry Raymond, who took up the cause with "greater vigor than he had ever shown before," proclaimed that "every vote given for Seymour is a vote for treason." At the Great [Republican] Union War Ratification Meeting at New York City's Cooper Institute on October 8, 1862, William Curtis Noyes, Daniel S. Dickinson, and Wadsworth's running mate, Lyman Tremain, pulled out all stops. Noyes began the meeting by assailing the Seymour Democrats as treasonous, while former senator Dickinson, the next speaker, bitterly compared the two gubernatorial candidates. Though both "were in the full maturity of natural life," Dickinson shouted, only "One bid adieu to his wife and children, turned his back upon his broad and fertile acres . . . [and] repaired to the theater of strife and danger."[18]

Captain Henry Wiley of the Wadsworth Guards, who had been introduced to Wadsworth as "John's son" from Springwater, spoke for many of New York's soldiers. Were he home, Wiley wrote, he would "work like a nailer for Wadsworth," who he believed "will be elected by a good majority." Moreover, he challenged the claim by "Democrats here and at Washington" that Wadsworth's election would constitute "an anti-McClellan victory." That is, despite Wiley's affection for McClellan—typical of most members of the Army of the Potomac—in the upcoming election he supported Wadsworth, who wanted to prosecute the war with energy.[19]

New York's Democrats, characterizing Wadsworth as a "malignant Abolition disorganizer," were just as certain that his election would be a disaster. They alternately put down Wadsworth as simply a deputy of the *New York Tribune*'s Horace Greeley, whose erratic views were now at the radical extreme, or as a toady to War Secretary Stanton. Whatever the case, the opposition believed that Wadsworth's defeat would pressure Lincoln to "smoke the radicals out of the Cabinet and Washington" and force him to appoint conservatives. Closer to home, the *Ontario Repository & Messenger* condemned Wadsworth as "of the black stripe, and would sooner give a dollar to a nigger than a white man, but would hesitate long before giving to either." His candidacy, according to the acerbic paper editor, "was no more than a millionaire's *simple duty.*"[20]

Also opposing Wadsworth was the restored Army of the Potomac commander. General McClellan confessed to a friend "a double motive for desiring the defeat of Wadsworth—I have so thorough a contempt for the man & regard him as such a vile traitorous miscreant that I do not wish to see the great state of N.Y. disgraced by having such a thing at its head." Goading McClellan, as if needed, was Wadsworth's former ally, "Prince" John Van Buren. In a campaign speech on October 13, Van Buren, New York's Democratic state chairman, had superciliously dismissed Wadsworth as a "mere militia major."[21]

Whether and to what extent Wadsworth was bothered by these criticisms cannot be determined, because for the most part he stuck to his resolve to attend to military matters rather than to campaign. However, he was hardly a passive spectator, even skirmishing on a different field of battle. In late October he had insisted on the removal of some Federal employees at the Brooklyn Navy Yard because of their activities on behalf of the Democrats. While possibly strategic, it showed pettiness on Wadsworth's part.[22]

Wadsworth was counting on his friends, *New York Times*'s Henry Raymond and *New York Tribune*'s Horace Greeley, to do the campaigning for him. However, early optimism had given way to doubt by late October, when the Union (Republican) State Committee, chaired by Henry R. Low, accelerated the campaign on behalf of Wadsworth and his running mate by mailing a broadside calling for supporters. Low and the committee exhorted supporters to remember "that the life of the Nation is at stake."[23]

Wadsworth's campaign managers had reason to worry. Even Lincoln's cabinet was split. According to Seymour's biographer, William H. Seward, "dead against" Wadsworth "all through the campaign," was working behind the scenes on behalf of Seymour. But there were other explanations for their anxiety. Despite an estimated 20,000 majority for Wadsworth, one of his allies from Bath, south of Geneseo, feared that attention would be paid to local candidates to the "neglect" of Wadsworth. Another fear was that Wadsworth's supporters "had been exhausted by the war excitement." They had to be awakened from their lethargy. Still another concern was that many men who would have supported Wadsworth were in the army. They might well have been correct on this score, for one New York regiment recorded a straw vote of 492–27 for Wadsworth! Unfortunately for Wadsworth the soldiers were unable to vote.[24]

Troubling too, Seymour was implying that Wadsworth's absence from campaigning indicated his unwillingness to debate the issues. In fact, Seymour was having a heyday debating with Wadsworth's stand-ins, including his running mate, Tremain, and Daniel Dickinson, a former state senator and at the time attorney general, who Seymour's biographer claimed "made vituperation a fine art."[25]

Wadsworth was advised that he had to do something directly for his cause, which induced him to travel to New York City for a mass meeting on October 30, sponsored by the [Republican] Union State Central Committee at the Cooper Union. Once more he encountered the ubiquitous Thurlow Weed. Unhappy on the sidelines, the undeterred Weed had entrained to New York City. Weed recalled that Wadsworth approached him in his hotel room. He greeted the candidate with "James, for the first time in my life, I am not glad to see you." Then he added by way of explanation, "you have been sent to make an abolition speech. You will do it, and thus throw away the State." Weed then urged Wadsworth to ignore the Republican committee's advice to "denounce . . . disloyal Democrats." Instead, Wadsworth should "leave the slavery question to take care of itself, and appeal to the friends of the Union, irrespective of politics, to rally in defense of the government." However, Weed's advice was to no avail; Wadsworth had set his course.[26]

He had already spelled it out in his letters to Smith, Raymond, and the Washington audience, but there in New York City he would have a much larger audience. He needed to energize and to prod supporters to spread the message, and he did not disappoint his campaign managers that Thursday night. Vigorously distancing himself from Seymour, he proclaimed: "The man who pauses to think of himself, his affairs, of his family, even when he has public duties to perform and his country lies prostrate, almost in the agonies of dissolution, is not the man to save it." Wadsworth reminded his listeners "that here in the State of New York—here, more even than in the Shenandoah and in the valleys of Kentucky—is the battle being fought which is to preserve our liberties and perpetuate our country."27

Wadsworth rhetorically asserted that he would not try to defend the administration, claiming rather disingenuously that he was "only its subordinate officer, its humble and, I trust, its faithful servant," which, according to reports, brought "great applause." Then he defended the administration, challenging the thievery and treason of the previous one, which had hopelessly wrecked the nation. Instead, now he saw men who "have labored faithfully and earnestly to save this country." What really bothered the Republican nominee was the bolder critics of Lincoln who preferred a revolution, but would not say so openly because their "infamy" would result in thousands of defections from the Democratic Party.

"Any honest patriot," Wadsworth continued, would "advise" Lincoln, "admonish him, if you will." Whatever one's opinions, the key was to "strengthen and sustain" the president. "Give him your lives and fortunes and sacred honor to aid his honest efforts to put down this rebellion." The key was to strike down slavery, "that institution which [was] dearer than life, than liberty, than country, than peace" to those who had sundered the Union.

Then, he focused on the real enemy: "the spurious aristocracy" of the South that had controlled the nation since its inception and that referred to the abolition of slavery as "some low, vulgar crime." The descendants of these aristocrats would one day look back at their ancestors and "blush for shame." Anti-war candidates (another slap at Seymour) want peace, "but, good God, what a peace!" That kind of peace means "eternal war!" Then Wadsworth urged his listeners to envision "this new and improved [United States] map of Seymour, Van Buren & Co., the map of these 'let 'em go' geographers." The result would be a nation permanently severed "by the slave line."

What were the alternatives? They were either join the so-called peacemakers who would preserve the Confederacy or "subjugate them to our laws and to our system." The latter was what the soldiers in the field, who may well "sleep in death forever," were committed to doing. "Have they been sacrificed in an unnecessary, as Mr. Seymour would say, and unprofitable war?" he asked rhetorically. He implored his listeners to not ignore the impending danger. For over a year he had seen "the sons of New York . . . flushed with victory . . . dismayed with defeat . . . sleeping on the frozen ground . . . suffering and dying in the hospitals." Yet these brave men were not about to surrender. Did his fellow New Yorkers propose to surrender or to "reanimate and encourage" those soldiers then serving their country?

Finally, candidate Wadsworth assured his listeners that as the election results began to come in there would be signs of alarm where voters have forgotten those soldiers and their cause, but ultimately the true patriots will "cry out: 'The country is saved!'" "The God of Justice" will prevail and "the glories of the Revolutionary period, even, will pale before the achievements of your soldiers and your statesmen." Central to Wadsworth's address was his assertion that he stood by Lincoln, because it was "just, it is holy so to do." The candidate's friends were delighted by his speech and the position so boldly stated.28

A historian later would note that Wadsworth's lack of "poise, phrase and deliberation" was compensated by the "fire and directness" of his speech, which caused the "loyal audience . . . to explode into long-continued cheering."[29]

Letters praising Wadsworth poured in. Barely two days after the address Martin F. Cogswell, writing from Albany, groped for words to "express to you the impression the speech has made upon me." He only regretted that his two sons were too young to vote, but they would honor Wadsworth "all their lives." An old family friend, Samuel A. Ruggles, wrote from New York City that his vote testified to the need to commit the state's executive authority to Wadsworth, "to hands unquestionably loyal."[30]

The most articulate testimony appeared in a letter that Wadsworth never saw—from John Lothrop Motley, diplomat, author, and friend, to his daughter Mary. Motley, still in Europe where Wadsworth had last visited him seven years earlier, found the "few speeches" Wadsworth had made to be "of the highest order of eloquence." Once Motley would have characterized Wadsworth only as "the agreeable man of the world, the liberal man of fortune, the thriving landlord, and now he turns out a hero and a statesman." The Brahman scholar had never been so "electrified" as he was by the course Wadsworth had taken.

> Nothing can be nobler or more heroic than [Wadsworth's] career ever since the breaking out of the war. Certainly these are times that prove the mettle men are made of, and not only does his character, but his intellect, shine forth most brightly since the great events in which he had been taking part have revealed what was in him.[31]

No doubt Wadsworth would have loved to have heard those words, though he would have scoffed at them publicly.

Many New Yorkers would have scoffed as well, for they were not so easily persuaded that Wadsworth reflected their views. Lincoln's "trial balloon of emancipation" and suspension of habeas corpus were proving quite unpopular with much of the population. The military defeats and deaths of so many of New York's young men also were causing anxiety among voters. The threat of intervention on the side of the South by Great Britain also hung heavily in the minds of many.

Nor did all soldiers share the candidate's passion for eliminating slavery. "The [Republican] radicals may possibly break Union, Constitution, Country, and everything else of a national character all to pieces," wrote Lieutenant George Breck of the 1st New York Light Artillery. "The emancipation proclamation," argued Breck, a Rochesterian, "I consider an ill-timed, mischief making instrument . . . uncalled for, except by a crazy lot of abolitionists, who are bent on destroying slavery, [even] if it costs the life of the nation, and sheds oceans of blood."[32]

Apparently others shared Breck's feelings about Wadsworth's radicalism. The 50,000 majority that Republican governor Morgan had enjoyed in 1860 was fast disappearing. At "the eleventh hour" Thurlow Weed was persuaded by Republican executive committeemen Abram Wakeman, James Terwilliger, and other Wadsworth supporters to help raise funds for their candidate.[33]

Tuesday, November 4, was "a beautiful, bright day, but destined to be memorable," wrote diarist George Templeton Strong from his New York City home. The "rather light" turnout in Strong's voting district seemed to portend "a fair prospect for the Wadsworth ticket," but a subsequent ride with Horace Greeley on the Fourth Avenue trolley to newspaper offices quickly dampened Strong's enthusiasm. Instead, he was encountering boisterous demonstrations against Greeley and Wadsworth: "Where's Greeley's 900,000 men?" "General Wadsworth can't run for governor, but he can run sometimes." The news "Downtown" was even worse: the likelihood of an "overwhelming defeat" of Wadsworth.34

Out of 602,546 votes cast, only 11,000 separated the two candidates. Seymour, the winner, took the Democratic strongholds of New York City and the surrounding counties as far north as Albany, Montgomery, and Schenectady, with the exception of Delaware. Seymour even grabbed a majority in Erie County (Buffalo). On the other hand, the 36-county rural vote, including Wadsworth's Livingston (which handed the Geneseoan a 1,400-vote majority) and its northern neighbor, Monroe County, went overwhelmingly for Wadsworth. Ironically, he even took Seymour's Cayuga County. These were the counties that had supplied the bulk of New York's volunteers. The absence of the soldiers' vote could well have made the difference, at least Wadsworth was so persuaded. But the editor of the Democratic paper in the county just east of Wadsworth's sarcastically crowed "NEW YORK—REDEEMED!" In much smaller print were the results: 568 for Seymour, 565 for Wadsworth, just a three-vote Democratic plurality. Upon being consoled after the election, the general is quoted by Provost Marshal Doster as replying, "Oh . . . that is no defeat in which two-thirds of the army is not engaged [disfranchised]."35

Other explanations for his defeat were also offered. Secretary of the Navy Welles blamed Wadsworth's defeat on Thurlow Weed, the deceitful and would-be kingmaker, Secretary of State Seward, and others. If "the gallant and patriotic" Wadsworth needed any consolation, it was that the momentary partisanship exemplified by Seymour and his supporters ultimately would be surpassed by the spirit of patriotism. Wadsworth's friend Judge Edwards Pierrepont wrote him to offer his explanation for the election results: Simply, the country was tired of the army's inaction. The same things that were making Wadsworth impatient were making the country impatient. It was not any "want of personal popularity or personal admiration."36

John Lothrop Motley's postelection explanation was that New York City, which had so strongly supported Seymour, "was pro-slavery, as it always has been." By comparison, "the really American part of [the state]," Motley claimed, "voted by a great majority for Wadsworth." The *Albany Atlas & Argus,* echoing the sentiments of other dailies in the East, exulted that Seymour's election had overthrown a "dangerous conspiracy." At bottom, Wadsworth's candidacy "concealed a plot for the overthrow of McClellan and the abolitionizing of the War." More analytically, supporter Henry Raymond, who earlier had predicted a 20,000-vote victory, offered his postmortem: Wadsworth's defeat could be

blamed on three classes casting their votes for Seymour. First were those opposing the administration, particularly its suspension of the writ of habeas corpus
and the Emancipation Proclamation. Second were die-hard Democrats, and the
third were Southern sympathizers. Into which class he would have placed the
very anti-Wadsworth Irish in New York City is unknown.[37]

Not so, claimed Thurlow Weed, who chose to let Horace Greeley's postmortem confession speak for both of them: "The worst battle lost to the Union
cause thus far was the New York State election." The Republicans had simply
chosen the wrong man; General Wadsworth's abolitionism was unacceptable.
His ill-considered extremism, Weed believed, had splintered New York into ir-
reconcilable factions and, consequently, had rent the North as well, just when
the South was becoming more united. Actually, the Wadsworth campaign experienced the same phenomenon that was occurring in New Jersey, Pennsylvania,
Ohio, and Illinois: growing distrust of the Radicals and Lincoln, who was perceived as selling out to the Radicals.[38]

Wadsworth, who had finally, and reluctantly, agreed to run for public office,
accepted the loss. Though his fortune was reduced by campaign expenses, his
principles and sense of worth remained intact. This was confirmed by an aide
who reported that "General Wadsworth came to my office door, stood erect,
and, holding his hand on his breast, said, 'Here is one person who thinks just as
much of General Wadsworth *after* the election as he did *before.*'"[39]

Chapter 12

"COULD NOT BE ELECTED GOVERNOR, . . . SO HE MUST HAVE A PLACE IN THE ARMY"

Wadsworth the New Division Commander

Wadsworth's postelection comments may not have been an accurate portrayal of his mood. Not only had he been defeated, but he was reported by Provost Marshal Doster "to suffer the mortification of being left without any command." Though still military governor, in reality Wadsworth no longer commanded any troops. This resulted from an organizational change begun in early September when General McClellan was restored to command, whereby the Military District of the Defenses of Washington was created and absorbed Wadsworth's Military District of Washington. The new organization included the Defenses South of the Potomac, four brigades commanded initially by Brigadier General Amiel W. Whipple; Defenses North of the Potomac, unbrigaded infantry and artillery serving under Colonel Joseph A. Haskin; and Wadsworth's District of Washington, which included only a provisional brigade under Major General Silas Casey.[1]

Doster recalled that "Wadsworth's staff officers were extremely loud and bitter in their denunciation. But the chief called them together and forbade them to say one word either in praise or in blame." While Wadsworth did not say anything then, and it would not be the only rebuff he would experience, this had to be a particularly difficult time for him.[2]

So now, with the election behind him and his military duties severely circumscribed, Wadsworth focused on the treatment of freed slaves, which was, in fact, an ongoing concern. The District of Columbia, where slavery had been steadily declining long before Lincoln and the Republicans arrived, was "a magnet for runaways." The runaways, and those freed later, wanted to join the nearly 12,000 Blacks living and working as common laborers and domestics in the capital, "the largest employer of former slaves and free-black people." Wadsworth could readily put them to work building fortifications, as he had done the past June in Maryland, as well as in policing hospitals and other jobs. The rub for many Washingtonians, however, was not only the unprecedented numbers of freed slaves and runaways, but the extent to which they replaced White hired laborers.[3]

Military Governor Wadsworth was caught in the middle. For example, William Wood, superintendent of the Old Capitol Prison, was struggling to find "situations" for former slaves with military or private employers. Further, the lodging of runaways and freed Blacks in the already overcrowded prison offended many, including an army doctor who urged for sanitary reasons that the Black inmates be "kept apart from respectable white people." Wadsworth agreed and ordered the inmates "relocated to Duff Green's Row, a cluster of tenements just east of the Capitol," with Wood in charge of them. As military governor, Wadsworth made policy daily, much as he had done when he skirmished with Marshal Lamon earlier. At issue then was whether civil or military authority controlled. Though Attorney General Bates ruled that the civil prevailed, Wadsworth's efforts to assist these "contrabands" continued unabated.[4]

The war accelerated the influx of runaways, and Washington represented not only personal liberty, but freedom to contract for employment. However, according to Ira Berlin et al., in *Freedom: A Documentary History of Emancipation, 1861–1867,* because of the deterioration of slavery "fundamental questions arose about the social order that would take its place" and the ongoing ad hoc military responses to the military situation. Army commanders quickly realized that former slaves could be employed to perform military tasks as well as debasing jobs that many Whites would not accept. "Practical-minded Republicans had no qualms about accepting fugitive slaves into federal lines," Berlin and associates claimed, "if only to punish the rebels." That is, Wadsworth and like-minded Unionists applied "abolitionist arithmetic: Every slave employed by the army or navy represented a double gain, one subtracted from the Confederacy and one added to the Union." No doubt this calculation underlay the Second Confiscation Act of July 16 and the Militia Act of July 17, 1862. The combined acts freed the slaves from disloyal owners and granted Lincoln the right to engage them against the Confederacy. Thus, by the fall of 1862, "the Union war effort rested in large measure upon the labor of former slaves."[5]

The Federal legislation offered Wadsworth an opportunity to pursue a personal agenda that combined his humanitarianism and practical business sense. His agenda was given added urgency by Lincoln's November 13 Order Concerning the Confiscation Act. The act authorized Attorney General Bates to seize and to confiscate property of "Rebels and Traitors" and to obtain the help of Wadsworth and other military commanders to carry out these responsibilities. As a result, the need arose to offer assistance to even greater numbers of former slaves, which led to more problems, not the least of which was equitable pay. It was a portent of the affirmative action policies of the next century, for, as Wadsworth noted, Black military laborers were receiving "nearly double the wages paid to farm laborers at the North." This was twice the $10 called for in the July 1862 Militia Act. When quartermasters tried to comply with the act, Black workers successfully demanded pay equal to Black co-workers freed earlier. Yet even the greater pay—$20–25 per month—was insufficient to make ends meet in inflated Washington. Makeshift hovels built by these workers provided little protection from the elements and none from eviction.[6]

Added to this combustible mixture was Julia A. Wilbur, agent of the Ladies Anti-Slavery Society of Rochester, New York, just north of Wadsworth's Geneseo home. She saw firsthand the dire results of lack of shelter, including the spread of smallpox, and appealed to Generals Banks and Wadsworth. Both sanctioned her offer "to act as matron, visitor, adviser & instructor to these poor women & children," but neither offered any direct help. Other officials were equally sanguine, but still nothing happened. In fact, Wilbur used just about every means to force the government into action. She even implored Lincoln to house these poor fugitive slaves in Alexandria, across the Potomac from Washington, but this led to more runaways wanting food and shelter. Charity was not the solution, but relief had to be provided.[7]

Beyond food and shelter, the greatest need for the newly freed slaves was employment. However, numerous problems resulted from attempts to employ them. One was that the jobs typically offered were so repugnant ("cleansing cesspools, scrubbing privies and policing the grounds") that no one with any choice would do them. A second problem was that military pay was delayed as long as three months, forcing the freed Blacks to rely on credit. Further, unscrupulous civilian employers charged the ex-slaves exorbitant prices for supplies, board, and room, or bilked the workers out of their pay. Wadsworth ordered an investigation by Provost Marshal Doster, but the lack of supervision over these former slaves and their lack of sophistication made it virtually impossible to monitor or remedy the situation. Still, Wadsworth persisted, ordering the superintendent of contrabands to report to him instances "in which persons under his protection have been defrauded of their wages, or otherwise maltreated." Wadsworth then promised to take "further action."[8]

Wadsworth not only attempted to offer the relief that Julia Wilbur and others demanded, but he sought to prove the "superior productivity of free labor." While by the Militia Act free Black military laborers were to receive $10 per month, less $3 for clothing and rations, in inflationary Washington the going rate for Black laborers generally was $25. But as Berlin et al. noted, "the vagaries of federal policy," which were implemented by "an array of politicians, bureaucrats, and military officers" (including possibly Wadsworth, though not named), resulted in conflict and confusion.[9]

For example, General Wadsworth proposed a solution that initially was supported by the War Department. On September 25, he wrote Secretary of War Stanton pointing out the discrepancy between the pay of Black laborers and Northern farmworkers. He asserted that many of the Black laborers "waste in dissipation" the wages they received because of their inability to handle money. This was coupled with the government's need to support "six or eight hundred [unemployed] women & children of the same class." So, Wadsworth recommended that

$5 be withheld from the Black laborers and teamsters and put away for them. Two days later Adjutant General Lorenzo Thomas ordered Quartermaster General Montgomery Meigs to adopt the policy.[10]

Reasonable on the surface, the policy produced an immediate backlash from laborers employed by special agreement to meet the urgent demand for workers. While it might well work in the South, where Union military force now applied, it would not serve in Washington, where workers were not hired under the Militia Act. The workers either left government employ or threatened to do so. Nor did it work for those less skilled who had been sent to Harpers Ferry to build fortifications for McClellan in September. The same $5 was deducted, although they were paid only 40¢ a day. What had seemed so sensible to Wadsworth, because it was analogous to his tenant system at home, had backfired.[11]

Necessarily, General Wadsworth, like the capital itself, came under particular public scrutiny. The flow of fugitive slaves, which corresponded to the intensity of military operations, had risen to high tide in September 1862 after Lee invaded Maryland. Concern for the welfare of the fugitive slaves led to the formation of the National Freedman's Relief Association of the District of Columbia and a number of relief agencies. Initially the agencies were a blessing to Wadsworth, who delegated authority to care for the former slaves to Methodist minister and former Chicago reform school administrator Danforth B. Nichols. Though this would prove to be only a stopgap measure, it offered Wadsworth some relief from a vexing problem.[12]

While General Wadsworth was exercising what little authority he could, General McClellan was positioning his army to confront Lee's troops, which had retreated from Maryland into northern Virginia, near Culpeper. In countering Lee, McClellan was relying upon Defenses of Washington commander Major General Heintzelman, rather than Wadsworth, who again was acting like an adjutant rather than a military commander. For example, on November 3, 1862, General Halleck had learned that Major General James Ewell Brown ("Jeb") Stuart with more than 1,200 cavalry was near Poolesville, Maryland, north of the Potomac and less than thirty miles from the capital, on his return from a raid on government stores in Chambersburg, Pennsylvania. "Old Brains" Halleck turned to Heintzelman, who then directed Wadsworth to check out the rumors. In turn, Wadsworth ordered Colonel James B. Swain, commanding "Scott's Nine Hundred" cavalry (the 1st U.S. Volunteer Cavalry), to do so. Swain then dispatched a detachment under First Lieutenant G. W. Smith. The result was conflicting reports, ranging from no Confederate troops to upward of 1,000.[13]

Not surprisingly, no one defending the capital knew what the Confederates' plans were. Yet Wadsworth apparently discounted the seriousness of an attack on Washington and revoked his previous order closing taverns. This brought the expected reaction from their denizens: Wadsworth was no longer considered "a horrible ogre" but was now "an agreeable and liberal man." Lincoln was less sanguine about the safety of the capital. Nor, despite the fact he had been prodding McClellan into action, was the president satisfied that McClellan was taking advantage of the good weather to mount some kind of attack.[14]

McClellan's failure to advance farther than Warrenton by the first week of November was the last straw. Lincoln's patience had long since been exhausted, despite his liking for McClellan the man. On November 5, prodded by a majority of his cabinet, Lincoln issued orders relieving McClellan and appointing Major General Ambrose Burnside—he of the distinguished muttonchops, but known hereafter as sideburns—in his place. Major General David Hunter would assume command of Burnside's IX Corps, while recently recuperated Joseph Hooker would replace a McClellan favorite, Fitz John Porter, as V Corps commander. Interestingly and possibly not coincidentally, Wadsworth was in Secretary Stanton's office with General Halleck when Brigadier General Catharenus P. Buckingham was given two envelopes containing orders—one relieving McClellan, the other appointing Burnside in his place. But there was no immediate indication of what this change would mean for Wadsworth—still angling for a field command.[15]

Wadsworth's future was still uncertain when fellow New Yorker Brigadier General John H. Martindale was appointed to replace him on November 19 and he was granted a leave of absence by Stanton. Over three weeks later, on December 7, the frustrated general wrote his youngest son, James: "I do not know what I am to do . . . whether to remain here [in Washington] or go into the field." By contrast, Wadsworth's middle son, Craig, had "gratefully accepted" Major General John F. Reynolds's appointment as aide-de-camp in early October. (Craig's father was equally satisfied.) Meanwhile, Wadsworth reunited with his oldest son, Charles Frederick, who had wrangled a leave through his father. But he found time to recommend to New York's Governor Morgan the promotion of Captain Augustus Funk of the 38th New York to major. Funk had impressed Wadsworth with his gallantry in the Peninsula campaign "under very trying circumstances."[16]

Realizing that his promotion was based no little on McClellan's inactivity, on November 15 Burnside promptly began to move the Army of the Potomac from Warrenton eastward toward Falmouth, on the opposite side of the Rappahannock River from Fredericksburg. The genial 1847 West Point graduate hoped to force a crossing before General Lee could concentrate his troops at Fredericksburg, but unfortunate delays of pontoon boats enabled Lee to pull together his far-flung infantry corps. Thus, on December 13, Burnside ended up attacking the entrenched Confederates on the heights behind Fredericksburg with predictably dismal results.

News about the expedition began filtering into Washington, then came the wounded. Fredericksburg was not just a Union defeat; it was an unmitigated disaster: "The rebs pored shell and grape in and our men fell thick and fast. . . . The rebs had all their own way and it was awful how they Slautered [*sic*] our men," reported one Pennsylvania soldier. Burnside's repeated assaults had led to the killing and wounding of almost 13,000 Union troops, compared to just over

5,000 Confederate casualties. On December 15, the demoralized Army of the Potomac retreated to the north bank of the Rappahannock.[17]

On the other hand, exactly a week after he had despaired over his future, an upbeat General Wadsworth rode alongside I Corps commander John Reynolds near the Old Richmond Road outside Fredericksburg. With Wadsworth was his former aide, Brevet Lieutenant Colonel John Kress, for whom he had double-barreled news. Kress's promotion was for heroics at the battle of Fredericksburg *and* he was expected to join Wadsworth, who was to command the I Corps' 1st Division, as the division's inspector general.[18]

Official notice of Wadsworth's appointment came on December 16, when he was assigned to duty under Major General William Franklin, the left grand division commander. Six days later he was officially named commander of the 1st Division of General Reynolds's I Corps, replacing Brigadier General Abner Doubleday, one of the Fort Sumter heroes, who had been temporarily commanding the division. Apparently Wadsworth's behind-the-scenes efforts, of which there is no written record, had borne fruit—he now had a field command. Better yet, he had a division. This was heady stuff, though there is no evidence that he behaved any differently upon learning the news. First, however, he had to complete some unfinished business. He was called to testify on behalf of his old commander, Irvin McDowell, who had sought a court of inquiry to counter what he considered unfounded criticisms of his conduct going back to First Bull Run. True to form, Wadsworth stuck by his old commander, who, nonetheless, was relegated to minor duties.[19]

On December 27, Wadsworth issued his first orders from camp at Belle Plain, Virginia. It was typical Wadsworth, a simple notification that he had assumed command and that Major Clinton H. Meneely and Captain Timothy E. Ellsworth were his aides-de-camp. Also, as Wadsworth had indicated earlier, Brevet Lieutenant Colonel John Kress was appointed his inspector general and, in fact, had begun his duties two days earlier.[20]

The new division commander, who ranked twentieth in seniority among the army's brigadiers, was not entirely unknown to the troops he now commanded. In fact, a Wisconsin soldier cynically declared that Wadsworth "could not be elected Governor, . . . so he must have a place in the army." Though less cynical, Lieutenant Colonel Rufus Dawes, commander of the 6th Wisconsin, which had survived Antietam and Fredericksburg, was not pleased either: "This army seems to be overburdened with second rate men in high positions, from General Burnside down," he wrote home. "This winter is, indeed, the Valley Forge of the war." While he did not mention Wadsworth by name, it appears Dawes did not exempt him from the criticism.[21]

In time Dawes came to admire Wadsworth, but Colonel Charles Wainwright, the wealthy 36-year-old corps chief of artillery, did not. Wainwright's appraisal was characteristically blunt: "I know nothing of his [Wadsworth's] natural ability, but it ought to be very great, as he knew nothing of military matters before the war, is not a young man, and has had no experience in battle to entitle him to so high a position." Yet Wainwright and Wadsworth had much in common, possibly too much. Wainwright was a physically powerful gentleman with fine tastes, including his reading matter. His wealth and membership in the New York State Agricultural Society alone should have helped him identify with Wadsworth. However, Wainwright had been a staunch Seymour supporter in the past gubernatorial election, and he deeply admired McClellan. Even more irksome to Wainwright, the inexperienced Wadsworth temporarily served as acting corps commander during Reynolds's brief leave of absence. Unfortunately, Wainwright's highly unfavorable impression of Wadsworth would continue and would produce a damaging relationship between them.[22]

There was no immediate reaction from Doubleday, an army regular who had commanded the division at Antietam and Fredericksburg. However, his replacement by Wadsworth, a volunteer with political influence, foretold a stormy relationship that affected their performances barely seven months later. In fact, Doubleday's assistant adjutant general, Eminel Halstead, was openly critical of Wadsworth. Ironically, this animosity did not carry over to Captain Craig Wadsworth, Reynolds's aide-de-camp.

These mixed reactions, indeed criticisms, of Wadsworth's appointment were not unwarranted. As the Wisconsin cynic noted, he was a political appointee, and, as Wainwright correctly recorded in his diary, he lacked experience commanding troops in fearful battles like Antietam or Fredericksburg. His concern for men serving under him, his ability to manage others, and his natural intelligence would have to compensate. Also, he seemed to have Major General Reynolds's support.

☆   ☆   ☆

On January 7, 1863, the new division commander rudely introduced himself to the 7th Indiana by citing the "bad condition" of the regiment's arms and camp. Similarly, he reported that Colonel Chapman Biddle's 121st Pennsylvanians "are personally very dirty, their arms in bad condition, and the camp of the Regiment badly policed. There are not log huts for quarters nor any appearance of a desire to make the men comfortable." Biddle was warned to expect another inspection soon. Regular division inspections would be conducted under the supervision of Lieutenant Colonel Kress by four newly named brigade inspectors. Wadsworth also wanted regular reports of men present for duty. Further, he requested horses and harnesses for the corps artillery, because the infantry had been increased enough to "support Batteries of 6 guns each." Finally, after being relieved, pickets were "to discharge their pieces at two P.M. daily in the vicinity of their respective camps."[23]

It was as if the old man were managing his "Home Farm"— juggling as many tasks as humanly possible. One day he was upbraiding men for the "enormous loss of arms," which he attributed to the "gross carelessness" of their officers. The next he was upbraiding brigade commanders for the loss of thirty to fifty horses per week due to starvation. Another day he was concerned about the inability of corps headquarters to sort mail by regiments and commands. Still another day he was criticizing the inefficient cavalry for failing to arrest a private for smuggling liquor into the camp and for not capturing civilians who were helping soldiers to desert to Maryland. Dissatisfied with the cavalry, on January 30 Wadsworth issued two separate orders. The first went to Brigadier General Solomon Meredith to take his 4th Brigade outside the picket lines to arrest civilians abetting deserters. A similar order was issued to the 24th Michigan's Lieutenant Colonel Mark Flanagan, a sturdy, 6-foot, 4-inch-tall former Wayne County, Michigan, sheriff. Flanagan and his Wolverines obtained results, but General Wadsworth found himself having to make more decisions. Two of the civilians nabbed that day demanded their money back from their captors, $335 and $48.31, respectively. The general allowed the civilians to have only "what was needed for their comfort until their cases were disposed of."[24]

The civilian general was uncharacteristically concerned with details, including settling accounts of the division quartermaster. Wadsworth sought permission for his assistant aide-de-camp and quartermaster, Lieutenant Clayton Rogers, to travel to Dayton, Ohio, to locate vital records, because the former assistant quartermaster, Captain Fielding Lowery, had "left the business of his Dept in great confusion. . . ." Wadsworth also felt "constrained" to check on the "fitness for command" of Colonel George F. Biddle of the 95th New York and recommended Brigadier General Gabriel Paul, Colonel Walter Phelps (22nd New York), and Colonel James Gavin (7th Indiana) to constitute the examining board. And the division commander gently reprimanded General Paul for ordering his staff to ignore orders from division headquarters unless they knew it was from someone identifiable on Wadsworth's staff. He was demanding that the chain of command be followed, something that he was known to circumvent on occasion and would do in the future.[25]

It was a difficult time for Wadsworth. In early January many soldiers were sick, suffering from want of food and clothes, which the 24th Michigan's historian blamed on the collusion of "rascally government contractors and inspectors." Shoddy shoes were an example. Frequently the soles were nothing more than scraps of leather glued together, which fell apart after a muddy or rainy day's march. The soldiers' clothing was scarcely better, falling to shreds after only a short time. Rain was another problem General Wadsworth and his men encountered. Reportedly, in late February a driving rain fell for fourteen straight hours. The extremely inclement weather even made it difficult, if not impossible, to forward provisions by roads and led to orders to use Aquia Creek instead. For some of the troops liquid spirits were an antidote, but Wadsworth would put a stop to that practice and to gambling. To maintain battle readiness, occupy time, and improve the soldiers' health, the tiresome and numbing drill was stepped up.[26]

It was also a difficult time for Army of the Potomac commander Burnside. He was the subject of an intrigue to force his dismissal. Then Lincoln refused to accept his resignation. Burnside felt he had to do something, which became a mid-January plan to cross the Rappahannock River on pontoon bridges up-stream from Fredericksburg and to sweep down on Lee's troops behind the town.[27] Unfortunately, he had to depend on openly critical subordinates, a dispirited army, and unpredictable weather, none of which cooperated.

However unfortunate for Burnside, the operation offered Wadsworth's men an opportunity to see another side of their new commander. On January 19, a "bracing, not too cold" day, with Wadsworth's division in the lead, Burnside's Army of the Potomac began its intended crossing of the Rappahannock. By 3:00 P.M. a torrential rain turned the once-frozen ground into a bottomless quagmire. The axles of wagons were buried, while horses and mules were up to their bellies in mud. The movement was called off, but the problem then was how to return to their camps, including crossing a deep ditch through which ran a swift stream. Wadsworth hollered to members of the 7th Indiana, "Men, shall we go around or put down a foot bridge?" Hearing "footbridge," Wadsworth "promptly dis-mounted, hung his sword on the pommel of his saddle and gave the reins to an orderly." Then, as he had done as a much younger man in a similar situation, General Wadsworth plunged "into the water and slush up to the tops of his Napoleons [boots], seized hold of one end of the logs as they were brought in, and placed it in position." For two days "Old Corduroy," as the soldiers fondly dubbed him, and his troops corduroyed roads, which required cutting logs, haul-ing them to the road, and placing them lengthwise across it. It was vintage Wadsworth.[28]

Despite outward appearances and a coveted field command, Wadsworth was himself dispirited, according to his political ally *New York Times* editor Henry Raymond. The editor had come to Wadsworth's camp, following up on what proved to be a false report of Raymond's brother's death. The general treated Raymond "with great kindness," including feeding him and locating his suppos-edly dead brother. Raymond then inquired why his host endured uncomfortable quarters and an absence of servants, forsaking the luxury one would expect for a division commander, particularly a wealthy one. Wadsworth's reply is revealing of his leadership style: He wanted to be an "example of plain living for his subor-dinate officers." Raymond doubted that it would have the intended effect.[29]

As a good reporter, Raymond probed for news. Wadsworth was unusually restrained. Eventually the *Times* editor elicited from Wadsworth that the prob-lem was disaffected officers who remained loyal to McClellan and undermined Burnside. But Wadsworth "had resolved to hold his tongue for the future," be-cause a year earlier "he had been so much censured" for speaking too freely about some of these same officers. In fact, Raymond found that the general was being excluded from discussions of details at command headquarters and complained about it. Not surprisingly, the division commander wanted his "general senti-ments and interest in the war . . . brought to bear more directly upon the coun-cils of the campaign."[30]

Raymond also visited Burnside, whose lack of confidence was as paralyzing as the muddy roads. He intended to offer his resignation and take the disloyal officers down with him. By contrast, upon his return from visiting Burnside and other officers, Raymond found that Wadsworth's confidence had been restored. In fact, Wadsworth, then occupying a small wood-frame house in an advanced position, was in surprisingly good spirits, even asking the editor to tell his wife, Mary Craig, that he was heating his own water for shaving. Further, he made it clear that he would not have abandoned the plans to attack Lee, despite the heavy rains that had bogged down the Union army. He countered Raymond's objection that the cannons could not be moved on the roads by arguing that the Confederates were in the same fix. He would attack with infantry alone.

But Wadsworth was clearly in the minority. Burnside was beset on all sides, and on January 25, he was gone, replaced the next day by Major General Joseph Hooker, "the blond war god." The two generals who outranked Hooker, Right and Left Grand Division commanders Edwin Sumner and William Franklin, also were relieved of their army commands, Sumner at his request.[31]

The boastful Hooker, who had undermined Burnside and whom Stanton distrusted but could not discount at this point, soon made his presence felt. Until now, his career had been uneven in the extreme. His bravery in the Mexican War as a lieutenant had been rewarded by brevets to the rank of lieutenant colonel, but he had resigned to take up farming and was eking out a living when the war began. At Williamsburg in the Peninsula campaign the press had dubbed him "Fighting Joe Hooker," which seemed to arouse his ambition and offer Radicals, like Chase, a standard bearer.[32]

General Hooker's appointment was greeted with mixed reactions by the soldiers he commanded, but shortly after assuming command he captured their confidence and reinvigorated their spirits by rapidly issuing a series of orders. One was to increase drill and field exercises, which not only offered the soldiers something to gripe about, but also greater fitness and health. Another systematized absences for officers and enlisted men. While only token leaves were granted, there was at least some regularity and fairness. Medical supervision was enhanced, and what we would today regard as elementary notions of sanitary conditions were instituted. This included the issuance of vegetables ("onions and potatoes," according to the 6th Wisconsin's chronicler, Rufus Dawes). More important in terms of purely military affairs, Burnside's grand divisions were abandoned, which seemed to garner universal approval. Instead, the more familiar corps structure was reinstituted. However, the act that probably had the greatest effect was the adoption on March 21 of the late Phil Kearny's idea of distinctive corps patches. Its purpose was twofold: to achieve accountability (straggling soldiers would be easily identified) and to raise morale. Wadsworth would shortly wear a red spherical patch, designating his 1st Division of the I Corps.[33]

Wadsworth too was getting acquainted with his command; reacquainted in some cases. He had already met Colonel Edward Fowler's 14th Brooklyn (the 84th New York), Colonel Lucius Fairchild's 2nd Wisconsin, which had confused other Union troops with their gray uniforms at First Bull Run, and the 6th Wisconsin.[34]

The 14th Brooklyn traced its origin to the early 1800s as the Militia of Kings and Richmond Counties, which was designated the 2nd New York State Division. The regiment's distinctive uniform, blue caps "trimmed with red, a blue coat with two rows of bell buttons, red pants, white gaiters, and a red breastpiece with one row of bell buttons," would make its members stand out anywhere and would lead to their nickname "The Red-Legged Devils." Wadsworth had become acquainted with them at First Bull Run, after which they had fought at Antietam, South Mountain, and Fredericksburg. The result was "a peculiar comradeship between him [Wadsworth] and the Brooklyn boys, who . . . [proved] ready and willing to perform any special duty he might ask, no matter how dangerous."[35]

The 2nd and 6th Wisconsin, along with the 7th Wisconsin, the 19th Indiana, and the 24th Michigan, belonged to the famous Iron Brigade, which shortly would be commanded by Brigadier General Solomon Meredith. The brigade's nom de guerre purportedly derived from an exchange between Hooker and McClellan during the battle of South Mountain on September 19, 1862. When McClellan asked who these men were who were "fighting against great odds," Hooker is supposed to have replied, "General Gibbon's Brigade of Western Men." McClellan countered that "They must be made of *iron*." Hooker, who had observed them at Second Bull Run, exulted, "By the Eternal *they are* iron."[36]

The brigade owed its reputation as a fighting unit to General John Gibbon, who, in turn, owed his star to Wadsworth's intercession. Upon assuming his first brigade command, West Pointer Gibbon had found these Westerners wanting. Vigorously drilling them and instituting discipline was only a part of his strategy. Though firm, like any army regular, he also relied on what today would be called behavior modification (rewarding expected behavior without advance warning), a technique he chanced upon during one of his first inspections.[37]

Gibbon also forced his brigade to adopt the regular army uniform, even the white leggings and white cotton gloves. "But most distinctive was the hat. In place of the kepi, worn by most volunteers, the men donned the black felt Hardee hat of the Regular Army, ordinarily worn turned up on the left side with a great black plume on the right side." They were thus transformed into the now familiar "Black Hats." However, their personal bravery—modeled after their first commander—the brigade's genuinely distinguishing feature, came later, at the battle of Groveton in the Second Bull Run campaign. They had been "suddenly, unexpectedly, and viciously" thrown into battle "in circumstances most likely to stampede soldiers unaccustomed to battle." Nonetheless, "they had not wavered then or thereafter."[38]

The 2nd Wisconsin had answered Lincoln's first call for volunteers, had rendezvoused at the state capital, Madison, and was mustered into Federal service June 11, 1861. Before the month was out the regiment was in Washington. Less than a month later, wearing its gray uniform, it formed part of Colonel William T. Sherman's 3rd Brigade at the battle of First Bull Run. After the battle the 821-man Badger regiment came under General Wadsworth's command in the defense of Fort Corcoran near the Aqueduct Bridge. On August 25, it was transferred to the brigade of Wadsworth's political ally, General Rufus King, which consisted of itself, the 5th Wisconsin (soon to be replaced by the 7th), the 6th Wisconsin, and the 19th Indiana.[39]

Commanding a fellow brigade in McDowell's division in early 1862, Wadsworth had become acquainted with the 6th Wisconsin, the regiment that probably gained the greatest renown of the brigade. These Badgers also rendezvoused in Madison, at Camp Randall, on June 25, 1861, and were mustered three weeks later. The regiment was commanded by Colonel Lysander Cutler, a contemporary of Wadsworth, who would as a brigadier general command Wadsworth's 2nd Brigade at Chancellorsville and Gettysburg. The 6th arrived in Washington on August 7 and, like its sister regiment, the 2nd, would see duty in the defenses of Washington, becoming part of the Iron Brigade in June 1863. Frank A. Haskell, Dartmouth College alumnus who left his law practice to become the 6th's adjutant, subsequently served as General Gibbon's aide and authored a highly acclaimed narrative of the battle of Gettysburg.[40]

Another member of the 6th Wisconsin illustrated the independence of these Westerners. As James P. "Mickey" Sullivan told the story, he had carefully modified his Springfield rifle so that it "worked almost as easy as a squirrel gun." At a general inspection Wadsworth questioned the modification, to which Sullivan replied, "So I can hit a canteen at one hundred yards." His division commander, a man who was known to bend rules and regulations, asked Sullivan "no more questions."[41]

The third (and largest) Badger regiment, the 7th Wisconsin, commanded by Colonel William W. Robinson, followed a similar course to Washington and to the Iron Brigade, which was bloodied at Antietam. The fourth regiment of Westerners, the 19th Indiana, was commanded by 52-year-old Solomon Meredith. At age 19, the 6-foot, 6-inch North Carolina native had moved to Indiana, where he served as county sheriff, four-term state legislator, and later U.S. marshal. He was appointed the 19th's colonel shortly before the regiment moved to Washington in August 1861. Meredith, a strong supporter of McClellan and opponent of employing Blacks as soldiers, would also fight political battles with Congress and with Secretary of War Stanton, just as he had done in his adopted state. Though his military training was scarcely better than his regiment's initially, he and the regiment would prove their mettle. Also despite their political differences, Wadsworth could trust Meredith, whose aggressiveness resembled his own.[42]

The final member of the much-heralded brigade was the 24th Michigan, which had answered General Gibbon's call for Westerners. (He is supposed to have sought a regiment from Wisconsin or Indiana, but accepted one from Michigan.) The Wolverines, commanded by Colonel Henry A. Morrow, joined the brigade on October 9, 1862. The Virginia-born Morrow was the third Southern commander in the brigade, along with Gibbon and Meredith. Because the 24th Michigan was reinforcing the brigade and because it was from a state Gibbon had requested, albeit his last choice, the regiment expected to be received favorably. Instead, it was met by stony silence when it was drawn up before the brigade in its well-worn outfits. The Michiganders, a number of whom were members of the Detroit Typographical Union, would have to prove themselves to these veterans of Second Bull Run, South Mountain, and bloody Antietam. Two months later, at Fredericksburg, they, like their commander, a

Mexican War veteran and judge in his adopted Detroit home, would secure the reluctant approval of their Iron Brigade comrades. There, according to Lieutenant Colonel Rufus Dawes of the 6th Wisconsin, "they showed themselves of a fibre worthy to be woven into the woof of the 'Iron Brigade.'"[43]

While other brigades in Wadsworth's division would not gain the same recognition, they either had already proved or would prove their mettle, including Colonel Walter Phelps's 1st Brigade (22nd, 24th, 30th, and 84th New York, or 14th Brooklyn), General Cutler's (formerly Colonel James Gavin's) 2nd Brigade, consisting of the 7th Indiana, 76th New York, 95th New York, and the 56th Pennsylvania, and Brigadier General Gabriel R. Paul's 3rd Brigade (22nd, 29th, 30th, and 31st New Jersey, the valiant 147th New York, which would take an awful beating at Gettysburg, and the 137th Pennsylvania).[44]

Finally, Brigadier General James S. Wadsworth had the field command he had so ardently sought. Soon he would be called to lead these men into some of the fiercest battles of the war. But now he had to learn the ropes on the battlefield and to gain the respect not only of these men but of the officers he thought had once censured him for speaking too freely.

Chapter 13

"HE'LL BE KILLED BEFORE [THE WAR] CLOSES"

The War Takes a New Turn Under Hooker

After the defeat at Fredericksburg and the "mud march" in its aftermath, the Army of the Potomac, numbering approximately 132,000, settled in north of the Rappahannock River for the remainder of the winter of 1862–1863. General Reynolds's I Corps held the extreme left at Stoneman's Switch on Potomac Creek, not far from White Oak Church, with Major General John Sedgwick's VI Corps, the largest corps, nearby. The II and III Corps, commanded respectively by Major General Darius Couch (replacing the recently deceased Edwin Sumner, who had resigned previously) and Major General Daniel Sickles, were camped near Falmouth. Prickly Major General George G. Meade's V Corps lay on the Richmond, Fredericksburg, and Potomac Railroad, while the XI Corps, with Major General Franz Sigel commanding (but soon replaced by Major General Oliver O. Howard), was near Brooke Station. Major General Henry Slocum's XII Corps, the smallest, was near Stafford Court House. The Union's picket line formed a rough triangle from near Belle Plain on the Potomac, down to the Rappahannock, up the left bank to near Falmouth, and back southeast to Belle Plain. The three divisions of the newly created Cavalry Corps, under the command of Major General George Stoneman, a classmate of McClellan and Stonewall Jackson, were scattered between Stafford Court House, Brooke Station, and near Belle Plain, an almost hundred-mile-long line.[1]

Hooker, the new commander, not only initiated a number of necessary changes to restore the soldiers' morale, he also appointed political generals to important posts that raised eyebrows. His selection of Brigadier General Daniel Butterfield, a former New York militia officer, as chief of staff, proved to be a good appointment. Butterfield was not only compatible with Hooker (and later Meade), but he was also an able administrator. However, Hooker's choice of the notorious Daniel Sickles to command the III Corps was a different matter. Sickles had emerged from New York City's infamous Tammany Hall to become a state assemblyman, Manhattan corporation counsel, congressman, and exonerated killer of the son of Francis Scott Key. "Whether he was drinking, fighting, wenching or plotting," wrote Civil War historian Bruce Catton, "he was always operating with the throttle wide open." In short, he was a man Hooker could genuinely enjoy.[2]

The new depot, handling enormous amounts of army supplies, was at Belle Plain, a desolate region bereft of even houses and approachable only by wagons. Passable roads were a necessity. General Wadsworth, who had plunged into the mud to help corduroy roads in mid-January near Falmouth, would reprise his role here, but his ingenuity would be taxed in other ways, as well. Hooker had substituted mules for packhorses, but mules' hooves cut right through the mud and mire. The practical Wadsworth simply substituted oxen, which were then stabled near his headquarters. "It was a rare treat to our men to see the old General take a gad [stick] and 'whisper to the calves,'" recalled the 6th Wisconsin's Rufus Dawes. "He took great interest in the oxen and was often seen at the landing giving them instructions and driving them." Wadsworth, in mud to his boot tops, would point to an ox and say, "That is an off ox"; another he would identify as the ox that "works the nigh side, don't you see his left horn." Dawes, who had rather summarily dismissed Wadsworth's appointment, was coming to appreciate him as "an intensely practical commander, indefatigable as a worker, and looking closely after details. No commander could do more for the personal comfort of his men."[3]

Though the new division commander could prove tough, he needed to be equally solicitous of the soldiers. "The recent disastrous failure and abortive movements, as well as the changes of commanders," claimed the 24th Michigan's historian, "produced their effect upon the *morale* of the army, and there was considerable despondency or dissatisfaction among the troops, as 200 desertions a day from the army proved." The Virginia weather with its alternating "frost, rain, snow, slush and mud" was another factor. The 24th Michigan alone reported twenty-five of its members "missing." Camp guards, three-a-day roll calls, courts-martial, and search parties resulted in the return and punishment of some deserters and squelched other disappearances. Seven brigade deserters were "sped out of camp [with] a cold wind blowing upon their shaved heads February 21." But something positive was needed. Promotions, where possible, represented a positive step. Fifteen-day furloughs for two of every hundred men (with married men given preference) was another.[4]

The biggest need for men and animals was food. To this end Wadsworth was forever ordering out (or leading) foraging parties. For example, the first week of February he personally led an expedition down the neck of Potomac Creek to Westmoreland Court House. He had returned with "about a hundred horses and mules, of very little value," the stuffy, hypercritical Colonel Wainwright noted in his diary, but "a goodly number of contrabands." Wainwright dismissed the general's exertions with the comment that "Wadsworth is one of the nervous sort, who must be doing something all the time which will show." "Quiet, unostentatious preparation," Wainwright sneered, "he does not appreciate."[5]

Seemingly oblivious to the artillerist's judgment of him, Wadsworth was particularly excited about an expedition resulting in the seizure of another seventy slaves the following week. Lincoln's Emancipation Proclamation, signed on New Years Day and declaring all slaves in rebellious states free, had effectively unshackled him. Every freed slave was another source of labor for the North and one less for the South. However, by early April the flow of contrabands, employed mostly as servants, had dwindled to a trickle.[6]

Then for ten days in late February Wadsworth again temporarily commanded the I Corps and requested his oldest son, Charles F., to serve as acting aide-de-camp. The request was denied by army general-in-chief Halleck. Knowing the ropes, the acting corps commander went directly to the president. The request languished until late March, when Wadsworth wrote to find out what happened to it. Lincoln then forwarded it to War Secretary Stanton without action.[7]

Shortly after commanding the corps, General Wadsworth himself took a week's leave, but was in harness again on March 9, when he rejected the findings of a general court-martial and demanded punishment in the case of a private absent for almost a year. Thereafter he stopped long enough to write his 16-year-old son, James Wolcott Wadsworth. The letter revealed not only the casualness with which the civilian-general accepted the risks of war, but his amazing vigor. He had just completed a sixteen-mile ride the previous day and had ridden "forty odd miles" two days before that. The general assured his youngest son that he would introduce him to war as an aide, as he had done with his two older brothers. But "Jimmy" would have to wait until fall, when the risks of fever had subsided.[8]

The next day, just as "stormy and disagreeable" as the previous day was balmy, Wadsworth helped celebrate the I Corps' anniversary dinner. Past and present corps' commanders, including McDowell, Hooker, Meade, and Reynolds, were invited to dine in the headquarters tent. (Meade was unable to attend due to the weather, and Hooker was answering a summons from Washington.) Division commanders Wadsworth, Robinson, and Doubleday, Hooker's chief of staff Butterfield, and other officers enjoyed a real spread prepared by Captain James Sanderson, the former New York City chef and now Wadsworth's commissary of subsistence. Ironically, eight to ten "contrabands," dressed in "white chokers [cravats] and thread gloves," served the diners much as they might have served their former masters.[9]

In his inimitable style, Wainwright, the corps' artillery commander, used the opportunity to assess the division commanders dining with him:

> It would be pretty hard to find three poorer division commanders than we have in this corps. . . . Doubleday knows enough, but he is entirely impractical, and so slow at getting an idea through his head. Wadsworth is active, always busy at something, and with a good allowance of common sense, but knows nothing of military matters. Robinson appears to be one of those old regular officers who have made no progress since they left West Point, and whose main exertions are expended in grumbling at and trying to get around whatever order they may receive from their superior.

This was not a good omen, considering the situation in which the corps artillery commander and the three division commanders would find themselves less than three months later.[10]

Wainwright certainly would have questioned General Wadsworth's rejection of requests by his four brigade commanders for a number of items that the general felt were "encumbrances," including thirty copies of General Silas Casey's two-volume *System of Infantry Tactics*. Nor did the division commander believe that more work animals were needed. In fact, there was insufficient forage for many more animals. Also "Commissary supplies are ample," including the five to eight days' rations each brigade had on hand. However, he agreed that two or three regiments were deficient in arms, and just over a week later he noted the need for corn for the oxen used to draw wagons. That meant ordering yet another foraging expedition.[11]

This was the side of Wadsworth that the 6th Wisconsin's Lieutenant Colonel Dawes saw: "a strong character," a commander who attended to the health and comfort of his men by sending out (or escorting himself) foraging parties. Dawes may even have been aware of a scheme General Wadsworth proposed to General Hooker's chief of staff Butterfield by which he would equip 8,500 men loaded on five or six wagons and 815 pack animals to forage in a wealthy area south of Belle Plain. While disallowed by Hooker, it illustrates characteristic concern for his troops as well as the restless Wadsworth's thinking. It may also reveal Wadsworth's disposition to satisfy his tastes. An amusing anecdote has it that "Gen. Wadsworth was himself badly disappointed" when some choice, cured Virginia hams, confiscated from a nearby plantation, fell into the "ruthless hand of the soldiers" rather than into his, as the expedition's officers had intended.[12]

On the other hand, how Wadsworth would have reacted to Colonel Adrian Root's discovery is unknown. As Officer of the Day, the 94th New York's Root (Kress's friend) had recently encountered a corporal on picket duty complaining of not feeling well. The picket's pain and other symptoms of severe indisposition increased, becoming so evident that officers had the picket carried to a nearby farmhouse. There the worthy corporal "was safely delivered of a fine, fat recruit."[13]

Nor was this the only woman in the I Corps. In fact, another had already established a reputation and was serving as matron of Wadsworth's 1st Division. Forty-three-year-old Mrs. Elmina Keeler of Oswego County, New York, a teacher in Oswego with her husband, a member of the 147th New York, had just joined the division. When her husband, an anti-war Democrat, enlisted after Antietam, Elmina took it upon herself to nurse the wounded. Her husband, stricken with sunstroke to which he was prone, was appointed ward master of the regiment's hospital, while his strong wife became matron. Thereafter, until her division appointment, she had attended to the sick and dying in Washington and had gathered medical supplies in the capital and her Oswego hometown. Her greatest fame still lay ahead of her. (The 76th New York made a similar claim: that Ann Redmond marched with the regiment, ministered to the sick, washed their clothes, and contributed "mirthful conversation and [a] hearty laugh.")[14]

However, General Wadsworth had other things on his mind. On March 22, anticipating battle, he telegraphed corps commander Reynolds at Willard's Hotel in Washington. Wadsworth wanted Reynolds to obtain a star for Lysander Cutler, temporarily commanding an I Corps brigade, as a reward for his services at the battle of Fredericksburg in December. Also Wadsworth wanted the tough Midwesterner for the upcoming battle. Likely, the division commander saw in Cutler, the 6th Wisconsin's first commander, a kindred soul. Despite his lack of military training, spare frame, 56 years, and uneven step as a result of an earlier wound, Cutler inspired confidence. The dark eyes beneath iron-gray eyebrows, and the grave appearance, were, the 6th Wisconsin's Dawes claimed, softened by a "genial manner." Cutler would be promoted shortly and rejoin the division as 2nd Brigade commander.[15]

About this time, late March, the telltale signs of "hard campaigning" to come were recognized by the veterans: No leaves of absence were issued, officers' wives were sent away, and rations were issued for ten days, not two or three. But, shortly thereafter, the issuance of a limited number of leaves and the return of officers' wives left the men guessing again. Not even reviews by Major General Hooker on April 3, after which he complimented Wadsworth's division about its "soldierly bearing," and six days later by President Lincoln offered any clues as to what lay ahead.[16]

The highly ceremonial inspection by Lincoln on April 9 was not simply a complimentary visit; he wanted to know what Hooker was doing with his 133,868-man army. All he got from Hooker was "When I get to Richmond." This boastfulness did not reassure Lincoln any more than it did the troops serving under him. Yet, despite "the Apollo like presence," "vain glorious manner," and "haughty criticism of others," the soldiers had come to admire Hooker, who Rufus Dawes observed had "the true Napoleonic idea of the power of an 'Esprit de Corps.'"[17]

The quality that artillery commander Wainwright felt Hooker lacked, namely, understanding of tactics, seemed to have been found by the end of April. Unlike Burnside, who had frontally attacked Lee's army, Hooker intended to cross the Rappahannock above Fredericksburg and turn the Confederate left. First, however, General Stoneman's cavalry was to cut Lee's supply lines and position itself on the Army of Northern Virginia's communication lines roughly thirty miles north of Richmond. With Lincoln's approval on April 12, General Hooker ordered preparations for a movement. The next morning General Stoneman was dispatched, and the rest of the army made ready.[18]

The troops were reminded not to burn camps "when ordered to march or mak[e] any unusual sign or indication that a movement is in progress." Sick soldiers were ordered out of camp and onto boats to transport them to hospitals in Washington. Discipline took on added importance as well. On April 18, Wadsworth arrested and brought charges against a lieutenant and private in the

7th Wisconsin. The former was charged with buying and appropriating a government horse, whereas the latter, who was placed in irons, was charged with knowingly selling the horse.[19]

The following day Wadsworth ordered his division to turn out for a heavy marching drill at 9:00 A.M. That meant donning knapsacks, haversacks, greatcoats (the heavy winter overcoat), blankets, shelter tents, and filled canteens. Before they could do so, Wadsworth recommended that the confused soldiers store their greatcoats at the forage dock to be forwarded to Washington.[20]

Orders were for each man "to carry ten day's rations, one hundred cartridges [more than double the usual], extra shoes, an overcoat, a blanket, a tent, a canteen, and a musket," the total of which has been estimated to weigh anywhere from forty-five to ninety-five pounds.[21] Division commander Wadsworth, living up to his reputation for attending to his soldiers' welfare, decided to determine for himself how heavy an enlisted man's load was. The following is drawn from a regiment history published in 1867:

> "Orderly!" said the General, "pack a knapsack, canteen, haversack, and cartridge-box, and roll the tent and overcoat and place them upon the knapsack, according to orders, and put the whole rig on me and hand me a gun. I am going to see if this order can be obeyed by the men"; and for nearly an hour the General paced his tent carrying the load of a soldier. At the end of that time, perspiring at every pore, he commenced unloading, declaring as he did so: "No man can carry such a load and live; it is preposterous!" He was obliged to promulgate the order, but to the General's credit be it said, no inspector came around to see that the order was obeyed.[22]

Then tents and blankets, oilcloths, extra shoes, woolen shirts, and a bag of corn were loaded onto the transportation mules. Officers packed valises, arranged papers, cleaned pistols, stored tourniquets, and paid debts before checking ammunition supplies and conditions of weapons. Finally they inspected the enlisted men's knapsacks for "superfluous articles, such as bibles and playing cards," which were thrown away.[23]

Still they waited, for the cavalry seemed to take forever to slog through the rain and muddy roads. The first phase had failed, so Hooker was thus forced to modify his plans. The cavalry would still try to get around the rear of the Confederates, but the infantry would be moving simultaneously. Unfortunately, incessant rain prevented any large-scale movement until the 28th.[24]

Meanwhile, on Wednesday, April 22, General Wadsworth was ordered by corps commander Reynolds to feint a movement down to Port Royal, southeast of Fredericksburg. Like General Doubleday's feint the previous day, this was intended to force Major General Jackson to strengthen his forces there. Wadsworth detailed the 24th Michigan and 14th Brooklyn, with Colonel Henry Morrow to command the expedition. After chasing away two cavalry units the regiments found the town "depopulated of whites," but hauled back some contrabands and received their division commander's commendation on their return, the 26th. Doubleday claims these movements forced Jackson to "strengthen his force in that quarter."[25]

Hooker was now ready, but his penchant for secrecy had left even his corps commanders in the dark about his plans. Booming cannon alerted the anxious men to a pending engagement, and a march order was issued at noon on Tuesday, the 28th. Wadsworth was confident of three of the four brigades he commanded, but Colonel Walter Phelps's 1st Brigade, the 22nd, 24th, 30th, and 14th Brooklyn, would prove problematic. There are two versions of this episode.

One has it that they all claimed their enlistments had expired and refused to march or to carry their rifles. Wadsworth informed them that government records indicated they had two more months to go. Then after breakfast one morning Wadsworth directed the mutinous troops to form in line near their stacked rifles in the camp's parade ground. The brigade continued to refuse to take their rifles, so the determined commander ordered an artillery battery to halt, unlimber, and load its guns barely eighty yards in front of the recalcitrants. Then two infantry regiments were formed on either side of the guns and told to load their weapons. By contrast, nearby was a brigade ready to take up the march. According to Wadsworth's inspector general, John Kress:

> General Wadsworth then rode to the front and center of the mutineers' line and told them they had placed themselves in a very perilous position, one in which the safety of the Government and the Army required should be settled at once by the strong arm of military power, and he would give them twenty minutes to take arms from the stacks, if they did not, the troops in line would fire on them.

The formerly mutinous soldiers promptly grabbed their weapons and prepared to march.[26]

In another version of this incident, Lieutenant Colonel Dawes of the 6th Wisconsin recalled that the affair was begun about noon on the 28th by a few two-year men of the 24th New York, who claimed their time was up. Wadsworth promptly dispatched his aide, Lieutenant Clayton Rogers, formerly of the 6th Wisconsin. A mounted Rogers galloped over to the 6th and 7th Wisconsin and ordered them to load their weapons and file near the small bank of mutineers. "A few pointed remarks by General Wadsworth, rendered pungent by the presence of our regiment with loaded muskets, brought them to their senses and they quietly fell in."[27]

Fighting anxiety and a pelting rain, Reynolds's I Corps and Sedgwick's VI Corps, forming the Union left, moved out. They were to cross the Rappahannock below Fredericksburg and make a "strong demonstration" downstream to distract Lee. The bulk of the army, the V, XI, XII, and Cavalry Corps, would move up from Fredericksburg, cross the Rappahannock at Kelly's Ford, then split, with Meade's V Corps moving down toward Chancellorsville across the Rapidan River by way of Ely's Ford. Howard's XI and Slocum's XII Corps would move farther

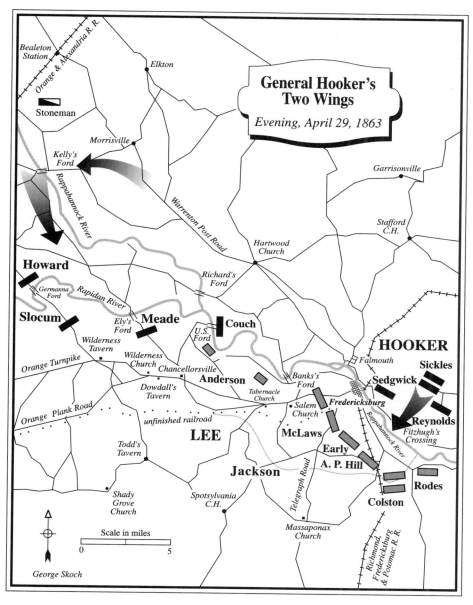

General Hooker's Two Wings

Evening, April 29, 1863

General Hooker's two wings (by George Skoch)

west, cross the Rapidan at Germanna Ford, and take the Plank Road through the Wilderness. Major General Darius Couch would send two of his II Corps divisions to Banks's and U.S. Fords and hold another near Fredericksburg. Sickles's III Corps would be in reserve. Thus, while trying to fool General Lee, Hooker would envelop Fredericksburg, forcing Lee's army to retreat toward Richmond, with both wings of the Army of the Potomac in pursuit. Even Hooker's harshest critics would have to give him credit.[28]

Wadsworth's four-brigade division, followed by Robinson's and Doubleday's, mushed through the mud until dark on April 28, bivouacking briefly two miles short of Fitzhugh's Crossing, three miles below Fredericksburg. Between 11:00 P.M. and 1:00 A.M. Wadsworth put just the Iron Brigade into motion again. At daybreak on the 29th, the brigade arrived at the river, obscured by fog. There, in range of Confederate sharpshooters, they waited apprehensively for division engineers to lay pontoon bridges. Like so many plans in this war, this one had unraveled, for which Wadsworth came under criticism.

The bridges were to be built under cover of darkness and completed by 3:30 A.M. to avoid alarming Confederates across the river. At 11:30 P.M., before they had advanced very far, Wadsworth's division was ordered to help with the bridge building. It was assigned the task of carrying pontoons, forty heavy boats, nearly a mile to the river, so that 6,000 men could make a single crossing. Wadsworth called on his 1st Brigade, and Colonel Phelps promptly detailed all but the 14th Brooklyn, which acted as skirmishers. Carrying the boats proved impossible; men collapsed under the weight of the heavy boats. Wadsworth decided to put only twenty boats on wheels and drag them. With the delays, he did not order the sixty men per boat to cross the river until 4:30 A.M., an hour after the bridges were to have been built.[29]

Hooker's chief of engineers, Brigadier General Henry Benham, frustrated by the task, enraged by the serious delay, and quite possibly bolstered by alcohol, unleashed his wrath on Wadsworth. Benham cited the success of Brigadier General Calvin Pratt, commander of the 1st Brigade, 2nd Division, VI Corps, which had just performed a similar task "in excellent time" with half the recommended number of men. Division commander Wadsworth apparently ignored this rebuke, though he may have been equally frustrated at the delay, for he had anticipated completion of the bridges earlier.[30]

Not only time, but the element of surprise, had been lost. Four hours earlier enemy signal lights and boats coasting along the opposite shore indicated that the Union movement had been detected. Now, at daylight, the sound and fury of musketry hammered at them, causing panic among the Blacks and extra-duty men helping to transport the pontoon train. Wadsworth became worried about his men being exposed to fire from "heavy bodies of rebel infantry moving toward your [Reynolds] right, two brigades, apparently." He also notified Reynolds that he spied a battery "coming into position." Whether Chief of Artillery Henry Hunt's guns posted near Pollock's Mill and commanded by Colonel Wainwright could counter the latter was questionable. The 14th Brooklyn and 22nd New York, directed by Lieutenant Colonel Kress, Wadsworth's aide, were positioned near the bank to reply to the sharpshooters across the way, but they had limited success. The plans to build bridges had to be abandoned temporarily. The alternative, crossing by boat, seemed equally suicidal. In fact, the 1st Division commander viewed the whole plan as suicidal. "It was all wrong from the first,"

Wadsworth wrote his eldest daughter, Cornelia. Hooker was ordering the Union corps "thrown across on one side of the enemy & form[ed] on the other[,] giving [Lee] a chance to crush first one & then the other."[31]

About the same time Generals Reynolds and Wadsworth viewed the developing action from heights above Pollock's Mill Creek (or Fitzhugh's Crossing), overlooking the river, and discussed what to do. The answer came from Brigadier General Benham, with orders from Hooker via Sedgwick, directing Reynolds "to cross the river at once, at all hazards." The swollen eye and blood trickling down Benham's face from his earlier collision with one of the pontoon boats accentuated his normally stern appearance. (Artillery chief Wainwright claimed that a whiskey-induced fall from a horse had caused Benham's injuries.) His fury at the delay and Wadsworth's alteration of plans was painfully apparent, but he had no time to argue or to threaten arrest, as he had done with another commander. Brigadier General Solomon Meredith's Iron Brigade was directed to make the hazardous crossing. Kress hastily improvised instructions while galloping down to the river. It was critical that the Union troops make it look like Fredericksburg was Hooker's objective and so hold the Confederates in Sedgwick's front.[32]

General Meredith deployed the 6th Wisconsin, the 24th Michigan, and Companies B, D, and E of the 2nd Wisconsin as skirmishers while the rest of the brigade provided cover fire. They ran across a field and down the bank for all they were worth, hollering like demons. Then General Wadsworth's son, Captain Craig ("Tick"), and others piled into the boats, one company apiece. Throwing "themselves upon the bottom of [the boats] as they had been instructed," they either poled their way across or used their rifle butts as oars. Wadsworth and Reynolds, seemingly unconcerned about the small-arm and artillery fire, calmly smoked cigars on the far bank.[33]

When the 6th Wisconsin and the 24th Michigan completed their crossing, they faced the 6th Louisiana and the 13th Georgia peering out of rifle pits. Undaunted, the men landed waist-deep into the muddy river and began their assault. In seven chaotic minutes they clambered up the steep south bank protected by underbrush and an abatis, charged straight into the severe fire of the Confederate sharpshooters, and overran them. The victors' prize was 103 prisoners, including three officers and some cannon. The boats were then poled back for the 19th Indiana and the 2nd and 7th Wisconsin to make the crossing.[34]

Loathe to force others to do what he would not, General Wadsworth "cried out, 'Hold on.'" Throwing his horse's lines over the animal's head, "he sprang into the stern of the boat." His horse hesitated to take "an icy bath so early in the morning, but the general said . . . 'Push him in, lieutenant.'" Into the river went the horse, trailing the boat. Then Wadsworth, defying orders to lie down, imitated Washington crossing the Delaware. After crossing, the "old gentleman" jumped out and "landed in the water," but he reached the crest "about as quick as any of us." Ashore, "he went from company to company, thanking the men for their brave assault." The incredulous men noted that the foolhardy Wadsworth had not come through completely unscathed; his cap sported two bullet holes. He was living a charmed existence, though one observer recalled thinking that "he'll be killed before [the war] closes." On the other hand, General Wadsworth believed that he had not exposed himself "unnecessarily." It was, he wrote a daughter, simply that he had a "very difficult task assigned" to him; it was his "place to organize and direct [the men]."[35]

During this episode Colonel Phelps's 1st Brigade was responsible for launching and unloading the boats, during which it faced continuous fire from rifle pits across the river still occupied by Confederate pickets. Around 10:30, after all the bridges had been laid, mostly by Phelps's 22nd and 24th New York, the rest of Wadsworth's division began to cross. Once on the other side, the division began digging rifle pits with Phelps's brigade forming on the brow of a small hill. Cutler's 2nd Brigade formed to Phelps's right, resting near the Pratt house, with Meredith's brigade to his left and Brigadier Gabriel Paul's 4th Brigade in the rear "under the hill." The 19th Indiana found it ironic that they had landed on ground they had occupied the previous December in the Fredericksburg debacle.[36]

For the remainder of the day, April 29, the other two I Corps divisions, under Robinson and Doubleday, lay in readiness still across the river, ducking occasional shells and watching the Confederates entrenching. As far as it went, the movement was a success. I Corps losses were minuscule: five men killed, sixteen wounded. Despite the dangerous assignment and crossing, Wadsworth's division lost only one man killed, with four wounded.[37]

☆ ☆ ☆

The rest of the Army of the Potomac had been even more successful. The V, XI, and XII Corps had completed a long, circuitous march to Kelly's Ford above Fredericksburg and down across the Rappahannock and Rapidan Rivers to Chancellorsville. By 2:00 P.M., with two-thirds of his army (more than 50,000 men) near the crossroads at Chancellorsville, an ebullient Hooker could boast that victory was virtually at hand.[38]

However, by this time Lee had deduced that the real danger to his army was on his left flank in the direction of Chancellorsville, not Fredericksburg. The Confederate commander had to find a way to outmaneuver Hooker or face a force that outnumbered his by roughly two to one. Imitating Hooker, Lee split his army. He left Early's Division of Jackson's Corps, along with Barksdale's Brigade of McLaws's Division (Longstreet's Corps), at Fredericksburg to screen the Confederate movement and to occupy Hooker's left wing. He then sent McLaws's and Anderson's Divisions and the balance of Jackson's Corps to the west on a collision course with Hooker's right wing.[39]

While General Lee was preparing his movements, Hooker, headquartered at the Chancellor House, was poised for the turning point of the war that he had predicted. On May 1, he advanced from Chancellorsville in three columns: Howard's XI and Slocum's XII Corps moved east on the Plank Road, Sykes's V Corps and Hancock's II Corps divisions followed the Turnpike, running parallel to the north. Humphrey's and Griffin's divisions of Meade's V Corps marched farther north along the south bank of the Rappahannock. By late morning the Union forces had advanced some two miles beyond Chancellorsville, where they made first contact with the enemy.

Then, strangely, despite still holding the upper hand, Hooker seemed to lose his nerve, as it has been commonly described. For thirty-six long hours Wadsworth's division, anticipating orders to move, to attack, to do something, waited. It was a "great mistake," Wadsworth observed, "We . . . could have driven the enemy." That is, by late afternoon on May 1, Hooker countermanded the order to advance and directed his men to reoccupy and strengthen positions of the previous night. Thus, the initiative passed to Lee. Finally, sometime after 7:00 A.M. on May 2, orders were given for Wadsworth's men to prepare to re-cross the Rappahannock and, following the other two divisions, to head toward Chancellorsville.[40]

The march began routinely, with the first regiments of Paul's brigade in the lead. But, when the Confederates spied the 137th Pennsylvania crossing, they began shelling, which destroyed a pontoon and killed and wounded a number of men, causing the remainder to duck for cover. General Reynolds ordered Wadsworth to abandon the movement as "impracticable," but the latter remonstrated. He called on Captain John A. Reynolds's Battery L, 1st New York Light Artillery, to counter the Confederate shelling. This led to an hour and a half duel, during which time the crossing resumed, though with the loss of "about 20 killed & wounded" and a roughly equal number of horses. After the remaining regiments, pickets, and skirmishers had crossed, and Reynolds had extricated his guns and animals, Wadsworth calmly rode across.[41]

The division, despondently viewing this as a retreat, recrossed the river without incident, except for delays on the crowded road. In a scorching sun it followed the river north and west to U.S. Ford, with only a brief halt. At 10:00 P.M., roughly fifteen miles (and hours) later, Wadsworth's four small brigades dropped to the ground still short of their destination, Hunting Run. They enjoyed a short nap, if any.[42]

However, their division commander was not allowed to rest. Instead, he searched for General Reynolds in order to receive orders as to the exact position his troops were to occupy. The bright moonlight did little to dispel the darkness that characterized this mysterious Wilderness, but as he pushed on down the narrow road he began encountering the routed troops of the XI Corps. (In one of the most daring moves of the war Lee had again divided his forces, sending Jackson off beyond the right end of the Union line, flanking the immigrant corps and sending them into pell-mell retreat.) At last Wadsworth found General Reynolds, who directed him to join the other two divisions and to form a second line. This line would stretch south approximately two miles from the Rappahannock along Hunting Run to Ely's Ford Road south of the Rapidan River and link with Meade's V Corps. Then the 1st Division commander made the return trek and roused his men.[43]

At approximately 4:30 A.M. on the 3rd, Wadsworth personally began positioning his four brigades, which was completed by about 6:00. General Reynolds

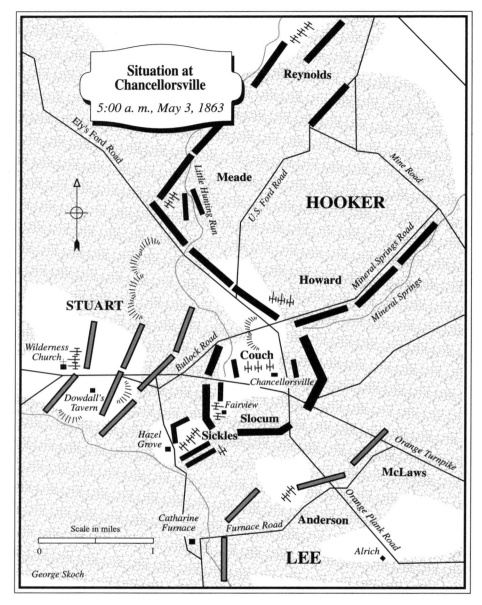

Situation at Chancellorsville (by George Skoch)

now had his corps in the line of battle on the extreme Union right in support of
Meade's V Corps. Once more, after throwing up breastworks, Wadsworth's men
dropped to the ground and waited.[44]

A battle was raging "left, right and center." The Union corps of Sickles, Slocum, and Couch were formed in a rough U. Sickles's corps squarely faced Jackson's, now commanded by "Jeb" Stuart after Jackson's mortal wounding the previous night. Now Slocum's XII Corps, facing almost directly south, and Hancock's division of Couch's II Corps, facing east, were busily defending against Anderson's and McLaws's Divisions. Yet, while pickets were trying to pick each other off, neither Reynolds's nor Meade's corps was engaged. "It was," according to Wadsworth, "the universal opinion that we [the I Corps] should have attacked."[45]

The battle sounds now became sporadic. Rumors flew. No fires were allowed, and an order was given to stop unauthorized discharge of arms, because it was impossible to tell whether pickets were advancing. Then, on May 4, despite the cannonading in the distance (Sedgwick's VI Corps was battling the Confederates at Salem Church), the fighting had generally subsided and the men were allowed to unsling their knapsacks and boil coffee in a drizzling on-and-off rain. However, throughout that long day and night they heard heavy volleys of musketry and constant alarms. Strangely, the next day whiskey rations were distributed, enough, combined with the heat, to "make the whole [6th Wisconsin] regiment drunk." It was, according to Rufus Dawes of the 6th Wisconsin, a long, hot day of "frustrating inaction."[46]

During the day, however, after Hooker's unnecessary council of war with his senior generals (Hooker had already decided he'd had enough), the Federals began to withdraw in a heavy rain toward the Rappahannock, with Wadsworth's division acting as rear guard.

The audacious Lee–Jackson combination had once more pulled off the impossible, forcing the Union Army of the Potomac to retreat, albeit at the cost of Jackson's death after his successful rout of the XI Corps. Many of Hooker's subordinates, prepared to renew the battle, were incredulous when Hooker chose to withdraw.

Wadsworth was among them: "So far as I could judge of the spirit and temper of the officers and men of the army, they were ready to take the offensive. . . . I think we should not have withdrawn. I think the enemy was whipped; although they had gained certain advantages, they were so severely handled that they were weaker than we were. . . . [W]e ought to have crushed the whole Rebel army." Nor was he convinced, as some argued, that Hooker, who had sustained a serious head injury, was not himself. The division commander had ridden along the line with Hooker just "a few hours" after the injury.[47]

The battle would be refought in dispatches and testimony by participants, with varying explanations for still another Union failure. Correspondent-historian William Swinton's summary is probably as good as any: The Army of the Potomac was not beaten, its commander was. A modern historian is just as blunt: Hooker lost his nerve and Lee capitalized on the fact.[48]

General Reynolds directed Wadsworth's inspector general, John Kress, to find a route for the corps' retreat on the evening of May 5. It was no easy matter.

"It was a gloomy, anxious, miserable night," Wadsworth later wrote to his eldest daughter, Cornelia, "all soaked to the skin and splashing about in mud and water of unknown depth." The only good thing was the Confederates did not follow or try to harass the retreating Union troops. Finally, the men were on their way again, crossing the Rappahannock during the morning. But the weather had become decidedly colder, numbing the tired soldiers, who had not been permitted to build any fires along the way.[49]

Wadsworth's division encamped that night at Hamet's on the Warrentown Road. By afternoon of the next day, May 7, the entire corps was assembled virtually back where their engagement had begun, with 292 fewer men. Wadsworth's division had come through relatively unscathed, reporting only eighteen losses: one enlisted man killed, one officer and fourteen men wounded, and two men captured or missing. Yet for ten miserable days they had marched, lived on hardtack and coffee, slept on wet ground, retraced their steps, and risked their lives— to no end. In fact, they had been virtual bystanders.[50]

Two days later General Wadsworth, "availing himself of the temporary repose" at Camp Wadsworth, thanked the troops he commanded. Wadsworth came in for praise as well. The *Detroit Tribune* pronounced that "Those who have known General Wadsworth, will describe him as a man of great deliberation and very few words, from whom a line of praise is more valuable than volumes from others."[51]

Despite Chief Engineer Benham's rebuke, division commander Wadsworth's daring (or foolhardiness) attracted the attention of other newspaper correspondents, particularly for his hazardous boat ride. Yet, as he had written his daughter Cornelia, he did not think he had taken unnecessary risks, but simply taken his "place" among his troops.[52]

The next eight days at Camp Wadsworth entailed the usual camp life. The Army of the Potomac would again back off and lick its wounds. Wadsworth's weariness and frustration spilled over into his circulars to brigade commanders. Charges against stragglers in the recent engagement were to be "disposed of without appeal to a General Court Martial." Instead, punishments would be "promptly adjudged and carried out" by other tribunals. The gambling had resumed, much to his and commander Reynolds's displeasure. The civilian-general knew his men needed to relax, but gambling only resulted in greater loss of morale and harm to the families of some of the men. Regimental commanders were ordered to go through the camps twice a day at different hours to arrest and put gamblers under guard, pending trial. Wadsworth also threatened to arrest a field officer of the 97th New York for attempting to appropriate for himself a house in which the regimental surgeon was caring for the sick.[53]

On Friday, May 8, the weary division commander requested a ten-day leave "to attend to important family and private business, and to visit my family." Initially his request was denied on grounds that "impending movements would not allow it." However, a week later he reapplied and a leave was granted when it appeared that no movement by Hooker was imminent.[54]

In fact, nothing was happening, though President Lincoln, concerned about the morale of his Eastern army, had visited Hooker's camp a week earlier and had met with the corps' commanders. The commanders were virtually unanimous that Hooker had blundered. "Hooker has lost the confidence of the Army," Wadsworth wrote his daughter, and we "are all humiliated at our retreat & discontented with conduct & the movement."[55] Hooker would have to be replaced. But by whom? Major General Meade's name was suggested, but he demurred, as did Wadsworth's commander, Reynolds. The disgusted II Corps commander Darius Couch used health as an excuse to remove himself. And so the matter stood.[56]

Now back near White Oak Church, General Wadsworth's division drilled and performed the inevitable, but irritating, picket duty, all the while griping about Hooker's being "outgeneraled and defeated." They also worried about being "materially weakened" by the daily departures of two-year and nine-month troops. Not surprisingly, courts-martial were on the increase, partly due to the soldiers' relative inactivity and ability to obtain alcohol.[57]

Commander Wadsworth returned to his division around May 25, after receiving a three-day extension of his leave, a message his son Craig no doubt enjoyed telegraphing him. During his absence, minor expeditions generally resulted only in opportunities to fraternize with the enemy pickets. However, one 105-mile foray by members of the Iron Brigade resulted in a problem—a large number of emancipated slaves trailing the returning soldiers and hauling their only possessions, including even featherbeds and stoves. How Wadsworth handled this influx is unrecorded.[58]

An end-of-the-month I Corps review clearly revealed the depleted state of the Army of the Potomac. Formerly 14,361 strong, now there were only 9,403 men in the corps, making it the smallest of the Army of the Potomac. Accordingly, on May 20 Wadsworth's division had been reduced to three brigades, and on June 16 it was cut to two. The departure of two-year men from Colonel Phelps's and General Paul's brigades had hacked the number of Wadsworth's regiments from nineteen to eleven. General Meredith's Iron Brigade, which was unchanged, now carried the white triangular flag with the corps' red sphere in the center, reflecting its status as 1st Brigade, 1st Division, I Corps. The venerable General Cutler commanded the new 2nd Brigade (7th Indiana, 56th Pennsylvania, 76th New York, 95th New York, 147th New York, and the 14th Brooklyn). With only 4,000 men, General Wadsworth commanded barely half the number he had prior to Chancellorsville. Even these regiments were depleted, when only men present for duty were counted.[59]

Roasting in the Virginia heat, the Union troops began hearing rumors of mysterious movements across the river and, according to the 6th Wisconsin's Dawes, were convinced that "Something important is impending." At the end of the first week in June he believed that "both armies are moving," but four days later the rumors were mistakenly dismissed as just more "alarms, orders and counter-orders."[60]

In fact, there was movement. By June 10 Hooker's reconnoitering balloons (Professor Thaddeus Lowe's hot air observation balloons) and General Sedgwick's VI Corps, which had probed the Confederate lines near Fredericksburg, had confirmed that Lee's troops were on the move. Three days later General

Hooker, convinced that Lee was headed toward the Potomac, ordered his army to be on the move as well. Once more civilians were ordered out of the camp, extra baggage was sent to the rear, and men were stripped to the essentials, and before daylight on Friday, June 12, the I Corps was on the march, headed for Deep Run in support of the III and V Corps.[61]

The men were sad to leave the pretty spot with its spring blossoms. Sadder still was Wadsworth's order for each regimental commander in the division to detail two officers and twenty "wholly reliable men" to report to the division Provost Marshal Clayton E. Rogers "to execute the sentence of death, etc."[62]

So, during a noonday halt for dinner, Wadsworth's division formed a hollow square. Then Private John P. Woods, a deserter from Company F of the 19th Indiana, sitting atop a rough, wooden coffin with his hands cuffed and feet shackled, was hauled by an ambulance wagon to the center of the square where a hole had been dug. General Wadsworth briefly addressed the soldiers before the dozen executioners took their place, roughly ten feet in front of Woods, and guards handed loaded weapons to the firing squad. After the chaplain spoke quietly to Woods, Lieutenant Rogers, Wadsworth's aide, gave the order to fire. Unfortunately, only four bullets struck the blindfolded prisoner, who fell backward. Another round to the head at close range was required to finish the gruesome job. Then, as if nothing had happened, the division resumed its march.[63]

This was the first time most of the men in the division had seen an execution. "The sympathetic part came in an hour later, when his [Woods's] aged father came to head-quarters bringing a pardon signed by President Lincoln."[64]

Now, on the march and with the execution behind them, the men could only speculate about what lay ahead. Odds were that they were to intercept Lee in Maryland or even Pennsylvania. Once there, "if we can not defeat them," the 6th Wisconsin's acting commander Dawes predicted, "we can never crush the rebellion."[65]

Chapter 14

"CLOSE UP, MEN, CLOSE UP!"

The Road to Gettysburg

In early June of 1863 the Army of the Potomac was on the march because the Confederates had once more taken the initiative. General Pleasonton, commander of the Army's Cavalry, had reported a Confederate advance on Harpers Ferry northwest of Washington by the corps of Lieutenant Generals Ewell and Longstreet. Yet General Hooker was still in the dark as to the Confederates' intentions as late as June 22, though a major offensive by Lee was anticipated almost a month earlier. All Hooker knew was that Maryland was being invaded. Boldly, General Lee was taking the war north, hoping to draw the Army of the Potomac out from its strong defensive position opposite Fredericksburg and in the process threaten Washington. Lee's campaign promised additional benefits to the Confederacy, including inspiriting its men and relieving beleaguered Virginians while benefiting from the rich granaries of Pennsylvania. Even further, a successful invasion would bolster arguments of Northern peacemakers and perhaps gain European recognition for the Confederacy.[1]

General Lee was aware that the Army of the Potomac had been diminished by the mustering out of two-year troops while his own army was enlarged by conscripts. More importantly, General Longstreet's Corps had returned from detached service south of the James River. Lee had three corps, numbering close to 80,000 men. At the outset of the march north they stretched for almost one hundred miles. Now it was up to Hooker not only to divine Lee's intentions, but to counter the resulting moves. Hooker was quickly disabused of the notion of marching on Richmond by President Lincoln, who urged him to make Lee's army, not the Confederate capital, his objective.[2]

By June 16, after Major General Jubal Early had driven in Federal outposts at Winchester and had begun to cross the Potomac River, Hooker realized the nature of the threat. He then began pushing his troops northwesterly so he could concentrate them and cover the approaches to Washington. Wadsworth's division, like others in the Army of the Potomac, felt the urgency with which they were being marched. The command to "Close up, men, close up!" rang in their ears. The I Corps initially had followed the Rappahannock by back roads. By the time Early was crossing the Potomac, they had marched more than sixty miles in nearly eighty hours. As the weary soldiers dropped to the ground near Centreville, they were, according to Lieutenant Colonel Rufus Dawes of the 6th Wisconsin, "tired, sore, sleepy, hungry, dusty and dirty as pigs." Yet, in its inscrutable way, the Union army command seemed more concerned about their appearance rather than their fatigue, ordering an inspection "with reference especially to the condition of their Under Clothing."[3]

The veterans knew the route ("our annual visit to Bull Run"), having taken it southward earlier, but they had never hurried like this before. Though it seemed impossible, they picked up the pace on the 17th, while the sun beat on them like a furnace and the dust from so many footsteps on the road choked their parched throats. "The day was extremely hot . . . roads were filled with wagons, batteries, cavalry, infantry, artillery, all rushing, halting, sweating," recalled a member of Cutler's brigade. "The dust arose in suffocating clouds, was inhaled at every breath, and settling upon faces from which the perspiration flowed at every pore." The dense scrub pine through which they had marched not only cut off any breeze, but it seemed to concentrate the heat: "Many a poor fellow marched his last." Frantic for water, they found only "some mudhole or slimy frog marsh." Some of the regiments even took a wrong turn just outside Centreville and had to retrace their steps.[4]

General Wadsworth showed his customary concern for the men: "There was an ambulance loaded with the valises of the officers serving on his staff. These valises the old General ordered thrown out, and the ambulance filled with the knapsacks and muskets of the exhausted soldiers." Characteristically, according to Rufus Dawes, this meant the impatient division commander also had tossed out papers from division headquarters, as well as his own valise, which subsequently had to be retrieved.[5]

Slowly word about their objective filtered through the ranks of the Union marchers. Near Leesburg, where they camped in "copious showers of rain" on June 18 and 19, a brigade newsboy had somehow managed to obtain and distribute newspapers with headlines proclaiming "Rebels in Pennsylvania." In a letter home Lieutenant Colonel Dawes professed his dread of another Antietam and alerted his future wife that if there was to be a battle, to "watch the papers to see if General John F. Reynolds and General James S. Wadsworth figure in it."[6]

On June 20, after two days' rest, the corps resumed its march, crossed Broad Run, and bivouacked again for the next six days. However, it was anything but dull there at "Frying Pan, Va.," a deserted place in a pine forest some seven miles from Centreville that did not even deserve a name. While many of Wadsworth's exhausted men simply rested, some members of the 56th Pennsylvania (Cutler's brigade) played a game of baseball on June 24, and other division members, ignoring the threats of guerrillas, pillaged at nearby farms, where chickens were particularly attractive targets. The poaching led to a warning by Wadsworth to his brigade and regimental commanders to keep their men in camp and to prevent "marauding and pillage by them." Officers would be "held personally responsible for all injury to property or wrongs to persons." He then ordered a "Brigade Guard" to surround his division. The guard served a double purpose—to protect from without (guerrillas) and from within (poachers). For now, the soldiers could indulge in fresh food, almost anything except fruit. Meanwhile the restless general busily superintended the construction of a makeshift bridge across Goose Creek, the shortest route to Edwards Ferry, across the Potomac.[7]

The I Corps' bivouac was about to end. By midafternoon on June 25, General Hooker had learned that part of Ewell's Corps had advanced to Chambersburg, Pennsylvania, on its way to Harrisburg, the state capital. Ewell had waited until newly promoted Lieutenant General A. P. Hill's recently created III Corps had caught up with Longstreet's Corps and was crossing the Potomac. Though Hill's Corps took three hours to pass through Boonsboro near Harpers Ferry, Hooker's twenty-four hours of irresolution meant forced marches by the Union army to catch up with the Confederates.

Finally, Hooker was all action. One of his first moves was to appoint General Reynolds to command the advance wing of the Army of the Potomac (I, III, and XI Corps and Major General Julius Stahel's cavalry), while he directed the other wing, the II, V, VI, and XII Corps. Hooker emphasized that it was imperative for Reynolds to seize and to hold Turner's Gap and Crampton's Pass, north of Harpers Ferry. After that the bulk of Reynolds's command was to head northeast to Middletown, Maryland, on the old National Road, march past Catoctin Mountain, then aim almost straight north. After bivouacking at Barnesville, the I, III, and XI Corps resumed the march at daylight on the 26th, in a drizzling rain, while the other four corps crossed the Potomac. Reynolds's command stopped in midafternoon after a short but arduous march over Catoctin Mountain (between five and nine miles) at Jefferson, just south of Middletown.[8]

Lieutenant Colonel Dawes described to his future wife the ordeal he and his troops were undergoing:

> What do you think of trudging along all day in a soaking rain, getting as wet as a drowned rat, taking supper on hard tack and salt pork, and then wrapping up in a wet woolen blanket and lying down for a sleep, but waked during the night three or four times to receive and attend to orders and finally turning out at three o'clock in the morning to get the regiment ready to march?[9]

If it was tough for this relatively young man, we can only imagine what it must have been like for General Wadsworth, only four months shy of his 56th birthday.

At about noon on June 28, Reynolds was ordered to resume the march and to loop back east to Frederick, Maryland, some thirty miles south of Gettysburg. This ten-mile hike briefly united his wing with all but the III Corps of the Army of the Potomac. Wadsworth's division furnished the rear guard to round up stragglers "who are roaming about the country in great numbers." More than a few marchers would overindulge in alcohol in and near Frederick and help themselves to civilian property. Wadsworth was irritated and ordered "this discreditable business of discipline . . . stopped at once." He had plenty of reasons. Major General Doubleday, acting corps commander, had ordered him to "pay Mr. Wm. Dixon thirty-five dollars for wood and rails taken as wood, by this Division in the night of the 28th inst [that month]."[10]

✭   ✭   ✭

Meanwhile a major change in army command had occurred, generally without the knowledge of the men. On June 27, General Hooker was replaced by Major General George Gordon Meade, formerly V Corps commander, whose place was taken by Major General George Sykes. As to when General Wadsworth was actually informed and what his reaction was are unknown. However, given his later testimony about Hooker's conduct of the battle of Chancellorsville, it is likely that he was not displeased. The formal cause of the change was that Hooker wanted more troops and had argued unsuccessfully with General-in-Chief Henry W. Halleck for the force guarding Harpers Ferry. In fact, Hooker had lost the administration's support, which was confirmed when Halleck granted Hooker's request for release from command.[11]

Despite Hooker's failure at Chancellorsville, criticism arose not only over the timing of his removal, but also of its fairness and impact on the army on the eve of a battle. Moreover, the 47-year-old Meade had been jumped over Generals Couch, Slocum, and Sedgwick, albeit with their support, particularly that of Couch, who had recommended Meade to Lincoln earlier. Command of the Army of the Potomac was literally thrust upon the reluctant Meade's two-starred shoulders. Though personally courageous, the short-tempered Meade seemed an unlikely choice, because his experience following graduation from West Point in 1835 to the beginning of the war was largely as an engineer captain. However, since then he had distinguished himself as a businesslike, competent, if not skillful, officer, unwilling to participate in political intrigues. The latter may have appealed to the administration as much as his reluctance to make "promises or pledges," unlike his boastful predecessors Pope and Hooker.[12]

The new commander faced the awesome task of coordinating an army that had been rejuvenated and led by an inspiring Hooker. Aware that the Confederates were concentrating near Gettysburg, Meade had to move closer to Lee's army, but remain in a position to defend Washington. First Meade concentrated his command at Frederick. Then he sought to develop a net to intercept Lee. The net required establishing a front, arcing from Emmitsburg, Maryland, about ten miles southwest of Gettysburg, to Westminster, Maryland, almost twenty-five miles southeast. It would face northeast toward Carlisle and York, Pennsylvania, between which Ewell's Corps was spread. Meade also had to prepare to meet Longstreet's and Hill's Corps, which were nearing Chambersburg almost twenty miles directly west of Gettysburg.[13]

Thus, General Meade not only had to develop a plan, but he had to orchestrate the advance of his seven corps on different roads to avoid dangerous congestion and delays. He counted heavily on reliable John Reynolds who was commanding the advance wing, while Meade retained command over the other wing (II, V, VI, and XII Corps).

The paths Meade's army had taken so far could have been traced by the clothing scattered along roadsides. The waste was appalling. "Knapsacks are piled," wrote Quartermaster General Montgomery Meigs, "blankets, overcoats, and other clothing thrown off." Imagine Meigs's feelings when a request, carefully couched to appeal to his patriotism, came for the issue of "10,000 pairs of bootees and same number of socks" to the troops passing through Frederick. Despite his misgivings, and recognizing that the weary soldiers' shoes were wearing out, Meigs agreed to do so.[14]

General Wadsworth's men needed those shoes, for they still had a way to go. Commander Meade had ordered the I Corps to make another long march (keeping to the left of the road to allow the XI Corps to march parallel with it), to Emmitsburg, on the Pennsylvania border, close to thirty miles. True to form, Wadsworth was concerned about his shoeless men "plodding over the stone and through the mud, barefooted." He determined his men would have shoes *now* and "ordered the seizure of boots or shoes suitable for our needs," even from civilians, and "transferred immediately to those in great need of them."[15]

General Wadsworth's aide, John Kress, recalled one incident that was particularly revealing of the impatient, and occasionally imperious, civilian general:

> In one of the Maryland villages through which we passed we noticed a large flour mill built of stone, the proprietor and his employees sat on the front steps of the mill, enjoying the military display. General Wadsworth and staff rode up, pleasantly greeted the party and inquired as to the possibility of getting any footwear in the village or its vicinity. The reply of the proprietor was so surly and ungracious that the General's ire was aroused, he said, "You have a good pair of boots on your feet, give them to one of my soldiers" The miller refused, whereupon the General directed an orderly to dismount and take possession of them, and it was quickly done.[16]

The general had shown the same concern at Barnesville, Maryland, where his division camped in a cornfield with water over their boots. "With characteristic kindness," he bought straw from a nearby farmer for his men to sleep on. Similarly, he ended up paying $35 for fence rails to build fires by means of which the men could dry their clothes.[17]

On the march, despite their weariness, the soldiers of the 76th New York had a good laugh. A disbelieving old farmer, standing on a private lane, could not convince the marchers that "Dare is no road up dis way!" The regiment had purposely chosen that path to avoid the crowded main road, and each passing officer was confronted by the Pennsylvania Dutchman's: "My Got, you can't go dis way!" "Tare ish no road dis way!" In time, however, the private lane became a "very wide road." At sunset on June 29, Wadsworth's division camped

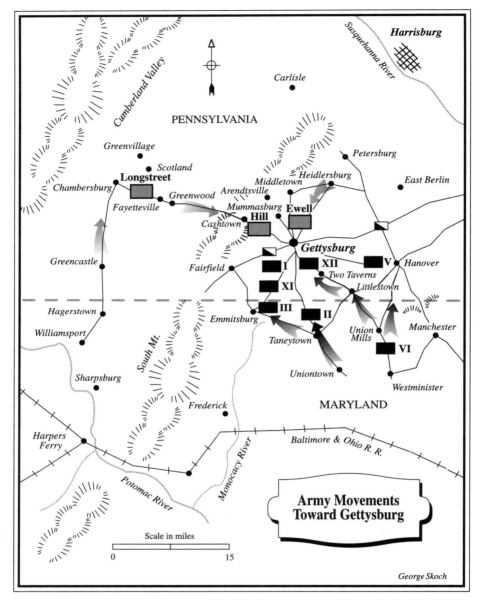

Army movements toward Gettysburg (by George Skoch)

at Emmitsburg, where St. Joseph's Academy, under the charge of the Sisters of Charity, was located. It was to be the last truly peaceful night for the marchers and for the Sisters. Soon the Sisters would find themselves administering to many of these same men.[18]

awaited further instructions from General Reynolds himself. Captain Craig Wadsworth, additional aide-de-camp to Reynolds, was detailed to act as liaison between Cutler's and Meredith's brigades.[33]

After Cutler's brigade hurriedly left the road, the Iron Brigade picked up the pace. A halt was called near the Peach Orchard (site of bloody combat the next day) to close up the ranks and to rest the men briefly. Near the Codori house, Meredith's brigade followed the broken fence line north, still trying to catch up with Cutler's marchers, who had discarded their knapsacks. Then the 2nd Wisconsin, the lead regiment, broke into a run and it too "stripped for action."[34]

The battle of Gettysburg, which had started with a solitary shot only a few hours earlier, would be a test even for these veterans. Still, they may have shared the feeling of Wadsworth's chief staff officer, John Kress:

> It is curious . . . how men reason at the commencement of a battle; they look around and think, "There goes Jones, poor fellow, he may be a dead man in a few minutes." They very seldom think, "I may be a dead man." The faculty of ascribing possible misfortunes to others and not seeing the application of the same argument to yourself, the offspring of a kind of selfishness, makes many a man carelessly brave who, if without it, might turn his back to the foe.[35]

Recalling Brigadier General James S. Wadsworth, calmly smoking a cigar while shells were falling all around him at Chancellorsville, Kress reflected: "Fortunate indeed is the man, who, when bullets fly about his ears, has something to do demanding mental and physical attention,—the officer must think of his men . . . think of everything except himself."[36]

Chapter 15

"HE WAS OF VENERABLE AND COMMANDING APPEARANCE"

Morning at Gettysburg, July 1

General Wadsworth was almost as much in the dark about the positions his division would occupy and what they faced as his men were. According to his later testimony, General Reynolds, who "was generally very particular in communicating his orders to his division commanders . . . communicated none if he had any." In fact, Wadsworth remembered that earlier in the day Reynolds had ridden to his headquarters asking what orders he had received from General Doubleday, acting commander of the I Corps. Wadsworth could only reply that he had been waiting for the other two divisions to pass, so Reynolds ordered him to "move on directly." Vague plans were what most soldiers had come to expect, but it was perilous for a division commander, especially one untested in a critical situation such as this. Necessarily, his performance would be affected and would lead to criticism. But that was still ahead of him.[1]

For now he had to learn where Reynolds wanted him to position his division, the first Union infantry to reach the battlefield. They had only momentarily consulted about whether Wadsworth's division was to go into town or to take a position west of the town. The latter was chosen, Wadsworth recalled, because if "they went into the town the enemy would shell it and destroy it." The battle hinged on Buford's weary cavalry and Wadsworth's two brigades to hold back the large corps of A. P. Hill until other Union troops could arrive. Fortunately, as Major General Oliver O. Howard, XI Corps commander, noted, "He himself [Wadsworth], of large frame, always generous and a natural soldier, had under him two reliable brigades, Cutler's and Meredith's."[2] And obviously General Reynolds had confidence in the division commander.

Wing commander Reynolds had ordered General Doubleday to direct the balance of I Corps, Robinson's and Doubleday's divisions (Rowley commanding the latter), with four of Wainwright's field batteries, toward the Fairfield Road. Because Reynolds expected a Confederate attack from the Chambersburg (Cashtown) Pike and Fairfield Road, General Doubleday was led to believe the

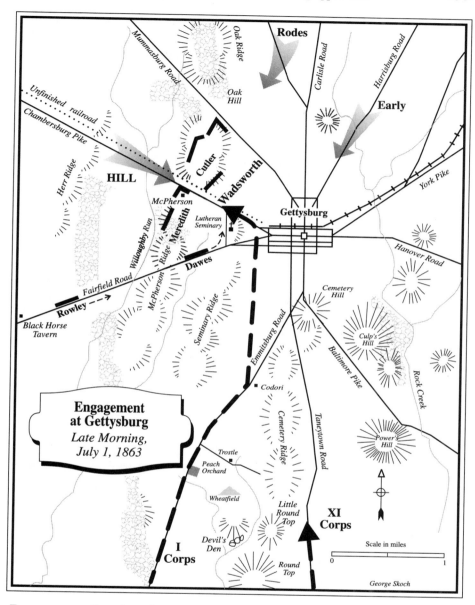

Engagement at Gettysburg: late morning (by George Skoch)

key to the Union defense was the woods between the two roads and would so act later.[3]

At approximately 10:00 A.M. Wadsworth's division hastened to support Buford's hard-pressed troopers. Reynolds and Wadsworth rode ahead with Captain James

Hall and positioned his 2nd Maine Artillery in the spot just vacated by Lieutenant Calef's Battery A, north of Chambersburg Pike on the westernmost of the two rises that constitute McPherson's Ridge. Hall's battery was to do as much damage as it could to Major William J. Pegram's Rebel artillery, which, according to Hall, had already begun a barrage from Herr's Ridge. Hall's guns also were to protect against Brigadier General Joseph R. Davis's 2,305-man brigade of Heth's Division. With skirmishers in advance, between 10:00 and 10:30 Davis's brigade had moved obliquely across Willoughby Run just north of the Chambersburg Pike toward Hall's right flank and was aiming for the cover of the railroad cut. An anxious Reynolds directed Wadsworth to "move a strong infantry support immediately to Hall's right for he is my defender until I can get the troops now coming up into line."[4]

While Reynolds and Wadsworth conferred, the 76th New York, 56th Pennsylvania, and 147th New York, the lead columns of Cutler's brigade, ducked "a shower of shells." For their protection (and to offer a brief respite) the 56th Pennsylvania's Colonel John Hofmann had the regiments drop to the ground to await Wadsworth's orders. Shortly Wadsworth ordered the three regiments to cross the pike and railroad cut. The 76th New York and 56th Pennsylvania, with roughly 560 men between them, did so and advanced beyond, approximately another 200 yards. It appears that Wadsworth intended to place them on West McPherson's Ridge, but they never made it. They were still in columns when artillery shells and rifle fire began to strike them, forcing Cutler to form them into battle line. In this haphazard operation, without an opportunity to perform a reconnaissance or to send out skirmishers, the two regiments formed roughly 300 yards north of the railroad cut facing northwesterly.[5]

General Wadsworth then turned his attention to the 14th Brooklyn and the 95th New York. Once they had moved around the Lutheran Seminary, Wadsworth directed Colonel Edward Fowler to deploy his 14th Brooklyn south of the pike and of Hall's battery. With the 95th New York on the right, the two regiments did a left face, which aimed them west. They then advanced to the crest of the eastern rise of McPherson's Ridge and were actually formed by General Reynolds, with the 95th New York to the 14th Brooklyn's right and next to the pike. The two regiments were virtually an island unto themselves, for woods to their left blocked any view to the south and the McPherson house and outbuildings obscured the regiments' view to their right, north of the road. Worse, while forming, some of Buford's cavalrymen warned them of the advance of Brigadier General James J. Archer's brigade of Hill's Corps. "Immediately the enemy opened fire upon us from a strong line of skirmishers in the woods to our left and front."[6] Archer's brigade was firing while advancing rapidly down the east slope of Herr's Ridge.

Apparently Wadsworth had expected the 147th New York, which had been in the middle of the brigade's march, to form with the 14th Brooklyn and the 95th New York south of the pike. However, the column's march was broken by the Seminary buildings and by Hall's battery, which had rushed forward through the column. Momentarily cut off and confused, Lieutenant Colonel Francis C. Miller halted them in the protection of McPherson's barn. Then, after getting instructions from Wadsworth, he formed his 380-man regiment into battle line and ordered them across the pike just beyond the railroad cut, where they settled into a small depression. Forming in this depression, out of sight of the rest of the brigade and of Hall, would prove nearly fatal to the 147th. Directly in front of them in a wheat field were the bobbing heads of the 42nd Mississippi, signaling an advance on Hall's battery. On the left of the 42nd was the 2nd Mississippi, and advancing obliquely in an effort to turn Cutler's right flank was the 55th North Carolina.[7]

The 147th's isolated and vulnerable position became the subject of controversy and led to criticism of Wadsworth. The first criticism was that General Wadsworth had not put out skirmishers, but there had been no time to do so. Second, the 147th ended up just to the right of Hall's battery, not forward to the western part of McPherson's Ridge to intercept the Confederate skirmishers before they could take advantage of the railroad cut, which intervened between Hall's battery and the 147th. Third, the regiment was "up in the air" (both flanks exposed) about 300 yards in front of the 56th Pennsylvania and 76th New York. Finally, the depression in which the 147th was placed did not allow them to be seen by other regiments in the brigade nor did it allow them to see the Confederates advancing through the ripening wheat field until too late. In short, according to General Doubleday's highly critical aide, Eminel P. Halstead, "Wadsworth seems to have formed line too hastily without a proper reconnaissance[,] for Davis' Brigade outflanked him."[8] On the other hand, because of the Confederate attack and confusion accompanying the 147th's advance, Wadsworth had no time to reconnoiter or to select a better placement.

By Halstead's reckoning Wadsworth should have formed on Seminary Ridge, where the woods and stone fences would have offered cover for a charge. Further, Wadsworth should have extended the intervals between regiments to equalize his front and to protect his right flank. Somehow this claim does not ring completely true. Wadsworth made no pretense to be a tactician, but he had been ordered to protect Hall's battery, which was well in advance of the woods.[9]

It remains that initially none of the three regiments, not yet fully formed into battle line north of the pike, had a good view of the enemy approach. Nor, because of the heavy haze that morning, did Wadsworth, who established his headquarters to the right of the 76th New York, approximately where his monument is now on Reynolds Avenue. Sometime between 10:20 and 10:30 A.M., through the haze and smoke of cavalry and artillery fire, Cutler's brigade spied only the 640-man 55th North Carolina, which was trying to turn the Union right flank. Colonel Hofmann of the 56th Pennsylvania then ordered his small, 282-man regiment to direct an oblique fire, which was answered by the North Carolinians. The battle of Gettysburg had now opened for Wadsworth's men.[10]

Scores of blue and butternut soldiers began falling. The 76th New York still could not see the 2nd Mississippi, "concealed in tall grass" less than 200 yards directly in front of them. The New Yorkers suffered several minutes of murderous musketry before they realized that this was not friendly fire. Even before that they had unsuccessfully ducked the rounds Pegram's battery was pouring in on them.

Hall's battery, which was trying to counter those guns, was unaware of the rapidity of the approach of Davis's Brigade. The latter had taken advantage of the withdrawal of Lieutenant John H. Calef's four-gun battery of horse artillery, which had been supporting Buford's cavalrymen before Hall's battery was brought up.[11]

The "close proximity of the combatants made the fire most destructive and deadly." Men lay "in ranks," wrote the 147th's surgeon, "as they had been formed in line of battle." The 76th New York was in a particularly perilous position when Colonel John K. Connally's 55th North Carolina performed a right wheel and charged with bayonets drawn. More officers and men fell as the North Carolinians moved perpendicular to the 76th. The New Yorkers were then caught in a cross fire delivered by the 55th North Carolina and the 2nd Mississippi. In this short, 15- to 30-minute encounter, Cutler reported that 45 percent (169 of 375) of the officers and men from the 76th New York were killed or wounded. The 56th Pennsylvania suffered just as badly, with an estimate of 130 casualties out of 252 men. These two regiments were not only "neutralized" as fighting forces, they were virtually eliminated as military units.[12]

Sensing that the three outnumbered regiments risked *total* annihilation, Wadsworth wanted them withdrawn. He urgently dispatched Captain Timothy Ellsworth to inform General Reynolds of the desperate position of his three regiments north of the Chambersburg Pike, but Ellsworth found Reynolds near death, which was promptly reported to Wadsworth. The latter, unaware that Doubleday was now commanding, took the initiative. He directed Cutler to order the 76th New York, 56th Pennsylvania, and 147th New York to pull back "to the shelter of the woods on Seminary Ridge."[13]

While Cutler's brigade was fighting for all it was worth, Wadsworth's other brigade, Meredith's Iron Brigade, had been deployed by Reynolds himself to halt the charge of General Archer's 1,197-man brigade (7th and 14th Tennessee, 13th Alabama, 1st Tennessee, and 5th Alabama). Archer, fearing his light brigade was at risk, had reluctantly advanced his men under cover of the woods on the McPherson farm just east of Willoughby Run.[14]

The only Union troops (fewer than 600) in position as Archer approached from Herr Ridge were the remaining two regiments of Cutler's brigade, the 95th New York and the 14th Brooklyn. Wadsworth had personally directed the 14th's Colonel Fowler to where he wanted them positioned at about the same time he had deployed Cutler's other three regiments across the pike. The 95th rested its right on the Chambersburg Pike (about 100 yards south of Hall's battery), while the 14th Brooklyn was stretched even more thinly from the 95th's left to McPherson's woods. Colonel Fowler's command had not completely formed when General Archer's skirmishers struck, wounding Fowler and the 95th's Colonel George Biddle.[15]

While General Wadsworth and Lieutenant Colonel Kress were standing on Chambersburg Pike, Kress called Archer's movement to his commander's attention. Wadsworth then directed him to form Meredith's Iron Brigade. Another version has it that Reynolds, wanting to hold on to the Fairfield Road, believed that Archer was close to turning the Union's left flank and directed

Wadsworth to order Meredith's lead regiment, the 2nd Wisconsin, to support the 14th Brooklyn's left.[16]

Regardless of which account is correct, General Wadsworth dispatched Kress to tell the 2nd Wisconsin's Colonel Fairchild, heading the long column of Meredith's brigade, to order an advance. Fairchild's regiment was to form to the left of the 14th Brooklyn and to get to the woods at the top of the slope of McPherson's Ridge. Kress did not even allow the 2nd Wisconsin to load their weapons. Instead he directed Fairchild to "Let them fix bayonets as they move ... you have not a minute to lose; the enemy is almost upon you." Then Kress moved down the line, repeating the message to each regimental commander.[17]

The Badgers advanced about a hundred yards and halted momentarily. Then they ran through the swale west of Seminary Ridge to the crest of the easternmost of the two ridges that constituted McPherson's Ridge, loading on the run. They were hit almost immediately by a volley of musketry from the 7th Tennessee, barely fifty yards away. Colonel William Robinson's 7th Wisconsin, also loading on the run and following on the heels of the 2nd Wisconsin, halted near Herbst Woods. Like its fellow regiment, it encountered a heavy fire, but, through the dense smoke, its commander was uncertain whether the Confederates or its fellow Badgers were firing on them. Just then Captain Craig Wadsworth affirmed that it was, indeed, the enemy and that General Wadsworth wanted the enemy driven out. Robinson immediately formed the 7th Wisconsin to the left and slightly behind the 2nd, following the ridge line. The 19th Indiana formed to the 7th Wisconsin's left, while Colonel Morrow's 24th Michigan closed to the left of the 19th. The 6th Wisconsin and the 100-man brigade guard had been halted by Doubleday before it could form. In concert, but not as one, the four remaining regiments of the Iron Brigade charged toward Willoughby Run.[18]

Because there are so many confusing accounts of this confusing battle, it is useful to return briefly to the 2nd Wisconsin's charge and one vital incident that affected what transpired thereafter. When the 2nd Wisconsin was hit by the volley of the 7th Tennessee, it was stunned and deflected to the right, desperately trying to hold on. Worse news followed. General Reynolds, behind the Badgers, was killed by a stray bullet. This was unfortunate on a number of counts. Reynolds had sized up the area and had a battle plan. Second, Reynolds was greatly respected, whereas Doubleday, now the senior officer on the field, was much less inspiring. Additionally, there was confusion over commands until General Howard came up. Wadsworth initially believed he was corps commander, for he did not yet know that Doubleday was on the field. (Colonel Gates of the "Ulster Guards," for one, believed Wadsworth "had succeeded to the immediate command of the I Corps, and in this instance nothing could have been better or more satisfactory. Brave, cool, zealous in the cause, and believing that the business of war is to *fight,* and beat your enemy as badly as possible.")[19]

In his first genuine engagement as division commander Wadsworth now labored under two handicaps. First, he had to coordinate his two brigades separated by the Chambersburg Pike. Second, he did not have a good relationship with Doubleday, upon whom corps command, in fact, had devolved. Wadsworth, a civilian volunteer, earlier had replaced Doubleday, a regular and West Pointer, as 1st Division commander, which temporarily demoted Doubleday to brigade commander. Also Wadsworth had twice served as acting corps commander. More importantly, after Reynolds's death "matters seemed to be at times, very much at 'loggerheads,'" claimed Lieutenant George Breck of the 1st New York Light Battery, "lacking a controlling, directing head in the movements and dispositions of our forces." Thus, this was a particularly critical moment for the Union and for Wadsworth, the civilian general, who now had the field command he had so ardently sought. For two hours his two brigades "alone" contended with a much larger force.[20]

On the other hand, during that time—in fact, in little more than an hour—Wadsworth's 1st Brigade, the "Black Hatters," with only a slight numerical advantage, had inflicted heavy casualties on Archer's Brigade and had captured its commander. Now, sometime after 11:00, having once more proved their worth, the Iron Brigade enjoyed a pause. By contrast, the 6th Wisconsin and the 100-man guard, which Doubleday had held in reserve, was just getting into action. It was being called on to stop Davis's Brigade, which was now about to pounce on the isolated, and apparently forgotten, 147th New York.[21]

The 76th New York and the 56th Pennsylvania had been withdrawn by Wadsworth for their survival. It remains a question whether they withdrew "in good order," as Wadsworth claimed, or "in great disorder," as General Davis recalled. The result of their withdrawal was that Hall's exposed battery was now supported only by the 147th New York, though neither Hall nor the 147th knew it immediately. Wadsworth's order to retire never reached the 147th. Its commander, Lieutenant Colonel Miller, was struck by a bullet before he could comply. This led to a confrontation between Wadsworth and battery commander Hall.[22]

Captain Hall, who had been assured by Reynolds that his battery was only temporarily posted, found himself facing skirmishers from the 42nd and 2nd Mississippi regiments, which "rose up [out of the railroad cut] . . . at a distance of not more than *fifty yards*." He turned his guns to the right and "opened with double shotted canister," which he dryly observed later "broke" the Confederate charge. (Canister, a tin can filled with iron balls, which disintegrated and flung the balls in every direction, would rip through anything in its path.) However, Hall's relief was only temporary, for he then discovered that the 76th New York and 56th Pennsylvania had been withdrawn and thought he was totally unprotected. Immediately he dispatched Lieutenant William Ulmer with his two-gun section back to the next "crest" not only to save his guns, but to fire on Davis's men in the railroad cut. However, even before unlimbering and positioning his guns, Ulmer's horses were killed and "a raking fire" swept over his guns, forcing their abandonment. Hall realized then that he had to extricate his remaining guns, but that meant he had to duck musketry from the cut and vault a fence. None of the horses that were to pull his last gun survived the awful fire from the fast-charging Mississippians and North Carolinians. Captain Hall looked in vain to the infantry to protect him, his men, and only three guns, one of which had lost a wheel.[23]

An angry Hall met General Wadsworth back at the intersection of Seminary Ridge and the pike and challenged Wadsworth's "cowardly" action in leaving Hall's guns and men unprotected. Though later the artilleryman would claim it was an unfortunate mistake, Wadsworth ignored the insubordination and shouted "Get your guns back, to some point to cover the retiring of these troops." Hall remonstrated that the proper place for his three remaining guns was where he had withdrawn them, albeit without orders, just in front of Seminary Ridge. "Oh, no," Wadsworth replied, "go beyond the town for we cannot hold this line." Captain Hall then shouted that he wanted to retrieve one of his guns, which "was in jeopardy" of being captured by the Confederates. Wadsworth "snappishly" told him to "Loose [sic] no time in getting your guns in position to cover the retreat." Hall did so, running through town to the cemetery south of town. No sooner had Hall begun to set up than Wadsworth ordered him to return to Seminary Ridge, where Wadsworth intended to make another stand. Hall later took some small satisfaction from this affirmation of his judgment, but Colonel Charles Wainwright indirectly concurred with Wadsworth's initial judgment—Hall's battery was in no condition to remain on the field. Indeed, once safely off the field, he would have to reorganize if he were to be of any help again.[24]

The incident was indeed unfortunate. First, Hall had been placed temporarily in an exposed position by Reynolds, who intended to withdraw him in due time. Second, as Gettysburg historian Edwin Coddington observed, this "was an instance of a conflict between two good officers, one an infantryman and the other an artilleryman." Wadsworth apparently let the matter drop momentarily, for he had other things on his mind, specifically the 147th New York's predicament.[25]

The regiment, recruited principally in Oswego, New York, north of Syracuse, was, for all intents, untested. It had joined the I Corps in January 1863 after serving in the defenses of Washington and on provost guard, but it had seen virtually no combat at Chancellorsville. Initially here at Gettysburg it was led by Lieutenant Colonel Francis C. Miller, rather than its disabled commander Colonel John Butler. Early in the battle the 147th had become separated and found itself in a depression virtually invisible to Hall's battery barely a hundred yards to its left across the railroad cut. Now, at the height of the charge and after the withdrawal of the 76th New York and 56th Pennsylvania, the 147th faced most of three Confederate regiments—the 42nd Mississippi, which had previously fronted Hall's battery; the 2nd Mississippi, which was moving obliquely toward the 147th; and the 55th North Carolina, which was on the right in a position to cut off any retreat.[26]

Lying prone, the New Yorkers were being struck in the head or upper body with fatal regularity by the Confederate fire, which was less than a hundred yards in front of them. The isolated regiment risked imminent capture. Wadsworth, who was returning to his headquarters near the woods on Seminary Ridge north of the pike, spied the heavily enveloped, but undaunted, 147th New York. He asked Assistant Adjutant General Timothy Ellsworth why it had not retreated with the 76th New York and 56th Pennsylvania when ordered to do so and dispatched Ellsworth to withdraw the imperiled regiment. Major George Harney, now commanding in place of the wounded Miller, had to be convinced that Wadsworth approved the regiment's withdrawal. Ordered to "divest themselves of everything but" their rifles and cartridge boxes (including their rations), the men wasted no time trying to free themselves.[27]

Davis's 2nd and 42nd Mississippi and 55th North Carolina were equally determined to cut off the 147th's retreat. But the 6th Wisconsin, 14th Brooklyn, and 95th New York mounted a rapidly improvised countercharge.[28] (An aide of Cutler's had hollered, "Go like hell!")

Another, more romantic, postbattle version has it:

> *When our lines they were broken, and backward did lag;*
> *And old 'Daddy Wadsworth,' rushed up to Bragg,*
> *Saying the Rebs were triumphant, you must save the day,*
> *They charged like a whirlwind, old Company K.*[29]

This is another instance where Wadsworth's role is unclear. As the doggerel suggests, Wadsworth may have ordered the 6th Wisconsin's Colonel Bragg to mount a charge, but Lieutenant Colonel Rufus Dawes of the 6th Wisconsin claimed to have initiated the counterattack with the approval of the 95th's acting commander, Major Edward Pye. On the other hand, the 14th Brooklyn's Colonel Fowler reported that he coordinated the attack directed at the railroad cut. Major Pye, like Wadsworth, offers no details in his report, and the hypercritical Eminel Halstead denies Wadsworth gave any orders. The truth will probably never be known.[30]

The counterchargers, from left to right the 14th Brooklyn, 95th New York, and 6th Wisconsin, were aimed between the 2nd and 42nd Mississippi and a contingent of the 55th North Carolina, in what has been called the railroad's "Middle Cut," where it was particularly deep. During this frantic charge, "old Daddy" Wadsworth was anxiously watching. Almost half of his men were in great peril. Thus began the heralded attack that would enter into legend. It ended, according to Dawes, with "a general cry from our men of: 'Throw down your muskets. Down with your muskets.'"[31]

While all of the participating regiments would claim credit for the victorious charge, Wadsworth, closest to the 6th Wisconsin whose raised national flag was plainly visible, exclaimed, "My God, the 6th has conquered them." Indeed, the three regiments, trapped in the railroad cut, counted close to 300 prisoners, including the 2nd Mississippi's Major John Blair, the 2nd's regimental flag, and an estimated 1,000 muskets.[32]

The surrender or retreat of the remaining regiments of Davis's Brigade occurred sometime around 11:30 A.M. and ushered in a lull in the day's battle. Cutler's brigade, now located in the woods on Seminary Ridge north of the railroad cut, counted its losses and reorganized. It had been a savage morning.

Nearly one-third of Wadsworth's men had been killed, wounded, or captured. In thirty minutes of desperate fighting the 147th New York had lost 60 killed, including 12 mortally wounded, and 136 wounded out of 380 officers and men, a casualty rate of 52 percent. Only 75 of the New Yorkers managed to retire to the eastern slope of Seminary Ridge. The 6th Wisconsin estimated that it lost more than half its men, including seven company captains, during the charge on the railroad cut.[33]

Notwithstanding the withdrawal of the bulk of Cutler's brigade, whether or not orderly, "Wadsworth's small division had thus won decided successes against superior numbers," according to Army of the Potomac Artillery Chief Henry Hunt. South of the Chambersburg Pike Meredith's Iron Brigade (minus the 6th Wisconsin), along with the 95th New York and 14th Brooklyn, had repulsed Archer's Brigade in a hard-fought duel. On the north side of the pike the rest of Wadsworth's division had relieved Buford's gallant cavalry and had held onto the ground as long as it could. In the process, Davis's Brigade had been so severely treated that it would not be a factor during the rest of the battle.

However great the losses in Wadsworth's division, it had borrowed time for the other two I Corps divisions and Howard's XI Corps to get to Gettysburg. And the 1st Division commander had secured a reputation: "The activity, efficiency, and, if I [Lieutenant Colonel Dawes] may so express it, ubiquity, of General James S. Wadsworth in the battle was remarkable. He was of venerable and commanding appearance, and was absolutely fearless in exposing himself to danger."[34]

Chapter 16

"WE ARE GIVING THE REBELS HELL WITH THESE GUNS"

Afternoon at Gettysburg, July 1

Near 11:30 A.M., both sides paused and assessed the situation. "The temporary repulse of Cutler and the defeat of Archer and Davis had produced
a feeling of caution on both sides," recalled Major General O. O. Howard, "a period of delay before any organized assault was attempted again." Wadsworth's
small division had relieved Buford's beleaguered cavalry, which had made a
heroic stand against numbing odds. But, while paying a terrible price, Wadsworth's men had only bought time by delaying and harassing Heth's Division.
The 147th New York had barely seventy-five able men left, less than a full-
strength company. The 76th New York assembled 141 men, barely a company
and a half, while the 56th Pennsylvania, with only 174 survivors, was not quite
two regular-strength companies. The 14th Brooklyn, which had lost between
125 and 150 of its 318 officers and men, and the 95th New York, which suffered
the loss of almost a third of its men engaged, were little better off.[1]

Though he would despair over the losses, Wadsworth remained confident of
his command. Meredith's brigade held McPherson's Ridge and Herbst's Woods
south of Chambersburg (Cashtown) Pike. North of the pike Cutler's decimated
brigade had held off Davis's Brigade, and now rested near Seminary Ridge.
Wadsworth and his battered division knew it was only a matter of time until the
battle resumed.

The sun beat on them as they lay where they could view dead comrades.
More disconcerting, they heard the rumble of artillery and saw more Confederates lining the field in their front. It was a tense time for Wadsworth and his men.
General Reynolds, who had initiated the battle and who could have articulated
strategy, was dead. Before the fatal round he had ordered up the III and XI Corps
to support the I Corps, now commanded by Brigadier General Abner Doubleday.
Though regular army and the ranking Union officer on the field, the acting corps
commander had been dubbed "Forty-eight Hours" Doubleday by critics for his

alleged inability to size up situations and to make decisions. Now he was being tested by an especially daunting situation: A. P. Hill's Corps was advancing from the west and Ewell's was reported north of Gettysburg. To counter them he had only Buford's cavalry division, Wadsworth's division, and two full field batteries, Captain James B. Stewart's Company B, 4th U.S. Artillery, and Lieutenant John B. Calef's Company A, 2nd U.S. Horse Artillery, and Captain James Hall's battery remnant. (Robinson and Rowley were not yet on the field.) Because Heth still had a numerical advantage, Doubleday felt he had ample justification for retreating, which the Army of the Potomac had been doing with agonizing regularity after bloody engagements. But he shared Reynolds's opinion that a stand must be taken here and now. A retreat would mean one more demoralizing experience for the troops. The war would never end until the Confederates' main army was defeated. The key was whether Wadsworth's diminished division could hold on until the other Federal corps arrived. Colonel Wainwright gloomily summed up the situation: A strong enemy force "would eat us up piecemeal."[2]

Taking a more optimistic view, at 12:10 P.M. Wadsworth reported that he thought "the enemy are retiring, and that we should advance promptly upon them." Given the situation as others saw it and the battered condition of Cutler's brigade, it is surprising that General Wadsworth would make such a suggestion. He may have been confident of his division, based on the strong leadership of brigade commanders Meredith and Cutler and the success of the Iron Brigade that morning. Also he had realigned (probably at Doubleday's direction) the Iron Brigade, minus the 6th Wisconsin, to enjoy the protection of Herbst's Woods while the other two divisions of the I Corps were positioned.[3]

The 24th Michigan was pulled back and exchanged positions with the 19th Indiana, whereby the 19th was now on the Union left and the 24th to its right. Unfortunately—and perilously—the 24th formed an obtuse angle, its right bent back toward the 7th Wisconsin and its left angling toward a deep hollow. This caused Colonel Morrow to protest (without effect) that it was impossible for both wings to view each other. The 2nd Wisconsin flanked the 24th on the right, and the 7th Wisconsin occupied the extreme right nearest the Chambersburg Pike. The men were directed to lie down and rest. Momentarily, the 6th Wisconsin and the 14th Brooklyn were aligned north of the pike facing west, but, based on information of an impending attack by Ewell's II Corps, fell back to support Cutler. The other four regiments of Cutler's badly cut-up brigade were in the woods just in front of Seminary Ridge to the right, but split off from the 6th Wisconsin and 14th Brooklyn. Necessarily, General Cutler spent some time collecting the six regiments he was commanding. Then he re-formed them in battle line just in front of the woods perpendicular to the railroad cut, with the 6th Wisconsin on the left.[4]

Shortly, Cutler's brigade seemed to be the target of Major David McIntosh's sixteen-gun artillery battalion. As if announcing the forthcoming Confederate attack, McIntosh, who had formed on Pegram's right in a line perpendicular to the pike, was shelling the Federals with increasing intensity. This prompted

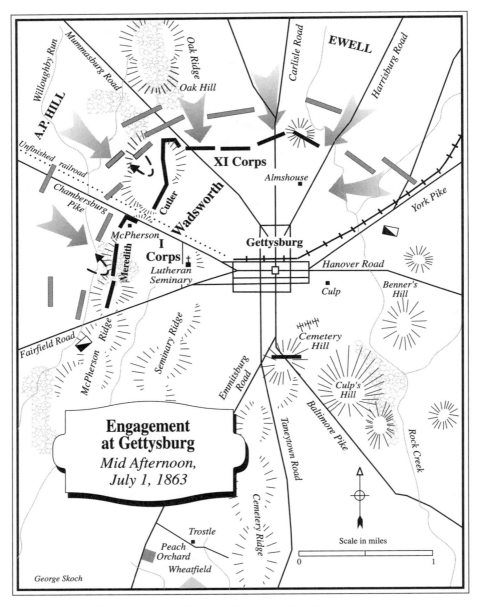

Engagement at Gettysburg: midafternoon (by George Skoch)

Wadsworth to call for Captain Hall's battery to return to its original position north of the Chambersburg Pike on McPherson's Ridge. However, Colonel Wainwright declined to order the battery up, claiming that Wadsworth "kept interfering with the proper placing of the guns." Once again—and it would not be the last time—the two headstrong officers butted heads, though Wadsworth ignored the incident in his official report.[5]

Undeterred, the division commander dispatched Lieutenant Colonel Kress to retrieve Hall and to guide the battery back through town to Seminary Ridge. Hall began advancing his badly beat-up battery, but decided to check out the situation himself. Skirmishers revealed an advance by firing on Hall, who promptly "countermarched" his battery back toward town, with the approval of Doubleday.[6]

The provoked Wadsworth simply ordered up the nearest guns to substitute for Hall's, the six 3-inch rifled guns of Lieutenant Calef's Company A, 2nd U.S. Artillery (Buford's cavalry). However, the young lieutenant also refused the order to return to his former position, invoking Wainwright's rationale that the position was too exposed. Wadsworth exploded at this second instance of insubordination and ordered Calef arrested and sent to the rear. Then Wadsworth overrode Calef and appropriated two of his gun sections to try to counter the destructive Confederate shelling, but it was an unequal battle from the start. They were met almost instantly by three four-gun Confederate batteries on their front and right (north), forcing Wadsworth to shift the 6th Wisconsin and the 14th Brooklyn between 100 and 130 yards behind and in support of his battery.[7]

Encountering artillery fire from the north and following Wadsworth's orders to use his judgment, Cutler wheeled the four regiments right so they faced the Confederate guns, an alignment that General Doubleday subsequently "sanctioned," and ordered the men into a prone position. Thus, barring a flanking movement, General Cutler's men were prepared for a frontal attack.[8] Because the woods behind offered no room to maneuver, it was the best he could do for now. The key was whether Howard's XI Corps could protect his right flank.

The foregoing battle of wills is characteristic of the two principal antagonists, James S. Wadsworth and Charles Wainwright. Given their personalities, these civilian soldiers were bound to clash. They reflected the sociogeographic split in New York State: Wadsworth, the upstater, versus Wainwright, the downstater. They also differed politically: Wadsworth was a belated, but thoroughgoing, abolitionist; Wainwright was a "Peace Democrat." Also they differed militarily: Wadsworth was infantry; Wainwright was artillery. Moreover, Wadsworth's military skills were suspect in Wainwright's eyes, and, whatever the necessity, Wadsworth was acting imperiously, more like the manager of his vast estate. He wanted artillery support for his troops that were threatened by Confederate fire and, without authority, he simply grabbed the nearest guns. This would not be the only time Wadsworth would take matters into his own hands, nor would this be the last time that he would be criticized for it. Before the day's fighting had subsided he would take a similar tack, which would inspire his men, but would expose himself and others to possibly unnecessary danger. Yet his actions symbolized the man—impetuous, courageous, selfless.

★　　★　　★

Confederate General Heth now knew he faced veterans, not militia, and formed his division in line of battle south of Chambersburg Pike: Archer's Brigade (Colonel Birkett Fry of the 13th Alabama commanding) on the Confederate right flank, Brigadier General James Johnston Pettigrew's Brigade (11th, 26th, 47th, and 52nd North Carolina) in the center, and Colonel John Brockenbrough's (Heth's) Brigade (40th, 47th, 55th, and 22nd Virginia) on the left. Davis's shattered brigade was left behind to collect stragglers. Major General William D. Pender's Division (the brigades of Colonel Abner Perrin and of Brigadier Generals James H. Lane, Edward L. Thomas, and Alfred M. Scales) was to support Heth's second attack of the day.[9]

The Union was better prepared now, as well. Wadsworth's badly bruised, but undaunted, division was joined by Robinson's and Doubleday's divisions (Rowley commanding). The two brigades of Rowley's division were positioned on either side of the Iron Brigade (minus the 6th Wisconsin) on the eastern slope of McPherson's Ridge, facing west. Colonel Chapman Biddle's brigade (80th New York, 121st, 142nd, and 151st Pennsylvania), after a number of shifts, was eventually placed to the left and rear of the Iron Brigade. Colonel Roy Stone's 2nd, or "Bucktail," Brigade (143rd, 149th, and 150th Pennsylvania) was to the right (north) of the Iron Brigade and initially formed at a right angle to the pike. Robinson's two brigades, just arriving, were separated some distance from each other on either side of the pike. Brigadier General Henry Baxter's 2nd Brigade (12th Massachusetts, 83rd and 97th New York, 11th, 88th, and 90th Pennsylvania) would eventually be aligned to the right of Cutler's brigade, facing north. Initially, Brigadier General Gabriel R. Paul's 1st Brigade was held in reserve straddling Fairfield Road, which Doubleday still thought to be the direction from which Reynolds had expected a Confederate attack. It was soon moved to the woods in front of the Seminary, where the men built breastworks of rails.[10]

At approximately 2:00 P.M. Wadsworth briefly conferred with General Howard, now the ranking officer, who had come on the field during the lull in the fighting. Wadsworth was told "to hold Seminary Ridge as long as possible," then, when necessary, withdraw to Cemetery Hill. Unfortunately, General Ewell's Corps had made its appearance on the field. Wadsworth had spied a Confederate battery setting up on Oak Hill, higher ground north of the Mummasburg Road and facing Cutler's brigade, forming south of the road. The guns threatened to enfilade the whole Union line. Wadsworth reported this to General Doubleday, who instructed Wadsworth to send Baxter's brigade "beyond the northern end of" the Union line, facing west, which he did.[11]

Baxter's brigade had scarcely been posted when they were hit by artillery and musket fire that created havoc not only for the men but for the trees near them. Wadsworth had feared just such an attack and during the pause in the fighting had warned Howard. In fact, the division commander correctly believed that the relatively weak force in his front indicated that the real Confederate movement would come from his right flank, as Oak Hill to the north, cresting on Oak Ridge, offered a commanding position to the first taker. General Howard had then ordered acting XI Corps commander Carl Schurz to guide his 1st and 3rd Divisions to Oak Hill before the Confederates held it in force, but he was too late. Major General Robert Rodes's Division, the first of Ewell's three divisions to reach the battlefield, had advanced and occupied the vital high ground.[12]

The double-barreled attack on the greatly outnumbered I Corps had begun. Wadsworth and his men faced troops from the west, with which General Doubleday had been most concerned, and now from the northeast. Heth was again approaching from the west with 4,752 troops along with Pender's 6,735-man division; from the north came Ewell's Corps, some 14,000 strong. The situation was becoming particularly desperate for the I Corps, with less than 12,000 men engaged, for Howard's 9,000-man XI Corps was not in place until almost 2:00 P.M.[13]

General Howard had to coordinate the scattered Union forces, but, unfortunately, he had already reported to Meade that Wadsworth's division had fled the field in total disorder. Not only was this totally inaccurate and embarrassing to Wadsworth, which Howard would belatedly acknowledge, but this caused more confusion. Meade, who disliked Doubleday (and blamed Doubleday for what Howard claimed was happening), would later order II Corps commander Major General Winfield Scott Hancock to assume overall command of what had been Reynolds's wing. The only hope was that the I Corps could beat back Hill's Corps before Ewell's Corps could mount a full-scale attack.[14]

Meanwhile, well before 2:00 P.M., the whole I Corps north of the Chambersburg Pike was engaged and under heavy Confederate fire. The two sections of Calef's battery, which Wadsworth had appropriated and positioned where Hall's battery had been earlier, had come under rifle and cannon fire even as it unlimbered. It was at this time that Wadsworth ordered the 6th Wisconsin forward to support the horse artillery. The Badgers too felt the force of the artillery shelling, leading Wadsworth to order up the 14th Brooklyn. Calef's two sections, no longer alone, would temporarily provide some protection to the I Corps troops north of Chambersburg Pike. But within fifteen minutes, the artillerymen were hit by an enfilading fire from a Confederate battery and had to withdraw closer to the protection of the woods near Seminary Ridge.[15]

General Buford, fearing for Calef's men, insisted to Doubleday that their guns be withdrawn completely and that a battery from the I Corps replace them. Wainwright, present during this exchange, realized just how irritated Wadsworth was with his earlier refusal to recall Hall's battery and agreed to substitute Captain Gilbert Reynolds's Battery L, 1st New York Light Artillery. But Wainwright conditioned this concession: Reynolds's battery was *not* to report to General Wadsworth, to which Doubleday acceded, and the battery was promptly moved up. At about the same time Lieutenant James Stewart's Battery B, 4th U.S., was positioned so it straddled the railroad cut on Seminary Ridge. Wadsworth may have been unaware of Wainwright's little ploy, for he did not mention Wainwright's one-upmanship in his report or in his later testimony to the Joint Committee on the Conduct of the War.[16]

Thinking he had taken care of the north side of the pike, Wadsworth asked for artillery support on the Union left. Wainwright responded to the newest request from Wadsworth by posting Lieutenant Benjamin Wilber's section of Reynolds's battery south of the pike between Herbst's Woods and the McPherson farm buildings, where its flank was protected. Previously Wainwright had placed James H. Cooper's Battery B, 1st Pennsylvania Light Artillery, on the far left, north of Fairfield Road on McPherson's Ridge, where he expected the division line to be. Cooper's battery was in support of Biddle's brigade of Rowley's division, which Wadsworth had ordered forward to Willoughby Run to protect the left flank of Meredith's Iron Brigade, now four regiments. However, Colonel Biddle had no sooner advanced than his brigade was hit by fire from Pettigrew's Brigade, which was concealed in a wheat field on the eastern slope of Herr Ridge, forcing Biddle to withdraw hastily.[17]

Roughly twenty minutes later Wadsworth became concerned about the Harman house and barn, approximately 500 yards beyond Willoughby Run. It was "crawling with Confederate skirmishers" who were threatening Cooper's battery. Again, bypassing the usual command structure, Wadsworth ordered Colonel Theodore Gates of the 20th New York State Militia ("Ulster Guards") of Biddle's brigade to clear out the troublesome skirmishers. In turn, Gates dispatched Captain Ambrose N. Baldwin of Company K to do the irksome and dangerous business. Captain John D. S. Cook vividly recalled the experience: Despite "needless exposure . . . General Wadsworth, who had been our first brigade commander, . . . had recommended us for the duty; that he knew our regiment would go where it was sent and stay where it was put. This story spread quickly all along the line and whether true or not, I know it helped to console us for the exposure to which we were subjected." Their selection by the "General whom we all loved and honored, compensated" for the danger. After a heated struggle the skirmishers captured the house and barn and held on for possibly two hours, until finally forced to retire when surrounded on three sides.[18]

True to form, once more James S. Wadsworth had taken matters into his own hands. That is, as historian David Martin wrote, "Wadsworth did not hesitate to give orders to troops not belonging to his division." Still, the ubiquitous Wadsworth continued to fear a full-scale movement from the north. General Howard was uncertain about the seriousness of the threat from Ewell's Corps. With his XI Corps up and temporarily having a numerical superiority, he could mount an advance. On the other hand, he (and apparently Doubleday) was more inclined to opt for a delaying action to permit the other corps to arrive.[19]

Wadsworth had been ordered by General Howard to hold Seminary Ridge, but Rodes's advance from Oak Hill made this a particularly difficult assignment now. Shortly, Wadsworth had even more reason to be concerned. Not only did Cutler's brigade face troops from Rodes's Division from the north, but Heth's and Pender's Divisions threatened his Iron Brigade from the west. In fact, when Biddle's brigade retreated pell-mell for the protection of Seminary Ridge, the 19th Indiana and 24th Michigan were exposed to a flank attack. As the fighting progressed, each of the units seemed to be fighting alone—in places where the opposing lines were less than forty yards apart.[20]

Between 3:20 and 3:45, Wadsworth asked Howard for reinforcements, but they were too little, too late. Fighting obstinately, a third, fourth, even a fifth line was attempted by the 19th Indiana and 24th Michigan. Eventually they withdrew, firing all the while, to Seminary Ridge. But their division commander was proud of their obstinacy, which he felt saved the day. "Colonel Morrow [24th Michigan]," Wadsworth is quoted as saying later, "the only fault I find with you is that you fought too long, but God only knows what would have become of the Army of the Potomac if you had not held the ground as long as you did."[21]

Initially Colonel Stone's brigade on the left of Chambersburg Pike checked Brockenbrough's Confederate brigade, then it was fighting on two fronts, and it too began to fall back. Like the 19th Indiana and 24th Michigan had earlier, the 7th and 2nd Wisconsin now bore the brunt of the Confederate attack, primarily from Scales's fresh brigade, composed of five North Carolina regiments (1,405 officers and men) in relief of General Brockenbrough's. The stubborn, battered remnants of the two Wisconsin regiments held on as long as they could, but they too were overpowered. Both regimental commanders had been severely wounded trying to inspire their men. The Badgers continued to resist until eventually, close to 3:30, they began to run out of ammunition. Then they, the last Union units on McPherson's Ridge south of the pike, withdrew to the center of Seminary Ridge between Chambersburg Pike and Fairfield Road.[22]

Despite the threat from Ewell's Corps, Wadsworth remained persuaded that the part of Cutler's brigade back on Seminary Ridge could defend itself. The ridge, about a half mile west of the town and running nearly north and south, was formed by an outcropping of rocks. It stretched more than a mile and a half, with the portion north of Chambersburg Pike ending at Oak Ridge, "a broken, rocky knoll some 300 yards to the right [of the Lutheran Seminary]." Woods fronted the seminary itself and another belt of trees ran along Oak Ridge. The position could be held temporarily, barring an enveloping movement by two Confederate corps.[23]

The key now was the north sector, specifically the XI Corps, which was to the I Corps' right. General Cutler originally had formed his brigade across the railroad cut facing west, but he had been forced to turn his troops to face almost due north. The problem was not with Wadsworth's troops; it was the fearful gap of close to 400 yards that separated Baxter's brigade from the XI Corps. General Howard had been unable to make a junction due to the presence of Rodes's Division on Oak Hill.[24]

The Union right, facing Ewell's Corps, had initial success, repulsing attacks by Rodes's three brigades with the support of Baxter's brigade and the XI Corps left. However, Cutler was forced to withdraw to the woods on Seminary Ridge, where part of his brigade rested near previously constructed breastworks, and awaited cartridges. After their ammunition was replenished, the men continued to wait, but not for long.[25]

Wadsworth recalled that as early as 2:30 the XI Corps had fallen back, thereby exposing his right flank, and ordered the 14th Brooklyn and the 147th and 76th New York also to withdraw to Seminary Ridge to support the rest of the brigade and batteries there. Scales banged at Cutler's restored brigade two or three times, but was repulsed each time by it and by Stewart's Napoleons, which, double-shotted with canister, had the expected effect.[26]

Shortly before 4:00 P.M., Cutler's brigade began to see a wild retreat by the XI Corps, exposing the brigade's right flank. Still, Wadsworth inaccurately believed he "could have continued to hold" Seminary Ridge. He counted on his artillery, "some six or eight Napoleon 12-pounders throwing grape and canister" to maintain his position against the advance of Heth's and Pender's Divisions. However, at 4:10 General Howard realized that the Federals could not hold out any longer and directed the I and XI Corps "to fall back gradually, disputing every inch of ground, and to form near my position, the Eleventh Corps on the right and the First Corps on the left of the Baltimore pike."[27]

Doubleday attempted to give the order to Wadsworth, who was in his element, helping Stevens's 5th Maine Battery fire canister into the advancing Confederates at close range. In fact, Wadsworth is said to have remonstrated, "Tell General Doubleday that I don't know a damned thing about strategy, but we are giving the rebels hell with these guns, and I want to give them a few more shots before we leave." While possibly apocryphal, Wadsworth's reply has a ring of truth to it.[28]

Given Wadsworth's order to withdraw, Cutler's men, minus the 6th Wisconsin, which took a more northerly route, followed the railroad embankment toward Gettysburg. Wadsworth's troops could only marvel that the Confederate artillery had not done more harm than it did to Cutler's brigade as it retired eastward. However, the 7th Wisconsin, the rear guard, suffered heavily from rifle fire striking their front and flank. In fact, Wadsworth's division was lucky to escape at all. "Finding myself outflanked on both right and left, heavily pressed in front, and my ammunition nearly exhausted," Wadsworth had reluctantly given the order to withdraw. By Wadsworth's count he had 1,600 men out of "about 4000 men that went into the action."[29]

While claims were made that the I Corps moved in an orderly fashion through town, there are a number of counterclaims, including that of the 6th Wisconsin's Dawes, who reported running into Confederate troops en route to Cemetery Hill. It was amazing that there was not more disorder as the two corps trod their paths on either side of the narrow, unfamiliar streets filled with ambulances, artillery, and wagons, as well as Confederates. One consolation was that the weary, battle-scarred troops enjoyed food and drink from sympathetic townspeople. The biggest threat was Confederate artillery, which was shelling the retreating Union forces. Where Wadsworth was during this tumultuous episode cannot be determined.[30]

By 5:00 P.M., after a wild retreat (as most recalled it) through the narrow, crowded Gettysburg streets, most of the I Corps had made it to Cemetery Hill, the spot where Howard figured a stand would have to be taken. But the corps was reduced by half, the most any Union corps suffered in the entire battle. Wadsworth's 1st Division was shorn of 2,155 rank and file. The 24th Michigan

JAMES WADSWORTH'S
COUSIN JEREMIAH
*(Pearson, Henry G.
James S. Wadsworth
of Geneseo. New
York: Charles
Scribner's Sons,
1913)*

THE GENERAL'S UNCLE,
WILLIAM WADSWORTH,
IN OFFICER'S UNIFORM
DURING THE WAR OF 1812
*(Pearson, Henry G. James S.
Wadsworth of Geneseo. New York:
Charles Scribner's Sons, 1913)*

THE GENERAL'S FATHER,
JAMES WADSWORTH
(AN ENGRAVING)
*(Courtesy, Livingston County
Historical Society, reproduced
by Ronald Pretzer)*

GENERAL WADSWORTH'S
SISTER, ELIZABETH
WADSWORTH MURRAY
(Pearson, Henry G. James S.
Wadsworth of Geneseo. *New York:
Charles Scribner's Sons, 1913)*

GENERAL WADSWORTH AS A YOUNG MAN
(Private collection, reproduced by Ronald Pretzer)

FOYER OF THE GENERAL'S
HARTFORD HOUSE
(Courtesy of Stuart Symington, Jr.)

THE GENERAL'S BROTHER,
WILLIAM W. WADSWORTH
*(Courtesy, Livingston County Historical
Society, reproduced by Ronald Pretzer)*

THE WADSWORTH'S
OFFICE IN GENESEO
(Photo by author)

THE GENERAL AS
A BUSINESSMAN
*(Courtesy, Livingston
County Historical
Society, reproduced by
Ronald Pretzer)*

STAMP FROM GENESEE VALLEY NATIONAL
BANK WITH GENERAL WADSWORTH'S LIKENESS
(Courtesy of Larry Turner, Groveland Town Historian)

GENESEO, N.Y. _____19_____ No.

GENESEE VALLEY NATIONAL BANK 50-741
AND TRUST COMPANY

PAY TO THE
ORDER OF_____ $_____

_____ DOLLARS

SAFETY DEPOSIT BOXES
TO RENT.

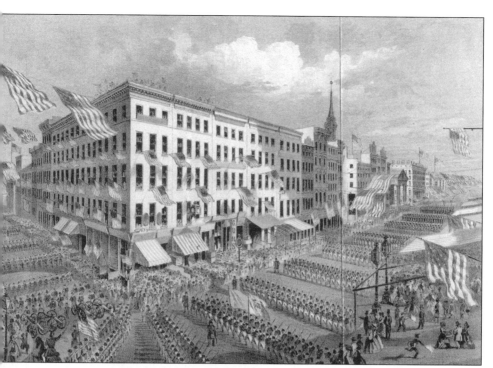

DRAWING OF "DEPARTURE
OF THE 7TH NEW YORK"
*(Lithograph of Sarony, Major &
Knapp, 449 Broadway, N.Y.,
Author's collection)*

MAJ. GEN. IRVIN McDOWELL
*(Massachusetts Commandery Military
Order of the Loyal Legion and the U.S.
Army Military History Institute)*

GENERAL WADSWORTH
EARLY IN THE WAR
*(U.S. Army Military
History Institute)*

THE GENERAL'S MIDDLE SON,
CAPTAIN CRAIG W. WADSWORTH
*(Courtesy, Livingston County Historical
Society, reproduced by Ronald Pretzer)*

THE GENERAL IN
HEROIC POSE

BREVET MAJOR CHARLES F. WADSWORTH.   BREVET COLONEL CRAIG W. WADSWORTH.

BREVET MAJOR JAMES W. WADSWORTH.   BREVET MAJOR MONTGOMERY RITCHIE.

SONS AND SON-IN-LAW OF JAMES S. WADSWORTH.

THE GENERAL'S SONS
AND SON-IN-LAW
(Pearson, Henry G. James S.
Wadsworth of Geneseo. *New York:
Charles Scribner's Sons, 1913)*

THE GENERAL NEAR WASHINGTON
*(Massachusetts Commandery Military
Order of the Loyal Legion and the
U.S. Army Military History Institute)*

CAMPAIGN FOR THE UNION, 1862.

FOR GOVERNOR,
JAMES S. WADSWORTH.

FOR LIEUTENANT-GOVERNOR,
LYMAN TREMAIN.

FOR INSPECTOR OF STATE PRISONS,
ANDREAS WILLMANN.

FOR CANAL COMMISSIONER,
OLIVER LADUE.

FOR CLERK OF THE COURT OF APPEALS,
CHARLES HUGHES.

UNION STATE CENTRAL COMMITTEE.

JAMES KELLY, New York.
ISAAC SHERMAN, New York.
ABRAM WAKEMAN, New York.
CHARLES JONES, Brooklyn.
J. C. FERGUSON, Westchester Co.
R. C. McCORMICK, Jamaica, Queens Co.
HAMILTON HARRIS, Albany.
CHARLES P. RICHARDS, Troy.

HENRY R. LOW, Monticello, Sullivan Co.
E. M. MERRIAM, Ogdensburgh, St. Lawrence Co.
EDWARD DODD, Argyle, Washington Co.
HENRY CHURCHILL, Gloversville, Fulton Co.
P. V. ROGERS, Utica.
FRANK HISCOCK, Syracuse.
M. S. CUSHMAN, Oswego.
W. S. LINCOLN, Newark Valley, Tioga Co.

WILLIAM GLEASON, Delhi, Delaware Co.
FREDERICK JULIAN, Greene, Chenango Co.
D. D. S. BROWN, Scottsville, Monroe Co.
JAMES C. JACKSON, Danville, Livingston Co.
ISAAC FULLER, Seneca Falls, Seneca Co.
WALTER L. SESSIONS, Panama, Chautauqua Co.
WILKES ANGELL, Angelica, Alleghany Co.
BEN FIELD, Albion, Orleans Co.

EXECUTIVE COMMITTEE.

Henry R. Low, Chairman.
Isaac Sherman, Treasurer.
Ben Field, Secretary.

Abram Wakeman.
Charles Jones.
Hamilton Harris.

Chas. P. Richards.
Walter L. Sessions.
W. S. Lincoln.

Astor House, N. Y., October 24th, 1862.

Dear Sir:

The Union State Central Committee desire to address you a few words upon the approaching election.

So important an issue has never before been presented for your decision—the unity of the Republic may depend upon the result.

Our free institutions and democratic form of government are upon trial, and the issue of this election may determine the verdict one way or the other. The truth of this remark will be apparent to you, when you remember the following facts:

I. The State of New York is the very backbone and principal support of the General Government in its efforts to suppress this wicked rebellion.

II. It furnishes nearly one-fourth of the men, and one-half of the money, used in the prosecution of the war.

III. As the General Government acts through the State authorities, to render the support of the State effective its constituted officers should be true, loyal, and friendly to the General Government and the Administration; otherwise the support and resources of the State are lost to the country.

IV. Besides, we elect thirty-one members of Congress in this State, and the character of the next House of Representatives will depend upon the result here.

From the above considerations, we earnestly appeal to you for support, and press upon your mind the conviction that the success of the Union ticket in this canvass is vitally important. As a citizen, patriot, and loyal man, therefore, we urge upon you to spare no effort, to shrink from no labor to render this work certain.

Be vigilant, be active, be faithful.

We have everything to encourage us in the indications from all parts of the State. A glorious victory can be lost only by the indifference, inactivity, or the contentions of our friends.

Go *personally*, and arouse the voters in your locality, and let no one be left at home. We ask, also, that you will use your best efforts to reconcile disputes and heal differences among Union men. *Let it not be said that any two of our friends are opposing candidates on the day of election.* It brings odium on our cause and is full of danger to the country. Patriotic men who cannot reconcile their claims, will surrender them rather than to stand in the way of the Public Good. Let there not be *two Union men* candidates for Congress in any one district of the State.

In conclusion, we sincerely trust that no loyal man will be diverted from the support of any *Union candidate* upon our ticket by any considerations or for any purpose, remembering that this is not with us a political contest, but that the life of our Nation is at stake.

Very truly, your friends,

H. R. LOW, Chairman.
BEN FIELD, Secretary.

CAMPAIGN POSTER FOR
GUBERNATORIAL ELECTION 1862
*(Courtesy, Genesee Valley Collection,
Milne Library, State University
of New York-Geneseo)*

COLONEL CHARLES WAINWRIGHT
*(Roger D. Hunt Collection at U.S. Army
Military History Institute)*

MYLES W. KEOGH
Major A.A.D.C. - Bvt. Lt. Col., U.S.V. - Capt. 7th Cav. U.S.A.
Killed June 25, 1876

Capt. P. Penn Gaskill
1st N.J. Cav.

Major Gen. J. Buford

C.W. Wadsworth
Capt. # A.A.D.C., U.S.V.

A. P. MORROW.
Lt. Col., 6th Penna. Cavalry
Lt. Col., 6th Cav., U.S.A.

GENERAL BUFORD AND STAFF,
INCLUDING CAPTAIN CRAIG WADSWORTH
*(Massachusetts Commandery Military Order of the Loyal
Legion and the U.S. Army Military History Institute)*

LUTHERAN SEMINARY AT GETTYSBURG
*(F.J. Severence photo, Wadsworth Collection, Milne Library, State
University of New York-Geneseo, reproduced by Ronald Pretzer)*

THE RAILROAD CUT AT GETTYSBURG
(F.J. Severence photo, Wadsworth Collection, Milne Library, State University of New York-Geneseo, reproduced by Ronald Pretzer)

CHAMBERSBURG STREET DOWN WHICH I CORPS RETREATED
(F.J. Severence photo, Wadsworth Collection, Milne Library, State University of New York-Geneseo, reproduced by Ronald Pretzer)

MAJ. GEN. GOUVERNEUR WARREN, V CORPS COMMANDER
(Massachusetts Commandery Military Order of the Loyal Legion and the U.S. Army Military History Institute)

GENERAL WADSWORTH, SHOWING THE STRAINS OF WAR
(Massachusetts Commandery Military Order of the Loyal Legion and the U.S. Army Military History Institute)

PLANK ROAD, WILDERNESS WHERE GENERAL WADSWORTH WAS MORTALLY WOUNDED
(Massachusetts Commandery Military Order of the Loyal Legion and the U.S. Army Military History Institute)

THE GENERAL'S GRAVE IN GENESEO
(Photo by author)

DEDICATION OF GENERAL WADSWORTH'S MONUMENT AT GETTYSBURG, 1914
(In Memoriam, James Samuel Wadsworth, 1807-1864. Albany: J.B. Lyon Co., 1916)

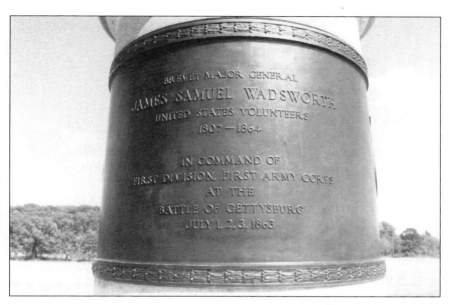

CLOSE-UP OF THE
INSCRIPTION ON GENERAL
WADSWORTH'S MONUMENT
AT GETTYSBURG
(Photo by author)

GENERAL WADSWORTH'S
MONUMENT AT WILDERNESS
(Photo by the author)

GENERAL
WADSWORTH'S SABER
(Photo by Ronald Pretzer)

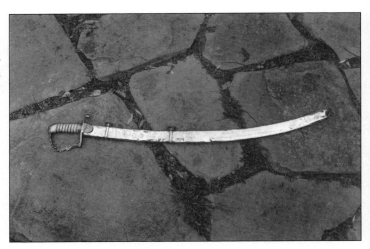

GENERAL ORDERS 197,
MAY 12, 1864, NAMING OF
FORT WADSWORTH IN
SOUTH DAKOTA
(Courtesy Dean North)

GENERAL ORDERS,
No. 197.

WAR DEPARTMENT,
ADJUTANT GENERAL'S OFFICE.
Washington, May 12, 1864.

The new posts recently established in the Department of the Northwest will be named as follows:

The post on James river .... FORT WADSWORTH.
The post at Devil's Lake .... FORT HAYS.
The post on the Upper Missouri .... FORT RICE.
The post on the Yellowstone river .... FORT STEVENSON.

BY ORDER OF THE SECRETARY OF WAR:

E. D. TOWNSEND,
Assistant Adjutant General.

OFFICIAL:

Assistant Adjutant General.

suffered heavily with 67 killed, 210 wounded, and 86 missing, out of 496 engaged, a casualty rate of 73 percent. The 147th New York had suffered even more, having lost 78 percent of its men, mostly defending Hall's battery in the morning. The 2nd Wisconsin reported the same percentage loss (233 out of 302 engaged that day, leaving for duty only 69 officers and men), but this cannot be substantiated. Lieutenant Colonel Dawes's official report lists 29 killed (two officers), 111 wounded (five officers), and 24 missing from the 6th Wisconsin.[31]

Both sides had paid a heavy price (an estimated 4,800 Confederate casualties versus approximately 5,900 Union) for the little piece of land on which this almost accidental engagement occurred that July 1.[32]

✦　　✦　　✦

Though he did not escape criticism, especially from Wainwright, the corps artillery commander with whom Wadsworth tangled again before leaving the battlefield, Wadsworth had passed his first real test as a division commander. His acknowledgment that he did not know strategy is only partly correct. Moreover, without an overall plan at Gettysburg, with the Army of the Potomac commander at a distance, and without the trusted Reynolds, for much of the battle Wadsworth had to rely on his generally untested judgment. He not only directed his small division to counter repeated Confederate assaults with some success, particularly on the south side of the Chambersburg Pike, but he allowed his trusted subcommanders necessary discretion. He had confidence in them and their troops, and they reciprocated.[33]

Wadsworth's appropriation of troops can be (and was) criticized, but he would not be the first commander to do so, nor the last. His altercations with artillerymen, particularly Wainwright, also led to criticism, but, again, such incidents were not unknown. Two days hence Major General Winfield Scott Hancock would override Army of the Potomac artillery commander Henry Hunt to protect his infantrymen. In fact, the struggle over the respective roles of the artillery and infantry would continue throughout much of the war.

Wadsworth certainly demonstrated the fearlessness that had characterized him, and he had coordinated his troops, under difficult conditions, about as well as anyone could have done so. He had been thrust into an exceedingly perilous position, leading two small brigades (the first Union infantry to reach the field) into battle against superior numbers without a plan—and without time even to load weapons. He had been, as more than one officer reported, everywhere on the field. As Doubleday reported, "General Wadsworth's division opened the combat, and defended the center of the line to the very last." Also Wadsworth's men were called on to cover the retreat from Seminary Ridge "by successive *echelons* of resistance." In between Howard asked Wadsworth to "hold out, if possible, awhile [*sic*] longer." Initially his command had been successful, including having driven back Archer's Brigade and having captured a number of prisoners, Archer among them. Similarly, north of the pike, Wadsworth's men had put Davis's Brigade out of action for the rest of the three-day battle.

As Gettysburg historian Edwin Coddington recognized, to achieve success the intricate Union movements required "highly trained soldiers and quick-thinking officers." Conspicuous among them was Wadsworth, who led "one of the crack divisions of the Army of the Potomac." Except for his reckless stand with Stevens's battery toward the end of the afternoon, he had acted like a division commander, and he and his men had helped stall the Confederate attack. "Wadsworth made up in courage," Coddington claimed, "what he lacked in skill, and he fought to the bitter end." Without doubt, this would be the high-water mark of Brigadier General James Samuel Wadsworth's military career.[34]

Chapter 17

"STILL FULL OF FIGHT"

Gettysburg, July 2 and 3

Late afternoon on that historic July 1, General Wadsworth despaired over the losses: "The severity of the contest during the day," he claimed, "will be indicated by the painful fact that at least half of the officers and men who went into the engagement were killed or wounded." The 1st Brigade commander, General Solomon Meredith, and the 24th Michigan's Colonel Morrow had been wounded. In fact, II Corps chief of staff Brigadier General Francis Walker considered the I and XI Corps virtually out of combat after their heroic stand earlier in the day. Confusion reigned. A relatively minor, but unsettling, example was 3rd Division commander General Rowley's aberrant behavior, allegedly due to drunkenness. During the withdrawal from Seminary Ridge Rowley gave "General Wadsworth's troops contradictory orders, calling them cowards," and raving. General Wadsworth's aide, Lieutenant Clayton Rogers, ordered the drunken brigadier's arrest, which was accomplished with the assistance of Lieutenant Colonel Dawes of the 6th Wisconsin. Fragments of units straggled through the town. One of the last Iron Brigade regiments to leave the field, the 6th Wisconsin, ran "full speed" and single-file through the village teeming with soldiers and wagons and up the slope of Cemetery Hill to find the colors of "a well-ordered line of men in blue" by a stone wall.[1]

Once there, the exhausted Badgers dropped to the ground among the gravestones with others from Wadsworth's division. Despite the terrible losses, they could console themselves that, as General Wadsworth later testified, "We who were engaged in that day's fight claim the credit of having held the enemy in check until General Meade concentrated his forces at Gettysburg." Meade agreed that the I Corps had maintained "its position with such tenacity as to inflict greater loss than it sustained. This, too, to its honor be it said, it managed to do notwithstanding the untimely death of REYNOLDS."[2]

The one-armed XI Corps commander, O. O. Howard, must be credited with posting the 73rd Ohio and 17th Connecticut and preparing a stand on Cemetery Hill even before the wild retreat from Seminary Ridge. His preparations included securing the Baltimore Pike, between the hill and town. Almost simultaneously he ordered General Doubleday to re-form the I Corps. Initially the corps took a position on the west side of Cemetery Hill, with the XI Corps to its right. Later Doubleday directed General Wadsworth to re-form his division, now numbering scarcely two regulation regiments, in a hollow east of the cemetery. The 147th New York counted only 79 on Culp's Hill, "a loss of 301 out of 380," while only 45 members of the 2nd Wisconsin, now commanded by Captain George H. Otis, answered roll call that night. The 24th Michigan could muster barely 27 officers and men. The only consolation, according to Wadsworth, was that "we punished the enemy so severely . . . that they were in no condition to continue the attack after we had retired to Cemetery Hill."[3]

The same confusion found among the infantry characterized the artillery, forcing Colonel Wainwright, the I Corps artillery chief, to sort out his batteries from those of the XI Corps. With an hour of daylight remaining, he had formed thirteen rifles and ten Napoleons (all but four from his own corps) on East Cemetery Hill. The guns faced northeast toward the advancing troops of General Early. Significantly the elitist artillery chief directed his officers "not to take orders from any man with a star on his shoulders who might choose to give them." There can be no doubt that he was referring to division commander Wadsworth, who had "borrowed" two sections of Calef's battery earlier in the day. Wadsworth's reaction, or even if he was aware of Wainwright's instructions, is unrecorded.[4]

It was an especially difficult time for the Army of the Potomac. General Howard later confessed that with his crippled army it was "impossible . . . to withstand Lee." But, some time after 4:30 P.M., Howard no longer bore responsibility for the wing that he inherited after Reynolds's death. As indicated, Meade had ordered Major General Winfield Scott Hancock, II Corps commander, to assume overall command of the troops on the field, replacing Howard, who outranked him. When "Hancock the Superb" arrived at Howard's headquarters, he assumed command and sent General Wadsworth and his troops back to Cemetery Hill.[5]

General Hancock quickly sized up the desperate situation. As he saw it, the XI Corps "was entirely unreliable and quite unmanageable," Howard was despondent, and Robinson's division of the I Corps was out of ammunition. On the other hand, Wadsworth "was still full of fight." Hancock considered the long ridge running south from Cemetery Hill to be the key to the Union defense, but he had to protect the Union right, which extended from Cemetery Ridge and curved around to the northeast, past East Cemetery Hill. Thus, he ordered Captain Stevens's 5th Maine Battery, with its six Napoleons, to climb Cemetery Hill and to occupy a knoll just east of the Baltimore Pike, facing north. However, this position exposed the battery's right to an attack from the east from Culp's Hill, so Hancock directed Doubleday to post a regiment to Stevens's right. After a brief verbal skirmish between Hancock and Doubleday, Wadsworth was ordered to shift the battered Iron Brigade. Now commanded by Colonel William Robinson of the 7th Wisconsin, the brigade was posted near the neck of Culp's Hill and was extended easterly and southward along the crest.[6]

Culp's Hill, some 700 yards southeast of Cemetery Hill, flanks Cemetery Ridge. It rises about 140 feet above the surrounding valley floor and offered the occupying troops a commanding position. Referred to by Confederates as a mountain, its highest point on the north gradually slopes southwest toward Rock Creek Hill. Heavily wooded, but free of undergrowth, it ascends to a rocky prominence, making it difficult for an attacking force to climb. In a postwar account Meade recalled the significance of Culp's Hill at this time:

> In my judgment, in the condition of the Eleventh and First corps, with their *morale* affected by their withdrawal to Cemetery Ridge, with the loss of over half their numbers in killed, wounded, and missing, . . . occupation of Culp's Hill [by the 20,000-man corps of Confederate General Ewell], with batteries commanding the whole of Cemetery Ridge, would have produced the evacuation of that ridge and the withdrawal of the troops there by the Baltimore Pike and Taneytown and Emmitsburg roads.[7]

Once Wadsworth had ordered the 6th Wisconsin to rejoin its weakened brigade and to entrench, he located his headquarters near the right gun of Stevens's battery. Of immediate importance to him was the appearance of the 7th Indiana, one of Cutler's regiments, commanded by Colonel Ira G. Grover. The regiment, which had been left behind to guard the corps' wagons, had been ordered forward by Grover, who took the initiative when he heard firing ahead. The Hoosiers arrived at Cemetery Ridge shortly before 5:00 P.M. Their reaction on seeing Wadsworth, while characteristic of the time, is worth quoting in full:

> Reaching there, we found General Wadsworth sitting on a stone fence by the roadside, his head bowed in grief, the most dejected woe-begone person one would likely find on a world-around voyage—a live picture of Despair: General Reynolds killed, the first corps decimated a full half, and its first division almost wiped out of existence. The General greeted us warmly, adding, "I am glad you were not with us this afternoon"; and, in response to General Cutler's claim that "if the Seventh had been with us we could have held our position," said "Yes, and all would now be dead or prisoners."[8]

Wadsworth promptly deployed the Hoosiers on Culp's Hill on the extreme right of the Union line in a rough, upside down, L-shaped formation. The foot of the L faced north and the leg faced east. Company B of the 7th Indiana was assigned the lonely and dangerous position on the leg. They quickly felled trees and, for the first time, built breastworks, using whatever they could lay their hands on.[9]

With the XI Corps on East Cemetery Hill running southeasterly along Baltimore Pike, the Iron Brigade entrenching to its right, and the III, V, and XII Corps slowly arriving, Meade would make a stand. It must have been particularly daunting for division commander Wadsworth, who had only the Iron Brigade to occupy Culp's Hill. General Cutler's broken brigade was still occupying the temporarily re-formed line on East Cemetery Hill, along with the XI Corps. The weary men hugged the breastworks, exchanged taunts with their Confederate counterparts, and ducked occasional shells cascading off the rocky prominence as dark approached. Then, at sunset an uneasy—and deceiving—quiet prevailed.

Shortly before midnight there was "quite a gathering of officers at the cemetery gate," including Generals Wadsworth, Howard, Schurz, Sickles, and Doubleday, when Meade arrived. Meade promptly reassured Howard that he had performed ably, checked with artillery chief Henry Hunt and topographical engineer Major General Gouverneur K. Warren, and now felt assured of the defensive deployment of the Union troops.[10]

The uneasy silence was broken during the night by a chance encounter between a reconnoitering party from Major General Edward "Allegheny" Johnson's Division of Ewell's Corps and a scouting party from Colonel Grover's 7th Indiana. After a brief skirmish and the capture of some Confederates, Johnson was persuaded that Culp's Hill was too strongly occupied for him to attack it. Thus ended the I Corps' first day at the little college-seminary town in south-central Pennsylvania, but two more bloody days lay ahead.[11]

It would be a long night for Lee, who had to make a critical decision. Among his alternatives were whether to withdraw, prepare a defense for a Federal attack, turn the Union left (which would force the Federals to attack), or renew the assault begun earlier in the day. After conferences with his various commanders, particularly Ewell, Lee decided to direct the main Confederate thrust at the Union left, near the Round Tops. He ordered Ewell, who did not want to give up what he believed to be the advantage of superior numbers and position, to hold in reserve two regiments while Allegheny Johnson attacked the badly outnumbered I Corps division on the hill.[12]

The Union commanders examined their options too; the primary one was where to focus their defense. The Federals had the shorter lines. It was a matter of getting the troops up and deployed on the so-called "fishhook," which curved around from East Cemetery Hill to lower Culp's Hill, the "barb." Holding on to Culp's Hill was vital, for it protected the rear of the Union troops on Cemetery Ridge and Cemetery Hill. As it was on that long night, Culp's Hill, defended by Wadsworth's thin line, was still exposed to attacks by Ewell's Corps from the north and east.

Wadsworth's tired soldiers were rudely awakened at 3:00 A.M. on July 2 by commanders fearful their men would not be ready for an attack by a force equal, if not superior, to their own. Ewell's Corps still threatened the Union right, with General Johnson's three brigades, roughly 6,400 officers and 16 guns, facing Wadsworth's exposed east flank. (The Stonewall Brigade had been sent to deal with Brigadier General David Gregg's cavalry, picketing the Union right.) There Wadsworth's only fresh troops, the 7th Indiana, huddled behind their breastworks.[13]

Sometime around 7:00 A.M., Wadsworth's hungry, anxious defenders on Culp's Hill began seeing reinforcements. The first to arrive was the rest of Cutler's decimated brigade, which had supported the XI Corps on East Cemetery Hill during the night. Wadsworth deployed them immediately. The 76th New York, 56th Pennsylvania, and 95th New York extended the 7th Indiana's line, facing north along the west slope of the ridge of Culp's Hill that had been protected through the long night by the 7th Indiana's Company B. The remnants of the 14th Brooklyn and the 147th New York formed a second-line reserve. General Wadsworth's sadly diminished division was once more united. The other two corps divisions, Robinson's and Rowley's, the latter now commanded by Doubleday, remained attached to the XI Corps at the base of East Cemetery Hill. For all intents and purposes, Wadsworth's division was now the I Corps.

The next reinforcement was the XII Corps, which General Slocum had advanced around 3:40 A.M. Brigadier General George S. Greene's 3rd Brigade, 2nd Division, which had spent the short night just north of Little Round Top on Cemetery Ridge, extended the line formed by Cutler's brigade and faced east. Emulating their compatriots, they began felling trees, piling cordwood to batten their logworks, and strengthening them with dirt on the south slope. They completed their task about 10:00 that morning. By late morning, with five corps in various stages of arriving, posting, and strengthening their lines, the Federals felt more secure. As Wadsworth recalled: "Every man in the army was available . . . concentrated on about three miles square. . . . The position was such that the enemy could not attack on our right and left simultaneously; and that left our right at liberty to re-enforce the left, if necessary, or *vice versa.*"[14]

About noon Wadsworth, enjoying a respite, was visited by George W. New, the 7th Indiana's surgeon, who had taken possession of a small church on Baltimore Pike to treat the wounded. After complimenting New for feeding the wounded, the general confessed that hunger had "compelled him to take some persons milch cow for dinner for himself and Staff." Surprisingly, the battle-scarred, middle-aged commander did not complain of fatigue.[15]

Throughout the long July 2 afternoon on Culp's Hill, observers with field glasses spied large Confederate columns marching toward their right and forming beyond Rock Creek, east of the Baltimore Pike, in preparation for an attack. However, nothing happened until approximately 4:00 P.M. when, from west of Cemetery Hill, "artillery and musketry thundered and crashed together." Then the distinctive Rebel yell rent the air. The immediate assumption of Wadsworth and others of his small force was that a Confederate advance on their position had begun. In fact, it was supposed to have begun even earlier.[16]

General Lee had ordered a simultaneous attack on both Union flanks. He had directed Ewell's Corps to make a diversionary demonstration—unless the opportunity to mount a full attack presented itself—against the Union forces on Culp's Hill, while General Longstreet struck the Union left. For a variety of reasons the movements had been delayed for approximately seven hours and, even when begun, they were not well coordinated. Lee's style was to express his intentions and entrust tactics to his commanders. Unfortunately, here his three corps failed to act in concert. General Hill's performance suffered from an undisclosed illness, General Ewell vacillated, and General Longstreet could be stubborn.[17] The anxious men in "old Daddy" Wadsworth's division soon "became absorbed by the awful combat on our left [rear]," the much-delayed attack by Longstreet's Corps against the Union left flank, the much examined battles at the Peach

Orchard, wheat field, and Little Round Top. Though not directed at Wadsworth's men, the tension increased, for the sounds from the battlefield led them to believe the Confederates were gaining the upper hand. Wadsworth was particularly concerned and asked Colonel Wainwright to direct artillery fire into the woods to the west front. The artillerist remonstrated that he

> could not without endangering our own men. Wadsworth then came over himself, and pointed out the spot where he said the rebs were and where he wanted to fire. I still insisted that it was within our lines, but he said that he had just come from there, and knew exactly where our lines were. I had been over there in the morning and thought differently. But not wishing to be ugly, I had one of "L" Company's guns pointed there, and then insisted on Wadsworth's aiming himself at the point he wanted to hit. So soon as he had seen one shot fired, he galloped off, quite happy. I had that gun fire slowly, watching it myself, for I could not believe I had made so great a mistake in spotting our position on the hill. We had not fired half a dozen shots when a major of the Twelfth Corps came over and said that we were dropping every shot directly into their line, and had already disabled half a dozen men. It was just as I supposed, the rebs were around the corner, where I could not get at them.[18]

There might have been a grim smile of self-satisfaction on the artillerist's face as he proved his antagonist wrong, in what seemed to be his game of one-upmanship. Of course, it is possible that Wainwright's cannoneers had the right deflection, but the wrong elevation. On the other hand, General Wadsworth was not an artillerist. Further, Wainwright was feeling his oats, for throughout the day he had "been allowed to run my own machine."[19]

Still safe behind their breastworks and shaded by oak trees, the men of Wadsworth's division listened to the din of battle raging to their left rear where "twenty or thirty regimental banners" were seen headed toward the Confederate charge. It was a welcome reprieve, allowing them to observe, rather than to exchange, gun fire.[20]

The division's respite came to an end between 7:00 and 8:00 P.M., when the all-too-familiar Rebel yell rose out of the woods to the Union right, followed by the crack of rifles. It was the much-delayed attack by Ewell's Corps, with Early's Division aimed toward Cemetery Hill. Though not in concert, the seventeen-regiment division of rough-hewn, profane Edward Johnson approached from the east. Johnson's attack was directed against General Greene's 3rd Brigade, Geary's division, of the XII Corps. The rest of the corps, Williams's and Geary's divisions, had been ordered to help meet the attacks of Longstreet's and Hill's Corps on the Union left at the Round Tops and the Peach Orchard.

General Greene's lone brigade could not defend against almost six-to-one odds without help. Shortly before 8:00 P.M. he called on Generals Wadsworth and Howard for that help. Though threatened by Early's attack across nearly his entire left front, Wadsworth summoned Dawes's 6th Wisconsin, Colonel Fowler's 14th Brooklyn, and Major Harney's 147th New York, a 355-man con-

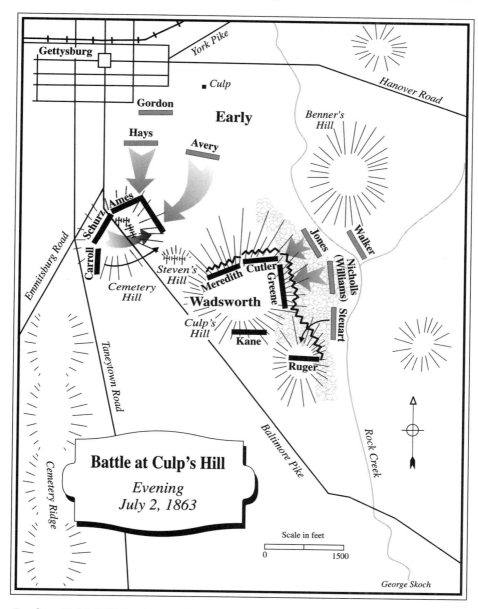

Battle at Culp's Hill (by George Skoch)

tingent, to report to General Greene. XI Corps commander Howard also sent three regiments, approximately 400 officers and men. In turn, Greene directed Wadsworth's three regiments to occupy what were thought to be unoccupied breastworks. Then all hell broke loose.[21]

Adjutant Henry H. Lyman of the 147th New York recalled that

> this night fighting in the dense darkness of the rocky forest was a feature of the
> battle most terrific and appalling. In advancing, no alignment could be main-
> tained; men stumbled and fell over the rocks and over the bodies of the dead and
> wounded; and as the opposing forces closed in and became intermixed, friends
> and foes could only be distinguished by the dancing flames from the muskets.[22]

Before long Wadsworth's whole division was involved, plugging holes in the severely stretched line of Union breastworks that represented the only defense of
Culp's Hill. If they failed, Cemetery Hill, and then Cemetery Ridge, would be
exposed. What had seemed so secure only hours earlier was now imperiled.

Despite the danger, a member of the 7th Indiana recalled that Wadsworth
"rode up in the rear of the [7th], pulled his hat down as if to shelter his face from
the rain of min[ié] balls that were coming in almost a solid sheet." Colonel Kress
was even more explicit, claiming that "in order to encourage the men, amid the
hottest of the firing [Wadsworth] seated himself on a rock immediately in rear of
our front line and above it. Bullets rattled against the rock continually but no inducement or plea from his staff officers could persuade him to quit the place until the enemy ceased the attack."[23]

Just as he had done at First Bull Run, then at Chancellorsville, the civilian general had inspired his men by his bravery, but one has to wonder whether his
recklessness was simply the ingrained impetuousness against which his father
had repeatedly warned him years earlier. Or, as Colonel Kress had observed,
Wadsworth, like many another soldier, ascribed death only to others. In
Wadsworth's case, given his cavalier response to his daughter in which he
sloughed off the danger of standing upright in a boat at Chancellorsville, it may
be that the civilian general felt he was simply demonstrating leadership, thinking
of everything except himself. Likely, we will never know what motivated the
civilian general to exhibit such disregard for his life.[24]

Once more Wadsworth's men had been engaged, particularly the 6th Wisconsin,
14th Brooklyn, and 147th New York, when Johnson's Division advanced. Fortunately for Wadsworth's and Greene's men, the return of the rest of the XII Corps
and darkness helped blunt Johnson's attack, but not before his men occupied the
lower summit. Similarly Wadsworth's troops were spared further harm when the
Federals repulsed the attack by Early's Division at Cemetery Hill.

After the battle Wadsworth not only refrained from singling out any individuals or regiments for fear of doing injustice to others, but he could not even

recall which regiments he had forwarded to Greene's defense. Others from his division, particularly the 6th Wisconsin's Dawes and the 56th Pennsylvania's Colonel Hofmann, were not so reticent. It remains that what was left of Wadsworth's division had again performed well.[25]

Once more quiet prevailed. However, Wadsworth's three regiments continued to support the XII Corps until sometime after sunrise on Friday, July 3, when they were replaced by an equal number of regiments from an independent Maryland brigade.[26]

Around 9:00 P.M., during the lull, Meade had convened a council of war with his corps commanders in the close quarters of the tiny house serving as his headquarters. He posed a series of questions to the assembled generals and over the next two hours received, in turn, their respective views. The upshot was that they were there to stay and defend themselves. Meade speculated that the Confederates would hit the Union center because they had unsuccessfully tried the Union left and right. Fortunately, he guessed right.[27]

First, however, the XII Corps would have to dislodge elements of Johnson's Division that had occupied parts of that corps' line at the bottom of Culp's Hill during the fighting that night. The task, Colonel Kress recalled, would require "very hard fighting." At approximately 4:30 A.M., the XII Corps' artillery opened with a barrage preparatory to the advance by the infantry. But, despite the cannonading, General Johnson's troops held their ground, and even advanced. Wadsworth responded by positioning two XI Corps regiments General Howard had sent over to help clear the trenches on the Union right that had been vacated by the XII Corps earlier. The danger they faced was revealed subsequently by the trees in the area of the Union advance, which bore the scars of rifle and cannon fire.[28]

Then Wadsworth ordered the 14th Brooklyn and the 147th New York to plug a breach immediately to the left of the big rock less than a quarter mile east of the Baltimore Pike. They dug in and resisted repeated assaults by General Johnson's "heavy columns." Shortly the pattern was to fire, race back for more ammunition, and return to the lines. Bodies fell all around them. "Before 10 a.m. of the 3d, every man and officer [of the 147th New York] present had fired 200 rounds and the numerous dead in their front showed with what effect." By 11:00 A.M., however, the firing on the east of Culp's Hill had ceased.[29]

General Johnson's attack, in fact, three attacks, had failed. The Union commanders across the hill, on Cemetery Ridge, were relieved. However, they acknowledged "we felt no apprehension for this part of the line [Culp's and Cemetery Hills], for . . . the 12th Corps, and the 1st Division [Wadsworth's] of the 1st [Corps], could be trusted."[30]

Once more there was quiet along Culp's Hill, and General Wadsworth's further depleted, hungry division rested. The general and his staff circled around a

> cracker-box table, in a clump of trees near our line of trenches, hoping to leisurely partake of a camp meal, when the enemy commenced that terrific cannonade preceeding [*sic*] the grand charge of Picket's [*sic*] Virginia Division. A

dozen shells burst at once in our vicinity, covering our dinner with dirt. There
was a grand rush for our horses, and all joined the General who had gone to the
best point of observation on Culp's Hill.[31]

From their vantage point Wadsworth and his staff then watched what became a
duel between more than 250 opposing guns. It was a "a volcano in eruption,"
according to Confederate colonel E. Porter Alexander, artillery chief for
Longstreet's Corps and one of the key participants. It was the most terrific cannonading the opposing armies had ever experienced. Unfortunately for the
Union troops on Culp's Hill, many of the Confederate guns, overshooting their
mark, landed shells among them.[32]

Some two hours later the Confederate guns stopped firing, and Wadsworth
and his staff caught sight of the mile-long, gray lines crossing the plain in front
of Cemetery Ridge. While General Hunt's guns created gaps in the Confederate
ranks, the Southerners remained aligned and aimed at the Union soldiers
crouched behind the stone fences in front of Cemetery Ridge. "General
Wadsworth could not restrain his desire to be useful," according to Colonel
Kress, and directed Kress to "go to General Meade at top speed, and ask if he did
not want our Division." The Army of the Potomac commander received General
Wadsworth's offer "with evident pleasure," but declined it, claiming "we are all
right."[33] Indeed, they were. "Pickett's Charge" was shattered, with as many as
half of its participants killed, wounded, or missing. Shattered too were Lee's
hopes for a decisive victory on Northern soil.

By 4:30 P.M. on July 3 the battle of Gettysburg had ended, though sporadic
firing would be heard for another twenty-four hours. Men who had lost their rations beating a hasty exit from Seminary Ridge on the first day had received only
"small issues of fresh beef which was eaten without salt," and realized just how
hungry they were. They had to listen to their stomachs growl until 5:00 P.M. on
July 4, when the Confederates had disappeared. Still, General Wadsworth was impressed by the morale of his men: "The slaughter had been terrible; but the spirit
of the troops was unimpaired, and, in my opinion, our troops were in good condition to have taken the offensive, and they would have taken it with alacrity."[34]

"At dark [of the 3rd], when all was once more quiet," recalled Colonel Wainwright, "a great relief seemed to rest on the minds of everyone; a sense, as it were,
that the worst was over. Not a certainty that the fight was done, or even that Lee
might not try it again tonight or tomorrow, but a feeling that he had done his
worst and failed." The weary Federals remained in their lines that night listening
to the moans and cries of the wounded from both sides. Though curious about
the results of their three days of fighting, few dared venture out for fear of becoming the target of any remaining sharpshooters.[35]

Chapter 18

"COULD THE GENERAL INFUSE HIS OWN COURAGE"

In contrast to the preceding three days' awful heat, punctuated by rifle and cannon fire, Saturday July 4 dawned "clear, and the air fresh and exhilarating." Better yet for the Union side, cavalry reported that the Confederates had withdrawn. In midmorning General Wadsworth accompanied Colonels Hofmann and Grover into the village. Wadsworth had ordered Hofmann, commanding his 56th Pennsylvania and Grover's 7th Indiana, to "advance through the town" to recover wounded Union soldiers. The party reached town by way of Baltimore Street to York Street, where they filed through the square, drawing sniper fire, which killed a member of the 7th Indiana. Whether this was enough to persuade General Wadsworth that the fighting was not yet over is unknown. At any rate, after half an hour the two regiments were ordered back to their positions on Culp's Hill.[1]

On the hill, burial parties from the I Corps were interring the dead at "the largest funeral" the Union soldiers had ever witnessed. In front of the 7th Ohio the bodies of 200 Confederates were discovered in "perfect lines of battle," behind rocks and logs and in front of breastworks. Colonel Wainwright claimed that a total of 1,200 bodies lay in the vicinity of Culp's Hill. Many of them, swollen and bloated in the hot July sun, were virtually unrecognizable. Individual attention was given to the Union dead, while the Confederates were placed in long trenches.[2]

It was worse on the battlefields west and north of town, where an estimated 5,000 Confederate dead were buried, twenty or more to a ditch, with barely two feet of earth to cover their mass, unmarked graves. Similarly, near the "angle" on Cemetery Ridge, where the Confederates made their farthest advance, "the dead lay in heaps." Gettysburg residents courageous enough to step outside were appalled by "the sickening, overpowerful, awful stench." It seemed to one resident that "every breath we draw is made ugly by the stench."[3]

From another time and another war, a combat veteran described soldiers in combat: "the inevitability of it takes over. . . . They immediately become callused to the smell of death, the bodies, the destruction, the killing, the danger. Enemy bodies and wounded don't affect them. Their own wounded and the bodies of their dead friends make only a brief impression, and in that impression is a fleeting feeling of triumph or accomplishment that it was not them." Once the battle is over, however, they "begin to think. They remember how their friends were wounded or killed. They remember times when they were inches or seconds from their own death. . . . With these thoughts men become nervous about going back in." Now, with silence descending on them, the men at Gettysburg had time to think about the awful bloodletting. And of their own narrow escapes.[4]

Wadsworth and other officers were ordered to send the list of casualties, naming officers. Official reports listed the casualty total as 23,049 officers and men of the Army of the Potomac: 3,155 killed, 14,529 wounded, 5,365 captured or missing (24 percent of those engaged). With 6,059 casualties, the losses of the I Corps clearly outnumbered those for the other corps engaged. The I Corps lost 25 percent more than the II Corps, which had the next highest losses, and had suffered almost six times the casualties of the XII Corps, which it had supported on July 2 and 3. General Wadsworth's division alone suffered 3,846 casualties, a gut-wrenching rate of 56 percent.[5]

Not only had many of Wadsworth's troops given their lives, but over the three days they had expended 80,000 rounds of rifle ammunition—60,000 Springfield .58 caliber, 4,000 Remington .54 caliber, and 16,000 Enfield .57 caliber—defending themselves. The results showed up in Confederate casualties. Overall, the Army of Northern Virginia suffered approximately the same number of casualties as the Federals, 22,557, with General Henry Heth's Division experiencing 3,348 casualties, or a 45 percent loss. Rodes's Division of Ewell's Corps, against whom Wadsworth's division also was engaged the first day, suffered losses of 3,116 (39 percent) for the three days. Allegheny Johnson's Division, whose attacks Wadsworth's troops had withstood on the second and third days, lost 30 percent, or 1,936 men.[6]

Whatever the benchmark used, the three-day battle in this little Pennsylvania town, the so-called "high water mark of the Confederacy," was a terrible slaughter. It would be refought in postbattle analyses, but the immediate dispute in its aftermath was whether Meade should have taken the offensive on that historic July 4th rather than allow Lee's army to withdraw virtually uncontested. Wadsworth was one who believed that "our troops were in good condition to take the offensive." He suggested that because "General Meade's headquarters were almost in line of battle, and were surrounded by great havoc," the Union commander "did not, perhaps, appreciate fully the completeness of his victory." Wadsworth was "sure [the slaughter of the enemy] was [greater] on the first day; I know we almost annihilated one or two brigades that came against us." Regular army Major General David B. Birney, commander of the 1st Division, III Corps, shared his opinion. So too, it appears, did General Lee, who did not hazard a renewal of the battle, given the strength of the Union position, his reduced supply of ammunition, and the concern for supplies. But Wadsworth and Birney were clearly in the minority.[7]

In time, General Wadsworth's conduct at Gettysburg would also come under scrutiny, but among his admirers was Major General Winfield Scott Hancock. In a postwar letter to Gettysburg historian John Bachelder, General Hancock wrote that in a proposed engraving "you must fit [in] all the *important* characters." Hancock identified only two division commanders: Brigadier General Alexander Hays, a West Point classmate of Hancock whose II Corps division vigorously defended Cemetery Ridge on July 3, and General Wadsworth. (Ironically, their fates would be linked again at the battle of the Wilderness less than a year later.) Meade too praised Wadsworth's conduct, which William Doster, Wadsworth's provost marshal in Washington, brought to Wadsworth's attention shortly after Gettysburg. But according to Doster, "he had never read it,—so careless was he of fame."[8]

On Sunday, July 5, the Federal pursuit of the Army of Northern Virginia began slowly. The I Corps was the last to move. The 7th Indiana's historian, contradicting Wadsworth's assessment, believed the corps "had been rendered ineffective for active service, by reason of its first day's work [losses sustained on July 1]." Before they could go far, however, they needed shoes. Unfortunately, the few available were at Westminster, Maryland, almost thirty miles southeast of the route they were taking. Characteristically, General Wadsworth once again "requisitioned" shoes:

> [W]hile passing through Maryland General Wadsworth espied a well appearing citizen standing by the roadside, looking upon the passing lines. Riding up to him this brief colloquy ensued: General—You live here? Citizen—Yes sir. General—Own this farm? Citizen—Yes sir. General—Take off your shoes and give them to that bare-footed man. Citizen did as ordered, but his demeanor betrayed him.[9]

The I Corps' route down the Emmitsburg Road was decided by Meade's need to cover Washington from an attack by the retreating Confederates and to shorten his supply line. Because the I Corps was detailed to bury the dead, it was slow to begin the march and made it barely south of Round Top that day. Then came a rapid, tiring march south to Emmitsburg and thence west through Middletown, covering over thirty-five miles in three days, despite heavy downpours, darkness, and having to clamber over rocky peaks. Wadsworth's men, subsisting solely on coffee and hardtack, finally stopped long enough to dig in at Turner's Gap in South Mountain, where the Iron Brigade had earned its sobriquet.[10]

Not even the frantic pace to Gettysburg matched this hike. Yet, like Wadsworth, many shared the itch of Rochesterian Lieutenant George Breck, of Reynolds battery, to catch up with the Confederates before they escaped back into Virginia and to "crush this horrid rebellion." And they picked up rumors that General Meade was being removed.[11]

On July 12, the division's march (in new shoes and socks, finally issued on the 9th) took them cross-country to Funkstown, near Antietam Creek, where nine months earlier the landscape had turned red with blood. Once more they entrenched in a rain that offered relief from the heat that had drained their energy—and behind their formidable entrenchments they waited and wondered.

What they did not know was that their path was taking them directly toward Williamsport, Maryland, and Lee's retreating army, stalled there by the rising waters of the Potomac River. Would a battle ensue? Was this the moment that army commander Meade had sought? This was the question uppermost in the minds not only of the men who had to do the fighting, but also their leaders.

Among those mulling their fate was I Corps' artillery chief Colonel Charles Wainwright. He "fully expected that we should have a fight this morning [July 13], but the whole day has passed without one."[12]

The question of whether to attack Lee's Army of Northern Virginia arose in no little part from Lincoln's prodding by way of General Halleck. With Lee trapped by the swollen Potomac, this seemed to be the moment the anxious president had long awaited. Meade too seemed to want to attack. But to do so he needed to concentrate his moving forces, which eventually he succeeded in doing near the turnpike leading from Sharpsburg to Hagerstown. His right, the XI Corps, lay nearest Hagerstown, while the left, the XII Corps, was near Jones' Crossroads. Barely six miles separated the Federals and the Confederates, the latter with their backs to the Potomac, which II Corps staff officer Frank Haskell recalled "was boiling and swift, and deep, a magnificent place to have drowned all this Rebel crew."[13]

"It was my desire to attack," Meade claimed, "[but] knowing that if I were defeated the whole question would be reversed, the road to Washington and to the north open, and all the fruits of my victory at Gettysburg dissipated I did not feel that I would be right in assuming the responsibility of blindly attacking the enemy." He was all too aware that his corps commanders, whom he had led for only twelve days, would have "to execute this duty." Therefore, according to Wadsworth's recollection, between 8:00 and 9:00 P.M. on Sunday, July 12, General Meade held a council of war. Present were acting I Corps commander Wadsworth, in place of the ailing General Newton (replacing the deceased Reynolds); Brigadier General William Hays, a West Point classmate of General Ewell, substituting for the wounded Hancock; and Major General William H. French, succeeding amputee General Sickles as III Corps commander. Generals Sykes, Sedgwick, and Howard represented the V, VI, and XI Corps, respectively. The final attendee was General Pleasonton, commanding the Cavalry Corps.[14]

General Meade told his assembled commanders that he lacked "knowledge of the ground," so he could not indicate "any precise point of attack . . . [and] would not do it [attack] unless it met their approval." Only three of the eight favored an attack: Generals Wadsworth, Howard, and Pleasonton. But their opinions were discounted, according to Lieutenant Haskell, Gibbon's aide-de-camp: Wadsworth "only temporarily represented the 1st Corps . . . ; Pleasonton, with his horses, would have been a spectator only; and Howard, with the '*Brilliant 11th Corps,*' would have been trusted no where, but a safe distance from the enemy." Haskell was quick to clarify that it was not Howard himself, "a brave and good man," but his troops who were suspect. Wadsworth tersely recalled that the other corps commanders were "decidedly against the attack." Meade "yielded," but ordered an examination of the Confederate position.[15]

Wadsworth returned to corps headquarters talking "very freely on the subject, and loudly against the decision." His aide, Major Clinton H. Meneely, who had waited "in a hard rain on that dismal night to guide General Wadsworth back to our head-quarters," was particularly struck by his superior's mood. "I do not think that I ever heard any person in high position express so much regret at a positive mistake [such] as was made by the meeting and where different action had such splendid promise of success." Noah Brooks, *Sacramento Union* correspondent and Lincoln friend from their Illinois days, recalled that two days later Wadsworth "almost shed tears while he talked to us about the escape of the rebel army." Even the hypercritical Wainwright had to admire "the old man's earnestness." Indeed, Wainwright wrote in his diary: "Could the General infuse his own courage and spirit of fight into each of the men, it would be well enough to drive ahead without taking anything into consideration. But there are very, very few, among officers or men, who have it." Yet Wainwright himself demurred. It was alright for Wadsworth and "did it concern no life but his own, it would be grand. *His only idea seems to be that war means to fight*" [italics added].16

The intrepid general must have conveyed this attitude at the meeting with those regulars who advised against an attack. He was unimpressed by the fact that four of them "were the ranking officers of the army" and boldly asked their reasoning. He recalled that General Sedgwick rather generally stated that he did not want to "jeopard [*sic*] all he had gained by another battle at this time," while Generals Sykes and French feared that a loss would open Washington to attack. Wadsworth countered that the line of breastworks along Antietam Creek and South Mountain offered sufficient defense if an assault on Lee's forces were repulsed.17

The whole argument became moot by July 14, when Meade discovered that Lee's army had escaped across the now-subsided Potomac by fording it at Williamsport or by marching on the rapidly built pontoon bridge at Falling Waters. Meade's belated pursuit resulted only in the capture of some guns, small arms, and probably fewer than 1,000 men. The Gettysburg campaign was over, except for reports and the congressional hearings brought on by disputes between participants and their supporters and detractors.18

At first glance Wadsworth's behavior subsequent to Gettysburg might seem hypocritical. Only eleven days earlier, at Culp's Hill, when counting casualties he was described as "woebegone." Here, countering senior officers, West Pointers, he pressed for an attack with barely a brigade. How could he even suggest the sacrifice of more men of whom he seemed so solicitous, commandeering not only shoes, but an artillery battery, to assure their safety and welfare? Because Wadsworth left no contemporary paper trail, we can only speculate. Certainly Colonel Wainwright, no friend of Wadsworth's, gives a clue: "His only idea seems to be that war means to fight."

On the other hand, his postbattle testimony before the Joint Committee on the Conduct of the War reveals some of his thinking. This was his second appearance before the politically charged, bicameral committee, which sought to fight the war in the halls of Congress. Earlier the committee had questioned Wadsworth about McDowell's conduct after First Bull Run. This time the focus was General Meade's post-Gettysburg conduct. Wadsworth asserted, as he had to those senior officers earlier, that "I did not believe that the enemy had ever come there [Williamsport] to fight a battle; that so good an officer as General Lee never would take a position with his back on the river to fight a battle." Wadsworth's conviction had increased since then, because "most of the officers I have met think it [an attack] should have been made." Consistent with his argument at Meade's war council, he testified that he doubted that Washington and Baltimore would have been jeopardized. Rather, he believed that "the enemy were demoralized by their retreat, and were short of ammunition." He was convinced of the latter from the fact that the Confederates were "using it [ammunition] so profusely there [at Gettysburg], that they had staked everything upon that battle. The whole army of the enemy was so handled as to show that they staked everything on that struggle."[19]

The general disclaimed any inside information into Lee's or Meade's plans by virtue of "his position in the army." Instead, he explained that he based his opinions on the fact that General Ewell's Corps had made three or four assaults on the morning of the third day and had been "repulsed with terrible slaughter; the ground was covered with their dead." In fact, he was "satisfied" that the Confederate force was spent "when they did not renew the attack on the morning of July 4. Had they intended to renew the attack, they would certainly have done it by daylight that morning. They were short of provisions, had no chance of getting up reinforcements, and had nothing to gain by delay [that is, not attacking again], and we had everything."[20]

But General Wadsworth clearly was in the minority. General Meade himself later testified that his subsequent examination of the defensive position of the Army of Northern Virginia after it had crossed the Potomac convinced him that an attack would "have resulted disastrously to our arms." Similarly, though admiring "the old man's [Wadsworth's] earnestness," diarist Wainwright offered the "opinion . . . that we could not carry it [the Confederate position]."[21]

Scarcely two days after Lee successfully crossed the Potomac, a fuming Wadsworth had tendered his resignation and was in Washington. At late afternoon tea he encountered Lincoln's secretary, John Hay, and others. When asked by one of the attendees why Lee had escaped, Hay recalled in his diary that Wadsworth replied "rather gruffly," "'because nobody stopped him.'"

Then, according to Hay's diary, the following conversation occurred, with Wadsworth the source:

> On the question of fight or no fight, the weight of authority [Meade's council of war] was against fighting. French, Sedgwick, Slocum, and Sykes strenuously opposed a fight. Meade was in favor of it, so was Warren, who did most of the talking on that side, & Pleasonton was very eager for it, as also was Wadsworth himself. The non-fighters thought, or seemed to think, that if we did not attack, the enemy would, & even Meade thought he was in for action, had no idea that the enemy intended to get away at once. Howard had little to say on the subject.
>
> Meade was in favor of attacking in three columns of 20,000 men each. Wadsworth was in favor of doing as Stonewall Jackson did at Chancellorsville,

double up the left & drive them down on Williamsport. . . . Wadsworth said to [Brigadier General David] Hunter, who sat beside him: "General, there are a good many officers of the regular army who have not yet entirely lost the West Point [idea] of Southern superiority. That sometimes accounts for an otherwise unaccountable slowness of attack."[22]

Later the exasperated Wadsworth made essentially the same argument to Navy Secretary Gideon Welles, upon whom he had called, adding that "Meade hesitated and delayed till too late. Want of decision and self-reliance in an emergency had cost him and the country dear, for had he fallen upon Lee it could hardly have been otherwise than the capture of most of the Rebel army."[23]

However, Wadsworth's resignation letter was much more restrained:

> I beg leave respectfully to state that in consequence of the considerable reduction of the numerical strength of the army & the simultaneous increase of general officers, it appears to me that I may now leave the service without detriment to it.
>
> In the 1st Corps, for instance, in which I have the honor to serve there are about nine thousand muskets [men] (the terms of service of several Regts have expired) and eleven general officers [here?] for duty.
>
> Under these circumstances, I am constrained to think that by continuing in the service I become a burthen rather than an aid to it and I accordingly respectfully tender my resignation of the commission which [I] hold, and ask the early action of the appointment thereupon.[24]

General Newton, commanding the I Corps, approved and forwarded the request to Meade the same day; Meade promptly forwarded it to Secretary of War Edwin Stanton. Meade added that he took "pleasure in bearing testimony to the zeal and efficiency with which he [Wadsworth] has at all times discharged the duties of his office," and expressed regret at losing "his presence and services."[25]

The troops Wadsworth had led also expressed their regret. "No better or more patriotic man ever shouldered a musket or carried a sword," wrote the 76th New York's regimental historian, who recalled his division commander's departure. "On leaving he shook the hand of each officer and man in the Seventy-sixth, as though they were brothers." Perhaps the fact that he could shake each hand (because of the greatly reduced numbers) reaffirmed his resolve to have the regiment sent on detached service to recruit. "I cannot bear to see the small remnant of the brave old Regiment put up to be shot any more," the regimental historian heard Wadsworth to say.[26]

It is difficult to assess Wadsworth's motives. It could be argued (wrongly) that he did not have the stomach for war and killing. Also he could be accused of backstabbing. The timing of his resignation strongly suggests a lack of confidence in Meade. Or it may also be that he could have more influence over the direction of the war if freed from command responsibility. Clearly, his highly vocal criticism of Meade's actions played into the hands of the Lincoln administration, which had already indicated dissatisfaction with Meade's failure to engage Lee before he escaped across the Potomac.

On the other hand, like his father, he tended to act on principle. It would be unseemly to criticize Meade while continuing to serve under him. Moreover, though Wadsworth could be disingenuous at times, the rationale he offered in his resignation letter is supported by a private conversation he had with his former provost marshal, William Doster. Doster recalled that Wadsworth believed "the tide had now turned in our favor." The need now was for more privates, not more officers, Wadsworth had told Doster. Officers who assumed "the duties of citizenship at home" should be praised, not criticized. And it is possible that Wadsworth was simply worn out, like his middle son, Craig, who was granted a four-day leave about the same time.[27]

Also there is an unsubstantiated account that other plans were afoot, namely, that General Wadsworth had been considered to lead Federal troops to put down the draft riots that had just erupted in New York City over the March 3, 1863, Enrollment Act, which asked Northern governors to supply 300,000 militiamen to serve nine months. It is interesting to speculate on whether Wadsworth was ever approached, and if so, what his response would have been. If he had been inclined, it would have been a chance to twist the nose of Peace Democrat Seymour, his successful gubernatorial opponent nine months earlier, as well as to demonstrate his strong principles and patriotism. But it would have meant leading unfamiliar troops in a bloody confrontation with civilians.[28]

Likely, critics might challenge Wadsworth for the timing of his resignation and for returning so quickly to politically charged Washington, where he made his views known. Yet his rationale seems plausible and consistent with his personality. He wasn't going to serve where he was not needed, and the number in his sadly diminished division did not justify the collection of officers then serving. Only this complex man himself could clarify his intentions, and there is no record of his having done so.

Although the general believed himself a civilian once more, he was not. Secretary Stanton refused to accept his resignation "because the Department is unwilling to dispense with the services of an officer so distinguished for patriotism and gallantry as General Wadsworth." Stanton intended to call on Wadsworth again, though there were no immediate plans to do so.

Chapter 19

"TO INSPECT COLORED TROOPS . . . CAMPS, POSTS"

General Wadsworth Tours the Mississippi Valley

While James Samuel Wadsworth, ex-division commander, pondered his post-Gettysburg fate, news filtered back of an equally important battle on the Mississippi River. The western armies under Major General Ulysses S. Grant had won a stunning victory at Vicksburg, Mississippi. It had taken a number of maneuvers, the loss of many lives, and eight and a half months, including a month-and-a-half-long siege, to split the Confederacy.

Reactions to the two Union victories were predictable. Wealthy New York diarist George Templeton Strong enthused that the "[U.S.] Government is strengthened four-fold at home and abroad." The Confederates' chief of ordnance, Josiah Gorgas, anguished that "Yesterday we rode on the pinnacle of success—today absolute ruin seems to be our portion." The immediate consequences of the fall of Vicksburg seemed clear, but the long-run impact was much less certain, and it would involve General Wadsworth.[1]

However, Wadsworth's whereabouts from mid-July to early October are unknown. He could have been in any one of four places: Washington; Geneseo, where the harvest on his farms would be in full swing; New York City in his lower Fifth Avenue town house; or Philadelphia, where his wife's family lived.

That Wadsworth expected no command immediately was suggested by his September 4 recommendation of Lieutenant Colonel John Kress, his faithful aide, to the army ordnance chief. Kress was in Washington examining applicants for commissions in Black regiments then being raised. He hoped for a regular army appointment in the Ordnance Department. He ignored Wadsworth's advice to take an appointment commanding volunteers, including possibly one of those Black regiments, whereby he could rise faster and enjoy a higher postwar regular army rank. Wadsworth even offered to help him, especially if the general should receive another command later. Kress politely demurred: "I replied that if he should be alive I knew he would aid me, and it might be better," but the prophetic Kress "*had grave fear he would not survive, I had seen him take so many unnecessary risks*" [italics added].[2]

The former division commander's repose came to an end on October 9, 1863. By Special Orders No. 452, from Adjutant General Lorenzo Thomas, "Brigadier-General J. S. Wadsworth, U.S. Volunteers, is assigned to special duty under the War Department." Per instructions from Secretary of War Stanton, the first part of his assignment, spelled out that same day, was

> to inspect colored troops that have been raised or are being raised and orga-
> nized in the Mississippi Valley, and also to inspect all camps, posts, plantations,
> towns, cities, and other places whatsoever where colored troops are being raised
> or where there is a colored population from which such troops may be raised.[3]

This assignment came about largely because of the Union victory at Vicksburg.

Less than a month after Vicksburg, President Lincoln asked "Unconditional Surrender" Grant about "raising [100,000] colored troops . . . [and] relieving white troops to serve elsewhere." Lincoln was applying the abolitionist logic that employment of freedmen "works doubly, weakening the enemy and strengthening us." Grant agreed with Lincoln about emancipation and "gave hearty support" to arming Blacks. Lincoln had already sent Adjutant General Thomas to the Mississippi Valley to look into the matter of arming the freedmen.[4]

Mobilization of former slaves was only half of the equation. Lincoln also was becoming increasingly aware of the need to care for the newly freed Blacks in the Mississippi Valley. The task of "constructing free labor upon the ruins of slavery" was particularly vexing. Increasingly slaveholders were abandoning their estates and their slaves in the face of advancing Federal troops. Former slaves had to fend for themselves or seek safety in Federal camps from marauding guerrillas. Federal policy had to be developed quickly. As Ira Berlin et al. noted in their history of emancipation:

> Although united in their determination to free the slaves and transform the
> South, antislavery Northerners did not share a vision of the social order that
> would replace the slaveholders' regime. They agreed that abolishing property
> rights in man and substituting the discipline of voluntary contracts for that of
> the lash were necessary conditions for a free South. But they disagreed about
> whether those steps were sufficient.[5]

The Lincoln administration had been wrestling with the issue since April 1862, when Major General Benjamin Butler occupied New Orleans and the Louisiana parishes from New Orleans to the Gulf of Mexico. The labor of former slaves clearly bolstered the Union war effort there. As noted earlier, the Militia Act of 1862 authorized the mobilization and payment of former slaves: $2 per month in southern Louisiana and $7 per month in the Mississippi Valley. Now, with emancipation, "Putting the freedpeople to work on abandoned plantations promised to solve many of the problems created by fighting a war for both national unity and universal liberty. By providing former slaves with a way to earn their own food, clothing, and shelter, it would reduce federal expenditures for relief."[6]

This was easier said than done. In the Mississippi Valley the Federal government had begun leasing captured and abandoned plantations to Northerners, Unionists, and Southerners who took loyalty oaths with the promise they would hire former slaves. An important goal was to find work for the freedmen to help them become more self-sufficient, like Northern laborers. However, the freed-people on plantations fell prey to different kinds of foes: guerrillas and unscrupulous plantation operators. Confederates responded to Vicksburg by conducting devastating raids on former slaves and reconstructed Southerners who were operating plantations in the Mississippi Valley. These raids, which killed, captured, and re-enslaved former slaves and terrorized the White plantation operators, were creating havoc with the plantation-leasing system. In addition to this quasi-military problem confronting Secretary of War Edwin Stanton, he was receiving complaints and advice from "knowledgeable observers," including Brigadier General John P. Hawkins. Hawkins charged that the leasing system in his command, the District of Northeastern Louisiana, was "a travesty of free labor." Unscrupulous "adventurers," including Northerners, were hiring the former slaves, but, unfortunately, they were paying unspecified sums that Hawkins regarded as only meager and insufficient wages.[7]

Secretary Stanton realized that he needed the advice of someone whose views he could trust. That someone was the general whose resignation he refused to accept, the former Squire of Geneseo. Exactly when Stanton reached this decision is unknown, as is the extent to which he had consulted with Wadsworth before appointing him.

From his posttrip report and subsequent testimony, it is clear that Wadsworth focused largely on the second part of his charge: to examine the "condition of the women, children, infirm, and sick of the colored people." After a personal inspection he was to report directly to Secretary Stanton what in his judgment were the means "best adapted to the protection, maintenance, employment, and comfort of the colored population not organized into troops, and generally to examine into and report upon any subject connected with the proper management and welfare of" that group. This was right up Wadsworth's alley, an opportunity to observe directly the early effects of Lincoln's policies and to express his abolitionist views.[8]

Stanton directed Wadsworth to report to Adjutant General Lorenzo Thomas and to begin his trip at Cairo, Illinois. He was to "proceed thence, if you deem proper, to New Orleans, or in any direction that, in your judgment, will enable you to investigate and report." It was as if Wadsworth had written the instructions himself. He could pretty much go where—and do what—he wanted. The Secretary of War either had complete confidence in the Radical New Yorker or he knew that Wadsworth was not likely to feel constrained by bureaucratic red tape.

Upon his departure from Washington on October 9, General Wadsworth called on a paymaster, identified only as "Rochester," for expense money. When the paymaster handed Wadsworth the money, he informed the general that in New Orleans the latter could obtain additional expense money from "Paymaster Vedder." Wadsworth replied, "No, sir . . . I shall not apply to Major Vedder. While I am in the service I shall be paid only by you." The general's reason was that he wanted an accounting from only one paymaster, so that he would have "an accurate statement of all the money I have received from the United States." Then, after the war he would donate that money to a disabled soldiers' home, claiming that "This is the least invidious way in which I can refuse pay for fighting for my country in her hour of danger."[9]

Wadsworth arrived at Cairo late in the evening on October 18. With him were Captain Timothy E. Ellsworth, his valuable aide-de-camp at Gettysburg, and his youngest son, James Wolcott, who had just turned 17 and was anxious to follow his brothers into the service. From Cairo young "Jimmy" wrote his mother:

> We arrived here safely this morning at two o'clock after a very tedious & dirty journey. We came to this hotel, the St. Charles, & at first could get no rooms, but at last the man concluded to give us a bed. So we went up stairs, & were put in a room with three others (the windows were closed & the air was delightful). Nevertheless, we went to bed. The sheets looked as if an army had slept on them. The windows & the window sills were covered with spots of blood where some poor, tormented fellow creature had waged war against three destroyers of sleep, commonly called mosquitoes. We woke up in the morning dirty & tired. On examining our premises, we found that to six persons there was but one basin & one pitcher, half full of water & no towels. We rang the bell for some. The man brought us some dirty Ohio river water, but said he could not get any towels, the housekeeper being out. What a hotel! the dirtiest & filthiest place I ever was in. The table corresponded with the rest.[10]

The young man was getting a taste of the austere conditions to which his father had become more acclimated over the years. Even the comparative comfort of an inspection tour took some getting used to by young Wadsworth, which might explain why "Jimmy" was permitted (or likely, invited) to accompany his father.

By contrast, in the afternoon of their arrival they paid a visit to Admiral David Dixon Porter, with whom they dined more comfortably, returning late in the evening. The next leg of their trip was a short jaunt downriver on a steamboat to Columbus, Kentucky, where they traveled "into the country to see the prairies." Then it was on to Island No. 10, past Memphis, and then far downstream to Natchez, Mississippi. There, on October 30, Wadsworth and his party met up with Lorenzo Thomas. The adjutant general enthusiastically welcomed Wadsworth, whom he deemed "a competent officer," and sought his judgment regarding regiments to be raised in Texas and Pensacola, Florida. Thomas escorted Wadsworth's party back upriver to Vicksburg and Goodrich's Landing, just above Vicksburg.[11]

Wadsworth's Mississippi Valley tour (by George Skoch)

There was no immediate reaction about their excursions from Inspector Wadsworth, but he may have shared his son's feelings. Jimmy wrote home that he was appalled by the towns, "miserable little holes," they visited:

We have visited 4 or 5 negro colonies. Those at Cairo, Columbus & Island 10 are very comfortable & healthy, but at Memphis & Vicksburgh [*sic*] they are in a deplorable condition. At the last two places they are dying off like sheep owing to bad management. I saw two little children who had died the night before, on account of sheer carelessness on the part of the physician. Father gave it to them strong, & I think they will do better hereafter if talking to them does any good. These colonies are composed of women & children & old & broken down men, all the able bodied men are put into the army. They are meant to be self-supporting institutions, by cutting wood for the government boats & raising vegetables for the market, but they are far from it now.[12]

Jimmy was also appalled by the inflated prices, including "15¢ for an old newspaper," driven up by speculators and others taking advantage of their oligarchic position.

Nor was the young man particularly impressed by the military situation, though this simply may have stemmed from his youthful ignorance. He found Island No. 10's fortifications washing away, but he was impressed by the immensity of those at Vicksburg. Possibly taking a page from his father's book, he had reservations about the discipline shown by western soldiers. Though "a splendid body of men . . . . They never touch their hats, nor even present arms to a general-officer."[13]

General Thomas wanted the inspector to "see everything possible," so Thomas not only accompanied Wadsworth, but put "my little steam-boat at his control." Thomas was concerned that the New Yorker "had not allowed himself more time to look minutely into everything." So he made sure that Wadsworth made sufficient stops, including visits to Natchez, Port Hudson, and Baton Rouge. Having done so, they steamed downriver to New Orleans and "west to Brashea [Brashear] City and Southerly along the banks of the River some Seventy-five miles." Still, the adjutant general regretted that Wadsworth was spending barely a month [traveling over 500 miles on the twisting Mississippi River], when "an inspector could be profitably employed for the next three months." On the other hand, General Wadsworth claimed that he visited "all Military Posts & other places where Colored Troops were stationed & had been, were being or might be raised, all camps or collections of colored Refugees & many plantations on which they were employed, making the inspections required by my orders."[14]

Inspector Wadsworth and his party returned to Washington by way of New York City, where he spent two weeks, arriving in the capital on December 3. Over the next two weeks the general prepared his report to Secretary Stanton, which served as the basis for his later testimony before the Freedman's Commission. He later acknowledged that in that report he may "have deliberately understated the extent of suffering, for fear of putting 'ammunition in the hands of the copperheads.'" And he stressed that it was important to realize that there was real suffering and a high mortality among the freed slaves in the camps and depots under military control. The suffering was the result of the "heartless course pursued by the large Slave holders." They had taken the most able-bodied slaves to

Georgia, Alabama, and Texas and had left only women, children, and the infirm, who were then "exposed to the depredations of Guerrillas & other wandering outcasts." Moreover, "these evils will continue until the people thus gathered together can be removed on to [*sic*] Plantations where they will find comfortable houses, gardens & Employment."15

Wadsworth made a number of recommendations, the three most important of which were: to get the ex-slaves out of the unhealthy depots; to develop a system of leasing "Abandoned Plantations" under Union military protection; and to arm the freedmen to protect themselves and the women, children, and infirm from depredations. In the long run the most efficient way to "elevate" the freed Blacks was "to educate the children, & place arms in the hands of the Adults." So no one would miss the point, he underscored it by adding that supplying arms would infuse "into the freed people a manly self dependence for the maintenance of their rights."16

General Wadsworth foresaw a system of leasing that, once developed, would eventually lead to "peasant cultivation." Lessees would make medical care available to the sick, open schools with reading matter for the children, offer religious instruction, and assure wages sufficient to enable workers to make a decent living and, in time, to own their own small farms. He emphasized that "This Government can not recede from the step which it has taken. To do so would be an act of infamy unparalleled in history." Unfortunately, the key would be the "white population of the Cotton Region." Their land could not be confiscated. Rather, the Southerners would have to sell the land, or the government would have to find "some Northern man who will lease your estate, and take a lease from the Gov't too, which will protect him." He summed up his report on a positive note. If his recommendations were followed, in five years (an extremely rosy prediction) he envisioned a profitable culture, a healthy country, and "an attractive character of the labor." That is, "a cultivation & production which never could have been attained under the old System."17

★　　★　　★

In January 1864, the American Freedmen's Inquiry Commission invited Wadsworth to elaborate on his report. Anticipating postwar reconstruction, in March 1863 Secretary Stanton had empaneled the commission, which included James McKaye, Robert Dale Owen, and Dr. Samuel G. Howe, three men who were well known to favor emancipation. Wadsworth readily admitted to the commissioners that when the war broke out he "was hardly a Republican." In fact, he had believed that "sudden emancipation was impossible," for it would result in "enormous sacrifice of life." He had now come around 180 degrees. He had been persuaded by reflecting on the 80,000 Blacks in his home state, which amply illustrated that "no portion of the population keeps so clear of the poor house & the jail as the blacks." This opinion was reinforced by his observations in Washington as military governor. A look at the statistics regarding Blacks there "would settle the whole question of slavery."18

Wadsworth testified that his report on conditions in the Mississippi lease system was "apologetic." In fact, under government control, the system was "folly." Close to 12,000 unfortunate freed slaves were suffering extensively, and fully a quarter of them were dying each year. The government's first task was to assure the safety of the "colored population." Then the government should begin a system whereby freedmen would learn and be able to bargain with lessees for wages. Unfortunately, now the ex-slaves were paid a subsistence wage by the government, which simply perpetuated their bondage.[19]

The general even suggested a contract with the freed Blacks to lease the land. Lessors would agree to "furnish suitable quarters and subsistence" and pay men $10 per month, women $6. Children between 12 and 16 would earn $2. For extra work they would receive additional pay, but the cost of their clothing was to be deducted from their pay. It was important also to provide rations for children under 12, which would include salt pork, meal, and molasses each week with "perhaps fish or fresh meat once in two weeks." The laborers would pay for their own "medical attendance" at a stipulated price. Wadsworth even prescribed gardens for each family to work, though he left the size of the gardens undetermined. Finally, he would require specific criteria for rating field hands.[20]

Wadsworth acknowledged that there was a "collision" of authority between the War and Treasury Departments, with Treasury responsible for the land and War responsible for the ex-slaves. He favored one authority, with Adjutant General Thomas, "a very thorough and honest" man, in charge, but he would not object to control by a "Bureau of Emancipation." On the other hand, General Wadsworth believed Secretary Chase did not want to relinquish "the great power and patronage it placed in his hands."[21]

A far greater fear for Wadsworth was that the whole enterprise would follow the system General Banks had instituted in Louisiana as commander of the army there. Banks had made the ex-slaves *adscripti glebae,* that is, property that followed the "land when it was legally transferred." Wadsworth argued that Banks's system "retained certain features of the old regime. Plantation laborers continued to be organized into gangs whose composition was determined by the operator of the estate, not by the workers." He protested that General Banks had created "a police system in the country." In fact, Wadsworth had remonstrated with Banks that "You are going to hand over these people to your successors [the reconstructed Southern states]—who will be but half-converted, at the best—not freedmen, but as serfs." He insisted that the freedmen must be permitted to bargain for wages.[22]

A more immediate need, General Wadsworth charged, was to save "these people from perishing." He was more concerned with getting the system working than with who controlled it. In fact, once the system was working, control would pass to the lessees and the freedmen who worked the farms and ultimately would become self-sufficient. His ideal was the land system his father and uncle had worked out over half a century earlier. If he had his way, "I would want no better business than to go back to Livingston Co. [New York], and select twenty young men of character and industry, and go back to Natchez, and put these men on abandoned plantations, and say to them—'I will furnish you with capital, and you must give me one-half the net profits. I will have a bookeeper [*sic*], to see that the accounts are all right, and the cotton must be sent to me to sell.'"23

Whatever was done, Wadsworth argued, it should not be hurried. The "excessive docility" of the Blacks demands "that we must exercise a certain guardianship over them, and suspend reconstruction until we have thoroughly emancipated them, and got the idea of freedom into their heads so that they cannot be reenslaved." Realistically, the New Yorker testified that the issue could be "settled" only when the U.S. Supreme Court recognized "the rights of the blacks."24

✳   ✳   ✳

By his report and testimony the general demonstrated his thoroughgoing abolitionism. When Rice University professor Harold Hyman, a twentieth-century Lincoln scholar, was asked whether Lincoln was a "liberal," Hyman replied, "Yes." Pressed to define liberal, Hyman turned the question around: What would you call a man who would arm Blacks, which would enable them to turn their guns on Whites? James Samuel Wadsworth certainly fit this definition as well. Yet Wadsworth was also employing the common sense for which he was noted by contemporaries. He realized that nothing immediate was going to change attitudes formed over two centuries. It would take the force of arms and the Federal government, including the Supreme Court, to assure the rights of the freed population. Moreover, he recognized that segregation would long remain. When asked by members of the Freedmen's Commission whether he had any doubt that "these two races can live amicably together," the general answered "No." But he attached a prophetic caveat: when "they *have* lived amicably together over a hundred years."25 That is, after freed Blacks and Whites had lived together one hundred years, future relations could be amicable. More important to Wadsworth was the implementation of a system of free labor, a system his father had developed in western New York. The ultimate goal would be free laborers working their own land, based on fair rental terms until they were able to buy the farms. The general had seen it work. The result was independent productive farmers who contributed to the general prosperity through the payment of taxes and assumption of civic projects. Once this happened, there would be no turning back, and the whole country would benefit. It would take patience, careful planning, and monitoring for five years. Again, Wadsworth showed his inveterate optimism. Once the Blacks were truly independent (and could protect themselves), the government would no longer need to provide any guardianship. It is worth noting that Wadsworth was viewing the situation as a Northerner, an abolitionist no less, and ignoring the "system of free labor" that existed for the poor Whites in the South. It would have been difficult for Wadsworth to be so optimistic about the future for freed Blacks if the sharecropping farming system, which trapped many Whites in poverty, were to become the model. How seriously Wadsworth's suggestions were considered is unknown; they had little immediate effect.26

✷   ✷   ✷

A rather curious—and much debated—footnote to history is alleged to have occurred about this time. In a letter purportedly written by President Lincoln to
General Wadsworth, the president laid out his thinking about reconstruction.
Claiming that the general knew his "private inclinations," Lincoln is supposed to
have written that, if the South loyally and cheerfully submitted and he (Lincoln)
granted "a universal amnesty," how could he "avoid exacting in return universal
suffrage [including of freed Blacks], or, at least suffrage on the basis of intelligence and military service." The significance of the letter is that Lincoln purportedly pledged that reconstruction "must rest upon the principle of civil and
political equality." The timing would have been appropriate (that is, after
Wadsworth's report on the conditions of freed Blacks in the Mississippi Valley)
and the statement does seem consistent with Lincoln's public and private statements. However, there is serious doubt about the letter's authenticity.[27]

While Wadsworth was ensconced at Willard's Hotel in the capital, where he
was writing his report, the general's middle son, Captain Craig, contacted him.
A glimpse at the nature of their relationship is offered in a December 4, 1863,
telegram from "Tick," at Culpeper, Virginia, to his father: "I have received three
(3) days leave but will not use it without you [sic] wish particularly to see me."
The father immediately telegraphed Major General Andrew A. Humphreys, who
may have been related to his wife, Mary Craig Wadsworth: "I should be glad to
see my son [undecipherable] for a day or two if not inconsistent with interests of
service." Whether father and son linked up is unknown.[28]

In mid-December, after completing his report, the general requested a leave
of absence, which was granted by the secretary of war "until further orders."
Shortly thereafter Craig too requested a leave. There were at least a couple of
reasons for granting leaves and extensions, though not necessarily to the
Wadsworths. One was that both armies were in winter camp. Another reason
was the need to secure reenlistments. In fact a winter-long, almost total reorganization of the army was necessary. Granting the men their promised furloughs
would aid the recruiting effort. Inducements to reenlist were substantial: credit
for an additional year for men who enlisted for three years but had served only
two, and a $300 bounty from the Federal government plus state and local boun-
ties. General Wadsworth's nemesis, Colonel Wainwright, labeled the bounties
"something enormous," in some cases as much as $1,000 (close to $10,000 in
today's dollars).[29]

What Wadsworth did during his first extended leave since the spring of 1861
is unknown. It is unlikely that he spent much time at his Hartford House and
"Home Farm," for there was generally little activity at this time of the year. Moreover, in the winter its residents tended to vacate the drafty house with its high
ceilings. Philadelphia had been a common destination for the general in earlier
years, though his New York City house seemed to attract him now. Wherever he
was, it appears that the Squire of Geneseo was spared the unusually cold tempera-
tures in Virginia that winter, which plunged to below zero on January 1, 1864.[30]

Nonetheless, he managed to make some needed improvements in the village of Geneseo, which, more than likely, he had his farm manager undertake for him. The January 21, 1864, *Livingston Republican* reported that he opened and enlarged the springs on Temple Hill, near the academy his father had helped found, and built a quarter-mile-long, log water main to Main Street. He also had constructed three reservoirs on Main Street, two on Second Street, and one on Center Street. The cost, which he bore, was approximately $4,000 (greater than $40,000 today).

On January 8, 1864, President Lincoln detailed General Wadsworth to sit on a court of inquiry. Special Orders 13 from the War Department directed him to join Major General David Hunter, Major General George Cadwalader, and Colonel Edmund Shriver, inspector general and recorder. The order required the court to investigate charges brought by Brigadier General Thomas J. Wood against Major Generals Alexander McD. McCook, Thomas L. Crittenden, and James S. Negley, stemming from the battle of Chickamauga. Wood, who claimed he was being made the scapegoat for the disastrous results there, was challenging the after-action reports of Generals McCook, Crittenden, and Negley.[31]

The court convened on January 29, 1864, in the St. Cloud Hotel, Nashville, Tennessee, and spent a long day hearing the testimony. Finally, on February 23, 1864, after the twenty-first session, the court concluded its work. It simply expressed a "marked condemnation" of General Wood for causing "vexatious and unprofitable investigations prejudicial to the service," and for his "coarse and offensive epithets" toward General Negley. While the court was not officially dissolved until April 9, 1864, General Wadsworth was back East and much more active by then.[32]

During the court's sessions General Wadsworth took time out to write his youngest son, with whom he had inspected the Mississippi Valley. It could have been old James writing him almost forty years earlier, even to the closing.[33]

My Dear Son:—

I recd some days since your letter by the way of Nashville. I am very glad to hear that you have made satisfactory arrangement for prosecuting your studies at N. Haven [Yale], and that you have gone at your work with good courage. You will never regret the sacrifices you make now to secure a good education. I have often deeply regretted that my own education was so deficient, especially in the classics. It has been a great barrier to my progress in other studies, especially the natural sciences, which I could not master thoroughly from want of some knowledge of the languages from which the technical terms were derived. I hope you will resolve to stick to it until you master them. Tho' if I get a command I shall keep my promise and take you with me. There is now little or no prospect of this coming to pass. . . .

I hope you will be careful as to what acquaintances you make— & what company you keep. Now is the time for study. The harder you work the sooner it will be over, and the sooner we shall all be together at our dear home, where we have so much to interest and amuse us. If you get into gay company & neglect your studies it will only add a year or two to your exile. . . .

Your Affectionate Father,
Jas S. Wadsworth

"Jimmy" listened to the advice about as well as his father had, and like his father, never completed his undergraduate education. He read only that he might get his chance to serve when his father obtained another command.

Events already transpiring would lead to that command.

Chapter 20

"GENERAL WADSWORTH NOW RETURNED TO ASSUME COMMAND"

While the restless general was bored with his duty on the court of inquiry, there was activity elsewhere. The depleted Union army had experienced limited success filling the ranks through recruitment and conscription. This led to morale problems. Only a small percentage of the veterans were allowed leaves to encourage reenlistments and to recruit. Those left behind grumbled. New arrivals introduced other problems, the most serious of which was desertions.

> At this time the abuses of the conscription system were made manifest to the men at the front by the character of too many men drafted for service or enlisting only for the bounty. The professional bounty-jumper and the kidnapped emigrant and street boy, who were "put through" the enlistment offices in New York and elsewhere, came in large numbers, the professionals with the intention of deserting at the earliest opportunity and repeating the profitable experiment by enlisting for large bounties.[1]

In fact, desertions became such a problem during the winter of 1863–1864 that "scarcely a Friday passed . . . that some of these deserters did not suffer the death penalty." Clearly, the rationale for every corps to provide gallows or firing squads was the need to assure dedicated men ready for the spring campaign. The earlier policy of leniency, tightened by General Hooker the previous January, still generally resulted in deserters being casually restored to duty. The new policy included not only a call for executions, but for placing individuals accused of desertion or absence without leave, for which charges had not already been forwarded, under arrest while continuing to perform regular duties.[2]

No doubt one reason for desertion was the unusually cold weather that forced the men to huddle in their shanties, where fireplaces alternately flared or died out. Cold wind gusts penetrated even their heavy wool overcoats. Irksome too were the all-too-familiar picket and guard duty, during which the Federal troops could occasionally overhear their Confederate counterparts performing similar duty across the Rapidan River, the dividing line between the Army of the Potomac and the Army of Northern Virginia. The Army of the Potomac, approximately 81,000 strong, was tightly concentrated in a small, V-shaped tract of land between the Rapidan and Rappahannock Rivers, roughly midway between Washington and Richmond. The I and III Corps were about two miles in advance of Culpeper Court House, the II Corps was near Stevensburg, the VI Corps rested on the Hazel River, and the V Corps guarded the Orange and Alexandria Railroad from the Rappahannock to Bristoe Station.[3]

The Army of Northern Virginia, relying on the corps of Generals Hill and Ewell, was entrenched on the Rapidan from Barnett's Ford, west of the Orange and Alexandria Railroad, to Morton's Ford, about twenty miles to the northeast. (Longstreet's Corps had been detached to Tennessee.) Pickets occupied the posts nearest the river, with the main body ready to move wherever needed to meet an enemy attack. For the time being General Lee's troops took advantage of the river and zealously guarded the railroad, their supply lifeline to Georgia and the Carolinas.[4]

Miserable weather, including thunderstorms, continued into February, when the primary activity of the winter occurred. Politico and Major General Benjamin Butler proposed a harebrained scheme for his Department of Virginia to capture Richmond. Reluctantly agreed to by the administration, this required the Army of the Potomac's I and II Corps to detain Lee's army by demonstrations across the Rapidan on February 6. While the inept Butler's movement up the peninsula was a failure, the II Corps' troops, primarily Brigadier General Alexander Hays's division, had initial success at Morton's Ford. But a combination of reinforcements and artillery proved how strongly entrenched the Confederates were. Acting corps commander Major General Gouverneur K. Warren, instructed not to bring on a general engagement, soon called off the movement and recrossed the river.[5]

The primary lesson from this relatively minor engagement was that General Lee's army was not going to be dislodged easily. It would take another tack—and, ultimately, another leader. The new tack began on March 4, 1864, when General Meade, responding to the loss of experienced officers, recommended to Secretary of War Stanton the consolidation of the five depleted Army of the Potomac corps into three. Before this change occurred, however, the Union armies would have a new commander. Ulysses S. Grant, the hero of the West, was commissioned Lieutenant General on March 10. Grant's elevation to the rank formerly held only by George Washington and his assumption of command of the armies of the United States signaled a major change. General Halleck would continue as chief of staff, while General Meade, who retained command of the Army of the Potomac, would report to Grant rather than to Halleck. Seemingly this move would serve both Grant and Meade well, for the latter, however prickly and unsure of Grant, was a trustworthy subordinate and would remain with troops he knew and trusted.

General Grant visited the Army of the Potomac's headquarters at Brandy Station on March 10 to confer with its commander and to appraise the situation. Shortly thereafter General Meade ordered "Ladies other than under Special Authority of the War Department or members of the Sanitary Commission or other Charitable Associations" out of camp, which the officers correctly assumed "meant business."[6] Yet nothing happened immediately.

☆   ☆   ☆

Given his early March testimony at the court of inquiry regarding Meade's conduct of the battle of Gettysburg, his access to the inner circles in Washington, and his temperament, Brigadier General James S. Wadsworth undoubtedly was aware of what was happening—and wanted to be a part of it. His cause may have been aided by "Count" Adam Gurowski, who then held a minor State Department post and still enjoyed some influence in Washington. Merciless in his criticism of "knaves or fools or both" in Washington, Gurowski had taken a liking to General Wadsworth and touted his military aggressiveness.[7]

Also the general may have been assisted by the Union League Club of New York, which had been supportive of the Union cause from the outset. The influential league had helped sponsor the enlistment of the 20th U.S. Colored Troops, which received its colors at the League House on Sunday, March 6. Among the 100,000 spectators was General Wadsworth, who watched out the window of the club's office at 823 Broadway and estimated that the troops were "not below the average of new regiments."[8]

Likely, seeing these recruits reminded the old man of the men he had commanded who were now prisoners in Richmond. This led to his visiting Henry Bellows, head of the U.S. Sanitary Commission, at his office and asking Bellows to extend the commission's efforts on behalf of these soldiers. Bellows recalled that Wadsworth "drew his check for $3000 & put it into the hands of our Treasurer, to be expended under my direction, for the relief of these poor fellows." Bellows was unable to comply, because his contacts with Richmond had broken off, so he returned the check to the "disappointed" general.[9]

Possibly the general wrote another check, as well, for Bellows's account is at variance with the testimony of Lieutenant Colonel James M. Sanderson, I Corps' commissary of subsistence, on two counts, the amount of the check and whether it was delivered. To an 1865 committee investigating the conditions suffered by Federal prisoners of war Sanderson claimed full delivery of Northern clothing and supplies to inmates of Richmond prisons. It appears that he was counting General Wadsworth's $2,000 draft on the New York City firm of Fitzhugh & Jenkins, which Sanderson and Major William Russell, Jr., I Corps assistant adjutant general, acknowledged receiving in a December 18, 1863, letter to the firm. It remains that, true to form, Wadsworth even tried to comfort his men from a distance.[10]

On the other hand, things were going well at the Home Farm in Geneseo. In fact, the local newspaper editor reported that Wadsworth's gardener, Mr. Hanby, had brought to the paper's office "good size" strawberries and "a quantity of string beans," both "far ahead of the season."[11] With affairs at home in good hands and with his wife safely ensconced at their brownstone in New York City, the general had no compelling reason not to resume his active military service.

★   ★   ★

Whatever the reason, on March 15, 1864, Special Orders No. 118 from the War Department directed Wadsworth to report to Army of the Potomac commander Meade on or before the 25th. Anticipating his assignment, at 10:05 A.M. on March 20 Wadsworth ordered I Corps Adjutant General Kingsbury to send three saddle horses and an ambulance (a springless, four-wheel wagon to transport wounded, but here to haul Wadsworth's luggage) to him at Falmouth, Virginia, by noon the next day. On the appointed day Brigadier General James S. Wadsworth duly checked in with General Meade and was then ordered to report to Major General Gouverneur K. Warren, commanding the V Corps, who appointed him to command the corps' 4th Division. Wadsworth quickly filled positions on his headquarters staff, but he was minus his trusted aide-de-camp, Lieutenant Colonel John Kress. The general's request of Kress was denied because he was needed by Major General Benjamin Butler.[12]

Taking up the reins, General Wadsworth scheduled a division review by Lieutenant General Grant on March 24, with his men to appear in their greatcoats and light marching order. The review came off, but foul weather forced cancellation of General Grant's appearance. The civilian general was glad to be back, but, like his men, he was unhappy with the consolidation, which reduced the army to three corps, the II, V, and VI.[13]

A member of the old I Corps may well have summed up the feelings of his comrades: "It is no more; the deed is done; the fiat has gone forth, and the First Army Corps has ceased to exist." Yet the men were urged to remember their duty to the Union. "Let every man who belonged to the old First Corps register a vow to faithfully perform his duty in the Fifth. Let it never be said that the men who have made their names glorious with Doubleday and Wadsworth, Meredith and Robinson, turned their backs to their country's foe, and stained their fair name."[14]

These sentiments were particularly pronounced among those who had worn the red sphere of Wadsworth's 1st Division of the I Corps. They had been ordered to turn in their old corps flags to the quartermaster, a particularly sad and poignant symbol of the change. General Humphreys, now General Meade's chief of staff, was particularly frank about the morale problem: "The history and associations of these organizations were different, and when they were merged in other organizations their identity was lost and their pride and *esprit de corps* wounded." The 76th New York's historian recalled that long after Gettysburg, when members of the regiment were asked to what corps they belonged, they proudly responded "To the old First." Likely, because of this practice and to counter discontent, the veterans were permitted to retain their old division and corps badge.[15]

The good news was that "Old Daddy" Wadsworth was back. In fact, the quartermaster of the 76th New York professed that the "heroic and patriotic" general's return helped greatly to compensate for losing their I Corps designation. "His disinterested patriotism in leaving his large and lucrative business to fight for principle without pay; his gallant conduct in crossing the river at Fredericksburg, in the face of the enemy; his kind care of his troops, all tended to give him a firm lodgment in the heart of each man in his command." Civil War scholar Ezra Warner claimed that Wadsworth's appointment was a "tribute to his soldierly qualities considering the number of brigade and division commanders rendered supernumerary by the reorganization of the army."[16]

Brigadier General James Samuel Wadsworth now commanded three brigades in the newly designated 4th Division. The 1st Brigade, the old Iron Brigade (7th and 19th Indiana, 2nd, 6th, and 7th Wisconsin, 24th Michigan), plus the 1st New York Battalion Sharpshooters would remain under the command of Brigadier General Lysander Cutler, though this reduced him from division command. The 2nd Brigade (76th, 95th, and 147th New York, 14th Brooklyn, and 56th Pennsylvania) would continue to be commanded by Brigadier General James C. Rice, while the 3rd Brigade (121st, 142nd, 143rd, 149th, and 150th Pennsylvania) was led by Colonel Roy Stone. Rice, originally from Massachusetts and an early enlistee, had advanced from first lieutenant of the 39th New York to colonel of the 44th New York, and then was promoted to his current rank shortly after Gettysburg. The 28-year-old Stone had helped form the 13th Pennsylvania of which he was major. Then, on August 30, 1862, he became colonel of the 149th Pennsylvania. These officers had all shown the necessary leadership at Gettysburg.

On March 28 General Wadsworth announced another division review, this one to take place on the 30th or 31st if the "weather was favorable." Unfortunately, a torrential rain fell, which penetrated the soldiers' tents and wool blankets and forced General Grant and other notables to ride the length of the lines rather than have the men march in review. The new commander's presence drew expected responses from some of Wadsworth's men: "The old hero looks better than I supposed," "His pictures belie him," "Where the divil is his pipe?"[17]

In fact, Grant was a "mystery" to the soldiers he now commanded, even to those who viewed him up close, such as staff officer Morris Schaff. Schaff had expected "the chieftain-type, surveying the world with dominant, inveterate eyes and a certain detached military loftiness." Instead, he discovered "a medium-sized, mild, unobtrusive, inconspicuously dressed, modest and naturally silent man." Nor did his "low, gently vibrant voice and steady, thoughtful, softly blue eyes" give any hint of the reason for his successes at Fort Donelson, Vicksburg, and Missionary Ridge. Rather, his natural reticence was magnified by his reclusiveness. By contrast, Colonel Theodore Lyman, one of General Meade's staff, saw another Grant, one who "habitually wears an expression as if he had determined to drive his head through a brick wall, and was about to do it."[18]

Two days later, just as the men began to dry out, a wet snow fell. Timber that had seemed so plentiful earlier was now reduced to stumps, which the frustrated soldiers tried to chop for wood.

Complaints also accompanied the easily recognized signs of preparation for a spring campaign. Despite the foul weather, buglers now sounded reveille at 5:30 A.M. (not 7:00, as before). Their call was preceded by the drummers' call five minutes earlier. Other signs of impending action were General Wadsworth's orders to brigade commanders to report by regiment the number of officers and men present and to assure that noncommissioned officers "habitualy [*sic*] wear the insignia of their rank, more especially Chevrons, and if not, [explain] why not." He also reported to the adjutant general the names of those added to his staff, which included Captain Craig Wadsworth as additional aide-de-camp, who was scheduled to report on April 7.[19]

There is no evidence that Craig served as his aide, but on April 7 the general dutifully telegraphed his wife that his son "Tick" and he were "quite well." This was a change. Less than a week earlier, responding to a recent letter from his "dear Wife," he had written that "I am quite well, except that I have taken a cold in my right eye & the Dr. forbids writing by candle light. It is not painful, but very weak and somewhat inflamed." He was taking quinine and reassured Mary Craig that "I can not think it will seriously trouble you."[20]

Nor did the cold in his eye (likely neuralgia) prevent him from taking time to write 23-year-old Jessie Burden, to whom his eldest son, Charles Frederick Wadsworth, five years her senior, had become engaged. She would be a good catch, given the Wadsworth males' penchant for selecting attractive and wealthy mates. Jessie's father, founder of the Burden Iron Works in Troy, New York, had developed horseshoe- and railroad-tie-forming machines. While the general humorously trotted out some of Charlie's faults, he, like his own father, revealed his deep affection for his family.

> I have just recd. a letter from my son informing me that he has offered you his hand and heart, and that you have referred him to your father. Without waiting for his decision, which however must of course be conclusive, allow me to assure you that no event could give us more pleasure than to welcome you to our family, and that Mrs. Wadsworth and myself would find our greatest joy in watching over your happiness. You have already made quite as complete a conquest of Mrs. W. as of our dear Charlie. Before she was aware that he was interested in you, she spoke of you to me in the highest terms.
>
> It is not for us to speak of our son except to tell you of his faults, and I must accordingly say to you, for there should be no concealment in such a case, that you are not his first love—tho' I am sure you are his second. He has been for some years devotedly and tenderly attached to *Iron*. If any one could wean him from this passion and make him think a little more of science, literature, and cultivated society, I think they would make a very good fellow of him. I am sure you can do this good work better than any one else.
>
> I can only say further, dear Miss Burden, that if your destinies should be united with those of our son, you will divide with him the parental care and affection with which we have watched over him, and which he has always dutifully returned.[21]

Though he found time to take care of personal affairs, General Wadsworth was fully occupied with military matters. On April 4, Lieutenant Colonel Rufus

Dawes of the 6th Wisconsin wrote his wife that the general "is now in command of our division, and we begin at once to feel the old fellow is trying in his own level headed way to ferret out abuses. For instance: 'All officers applying for leave of absence must state the date and length of their last leave.' He is a thorough and able commander." Four days later in another letter to his wife, Colonel Dawes was again praising the general, who had informed his commanders of an inspection that day, the result of which was that "every man is busy polishing his gun and brasses and blacking his shoes."[22]

The brigade and regimental officers were equally busy—with reason. A couple of weeks later their division commander informed them that he would "publish in general orders, the regiment in his division that stood first in soldierly qualities, discipline, cleanliness, and condition of arms." But he was not about to disclose when the inspections would occur.[23]

True to his word, General Wadsworth published the results of the inspection. The 6th Wisconsin, having surreptitiously obtained advance notice, was reported to excel in "neatness of clothing and appearance," with the 150th Pennsylvania and 147th New York just trailing. The 95th New York, 24th Michigan, and 121st Pennsylvania were condemned for having arms and equipment in the "worst condition." The 7th and 19th Indiana and the 150th Pennsylvania were praised for demonstrating the "best condition" of their transportation, whereas the 7th Wisconsin and 121st and 143rd Pennsylvania were criticized for showing the "least care." The intended results, encouraging competition among the regiments to perform well, apparently occurred, causing men in the 150th Pennsylvania, the "Bucktail Regiment," to complain that the 6th Wisconsin had the advantage of a more recent clothing issue.[24]

While "Old Corduroy" was preparing his men for the discipline needed to wage a campaign, it is not unlikely that he was also reacting to the new army commander. Perhaps he recalled his son Jimmy's reaction to the sturdy, but undisciplined, Western troops he observed during the Mississippi Valley trip with his father. Possibly the father wanted to impress General Grant with the discipline among these Easterners who had not enjoyed the successes—or acclaim—of the Westerners. Clearly a military air was returning to the camps of the Army of the Potomac. Drills were increased, and orders were coming down daily: Pickets were to return in the same order as they went out, the teamsters were to be exempt from bearing arms, and those considered unfit for combat were transferred to the Veteran Reserve Corps. Officers were being "held to a rigid accountability," including responsibility for turning in unserviceable shoes. Even such minor matters as the time of day for submission of papers requiring the commanding general's action were pushed up a half hour. By the end of the month it seemed as if orders to brigade and regimental commanders were being issued hourly.[25]

The creation of a disciplined army, with which the men can identify in both body and spirit, demands a closeness and trust generally unknown—and likely unattainable—at other times. A modern military historian has observed that: "At its height, this sense of comradeship [common in war] is ecstasy. . . . Men are true comrades only when each is ready to give up his life for the other, without reflection and without thought of personal loss."[26]

"[E]verything betokened an advance of the army." Anxiety gripped everyone, from the newest recruits to the veterans. Pop-eyed, dyspeptic 49-year-old Major General George Gordon Meade may have been the most apprehensive. Though he continued to command the Army of the Potomac, he was uncertain of what that meant. General Grant had planted himself near the Culpeper rail station in a plain brick building reflecting the style of its occupant, rather than in Washington or back in the Western Theater. Meade could be sure only of his three corps commanders, Major Generals Winfield Scott Hancock (II Corps), John Sedgwick (VI Corps), and Gouverneur Kemble Warren (V Corps).[27]

Morris Schaff recalled that Hancock was a "very handsome, striking-looking man . . . symmetrically large, with chestnut hair and rather low forehead" who exuded authority, as well as a stormy temper, which gave vent to his legendary profanity. Short, stocky "Uncle John" Sedgwick was slow, but reliable, having long since earned the confidence of his men by his "gentleness and sweetness." And youthful-looking, black-haired Gouverneur Warren, with all his idiosyncrasies and strongly voiced opinions, had demonstrated leadership and dependability defending Little Round Top. In fact, at this time General Grant judged that "Warren was the man I would suggest to succeed Meade, should anything happen to" him.[28]

The division commanders were also equally reliable. In addition to General Wadsworth, the V Corps now counted on Major General Charles Griffin, absent from Gettysburg, but idolized by his men despite his hardness, to command the 1st Division. Griffin had distinguished himself earlier with General Sickles's III Corps. The 2nd Division was commanded by Major General John C. Robinson, "the hairiest general . . . in a much-bearded army." Though he had been dismissed from West Point his sophomore year, four years later he was commissioned a regular army second lieutenant and had proven his bravery many times, including at Gettysburg. Brigadier General Samuel W. Crawford, who had proved his leadership and courage at Cedar Mountain, Antietam, and Gettysburg (the latter as a division commander in Sickles's III Corps), commanded the 3rd Division.[29]

The drills, reviews, distribution of camp and garrison equipment, return of quartermasters' stores, and the "necessity of greater attention to the cleanliness of the troops and their tents or huts," including the daily airing of bedding, seemed to confirm that a campaign was imminent.[30] Still nothing happened. Grant was not ready. He wanted to become acquainted with those in command, but he also had to be sure that his forces in the West, now under Major General William T. Sherman, as well as General Butler's peninsula command and other commands, were coordinated. And lastly, he wanted the Virginia roads to dry out.

Nor was General Robert E. Lee ready. He expected a movement by Grant, so he had disallowed General Pickett's request to make an expedition to North Carolina to keep the railroads operating. In fact, Lee had just recalled newly promoted Major General Robert Hoke from his expedition to New Bern, after his successful capture of Plymouth, North Carolina, on April 20.[31]

Yet there was no denying that the new Union commander intended to engage the Confederates, whether or not either side felt completely prepared. Lincoln had called upon General Grant because Lincoln regarded him as a fighter. He might lack finesse, but not a coherent strategy or determination. As one close observer of the commander reported, "Give General Grant men enough of the tried valor and experience of this fighting army of the Nation and I think he can go to Richmond . . . and crush the rebellion." Grant's unaffected manner led the soldiers to realize that "Grant wants soldiers, not yaupers."[32] The veterans were particularly aware of the imminent battle:

> Our time is drawing to a close. We have been to the top run [*sic*] of the lader [*sic*] & are now going down the other side. Every day draws us one step near[er] the end. . . . I suppose you folks at home think that the Rebs are nearly whiped [*sic*], but I tell you what, they can fight yet & so *can* we & *will* until they lay down their arms & I hope that will be soon. They must do it sooner or later & the *sooner* they do it the better it will be for them.[33]

Warm weather on Sunday, May 1, which seemed to inspire the grass to grow and the peach and plum trees to bloom, may also have led to reflection. A member of the II Corps almost wished for rain, "for every day of fine weather brings us nearer to the terrible battle which must be fought here in Virginia." He had reason to want rain, because "the more battles a person gets in the more he dreads the next. The only wonder to me now is, how anyone escapes unharmed." The 56-year-old, white-haired general from Geneseo might well have written these words, but there is nothing to suggest he was engaged in any reflection or had any fears.[34]

Even if he had been so inclined, Wadsworth had little time to reflect. Orders and circulars were being initiated, transmitted, and received with increasing regularity. It was now not a question of whether, but when, the campaign would begin, which depended on how Grant sized up the situation.

Lee's 62,000-man Army of Northern Virginia was still thinly stretched along the Rapidan River from Barnett's to Morton's Fords, some eighteen to twenty miles. Lieutenant General Powell Hill's Corps tenuously held the upper half, and General Ewell's, equally tenuously, patrolled the lower. Lee had ordered the return of Longstreet's Corps (minus Pickett's Division) from East Tennessee in anticipation of a Union movement across the Rapidan at Germanna or Ely's Fords.[35]

Lee's army was the objective of the Army of the Potomac, not Richmond, as Grant's instructions to Meade on April 2 had made clear. However, Richmond was still a prize to be had, so Grant directed Major General Benjamin F. Butler, commanding the newly created Army of the James, to move to City Point on the south bank of the James River near Petersburg, while Meade occupied Lee to the north. If Butler could not take Richmond and Lee fell back, both Union armies would link up and become a single unit. To put more pressure on Confederate resources, Major General Franz Sigel's Department of West Virginia would move in two columns, one to destroy the East Tennessee and Virginia Railroad, the other to destroy railroads in the Shenandoah Valley. After reuniting, the columns would join the Army of the Potomac by way of Gordonsville.[36]

Grant's task was to interpose his troops between the Army of Northern Virginia and its communications and supplies. Moving by the Union left flank would take three corps of greater than 25,000 men each, with 4,000 trailing wagon trains, through approximately fifteen miles of mostly forest and "impenetrable growth" known as the Wilderness. This required a midnight departure and a rapid march beyond the Rapidan on the first day. The three corps would have to pass through this desolate area before General Lee could organize for an engagement: a thirty-mile tramp in twenty-four hours or less. Thus was set in motion another of the many unanticipated and disastrous engagements that characterized this long, bloody war.[37]

On Monday, May 2, 1864, General Meade issued orders to move two days hence. Two cavalry divisions would take the lead, with Brigadier General David Gregg's 2nd Cavalry Division moving toward Ely's Ford and newly arrived, youthful Brigadier General James H. Wilson commanding the 3rd Cavalry Division, headed toward Germanna Ford. After they arrived at their destinations they would send out "strong reconnoissances [*sic*] . . . until they feel the enemy."[38]

Whether it was the comfortable spring weather or the portent of battle, the former Squire of Geneseo momentarily turned his attention to his correspondence. Characteristically, he was able to shift his focus from military to business to personal matters. He had just made a judgment call regarding two "culprits" from the 6th Wisconsin who "begged piteously" to rejoin their regiment, even at the risk of being killed, rather than being shipped off to New York State's Sing Sing Prison. General Wadsworth granted their requests.[39]

Amid the "bustle and confusion" resulting from orders to move out at midnight on May 3, and after writing to a business associate, the general took time to "withdraw my mind from the Scene & the duties of the hour for a few minutes." He assured his "dear Wife" that he and their middle son, "Tick," were well "and in the best spirit." Moreover, he felt "sure of victory." Then in an unusually reflective mood, he spelled out his affection for his wife and family and—reminiscent of his father—underscored the significance of the Wadsworth name.[40]

> I wish I could tell you how much I love you & our dear children, how anxious
> I am that all should go well with you, that you will all live in affection and
> kindness, and that none of our dear children will ever do anything to tarnish

the good name which we hold and we hope to maintain. . . . write a kind letter to dear Jimmie if he is not with you, with all the love and affection I can express. Kiss _____ and Lizzie and believe me[,] my dear wife _____ & truly Yrs. J. S. Wadsworth

Despite his assurances, there is a hint of his mortality that had not been present earlier. It was not unusual for veterans to consider their odds of survival reduced with each battle, but this was uncharacteristic of James Samuel Wadsworth. With the exception of a short spell in his early adulthood, he had demonstrated the unbounded optimism of those who blazed trails to western New York. Perhaps he sensed that the appointment of General Grant signaled a dramatic change in the conduct of the war. Iron Brigade historian Alan Nolan aptly captures the difference:

It was to be like no other campaign that army had ever experienced. Gone were the years of sporadic fighting, the recurring episodes of great preparation, climactic battle, and prompt disengagement. The *constant* war had begun, war which the officers' reports could only identify by "epochs," during which "two great armies marched and fought for 11 months . . . without ever being out of gunshot."41

Chapter 21

"FIND OUT WHAT IS IN THERE"

Wadsworth Enters the Wilderness

According to General Meade's orders, the V Corps was to begin its movement at midnight on Wednesday, May 4, 1864. Tension built by the hour, causing Colonel Charles Wainwright to complain that "Orders have been coming in thick and fast all day; an army is as bad as a woman starting on a journey, so much to be done at the last moment." General Wadsworth was one of those transmitting and initiating orders. Among them was one making clear that only officers or men "temporarily disabled or exhausted" would be allowed to ride in spring wagons or ambulances. Proof of disability or exhaustion required a surgeon's certificate or a division or brigade commander's order. Only "a few light packages not exceeding in all, one hundred pounds" were to be carried in the wagons.[1]

Of particular concern was the status of the men who were to do the fighting. Those whose service was to expire were reminded that, nonetheless, they "would be shot without trial if they do not step out to the music." Among those short-timers were the 2nd Wisconsin and the 14th Brooklyn, two regiments that had been tested virtually from the start of the war. Additionally, General Wadsworth notified his brigadiers that they were "authorized to restore to duty any officers or men who may be in arrest in their respective commands."[2]

True to form, on May 2, the general was actively involved in preparations, during the course of which he encountered the corps artillery commander, Colonel Wainwright, who was inspecting the redoubts under construction south of Culpeper. "The old gentleman [Wadsworth] was talkative as usual," Wainwright wrote in his diary, "and said that he did not know very much about engineering, though he did claim to be otherwise pretty well up on military matters." Never passing up an opportunity to put down Wadsworth, Wainwright "agreed with him perfectly as to his ignorance of engineering, and thought he would be wiser not to attempt to use terms belonging thereto." In fact, the "old gentleman" did know something about engineering from his experiences working with his uncle and farm managers. On the other hand, at least Wainwright appeared to credit Wadsworth with knowledge of "military matters," albeit in a back-handed way.[3]

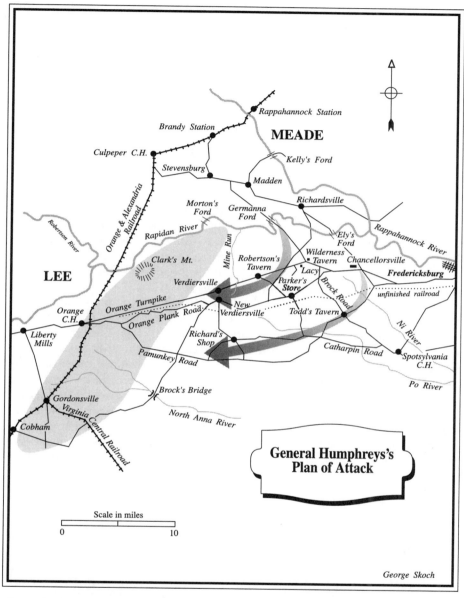

General Humphreys's plan of attack (by George Skoch)

It was an especially busy time for quartermasters. Lieutenant Morris Schaff, a member of General Meade's staff, recalled that "Trains were backing in to be loaded with surplus stores; fresh troops, infantry and cavalry, were arriving and had to be supplied at once, whole regiments in some cases, with arms and equipment.

Teams stood, waiting, the drivers clamorous for their turn to load with ammunition or delayed supplies."[4]

Amid the hurly-burly of preparations, General Warren called his division commanders and Wainwright to his quarters in the late afternoon of May 3. Warren showed his orders to the assembled commanders and explained the next day's movement. The V Corps was to begin its movement at midnight. General Griffin's 1st Division would lead off, with Crawford's 3rd Division close behind, and then the corps artillery. Wadsworth's 4th Division would move out next, followed by Robinson's 2nd Division. "Uncle John" Sedgwick's VI Corps would follow the V Corps' route, starting four hours later. The route would take them from Culpeper, almost directly east along the south side of Mountain Run, to Stevensburg. Then they would head south and east again on the Germanna Plank Road to Germanna Ford. General Hancock's II Corps was to coordinate its move with General Warren's. To avoid delay at the Rapidan the II Corps was to cross at Ely's Ford, farther east, and make a wide sweep southwest to the Catharpin Road, below the Orange Plank Road. At Shady Grove Church the II Corps would extend its line to meet Warren's corps. Warren's and Sedgwick's corps would form the army's right flank and Hancock's the left. Cooperation and timing were the keys to success.[5]

Only enough wagons for five days' forage would accompany the infantry; The rest of the wagons were to be sent off to Chancellorsville. The men would receive fifty rounds of ammunition, three days' rations in their haversacks, three days' bread and small rations in their knapsacks, and three days' beef on the hoof. No fires were to be built enroute. The marchers would stop for breakfast once they had crossed the Rapidan at Germanna Ford. Later the V Corps would continue southward along the Germanna Plank Road toward the Wilderness Tavern, where the divisions of Crawford, Robinson, and Wadsworth would position themselves. Griffin's division, in the advance, would head west beyond the tavern along the Orange Turnpike toward Mine Run, behind which Grant expected to find Lee's Army of Northern Virginia digging in, as it had in February.[6]

The Army of the Potomac was headed for familiar surroundings, where it had fought the unsuccessful battle of Chancellorsville almost exactly a year earlier. Ironically, at this very moment, General Lee was headquartered less than six miles away from that battlefield. Perhaps he was mulling over that same battle and its results. On this soft, cloudy May night, Colonel Wainwright found Wadsworth alone at corps headquarters speculating about whether the move was to take them "around Lee's right or left." The artillery chief superciliously informed Wadsworth that he held no opinion. Rather, chiding the civilian general, Wainwright "declared I must be a regular." That is, regular army men, with whom he identified, were not expected to "give an opinion on subjects they knew nothing about." Again, there is no record of "the old gentleman's" reaction to still another put-down from the ever-critical Wainwright.[7]

However, the battle-tested general must have recalled his disappointment over the army's lack of success on the Chancellorsville battlefield, when he had recklessly escorted members of the Iron Brigade across the Rappahannock under heavy enemy fire. As he had written in a postbattle letter to his daughter Cornelia, "we ought to have crushed the whole Rebel Army." Yet, he must have had a foreboding, which was suggested by the letter he had just written Mary Craig, in which he seems finally to have become aware of his mortality. He was tired; that much was evident to those close to him.[8]

☆　　☆　　☆

The bugle sounded the "fall-in call" at midnight. Two hours later Wadsworth and others received orders to move out. "There is a kind of weird excitement in this starting at midnight," Colonel Wainwright recalled. "The senses seemed doubly awake to every impression." In the dark, a Massachusetts soldier remembered, every sound was impressed in memory, particularly "the hum of moving troops and the peculiar rattle of cup and canteen which is heard only in war." The marchers, stretching in a line close to four and a half miles long, kept a steady pace as they trod along the narrow roads that characterized the area. While there was an air of confidence and hopefulness, the soldiers, according to a II Corps officer, realized that "hard and bloody work was before them."[9]

Just before the corps crossed the Rapidan at Germanna Ford, it halted. Generals Warren and Wadsworth sat mounted, the latter on his iron-gray horse, and were attended by their staffs at the top of the north bank. Lieutenant Porter Farley of Monroe County's 140th New York would long recall observing "the gray head and benign but determined face of General James S. Wadsworth." Farley admired "the brave old man who left the comforts of a princely estate for the hardships of war . . . for the cause which he had so ardently espoused."[10]

By 5:00 A.M., in the early morning light, the men began to catch glimpses of the roads crowded with infantry columns, dipped flags, wagon trains, and the reflections of the corps' shiny brass Napoleons. It all seemed so incongruous that spring day to be marching past flowering dogwoods, violets, azaleas, and primroses that gave off a welcome scent. In fact, years later a Confederate veteran marveled at the beautiful Wilderness Run valley: "The fields stretch away to the forests on every side and are as green as a well-watered, fertile soil can make them. Instead of wilderness the country seems a paradise."[11]

Sometime after 9:00 A.M., after crossing the river, the weary but relieved soldiers dropped to the ground and breakfasted. General Grant was even more relieved. His "most serious apprehensions . . . of crossing the river in the face of an active, large, well-equipped, and ably-commanded army" had not been realized. Then, abruptly, near Wilderness Tavern the Army of the Potomac once more found itself in the 20,000-acre forest forever and infamously known as the Wilderness.[12]

It was forbidding, Lieutenant Morris Schaff vividly recalled years later:

> a vast sea . . . of dense forest—a second growth more than a century old. It is
> made up chiefly of scrubby, stubborn oaks, and low-limbed, disordered, hag-
> gard pines,—for the soil is cold and thin,—with here and there scattering
> clumps of alien cedars. Some of the oaks are large enough to cut two railroad
> ties. . . . But generally, the trees are noticeably stunted, and so close together,
> and their lower limbs so intermingled with a thick underbrush, that it is very
> difficult indeed to make one's way through them.[13]

Once in what Schaff called this "vast sea . . . of dense forest" a spell seemed to
come over the soldiers, who soon realized that individual courage would count
for more than tactics.

It is useful to give a brief overview of the locale of this jungle of scrub pine in
which Wadsworth's division now found itself and which would result in his undoing. The twelve-square-mile area lay directly south of the Rapidan River between Chancellorsville to the east and Mine Run, a northward flowing tributary
of the Rapidan, to the west. Two roughly parallel roads, the Orange Turnpike, a
post road of its day, and the Orange Plank Road, ran through the forest, otherwise almost totally bereft of clearings. The two roads (actually one that split)
linked Fredericksburg on the east and Orange Court House some thirty to
thirty-five miles to the west. They also intersected two other roads that ran in a
southeasterly direction, the Germanna Plank Road, which ended at the Plank
Road, and the Brock Road, running just east of the Wilderness Tavern on the
Turnpike and extending beyond the Plank Road.

Once Griffin's division, in the lead, reached the Wilderness Tavern, it turned
west on the Turnpike and, after a mile, bivouacked in the woods near the Lacy
farm. It was followed by the rest of the V Corps, which still had to cross Flat
Run, an even smaller tributary of the Rapidan that was fast becoming a mud
hole. Crawford's 3rd Division, next in line, marched along grassy Parker's Store
Road and also halted near the Lacy farm, about a half mile south of the Turnpike. At 3:05 P.M. General Wadsworth, the "large man . . . with silvered hair and
nobly carved features," bivouacked his division east of Wilderness Run, opposite
Crawford's division. Then he promptly dispatched the 2nd Wisconsin of Cutler's
brigade for picket duty. The regiment's picket line strung out about three miles
toward Chancellorsville along a gravel road near the junction with the Plank
Road. The pickets were surprised and sobered to find "the debris of war—knapsacks, belts, bayonets, scabbards, etc." that marked the battlefield of the previous
May. General Robinson's division dropped to the ground on the Germanna
Road near Caton's Run.[14]

Virtually the whole Army of the Potomac was now across the Rapidan on
schedule. Warren's V Corps was massed around Wilderness Tavern; Hancock's II
Corps lay at Chancellorsville; Sedgwick's VI Corps was camped immediately
south of the Rapidan along the Germanna Plank Road; Wilson's Cavalry Division, which had preceded Warren's corps, was deployed around Parker's Store;

and Gregg's Cavalry Division, having crossed at Ely's Ford in advance of Hancock, was deployed between Chancellorsville and Todd's Tavern. Only Burnside's IX Corps, which was advancing by forced marches from Brandy Station and Manassas Junction, had yet to join Grant's troops.

At sunset General Wadsworth's men, clearly visible from corps headquarters near the Pike, prepared their supper, such as it was, as the smoke from their fires wafted over them. Then after supper some of them washed their feet as the division settled in for a good night's rest, despite some rain that evening. But Wadsworth and his fellow commanders did not enjoy a similar respite. They received orders from General Warren at 8:30 P.M. In addition to prescribing the next day's order of march, Warren instructed them to close their columns and post flankers when passing intersecting roads.15

Meanwhile at Orange Court House General Lee, roughly eighteen miles west, was trying to determine when and where the Union attack would come. The first indication of a Federal movement was the "unusual quantity of smoke in the day time and moving of lights by night" on May 2. The veterans were all too familiar with the routine: "The last thing a soldier does on breaking a camp, is to make a bonfire of his surplus wood and winter 'fixings,'" recalled an aide to Brigadier General George H. Steuart. Suspicions were confirmed the next day, May 3, when "a cloud of dust . . . floating over the woods in front . . . the white covers of wagons and glistening bayonets . . . passing in endless succession [left] no doubt the Union army was moving to cross one of the fords below, Germanna we rightly supposed."16

General Steuart promptly notified Confederate signalmen atop Clark's Mountain, who were already aware of the movement and had informed General Lee. In turn, Lee sent a dispatch to General Braxton Bragg in Richmond. "Reports from our lookouts seem to indicate that the enemy is in motion. The present direction of his column is to our right." Brigadier General John Imboden also reported General Sigel's advance from Winchester up the Shenandoah Valley, "with wagons, beef cattle, etc." Lee, who envisioned a flanking maneuver against Grant to pin his troops down, put his men in motion. Ewell started his three divisions (17,000 men) east on the Orange Turnpike toward Wilderness Tavern. Instructed not to bring on a general engagement until General Longstreet's Corps was up, Ewell halted at Robertson's Tavern (Locust Grove) almost six miles from the Wilderness Tavern. Almost simultaneously, A. P. Hill's Corps, well ahead of Longstreet's, was moving east parallel to Ewell's on the Orange Plank Road, with Major General Harry Heth's Division in the advance. Heth halted near Mine Run, between seven and eight miles west of Parker's Store. Longstreet's Corps, which did not begin its advance until about 4:00 P.M., bivouacked that night at Brock's Bridge, some ten miles from its starting point at Gordonsville, with another eighteen miles to go to meet up with General Hill.17

The next morning, Thursday, May 5, the V Corps started "punctually" at 5:00 A.M. General Crawford's division took the lead, followed by Wadsworth's. The divisions of Generals Robinson and Griffin brought up the rear. Soon

Wadsworth's division was stretched out on a narrow north–south road leading through a dense wood. It was headed south for Parker's Store on the Orange Plank Road, about four miles southwest of the Wilderness Tavern. Then roughly two hours later "the old gentleman," as Colonel Wainwright was disposed to call him, was halted by a courier with a dispatch from Warren to reverse course. Wadsworth was to unite with General Griffin on his right, because Griffin's pickets, on the Orange Turnpike, were being fired upon.[18]

Once more the Federals, like their Confederate counterparts, had to gird up their courage. The process included, as Paul Fussell subsequently wrote about World War II soldiers, a good degree of rationalizing: "It *can't* happen to me . . . [which] erodes to . . . It *can* happen to me . . . making inevitable the third stage of awareness: It is going to happen to me, and only my not being there [on the front lines] is going to prevent it." Yet something internal typically overcomes that "dreadful realization." At times it is only a feeling of comradeship: "I can't let my buddies down" or "I can't appear a coward in front of" the men with whom I have eaten, slept, and marched. As noted earlier, upon becoming a brigade commander John Gibbon realized that punishment was a much less effective motivator than conscience or esprit de corps.[19]

At first Warren was not disposed to consider the firing anything more than a demonstration and kept his divisions moving. Further information confirmed that the Confederates, who were supposed to be in a defensive position behind Mine Run to the west, were advancing east in force along both the Turnpike and the Plank Road. This prompted Meade to suspend the march and to direct Warren to attack, which would prove a mistake. Meade also ordered Hancock not to advance beyond Todd's Tavern, barely four miles southeasterly of the Orange Plank Road. This fit Grant's desire to pitch into Lee's army there and now, even without disposition. Warren, still uncertain about what he faced as late as 8:00 A.M., rode over to Wadsworth, who was forming his division near the Lacy house on the west side of Parker's Store Road. Looking into a deep woods, Warren said to Wadsworth, "Find out what is in there."[20]

Morris Schaff, ordnance officer at General Meade's headquarters, recalled this moment as a turning point. Had Warren himself continued south to Chewning Farm, the good defensive spot General Crawford had secured, he would have ordered Crawford's division to hold on. The result, Schaff maintained, would have been analogous to Warren's "brilliant coup on Round Top by bringing Wadsworth right up to hold it."[21] Instead, the V Corps commander later would order Crawford to connect with General Wadsworth's division.

Meanwhile, Wadsworth shifted his division toward General Griffin's left. This placed the New Yorker's men in an opening about a half mile up the road from Crawford's division, which was nearing Parker's Store. One of Robinson's brigades was to form on Griffin's left also, while the rest of Robinson's brigades were held in reserve.[22]

The success of the Union movement now depended upon whether Warren could unite the separated V Corps divisions and hold the Turnpike until the VI Corps arrived from Germanna Ford. Equally important, Brigadier General

George Washington Getty's VI Corps division would have to advance to the Plank Road and hold its intersection with the Brock Road until Hancock's corps arrived to counter Hill's Corps, which before noon had driven away the Union cavalry. However, orders did not reach General Getty until 11:00, too late to influence the struggle beginning to ensue. Union success also depended on Brigadier General Horatio G. Wright's division. It would have to head down the Culpeper Mine Road from the Germanna Plank Road, slanting southwest toward Warren's right flank, and, in a timely manner, connect with Griffin's division, straddling the Turnpike. This did not occur either.

Wadsworth still had to make the connection with Griffin's division. He had spotted a woods road leading from the opening to where he heard Griffin's division firing at Ewell's attackers. By taking the route, he believed he could strike the flank of Major General Robert Rodes's Division, which was forming north of the Turnpike. However, this put Wadsworth's left flank in the air, because General Crawford's division was still about a half mile south at the Chewning Farm. At 8:30 A.M. General Wadsworth rather vaguely reported to General Griffin that he had found an opening for one brigade and a "tolerable position for [his two batteries of] artillery about 1 1/2 miles from Lacy's house." He also had another brigade "stretched thinly through a piece of very thick woods" and a third brigade near Griffin's left. Battle lines were forming, facing west. Once the lines were formed, the men were allowed to lie down to await the order to advance. Paradoxically, while a fierce battle would soon be raging, the soldiers heard the "twitter of birds," of which the woods were full, and the officers of the 6th Wisconsin "were chattering and chaffering in the highest spirits."[23]

At 10:30 A.M., almost two hours later and over three hours after the V Corps' initial contact with Ewell, Wadsworth received the call to advance. His division headed "due west," but a compass was useless in those tangled woods, underbrush, and briar-tangled ravines. His men also contended with the acrid smell of the musket fire and the awful noise—one "endless concussion." Skirmishers from the 6th Wisconsin and 150th Pennsylvania were pushed forward, followed by the main battle line. A deadly struggle soon ensued between unseen combatants—and, with it, an unfortunate delay.[24]

The delay, according to Wilderness historian Gordon Rhea, resulted from Wadsworth's "showing no inclination to hurry." While the Union delay may well have proved costly in terms of casualties and ultimately the battle, it is unfair and inaccurate to single out for blame General Wadsworth. Whatever his many faults, hesitancy was not one of them, and, in fact, Rhea speculates that Wadsworth was following Griffin's example. Griffin wanted the support of Wright's VI Corps division before launching an attack.[25]

Once under way, Wadsworth's division followed a path that took them through a tangled thicket, forcing the commander to leave two artillery batteries (twelve pieces) behind. It was not humanly possible to move in a straight line through the tangled undergrowth. Almost immediately the division was in "serious trouble." When it passed over Denison's Maryland brigade, his men lost direction, and individual units lost contact with each other. Increasingly the dense

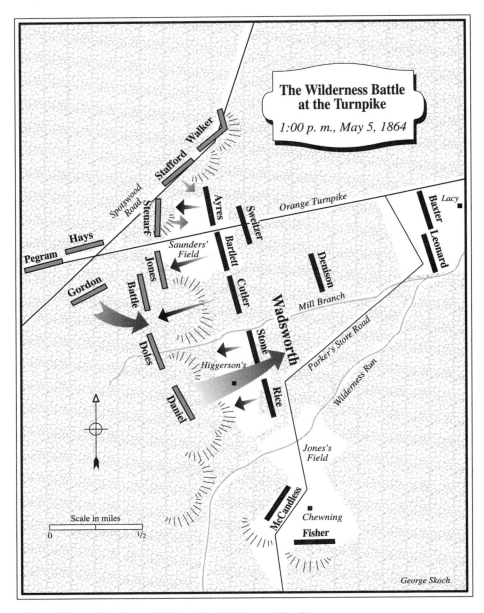

The Wilderness Battle
at the Turnpike

1:00 p. m., May 5, 1864

The Wilderness battle at the Turnpike (by George Skoch)

Wilderness itself became as much the enemy as the opposing forces firing on them. The division eventually found its way to a spot between Griffin's division, which straddled the Turnpike, and Crawford's, which bent back toward the Plank Road. Unfortunately, as Wadsworth's division wended its way through the entangled brush, individual units swung north, at an angle to General Griffin's division. This would prove the undoing of Wadsworth's small division.[26]

Brigadier General James Rice's brigade, previously Cutler's (the 76th, 95th, and 147th New York, the 14th Brooklyn, and the 56th Pennsylvania), was to anchor the left, just east of Higgerson's Field and at the angle in Parker's Store Road. The center was to be held by 28-year-old Colonel Roy Stone's Pennsylvanians (the 121st, 142nd, 143rd, 149th, and 150th). General Cutler's Iron Brigade (2nd, 6th, and 7th Wisconsin, 1st New York Sharpshooters, 7th and 19th Indiana, and 24th Michigan) was deployed on Stone's right and about 500 yards from Griffin's left. Momentarily the left, just south of the Pike, was secured by Brigadier General Joseph Bartlett's brigade of Westerners, downeasters, and Pennsylvanians. As well as can be determined, these were the dispositions at approximately noon, on May 5.

In the woods in front of Cutler's brigade and digging in were Brigadier General John M. Jones's Virginians (the 21st, 25th, 42nd, 44th, 48th, and 50th Virginia) of "Allegheny" Johnson's Division. Brigadier General Cullen A. Battle's Alabamians (3rd, 6th, 12th, and 26th, with the 5th acting as provost guard) of Major General Robert E. Rodes's Division backstopped the Virginians. Colonel Stone's brigade faced Brigadier General George Doles's three-regiment Georgia brigade (4th, 12th, and 44th), while General Rice's brigade would encounter Brigadier General Junius Daniel's Tarheels (32nd, 43rd, 45th, 53rd, and 2nd North Carolina). Fast approaching was the Georgia brigade of fiery, ramrod-straight Brigadier General John B. Gordon. What would soon be of more importance, however, was the half-mile gap between Crawford's right and Wadsworth's left.

Cutler's brigade formed up along the southern edge of Saunders' Field, one of the few clearings in the Wilderness. In the front line were the 7th Wisconsin (on the right), the 2nd Wisconsin, 19th Indiana, and 24th Michigan, with the 7th Indiana directly behind the 7th Wisconsin and the 6th Wisconsin in the second line. Along with Bartlett's brigade the Westerners hit Jones's Virginians head-on, causing that portion of the Confederate line to collapse. Cutler's troops exuberantly pushed ahead and captured 289 prisoners and three battle flags, imitating their success at Gettysburg on July 1. Unfortunately, their enthusiasm contributed to their undoing, for in the process the Iron Brigade drifted dangerously to the left. Now separated from Bartlett's men, they became exposed to a flank attack by Doles's Georgians and Battle's Alabamians.

Worse, General Gordon's Georgians emerged out of the woods and plugged a hole between Doles and Battle. Then, as Cutler reported, "Stone's brigade [on their left] gave way soon after meeting the enemy, thus letting the enemy through the line." The Iron Brigade was now exposed to a murderous cross fire from the Confederates back in the woods by the Turnpike, as well as from those overlapping on their left. Before a correction could be ordered, the 6th Wisconsin, which had originally been following the 7th Indiana, became isolated and lost nearly fifty men. Only the brush saved the others who, guerrilla-style, fired on the concentrated Confederates from behind any protection they could find.[27]

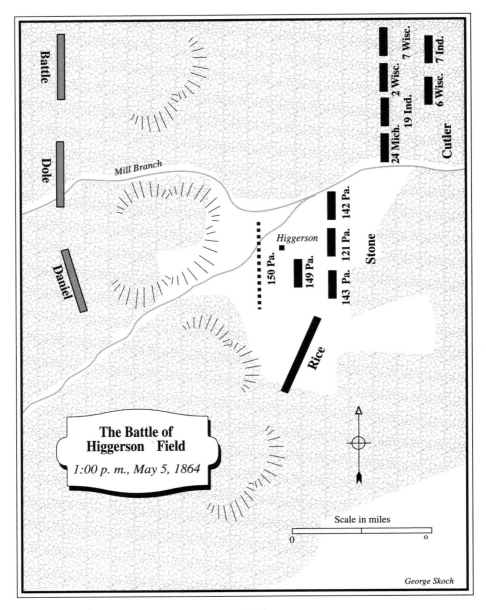

Battle

Dole

Mill Branch

Daniel

24 Mich.   19 Ind.   2 Wisc.   7 Wisc.

6 Wisc.   7 Ind.

Cutler

142 Pa.

121 Pa.

Higgerson

150 Pa.   149 Pa.   143 Pa.

Stone

Rice

**The Battle of
Higgerson   Field**

1:00 p. m., May 5, 1864

Scale in miles

0   o

George Skoch

The Battle of Higgerson's Field (by George Skoch)

The Federals were firing blindly in the general direction from which the opposing fire was coming. "At this point," the 19th Indiana's historian noted, "the battle of the Wilderness more closely resembled a riot than a battle." The noise alone was overwhelming. Flags, the guides for formations, were falling, lines of communication were breaking down, and higher-level commanders were unable to direct the engagement. The noise of battle drowned out shouted commands. Maneuvering was out of the question, for commanders were often hidden from sight. In fact, Wadsworth's aide, Captain Robert Monteith, claimed that "no officer could see ten files [two ranks of ten men] on either side of him." Blinded by thickets, brigades soon became isolated units. "A strange lethargy," an unnatural hesitancy, seemed to grip otherwise courageous men who became alarmed at invisible antagonists firing all around them, even, at times, in their rear.[28]

The vaunted Iron Brigade collapsed under the onslaught, which caused a general retreat. Not even the intrepid General Wadsworth, seemingly unconscious of his personal welfare, could restore order. "Where is my second line?" the old man hollered, "Bring up my second line," meaning Colonel Denison's Marylanders. Unfortunately, Denison, who had not budged, was still a mile back.[29]

Wadsworth's various regiments and brigades tried re-forming twice or three times. The 76th New York of General Rice's brigade, which had become mired in a swamp, found itself in some situations that sound almost apocryphal in their retelling. Its skirmishers were overrun, it milled about, conducted two councils of officers, was captured and released and got lost. Three companies, nearly all of the brigade's skirmish line, were captured. By 2:15 P.M., Chief of Staff Humphreys had reported that "Wadsworth's Division, on Griffin's left, has been driven in, and Crawford's Division has been called in so that his line is thrown back considerably. His left must be more than a mile in the rear of where it was before."[30]

Griffin's brigades were experiencing a similar fate. The Confederates had not only stopped the Union movement through the Wilderness, they were decimating the blue-clad soldiers. One soldier, experiencing his first battle, recalled hearing bullets spatting against a large oak tree protecting him, which caused his heart to pump and his throat to dry. At his feet lay a dead sergeant "with a hole in his forehead just above his left eye. Out of this wound bits of brain oozed, and slid on a bloody trail into his eye, and then over his cheek to the ground." Others would suffer even more grisly fates, suffocating from the smoke coming out of the dry grass set afire by the musketry and shelling or being roasted by the fires that were popping up all over.[31]

The "fearful confusion [and the] calamity spread to all the troops in that region," Lieutenant Colonel William Swan, an aide to General Ayres, recalled, yet "every soldier . . . seemed to know the way to the Lacy house." Still, Swan observed, it was "not altogether a disgraceful retreat." Cutler's brigade "came back in pretty good order," bringing with it the flag of the 50th Virginia, which a member of the 7th Indiana had grabbed.[32]

Then the pursuit let up, and the soldiers lay flat, hoping to escape any more damage. Eventually, in the open ground near the Lacy house, the V Corps was re-formed, but this was the first time members of the Iron Brigade could remember being routed. On the other hand, Colonel John W. Hofmann, commander of the 56th Pennsylvania, apparently wanted to re-form for a counterattack, "but General Wadsworth, who had a remarkable capacity for keeping a clear head in the most trying situations," dissuaded him. It would be futile, according to the general.[33]

The entire V Corps' attack had collapsed. The advance of Brigadier General Romeyn B. Ayers's brigade (Griffin's division) north of the Turnpike was stopped by the brigades of Brigadier Generals George H. Steuart and James A. Walker, as was a furious counterattack, in which Ayres was supported by Colonel Jacob B. Sweitzer's brigade. Brigadier General Joseph J. Bartlett's brigade, supported by Sweitzer and Cutler, initially had been successful, but it too was driven back. As noted, Stone got bogged down in a swamp; and Rice's oblique advance had been counterattacked and repulsed by Gordon's and Daniel's Brigades.

Earlier, around 11:15 A.M. Crawford had asked Warren's assistant adjutant if he should abandon his position near Parker's Store so he could connect with General Wadsworth's division. General Warren unhesitatingly answered yes. However, Crawford had delayed, for he felt his position on Chewning Heights commanded the Plank Road. It appeared the whole line of battle would be turned. A half hour later General Warren instructed General Crawford that "you must connect with General Wadsworth, and cover and protect his left as he advances." But the order was too late to prevent Warren's repulse, as was the arrival of the VI Corps. Unfortunately, also, when Crawford abandoned the Chewning Farm, Heth's Division was allowed to gain the upper hand on the Plank Road. As Warren and other frontline officers had felt from the beginning, they had begun the battle before they were ready and without necessary support.[34]

By 2:30 P.M. the V Corps was virtually back where it had started, at the Lacy house, and sadly at an awful price. For example, the 2nd Wisconsin suffered two officers and six men killed, four officers and fifty-four men wounded—with just over a month to go on their three-year enlistments. The 147th New York lost fifteen men killed, four officers and eighty-six men wounded, plus two officers and sixty-four men missing. The 7th Indiana reported one officer and fifteen men killed, three officers and eighty-nine men wounded, and four officers, including regimental commander Colonel Ira G. Grover, and fifty men missing.[35]

"Deeply mortified and in high temper," General Wadsworth rallied his division "with great exertion." Despite the obstacles and the unexpected retreat, it seemed that "it only took a moment" to revive these battle-hardened soldiers, recalled ordnance officer Morris Schaff. "[O]nce out of the woods and where they could see their colors, all rallied save now and then a man whose heart was not made for war." Unfortunately, there was no breather for the survivors, who were put to work building log breastworks.[36]

With the battle on the Turnpike winding down, General Grant had to determine what to do next. He could go at General Ewell's Corps again, but that would require concentrating his scattered corps. He had already seen the brutal result of sending in one division or one brigade, even one regiment at a time, instead of massing the troops. Additionally, to renew the attack would mean pushing the battered V Corps troops into the fray again. A reconnaissance by Generals Grant and Warren through the musket-induced haze near Saunders' Field and past the mangled units tended to clinch the decision not to renew the fight there.

However, about this time sturdy General Horatio Wright's much-delayed VI Corps division arrived. It had finally made the trek through the Wilderness along the Culpeper Mine Road, which came in from the northeast on a diagonal and intersected with the Turnpike. Wright quickly formed three of his four brigades north of the Turnpike facing west. (General Shaler's brigade was left to guard river crossings.) The brigades of Colonel Samuel Leonard and Brigadier General Henry Baxter of Robinson's division, kept in reserve earlier, took positions along the Pike facing south. They connected with the right of Denison's brigade, which was south of the Pike facing west. Extending the line south of the Pike were the three brigades of Griffin's division and then Crawford's two brigades. Wadsworth's division remained in reserve near the Lacy farm. Wright attacked the Confederates sometime after 3:00 P.M. and the fighting continued for almost two hours, as Sedgwick and Ewell fed in additional troops—with virtually the same results as the earlier clash on the Turnpike.[37]

The picture to the south, on the Orange Plank Road, was a little brighter for the Federals, though the battle had begun inauspiciously. General Getty's orders directed his VI Corps division to secure the intersection of the Plank and Brock Roads until Hancock's corps arrived and then to link the two Federal wings. By noon Getty's skirmishers had engaged Powell Hill's, but Hancock's corps, rerouted up the Brock Road, was still almost three miles away. Headquarters, mistakenly assuming Hancock's troops were near, ordered Getty to make an assault. General Hancock rushed three divisions forward. By 4:15 General Getty, under Hancock's orders, was heavily engaged, and another deadly struggle ensued.[38]

Between four and five o'clock, Grant and Meade, near Warren's headquarters at the Lacy house, learned that Major General Cadmus Wilcox's Division, trying to link Ewell's and Hill's Corps, was moving to reinforce Heth on the Plank Road. Birney's and Mott's divisions of Hancock's corps, which finally arrived in support of Getty, were pitched into the struggle, but they too were driven back by Heth. Mott's division was routed. Gibbon's division, which had raced up from the south, stopped the rout. However, Wilcox's attack led to a furious battle by his and Heth's divisions against the divisions of Getty, Mott, Birney, and Gibbon from approximately 6:30 to 7:30, when finally Hancock's last division, Brigadier General Francis Barlow's, converged on the melee from the south. Meanwhile, it appeared to Grant and Meade that throwing more Federal troops against the Confederates would tip the scales in their favor. So General Grant ordered Warren to attack Hill's flank and rear. "Wadsworth, terribly chagrined over the conduct of his division in the attack up the Pike, was anxious to retrieve the reputation of his troops, and asked to be sent against Heth."[39]

At roughly 6:00 P.M. General Warren acceded and ordered General Wadsworth to arouse his mauled troops, minus General Rice's battered brigade, which was held in reserve, to support the Federal attack on the Plank Road. Wadsworth directed his commanders and General Baxter, whose brigade was to accompany Wadsworth's division, to move out southeasterly to strike the flank of Hill's Corps. After traversing a torturous path through almost impenetrable woods the New Yorker halted Baxter's and Stone's brigades in line of battle, with his left about 800 yards west of the Brock Road and flanking Hill's Corps on the Plank Road. Cutler's brigade formed a second line, while Rice's brigade brought up the rear.[40]

Cutler's, Stone's, and Baxter's brigades were quickly thrown into the fray. They got into action in the nick of time, driving back skirmishers on the left of Wilcox's Division, just as Barlow's division of Hancock's corps struck Wilcox's line on the right. Hill's entire line was threatened, but a gamble by "Little Powell" Hill—and darkness—ultimately turned the tide in favor of the Confederates.[41]

In the dusk Major General J. E. B. Stuart and Colonel Charles S. Venable, cautiously surveying the area near Hill's left through the thick smoke, were startled to see Wadsworth's division advancing upon them. "If night would only come," Venable quietly whispered to his companion and rode off to inform Lee. General A. P. Hill, busily trying to restore some order to his troops, spotted the 125-man 5th Alabama Battalion, the corps' provost guard. Pointing with his weapon, he ordered them to "Rush ahead firing and give the rebel yell, as though you are followed by brigades." Led by Major A. S. Van de Graaff and Captain Wade Ritter, members of this minuscule outfit charged forward screaming at the top of their lungs. Until then the brigades of Baxter and Stone had only run into pickets, which they had driven back. However, in the denseness of the woods and the fading light, upon seeing the fire on Baxter's skirmishers, Stone's brigade broke in what Wadsworth's adjutant claimed was a "disgraceful manner." Only the brigade officers' "exertions . . . and Cutler's bayonets" from behind stopped any of the fleeing soldiers.[42]

The din of the battle alone would have been enough to disorient, if not frighten, even Wadsworth's experienced soldiers. Throughout that long day the noise had been deafening. Soldiers groped for words to describe the "unbroken, maddening" sound of rifles being fired as rapidly as humanly possible until the discord had "approached the sublime." Now, once again, both sides were called upon to fight an enemy visible only by the flash and crack of rifles. The two sides battered at each other at close range along a half-mile-long line, bereft of entrenchments and artillery or cavalry support. It was simply "close, square, severe, face-to-face volleys of fatal musketry," in the words of a correspondent. In this late-day conflict the 97th New York of Baxter's brigade, in the front line, lost approximately sixty men killed and wounded. Even the staff of the colors showed the results—"one-third of it was splintered off."[43]

Night finally came. For Wadsworth's and the other Union troops the day had been a bloody, frustrating stalemate, another embarrassing setback. Hancock felt that only darkness had blunted what could have been such a successful attack that evening by the forces of Generals Wadsworth and Barlow. Similarly,

General Humphreys claimed that "an hour or more of daylight and he [Hill] would have been driven from the field." As historian Scott Price put it, "A golden opportunity [for the Union] had been lost . . . the war would drag on for nearly another year."[44]

In the unnatural silence of the night it occurred to the exhausted troops that throughout most of the battle they had not heard the booming of cannon, for generally the artillery had been rendered ineffective in the dense Wilderness. Then in the darkness they caught the voices of their enemies, even "drew water from the same brook." In fact, some of Wadsworth's troops, in a line perpendicular to General Heth's and to the right of General Hancock's, lay almost in reach of Hill's outposts. There, among the dead and wounded, they heard the particularly distressing moans and cries of the wounded ("My God, why hast thou forsaken me?") and tried to provide succor where possible. Before long the gloom of the Union troops gave way to restlessness due to rumors that General Longstreet's Corps had caught up and was now directly in front of them. (He would not arrive until early on May 6.)[45]

There was concern at Union headquarters also. Instead of marching through this Wilderness, the Army of the Potomac was trapped by an army with inferior numbers. Grant had drawn criticism for mounting an attack before his subordinates were ready and feeding too many Federal units into the attack singly or in smaller configurations. Union victory would now depend on superior numbers and an early-morning pincer attack on Hill's Corps. Wadsworth's badly battered, but still tough, division north of the Plank Road and Hancock's II Corps straddling the road would have to beat Longstreet's Corps to the punch.

At a late-night conference Grant told Meade he wanted Hancock to begin the attack at 4:30 A.M. the next morning. The onus would rest on Hancock's II Corps, supported by Wadsworth's division and by two divisions of General Burnside's corps, which had crossed the Rapidan and massed on the Germanna Plank Road. Burnside's task took on particular importance; he was to aim for the Chewning farm in hopes of crashing into the rear of Hill's troops. Much hinged on the coordination and concentration of troops, something that had not occurred so far and that this dense forest would make nearly impossible.[46]

Sometime before 10:30 P.M. Meade met with his corps commanders, who induced him to request a 6:00 A.M. start. Their tired men were badly scattered in the dense thicket, and daylight was needed "to properly put in re-inforcements." General Grant grudgingly agreed to delay the attack to 5:00 A.M., fearing that the later start would enable the Confederates to take the initiative. In fact, that is exactly what General Lee planned. General Ewell's troops would hit the Union troops north of the Plank Road, while the rest were bottled up fighting Hill's and Longstreet's Corps.[47]

The order for Wadsworth's advance reached his headquarters sometime after 12:15 A.M. on May 6. He was ordered to "set your line of battle on a line northeast and southwest, and march directly southeast on the flank of the enemy in front of General Hancock." When the old man should have been getting some rest, duty forced him to prepare for renewal of the battle. To this end, he dispatched his aide, Robert Monteith, on what turned out to be a harrowing excursion to obtain 20,000 rounds of ammunition. Monteith recalled this as the "most anxious night spent during my service."[48]

It's doubtful the 56-year-old general got any sleep that night. Certainly, fatigue was sapping his legendary energy.

Chapter 22

"MY GOD, COLONEL, NOBODY COULD STOP HIM"

The Wilderness, May 6, 1864

While Grant reluctantly agreed to postpone the attack until 5:00 Friday morning, May 6, his decision was rendered moot. "At daybreak the most furious musketry commenced that I ever heard," wrote an officer of the 126th New York Infantry, II Corps. "Oh! how it did rattle." Lee had told Ewell the previous night that he would take the initiative. Anticipating Grant's move, Ewell's Corps, which had been reinforced during the night, would attack Sedgwick's troops at the starting time Grant had initially directed. While Lee's orders appear rather vague, at a minimum he wanted Ewell to keep Sedgwick and Warren occupied. This would relieve the pressure on Hill's Corps while Longstreet established his troops along the Orange Plank Road.[1]

Ewell's men duly launched a probing assault along the Pike, and initially General Sedgwick's right "flung [them] back with a vengeance." Subsequent Union attacks by Griffin's division of the V Corps and Seymour's men from Sedgwick's VI Corps were blunted by the Confederates making good use of their entrenchments. Heavy Union losses resulted. For most of the remainder of the day, the fighting on Warren's and Sedgwick's front settled down to skirmishing against Ewell's troops.[2]

Union forces near the Plank Road were not ready to attack at 4:30 A.M., Grant's usual starting time, and concerns mounted. Only Brigadier General Robert B. Potter's division of Burnside's IX Corps, which had been put in motion at 2:00 A.M., was up. Potter's men were trying to find their way through the woods toward Hill's flank. A more immediate concern was a report General Hancock had received that General Longstreet's Corps "was passing up the Catharpin road to attack my left flank."[3]

Nonetheless, promptly at the sound of the 5:00 A.M. signal gun, General Hancock sent out skirmishers. The main body of II Corps' attackers, commanded by Major General David Birney, headed westward along the Plank Road. Birney's division was in the lead, followed by the divisions of Brigadiers Gershom Mott,

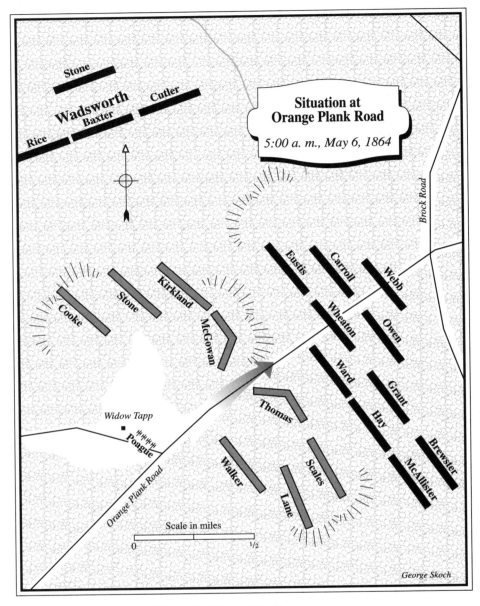

Situation at Orange Plank Road (by George Skoch)

John Gibbon, and George Getty (VI Corps). Birney's task was to drive back Hill's disorganized units before General Longstreet's Corps could arrive.[4]

As planned, the other prong of the anticipated pincer movement was General Wadsworth's force, which first had to fight its way "through the dense, trammeling woods." Baxter's brigade (Robinson's division) occupied the center of the battle line, with Rice on the right flank and Cutler on the left. Colonel Stone's brigade, commanded by Colonel Edmund Dana of the 143rd Pennsylvania, remained behind Baxter's. Well before 6:00 A.M. the four brigades, moving in a southerly direction toward the Plank Road, had advanced almost a mile. Wadsworth could be pleased thus far, for his men had to make a 90 degree turn, a particularly difficult movement.[5]

Ahead and on a slight diagonal to Wadsworth's right lay the left flank of the divisions of Confederate Generals Heth and Wilcox, which had become acutely intertwined the previous day. They were now sprawled in all directions, making their commanders anxious. North of the Plank Road and almost directly in the path of General Wadsworth's division was the left flank of General Heth's troops, with Samuel McGowan's Palmettos mixed in. South of the road and facing the left side of the Union II Corps advance was Wilcox's command, along with Henry Walker's Brigade from Heth's Division.[6]

Wadsworth's men, as if to redeem themselves from the previous day and seemingly oblivious to the combined Confederate shelling and musket fire, rushed forward. "Sweeping in from the right," Wadsworth's division smacked into General Kirkland's North Carolinians, "driving [them] in great confusion." Only Colonel John Stone's Mississippians and Brigadier General John Cooke's Tar Heels, who had managed to entrench themselves, were able to offer any resistance, and they bloodied General Rice's troops.[7]

Just as relentlessly, Birney's command, with the assistance of General Getty's division of the VI Corps, had shoved the Confederates over a mile back west along the Plank Road to the northeastern slopes of the Tapp field. Lieutenant Colonel Hazard Stevens, a member of Getty's division, described it as "blind bushwhacking." In the process they had leaped a Confederate breastworks and, after a charge of close to 400 yards, did the same over a line of rifle pits. It was a close, savage contest. Then the two prongs, Wadsworth's and Birney's men, bearing west on both sides of the road, linked in pursuit of Wilcox's and Heth's Rebels, which were falling back in confusion.[8]

Until then, Hancock, whose eyes blazed at the sound of combat, had been unusually subdued. His style was to command personally, an almost impossible task in this vast woods. At roughly 5:30 A.M., only a half hour after the initial attack, he was "radiant." His face "wreathed with smiles," Hancock hollered to Colonel Theodore Lyman of Meade's staff, "We are driving them, sir; tell General Meade we are driving them most beautifully." Grant's plans seemed to be coming to fruition.[9]

Experiencing success, the Union troops along the Plank Road rushed forward with abandon, scooping up prisoners as they went along. Unfortunately in the process, shortly after 6:00 A.M. the various units began to dangerously intermingle as they neared the Widow Tapp's farm. "The character of the woods," the increasingly desperate fighting, and the whining projectiles from the guns of Confederate Lieutenant Colonel William T. Poague, "masked by thick shrub and pines" on the Tapp farm and aiming straight at the Union troops, led to confusion. Again observers groped for words to describe it: "[T]here is scarcely the semblance of continuous and effective formation; regiments and brigades that started in the rear are now in the front and on different flanks; their commanders scattered through the woods in little detached, anxious groups, a staff officer or two, an orderly with the headquarters guidon."[10]

The II Corps historian recalled the close fighting: "In some cases [the Union troops] were heaped up in unnecessary strength; elsewhere great gaps appeared; men, and even officers, had lost their regiments in the jungles; the advance had not been, could not have been, made uniformly from right to left, and the line of battle ran here forward, and there backward, through the forest; thousands had fallen in the furious struggle; the men in front were largely out of ammunition."[11]

Compounding matters, Wadsworth's southward advance caused him to crash into the right flank of Birney's wing and crowd the latter toward the south. Birney called a halt of approximately half an hour to try to re-form his disordered troops. Simultaneously, Wadsworth attempted to disentangle his forces— amid the indiscriminately intermixed Union and Confederate dead and wounded—and to re-form his division north of the road.[12]

A participant believed that this halt "was a fatal mistake." Until then the Union troops had it their own way. "[G]ood fortune [was] on our side, and our men were in good spirits," the 97th New York's historian wrote, "while the Confederates were panic stricken, and fled beyond their works." Nonetheless, the Confederates had done their share of damage.[13]

Lieutenant Colonel Poague's guns, tossing short-range shells, had torn through the ranks of Wadsworth's men. The result was devastating and demanded that the general lead his men back into the protection of the woods. There he formed them, with Baxter's brigade in the front line with its left resting on the Plank Road. Directly behind were Cutler's and then Stone's brigades, while Rice's was deployed to the right of Baxter's. Wadsworth ordered them massed in the protected area to avoid the murderous Confederate artillery fire, which was pounding them "with deadly effect." Wadsworth's division was, in the words of Lieutenant Colonel William Swan, "in a worse plight, if anything," than the previous day; the losses were staggering.[14]

About this time Wadsworth also assumed command of Colonel J. Howard Kitching's 6th and 15th New York Heavy Artillery regiments. Kitching's raw gunners, who were placed on an angle to General Rice's right, had just been assigned to Wadsworth from General Hunt's corps artillery. The small (2,900-man) brigade had enjoyed relatively soft duty in Washington, but now acted as "foot artillery," or, less poetically, infantry. It was poorly prepared for what lay ahead.[15]

An equally appalling confusion characterized the reeling Confederates, but their salvation and the downfall of the hitherto victorious Federals began to appear about this time, 6:00 A.M. Longstreet's 10,000-man corps was now advancing eastward along the Plank Road. In the lead were Major General Joseph Kershaw's four brigades (his own, commanded by Colonel John Henagan, and those of Brigadier Generals Benjamin G. Humphreys, William T. Wofford, and Goode Bryan), which were to form south of the road on the right. Following close behind and expected to form on the left to confront General Wadsworth's command were Major General Charles W. Field's five brigades. These included Brigadier General Micah Jenkins's Palmettos, Brigadier General John Gregg's Texans and Razorbacks, Colonel William F. Perry's Alabamians, and Brigadier Generals George Tige Anderson's and Henry C. Benning's Georgians. Newly promoted Brigadier General E. Porter Alexander commanded Longstreet's three-battalion artillery. On their approach the Confederates observed "the sun, blood red, from the effect of the smoke of battle," and realized they were in for a "hot time."[16]

Perhaps aroused by General Lee's personal inspiration, Gregg's Brigade (3rd Arkansas, 1st, 4th, and 5th Texas) charged forward with abandon. Their shouts, intended to send chills down the backs of the skirmishers toward whom they were aimed, instead ushered in a murderous response from the first line of Wadsworth's troops. Gregg's pumped-up brigade exchanged fire that at times was as close as twenty yards. Eventually, however, Gregg's heroic, but outnumbered, troops fell back after attempting another charge and leaving more than two-thirds of their numbers on the ground. But they had done the job, halting and battering Wadsworth's troops.

Before Wadsworth's men could catch their breath, they were into another deadly struggle with General Benning's Georgians. Benning's Brigade met the same savage resistance as Gregg's. Then it was Colonel William Perry's turn. Commanding Law's Brigade, Perry split his five Alabama regiments, which charged at the double-quick. The 15th, 44th, and 48th Alabama veered left toward Wadsworth's somewhat scattered command. Unfortunately, in an attempt to concentrate his units, Wadsworth had shifted his men to form four lines, a one-brigade front. Inadvertently he had set up his men for a flank attack. The 4th and 47th Alabama regiments aimed straight ahead into Baxter's brigade, delivering a "most galling fire" and inflicting a disabling wound on its commander.[17]

Colonel Perry's left wing, with the support of some of Gregg's re-formed troops, quickly capitalized on the opportunity afforded by Wadsworth's realignment and smashed into his flank after the skirmishers found their quarry. The 15th Alabama, commanded by Colonel William C. Oates, first struck at Colonel Kitching's inexperienced artillerymen, now foot soldiers, and sent them scattering. The rest of Wadsworth's men tried to answer the swelling Confederate fire with their own. The Federal formation began disintegrating, opening the way for an attack on Cutler's brigade.[18]

The old Iron Brigade suffered heavy losses and, badly disorganized, also fell back. The 15th Alabama's Colonel Oates later claimed that Cutler's men "bolted." Cutler contended that he had tried to rally his men, but by the time he was able to create any order, they had retreated close to half a mile toward the Lacy farm. The defeat had to be particularly disheartening to the tough old Badger whose equally tough veterans had staved off attacks on July 1 at Gettysburg. Exacerbating the situation, the two staff officers Cutler had sent to obtain orders from General Wadsworth encountered Confederate skirmishers. Not even finding the division flag did any good, for Cutler located only two of Wadsworth's aides. Cutler, bleeding from an upper-lip wound, even supposed that Wadsworth had been killed, an impression reinforced by one of Cutler's staff. (It was later discovered that the supposition was based on the fact that the general's horse had been killed when Cutler's brigade broke.)[19]

Now Colonel Edmund Dana's brigade, formerly the wounded Colonel Stone's, was called on to meet the Rebel attack. Major George W. Jones, a member of the 150th Pennsylvania, attested to the fact that Wadsworth's death was (anticipating Mark Twain's quip) greatly exaggerated: "General Wadsworth, who was always at the front, called out in a paternal way, 'Come on Bucktails.'" With the general personally leading the way, the Bucktails charged, were driven back, then temporarily regained the lost ground, much as the other brigades had done. "Five times we traverse the same ground," the 150th's Sergeant Frey recalled, "led by General Wadsworth who sits on his horse with hat in hand, bringing it down on the pommel of his saddle with every bound as he rides at the head of the column." The intrepid general ignored the bullets striking like hail among them. Instead, he rode "slowly back in their midst, speaking kindly to them, with ever a smile on his pleasant countenance which shows no concern for the storm of lead and iron raging around him." Doggedly firing, Dana's troops contested "every inch of ground" as they followed Cutler's men to the Lacy farm.[20]

The continuous fighting had once again caused regiments and brigades, even corps, to become tangled and may have led General Meade to issue orders clarifying commands. By 8:00 A.M. the Confederates had mauled Wadsworth's fast-disintegrating units and had pushed them back to the Brock–Plank Roads intersection. There Meade directed Wadsworth to take orders from General Hancock and to expect two of Burnside's brigades to relieve him. Shortly thereafter Hancock ordered Wadsworth to take command of all the troops north of the Plank Road. They included General Webb's Pennsylvanians, brought forward from the reserve, and Colonel Sumner Carruth's brigade (IX Corps), which had just arrived at the intersection.[21]

Ordered by Hancock to attack on his front, General Wadsworth rode back down the Plank Road, with Carruth's and Webb's brigades in tow, to re-form his lines. The general sent his hodgepodge command forward around 8:50 A.M. He concentrated on connecting General Rice's brigade, the only one from his division still on the front line, to Webb's and Carruth's brigades, thereby extending the Union line to the right. For nearly an hour Rice's, Webb's, and Carruth's brigades fought Perry's Alabamians, which moments before had been bolstered by the brigades of Brigadier Generals Abner Perrin and Edward Perry of Major General Richard Anderson's Division, now attached to Longstreet's Corps. Anderson had finally arrived on the battlefield in the rear of Longstreet's charging divisions and had sent Perrin and Perry north of the Plank Road to support the attacking Alabamians there. The Union forces were now feeling the full brunt of General Longstreet's charge, which Longstreet personally directed.

Not only was the whole Union advance grinding to a halt, but new threats were developing near the Plank Road, the key to General Grant's plans. Confederates were reported to be less than a half mile from the Lacy house. In the meantime, the bulk of Burnside's IX Corps offered only minimal help. It had gotten lost, then was delayed by the Union supply train, and failed to connect with Hancock, despite prodding by General Grant. As late as 11:45 A.M., Grant's chief of staff, Brigadier General John Rawlins, reminded Burnside that Hancock had been "expecting you for the last three hours."[22]

By 10:00 A.M. there was a "lull all along the line . . . the ominous stillness that precedes the tornado." The Union and Confederate armies were like two battered, exhausted boxers, dropping their hands at the end of a round and staring at one another. General Wadsworth, "the old gentleman," snacked on hardtack and confessed to his aide, Captain Robert Monteith, that he was so unfit and tired that he "ought in justice to himself and his men, to turn the command over to Gen. Cutler." Ironically, it did not occur to Wadsworth that the Iron Brigade's commander was actually eight months older than he—and, likely, as tired.[23]

His fatigue was obvious to his son, Major Craig Wadsworth, who had obtained permission from 1st Division cavalry commander Brigadier General Alfred T. A. Torbert to visit his father during that lull. The young Wadsworth studied his father, whose dark eyes and sad face a photographer had so poignantly captured not long before. "Tick" expressed concern and urged his father not to be so reckless.[24]

In the eerie and unnatural quiet, the words of the general's father, "What will your ambition lead you to do?" may have rung in his ears. Just two days earlier he had set off under a "bending morning sky." The singing of birds and the dewy blossoms of dogwoods, violets, and azaleas reflected the "glad May air." He had taken time to write his wife, Mary Craig. In turn, she had forwarded to their youngest son the same advice that old James had offered the general in another age and time: not to "be led away & fall into bad habits . . . select your companions with judgment . . . [to make] your dear Father" proud.[25]

Instead of being home with his wife, Wadsworth was in the middle of a riot in thick, smoke-filled woods. Serving without pay, General Wadsworth had clearly proven his patriotism, courage, and leadership. A lieutenant colonel in General Alexander Hays's brigade recalled that Wadsworth's "presence on the field under the hottest fire inspirited [*sic*] and encouraged the men, and they will ever cherish with pride the memory of the chivalric bravery exhibited by [Wadsworth] in this battle." General Meade's chief of staff and later II Corps commander, Major General Andrew A. Humphreys, virtually gushed: Over these "two days of desperate fighting . . . he [Wadsworth] was conspicuous *beyond all others* for his gallantry, prompter than all others in leading his troops again and again into action. In all these combats he literally led his men, who inspired by his heroic bearing continually renewed the combat, which but for him they would have yielded."[26]

Why didn't Wadsworth turn the command over to General Cutler? Was it his fabled impetuousness? Did he have a death wish? His former adjutant general, Colonel John Kress, seemed to imply it: "I had grave fear he would not survive,

I had seen him take so many unnecessary risks." John Lothrop Motley, the diplomat-historian, claimed he always had "so deep a foreboding of his fate."[27]

"What will your ambition lead you to do?" was a good question. James Samuel probably had never sincerely tried to answer his father's question—really an admonition—and he had no time to do so now.

Aware of the firing on his left and a disturbing disorder, Wadsworth stirred himself, mounted his second horse of the day, and rode through the woods to the Plank Road. Halting at the edge of the road, he tried "to ascertain the location of the [II] corps with a view to concerted action." Before he could position his men, he observed "one of the strangest scenes of army experience," wrote the Philadelphia brigade's historian. "Without any apparent cause that could be seen," a mass of unidentified Union troops was falling back south of the road. They did not appear to be demoralized, nor acting under orders. Rather these troops, "indifferent to commands or entreaties," looked like "a throng of armed men who were returning dissatisfied from a muster."[28]

Alarmed, and granted authority over all the Union troops north (right) of the Plank Road, Wadsworth exercised it. He rode toward General Henry Eustis's 4th Brigade of the VI Corps, which were deployed on the right in the third line north of the Plank Road. Hoping to check the Confederate flank attack by positioning the brigade parallel to the road, Wadsworth made "a sweep with his arms from right to left to indicate to his regiments a half wheel." The 37th Massachusetts, approaching him before the movement began, was ordered to stem the Confederate advance. With Wadsworth leading the charge, the regiment faced a "deadly fire," but broke the first Confederate advance and struck the second before being virtually surrounded. The New Yorker then ordered the men to face the rear and fight their way back, subsequently praising the men for having "done all I expected a *brigade* to do."[29]

Wadsworth had discovered the cause of the wild disorder that he had observed previous to the charge: Another Confederate attack had broken through the Union left, south of the road. General Longstreet's aide, Lieutenant Colonel G. Moxley Sorrel, had secretly led the brigades of Brigadier Generals William "Billy" Mahone, George Thomas " Tige" Anderson, and William T. Wofford and Colonel John M. Stone (Davis's Brigade) around the Union left flank using an unfinished railroad cut. The maneuver was reminiscent of Stonewall Jackson's flanking movement at Chancellorsville the previous May. At about 11:00 A.M., Mahone's 12th Virginia, which rather miraculously had found its way through the thick underbrush ahead of the others, saw its opportunity while the Federals were trying to handle the divisions of Generals Field and Kershaw in their front. Deployed as skirmishers, the Virginians "dashed" across the field and struck the Union left. Sorrel's other Confederate brigades quickly followed suit. Before long they had rolled up Birney's flank south of the Plank Road and now threatened Wadsworth's command across the road. The

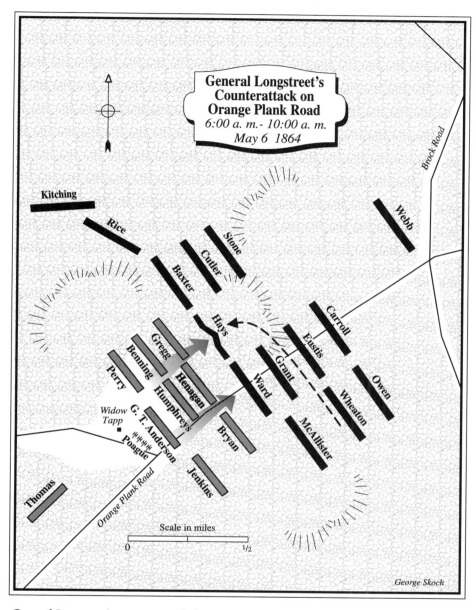

General Longstreet's counterattack (by George Skoch)

contradictory accounts of what happened thereafter are as confusing as the nature of the land itself.[30]

By most accounts General Wadsworth's amorphous command was hit hard. From the front, north of the road, came the divisions of Generals Field and Anderson. Then Kershaw came from the south, and finally Mahone's Brigade smashed from the left flank. It was chaotic, and the "old gentleman" mustered a reserve of energy to try once more to rally his men. First, he personally directed General Rice's brigade (76th, 95th, and 147th New York, the 14th Brooklyn, and the 56th Pennsylvania) to change front and to form parallel to the road facing south. The "object of the movement," according to Wadsworth, "was to take in flank the enemy as he came forward." (In fact, this movement would have aimed Rice's men directly at Mahone's.) Unfortunately, the maneuver exposed the right flank of Rice's command to the combined fire of guns and sharpshooters advancing along the Plank Road.[31]

While General Grant was trying to get General Burnside to "push in with all your vigor," the bulk of Burnside's corps was working its way through the woods between Warren's line on the Turnpike and Wadsworth's right flank. Burnside's troops were desperately needed, for the Confederates threatened to overrun General Wadsworth's lines. Mahone's 12th Virginia had rapidly advanced, accompanied by the rifle fire of the other flankers. Almost simultaneously Field's and Anderson's Divisions aimed straight at the Federals north of the road. Brigadier General Edward Perry's three Florida regiments (Anderson's Division) slightly overlapped Wadsworth's right. To their right were William Perry's Alabamians, while next to the road was Abner Perrin's Alabama Brigade, with Nathaniel Harris' Mississippians behind Perrin's.[32]

General Wadsworth quickly formed his Federals to confront them. Right to left in the Union front line were Sumner Carruth's Bay Staters and Webb's mix of Maine, Massachusetts, Michigan, and New York regiments, which had been battered earlier. In the second line were, right to left, Stevenson's and Rice's brigades. Behind them were the brigades of Brigadier Generals Henry Eustis and Frank Wheaton from the VI Corps. The Union front extended for something like a half mile.[33]

One of William Perry's 4th Alabamians regarded this as "the most critical moment of that awful, bloody, strenuous day's battle" for those Confederates north of the road. A countercharge (their second) was ordered, and it caused the Federals, including Carruth's brigade, "to scatter like partridges." Amid the "appalling disorder" and rising above the crash and roar of the battle were the "clear commanding tones" of General Wadsworth "as he attempted to resist the deadly torrent that was sweeping resistlessly forward." The impetuous general spied the 57th Massachusetts' color sergeant, Leopold Karpeles, and ordered him to post his colors. Karpeles, a 24-year-old Czech Jew, had emigrated to Texas, where as a teenager he rode shotgun for his brother's wagon trains before moving to Massachusetts.[34]

This was a desperate move in a desperate situation, but an inspired one. "[C]olors are very important to every organization in war," observed the 57th Massachusetts' historian. The colors not only mark the presence of the commanders of each distinctive command, but they direct troop placement. More important, "a regiment's flag was its soul." Thus, Wadsworth was appealing to the deepest emotions of the men facing an overwhelming charge while choking on the sulphurous smoke that enveloped them.[35]

General Wadsworth then called on the men "to rally around that standard and hold the ground until reinforcements could be brought up." Color Sergeant Karpeles bravely climbed on a stump and rallied forty others from the regiment. However, the charge of the Confederates quickly overran them, and "the colors were soon lost to sight amid the confusion." Karpeles, who would receive a Medal of Honor for his bravery, somehow managed to hold onto the flag as he and remnants of the regiment dropped to the ground and miraculously escaped capture. But the undaunted Wadsworth may have lost his second horse of the day.[36]

In the flowery language of the time, Lieutenant John Anderson of the 57th Massachusetts compared Wadsworth to "the first Napoleon, [who] possesse[d] powers of personal attraction that few could resist." He was able to draw "men around him who had never seen or scarcely heard of him before, holding them almost in the jaws of death and impressing them with his own lofty spirit of loyalty which rose above all fear of danger." In fact, Wadsworth's "Steady, boys, stand firm and we will soon whip them" still rang in Anderson's ears a quarter century later.[37]

Not everyone offered such an exalted view of the New Yorker. Certainly not regular army General Webb, who thereafter received what he considered "the most astonishing and bewildering order." General Wadsworth, in command of Webb's nine regiments, ordered Webb to "go to the left, find four regiments, and stop the retreat" of the troops fleeing toward the Brock Road. If Webb had been astonished by the previous order, he would have been even more so by the "old gentleman's" next one, which was given in Webb's absence.[38]

General Wadsworth had discovered Webb's 20th Massachusetts behind Confederate-constructed breastworks near the Plank Road, fronted by a ravine. Following instinct, he determined to plug the gaping hole in the Union line with them, a feat that required naked courage. He approached its commander, Colonel George N. Macy, and asked what troops these were and who commanded them. Macy replied they were his and that he had been instructed by General Webb to remain where he and the regiment were; that this was a critical defensive position. When Wadsworth ordered Macy to advance his regiment, Macy reminded Wadsworth that these were II Corps troops, not V Corps. By this time, Wadsworth's patience was exhausted. Perceiving that Macy was either insubordinate or fearful, he informed Colonel Macy that he would lead them himself. The general then "leaped his horse over the" logworks.[39]

The 1st Regiment of Berdan's U.S. Sharpshooters of the II Corps were just as startled—and disturbed. Wadsworth crossed over the Plank Road and rode "away ahead of anything on that particular field" to a line the Sharpshooters were trying to hold south of the road. Waving his sword, the excited general's "loud demands [and] peremptory orders" forced the Sharpshooters to surge farther forward, but they "met [the Confederates], coming with a rush—the balls hissing hot and low." Wadsworth rode ahead, with the 20th Massachusetts trailing.[40]

It was worse than foolish—a division commander leading a regiment in an assault—but it was quintessential Wadsworth. He would not order others to do something he would not do—in total disregard for his life. When his aide,

Lieutenant Earl M. Rogers, was asked by the 6th Wisconsin's Colonel Dawes why the general was allowed to ride "to certain death," Rogers replied, "My God, Colonel, nobody could stop him." Colonel Macy was convinced that Wadsworth "is out of his mind," but duly ordered his regiment forward.[41]

The Bay Staters tentatively moved out of the protection of the breastworks and into the woods behind the fast-charging Wadsworth. Colonel Swan claimed that the men of the 20th Massachusetts "had lost their dash, some of them being greatly disturbed by the change of front." Nonetheless, the attackers advanced to a point about three-quarters of a mile west of the Brock Road, just north of the Plank Road. Hereafter accounts differ according to the narrator. Lieutenant Schaff claims that the 8th Alabama, General Perrin's Brigade, lying in wait, rose and fired a fatal volley at the unsuspecting Federals. The impact was immediate and devastating, and the attack was abandoned. However, at this moment General Wadsworth's third horse of the day "panicked and bolted toward the Alabamians."[42]

Either the general, an expert horseman, or his aide, reportedly Lieutenant Rogers, attempted to rein in his horse. This caused the horse to turn and to expose the general to a bullet that tore into his skull and splattered his brains onto his aide. Rogers, who erroneously reported to headquarters that General Wadsworth was killed instantly, was forced to leave Wadsworth within the Confederate lines among the throng of dead and dying.[43]

Another version has it that a member of General William Perry's (Law's) Brigade killed General Wadsworth. P. D. Bowles of the 4th Alabama recalled that "a Federal officer [Wadsworth] came dashing up almost to my right. Whether this was a mere act of bravado or because he could not manage his horse I do not know, but just as he reached the opening on the plank road and was near a large tree, one of the men in my command shot him off his horse." This is certainly possible, but not corroborated.[44]

William T. Lowry, a 19-year-old member of Company D, 8th South Carolina Regiment of Kershaw's Brigade, also is credited with killing the general. Moreover, Lowry was supposed to have grabbed the general's field glasses, which were reported destroyed when Lowry's house burned around 1917. This account is both uncorroborated and unlikely. Further, the reference to the field glasses being burned up has been discounted.[45]

Purportedly, Second Lieutenant Arthur Jakeman of the 6th Virginia offered an even more detailed but, again, unsubstantiated, postwar account, which could have resulted in a different ending for the volunteer general. When the 20th Massachusetts broke, Wadsworth "was so near our lines that [Jakeman] ordered his men not to fire upon him, fearing that he was one of our officers." Just then a wind blew, disclosing the colors of the retreating soldiers. "The men fired without waiting for orders and General Wadsworth fell."[46]

The most detailed and unlikely version of Wadsworth's mortal wounding was offered by Private David Holt of the 16th Mississippi, General Harris's reserve brigade. Holt describes the Federals as coming out of the woods into an opening where they were unable to deploy their line, making them particularly

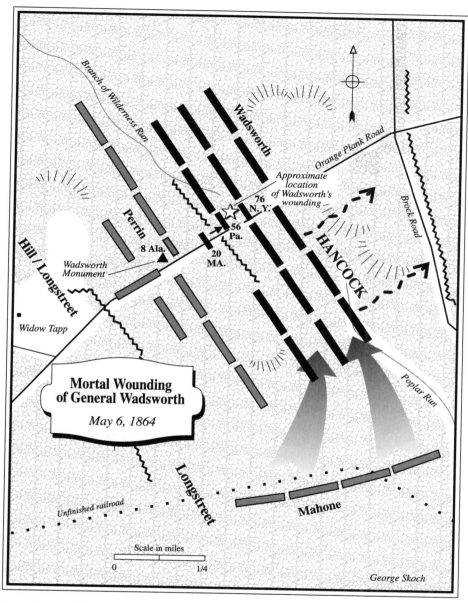

Mortal wounding of General Wadsworth (by George Skoch)

vulnerable. Surrounded and ordered to surrender, Wadsworth is supposed to have foolishly drawn a .38 caliber, silver-plated, pearl-handled Colt pistol, "a pretty toy," with one hand, while holding his sword with the other, when a companion of Holt's shot Wadsworth in the *side.*[47]

This account is contradicted in one important detail by Brevet Major Z. Boylston Adams, a member of the 56th Massachusetts. Adams, a surgeon who knew Wadsworth by sight and saw him again after he fell, recalled that "a musket ball had entered the top of his head a little to the left of the median line." This means Wadsworth was shot while leaning forward when his horse bolted. Or he was dismounted.[48]

In fact, Major George W. Jones of the 150th Pennsylvania, who challenged "most of the published accounts" of the general's fatal head wound, claimed that Wadsworth was dismounted. Jones recalled that General Wadsworth "was on the plank road at the time, *leading his horse,* having been persuaded to dismount by some of his officers . . . [to avoid] needlessly exposing himself to the fire of sharp-shooters" [italics added]. Jones purportedly relied both on his own observation and on "the testimony of a number of officers and men of the 150th," which he regarded as "conclusive." He also may have relied on Major Osborne of the 149th Pennsylvania, who reported that "I was sitting on my horse within two or three feet of the General, just in the rear of the front line, when he fell." If General Wadsworth was dismounted, it would have been possible for a bullet to enter the top of his head. But most reporters of the battle insist that he was riding his horse.[49]

Still another account claims that General Wadsworth was "shot by a rebel sharpshooter who was concealed in a tree."[50]

The most plausible account claims that "General Wadsworth and his horse . . . were both killed" by a volley from the 12th Virginia of Mahone's Brigade. Colonel V. D. Groner of the 61st Virginia Regiment, a member of the brigade, substantiates that account. He recalled that the brigade charged at right angles to the Plank Road "for some little distance, and then wheeled to the left." The 12th Virginia, on "the extreme right," crossed the Plank Road and drove straight into Wadsworth's tiny command and cleared "our entire front."[51]

Brigadier General James S. Wadsworth was counted among the more than 25,000 casualties of the battle of the Wilderness, which ended that night when the Confederates ran out of steam.

James Samuel Wadsworth, the intrepid warrior, who had enjoyed the companionship and respect of officers and men, college presidents, governors, cabinet members, even two U.S. presidents, now lay dying among the enemy in this godforsaken forest consumed by smoke and the annihilation of battle. As observers of his conduct in the war had predicted, the patriot's "ambition," in this case, unyielding commitment to the overthrow of slavery, had been his undoing.

Chapter 23

"WOULD RATHER HAVE LOST . . . [A] BRIGADE"

Wadsworth's Death

Reports of the wounding and capture of Brigadier General James Wadsworth, accurate this time, began filtering back to the rear of the Union lines almost immediately. The first reporter may well have been General Cutler, though he remained tentative. Earlier he had mistakenly reported his fear that the general had been killed. Instead, now he said "I don't know that General Wadsworth is killed. I know that he rode up the plank road while I was rallying the troops of the division." Cutler was relying on an officer who "informed me that he saw a general answering [Wadsworth's] description in every particular killed at the same place." Shortly thereafter the report was confirmed by Lieutenant Earl Rogers. Colonel Wainwright, the "old gentleman's" antagonist, hoped "that Wadsworth is not dead," and, in a rare moment of praise, confided to his diary that Wadsworth "and his men are said to have fought superbly." General Grant, upon learning of the V Corps division commander's fate, is reported to have remarked uncharacteristically "that he would rather have lost an entire infantry brigade rather than this brave and wise man."[1]

At 12:45 P.M. Major Edward Platt reported to General Humphreys that "An aide to General Wadsworth has just come in," claiming to have been with Wadsworth "when he was struck in the head about half an hour ago" and that "the body was left on the ground." In turn, Humphreys notified General Warren. "I felt his loss more keenly than anyone I know of," Warren wrote later, for General Wadsworth represented "the best and strongest friend in our country." Because General Hancock's forces were to pass over the spot where Wadsworth was reported to have fallen, Humphreys suggested to Warren "that some of General Wadsworth's staff, with a small party, follow" Hancock's men "to recover General Wadsworth's remains, should he have fallen." Two days later, Brigadier General James H. Wilson of the 3rd Division Cavalry notified Major General Philip Sheridan that a Confederate prisoner had informed him that General

Wadsworth was "not yet dead, though insensible from a wound in the head, and expected to die eventually."[2]

Confederate reports of Wadsworth's capture and supposed death were almost as prompt and numerous. At 8:00 P.M. on May 6, General Lee notified Richmond of the general's death. Almost simultaneously a telegram informed Montgomery Ritchie (Cornelia Wadsworth's husband) in Washington that his father-in-law had been killed and his body was in Confederate hands. Presumably Lee had ordered the telegram sent, based on a report from Brigadier General "Billy" Mahone, who had come upon the well-known New Yorker among "a large number of dead and wounded in our hands."[3]

One of many ironies in this sad episode is that previously General Wadsworth and II Corps brigade commander Alexander Webb had talked about head wounds. The young brigadier recalled telling Wadsworth that he had concluded from his observations that soldiers with head wounds could not survive, so he did not have these men carried from the field. He had argued that the wounded soldier "slowly lost his vertical position and was incapable of making a movement of his head from the ground." As it turned out, Webb's diagnosis proved correct in terms of General Wadsworth's wound, but not his own. Barely a week after Wadsworth was mortally wounded, a bullet passed through one of General Webb's eyes and out behind the ear. Contrary to his earlier conclusion, the brigadier found he could raise his head and realized he would live.[4]

As unclear as are the circumstances surrounding how General Wadsworth was hit, it is equally hard to determine who found him and where. Major John Cheves Haskell, one of Longstreet's artillery commanders, claimed to have been first to come upon the wounded general. "While we were advancing," Haskell later recalled, "I noticed a large, fine-looking man in the uniform of a general, who was lying on the side of the road in the dust and heat." Haskell detected breathing and instructed two orderlies to move the general. "They stuck some muskets up and spread a blanket over him as an awning, then got a surgeon to examine him. The surgeon did not think that he was conscious, and gave him some water and morphine."[5]

The May 10 *Daily Richmond Enquirer* credited Captains A. G. Morton of the 20th Georgia and A. C. Mott of General Benning's staff with finding the mortally wounded division commander. The *Enquirer* provided all the gory details: Wadsworth had been "shot in the crown of the head, the ball having penetrated the skull, leaving the brain protruding." Captains Morton and Mott "spoke to him, and finding him unconscious or unable to speak, endeavored to resuscitate him by administering a stimulant [likely whisky]. The wounded man seemed to appreciate the effort, but the remedy was ineffectual." Morton then "wrote the words 'General Wadsworth of New York' on a slip of paper, and pinned it to the lapel of his coat, and left him." Many years later Major A. R. H. Ranson, a Confederate ordnance officer, said that he had spotted the wounded general and the slip of paper, but recalled that it was attached to a cedar bush rather than pinned to his coat. Written on the "large piece of paper" were the words: "This is the body of General Wadsworth of New York. It is requested that every attention be given this distinguished officer."[6]

Haskell's account is partially substantiated by a letter from a John Lee Carroll of Baltimore to Mary Craig Wadsworth more than a year and a half after her husband's death. Carroll had checked with Colonel Charles Marshall, who was not only one of the most trusted of General Lee's staff (and may have actually written the letter), but was at Wadsworth's "side a short time after he was wounded." Mary Craig's husband was lying "about fifteen paces to the left [north] of the Plank Road, in the woods," from which Marshall inferred that the general fell trying to rally his men. However, Marshall may not have been aware that Major Haskell had directed his orderlies to move Wadsworth. Marshall found Wadsworth "lying on his back, his head supported by something which I do not now remember, and over him was extended a shelter tent, about three feet from the ground, the two corners at his head being attached to the boughs of trees. I think, the other two, and the sides being supported by muskets."[7]

Two things particularly caught Carroll's eye. The first was the general's "perfectly natural" appearance. The second was the way the unconscious man's "fingers played with the trigger" of one of the muskets supporting the shelter tent. Occasionally Wadsworth pushed the musket away at arm's length, but continued to grasp it. Longstreet's artillery commander, Porter Alexander, also recalled that Wadsworth "had gotten his finger on the trigger of one of the muskets & was picking & playing with it." Another observer remembered that Wadsworth also was "playing with the buttons on his coat," indicating that he "was so severely injured that his mind wandered."[8]

Carroll had supposed from the "calm and natural" facial expression and open eye that the dying man was conscious. However, when Carroll tried to talk to Wadsworth, he discovered that the latter "was unconscious of what was passing around him." At this point Carroll was called away and never saw Wadsworth again. He did learn from the Army of Northern Virginia's medical director, Dr. Lafayette Guild, that about noon the same day, the 6th, the mortally wounded general was removed to a Confederate field hospital, about a mile to the rear, with other Union and Confederate soldiers. Wadsworth was placed in an officer's tent erected "for his especial benefit" and was attended by Dr. James W. Claiborne, a surgeon in Mahone's Brigade.[9]

Major Ranson, who spotted the note identifying Wadsworth, claimed to have ordered the ambulance that carried the dying general to the field hospital. There Dr. Guild examined him and quickly concluded that nothing could be done for the New Yorker. However, quite at odds with other accounts, Ranson recalled a half century later that Dr. Guild discovered that the unseeing Wadsworth "talked incessantly," in fact, "freely and pleasantly," until questioned by Guild about the Union movements. Then "he emphatically shut up," leading Ranson to conclude that the general's reticence "was a remarkable instance of what *noblesse oblige* means to a dying gentleman and soldier."[10]

A subsequent report to Union army headquarters, apparently from a Union prisoner, mentions "one of *our* officers attending" Wadsworth in the Confederate field hospital. That officer was likely Captain Z. Boylston Adams, a young surgeon who was commanding Company F, 56th Massachusetts, when wounded and captured by the Confederates. He lay in the makeshift hospital with Wadsworth. Indeed, Adams offers the most detailed and intimate account of the general's condition and care. Regaining consciousness after an operation on his leg, Captain Adams became aware of a Union general ("shown by his shoulder star") lying on a stretcher under the same tent fly sheltering him. Adams recognized Wadsworth from having seen him re-forming troops earlier in the day: "He was rather tall, an eminently handsome man of commanding presence, but showing gentle breeding."[11]

Impulsively, Captain Adams applied his surgeon's training to diagnose the general's condition. Adams lifted the unconscious man's eyelids, but found "no speculation [capacity to see] in those eyes." Next he checked Wadsworth's pulse, which was regular, and listened to his labored breathing. Occasionally the mortally wounded general, whose "noble features were calm and natural," sighed deeply. Further examination revealed that "his right arm was evidently paralyzed, which indicated that the injury was to the left brain." Adams became fascinated by "one very singular fact." The general, who, from all appearances, was totally unconscious, would "frown and show restlessness" when someone grabbed the paper with his name on it. He would move his hand "to and fro as if in search of something, until the paper was put into his fingers." Once the paper was returned to his fingers, he "would grasp it and lay his hand quietly upon his breast." It appears that the scrap of paper with Wadsworth's name on it went from the cedar bush to Wadsworth's lapel and finally to his hand.[12]

Like a magnet, the famous Yankee attracted Confederates, who thronged the tent. They "crowded around, curious to see the dying man whose name and fame had reached their ears," and pounded his surgeon-tentmate with questions. "'Do you mean to say that this is James S. Wadsworth of New York, the proprietor of vast estates in the Genesee valley, the candidate for governor in 1862?' etc." Their curiosity led to an unsettling experience for Captain Adams. "Unmindful of the impress of dignity and nobility of character . . . of the dying man," into the tent burst a "vain young fellow much bedizened with stars and buttons and gold lace" and drunk withal. The inebriated Confederate indignantly labeled Adams a liar; the wounded general could not be James S. Wadsworth, the propertied Northerner. Union officers were "crazy abolitionists, mercenaries, low politicians, hirelings from foreign armies, etc." Adams remonstrated and, in the process, revealed that he was from Massachusetts. The young Confederate flew into a rage, then drew and cocked a revolver. Timely intervention by other Confederates saved Adams.[13]

On Saturday night, May 7, more than thirty hours after he was hit, Confederate surgeons "examined General Wadsworth's wound, removing a piece of skull, and then probing for the ball," which struck Adams as "bad surgery." They found the "ball had entered near the top of the head, had gone forward, and was lodged in the anterior lobe of the left side of the brain." Thus, Adams concluded that the general was either falling or bent forward "in anticipation of a volley from the advancing enemy."[14]

Attempts were made to feed Wadsworth, but he was unable to swallow more than a teaspoonful. Otherwise, the offering dribbled out of the corners of his mouth. One would-be caregiver was "a Virginian, not a soldier," who entered the tent by the rear. The Virginian wanted to know if the wounded man really was the person who had once saved his life. Then he introduced himself as Patrick McCracken, the 34-year-old native Irishman who had been released in 1862 by Military Governor Wadsworth after giving assurances that he was a farmer, not a spy, and would not assist the Confederacy. Now, ironically, McCracken was worried about being accused of aiding the Union wounded, according to Captain Adams. Still, he "would be happy" if Adams would give General Wadsworth a bottle of milk and some food. Told that the unconscious man could not swallow, McCracken offered the sustenance to Adams. However, John Lee Carroll wrote Mary Craig Wadsworth that on May 8, the day Wadsworth succumbed, he was offered some broth, "expressed his assent by slightly nodding his head" and "swallowed a few spoonfuls."[15]

A generation later, Captain David Augustus Dickert of the 3rd South Carolina, Kershaw's Brigade, poignantly recalled seeing the dying "multi-millionaire in an enemy's country, not a friend near to hear his last farewell or soothe his last moments by a friendly touch on the pallid brow."[16]

According to John Carroll, after Wadsworth's death Patrick McCracken "applied to the Medical officers of the hospital, for permission to take charge of his remains until they should be sent for." Writing Mary Craig from "Spotsylvania Court House, Va., near New Hope Meeting House, on Plank Road, going from Fredericksburg to Orange Court House, May 9, 1864," McCracken offers the most detailed and contemporaneous account of events subsequent to Wadsworth's death. About 3:00 on the 8th, McCracken returned to find the general dead "and in a box, ready for interment." The Virginian explained that he wanted to repay his benefactor and promised to make a coffin for the general and "bury him in a family burying ground." The head surgeon "cheerfully consented" to the removal of the body.[17]

However, when McCracken returned with the coffin, he ran into bureaucratic red tape. He recalled that General Lee had issued special orders to bury General Wadsworth "by a large tree, the tree to be cut low and his name marked on it." Captain Adams interceded and assured the head surgeon that McCracken could be trusted. McCracken "removed [the body] from the box to the coffin," which he asserted was "as good as any could be made in the country." Then, as promised, he buried Wadsworth in the McCracken family burying ground "with the clothing as he fell on the battle-field" and covered the coffin "with plank and then dirt." Afterward he had a "large plank planed and marked for a headstone," which he placed at the head of the grave. McCracken expressed his "pleasure in having [Wadsworth] moved through our lines to his friends" as soon as arrangements could be made by the Confederate authorities.[18]

Meanwhile Major General George Meade had attempted to contact Captain Craig Wadsworth to send him to the general's widow in Washington, but "we were then fighting and he [Craig] was reluctant to leave at that moment." Further, if Mary Craig preferred it, General Meade was prepared to place Craig on his staff "and under my eye, altho I know he will not like it as well as being with the cavalry." Though contrary to Craig's wishes, "I will nevertheless bring him back here." Then Meade, inconsistently, assigned him to Brigadier General Alfred Torbert, commander of a cavalry division and "a *gentleman* of high character."[19]

The very day her husband was shot Mary Craig Wadsworth had written her youngest son, James W., about her fervent hope that her husband and middle son, Craig, would be home for the summer, restored in health. Craig would, along with his brothers Charles and Jimmy, but not the man she had married three decades earlier. Now Mary Craig wrote General Meade that she wanted her husband returned to his native soil and used her influence on Secretary of War Stanton.

On May 12, Stanton telegraphed Army of the Potomac commander Meade asking him to make "every effort" to recover the remains of Wadsworth and other officers within Confederate lines.

Even before that, the same evening that McCracken was interring the general, surgeon Benjamin T. Kneeland of New York's 1st Dragoons (130th N.Y.) was ordered by General Grant's medical director to transport the wounded from both sides to Fredericksburg. Kneeland, who was carrying out that order, learned of General Wadsworth's mortal wounding from Craig Wadsworth and, subsequently, was told by Confederates that the general had been buried in Patrick McCracken's dooryard.[20]

Almost simultaneously Meade dispatched A. K. St. Clair, assistant surgeon of the 1st Michigan Cavalry, with a note requesting permission for St. Clair to pass far enough to obtain Wadsworth's remains, so they could be transferred "to his afflicted widow and relatives." Confederate commander Lee promptly informed Meade that he was "not at liberty" to permit surgeon St. Clair to "come within our lines." Instead, he would have Major General Wade Hampton convey the body to the Union lines. Hampton then notified Meade that he would order a flag of truce posted at the Wilderness Church on Plank Road at noon on May 17. At the appointed time Simon Baruch, the father of future businessman and statesman Bernard Baruch, remembered that "tattered men in gray bared their heads" as the ambulance bore "Wadsworth's body through the Confederate lines." The 1st Dragoons' Dr. Kneeland then ordered the body sent to Fredericksburg, where he met Major Montgomery Ritchie, the general's son-in-law, who confirmed Kneeland's identification of the general. Once there, surgeon Kneeland "made [the body] as decent as we could for sending home, and sent it."[21]

The general's effects were treated more cavalierly. Colonel G. Moxley Sorrel recalled that when "there was still some life left in the General," but before Confederate surgeons could reach him, "some of his valuables—watch, sword, glasses, etc.—had disappeared among the troops." Westwood A. Todd, an officer in the 12th Virginia, Mahone's Brigade, recalled that "Our men had gone through him before his rank was discovered by our officers." The results were obvious: "His hat and boots were gone and every button cut off his coat." Bob Archer of the 6th Virginia appropriated the general's pocketbook and $90, while John Bolote grabbed Wadsworth's gold watch, and an unknown (to this day) took his "elegant" and very expensive field glasses. One item that quickly reappeared was "a good general map of Virginia," which Colonel Sorrel made use of and which years later he returned with pleasure to the general's youngest son, then a congressman.[22]

Mary Craig Wadsworth had written Meade that she wanted not only the return of her dead husband's body, but also his effects. However, Meade wanted authorization from Grant. Upon Grant's instructions Meade contacted General Lee, who "directed inquiries" and assured Meade he would "take great pleasure in restoring them to his widow," if they could be found. Meanwhile, Meade wrote the grieving widow that Grant did not "think it expedient . . . at this moment" to seek a flag of truce, but "promises me" to do so "at the earliest possible moment."[23]

Almost a year later, when she still had not received any of her husband's effects, Mary Craig wrote General Lee directly, identifying the items she sought. Apologetically Lee replied that he had requested the officer in command where General Wadsworth fell to "take every step in his favor" to recover the requested items, but circumstances in that summer of 1864 made it impossible to comply "with her wishes." He reiterated his promise to restore the items she had requested, but more time would elapse before any of them found their way back to her.[24]

A *Daily Richmond Enquirer* report on Monday, May 9, was much less considerate as well as inaccurate: "This defunct son of Mars, we learn, was a son of an opulent citizen of Western New York. Prior to the war he was regarded as a person of some pretensions to decency. . . . He graduated at Yale College, in the same class with Hon. Allen T. Caperton, one of the Confederate States' Senators from Virginia, and perished ignobly on the battle field near Chancellorsville, last Friday."

By contrast, Secretary of the Navy Gideon Welles was heartbroken when on May 10 President Lincoln read the dispatch from General Grant about Wadsworth. "Few nobler spirits have fallen in this war," Welles recorded in his diary. Worse, Welles felt, the death was unnecessary. Wadsworth "should, by good right and fair-dealing, have been at this moment Governor of New York." He would have been, concluded Welles, except for the "perfidy of Thurlow Weed and others," including Welles's fellow cabinet member, William Seward. Now, the "single-minded patriot," who could have stayed home enjoying the comforts that wealth could provide, lay dead.[25]

President Lincoln was equally grieved, if not more so: "I have not known the President so affected by a personal loss since the death of [Lincoln's friend Edward] Baker," wrote Lincoln's secretary, John Hay, "as by the death of General Wadsworth." "No man has given himself up to the war with such self-sacrificing patriotism as Genl Wadsworth," concluded Hay, or was as "profoundly indifferent to popular applause."[26]

The patriot was now one of the many casualties of a campaign that had started so glowingly for the Federals, but had become a gloomy failure. Unforgivable lack of understanding of the geography (given the battle of Chancellorsville a year previous), lack of coordination, Burnside's delay, Confederate heroics, and the impenetrable forest had spelled a tie, if not another defeat, for the Union. Grant's initial handling of the army here in the East did little or nothing to suggest a change in the Union's fortunes.

Losses for the Army of the Potomac and the IX Corps were "enormous": 17,666, including 2,246 killed, 12,037 wounded, and 3,383 missing, or 17 percent of effective troops. Confederate losses are harder to obtain, but they are estimated at 7,750, or almost 13 percent. Including its fearless commander, Wadsworth's 4th Division sustained a total of 2,008 casualties, 10 percent of whom were killed. Compared to Gettysburg, the division's losses here in the Wilderness were less devastating, but, like many other units, it would never be the same again. In the eyes of many, the biggest loss was the inspirational division commander.[27]

✯   ✯   ✯

Barely a day and a half after Wadsworth expired, a public meeting was held at the American Hotel on Geneseo's Main Street to announce his death. County Judge Charles H. Carroll and *Livingston Republican* editor James T. Norton were appointed chairman and secretary, respectively, to plan funeral arrangements. "After brief, appropriate and feeling speeches" by Judge Carroll, W. H. Kelsey, and unnamed others, a seven-man committee was "appointed to report resolutions suitable to the melancholy occasion."[28]

On May 12 the general's hometown paper, the *Livingston Republican,* reported that the body of Geneseo's most distinguished citizen was due in Geneseo on Thursday, May 19, or Friday, May 20, with the funeral to be conducted on Saturday, the 21st. A week later it printed a note from an anonymous person who had a "presentment" that Wadsworth would be killed. Yet the writer was stunned, "for it was but a few days ago, at Willard's [Hotel in Washington], he took me by the hand and said, 'good-bye,'—and how often he has added 'God bless you.'" Other towns, including Geneva, also lamented the death of one of the conspicuous "citizens of the State."[29]

Almost simultaneously, by General Orders 197, the War Department honored Wadsworth by giving his name to a post constructed on the James River near the present city of Aberdeen, South Dakota. Thinking along the same lines, Major General John A. Dix, whose career often paralleled James S. Wadsworth's, recommended renaming "Fort Richmond" on Staten Island in Wadsworth's honor. The present name "suggests nothing to my mind but some passages in British history, and a city sheltering traitors in arrest against the Government," wrote General Dix. "If there is any reason why this name [Fort Richmond] can not be changed for another [Wadsworth] which is identified with our own history, at the most critical period of our existence, and adorned with the manliest virtues," then, Dix continued, name the fort at Sandy Hook in General Wadsworth's honor. At least one fort ought to "be made a medium for transmitting to posterity one eminently endeared to the people of this state." The recommendation was formally approved on November 7, 1865.[30] Fort Wadsworth still occupies a northeast corner of Staten Island, its grounds now bisected by the Verrazano-Narrows Bridge.

Also out of respect for Wadsworth, on May 10, New York State governor Horatio Seymour, Wadsworth's opponent in the 1862 gubernatorial race, had issued an order to display the national flag at half-staff on the state capitol and all the state arsenals. Seymour's accompanying message, announced "with painful feelings," had more than a few, possibly unintended, ironies. After pointing out the "wide influence" Wadsworth exercised "by the energy of his character," Seymour recalled that the dead general "was always decided and resolute in demanding purity of legislation and wise administration of the affairs of our own State," even to "periling his own person in upholding the principles which he advocated."[31]

In addition to flying the state flags at half-staff, Governor Seymour ordered the state's adjutant general, John T. Sprague, to travel to Washington to "receive" the general's remains and to "make such arrangements for transporting the body home as might be agreeable to the family of the deceased." On Saturday, May 14, William J. McDermott, recently paroled surgeon of the 3rd U.S. Infantry and 66th New York Volunteers, accompanied Wadsworth's body, "which had been interred by the order of Gen. Lee, in a neat coffin," through the Union lines. The general's remains, in the care of his son-in-law, Captain Montgomery Ritchie, and two others, would take a circuitous—and likely for the family, a tortuous—route home.[32]

The first stop was Washington, to which the coffin had been borne up Aquia Creek by the steamer *Mary Rapley,* on May 18. Son-in-law Ritchie, Major Cutter of General Augur's staff, and Dr. John Ross, assistant to the governor's embalmers, were the escorts. Dr. Ross had been sent on May 11 specially to exhume the body and to bring it home. However, Ross reported that "some of [General Lee's] officers did all in their power to thwart the party seeking [Wadsworth's] body by objecting to slight informalities in the arrangements for the flag of truce." The result was that the general's body was "so far decomposed that it cannot be embalmed." Instead, the body was placed "in a metallic coffin" before being escorted to New York City.[33]

The coffin bearing the general's remains arrived in New York City on May 19, aboard the 6:30 P.M. train. It was accompanied by Adjutant General Sprague, Dr. Fitzhugh, a six-man committee selected by the state's congressional delegation, per Governor Seymour's orders, and eight men chosen from the Veteran Reserves. "The remains were received at the foot of Cortlandt street by a detachment of the Third Regular Infantry under command of Lieut. [George K.] Pomeroy, and Company C, Seventh Regiment [National Guards], Capt.[George T.] Haws commanding." It seemed fitting to have the 7th New York ceremonially receive the body of the man who arranged out-of-pocket transportation for them to Washington barely three years earlier.[34]

A half hour later a procession formed and marched into the "Governor's room" in the City Hall, where the coffin remained until 3:00 P.M. on Friday, May 20. Reportedly "an immense concourse of citizens" visited the casket of the "prominent gentleman" as it lay in state on that balmy day. A New York musician, W. Charles, even composed a "Grand Solemn March," which was dedicated "To The Memory of The Brave General James S. Wadsworth." Whether the song, which mirrored the times ("How sleep the brave who sink to rest/By all their Country's wishes blest."), was ever played publicly cannot be determined. At the appointed time General John A. Dix, ex-governor Hamilton Fish, ten unidentified others serving as pallbearers, and the 7th Regiment escorted the body to the Erie Railroad Station.[35]

The next stop was Rochester, New York, where last-minute preparations for a civic ceremony were hastily made at 2:00 P.M. on the 20th in Mayor James Bracket's office. However, the large crowd at the city offices forced the organizers to shift the meeting to the Common Council Chambers, into which the famous citizen's body was escorted by D. W. Powers, George F. Danforth, and Samuel Wilder. At the meeting, an eighty-man delegation, headed by the mayor, was named to attend the funeral the next day in Geneseo. This was followed by resolutions honoring Wadsworth and directing the mayor to fly flags at half-staff and to have the city's bells rung during the funeral.[36]

Then, once more the coffin was put aboard a train, with members of the heroic, but badly decimated, 21st New York, the "First Buffalo Regiment, leading the procession." Fittingly, the 21st New York, a part of Wadsworth's brigade in Washington, escorted the body and refused Mrs. Wadsworth's offer to pay them for their services. The "old gentleman" was making his final trip home to his beloved Geneseo.[37]

The route of the train bearing the general's coffin often paralleled the Genesee River, southward through the rich farmland of the towns of Henrietta, Rush, and Avon, to the Village of Avon, where, on Saturday morning, May 21, "an immense number of people" met the 8:00 A.M. train. A Geneseo contingent, consisting of "a large number of personal friends, a suitable military escort," Adjutant General Sprague, and an individual identified simply as "Dr. McMillan of the regular army," then took charge of the funeral cortege as it headed down the Valley, or Geneseo, Road.[38]

Finally the cortege made its way to Hartford House, one of the largest in western New York, which Wadsworth had built for himself and his wife three decades earlier. Closed churches, businesses, and houses draped in black and flags hanging at half-mast attested to the solemnity of the occasion. In a special tribute to the deceased his photograph "encircled in a wreath of evergreen" was hung outside the *Livingston Republican* office by editor James Norton. At 1:30 P.M., the general's remains were moved to St. Michael's Church, the Episcopal church to which, tradition has it, the general's father and uncle had shifted their allegiance after a disagreement with the minister of the Presbyterian church. "The usual burial service" was conducted by "The Rev. Mr. Irish," whose homily proclaimed the deceased was "an aristocrat of the only aristocracy America will ever harbor."[39]

Following the church service, despite the family's wish "that there should be no display," a large procession was formed under the direction of E. R. Hammatt. The procession then wound its way down "thronged" Main Street to Big Tree Lane and up to Temple Hill, which crowned the rise to the east. Just outside the village limits lay the cemetery, which old James had set aside and which now was "neatly laid out in lots and walks, and carefully kept in order." Sturdy oaks and maples, which dot the Genesee Valley, here sheltered the graves of Geneseo's most prominent citizens, including Governor John Young, with whom the general had been allied politically, and the Wadsworth family plot.

The Squire of Geneseo, whose "ambition" led him to become an abolitionist, an ultra-ardent patriot, and an intrepid warrior, now joined his father, uncle, grandmother, mother, and two siblings, less than five months shy of his fifty-seventh birthday.[40]

Chapter 24

"HIS EXAMPLE STILL LIVES TO INSPIRE"

Memorials and tributes poured in to Mary Craig Wharton Wadsworth and the family. Particularly meaningful to the family was the one by which James Samuel was breveted Major General of Volunteers by Secretary of War Stanton. The brevet, dated June 27, 1864, recognized the general for "Gallant and distinguished Services at battles of Bull run [*sic*], Gettysburg and the Wilderness." Captain Craig W. Wadsworth "acknowledged" receipt of it on May 7, 1865, almost exactly a year after his father was mortally wounded. Significantly, Wadsworth's brevet was issued before a slew of them were awarded to volunteers in 1865.[1]

In another tribute to the fallen soldier shortly after his death, flagstaffs and banners bearing his and General John Sedgwick's likenesses were planted near the Washington Monument in June 1864. They recalled two Union generals who fell a month earlier during the bloody spring of 1864 campaign.[2]

More personal and meaningful was the note written to Mary Craig by Army of the Potomac commander Meade, who had come to regard General Wadsworth as a "personal friend to whom I had become warmly attached." Almost simultaneously, she received a letter from Major General Winfield S. Hancock: Though Wadsworth was "not a soldier by education," he was considered "so good that . . . each corps commander desired him as commander of [a] division."[3]

V Corps commander Gouverneur K. Warren wrote a particularly thoughtful and personal four-page letter. In less than two months the civilian general had made a distinct impression on Warren, "whose unbounded confidence he [Wadsworth] had gained." Above all, Warren wanted Mary Craig to know that her husband had not died in vain, "that his example still lives to inspire." Wadsworth, who had given up "the comforts . . . of a happy home, and the highest civil honors," had led by example: "in the thickest of the carnage, in the van of his troops, in the very teeth of the enemy he met a patriot's death." The Army of the Potomac's chief of staff, Major General Andrew A. Humphreys, was equally eloquent in a letter addressed to "Dear Cousin."[4]

Men who had served under Wadsworth were as likely to express the same sentiments. Even the hypercritical artillerist Colonel Charles Wainwright had to acknowledge his appreciation for Wadsworth's personal qualities, except for what Wainwright regarded as his talkativeness. Particularly heartfelt were the tributes paid to Wadsworth in the histories of regiments that had served under him and that recalled his leadership, bravery, and empathy for his men.

"The Fourteenth [Brooklyn] especially felt his loss," wrote the regiment's historian, "for there had been a peculiar comradeship between him and the Brooklyn boys. . . . This brave soldier was more than a patriot; he was a hero who gave his life, his sons and his fortune to the cause of liberty." Colonel Theodore Gates, commander of the 20th New York Militia (the "Ulster Guards"), recalled when the general rode into their camp months after he ceased to command their brigade: "there was a rush of officers and men to greet their old commander." His face lit up upon seeing "how universal and genuine was the esteem in which his old command held him." The 6th Wisconsin's Colonel Rufus Dawes especially remembered General Wadsworth's "great solicitude for the suffering men" making the weary trek to Gettysburg. "Among those who fell [in the Wilderness] none was more sincerely mourned by those who served under him" than Wadsworth, wrote the 7th Indiana's historian. "The division had other commanders whom it rightly honored, but none as it did 'Pap Wadsworth.'" Almost two decades after the war's end the thought of Generals Reynolds and Wadsworth "in their graves" still brought tears to Captain J. Volnay Pierce, late of the 147th New York.[5]

Memorials bore the mark of the New Yorker's civilian friends and associates as well. Wadsworth's death "was something that I had been constantly expecting yet dreading to hear," U.S. Minister to Austria John Lothrop Motley revealed to Mary Craig. In a long, eight-page letter to her Motley remembered "the handsome young man [at Harvard . . . who was] the most thoroughly American I ever knew." However, Motley admired Wadsworth even more now because the patriot "knew he was fighting to preserve the existence of the only free country in the world."[6]

The most widely published tributes were from Wadsworth's political associates. Typical was L. E. Chittenden's, which occupies almost half a page of his introduction to the much-delayed report on the 1861 Peace Conference, of which Wadsworth was an influential member. "Those of us who were associated with him politically, had learned to love and respect him." Even his opponents, Chittenden was quick to add, "admired his unflinching devotion to his country, and his manly frankness and candor." Similarly, New York City's Union Defense Committee paid tribute to one of its most famous members. Fittingly, on May 21, the committee's resolutions were read by Edwards Pierrepont, a political ally of the general. They noted that "by his devoted life and by his glorious death" Wadsworth left to "coming generations, a bright example for patriots to imitate."[7]

"Great events always discover and bring out great men," proclaimed a memorial in the *U.S. Service Magazine*. "Prominent among these [men]" was General Wadsworth. The memorial emphasized the general's service in the military, which came about because "the necessity of the country demanded it." The anonymous author recalled the fallen hero's "coolness, courage, and capacity" as an unpaid volunteer aide to Major General Irvin McDowell and as military governor. Important, too, Wadsworth "prevented wrong and outrage" in that part of Virginia where he had authority and offered "a refuge to the oppressed." While the patriot provided an example of unflinching courage at Chancellorsville, Gettysburg, and the Wilderness, it was through his dying that "he lives still" in the hearts of those who honor his "patriotism, philanthropy and self-abnegation."[8]

The tribute by the Century Association, the prestigious New York social group, of which the Squire of Geneseo was a member, probably most objectively summarized his life. Using background material prepared by Lewis F. Allen, William J. Hoppin emphasized that while Wadsworth's wealth was "as large as some German principality," he was free from "false pride." Yet Allen and Hoppin recognized his impetuousness, "his habit . . . of riding about the foremost line, even among his skirmishers, which somewhat unnecessarily exposed his life."[9]

Back in western New York, the New York State Agricultural Society closed its exhibition, held in Rochester, to pay tribute to its late president. The society's resolution was highlighted by anecdotes about the general from his son Craig and by Craig's reading of a letter from Patrick McCracken to Mary Craig. The Buffalo Historical Society and the Union Bank of Rochester also memorialized Wadsworth, as did his Genesee Valley neighbors, including the Livingston County Bar Association.[10]

In a rather surprising tribute, the Grand Army of the Republic Post No. 12 in Fredericksburg, Virginia, organized July 26, 1871, was named for the fallen general. The announcement was addressed to "Mrs. General" and signed by L. H. York, post commander, less than a week after the post was founded.[11]

Two other memorials to the general at this time stemmed from his unfulfilled wishes. The first, laid out originally in his father's will, was the Wadsworth Library. The Federal-style, brick building at the corner of Center and Second Streets in his hometown was built in 1867. With its vaulted ceilings, high arched windows, and copies of paintings of the general and his father looking down on library users, it still serves the village today.[12]

The second was the present-day State University of New York at Geneseo. Its founding as a normal (teacher education) school dates to 1871 and reflected the general's and his father's interest in public education. But two big obstacles faced the organizers of the school in 1871: money and land. Over strenuous objections (the village was in debt owing to two disastrous fires and construction of a water line and bridges), a scant majority of Geneseoans voted to appropriate $45,000 to establish the school. Additional money came from a $10,000 trust fund created for educational purposes by old James. The land was donated by the general's heirs, who deeded 6.73 acres, worth $2,019.60, to the town commissioners, who then turned the property over to the state for the nominal sum of $1 in 1871. The success of the institution, which first bore the name Wadsworth Normal and Training School, is one of the most lasting memorials to the general, his father, and his family.[13]

The 1880s saw a resurgence of interest in the Civil War; within a decade it grew into a full-blown movement to erect monuments to soldiers who had fallen in the conflict. In 1910, the New York State Legislature approved the expenditure of up to $10,000 for a monument at Gettysburg to honor General Wadsworth. At a cost of $7,788.28, the New York State Monument Commission erected an impressive tribute to Wadsworth on Reynolds Avenue, north of the Chambersburg Pike and the now-completed railroad. Begun in early 1912, the monument, designed by R. Hinton Perry and constructed by the Gorham Company of New York City, was dedicated on October 6, 1914. Atop the ten-foot-high, drum-shaped, "highly polished . . . dark Barre granite" pedestal stands the lifelike, nine-foot representation of General Wadsworth pointing toward the oncoming Confederates.[14]

The commission invited veterans from various regiments with which the general had been involved (including Geneseo's 104th New York that he had helped form) to attend the ceremony. The aging veterans were instructed to "appear in the uniform usually worn on Memorial Day." Among attendees were five members of the Wadsworth family: the general's youngest son, former congressman James ("Jimmy") W., and his wife, Maria; his grandson, James W., Jr., elected U.S. senator a month later; and his great-grandchildren, James Jeremiah, future U.S. ambassador to the United Nations, and Evelyn, who would marry Senator Stuart Symington. The youngest Wadsworths unveiled the monument, and the general's son and grandson both spoke briefly, recalling his unwavering devotion to duty.[15]

Another generation would pass before a second monument was erected to honor Brevet Major General James S. Wadsworth. The monument demonstrated two other Wadsworth traits—tenacity and obstinacy. According to an unidentified source, then Congressman James W. Wadsworth, Jr., "came to the Wilderness Battlefield in March 1936, where he found a Park Service sign concerning the general's demise." Dissatisfied with the plain marker, the general's grandson offered to erect a monument "at his own expense." This led to extensive research and a report by National Park Service historian Edward Steere, who determined that the general actually fell at a spot a short distance from the marker and outside the park boundary. Park Superintendent Branch Spalding tried to persuade Congressman Wadsworth to erect the monument on park land. The congressman countered with an offer to purchase fifty square feet bordering the Plank Road (Route 621), some 485–535 feet east of Hill–Ewell Drive, and to donate it to the park, which he did sometime in late 1936, over the strenuous objections of Spalding. Spalding apparently feared that future developments would threaten the small, isolated plot of land. The congressman countered again by promising to donate the plot where the monument would stand. Spalding's objections were "abrogated," which was followed shortly thereafter by the transfer of land. The final design by sculptor Carl S. Mose, bearing the approval of the Federal Commission on Fine Arts, on July 17, 1936, was a bronze tablet measuring 4 feet by 2 feet, 11 inches. The tablet, resting on a "rubble stone column," featured a "life-size left profile of the general and an appropriate inscription."[16]

The most recent and unusual ceremony involving Wadsworth was a funeral reenactment in the summer of 1989, coinciding with the Town of Geneseo's bicentennial celebration. It was conceived by James Wadsworth Symington, a former Missouri congressman, who had paid for the restoration of his great-great-grandfather James Samuel's monument in the Wilderness. He wanted to know more about the descendants of Patrick McCracken, who had buried Wadsworth's body on his property. Symington's interest led to a meeting and a joint photograph near the general's monument in the Wilderness with Terry McCracken, Patrick's great-grandnephew and Loudon County, Virginia, deputy sheriff. The two descendants met again at the funeral reenactment, where a service was conducted by Civil War reenactor Benedict R. Maryniak as Civil War Chaplain Philos G. Cook.[17]

EPILOGUE

Aquila Non Captat Muscas

Aristocrat. Husband. Father. Farmer. Lawyer. Investor. Corporate partner/director. Abolitionist. Gubernatorial candidate. Brevet Major General.

James Samuel Wadsworth seemed bigger than life. Everything about him was big—beginning with the large frame for which he was noted. Then there was the estate he inherited and subsequently enlarged, including the impressive house he built. Even the number and variety of his acquaintances and associates seem outsized. A listing of them would read like a Who's Who of nineteenth-century America. The traits that reflect Wadsworth's strong character include:

- the largesse of his many benevolences,
- his ambition and unstinting work ethic in business matters, even when money was tight,
- the single-mindedness and determination with which he pursued his interests in agriculture, civic service, and politics,
- the wave of his hand signaling an expansive gesture,
- the manner in which he won the respect, even affection, of others, particularly the soldiers in the ranks who were asked to die for the cause in which he believed at least as strongly as they,
- the strength to withstand daunting challenges in peace and war, and
- the unwillingness to compromise on important matters, particularly his unflinching conviction that slavery must be abolished.

Yet the general remains enigmatic in many respects. Largely, we know about him from his business records and from others; he reveals little in his own scanty writings.

Today, removed as we are from James Samuel Wadsworth by time and circumstances, to assess him and his impact on nineteenth-century America, particularly on the Civil War, is particularly difficult. Prudent assessment requires collecting, sifting, analyzing, and synthesizing an increasing amount of information to render a coherent whole. Inevitably gaps and contradictions result.

For example, Colonel Wainwright, a younger contemporary, charged that Wadsworth "knew nothing of military matters before the war, is not a young man, and has had no experience in battle to entitle him to so high a position [division commander]." Even allowing for Wainwright's prejudice, based no little on his political differences with Wadsworth, there are grounds for such an assessment—as far as it goes. On the other hand, the celebrated Winfield S. Hancock considered Wadsworth "so good that . . . each corps commander desired him as commander of [a] division." Respected Civil War historian Allan Nevins concluded that Wadsworth was "a man of great natural abilities, as his leadership in the Republican party indicated . . . [and] his gallantry at Gettysburg [demonstrated]." Are these contradictions? Might all the assessments be correct? While great natural abilities do not necessarily translate into specialized military skills, Wadsworth became a trusted commander.

General Wadsworth was born to lead. He inherited not only wealth, but a strict code of honor and a passion for life and causes. Still, he demonstrated very human frailties: youthful vanity and profligacy, brusqueness and impetuousness. He was educated largely by experience, his immaturity at the time having twice cut short a college education. However, the education he did acquire enabled him to undertake complicated investments and to improve upon the large agricultural estate his father and uncle had created. Further, like his father, he fostered education in his own village and New York State, serving the latter as a trustee on its educational policy-making body and as administrator of his father's educational trust.

James Samuel often demonstrated his father's moral certainty, but he also served as a lawyer-agent for the notorious Ogden Land Company, which scandalously bribed the Senecas out of their reservation land. Yet there is testimony to his sensitivity toward those same Senecas. Perhaps his sensitivity was simply evidence of his awareness of noblesse oblige. As with most phases of his life, he offered no explanation for his behavior during this brief, but relatively important, episode.

A gubernatorial candidacy, however reluctantly entered and pursued, violated his father's injunction to avoid the "vile business of politics." Perhaps it was the blood of his ancestors Captain Joseph and General James that drove him to become a Radical and ultimately to ally himself with those who were as instrumental in bringing on a fratricidal civil war as those he condemned at the 1861 Peace Conference.

When the war erupted, Wadsworth was a nineteenth-century Cincinnatus, dropping his plow and thrusting himself into the fray. Initially, he helped arm and transport soldiers to counter secessionist attempts to disrupt their travel to Washington, D.C. But that was not enough for him. The Wadsworth eagle stooped not to small things. At an advanced age he became an unpaid volunteer. His first assignment, possibly politically motivated, was to serve as an aide to Major General Irvin McDowell, who came to rely on his judgment and trustworthiness. Typically aides were younger, more expendable men who performed risky and physically demanding jobs. "Major Wadsworth" reveled in the assignment and assumed greater authority in the process. In fact, Provost Marshal William Doster, who observed Wadsworth closely for eight months, proclaimed that Wadsworth "won his star before wearing it."[1] However, like Cincinnatus, clearly Wadsworth did not seek authority for its own sake. Rather, he wanted to rid the country of those he regarded as traitors. We have no reason to doubt that when this was accomplished, he intended to resume plowing.

Next fate propelled him into the nation's capital as its military governor. However, even with all its intrigues and responsibilities—turning raw recruits into fighting men, accommodating contrabands, imprisoning secessionists, and obtaining military intelligence—this was not the ultimate test of his management skills or ambition. He believed he could command men and matériel as well, and actively sought a field command. His success in obtaining it is a tribute to his leadership and fighting qualities. He cannot be dismissed simply as a politically appointed general, like others, whose names readily come to mind.

Those who saw these qualities in Wadsworth included not only President Lincoln and Secretary of War Stanton, but army regulars John F. Reynolds, Winfield Scott Hancock, and Gouverneur K. Warren. For example, Hancock instructed Gettysburg historian John Bachelder to make sure he fit General Wadsworth into a proposed engraving of "all the important characters" in that historic battle. Even Union army commander Ulysses Grant commended his grit, earnestness, and sincerity. Men under Wadsworth's command showered "Old Daddy" with praise, even marveled at his pragmatism and his common sense. His willingness to perform mundane, even arduous tasks, such as corduroying muddy roads, which earned him the sobriquet "Old Corduroy," impressed those who served under him. And, though they could not help but laugh when observing him talking to the oxen he substituted for mules in the aftermath of the Fredericksburg "mud march," they had to admire his understanding of and experience with such everyday matters.

The civilian general learned quickly, relying on carefully picked young staff officers, like William Doster, his provost marshal in Washington, West Pointer John Kress, his closest aide, and brothers Clayton and Earl Rogers of the 6th Wisconsin, competent, battle-tested soldiers. He also wisely delegated, for example, giving wide powers to Brigadier Generals Cutler and Meredith, two equally tough volunteers, at Gettysburg. Never vainglorious, he was quick to praise others in his terse reports.

His admirers also included those against whom he had fought and ultimately who had taken his life. In fact, some Confederates were incredulous that a man who seemed to have it all would give it up so readily. Only Southern cavaliers like the wealthy plantation owner Major General Wade Hampton, with whom General Wadsworth can best be compared, were supposed to be willing to sacrifice their lives and fortunes for a cause. Yet the Union general, who died in a Confederate hospital tent, had done just that.

Characteristically, Wadsworth had his share of critics, including the controversial Major General George McClellan. Moreover, his critics probably had grounds for their views. He was guilty of mistaken judgments, made enemies, intrigued (possibly unconsciously), and occasionally preferred the grand gesture and impetuous action to extended analysis and reflection. He readily admitted his lack of military training, though he was not averse to offering advice on tactics as well as on the overall conduct of the war. His arrogance and impatience with protocol led him to assume authority, as he did at Gettysburg, and again at the Wilderness, where he lost his life.

He was "essentially a fighting general," William Doster recalled, "who thought strategy folly and who believed in giving hard blows."[2] Submitting his resignation when Major General George G. Meade chose not to pursue General Lee's Army of Northern Virginia after Gettysburg was vintage Wadsworth. But, so too was his ardor for preparing his men. "During the long drilling months which succeeded General McClellan's appointment to the command-in-chief," proclaimed an editorial in the May 21, 1864, *Harper's Weekly*, "General Wadsworth won for himself the credit, among the most experienced army officers, of having his brigade, long before the close of the year, in the most efficient condition, alike as to drill and discipline."

The confidence that the Lincoln administration placed in Wadsworth's managerial skills was matched by the assurance of his radicalism and dedication to the cause. More than once he pitted his judgment against others. He accurately challenged McClellan's intelligence chief, Allen Pinkerton, when the administration was trying to divine the numbers of Confederates facing Washington and occupying the Virginia Peninsula. Though his resignation after Gettysburg might be considered spiteful, rather than accepting it, War Secretary Stanton and Treasury Secretary Chase sought his opinion on the treatment and employment of freedmen in the Mississippi Valley. While confessing that at the beginning of the war he was "barely a Republican, that is, only opposed to the extension of slavery," Wadsworth later became a full-blown abolitionist. He was convinced that the Union must not only put down the rebellion, but it must also destroy the "base, selfish & degraded aristocracy" that capitalized on enslaving others. His written report and subsequent testimony concerning freed blacks, based on personal observations, illustrated the extent to which he had thought about not only the immediate problems faced by freedmen, but about reconstruction following the war. Not surprisingly, though he doubted that genuine integration could be achieved even in a hundred years, he offered a scheme for achieving independence modeled on his and his father's progressive tenant system by which land ownership could become a reality.

Wadsworth's wealth afforded him an envious independence, but it also could be a curse. Combined with his personal qualities, it drew him into the cataclysm that snuffed out his life and rent his family. The war-related stress his son Craig suffered may well have led to his premature death, just as his son-in-law's wartime death could be attributed to the hardships of service. Principle, or moral certainty, which he shared with his father, committed him to the Union cause and led to his untimely demise.

In retrospect, Brevet Major General James S. Wadsworth's life seemed fated by the ambition against which his father had admonished him. Yet this was not ambition as usually defined, not aspiration to hold office, to enjoy honors, or to bask in the affection of others. Rather, it was a propensity to court peril. His riding hell-bent-for-election at Harvard, investing in causes as well as business ventures, shunning compromise and charging into an entrenched enemy were manifestations of this ambition. He seemed fated to try to change the world, at least the part he could touch—and he had a large reach.

James Samuel Wadsworth, a bundle of contradictions, was the stuff of legend. Devoted to the cause and indifferent to petty criticism, he soared like an eagle. He was a natural aristocrat who practiced democracy, a reckless adventurer who became a successful businessman rivaling his father, an untrained civilian who commanded important divisions in three of the Civil War's major battles, and a leader who was deeply sensitive toward his men but rigorously demanding of himself. Above all, he was an unselfish patriot who left a legacy of commitment to public service that his descendants would follow well into the next century.

APPENDIX A

General Wadsworth's Command in Washington, March 1862[1]

CAVALRY

1st New Jersey Cavalry	Alexandria
4th Pennsylvania Cavalry	East of the capital

ARTILLERY AND INFANTRY

10th New Jersey Vols.	Bladensburg Road
104th New York Vols.	Kalorama Heights
1st Wisconsin Heavy Artillery	Fort Cass, Va.
Three batteries of New York artillery	Forts Ethan Allen and Marcy
Depot of New York Light Artillery	Camp Barry
2nd D.C. Vols.	Washington City
26th Pennsylvania Vols.	G. Street Wharf
26th New York Vols.	Fort Lyon
95th New York Vols.	Camp Thomas
94th New York Vols.	Alexandria
88th Pennsylvania Vols. (detachment)	Alexandria
91st Pennsylvania Vols.	Franklin Square Barracks
4th New York Artillery	Forts Carroll and Greble
112th Pennsylvania Vols.	Fort Saratoga
76th New York Vols.	Fort Massachusetts
59th New York Vols.	Fort Pennsylvania
88th Pennsylvania Vols. (detachment)	Fort Good Hope
99th Pennsylvania Vols.	Fort Mahan
2nd New York Light Artillery	Forts Ward, Worth, and Blenker
107th Pennsylvania Vols.	Kendall Green

54th Pennsylvania Vols.	Kendall Green
Dickerson's Light Artillery	East of the capital
86th New York Vols.	East of the capital
98th Pennsylvania Vols. (detachment)	East of the capital
14th Massachusetts (Heavy Artillery)	Forts Albany and Tellinghast, Richardson, Runyon, Jackson, Barnard, Craig, Scott
56th Pennsylvania Vols.	
4th U.S. Artillery (detachment)	Fort Washington
37th New York Vols.(detachment)	Fort Washington
97th New York Vols.	Fort Corcoran
101st New York Vols.	
12th Virginia Vols.	
91st New York Vols.	

APPENDIX B

Order of Funeral Procession, May 21, 1864[2]

Clergymen
Committee of Arrangements
Band
The N.Y. 21st Volunteers, under command of Col. Rogers, of Buffalo,[sic] with
arms reversed
Hearse
With guard of soldiers, and Pall-Bearers
Mourners in carriages
Carriages with Members of Congress, and other officers
Carriages with friends
Citizens of Rochester
Carriages of citizens

APPENDIX C

The Elusive Field Glasses
of General Wadsworth

In his August 23, 1985, letter to James Wadsworth Symington, Fredericksburg National Park Historian Robert K. Krick mentioned "an interesting encounter" with a South Carolinian about ten years earlier. The unnamed visitor informed Krick that "his grandfather [a soldier in General Kershaw's Brigade] had shot General Wadsworth." Though courteous, Krick was skeptical until the visitor ran to his car and grabbed "a pair of 19th-century field glasses with Wadsworth's name elegantly engraved on them." Unfortunately, the visitor not only showed no interest in donating the glasses to the park, but he insisted on remaining unnamed.[3]

Symington was excited about the prospect of learning more about the field glasses: What was the name of the South Carolinian who shot General Wadsworth? Was he part of Mahone's Brigade? "What do we know of Sorrel [G. Moxley Sorrel, who Horatio King claimed obtained the General's glasses along with his map]?" This precipitated another round of correspondence regarding the field glasses, including a letter enclosing an article from the *Richmond (Virginia) Examiner* of May 27, 1864. The article claimed that Confederate "Major McMullen" had "exhibited" the glasses in Richmond. Then it went on to describe them: "They are of the most unique, elaborate and expensive kind, being adapted either for the sea or field service. The power of the lense upon actual test, was found to be very great." The paper also claimed that the general's other effects, including $500 in greenbacks, "forty in gold, and a splendid gold watch," had been forwarded to the family.[4]

Two years later someone on Krick's staff located an article in the *Petersburg (Virginia) Daily Express* of August 1, 1864. ". . . [I]t was my fortune to see the magnificent field glass formerly used by Yankee Major Gen. Wadsworth," wrote a Richmond correspondent for the *Augusta (Georgia) Constitution*. "In one respect it differed so widely from any of the kind I have ever seen before that I cannot but mention it." Then follows a long description, the essence of which is that the lenses adapted, "without necessitating any alteration in the exterior of the glass," to three different uses: the theater, the field, and the sea. This was accomplished by "simply touching a spring." The correspondent struggled for words to express his amazement at the quality of the lenses, which allowed "for even the difference between terrene [*sic*] and oceanic atmospheres." At the time the glasses were being offered for sale in Petersburg at $600 (more than $5,000 today).[5]

Symington hoped the anonymous owner of the field glasses would sell them to the family occupying the house the general had built or to a museum of the owner's choice. Meanwhile, Symington contacted his cousin, Harry Wadsworth of Geneseo, who, with his mother, had a number of the general's effects, including his sword, field desk, epaulets, and stars, hoping he might be able to follow up on the search. Apparently the search still goes on.[6]

APPENDIX D

The Saga of the Wadsworth Monument at the Wilderness

The second monument erected to the memory of Brevet Major General James S. Wadsworth began when Congressman James W. Wadsworth, Jr., visited the Wilderness battlefield in March 1936 and came upon the marker designating where his grandfather had died. Dissatisfied with the plain marker, the general's grandson offered to erect a monument "at his own expense." This led to National Park Service historian Edward Steere's determination that Wadsworth actually fell outside the park boundary. Park Superintendent Branch Spalding tried to persuade Congressman Wadsworth to erect the monument on park land, which resulted in the congressman's counteroffer.[7]

This caused Superintendent Spalding to become "justifiably upset" and to object to the acting director of the National Park Service. Undeterred, "the Congressman and his sister erected the monument on an inadequate plot of land 109 yards from Park property on a public highway (State 621), against our advice, and now wishes us to take over the responsibility of its maintenance."[8]

So, sometime between September 24, 1936, and January 8, 1937, a monument, designed and fashioned over a period of four months in the late spring of 1936, had been erected. The form the monument was to take had been developed in the period from April to July 1936. Initially it was to be "a single unhewn boulder" with a tablet attached. The final design, bearing the approval of the Commission on Fine Arts, July 17, 1936, was a bronze tablet, designed by sculptor Carl C. Mose, measuring 4 feet by 2 feet, 11 inches, with a " life-size left profile of the general and an appropriate inscription." It was placed on a "rubble stone column" 8 feet by 5 feet by 3 feet on an "irregularly shaped rough rubble base." In 1940 "the prospective donation of surrounding lands abrogated" the Park Service's objections to maintaining it. On April 28, 1941, Harriet W. Harper, the congressman's sister, deeded the land (0.6 acres) to the Fredericksburg National Military Park.

That was not the end of the saga. In 1985, the general's great-great-grandson, James Wadsworth Symington, a Washington lawyer, former Missouri congressman, and chief of protocol under President Lyndon B. Johnson, discovered that the monument needed attention. Moss was growing on it, spider webs clouded it, and white streaks were discoloring the surface of the bronze tablet. He asked Susan Shaw of the National Trust for Historic Preservation whether maintenance could be performed on the monument that his grandfather had erected over the Park Service's earlier objections. Ms. Shaw forwarded Mr. Symington's request to the Fredericksburg and Spotsylvania National Military Park's Chief Historian Robert K. Krick. Krick recognized the need but saw this as second in the park's priority, "behind the even more deteriorated Humphreys Monument on Marye's Heights." Though the cost of cleaning the tablet (the monument itself was all right), "ought not to be too high," the park's budget was tight. Mr. Symington then offered to pay the cost of the monument's treatment.[9]

About three weeks later, on September 11, 1985, Park Superintendent James R. Zinck described what steps could be taken to clean the tablet at a cost of $450 and asked whether this would be acceptable to Mr. Symington. If so, work could begin a month after clearance from the President's Advisory Council on Historic Preservation. Less than ten days later the general's descendant agreed to bear the cost of the needed cleaning and preservation. Work was begun on October 24 and completed four days later.[10]

NOTES

PREFACE

1. Lewis F. Allen, *Proceedings of the Century Association in Honor of the Memory of Brig. Gen. James S. Wadsworth and Colonel Peter A. Porter: With the Eulogies Read by William J. Hoppin and Frederic S. Cozzens, December 3, 1864* (New York: D. Van Nostrand, 1865).
2. Curiously, there is not even any record of his height, weight, or eye or hair color. At best he is described as having a "large frame." A portrait of him as a seated young man shows him almost foppish, with dark brown to black hair and dark gray or blue eyes.
3. Henry Greenleaf Pearson, *James S. Wadsworth of Geneseo: Brevet Major General, U.S.V.* (New York: Charles Scribner's Sons, 1913).
4. Letter to James Samuel Wadsworth from Alfred Wilkinson, September 25, 1862, Wadsworth Family Papers (WFP).
5. Letter from James Samuel Wadsworth to David Dudley Field, Horace Greeley "et al.," September 14, 1862, WFP.

CHAPTER 1

1. Morris Schaff, *The Battle of the Wilderness* (Boston: Houghton Mifflin, 1910), pp. 58, 59.
2. Military units in descending order were armies, for example, the Union's Army of the Potomac, with two or more corps averaging 16,000 men, which, in turn, had two or more divisions (often 6,000 infantrymen), containing three to five divisions, each with three to five regiments of 1,000 men per regiment of ten companies. A battalion might have up to five companies of 150 men.
3. Schaff, *The Battle of the Wilderness*, p. 152.
4. Alexander Webb, "Through the Wilderness," in Robert Underwood Johnson and Clarence Clough Buel (eds.), *Battles and Leaders of the Civil War* (New York: Century Co., 1884, 1887, 1888), Vol. 4, p. 163.

    Schaff, *The Battle of the Wilderness*, pp. 39, 40, cautions every writer about claiming certainty about time or place of any movement or engagement and wonderfully illustrates it with a story. John Bachelder, the Gettysburg authority, told Schaff he believed he had "discovered how Joshua made the sun stand still." It seems Bachelder consulted with different members of the II Corps about events at Gettysburg on a particular day and found "no two regiments or brigades agreeing." But, each claimed "We were there, Bachelder, and we ought to know, I guess." Bachelder realized "that it would take a day of at least twenty hours instead of thirteen at Gettysburg to satisfy their accounts." Or the sun would have to stand still. The reader is cautioned to remember Schaff's advice: Times and places of unit movements and engagements are at best approximations.
5. Webb, "Through the Wilderness," p. 159; Schaff, *The Battle of the Wilderness*, p. 266.
6. Z. Boylston Adams, "In the Wilderness," in *Civil War Papers, Commandery of the State of Massachusetts, M.O.L.L.U.S.* (Boston: The Commandery, 1900), p. 389; Schaff, *The Battle of the Wilderness*, p. 236; James Longstreet, *From Manassas to Appomattox* (New York: Mallard Press, 1991), p. 562 (reprint).

7. Longstreet, *From Manassas to Appomattox*, pp. 562, 563; Schaff, *The Battle of the Wilderness*, p. 269.

8. Andrew A. Humphreys, *The Virginia Campaign of '64 and '65*, Vol. 6, Part. 2, *Campaigns of the Civil War* (New York: Thomas Yoseloff, 1963), p. 44 (reprint); Webb, "Through the Wilderness," p. 160.

9. Lewis F. Allen, *Proceedings of the Century Association in Honor of the Memory of Brig. Gen. James S. Wadsworth and Colonel Peter A Porter; With the Eulogies Read by William J. Hoppin and Frederic S. Cozzens, December 3, 1864* (New York: D. Van Nostrand, 1865), pp. 16, 18.

10. Benedict R. Maryniak, "Patroon, Soldier and Hero," "The Famous Long Ago," *The Courier*, Vol. 4, Issue 6 (Nov./Dec. 1989), p. 23.

11. Ibid., p. 24.

CHAPTER 2

1. Horace A. Wadsworth, *Two Hundred Fifty Years of the Wadsworth Family in America* (Lawrence, Mass.: Eagle Stream Job Printing, 1883), pp. 30, 31; Richard B. Morris and Jeffrey B. Morris (eds.), *Encyclopedia of American History* (New York: Harper & Row, 1976), pp. 41, 42. Horace, the family genealogist, speculates that William and his family followed Reverend Thomas Hooker from his Chelmsford, England, church, some twenty miles north of London, to a house in Cambridge, near Harvard Square, becoming part of an influx of 20,000 emigres to New England between 1630 and 1640. Christopher, or "Xtopher," Wadsworth headed what became the Maine–Massachusetts branch. The genealogist also distinguished the Wadsworths and others aboard the ship *Lion* from the Pilgrims, who landed a few years earlier, claiming the former were "Puritans," or "men of standing and influence."

2. Wadsworth, *Two Hundred Fifty Years*, pp. 16, 17, 31.

3. Ibid., p. 85.

4. Ibid., p. 87; Pearson, *James S. Wadsworth of Geneseo*, p. 3. His appearance before the Court of Assistants resulted from his having threatened "to knock down Mr. Ichabod Wells, sheriff of Hartford." Nor was he averse to threatening others, including Governor Fletcher of New York, who attempted to exercise his authority over the militia, of which Joseph was a member. When Fletcher attempted to read a proclamation, the captain is reported to have had the militia drums beat and warned Fletcher that if he continued to interrupt the drumbeat by reading his proclamation, he would "make the sun shine through you in a moment."

5. Pearson, *James S. Wadsworth of Geneseo*, pp. 3, 4.

6. Wadsworth, *Two Hundred Fifty Years*, p. 81; Pearson, *James S. Wadsworth of Geneseo*, p. 4, claims that from April 9, 1778, to January 1, 1780, Jeremiah served as "commissary-general of purchases" by congressional election.

7. To simplify understanding, the term "cousin" is used to describe the relationship between brothers James and William and Jeremiah Wadsworth and Jeremiah's son, Daniel. In fact, James and Jeremiah were second cousins "once removed," or cousins a generation apart; Terrick V. H. FitzHugh, *The Dictionary of Genealogy* (Totowa, N.J.: Barnes & Noble Books, 1985), p. 81; Shirley B. Goerlich, *Genealogy: A Practical Research Guide* (Sidney, N.Y.: RSG Publishing, 1984), p. 244. That is, James was a sixth-generation Wadsworth in America, whereas Jeremiah was fifth generation; Wadsworth, *Two Hundred Fifty Years*, pp. 196–202. Specifically, James and Jeremiah descended from William Wadsworth, whose son John had eight children, including "Major James," from whom James's grandfather, "Squire James," and father, John Noyes, were descended, and John, from whom Jeremiah's father, Daniel, was descended. Jeremiah's son Daniel, who was the same generation as James, is James's second cousin "twice removed."

8. Documents in Wadsworth Family Papers, Library of Congress, hereafter WFP. As justice of the peace and constable of Durham, father John Noyes handled the usual petty cases: removing transients, forcing the settlement of debts, enforcing a ban on card playing, fining a tavern keeper for selling "strong liquor" (French brandy) in lesser quantities than permitted by Connecticut law, and remanding individuals to jail for theft.

9. Pearson, *James S. Wadsworth of Geneseo*, p. 7, claims that Jeremiah's purchase was 25,000 acres bordering on the Genesee River; Orsamus Turner, *History of the Pioneer Settlement of Phelps and Gorham's Purchase, and Morris' Reserve* (Geneseo, N.Y.: James Brunner, 1976), pp. 325, 326 (reprint). Turner credits James Samuel Wadsworth for the use of the Wadsworths' papers to prepare his history.

Possibly their older brother, "Major" John Noyes, did not become part of the arrangement with Jeremiah because he was already established in the community and retained the Home Farm. The title "Major" stems from his appointment as ensign in a Connecticut infantry regiment, May 28, 1784, at age 26, and by 1793 he was regularly referred to in that manner; WFP.

10. The terms Indian and Native American will be used alternately, with Indian preferred for consistency with contemporary accounts.

11. Pearson, *James Samuel Wadsworth of Geneseo*, p. 7; Arthur C. Parker, *The History of the Seneca Indians* (Port Washington, N.Y.: Ira S. Friedman, 1967), pp. 133, 134; Robert W. Silsby, *The Holland Land Company in Western New York* (Buffalo: Buffalo and Erie County Historical Society, 1961), Vol. 2, pp. 1, 2.

12. By a June 1788 treaty with the Senecas on Buffalo Creek, Phelps and Gorham obtained the claim to about 2,600,000 acres running roughly from the Genesee River to Buffalo, the east side of the purchase; Parker, *The History of the Seneca Indians*, p. 134. However, these claims would be disputed later when Phelps and Gorham declared bankruptcy, as did Robert Morris, their successor to the title, and ultimately when the Holland Land Company, the successor to Robert Morris, claimed ownership.

13. Deed, April 9, 1790, WFP; Turner, *Phelps and Gorham's Purchase*, p. 325. There were seven, six-mile-wide ranges running from the Pennsylvania border north to Lake Ontario and from the preemptive line in Seneca Lake west to the present New York border, with fourteen townships, or tracts, six miles square in each range; E. Thayles Emmons, *The Story of Geneva* (Geneva, N.Y.: The Finger Lakes Times, 1982), pp. 50, 51.

   Dollar equivalents throughout this period are extrapolated from historical price indexes in John J. McCusker, "How Much Is That in Real Money? A Historical Price Index for Use as a Deflator of Money Values in the Economy of the United States," *Proceedings of the American Antiquarian Society*, Vol. 101 (1992), pp. 297–373; United States Bureau of the Census, *Historical Statistics of the United States* (Washington, D.C.: Department of Commerce, 1970), p. 212; and Alice Hanson Jones, *Wealth of a Nation To Be* (New York: Columbia University Press, 1980). Jones, p. 10, states that the U.S. dollar was not created until 1792. Thanks are due to Dr. David Martin, Management Science Professor, SUNY–Geneseo, for helping make sense of the indexes. However, the amount paid, over $40,000 in today's currency, seems far out of line with the price paid by Phelps and Gorham and with prices per acre quoted by James to Jeremiah, February 20, 1793, though there was a sharp deflation after 1792.

14. These 345 acres included all of Township No. 10, 7th Range, except for lots 87 (172 acres), 79 (123 acres), and 92.

15. Turner, *Phelps and Gorham's Purchase*, p. 326. Slavery still existed in Connecticut at that time.

16. For some reason only William was listed in the 1790 census as a head of family in the region west of the old Massachusetts preemption line. This was section 9, range 7; ibid., p. 479.

17. This story has gained greatest recognition through Alden Hatch, *The Wadsworths of the Genesee* (New York: Coward-McCann, 1959), pp. 36, 37, 39, 40. Hatch is a good, but not entirely accurate, storyteller. However, the legend of Jenny has taken on a life of its own.

18. For example, in 1791, James rode to Niagara, over seventy miles, to check on the likelihood of an Indian war. Though he encountered no difficulty, he confessed that "it was a most solitary ride"; Turner, *Phelps and Gorham's Purchase*, p. 78n. That same year, James rode to Whitestown, just outside Utica, some 160 miles from Geneseo, to attend a town meeting and to be elected town path master for building a road to Canandaigua, following the path he and brother William had traversed the previous year; ibid., p. 126.

   The only record of James's admission to the practice of law is found in *Phelps and Gorham's Purchase*, p. 333. Turner notes that Wadsworth was admitted to practice "to enable persons to sue out writs and bring actions, which at the present, for want of attornies [*sic*], it is impossible to do." Turner also claims that James was conducting business before the Court of Common Pleas and General Sessions in Canandaigua prior to 1794, (pp. 170–171). So far no records to verify this have been found.

19. James's letters to Jeremiah Wadsworth, February 20, and April 26, 1793, WFP; Pearson, *James S. Wadsworth of Geneseo*, p. 7. James's success in attracting Nutmeggers is described in Turner, *Phelps and Gorham's Purchase*, pp. 504–505, 510–511.

20. Paul D. Evans, *The Holland Land Company* (Buffalo: Buffalo Historical Society, 1924), pp. xi, 11, 12, 23, 26. One of the last sales by Phelps and Gorham (11,000 acres in Township 11, Range 5) was to Jeremiah Wadsworth, which his younger cousin, James, began selling for him at $1.25 to $2.00 per acre in June 1793; Turner, *Phelps and Gorham's Purchase*, pp. 530–531.

21. Letters to Jeremiah Wadsworth, January 24 and April 1, 1795, WFP.

22. Ibid., July 19, and December 7?, 1795; Evans, *The Holland Land Company*, pp. 209, 215. Though he found Burr's bill allowing aliens to buy land in the United States advantageous, James was contemptuous of Burr, whose conduct he claimed "would make . . . christians shudder"; letter from James Wadsworth to J. Savages, February 7, 1804, WFP. Earlier Wadsworth and Burr had corresponded frequently on matters ranging from politics and business to courtship and marriage, with Burr using ciphers rather than names; Turner, *Phelps and Gorham's Purchase*, p. 337n.

23. Letters of James to Jeremiah Wadsworth, June 9, August 16, 1796, and February 28, 1797, WFP. Turner, *Phelps and Gorham's Purchase*, pp. 336, 337, claims that in London James became agent for Sir William Pultney, for the sale of a 300-square-mile parcel west of the Genesee River to which would be added a commission to sell land closer to his own property in Geneseo. One of these sales apparently was to the celebrated painter Benjamin West, whom James Wadsworth had asked to use his influence to induce more confidence in American investments among Londoners. However, David Minor, of Eagles Byte Historical Research, dates the purchase by West as occurring January 7, 1800 (David_Minor@mlstand.com, August 17, 1995).

24. Letter from James to Jeremiah Wadsworth, September 29, 1797, WFP.

25. Evans, *The Holland Land Company*, pp. 216, 222. The unfortunate episode with Morris is not only rather vague, but beyond the scope of this treatment. James Wadsworth's version is that if there were any dishonest dealings, they were by Morris. Subsequent events tend to substantiate Wadsworth's position, for his reputation grew over the years, contrary to that of Morris.

26. Letters from James to Jeremiah Wadsworth, July 3, July 16, 1799, WFP. Apparently James was busy, for he had claimed pay for working Sundays, a claim that had been denied by an Ezra Brainerd, possibly a clerk for Jeremiah; letter to James Wadsworth from Ezra Brainerd, July 15, 1799, WFP. James followed up on his report of Morris's insolvency, but assured his cousin that his investments were protected; letter from James to Jeremiah Wadsworth from Albany, July 16, 1799, WFP.

27. Ibid., August 23, 1799, WFP.

28. Letters from James to Jeremiah Wadsworth from New York City, February 26 and March 18, 1801, WFP. More details can be found in Thurlow Weed, *The Autobiography of Thurlow Weed* (Boston: Houghton Mifflin, 1884), Vol. 1, p. 153, though the precise nature of the insults is never revealed.

29. It is unknown whether she died in Connecticut or in Geneseo. There is reason to believe that the sons may have brought her to Geneseo before her death, but this cannot be confirmed.

30. Letters from William and James to Jeremiah Wadsworth, October 8, and December 12, 1799, WFP.

31. Letters from James to Jeremiah Wadsworth, April 8, May 3, September 15, 1800, WFP.

32. A local authority, Charles Van Ry, claims that Bill lived in the cobblestone house on the Big Tree Farm, not what came to be called the Homestead. This may be later, after James married.

33. Frederick Mather, "Historic Homes: The Wadsworth House at Geneseo," *Magazine of American History*, Vol. 14, No. 5 (1885), p. 434.

34. John W. Barber and Henry Howe, *Historical Sketches of the State of New York* (Port Washington, N.Y.: Kennikat Press, 1970), p. 246 (reprint). Barber and Howe acknowledged that this was "extracted from a series of historical and descriptive letters published in the *New York Commercial Advertiser*, during the summer and autumn of 1840" by the editor, William L. Stone, ibid., p. 244.

35. Turner, *Phelps and Gorham's Purchase*, p. 346.

36. Notice to James, February 24, 1801, WFP; letter from James to Jeremiah Wadsworth, June 7, 1801, WFP; Lockwood L. Doty, *History of Livingston County* (Geneseo, N.Y.: Edward A. Doty, 1876), pp. 285, 286. The trip may well have been mostly by boat. For example, it is also reported that "In 1804 General William Wadsworth took two ark loads of oxen to Baltimore" from Arkport, south of Geneseo, down the Susquehanna; Ulysses Prestiss Hedrick, *A History of Agriculture in New York State* (New York: Hill and Wang, 1966), p. 254 (reprint).

37. One anecdote about William's military activities recalls the Black woman, Jenny, who accompanied William to Geneseo and ministered to the brothers during their illness. In preparation for one of then Captain Wadsworth's reviews of the militia in Canandaigua, she is reported to have been "queing and powdering" his hair when, in June 1795, Duke de Liancourt, "one of the most eminent noblemen of France," visited and spent the night at William's "small log house as dirty as any I have ever seen"; Turner, *Phelps and Gorham's Purchase*, p. 326; Doty, *History of Livingston County*, pp. 265–269; David W. Parish, Geneseo Town and Village Historian.

The full extent of Jenny's relationship to William will probably never be known, nor yet the details of her heritage, dates of birth and death, or burial site. There is one rather oblique suggestion of intimacy by a "city paper writer" who wrote that Jenny sired a daughter who married a lawyer (both unnamed) and moved to Liberia where the husband held a "high position"; "the Home of the Wadsworth's," *Livingston Republican*, November 29, 1864. Further, the unknown writer claimed that union resulted in a daughter who graduated third in her class at Genesee College (later Syracuse University). Then the writer cuts to the jugular: "How much of it [class ranking] is due to her mother's father's [presumably William Wadsworth] blood? Yet with all her aristocracy of birth, and manifest ability, she could not have full play for her powers . . . and has followed her parents to the foreign shore." While this has all the earmarks of an exposé, it does suggest questions that beg answers.

38. The total included 27,000 acres in Geneseo and north to the towns of Avon, Rush, Chili, and Henrietta, another 22,220 acres acquired by 1810, 12,900 more by 1820, and another 7,000 acres by 1835. Reportedly large droves of Wadsworth cattle were wintered in "Rush Bottom" (town of Rush), because the rushes provided food and protection; Turner, *Phelps and Gorham's Purchase*, p. 535; James Renwick, "Life of James Wadsworth," *Monthly Journal of Agriculture*, Vol. 2, No. 4 (October 1846), p. 150.

39. Neil A. McNall, *The First Half Century of Wadsworth Tenancy* (Rochester, N.Y.: University of Rochester, 1977), pp. 7, 9; James Wadsworth, Letterbook 61, p. 197; *Livingston Register*, August 27, 1827; letters from James to Jeremiah Wadsworth, September 15, 1800, June 7, 1801, WFP. By 1826, it was claimed that the Wadsworths' land debts were "so secure that they only required the occupier of the soil to pay the Interest every year, which is exacted with rigour; and are contented that what is due on Principal should remain"; report of Jacob S. Otto, land agent for the Holland Land Company in Robert W. Bingham (ed.), *Reports of Joseph Ellicott* (Buffalo: Buffalo Historical Society, 1937), Vol. 1, p. 414.

By 1830 responsibilities for their land holdings and the business were hanging heavy over the brothers, who were then in their sixties. They found themselves forced to hire an "Outdoor Clerk" or "Farm Agent," who supervised land to assure buildings were in repair, fences were "eight rail high, well righted up and made of oak or ash timber," and no "burdock, Canada Thistle or other noxious weeds [were] growing on the farm." Annual leases were replaced by life leases; McNall, *The First Half Century of Wadsworth Tenancy*, pp. 3, 4, 15, 17.

Other agents were hired to attend to the dairying, wheat and hemp raising, and the care of Merino sheep from the Livingstons that James had introduced to the land. The fine quality of the latter, an always saleable commodity, and the small expense required, made this a particularly good investment, one they could count on to pay bills. DeWitt Clinton's journal cited a visit to William Wadsworth in 1811, wherein he saw the latter's advertisement to let out his Merino rams for siring. Compensation for use of his rams was all the ram progeny and all but two of the ewe progeny, for which he would pay eight shillings cash; Hedrick, *A History of Agriculture in New York State*, pp. 372, 373. However, not long after William's death, prices of wool declined, and James, like most of his neighbors, turned more to dairying.

40. Letters from James to Jeremiah Wadsworth, February 6 and August 25, 1801, WFP. It is reported that shortly after the Wadsworth brothers had arrived at Big Tree, James had received a "tender epistle" from a woman in his native Durham, Connecticut, who recognized that his goal of "making a fortune" would probably supersede any marriage plans; Turner, *Phelps and Gorham's Purchase*, pp. 331, 332.

41. A very brief lineage is provided by Sally Wood, *Family History of William Perkins Wadsworth and Martha Doty Scofield* (Geneseo, N.Y.: Private printing, 1994).

42. Wadsworth, *Two Hundred Fifty Years*, p. 28.

43. James J. Wadsworth, *The Silver Spoon: An Autobiography* (Geneva, N.Y.: W. F. Humphrey Press, 1980), p. 17.

44. Weed, *Autobiography*, Vol. 1, p. 153; Wadsworth, *Two Hundred Fifty Years*, pp. 27, 29.

CHAPTER 3

1. David Minor, Eagle Bytes Historical Research, http://home.eznet.net/~Minor.

2. James's need to show and be the object of affection is particularly apparent in a letter to his older son at Harvard from May 25, 1827, wherein he hoped to find James Samuel and his brother William "affectionate sons. My sincere affection to William. Your Affectionate Father," WFP.

3. William J. Hoppin and Frederic S. Cozzens, *Proceedings of the Century Association in Honor of the Memory of Brig.-Gen. James S. Wadsworth and Colonel Peter A. Porter; With the Eulogies Read by William J. Hoppin and Frederic S. Cozzens, December 13, 1884*. New York: D. Van Nostrand, p. 12; letter from Wedworth

Wadsworth to John Noyes Wadsworth, October 16, 1812, WFP, that "Uncle William" had been so badly wounded that he wielded his sword with his left hand when his right arm was broken at the Battle of Queenston.

4. Letters from James to James Samuel Wadsworth, July 15, 1826, August 20, 1826, WFP. This appears to refer to a rather bizarre and potentially fatal incident in 1823, when some students dragged a small cannon from the village of Clinton, approximately a mile up the steep hill to the college and then up four flights of stairs to the hallway, where they fired it into the room of tutor William Kirkland. While the unpopular Kirkland was not hurt, his coat was "shredded," windows were broken, and walls and doors "shattered." Fragments from the blast soared through the roof and plummeted to the cellar; Walter Pilkington, *Hamilton College, 1812–1862* (Clinton, N.Y.: Hamilton College, 1962), pp. 93–94. What part, if any, James Samuel played in this incident cannot be determined, nor can his attendance be verified by Hamilton's Curator of Archives, Frank K. Lorenz, per letters to the author.

5. Letter to the author from James McCarthy, Curatorial Assistant, Harvard University Archives, Cambridge, Mass., January 12, 1995.

6. Josiah E. Kittredge, "Historical Sermon," in *The Centennial Celebration of the Geneseo Village Presbyterian Church, Geneseo, New York, 1810–1910* (Geneseo, N.Y.: Geneseo Presbyterian Church, 1910), pp. 55, 56. Ironically, though James Wadsworth was a big subscriber to the church, only his wife Naomi is listed as a member of the congregation, having been received on confession; ibid., p. 85. When James Samuel was growing up, there was a school on the first floor of the two-story Brick Academy, located at the corner of Center and Elm Streets (the second floor of which was used for religious meetings and for a court), according to an 1871 *Livingston Republican* article and F. W. Beers, *Atlas of Livingston County, New York* (New York: Author, 1872), pp. 20–21; Pilkington, *Hamilton College, 1812–1862*, pp. 70, 74.

7. Letters from James to James Samuel Wadsworth, July 15 and August 20, 1826, WFP; Jacob Rhett Motte, "A Southern Sport at Harvard," in William Bentinck-Smith (ed.), *The Harvard Book* (Cambridge: Harvard University Press, 1982), pp. 188–190.

8. Letter from James to James Samuel Wadsworth, August 20, 1826, WFP; William Wolcott Wadsworth would enter Harvard with the class of 1829, but there is no record that he graduated from Harvard; letter to the author from Brian A. Sullivan, Curatorial Assistant, Harvard University Archives, Cambridge, Mass., October 25, 1995.

9. Bernard Bailyn, "Why Kirkland Failed," in Bernard Bailyn et al. (eds.), *Glimpses of the Harvard Past* (Cambridge: Harvard University Press, 1986), p. 25; Oscar Handlin, "Making Men of Boys," in Bailyn et al., *Glimpses of the Harvard Past*, p. 50.

10. Oliver Wendell Holmes, "Of Cambridge and Female Society (1828–1830)," in William Bentinck-Smith (ed.), *The Harvard Book*, p. 167.

11. Bailyn, "Why Kirkland Failed," pp. 19–44, 25; Samuel A. Eliot, *Sketch of the History of Harvard College* (Boston: Charles C. Little & James Brown, 1848), pp. 110, 112–113.

12. Letters from James McCarthy and Brian A. Sullivan, Curatorial Assistants, Harvard University Archives, Cambridge, Mass., January 12, 1995, and October 25, 1995, and excerpts from "Fac. Rec. X."

13. Letter from James to James Samuel Wadsworth, August 21, 1826, WFP.

14. Letter from Cornelia to James Samuel Wadsworth, January 29, 1825, WFP. Elizabeth, in an August 27, 1845, letter to James Samuel confessed that "no happiness can atone for your loss [absence], Cheri. We miss you more than all beside!" Letter from William to James Samuel Wadsworth, November 26, 1831, WFP.

15. Letter from Cornelius C. Felton to James Samuel Wadsworth, June 8, 1828, WFP. Felton, who was later described as "the huge, hearty old-fashioned scholar" (or "the jolly giant"), was a close friend of many of New England's literary and political giants, including Longfellow, Sumner, Prescott, and the Peabodys, as well as Europe's finest scholars; Van Wyck Brooks, *The Flowering of New England, 1815–1865* (New York: E. P. Dutton, 1936), pp. 447, 165, 166. Felton would prove to influence James Samuel's politics at least indirectly.

16. Letter from Cornelius C. Felton to James Samuel Wadsworth, June 8, 1828, WFP.

17. Letter from James to James Samuel Wadsworth, November 29, 1843, WFP. Projects to which James devoted himself are almost too numerous to name, but they include donating approximately two and a half acres for a public square and almost two more acres for a courthouse and jail in 1821 (Doty, *History of Livingston County*, p. 352), opening his house and farm as "hospitals" in early winter 1825 when smallpox was plaguing Geneseo (James's letter to cousin Daniel, February 23, 1825), applying to the New York State Legislature for a new bank and subscribing $10,000 to get it off the ground, presiding over the board of direc-

tors of the Livingston County Bible Society, giving money to the Franklin Institute for the Improvement of Society in Rochester (hoping it "animates" other villages to follow suit), helping pay off the indebtedness of the county branch of the New York State Temperance Society, and putting $6,000 in trust on March 11, 1833, to be used to compile, print, and distribute to the trustees of each common school in New York State courses of popular lectures "adapted to the capacities of children" that could be "conveniently read in half an hour." He is best known for obtaining legislation to create district common schools and libraries within, for which no projects offered him greater satisfaction; Weed, *Autobiography*, Vol. 2, pp. 344–345. It remains, however, that Temple Hill Academy was his first true educational endeavor, which he recognized was an "experiment"; letters from James to James Samuel Wadsworth, May 25, 1827, June 18, 1827, WFP.

18. Letters to James Samuel Wadsworth from John T. Sargent, September 21, 1828; George Turner, September 14, November 26, December 3, 1828; and C. Jones Richards, June 30, 1828. It may well be that Sargent introduced Wadsworth to Miss Sullivan; letter to James Samuel Wadsworth from Sargent, September 8, 1828. Miss Sullivan was still "a candidate for the holy state" as late as March 7, 1831, according to Edmund Quincy's letter to Wadsworth on that date. Letters from James G. Rowe, July 27, 1828, and Thomas Giles, January 27, 1827, to James Samuel Wadsworth. Letters to James Samuel Wadsworth from George S. Hillard, July 28, 1828, Charles Terry, May 21, 23, 1832, and Jos. W. Lesesne, July 29, 1830. Terry's May 23, 1832, letter suggests Wadsworth's "promiscuous regard prompted" him to visit a prostitute, though a tear in the page at that point carefully deletes the name. All letters from WFP.

Levi Hubbell, a Canandaigua friend, dismisses James Samuel's prenuptial experiences as a young man's interest in sex; letter from Levi Hubbell to James Samuel Wadsworth, May 29, 1830, WFP.

19. An example of his taste in clothing appears in a letter from a New York tailor, Sam(?) Frost, May 30, 1830, WFP, noting James Samuel's dissatisfaction with articles ordered earlier and spelling out the day's fashions.

20. Letters from Thomas Giles to James Samuel Wadsworth, January 27, 1827; George Turner to James Samuel Wadsworth, January 26, 1829; January 18 and June 7, 1841; and from Nathaniel Parker Willis to James Samuel Wadsworth, January 4, 1829, WFP.

21. Letter from Naomi Wolcott Wadsworth to William Wolcott Wadsworth, June 1, 1827, WFP.

22. Letterbook, John T. Kirkland and correspondence, October 2, 1827, WFP.

23. Letter to the author from James McCarthy, Curatorial Assistant, Harvard University Archives, Cambridge, Mass., January 11, 1995. The other courses, for which there should have been grades, were Natural Philosophy, Latin, Composition, Modern Languages, and Themes.

24. Letter from James to James Samuel Wadsworth, October 17, 1827, WFP.

25. Letter from John T. Sargent to James Samuel Wadsworth, January 26, 1828, WFP.

26. Letter from John Lothrop Motley to Mary Craig Wadsworth, June 26, 1864, WFP; *Webster's Biographical Dictionary* (Springfield, Mass.: G. & C. Merriam, 1967); Brooks, *The Flowering of New England*, pp. 90, 119, 334–342.

27. James's involvement in the affair, though regarded as consultation, linked him and his older son to a number of prominent New Yorkers, including future governor and U.S. secretary of state William H. Seward, Francis Granger, son of the former postmaster general under Jefferson and Madison, and newspaper editor Thurlow Weed, a powerful national political figure.

There are any number of sources about the Anti-Masonic movement of the late 1820s through the 1830s, one of which is Weed, *Autobiography*, Vol. 1, especially Chapter 29 and again on pp. 299, 366, 343, 344. Weed shows "how peremptorily Mr. Wadsworth refused office" by quoting his October 1828 letter, p. 344. See also Doty, *History of Livingston County*, p. 393; *Livingston Register*, January 2, 1827, February 26, 1828, and April 8 and 27, 1829. One of his daughters claimed that "Papa has been offered very often the office of senator some five or six times & has been pressured very hard to accept"; letter from Cornelia and Elizabeth Wadsworth to William Wolcott Wadsworth, October 10, 1828, WFP. A short, recent account is Martin Naparsteck, "The Morgan Affair," *Genesee Country*, Vol. 2, No. 1 (April/May 1994), pp. 46–51. An account that paints the Masons more favorably is Ossian Lang, *History of Freemasonry in the State of New York* (New York: Grand Lodge of New York, F. & A. M., 1922).

James's willingness to be an anti-Masonic candidate, *Livingston Register*, April 8, 1829.

28. Very briefly, this convoluted series of transactions arose out of the Big Tree Treaty signed September 15, 1797, at Geneseo (Big Tree), whereby the Senecas sold their rights to the land west of the Genesee River to Lake Erie, less a mile-wide strip and 337 square miles retained for ten reservations, to Thomas Morris,

representing his father. The reservations were the subject of these negotiations between the Senecas and the Ogden Land Company, which wanted the land for resale. This précis is courtesy of David Parish, Town and Village of Geneseo Historian, in an untitled paper, which was prepared for a meeting of the Big Tree Treaty Commemoration Committee, January 25, 1995.

29. Parker, *The History of the Seneca Indians*, pp. 151, 152; U.S. Bureau of Indian Affairs, *Seneca Indians Who Will Be Affected By The Kinzua Dam Reservoir*, Report #175 (March 1963); Silsby, *The Holland Land Company in Western New York*, pp. 9–11; Bradshaw Snipes, "Friends' Relations With the Seneca Indians, 1838–1850," M.A. Thesis, Haverford College, May 10, 1949, p. 2; James Wadsworth's letter to T. L. Ogden, June 21, 1819, Letterbook, Shelf 27, pp. 546, 547, which indicates that a relationship with the Ogden Land Company existed at least as early as 1819; *Livingston Register*, November 13, 1827, and September 3, 1828; Evans, *The Holland Land Company*, p. 196; letter from James to James Samuel Wadsworth, October 22, 1827, WFP; Laurence M. Hauptman, "The Historical Background to the Present-day Seneca Nation–Salamanca Lease Controversy," in Christopher Vecsey and William Starna (eds.), *Iroquois Land Claims* (Syracuse, N.Y.: Syracuse University Press, 1988), pp. 102–103; James Renwick, "Life of James Wadsworth," *Journal of Agriculture* (October 1846), pp. 145–156. The letter about James Samuel's attendance at the Indian lands is from Elizabeth Wadsworth Murray to her brother William, September 9, 1828, WFP. James mentions headaches in a letter to his cousin Daniel Wadsworth, Jeremiah's son, June 23, 1828, WFP.

30. Letter from Cornelius Felton to James Samuel Wadsworth, April 26, 1828, WFP. Apparently Webster, to whom James and Naomi Wadsworth had introduced Carolyn LeRoy, his second wife, was a friend of the Wadsworths; letter from John P. Murray to James Samuel Wadsworth, November 24, 1829, WFP.

31. Letter from George S. Hillard, who would read law with Webster after James Samuel's departure, July 28, 1828; letter from George Turner to James Samuel Wadsworth, September 14, 1828, WFP.

The sometime law student was still pursuing Boston ladies, including requesting a love poem; letters from Edward B. Emerson, George Hillard, and George Turner to James Samuel Wadsworth, June 26, 1828, October 15, 1828, and September 14, 1828, respectively, WFP.

32. Letter from Cornelia Wadsworth to William Wadsworth, December 1, 1828; letters from Naomi Wadsworth to William Wadsworth, December 3, 1828 and March 1, 1839, WFP.

33. Letter from George Turner to James Samuel Wadsworth, January 26, 1829; letters from Nathaniel Parker Willis, January 27, and September, 1829, WFP; undated note from David W. Parish, Town and Village of Geneseo Historian.

34. Naomi Wadsworth also was concerned about her younger son, William, who had suffered a knee injury, forcing him to rely on crutches, and she, no doubt, was feeling lonely because her husband had enrolled Elizabeth, their youngest child, in a Philadelphia school on Pine Street, the name of which her husband had not bothered to inform her; letters from Naomi and from Cornelia Wadsworth to James Samuel Wadsworth, November 15, 1829, and February 8, 1830, respectively, WFP. One Harvard companion suggested excessive drinking had brought on James Samuel's illness about this time, his brother attributed the condition simply to homesickness, and still another friend saw no symptoms of any health problem; letter from C. Jones Richards, June 27, 1830; letter from James Samuel to William Wolcott Wadsworth, April 5–6, 1830; and letter from a friend identified only as "Sullivan," May 11, 1830, WFP.

35. Letter from John P. Murray to James Samuel Wadsworth, November 24, 1829, WFP.

36. Letter from James to James Samuel Wadsworth, December 26, 1829, WFP. Naomi Wadsworth reinforced her husband's concerns when she lamented about her older son's behavior, including her unintended collusion with the son when she believed he debauched in Rochester instead of seeing a doctor there, and his licentiousness—reading Byron and his ilk; letter to James Samuel from Naomi Wadsworth, January 31, 1830, WFP.

37. Letter from James to James Samuel Wadsworth, January 15, 1830, WFP. Pearson, *James S. Wadsworth of Geneseo*, p. 23, identifies the law firm as McKean & Denniston. Letters from Charles Terry and Edmund Quincy to James Samuel Wadsworth, July 14 and 29, 1830, and March 7, 1831, respectively; William Wolcott Wadsworth to James Samuel Wadsworth, January 2, 1831; James Samuel to William Wolcott Wadsworth, January 7, 1831, WFP.

38. Hoppin and Cozzens, *Proceedings of the Century Association*, p. 17.

39. Letters from James to James Samuel Wadsworth, October 29, 1830, and January 25, 1831, WFP.

40. Letter from James Samuel to William Wolcott Wadsworth, February 10, 1831, WFP.

41. Letters from James to Daniel Wadsworth, March 13, 27, 1831, WFP. Because death certificates were not maintained in the county until after 1870, the causes of death of Naomi and Cornelia are unknown. Strangely, Naomi Wadsworth's death is noted briefly in the *Dansville Village Chronicle*, March 8, 1831, p. 3, but not in Geneseo's paper, the *Livingston Register*. On the other hand, the *Register* did report Cornelia's death on March 30, 1831, though, again, without any details. However, on April 20, 1831, the paper carried a report from the *Albany Evening Journal* (Thurlow Weed's paper) that Cornelia died of "brain fever" brought on by her mother's death. As indicated earlier, tuberculosis may have been the cause of death for Naomi and Cornelia.

42. Letter from James to Daniel Wadsworth, April 10, 1831; letter from James to James Samuel Wadsworth, August 31, 1831, WFP.

CHAPTER 4

1. Thurlow Weed, the Albany newspaperman and behind-the-scenes politician, recalled this curiosity: "Just as the sun was rising one morning, when the [Asiatic] cholera was at its worst, the late General James S. Wadsworth, . . . called at my house [in Albany] and asked me to accompany him to the cholera hospital. On our way to the hospital we encountered three hearses with the remains of as many cholera victims, who had died the preceding night. I left my friend at the hospital door, not caring to visit its patients before breakfast"; Weed, *Autobiography*, vol. 1, p. 417.

   There were also a few letters of condolence, including one to "Tom" from C. Jones Richards, who considered himself more as a relative than friend because of their long acquaintanceship, July 8, 1831, and from Adrian Terry, now a doctor, who lamented the losses of James Samuel's mother and sister, June 20, 1831, WFP.

2. Letter from William Wolcott Wadsworth to James Samuel, May 10, 1831, WFP. Temporarily, following her mother's death, Elizabeth was placed in the care of her older sister, Harriet, and brother-in-law, Martin Brimmer, who reported to James that Elizabeth and Harriet, though feeble, "have recovered to a good degree their composure"; letter from Martin Brimmer to James Wadsworth, May 26, 1831, WFP.

3. Letter from James Samuel to William Wolcott Wadsworth, August 9, 1831; letter from John B. Church to James Samuel Wadsworth, August 29, 1831; letter from William Wolcott Wadsworth to James Samuel Wadsworth, September 1, 1831; letters from William Wolcott Wadsworth to James Samuel Wadsworth, September 2, 5, 14, 1831; letters from James Wadsworth per clerk, William Farmer, to James Samuel Wadsworth, September 5 and 30, 1831; letter from Elizabeth Wadsworth Murray to William Wolcott Wadsworth, September 25, 1831. All letters from WFP.

4. Letters from James to James Samuel Wadsworth, August 9, 17, 1831, WFP.

5. Weed, *Autobiography*, Vol. 1, pp. 389, 425; letters from Elizabeth Wadsworth Murray to William Wolcott Wadsworth, October 1 and 8, 1831, WFP; *Livingston Register*, February 9, 1831; letter from James Samuel Wadsworth to his uncle William Wadsworth, October 9, 1831, WFP. The Anti-Masonic Party, the first third party in the United States, would become absorbed by the Whigs after the election of 1836; Morris and Morris, *Encyclopedia of American History*, p. 204.

6. Letters from James to James Samuel Wadsworth, August 31, 1831, and one undated, but apparently about the same time when James Samuel was in New York City on family business, WFP.

7. Undated letter from James to James Samuel Wadsworth, but apparently sometime in August, when the latter was in New York City on family business, WFP. James Samuel's sister Harriet also was a bit surprised to learn that her brother was not obliged to be in Albany studying; letter from Harriet Wadsworth Brimmer, November 10, 1831, WFP.

8. Letter from James Samuel to William Wolcott Wadsworth, October 11, 1831, WFP. Livingston and Cass had only recently become part of President Andrew Jackson's reorganized cabinet. Livingston replaced Secretary of State Martin Van Buren and Cass replaced Secretary of War John H. Eaton, as a result of the cabinet split that erupted over Eaton's marriage to Washington barmaid Peggy O'Neale; Morris and Morris, *Encyclopedia of American History*, p. 203.

9. Letters from Elizabeth Wadsworth Murray to James Samuel Wadsworth, November 28, December 3, 1831, WFP.

10. Letters from James to James Samuel Wadsworth, December 2, 13, 23, 1831, WFP.

11. Letters from Charles A. Terry to James Samuel Wadsworth, December 30, 1831, and from Nathaniel Parker Willis, no date; letter from Elizabeth Wadsworth Murray to James Samuel Wadsworth, January 28, 1832, WFP.

12. Letters from James Wadsworth and Elizabeth Wadsworth Murray to James Samuel Wadsworth, February 7, January 23, 1832, WFP.

13. Weed, *Autobiography*, Vol. 1, p. 392. Weed claims that Wadsworth and Seymour were admitted as attorneys whereas Dix was admitted as a counselor. Apparently the distinction was between those newly admitted ("attorney") and those in practice who had passed a second exam ("counselor"), *Black's Law Dictionary*, rev. 4th ed. (St. Paul, Minn.: West Publishing, 1968), pp. 164, 418.

14. Letter from Elizabeth Wadsworth Murray to James Samuel Wadsworth, May 12, 1832, WFP. There is reason to believe that there has been some censorship of James Samuel's correspondence, possibly after his marriage. Names of females seem to be deleted from some letters to him, for example, but more importantly there are no letters to and from his wife Mary Craig Wharton Wadsworth during the period of their courtship and virtually no letters by James Samuel thereafter. By contrast, letters to and from James, who, admittedly, had a secretary, are quite extensive. This puts the biographer at a distinct disadvantage. Letter from Elizabeth Wadsworth Murray to James Samuel Wadsworth, March 12, 1832, WFP.

15. Letters from James to James Samuel Wadsworth, February 7, 14, 19, March 6, 9, 15,17, 1832, WFP; letters from James Wadsworth, Charles Terry, and William Farmer to James Samuel Wadsworth, March 19, April 23, and May 14, 1832, respectively, WFP. Piffard, a self-taught physician, was commonly called "Dr. Piffard." However, Geneseo Town and Village Historian David W. Parish questions why the Wadsworths, who were so interested in the latest treatments, consulted Piffard when there were more than sixty physicians in Livingston County at this time. Parish speculates that consultation with Piffard may have been an attempt to avoid any untoward publicity. Apparently James Samuel also had consulted a Philadelphia doctor recommended by the family friend Dr. Frederick F. Backus of Rochester; letter from Frederick Backus to James Samuel Wadsworth, May 29, 1832, WFP.

16. Letters from James to James Samuel Wadsworth, May 17, 18, 23, 1832, WFP. It is risky to speculate, but it may be that James Samuel was experiencing the effects of alcohol poisoning, as had some of his Harvard friends, though it is possible that he was suffering what is loosely called a nervous breakdown, for his father blamed the illness on his son's nervous system. Charles Terry's allusions to his promiscuity in a May 23, 1832, letter suggest another cause, but the letter is torn at a place that seems to reveal more about Wadsworth's affliction.

17. James had informed his cousin Daniel that a cholera epidemic in Albany and Boston made Harriet's health a real concern, leading a doctor to state that it was necessary for her to go to a warmer climate, such as Cuba, Italy, or France; James Wadsworth to Daniel Wadsworth, July 14, 1832, WFP. In early 1833 Harriet died in Havana; letter from Mrs. Henderson Inches, Jr., to James Samuel Wadsworth, January 20, 1833. Mrs. Inches, née Susan Brimmer, was the sister-in-law of Harriet Wadsworth Brimmer; Justin Winsor (ed.), *The Memorial History of Boston, 1630–1880* (Boston: James R. Osgood & Co., 1881), Part. 2, p. 555.

18. Doty, *History of Livingston County*, p. 362.

19. A copy of the document with New York Life and Trust Company lists the six areas that the lectures, intended to be read by the students themselves, would cover (application of Science for the Arts, Agriculture and Horticulture, Legislation, Political Economy, Astronomy, Chemistry, and other branches of Natural Philosophy to be determined by his trustees, his two sons, and three others with him James conducted business) and "intellectual, moral and religious instruction"; March 11, 1833, WFP. Ironically, five months later he denied a $213 request from Geneva (later Hobart) College to purchase a set of "classics" books, because "Our Colleges contribute so little to National education, so little to the sound instruction of public opinion." When they made themselves "useful," they would receive abundant donations; letter from James Wadsworth to Geneva College, August 5, 1833, WFP.

20. Attesting to Mary Craig Wharton Wadsworth's qualities are a letter from Adrian Terry to James Samuel Wadsworth, February 24, 1834, WFP, and from John Lothrop Motley, whose acquaintanceship with Wadsworth would be renewed shortly; Pearson, *James S. Wadsworth of Geneseo*, p. 24. Reference to the Sully painting of Mary Craig Wharton Wadsworth confirms opinions about her beauty.

21. Letters from James to James Samuel Wadsworth, January 12, 17, 1834, and an undated one that appears to have been written in January 1834; letters from John Van Buren to James Samuel Wadsworth, July 31, and September 29, 1834, WFP. The younger Van Buren, who would become New York's attorney general

in 1845, is supposed to have acquired the sobriquet "Prince" because "he had danced with the future Queen Victoria while his father was momentarily minister to England in 1832"; Stewart Mitchell, *Horatio Seymour of New York* (Cambridge: Harvard University Press, 1938), p. 103. Barnburner journalist Henry B. Stanton describes the aggressive John Van Buren as electrical, witty, and sarcastic; ibid., p. 74.

22. The moving story of this romance has been told by David W. Parish, "Elizabeth Wadsworth: Lily of the Valley," *Genesee Country*, Vol. 1, No. 3 (August/September 1993), pp. 29–31; Pearson, *James S. Wadsworth of Geneseo*, pp. 26–28. Another, less publicized visitor was British farmer-writer Patrick Shirreff, who was looking for land for his brother in late spring 1833. An experienced observer, Shirreff attested to the Wadsworths' knowledge of farming; Roger Haydon (ed.), *Upstate Travels: British Views of Nineteenth Century New York* (Syracuse, N.Y.: Syracuse University Press, 1982), pp. 5, 47.

23. Wadsworth, *The Silver Spoon*, pp. 17, 19; *Philadelphia National Gazette and Literary Register*, May 12, 1834. The Wharton family traces its roots to Thomas Wharton, a Quaker who came from Westmoreland in England to Philadelphia around 1683 and whose descendants became wealthy merchants. Little is known about Mary Craig, other than she was the product of a marriage between John Wharton and Nancy Craig, which produced three children: William Craig (1811), Mary Craig, and Thomas Carpenter Wharton (1819 or 1820); Anne H. Wharton, *Genealogy of the Wharton Family of Philadelphia, 1664–1880* (Philadelphia: Author, 1880). The Wharton family claims merchants, lawyers, and university presidents among its prominent members.

24. Letter from "John" to James Samuel Wadsworth, January 12, 1835; letter from James to James Samuel Wadsworth, January 11, 1835; letter from I. M. Andrews to James Samuel Wadsworth, April 6, 1835, WFP.

    Extrapolation from historical price index in McCusker, "How Much Is That in Real Money?" pp. 297–373, and U.S. Bureau of the Census, *Historical Statistics of the United States*, p. 212.

25. Letter from John Young to James Samuel Wadsworth c/o Barings Bros. & Co., London, March 9, 1835; letter from John Van Buren to James Samuel Wadsworth, April 12, 1835, WFP.

26. Letter from S. W. Singer, Secretary, Committee of the Travellers, May 20, 1835, WFP.

27. Alice Wadsworth Strong, *Hartford House, 1835–1985* (Geneseo, N.Y.: Private printing, 1985). While Mrs. Strong notes that James Samuel and Mary Craig Wharton Wadsworth returned to Geneseo and began constructing the house in the fall of 1834, it appears from letters to James Samuel that it was late spring 1835 when they returned from their honeymoon. Drawings of the original villa and the Geneseo house are included in the monograph. Details of the house are from John E. Squeri, "Hartford House," a paper prepared for the class Art History 280 at SUNY–Geneseo, December 10, 1979; Sidney George Fisher (Nicholas B. Wainright, ed.), *A Philadelphia Perspective: The Diary of Sidney George Fisher Covering the Years 1834–1871* (Philadelphia: Historical Society of Philadelphia, 1967), p. 217. The name given their new residence, Hartford House (without the adjective "the"), seems to have two derivations. One comes from the pronunciation of Lord Hertford's house, and the second stems from the Wadsworths' ancestral home in Hartford, Connecticut; videotaped interview of Mrs. Alice Wadsworth Strong by Dr. Martin Fausold, biographer of James Samuel's grandson, James Wolcott Wadsworth.

28. Invoices in WFP; Henderson Inches, Jr., to James Samuel Wadsworth, August 27, 1836, WFP. Henderson Inches, Jr., was the business associate and brother-in-law of Martin Brimmer; Winsor, *The Memorial History of Boston, 1830–1880*, Part 2, p. 555. James Samuel relied heavily on Brimmer and Inches. Prices were extrapolated from the historical price index in McCusker, "How Much Is That in Real Money?" pp. 297–373, and U.S. Bureau of the Census, *Historical Statistics of the United States*, p. 212.

CHAPTER 5

1. Fisher, *A Philadelphia Perspective*, p. 41.

2. Letters from James Samuel Wadsworth to I. M. Andrews, April 6, 1835, March 22, 1836, and to James Sperry, March 2, 1836; letter from William Short to James Samuel Wadsworth, September 16, 1836; codicil added to James Samuel Wadsworth's will, May 16, 1856, Livingston County Surrogate Court, Wills, Book 7, p. 1. The Ohio Counties were Defiance, Fulton, Henry, Lucas (Toledo), Paulding, Williams, and Wood. This tract was conveyed to him by Daniel H. Fitzhugh on November 25, 1855. It appears to have

been part of a previous agreement between the two, whereby he and Fitzhugh bought a much larger tract together, with the intent of Wadsworth ultimately owning the entirety, when he was less extended.

3. Letters from Benson & Lefferts to James Samuel Wadsworth, October 13, and November 15, 1836, and from E. R. Stammate(?) to James Samuel Wadsworth, undated, but sometime in early 1837; letter from Daniel Fitzhugh to James Samuel Wadsworth, March 5, 1837; letter from Nicholas Biddle to James Samuel Wadsworth, July 21, 1838, WFP. The younger Wadsworths already had been instrumental in obtaining legislative approval for a Livingston County Bank after a number of tries and, by mid-June 1830, they, with business associates William Spencer, Allen Ayrault, and Daniel Fitzhugh, had managed to obtain subscribers for the initial offering of stock in the amount of $100,000 at $25 per share; *Livingston Register*, April 29, May 5, 1829, and May 31, June 9, 25, 30, 1830. Congressman George W. Patterson from the nearby hamlet of Greigsville intended to induce influential residents of the village of York, just north of Greigsville, to support the Geneseo bank and suggested that James Samuel do the same in the village of Livonia, just east of Geneseo; George W. Patterson to James Samuel Wadsworth, May 28, 1839, WFP.

4. Letters to James Samuel Wadsworth from I. W. Andrews, March 22, 25, 1836, and Philo Fuller, March 22, 1839, WFP.

5. Letter from James to James Samuel Wadsworth, July 26, 1837, WFP.

6. Hauptman, "The Seneca Nation–Salamanca Lease Controversy," p. 103; U.S. Bureau of Indian Affairs, "Seneca Indians Who Will Be Affected By The Kinzua Dam Reservoir," p. 3; Parker, *The History of the Seneca Indians*, p. 133; *Livingston Register*, October 16, 25, and November 19, 1827. Sales included acreage from the Buffalo Creek, Cattaragus, Tonawanda, and Caneadea Reservations, while roughly a year later another 47,000 acres were put up for sale from the same reservations; *Livingston Register*, August 19, September 8, 31, 1828. Title to these lands was obtained from the Senecas in 1826. David A. Ogden, founder of the Ogden Land Company, had been "permanent counsel" to the Holland Land Company since at least 1802; Evans, *The Holland Land Company*, p. 245. Notice giving James Samuel power of attorney is dated December 14, 1837, WFP.

7. Letter from James Wadsworth to Thomas L. Ogden, June 21, 1819, Letterbook 61, Shelf 27, pp. 546, 547.

8. Bradshaw Snipes, "Friends' Relations with the Seneca Indians, 1838–1850," M.A. Thesis, May 10, 1949, pp. 2–5. It is ironic that the Iroquois, or Five Nations, as they were originally known, needed such protection, for New York's first constitution in 1777 recognized ongoing frauds being committed against the Iroquois and provided that "no purchases or contracts for the sale of lands made since the 14th day of October [1775]" or thereafter would be valid "unless under the authority and with the consent of the legislature of this state"; Gerald Gunther, "Governmental Power and the New York Indian Lands—A Reassessment of a Persistent Problem of Federal–State Relations," *Buffalo Law Review*, Vol. 8, No. 1 (Fall 1958), p. 3. Federal legislation dating less than twenty years later went so far as to make it a misdemeanor even to negotiate with Indians without the presence and approval of federal commissioners; ibid., p. 5.

9. Ibid., pp. 3, 15, 17. Gillet's role throughout this affair is generally considered conspiratorial, which seems substantiated by a number of sources, including Horatio Jones's letter to James Samuel Wadsworth, February 18, 1838, WFP.

10. Letter of Horatio Jones to James Samuel Wadsworth, February 16, 1838, WFP. As a young man Jones had been captured by the Senecas and voluntarily lived many years as one of them; Turner, *Phelps and Gorham's Purchase*, pp. 286–291. Jones's familiarity with the Senecas, indeed reputation among them and ability to interpret, made him a particularly valuable Ogden ally. Moreover, Jones had a vested interest, for he was appealing to Wadsworth to obtain President Van Buren's approval of Jones to serve as agent and superintendent for the removal of the Senecas; letters from Thomas L. Ogden and Joseph Fellows to James Samuel Wadsworth from mid-June to mid-July 1838, WFP.

11. Letter from James Samuel Wadsworth to Joseph Fellows and Thomas Ogden, December 6, 1838, Letterbook 1, Shelf 27, p. 44; letters from Thomas L. Ogden to James Samuel Wadsworth, July 9, 30, 1839, WFP.

12. Letters from James Samuel Wadsworth to H. B. Potter, August 29, 1839, and to "Messers Potter, Allen, Stryker, Wilcox," August 30, 1839, Letterbook 1, Shelf 27, pp. 2, 29; letter from James Samuel Wadsworth to Thomas L. Ogden, February 1, 1839, Letterbook 1, Shelf 27, p. 38.

13. Letters from Thomas L. Ogden and Joseph Fellows to U.S. Commissioner Ransom Gillet, October 2, 1838, and September 28, 1839, Letterbook 1, Shelf 27, pp. 35, 40; letters from Thomas L. Ogden and

Joseph Fellows to James Samuel Wadsworth, January 14, February 15, March 16, 1839, WFP; letter from James Samuel Wadsworth to Thomas L. Ogden, March 20, 1839, Letterbook 1, Shelf 27, p. 48.

14. Letter from James Samuel Wadsworth to Thomas L. Ogden, July 1, 1840, Letterbook 1, Shelf 27, pp. 58, 59. Author Snipes's claims about payments seem to support Wadsworth's accounting. For example, Snipes writes that pressures to obtain signatures to assure President Van Buren of the legality of the treaty led to payments of $2,000 to Seneca chief John Snow in 1837 plus a lifetime lease to the farm where he lived, and $6,000 to Chief Samuel Gordon that same year. Snipes concludes that "almost every one of the . . . 140 Seneca warriors" had been bribed some way or another; Snipes, "Friends' Relations With the Seneca Indians, 1838–1850," pp. 23, 24. For a more extended treatment of the role played by the Quakers, see New York State Assembly, *Report of the Special Committee to Investigate the Indian Problem of the State of New York, Appointed by the Assembly, 1888* (Albany: Troy Press, 1889), pp. 61–62. Letter from Asher Wright to James Samuel Wadsworth, October 8, 1840, WFP. The treaty was resubmitted to the Senate in 1842 after seventy-nine chiefs assented to its revision and called on the federal and state governments of Massachusetts and New York to ratify it. This did not end Ogden Land Company involvement, however, for it continued to "tamper" to obtain land on the Cattaraugus Reservation; Snipes, "Friends' Relations With The Seneca Indians, 1838–1850," p. 48. Nor did it end attempts by some Senecas to overturn it up to 1868, when a new constitution was written; New York State Assembly, *Report of the Special Committee to Investigate the Indian Problem*, p. 63.

15. Marc Friedlaender et al. (eds.), *Diary of Charles Francis Adams* (Cambridge: Belknap Press, 1986), Vol. 7, p. 258; *Livingston Republican*, December 5, 1837, p. 2.

16. Invoice, November 11, 1838, WFP; letters from John Colt, Clifton Wharton, and Benson & Lefferts to James Samuel Wadsworth, March 24, October 7, and December 5, 1837, respectively; letters from H. T. Dexter in Scottsville, William W. Wadsworth and Thomas M. Willing to James Samuel Wadsworth, September 27, 1838, July 3, 1839, May 9, 1839, respectively. Letters from W. S. Church to James Samuel Wadsworth, June 19, 1840, at 3:30 P.M. and later that day, and letter from Thomas Willing, December 29, 1840. All letters from WFP.

17. Letter from Nathaniel Parker Willis to James Samuel Wadsworth, November 5, 1837, WFP.

18. Letters from Martin Van Buren and Henry P. Gilpin to James Samuel Wadsworth, September 5, and November 15, 1838, respectively, WFP.

19. Pearson, *James S. Wadsworth of Geneseo*, p. 29.

20. Other incidents that might be cited include the story of Jenny, who had nursed his father and uncle to health that first year in Geneseo, his tour of Charles Carroll of Carrollton's plantation, and his own observations of Black Americans who had worked on shares at Big Tree and on the Carroll and Fitzhugh estates just south of Geneseo before slavery was outlawed in New York roughly ten years earlier.

21. Fisher, *A Philadelphia Perspective*, entry for February 6, 1840, p. 97; letter from Dr. Charles Meigs to James Samuel Wadsworth, May 9, 1841, WFP; James H. Smith, *The History of Livingston County* (Syracuse, N.Y.: D. Mason Publ., 1881), p. 119; Geneseo Town and Village Historian David W. Parish. The Wadsworths remained active in the society for years: James Samuel's second son, Craig W., served as president from 1865 to 1866, while Craig's younger brother, James W., became president five years later, and their cousin, William Austin (William's youngest son), was president 1877–1878.

22. Hedrick, *A History of Agriculture in New York State*, p. 63. He, his father, and brother had earlier paid the requisite $50 to become life members. Doty, *History of Livingston County*, p. 425; letters from Luther Tucker, secretary of the New York State Agricultural Society, January 26 and April 16, 1842, WFP. Certificate of election to the Philadelphia Society in WFP; Wadsworth's report to the secretary of state, *New York State Agricultural Society Transactions* (Albany: E. Mack Printer to the Senate, 1843), Vol. 2, pp. 5, 1, and Vol. 3 (1844), pp. 7–8.

23. *New York State Agricultural Society Transactions*, Vol. 3, pp. 21, 29, 34, 35, 53. The next year James Samuel won $13 for his bull, while Elizabeth was awarded $3 for her flowers; ibid., p. 670.

24. The 25-year-old Hammatt, who had come to Geneseo only five years earlier and who shared James Samuel's political bent, in time would manage not only the entire Wadsworth estate, but also the Martin Brimmer estate when James Samuel became an executor; *Livingston Republican*, September 17, 1839, January 9, 1844, August 22, 1884.

25. *Littell's Living Age*, No. 9, July 13, 1844; letters from James to James Samuel Wadsworth, November 21, 29, 1843, WFP.

26. Last letter from James to James Samuel Wadsworth, December 6, 1843, WFP.
27. Letters from William Wolcott Wadsworth to James Samuel Wadsworth, John W. Wadsworth, and William Cushing, March 31, 25, and 30, 1843, respectively; Letterbook of William Wolcott Wadsworth, Shelf 27. The reason for William's trip to Europe is unknown.
28. Letters from Elizabeth ("Lizzie") Wadsworth Murray to James Samuel Wadsworth in Philadelphia and Washington, February 3 and 5, 1844, WFP.

CHAPTER 6

1. Exemplified Copy of the Will of James Wadsworth, Esq., Deceased, prepared November 25, 1843, and entered into probate September 9, 1844, WFP. William Wolcott Wadsworth returned to Boston after a twelve-day ordeal sailing from Liverpool; letter to James Samuel Wadsworth from Martin Brimmer, September 1, 1844, WFP. Ironically, James Samuel's maternal grandmother, Jerusaha Wolcott, died this same year, but there is no mention of this in the Wadsworth Family Papers.
2. Ibid. James Samuel would also deal with more mundane matters, including consenting to a six-rod enlargement ("attuation") of South Street, which bordered his sister's Mansion House property, Order of the Town of Geneseo Highway Commissioners, March 16, 1845, WFP.
3. Examples are Thurlow Weed's *Albany Journal*, June 10, 1844; the *Albany Evening Atlas*, the same day; *Littell's Living Age*, July 13, 1844; *New York American*, August 23, 1844. Notice of nomination by James Rose, Clerk of the New York State Assembly and Esaac R. Elwood, Clerk of the New York State Senate, May 4, 1844, WFP.
4. Letters from Edwin Croswell, James Faulker, and Benjamin F. Angel to James Samuel Wadsworth, October 25, 1842, November 16, 1841, January 4 and 12, 1842, respectively, WFP.
5. Letter from Orville Hungerford to James Samuel Wadsworth, May 5, 1844, WFP; Doty, *History of Livingston County*, p. 428.
6. Pearson, *James S. Wadsworth of Geneseo*, pp. 36, 37; Doty, *History of Livingston County*, p. 528.
7. Letters from Elizabeth Wadsworth Murray to James Samuel Wadsworth, whom she typically addressed as "Cheri," August 10, 27, 1845, WFP. She also lamented that everything came to a standstill when he was gone; letter from Elizabeth Wadsworth Murray to James Samuel Wadsworth, September 14, 1845, WFP.

   Elizabeth, long dominated by her father (and by affection for James S.), was now alone in and mistress of the large house her father and uncle had built. She was settling into the role of spinster to which her father relegated her when he rejected suitor Charles Murray's request for permission to marry her. Yet from all accounts she entertained in the true Wadsworthian manner. For example, Richard Henry Dana, Harvard-educated lawyer, member of a socially prominent Massachusetts family, and author of *Two Years Before the Mast*, recalled being entertained by Elizabeth in July 1845. While Dana found James Samuel to be "a fine looking, frank, ready & pleasant man," he was enchanted by Elizabeth, "a truly lovely creature, sensible, pretty, unaffected & interesting. I don't know when I have been so charmed with any lady"; Richard Henry Dana (Robert F. Lucid, ed.), *The Journal of Richard Henry Dana, Jr.* (Cambridge: Belknap Press, 1968), Vol. 1, p. 309.

   Philadelphia socialite-lawyer Sidney George Fisher was equally captivated by Elizabeth. In 1848 on another trip to Geneseo Fisher found her "a very remarkable person . . . young, handsome, intellectual, cultivated, graceful & elegant, of most lovely, pure & elevated character, very rich & living alone . . . in a neighborhood where she has no equals or companions & managing her own household & estate." Yet he perceived that "she feels solitary, and that she is sensible that her life is without its best interest & purpose"; Fisher, *A Philadelphia Perspective*, p. 218.
8. Letter from John Van Buren to James Samuel Wadsworth, August 21, 1846, WFP. Prince John was raising $4,000 to keep the *Albany Atlas* (the Democratic Party organ at the time) afloat and claimed the $500 Wadsworth had contributed "acts like a charm upon the poor rich men."
9. Denis T. Lynch, "Party Struggles, 1828–1850," in Alexander C. Flick (ed.), *History of the State of New York* (Port Washington, N.Y.: Ira J. Friedman, 1962), Vol. 6, p. 76 (reprint of 10-volume set by Columbia University Press, 1934). Weed, *Autobiography*, Vol. 1, p. 534, offers another origin of the word "Barnburner," referring to the Dorr Rebellion in Rhode Island in 1842, wherein insurrectionists engaged in "highway robberies and the burning of farmers' well-stored barns."

10. Letters from Simeon B. Jewett and John Van Buren to James Samuel Wadsworth, June 20, 26, 28 and July 17, 1847, WFP.

11. The *Livingston Republican*, October 7, 1847, reported that "Mr. Wadsworth either lost his usual self complacency or else the defeat of Mr. Wright the year since has made a very lasting and heartfelt impression." Wadsworth was quoted as saying "It is too late, said he [Wadsworth] to do justice to that great and good man; but thank God, it is not too late *to do justice to those who stabbed him* (cheers, hissing, stamping and cries of order)."

12. Lynch, "Party Struggles, 1828–1850," p. 78; Pearson, *James S. Wadsworth of Geneseo*, p. 44. Pearson claims that it was the Hunkers who split into "Softs" and "Hards," whereas Mitchell (*Horatio Seymour of New York*) and Lynch claim that it was the Democratic Party itself, not just the Hunkers, that was so split after 1849. In either case the term Barnburner disappears as most become Free Soilers or anti-slavery proponents. Letters from John Van Buren to James Samuel Wadsworth, October 22 and 24, 1847, WFP.

13. *Livingston Republican*, December 1, 1846; Arthur J. May, *A History of the University of Rochester, 1850–1962* (Rochester, N.Y.: University of Rochester, 1977), p. 14. In fact, the "Wadsworth tract," north of Griffith Street, between Union Street and the present South Avenue, was one of three possible sites; Jesse Leonard Rosenberger, *Rochester, The Making of a University* (Rochester, N.Y.: University of Rochester, 1927), pp. 13, 48, 75.

14. *Western Literary Magazine* (Buffalo), Vol. 8, No. 4 (February 27, 1847), p. 63, quoting the *Albany Journal*; *Livingston Republican*, January 28, March 3, 11, and April 29, 1847. Geneseo's total, which included Wadsworth's donation, as of April 28, 1847, was reported to be $1,100; *Livingston Republican*, April 29, 1847. The firm of Grinnell, Minturn & Co., at an estimated cost of $500, freighted the corn free, according to the *Western Literary Magazine*.

15. Martin Brimmer, James Samuel's brother-in-law and former mayor of Boston, died April 25, 1847; Winsor, *The Memorial History of Boston, 1830–1880*, Part. 2, p. 555. Surprisingly, the Wadsworth Family Papers do not mention the event.

16. Letters from John Van Buren and Albert Lester to James Samuel Wadsworth, November 8 and December 27, 1847, WFP.

17. Letter from Reuben H. Walworth to James Samuel Wadsworth, December 3, 1847, WFP. Family lore and an obituary claim that William's mental condition resulted from a fall at the Street Farm west of Avon, which caused permanent injury; *Livingston Republican*, August 12, 1852. William had married Emmeline Austin of Beverly, Massachusetts, tenth child of Samuel Austin, clerk in the office of the Massachusetts secretary of state, and Abigail Winslow Austin, January 5, 1846. Emmeline was, thus, left to deal with the death of her father and the care of three children; Wood, *Family History of William Perkins Wadsworth and Martha Doty Scofield*.

   Ironically, less than a year later Walworth became the Hunker candidate for governor, opposing John A. Dix, whom Wadsworth supported.

18. Fisher, *A Philadelphia Perspective*, p. 206; letter from Francis P. Blair to James Samuel Wadsworth, June 28, 1848, WFP. Blair viewed the abolitionist just as much a "negro lover" as the slave propagandist. Each considered the slave property; political to the abolitionist, personal to the propagandist.

19. Letters from Horatio J. Stow and Andrew White Young to James Samuel Wadsworth, June 29 and July 20, 1848, WFP; Mitchell, *Horatio Seymour of New York*, p. 110; letters from Martin Van Buren and Preston King to James Samuel Wadsworth, August 7 and September 28, 1848, WFP.

20. Appointment letter from Governor Fish to James Samuel Wadsworth, April 20, 1849, WFP; Doty, *History of Livingston County*, p. 436. He was also being hit for money by others, including former Whig governor and fellow Geneseoan John Young, who needed Wadsworth to act as his surety so he could be appointed assistant treasurer for the City of New York; letter from John Young to James Samuel, May 25, 1849.

21. On October 10, 1853, Wadsworth was appointed by the Supreme Court as trustee for the estate of his brother William Wolcott and guardian of the three children, William Austin (age 6), Livingston (age 4), and Herbert (age 2); Grantee Index, Deeds, Book 50, p. 104, Livingston County Court House.

22. Fisher, *A Philadelphia Perspective*, pp. 215–217. It may well have been that Fisher had not given up an ultimately futile courtship of sister Elizabeth; David W. Parish, "A Glance Backward," *Livingston County News*, June 1, 1995, p. 5.

23. Parish, "Elizabeth Wadsworth: Lily of the Valley," pp. 29–31; Pearson, *James S. Wadsworth of Geneseo*, pp. 26–28; and Fisher, *A Philadelphia Perspective*, p. 250. Elizabeth wrote her sisters-in-law Mary Craig

Wadsworth and Emmeline Austin Wadsworth that she was delighted to see the way her brother ("Cheri"), who wore the heavy "gold chain" Elizabeth had given him, took to her husband; letters from Elizabeth Wadsworth Murray to Mary Craig Wadsworth and Emmeline Austin Wadsworth, December 20, 1850, WFP; passport issued to James Samuel, November 23, 1850.

24. *Livingston Republican*, February 20, 1851. Apparently James Samuel described the ordeal to his new brother-in-law, Charles Murray; letter from Murray to James Samuel, February 5, 1851.

25. *Livingston Republican*, March 6, 1851; letter from Martin Van Buren to James Samuel Wadsworth, March 3, 1851, WFP.

26. Letter from Azariah C. Flagg, March 8, 1850, WFP; letter to Henry S. Randall, November 2, 1851, C. E. French Collection, Massachusetts Historical Society. Randall, who had been defeated two years earlier for the same position, apparently was pleased with the outcome this time, for it made him ex-officio Superintendent of Public Instruction, whereby he could exercise influence over education, a long-standing interest; *Dictionary of American Biography*, Vol. 15, pp. 347–348. Randall is probably better known as the author of the still acclaimed, three-volume biography of the *Life of Thomas Jefferson*.

27. Doty, *History of Livingston County*, p. 449; Maryniak, "Patroon, Soldier and Hero: Brigadier General James Samuel Wadsworth of Geneseo, New York," "The Famous Long Ago," *The Courier*, Vol. 4, Issue 6 (November/December 1989), p. 23. Another venture, which was begun toward the end of the decade, proved beneficial not only to the Buffalo economy, but to the nation's. Incorporated under the title Palmer, Wadsworth, Thompson & Co., Buffalo Union Iron Works, Wadsworth was also able to engage his son, Charles F., now returned from France, as the first American to graduate from France's École des Mines (School of Mines), as a director. The business combined a large furnace and rolling mills in which the Wadsworth squire and George Palmer had invested, with a similar enterprise owned by Augustus P. Thompson and Edward S. Warren. It was, in fact, a complement to the Buffalo & State Line Railroad, in which Palmer and Wadsworth were also involved as president and director, respectively. By 1862 the iron furnaces were netting $500 a day for stockholders, and by 1863 had rolled out several fifty-foot-long rails, weighing twenty pounds per foot, for the Buffalo & State Line Railroad. They were claimed to be the longest rails produced up to that time; *Buffalo Evening News*, November 9, 1863.

28. Leona Lawrence, Sue Migliore, and Peggy Szczesniak, *100th Anniversary of St. Mary's Church* (Geneseo, N.Y.: St. Mary's Church, December 17, 1989). A similar version is offered by Wadsworth's great-great-grandson Stuart Symington, Jr., though the way he heard the story is that the worshippers were "huddled in a fence corner near Geneseo one rainy day"; letter from Stuart Symington, Jr., to author, August 15, 1994. Apparently Bishop Timon was a good friend of Geneseoans, including James Samuel, according to Geneseo Town and Village Historian David W. Parish.

29. The deed is recorded on August 28, 1854, Book 50, p. 104, Livingston County Court House.

30. Letter to Mary Craig Wadsworth from Elizabeth Wadsworth Murray, October 5, 1851; letters from Charles Murray to Mary Craig Wadsworth, November 19 and December 5, 1851, WFP.

31. William Wolcott Wadsworth died July 21, 1852, without a will. Letters of administration were issued to James S. Wadsworth, Daniel Fitzhugh, and Martin Brimmer, Jr., who posted performance bonds totaling $274,000 on October 26, 1852; Surrogate Record, Livingston County. Retired county judge Robert Houston states that typically the amount of the bond is twice the liquid assets of the deceased. James Samuel would be appointed trustee of William's estate and guardian of his three children; October 10, 1853, Book 50, p. 104, Grantee's Deeds, Livingston County Court House.

32. *Livingston Republican*, August 12, 1852, apparently adapted William's obituary from the *Rochester American*, August 10, 1852. Because no death records existed in the Livingston County Courthouse before the 1870s, it is impossible to determine the exact cause of death. William's second son, Livingston, would die at age 16, October 27, 1865, and be buried in his mother's family's plot in Beverly, Massachusetts; *Livingston Republican*, November 2, 1865.

33. Letter from Charles Murray to James Samuel Wadsworth, December 5, 1852, is mistakenly dated 1851, WFP. The New York State Legislature passed a special bill to authorize Charles James Murray to hold onto the land only for ten years after he became of full age unless he should become a U.S. citizen; document in WFP. Provision for his sister-in-law and nephews, including William Austin Wadsworth, Livingston Wadsworth, Herbert Wadsworth, Charles James Murray, and Martin Brimmer, Jr., would come in James Samuel's 1856 will. Why the purchase of the Mansion House, which Elizabeth had inherited, was considered by Charles A. Murray a bad bargain is unknown. It might well be that James Samuel had to sell other

lands in a hurry and at a lower price than he would have otherwise to obtain the money. At any rate, Murray made a new will leaving the same amount to James Samuel and his heirs as an act of justice and due regard for his lamented wife's affection for her brother.

34. Note on letter to Mary Craig Wadsworth from Elizabeth Wadsworth Murray, October 5, 1851, WFP.

CHAPTER 7

1. Morris and Morris, *Encyclopedia of American History*, pp. 250–254.
2. Letter from Horatio Seymour to James Samuel Wadsworth, May 19, 1852; letters from William Marcy to James Samuel Wadsworth, December 8, 1851; July 15, 1852; August 8 and 28, 1852, WFP.
3. Doty, *History of Livingston County*, pp. 461, 453. Wadsworth was being called upon to help finance other projects as well, many of which rebounded to his benefit. For example, on September 29, 1853, Wadsworth helped raise (through $50 dues) $8,000 capital for the Livingston County Association for the Importation and Improvement of Stock and was elected its president. One of his responsibilities was to send agents to Europe to buy prize stock that would be imported and sold at public auction, though stockholders would "have preference in the use of the animals, upon complying with the owners' terms."
4. W. W. Killip, "Reminiscences," in *Thirty-Fifth Annual Meeting of the Livingston County Historical Society— 1911* (Nunda, N.Y.: Sanders Printers, 1911), pp. 10–11.
5. Pearson, *James S. Wadsworth of Geneseo*, pp. 29, 30; passport issued to James Samuel Wadsworth, September 23, 1854, WFP. The party was diminished by two when Nancy and James W. "were left at school in Vevey." The others toured Naples, Rome, Milan, Bologna, Genoa, Dresden, and Cologne before visiting nephew Charles James Murray and Elizabeth Wadsworth Murray's grave in England.
6. Letter from Motley to Mary Craig Wadsworth, June 24, 1864, WFP; Pearson, *James S. Wadsworth of Geneseo*, p. 34.
7. *N.Y. State Agricultural Society Transactions for 1858* (Albany: Van Benthuysen, 1859), Vol. 18, pp. 299–300. Wadsworth was responding to a circular from the executive committee requesting information about the extent and effect of midge infestation.
8. Weed, *Autobiography*, Vol. 2, pp. 241, 233.
9. Appendix D, Pearson, *James S. Wadsworth of Geneseo*, pp. 299, 300.
10. DeAlva S. Alexander, *A Political History of the State of New York* (Port Washington, N.Y.: Ira J. Friedman, 1969), Vol. 3, p. 43 (reprint); letter from James Samuel Wadsworth to "Grover"(?), May 23, 1858, WFP; Weed, *Autobiography*, Vol. 2, pp. 246, 247.
11. Doty, *History of Livingston County*, p. 459; document naming Wadsworth elector, dated November 24, 1856, WFP. The Republicans polled almost as many votes as "the combined vote of two opposing parties [American and Democratic]," according to Doty; Weed, *Autobiography*, Vol. 1, pp. 472, 473; *Dictionary of American Biography*, Vol. 9, pp. 394–395. Hunt is probably best known as a U.S. Supreme Court associate justice from 1873 to 1882, though he is known to New Yorkers as the New York Court of Appeals judge who heard the case of Susan B. Anthony for attempting to vote. Field, who would gain greater fame as a jurist and civil rights reformer, has been described as rigid and unbending in politics, making him unsuitable to moderates; ibid., Vol. 6, pp. 360–362. He would play a particularly prominent role in the Peace Conference of 1861.
12. Letter from Joseph Blunt, August 14, 1858, to James Samuel Wadsworth, WFP. Blunt sought a new constitution granting power to the executive to name a judiciary more conducive to public confidence.
13. Morris and Morris, *Encyclopedia of American History*, pp. 263–264.
14. Letter from James Samuel Wadsworth to "My dear Grover"(?), May 23, 1858, WFP; letter from Joseph Blunt to James Samuel Wadsworth, August 14, 1858, WFP; Hoppin and Cozzens, *Proceedings of the Century Association*, p. 14; Kenneth Jackson (ed.), *The Encyclopedia of New York City* (New Haven: Yale University Press, 1995), p. 200.
15. Pearson, *James S. Wadsworth of Geneseo*, p. 48. Apparently Wadsworth's feelings about Seward were well known. In fact, one historian claims that Robert F. Paine, a supporter of another candidate, Ohioan Benjamin Wade, had "sounded out Seward's bitter foe, James Wadsworth of New York" about his willingness to run as Wade's vice president; H. L. Trefousse, *Benjamin Franklin Wade: Radical Republican from Ohio* (New York: Twayne Publishers, 1963), p. 123.

16. Pearson, *James S. Wadsworth of Geneseo*, p. 49.

17. Undated *Chicago Evening Journal*, Wadsworth file, Livingston County Historian, Geneseo, N.Y.. However, it appears to have been written at the time of Wadsworth's death, May 8, 1864.

18. Pearson, *James S. Wadsworth of Geneseo*, p. 50; Wadsworth's testimony before the Freedman's Bureau, in Ira Berlin et al. (eds.), *The Wartime Genesis of Free Labor: The Lower South*, Series I, Vol. 3 of *Freedom: A Documentary History of Emancipation, 1862–1867* (Cambridge, UK: Cambridge University Press, 1991), p. 492.

19. Charles A. Dana, *Recollections of the Civil War* (Lincoln: University of Nebraska Press, 1996), pp. 2, 3 (reprint). Apparently Dana accompanied Wadsworth and Carroll at the request of Horace Greeley, for whom Dana was then working.

20. Others named were David Dudley Field, William Curtis Noyes, William E. Dodge, and Greene C. Bronson from New York City; James C. Smith and Francis Granger (replacing "Judge" Addison Gardiner) from Canandaigua; Erastus Corning from Albany; Amaziah B. James from Ogdensburg; New York's first Republican governor, John A. King, from Jamaica; and old John E. Wool from Troy. It was a combustible mix, with Radicals barely outnumbering moderates; Maryniak, "Patroon, Soldier and Hero," "The Famous Long Ago," *The Courier*, Vol. 4, Issue 6 (November/December 1989), p. 23; L. E. Chittenden, *A Report of the Debates and Proceedings in the Secret Sessions of the Conference Convention* (New York: D. Appleton & Co., 1864), pp. 9, 465 (Appendix II). On his own hook, Chittenden, a Vermont delegate, kept notes throughout because of the controversy about having the debates made public. The New York delegation voted in favor of having the debates made public. Why other prominent New Yorkers, including Horatio Seymour, who was active at New York's recently concluded Peace Conference, were not appointed delegates is a bit of a mystery.

21. Robert G. Gunderson, *Old Gentlemen's Convention: The Washington Peace Conference of 1861* (Madison: University of Wisconsin Press, 1961), pp. 59, 72.

22. Chittenden, *A Report of the Debates*, pp. 600, 441. The Peace Conference report was forwarded to President Buchanan and to the House of Representatives, where on March 1 members voted 93–67 to suspend rules to receive it. This was referred to by some as a "test vote." Thus, lacking the necessary two-thirds in favor, the House voted not to receive the report, labeled "Memorial."

23. Martin L. Fausold, *James S. Wadsworth, Jr.: The Gentleman from New York* (Syracuse, N.Y.: Syracuse University Press, 1975), pp. xiii–xiv. Estate value is extrapolated from historical price indexes in McCusker, "How Much Is That in Real Money?" and U.S. Bureau of the Census, *Historical Statistics of the United States*. Wadsworth's will was entered in probate May 23, 1864; Wills, Book 7, p. 1, Livingston County Surrogate Court and WFP; Hoppin and Cozzens, *Proceedings of the Century Association*, pp. 16, 17. Shelby Foote, *The Civil War: A Narrative, Red River to Appomattox* (New York: Random House, 1974), Vol. 3, p. 160, flippantly (and inaccurately) described Wadsworth as a "Hudson River grandee." This brought a criticism from Livingston County resident and former public school librarian Mrs. Betty Minemier. Foote responded that he "simply" relied on *Webster's Dictionary*, which defined the term as "'a person of high rank; an important person,' which he clearly was"; exchange of letters between Mrs. Betty Minemier and Shelby Foote, no dates, courtesy of Mrs. Minemier. Ironically, Foote's wife had attended school in Connecticut with Wadsworth's great-granddaughter, Perky Wadsworth Lloyd, and had remained friends "for nearly forty years."

24. The only recorded activity was his April 8, 1861, recommendation of a candidate for Surveyor and Collector of the Port of New York, a plum that had been a constant source of conflict between New York's political parties; Roy P. Basler (ed.), *The Collected Works of Abraham Lincoln* (New Brunswick, N.J.: Rutgers University Press, 1953), Vol. 4, p. 325.

His 26-year-old son Charles Frederick was in Buffalo, serving as a director of the Union Iron Works. His daughter Cornelia, 22, had in 1858 married Montgomery Ritchie. Twenty-year-old "Tick" was in college, and 15-year-old James Wolcott ("Jimmy") was splitting his time between home and prep school. Before long 18-year-old Nancy would be married to Edward M. Rogers.

25. Benson J. Lossing, *The Empire State* (Hartford, Conn.: American Publishing Co., 1888), Vol. 1, pp. 522–524. In a year's time the committee hit on members as well as Wall Streeters to raise approximately $1,000,000, which it disbursed to equip forty-nine regiments. It is claimed that one of these regiments was the 7th New York Volunteers, which on Friday, April 19, had marched down Broadway to a "tempest of cheers two miles long"; Theodore Winthrop in the *Atlantic Monthly*, Vol. 7, No. 44 (June 1861), p. 745.

26. Pearson, *James S. Wadsworth of Geneseo*, pp. 56–60; "General James S. Wadsworth," *United States Service Magazine* (New York), Vol. 4 (July 1865), p. 20; Hoppin and Cozzens, *Proceedings of the Century Association*, pp. 22, 23; *Official Records of the Union and Confederate Navies in the War of the Rebellion* (Washington, D.C.: Government Printing Office, 1897) in 27 volumes, Series I, Vol. 4, pp. 331, 432 (hereafter Navy O.R.); Pearson, *James S. Wadsworth of Geneseo*, p. 56; *New York Times*, May 3, 1861, p. 1.
27. This discussion relies heavily upon James H. Whyte, "Divided Loyalties in Washington During the Civil War," in *Records of the Columbia Historical Society, 1960–1962* (Washington, D.C.: Columbia Historical Society, 1989), pp. 103–122. There was no "rallying point," according to Captain Charles P. Stone, who was to become Inspector-General of the District Militia. It was a daunting task: The Washington Light Infantry and the National Guard were firmly commanded by Unionists, whereas other militia companies were of doubtful loyalties. Not even the district police could be trusted. Further, former Maryland governor Lowe maintained that the District of Columbia would be reclaimed by Maryland, which, just over a half century earlier, had ceded it to the new government. Perhaps nothing indicated the divided loyalties more than Washington's well born, who held important government posts, but would in time join the Confederacy in equally important positions. Also there were those who held prominent positions and whose sons took up the Southern cause, including William Towers, chief clerk of the Government Printing Office, and William Hickey, chief clerk of the U.S. Senate. Of course, there were also those suspected of and accused of treason. Nor were the District churches exempt from these divided loyalties, especially the Episcopalians.
28. Letter from James Samuel Wadsworth to Governor Edmund Morgan, May 6, 1861, Governor Edmund Morgan Papers, New York State Library, Albany.
29. For clarification of the reference to New York troops already raised, see Frederick Phisterer, *New York in the War of the Rebellion 1861–1865* (Albany: L. B. Lyon Co., 1912), Vol. 1, pp. 14–21, 3rd edition. The thirty-eight New York regiments authorized (and subsequently raised for two years' service) by the New York State Legislature on April 16 were accepted by Secretary of War Cameron on May 3, which satisfied Lincoln's call that day for forty regiments to serve three years. Letters from James Samuel Wadsworth to Governor Morgan, May 20, Morgan Papers, New York State Library; the May 23 letter is in Pearson, *James S. Wadsworth of Geneseo*, pp. 61, 62.
30. The May 16, 1861, appointment from the Adjutant General's Office is located in WFP; File W.17.C.B.1963, National Archives, Washington, D.C.; *The War of the Rebellion: A Compilation of the Official Records of the Union and Confederate Armies* (Washington, D.C.: Government Printing Officer, 1880–1891), Series 3, Vol. 1, pp. 211, 241 (hereafter O.R., Ser. 1, unless otherwise identified).
31. Pearson, *James S. Wadsworth of Geneseo*, p. 63.
32. Letter from Governor Edmund Morgan to James Samuel Wadsworth, June 22, 1861, WFP.
33. Former governor John A. King offered "very sincere congratulations on this most judicious selection of a gentleman, who whatever he may lack in Military Experience, possess [*sic*] the great Elements of success, judgment, reason and Energy." King hoped Wadsworth would accept, for he had "the support of all who desire that gentlemen of high character and high position should lead in Military, as well as in Civil affairs"; letter from John A. King to James Samuel Wadsworth, May 17, 1861, WFP. Because Governor Morgan had sent regiments of the 1st Division of the State's Militia from New York City under the command of Major General Sandford to defend Washington, he was "apprehensive that [Dix and Wadsworth] may not be recognized at Washington." However, he pointedly reminded Secretary Cameron that New York had already "furnished forty-six regiments to the war" in addition to eleven sent in April to defend Washington. O.R., Series 3, Vol. 1, pp. 241, 246–247. Wadsworth's lack of "regret or hesitation" is in his letter to Governor Morgan, May 21, 1861, and his formal resignation was on June 23, 1861, Morgan Papers, New York State Library.
34. Hoppin and Cozzens, *Proceedings of the Century Association*, pp. 23–24.

CHAPTER 8

1. William C. Davis, *Battle at Bull Run* (Baton Rouge: Louisiana State University Press, 1977), pp. 9–12; James B. Fry, "McDowell's Advance to Bull Run," in Johnson and Buel, *Battles and Leaders*, Vol. 1, p. 171.
2. Pierre G. T. Beauregard, "The First Battle of Bull Run," in Johnson and Buel, *Battles and Leaders*, Vol. 1, p. 196. A particularly cynical explanation of the reason for the First Bull Run battle claims that McDowell

was ordered to Manassas "under pressure of public opinion, voiced by Brigadier Generals Horace Greeley and Murat Halstead and other generals of the editorial profession who laid out all the great campaigns of the war in their dingy sanctums"; Thomas S. Allen, "The Second Wisconsin at the First Battle of Bull Run," in George H. Otis (Alan D. Gaff, ed.), *The Second Wisconsin Infantry* (Dayton, Ohio: Morningside, 1984), p. 220.

3. Beauregard, "The First Battle of Bull Run," p. 196.
4. Fry, "McDowell's Advance to Bull Run," pp. 173–175.
5. *Report of the Joint Committee on the Conduct of the War* (Washington, D.C.: Government Printing Office, 1865), 37th Congress, 3rd Session, Part 2, p. 38; editors' notes in Fry, "McDowell's Advance to Bull Run," pp. 176, 167. Among, if not the gaudiest regiment was the 39th New York Infantry, the "Garibaldi Guards," a notorious, polyglot outfit that had already gained the attention of Washingtonians; Margaret Leech, *Reveille in Washington* (New York: Harper & Bros., 1941), pp. 85, 88, 93; William L. Burton, *Melting Pot Soldiers* (Ames: Iowa State University Press, 1988), p. 169.
6. Ezra Warner, *Generals in Blue* (Baton Rouge: Louisiana State University Press, 1964), p. 244, 514.
7. Beauregard, "The First Battle of Bull Run," p. 197.
8. Davis, *Battle at Bull Run*, pp. 52–53; Beauregard, "The First Battle of Bull Run," p. 198.
9. Fry, "McDowell's Advance to Bull Run," p. 175.
10. Testimony by James S. Wadsworth, *Report of the Joint Committee on the Conduct of the War,* 37th Congress, 3rd Session, Part 2, p. 48.
11. Fry, "McDowell's Advance to Bull Run," particularly pp. 179–191; McDowell's testimony, *Report of the Joint Committee on the Conduct of the War*, 37th Congress, 3rd Session, Part 2, pp. 39, 40, 41, 43.
12. In its first battle the 2nd Wisconsin, which would help the Iron Brigade attain its later reputation for courage and hard fighting, was as ineffective as any Union regiment with its "chunky" weapons, which kicked so hard men were knocked onto their backs; Otis, *The Second Wisconsin Infantry*, pp. 35, 36.
13. These totals from O.R. 2, pp. 327, 570, differ from those of William F. Fox, *Regimental Losses in the American Civil War, 1861–1865* (Albany: Albany Printing Co., 1889), pp. 543, 549, in terms of Union totals, with Fox reporting 470 killed, 1,071 wounded, and 1,793 missing. The quote is from Allen, "The Second Wisconsin in the First Battle of Bull Run," in Otis, *The Second Wisconsin Infantry*, p. 224.
14. Testimony by Colonel Edmund Schriver at McDowell Court of Inquiry in December 1862; O.R. 12, Part 1, p. 90. At this time McDowell's staff included Captain James B. Fry, assistant adjutant general, and three aides-de-camp: Wadsworth, 1st Lieutenant Henry W. Kingsbury, who would be killed at Antietam commanding the 11th Connecticut Volunteers, and Major Clarence S. Brown; O.R. 51, Part 1, p. 413. McDowell's comment on Wadsworth is in his postbattle report; O.R. 2, Part 2, p. 322.
15. General McDowell's postbattle report, ibid. Fry was a particularly well-respected regular army officer, West Point 1847, who after some controversy would be appointed to head the Bureau of Provost Marshal General by Grant, would achieve the rank of brevet major general, and would become postwar assistant adjutant general to Brevet Major General Winfield S. Hancock; Warner, *Generals in Blue*, pp. 162–163. Fry would show great affection for Wadsworth in his letter to the latter on leave after Bull Run; letter to James Samuel Wadsworth from James B. Fry, August 12, 1861, WFP.
16. C.V. Tevis and D. R. Marquis, *The History of the Fighting Fourteenth* (New York: Brooklyn Eagle Press, 1911), p. 150. This outfit would get to know Wadsworth even better within a year when he actually commanded them. McDowell reported the incident and quoted Wadsworth to the effect that he "called on the boys to *rally once more for the glorious flag*"; *United States Service Magazine*, Vol. 4 (July 1865), p. 21.
17. Heavy reliance for this aspect of Wadsworth's activities is placed on the account in Pearson, *James S. Wadsworth of Geneseo*, pp. 75–80, and *United States Service Magazine*, Vol. 4 (July 1865), pp. 20–21.
18. Elisha R. Reed, "Both Sides of Life in Rebel Prisons," in Otis, *The Second Wisconsin Infantry*, p. 159.
19. "Extract from Proceedings of Executive Committee," Union Defense Committee, August 20, 1861, WFP; appointment letter, August 9, 1861, WFP; letter from New York Senator Preston King to James Samuel Wadsworth, August 3, 1861, WFP, informing Wadsworth of his confirmation by the Senate after New York's congressional delegation had unanimously proposed him for promotion following Lincoln's "Memoranda of Military Policy"; Basler, *The Collected Works of Abraham Lincoln*, Vol. 4, pp. 457, 458.
20. Doty, *History of Livingston County*, pp. 476, 477. Wadsworth would present the colors in April 1862; Phisterer, *New York in the War of the Rebellion*, Vol. 1, p. 127.

21. Phisterer, *New York in the War of the Rebellion,* Vol. 3, pp. 1873, 1970, 1994, 2137, Vol. 4, p. 2860; O.R. 5, pp. 16, 454; Frank J. Welcher, *The Union Army, 1861–1865, Organization and Operations* (Bloomington: University of Indiana Press, 1989), Vol. 1, pp. 79, 245; Frederick H. Dyer, *A Compendium of the War of the Rebellion* (Dayton, Ohio: Morningside, 1978), pp. 188, 189, 193 (reprint; hereafter *Compendium*).

22. Stephen W. Sears (ed.), *The Civil War Papers of George B. McClellan* (New York: Ticknor & Fields, 1989), p. 116; George B. McClellan, *McClellan's Own Story* (New York: Charles E. Webster & Co., 1887), pp. 76–79, 103; Stephen E. Ambrose, *Halleck: Lincoln's Chief of Staff* (Baton Rouge: Louisiana State University Press, 1990), p. 206 (reprint).

23. Wadsworth's report on post–Bull Run activities, no date, WFP. Wadsworth also had to assure that his troops were armed, including recording the types of arms his brigade had and ordering 20,000 .69 caliber cartridges and 5,000 .58 calibre cartridges for his soldiers' Austrian, Springfield, and Enfield rifled muskets. Forage needs are found in "Report of Quartermaster Brigadier General Stewart Van Vliet," O.R. 11, Part 1, p. 157, and Russell F. Weigley, *Quartermaster General of the Union Army* (New York: Columbia University Press, 1959), p. 270. Forage totals from December 8, 1862, to June 30, 1865, were 2,787,758 bushels of corn, 20,997,289 bushels of oats, 43,311 bushels of barley, 269,814 tons of hay, and 8,243 tons of straw; ibid., p. 271.

24. It is unclear exactly when General Wadsworth returned from leave, but he claimed that he took command "at once" after his appointment, General Wadsworth's undated report on post–Bull Run activities, WFP.

25. Ibid.

26. John Kress, *Memoirs of Brigadier General John Alexander Kress* (Philadelphia: Author, 1925), p. 1. The Pennsylvania-born Kress had been appointed to West Point from Laporte, Indiana, after a short career with a railroad. Wadsworth's request to Governor Morgan, September 10, 1861, Morgan Papers, New York State Library. Pearson, *James S. Wadsworth of Geneseo,* p. 81, claims that an inducement to Wadsworth to serve as brigade commander was the promise of a West Point graduate to be his adjutant, and Kress was, it turns out, a fortunate substitute; O.R. 5, p. 18.

27. Letters from James Samuel Wadsworth to Governor Edmund Morgan, September 10, 15, 17, 1861, Morgan Papers, New York State Library; Phisterer, *New York in the War of the Rebellion,* Vol. 3, p. 1886, Vol. 4, p. 3358.

28. Letter from James Samuel Wadsworth to Governor Edmund Morgan, September 27, 1861, Morgan Papers, New York State Library.

29. Correspondence from General McDowell to James Samuel Wadsworth, October 20, 1861, WFP; Wadsworth's report on post–Bull Run activities, no date, WFP; correspondence from General McDowell to James Samuel Wadsworth, October 20, 1861, WFP; Theodore B. Gates, *The "Ulster Guards" (20th New York State Militia) and the War of the Rebellion* (New York: B. H. Tyrrel, 1879), p. 164. Wadsworth's inclination to take matters in hand regardless of general procedures led to two minor rebukes by General McDowell on November 4 and 8, 1861. The first dealt with Wadsworth's granting furloughs for disabilities without consulting headquarters, while the second stemmed from some suggestion Wadsworth had made, albeit with McDowell's endorsement; Record Group 393, Part II, 55/120,121, National Archives.

30. Enclosure in correspondence of General Beauregard to General Joseph Johnston, November 15, 1861, O.R. 51, Part 2, p. 379.

31. Gates, *The "Ulster Guards,"* p. 164.

32. Report of Wadsworth, O.R. 5, p. 437; report of Major Martin, O.R. 5, pp. 439, 440.

33. Report of Lieutenant Colonel Fitzhugh Lee, O.R. 5, p. 442; report of Lieutenant Colonel Edward Fowler, 14th Brooklyn (84th N.Y. Vols.), O.R. 5, pp. 441, 443.

34. Alan T. Nolan, *The Iron Brigade: A Military History* (Berrien Springs, Mich.: Hardscrabble Books, 1983), pp. 31, 34 (reprint), claims that King's Brigade went into winter quarters October 5, 1861; Hoppin and Cozzens, *Proceedings of the Century Association,* pp. 17, 18.

35. Craig had been commissioned September 19, but not mustered, 2nd Lieutenant in the 25th New York, the Kerrigan Rifles, a part of Porter's division, but shortly he became a captain and aide-de-camp; Phisterer, *New York in the War of the Rebellion,* Vol. 4, p. 3370, and Vol. 3, pp. 2017, 2026; Pearson, *James S. Wadsworth of Geneseo,* pp. 82, 83, 65.

36. Letter of Adrian Root to his mother, November 29, 1861, and footnote, courtesy of Benedict R. Maryniak.

37. Pearson, *James S. Wadsworth of Geneseo*, pp. 83, 84, citing the description of the Army of the Potomac by the 55th New York's commander, Colonel Regis de Trobriand, and p. 85, citing *London Times* correspondent W. H. Russell's *Diary*.

38. Gates, *The "Ulster Guards,"* pp. 152, 153.

39. Letter from Charles H. Upton to Horace M. Dewey of Mt. Kisco, New York, printed in *New-York Daily Tribune*, October 24, 1862. Copy at Livingston County Historical Society.

40. Statements dated February 3 and 21, 1863, in WFP.

41. Alan Nolan, *The Iron Brigade*, pp. 39, 40; John Gibbon, *Personal Recollections of the Civil War* (Dayton, Ohio: Morningside, 1978), p. 15 (reprint).

42. Gibbon, *Personal Recollections of the Civil War*, pp. 26, 27. General McDowell had met with President Lincoln on April 20 to recommend Gibbon personally; O.R. 51, Part 1, p. 70. For Wadsworth's attendance in Washington, see Record Group 94, Office of the Adjutant General, Generals Papers and Books, National Archives.

CHAPTER 9

1. Letter from Henry J. Raymond to James Samuel Wadsworth, February 9, 1862, WFP.

2. M. C. Meigs, "The Relations of President Lincoln and Secretary Stanton to the Military Conduct of the Civil War," *American Historical Review*, Vol. 26 (1920–1921), p. 292.

3. Allan Nevins (ed.), *A Diary of Battle* (Gettysburg, Penn.: Stan Clark Military Books, 1993), p. xiv (reprint); Leech, *Reveille in Washington*, p. 132; T. Harry Williams, *Lincoln and His Generals* (New York: Alfred A. Knopf, 1952), p. 57.

4. Dana, *Recollections of the Civil War*, p. 5.

5. Nevins, *A Diary of Battle*, pp. 15, 8.

6. War Department Order 2, O.R. 5, p. 18; Basler, *The Collected Works of Abraham Lincoln*, 5, pp. 149–151.

7. William E. Doster, *Lincoln and Episodes of the Civil War* (New York: G. P. Putnam's Sons, 1915), pp. 46–48, 11–12, 66, 113. Doster's appointment was dated March 20, 1862; ibid., p. 49.

8. Ibid., pp. 49, 50. See pp. 144–146 for other examples of Wadsworth's incorruptibility.

9. Abner R. Small (Harry A. Small, ed.), *The Road to Richmond* (Berkeley: University of California Press, 1939), p. 13; Benjamin F. Cooling, "Defending Washington During the Civil War," in *Records of the Columbia Historical Society, 1971–1972* (Washington, D.C.: Columbia Historical Society, 1989), pp. 317, 319.

10. War Department General Orders No. 25, March 15, 1862, O.R. 5, p. 759.

11. Whyte, "Divided Loyalties in Washington During the Civil War," p. 120; Doster, *Lincoln and Episodes of the Civil War*, pp. 162–169; Leech, *Reveille in Washington*, p. 141.

12. Doster, *Lincoln and Episodes of the Civil War*, p. 106.

13. Assistant Secretary of War Peter Watson to General Wadsworth, O.R., Series 2, 4, pp. 349, 461; Leech, *Reveille in Washington*, pp. 154–158. An example of what Wadsworth encountered occurred on August 7, 1862. Watson ordered Wadsworth to make a "strict investigation" after the *Evening Star* reported that Stanton's order to "keep her [Boyd] in close custody" had been violated. Wadsworth made an investigation that same day and noted that her only visitors were his aide, Major Clinton H. Meneely, who had visited the prison with a man from the Post Office Department, and "a Doctor Hale." No doubt Wadsworth breathed a sigh of relief in late August when Miss Boyd was released because no charges had "been lodged against her."

14. Louis M. Starr, *Bohemian Brigade: Civil War Newsmen in Action* (New York: Alfred A. Knopf, 1954), pp. 85, 87; O.R., Series 2, 2, pp. 246, 269.

15. McClellan's instructions to Wadsworth, O.R. 11, Part 3, p. 13; O.R. 12, Part 3, p. 6; Record Group 94, Office of Adjutant General, National Archives; McDowell's division, O.R. 5, p. 718, as of February 6, 1862. However, McDowell, ibid., p. 708, substitutes the 25th New York for the 35th and the 20th for the 12th, whereas Phisterer, *New York in the War of the Rebellion*, Vol. 3, p. 2137, lists the 12th and the 35th, respectively, until March 13, 1862. Special Orders No. 83 are in O.R. 11, Part 3, p. 13. Wadsworth's total command as military governor is listed in ibid., 5, p. 22, and in his undated, unaddressed, handwritten report on his activities as military governor, WFP.

16. Wadsworth's command listing, O.R. 5, p. 22; ibid., 11, Part 3, p. 60; and General Wadsworth's testimony at the court of inquiry requested by General McDowell, ibid., 12, Part 1, p. 113.

17. Cooling, "Defending Washington During the Civil War," p. 322. The report on the condition of the forts is by Barnard in O.R. 5, pp. 698–699.

18. McClellan had been commissioned major general of volunteers of Ohio, April 23, 1861, major general in the U.S. Army, May 14 (second only to General Winfield Scott), and commander of the Division of the Potomac (the Army of the Potomac), July 25; McClellan, *McClellan's Own Story*, pp. 1, 2; Warner, *Generals in Blue*, pp. 290–291.

19. Sears, *The Civil War Papers of George B. McClellan*, p. 97. The quotation from the draft of *McClellan's Own Story* was brought to the author's attention by McClellan biographer Stephen Sears in a January 4, 1996, letter to the author. The conversation between Stanton and McClellan is from McClellan, *McClellan's Own Story*, p. 226.

20. Ibid.; Doster, *Lincoln and Episodes of the Civil War*, pp. 52–53.

21. Pearson, *James S. Wadsworth of Geneseo*, pp. 102, 103.

22. James McPherson, *Battle Cry of Freedom* (New York: Oxford University Press, 1988), pp. 363, 364.

23. Stephen W. Sears, author of *George B. McClellan: The Young Napoleon* and editor of *The Civil War Papers of George B. McClellan*, supports this assessment of Wadsworth in similar words; letter to author, January 4, 1996. Hill's claim is found in Starr, *Bohemian Brigade*, pp. 123–124, 151–152. His sources included Secretary of the Treasury Chase and Senators Henry Wilson, James Grimes, and Charles Sumner. See also Doster, *Lincoln and Episodes of the Civil War*, pp. 52, 53.

24. Williams, *Lincoln and His Generals*, pp. 66–73; McClellan, *McClellan's Own Story*, pp. 195–196; Stanton to McClellan, March 13, 1862, in Basler, *The Collected Works of Abraham Lincoln*, Vol. 5, p. 157.

25. McClellan's instructions to Generals Banks and Wadsworth indicated that Washington's security could be assured by garrisoning the right (east) bank of the Potomac, establishing a covering force of 25,000 to occupy the left (west) bank, and leaving 40,000–50,000 troops for the city's defense, O.R. 5, pp. 55–56; Basler, *The Collected Works of Abraham Lincoln*, Vol. 5, pp. 157, 158.

26. Instructions from McClellan to Wadsworth, O.R. 5, p. 57.

27. Williams, *Lincoln and His Generals*, pp. 78, 79; McClellan's communication to Stanton, O.R. 12, Part 1, pp. 226–227; Wadsworth's report to Stanton, O.R. 11, Part 3, pp. 58, 60–61; Cooling, "Defending Washington During the Civil War," p. 323.

28. McClellan's report to Adjutant General Lorenzo Thomas, O.R. 5, pp. 60–61.

29. Wadsworth's report to Stanton, O.R. 11, Part 3, pp. 60–61, 62; Wadsworth testimony at McDowell Court of Inquiry, December 17, 1862, O.R. 12, Part 1, p. 113; Williams, *Lincoln and His Generals*, p. 74; Basler, *The Collected Works of Abraham Lincoln*, Vol. 5, p. 179.

30. McClellan's report to Adjutant General Lorenzo Thomas, O.R. 5, pp. 60–61; Sears, *The Civil War Papers of George B. McClellan*, p. 233.

31. Dispatch from Assistant Adjutant General Seth Williams to General Wadsworth, O.R. 11, Part 3, pp. 54, 55; General Wadsworth to General Sumner, O.R. 11, Part 3, p. 57; General Sumner to Secretary Stanton, O.R. 11, Part 3, p. 64; General Wadsworth to Stanton, O.R. 11, Part 3, p. 67; Microfilm 711, Adjutant General's Office, National Archives.

32. Welcher, *The Union Army, 1861–1865*, Vol. 1, p. 82; undated, unaddressed report by Wadsworth on his activities as military governor, WFP.

33. Order from Stanton to Wadsworth, O.R. 12, Part 1, p. 225; report of Assistant Inspector General Roger Jones to War Department, O.R. 12, Part 1, pp. 225–226.

34. McClellan's telegram to Stanton, O.R. 11, Part 3, p. 71; Basler, *The Collected Works of Abraham Lincoln*, Vol. 5, p. 182; Stanton dispatch to McClellan, O.R. 11, Part 3, p. 73.

35. McClellan also successfully wrestled Franklin's and McCall's divisions of McDowell's corps from Stanton, O.R. 12, Part 1, p. 220; "Confidential" dispatch to Lincoln in Basler, *The Collected Works of Abraham Lincoln*, Vol. 5, p. 195.

36. George C. Gorham, *Life and Public Services of Edwin M. Stanton* (Boston: Houghton Mifflin, 1899), Vol. 1, pp. 418–420, 426–432, 367.

37. Harry Williams also regarded Wadsworth a member of the "Jacobin cabal"; Williams, *Lincoln and the Radicals* (Madison: University of Wisconsin Press, 1969) pp. 82, 127–163; McClellan, *McClellan's Own*

Story, pp. 266, 267. McClellan's count to Lincoln was based on a total of 171,602 men in his command, from which he deducted 32,119 (McDowell's I Corps and artillery), Blenker's 8,616, Banks's 21,759, Wadsworth's 19,308, the I Corps' and Blenker's cavalry of 1,600 and 800, respectively, and the troops of Van Alen and Wyndham, 1,600, for a total of 85,792 men. Then he deducted another 23,796 men absent. McClellan was not alone in complaining, for IV Corps commander Erasmus Keyes complained privately in a long letter to Senator Ira Harris (ibid., pp. 267–270), but he wanted his concern about the number of troops brought to the attention of Stanton and Lincoln.

38. Edwin C. Fishel, *The Secret War for the Union* (New York: Houghton Mifflin, 1996), pp. 53, 102–105, 112–113.

39. Wadsworth's testimony at the McDowell Court of Inquiry, O.R. 12, Part 1, pp. 114, 115.

40. *Dictionary of American Biography*, Vol. 7, p. 46. Frothingham's handwritten, untitled editorial is in the Frothingham Papers, 21.2.1d 108, Massachusetts Historical Society. The document marked "Private" was from Colonel William B. Greene, 1st Massachusetts Artillery, who was part of the Defenses of Washington and had resigned October 11, 1862; Official Notice from Headquarters, Military District of Washington, April 1, 1862, Richard Frothingham Papers, Massachusetts Historical Society. For a sample of other attacks on Wadsworth see Williams, *Lincoln and the Radicals*, pp. 128, 130.

41. Frothingham's untitled, handwritten editorial, Frothingham Papers, 21.2.1d 108, Massachusetts Historical Society. Almost a century later a similar conclusion was drawn by Clifford Dowdey, whose flair for writing was matched only by his Southern bias: "No Confederate general could have accomplished more than did Republican Wadsworth with a letter that immobilized ninety-five thousand troops in three separate departments for the protection of Washington, with not one Confederate north of the Rappahannock River"; *The Seven Days: The Emergence of Lee* (Lincoln: University of Nebraska Press, 1993), p. 49 (reprint). Revealingly Dowdey dismisses Wadsworth as "a fifty-five-year-old farmer" and repeats Shelby Foote's earlier error in referring to Wadsworth as a "wealthy Hudson River patroon." (Foote called Wadsworth a "Hudson River grandee.") By contrast is Dowdey's description of Confederate Wade Hampton, with whom Wadsworth might well be compared: "the massive South Carolina grandee, was one of the richest men in the South, one of the most chivalric, and one of the toughest"; ibid., p. 121.

42. Letter to the Editor, *New York Times*, May 19, 1863. Wadsworth pointed out that troops were detached from his command, including regiments sent to Generals Richardson, Heintzelman, and Hooker plus two heavy artillery batteries, the 1st Connecticut and 3rd New York. Further, none of the troops General Banks commanded could have helped, because they were behind two ranges of mountains, and General Dix's small force at Baltimore was guarding railroads leading to Washington and Annapolis.

43. Thomas J. Rowland, "Heaven Save a Country Governed by Such Counsels!" *Civil War History*, Vol. 42, No. 1 (1996), p. 8; Williams, *Lincoln and the Radicals*, p. 82.

44. Oliver O. Howard, *Autobiography of Oliver Otis Howard* (New York: Baker & Taylor, 1907), pp. 171–172.

45. Doster, *Lincoln and Episodes of the Civil War*, pp. 48, 53.

46. This line of inquiry was suggested in part by phone conversations with Civil War historians Mark Snell, Director of the George Tyler Moore Center for the Study of the Civil War, Shephard College, and Joseph Harsh, Professor of History and Art, George Mason University.

47. Rowland, "'Heaven Save a Country Governed by Such Counsels!'" p. 8; Williams, *Lincoln and His Generals*, p. 80. Compare Williams's stance in 1941 in his *Lincoln and the Radicals*. Also compare Bruce Tap, *Over Lincoln's Shoulder* (Lawrence: University of Kansas Press, 1998). Tap, who claims to "steer a course between" Williams and revisionist Hans Trefousse, *The Radical Republicans: Lincoln's Vanguard for Racial Justice* (New York: Alfred A. Knopf, 1969), gives short shrift to Wadsworth's role in affecting actions by the Committee on the Conduct of the War toward McClellan.

48. Williams, *Lincoln and the Radicals*, p. xi. See also Fishel, who concluded that McClellan was undone by his own deception; Edwin C. Fishel, "Pinkerton and McClellan: Who Deceived Whom?" *Civil War History*, Vol. 34, No. 2 (June 1988), pp. 115–142; Doster, *Lincoln and Episodes of the Civil War*, p. 52.

CHAPTER 10

1. Letters of Captain (later Major) Henry A. Wiley to his brother Harper, April 4 and 13, 1862, courtesy of descendant Theodore Capron of Wayland, New York.

2. Record Group 94, Adjutant General's Office, Commission Branch, File W17 CB 1863, dated March 16, 1862, National Archives.

3. Undated, unaddressed report by General Wadsworth on his activities as military governor, WFP; Wadsworth's orders to Provost Marshal Doster, May 19, 1862, O.R., Series 2, Vol. 3, p. 554.

4. General Wadsworth's orders to William P. Wood, Superintendent, Old Capitol Prison, May 22, 1862; ibid., p. 571.

5. John Kress, *Memoirs*, p. 8.

6. Leech, *Reveille in Washington*, pp. 246–247.

7. Doster, *Lincoln and Episodes of the Civil War*, pp. 26–27, 162–169, offers examples of skirmishes between Lamon and Wadsworth, but it is unclear whether these refer to this affair. Undated, unaddressed report by General Wadsworth, WFP. Apparently District of Columbia police officers obtained fees for arresting contrabands, a practice against which Wadsworth later protested; September 9, 1862, M711, Roll 35, Adjutant General's Office, National Archives. Wadsworth also sent contrabands to scrub, scrape, and whitewash a filthy former transport, the steamship *Daniel Webster*, which had been turned over to the Sanitary Commission by Stanton for use as a hospital; Allan Nevins and Milton H. Thomas (eds.), *The Diary of George Templeton Strong: The Civil War, 1860–1865* (New York: Macmillan Co., 1952), Vol. 3, p. 220.

8. Letter to James S. Wadsworth from Senator Henry Wilson, May 14, 1862, WFP.

9. Adam Gurowski, *Diary from March 4, 1861 to November 12, 1862* (Boston: Lee and Shepard, 1862), Vol. 1, p. 246.

10. Undated, unaddressed report by Wadsworth on his activities as military governor, WFP.

11. Basler, *The Collected Works of Abraham Lincoln*, Vol. 5, p. 224.

12. Undated, unaddressed report by Wadsworth on his activities as military governor, WFP; Telegram, Record Group 94, Office of the Adjutant General, Microfilm 504, Roll 101, National Archives.

13. Undated, unaddressed report by Wadsworth on his activities as military governor, WFP.

14. Pearson, *James S. Wadsworth of Geneseo*, pp. 142, 143; copy of letter and census data from National Park Service Chief Historian Robert Krick to James Wadsworth Symington, James S. Wadsworth's great-great-grandson, October 1, 1985, courtesy Benedict R. Maryniak.

15. *Livingston Republican*, May 19, 1864. At the time of this item, anecdotes and memories were pouring in. They may well have elevated Wadsworth to sainthood, though there is a consistency to anecdotes about Wadsworth's concern for soldiers.

16. The purpose was "to provide a home and maintenance for officers and soldiers who have served, are now serving, or may hereafter serve, in the volunteer forces raised or furnished from" New York State. Occupants would be honorably discharged New York soldiers disabled by service wounds, decrepit, or homeless and unable to support themselves; Phisterer, *New York in the War of the Rebellion*, Vol. 1, p. 41.

17. General McDowell's dispatch to Secretary Stanton, O.R. 51, Part 1, p. 567.

18. Ibid., p. 589.

19. General McDowell's dispatch to Wadsworth, O.R. 12, Part 3, pp. 138–139.

20. Colonel Schriver's dispatches to Generals Geary and Wadsworth, ibid., pp. 170, 192; General Geary's dispatch to Wadsworth, ibid., p. 240; McDowell's orders to Geary, O.R. 51, Part 1, pp. 601, 616.

21. Dispatches between General McDowell and Secretary Stanton, O.R. 12, Part 1, pp. 499, 500.

22. Dispatches from McDowell to Wadsworth, O.R. 51, Part 1, pp. 622, 625, 629, 628.

23. Ibid., p. 628; Wadsworth to McDowell, O.R. 12, Part 3, pp. 215, 216.

24. Document in WFP, dated May 23, 1862. Craig W. Wadsworth had been commissioned 2nd Lieutenant and Aide-de-Camp of the 25th New York Volunteers in his father's brigade in November 1861, and was appointed aide to General Fremont on May 24, 1862, Military Service Papers, National Archives; Microfilm 711, Roll 35, No. 621, National Archives.

25. Dispatches between General McDowell, Lincoln, and Stanton, O.R. 12, Part 3, p. 269.

26. Dispatch from Stanton to Wadsworth, ibid., p. 241.

27. Dispatch from General McDowell to Wadsworth, ibid., p. 221.

28. Correspondence between General McClellan and President Lincoln, O.R. 11, Part 1, p. 33; Sears, *The Civil War Papers of George B. McClellan*, p. 278.

29. Dispatches between General McDowell and Secretary Stanton, O.R. 12, Part 3, pp. 267, 272, 292, 300.

30. Secretary Stanton's orders to General Dix, ibid., pp. 304, 305.

31. Report of Wadsworth's command, ibid., p. 313; Warner, *Generals in Blue*, pp. 486–487, 554.

32. Secretary Stanton's orders to Wadsworth, O.R. 12, Part 3, p. 408.

33. Ibid., pp. 448, 411, 414, 498. These included a British consul, a French visitor, and "bushwhackers" from General Ewell's division, O.R., Series 2, 3, p. 665. "Scott's Cavalry," also known as "Scott's Nine Hundred," was the 11th New York Cavalry (1st U.S. Vol. Cav.), Phisterer, *New York in the War of the Rebellion*, Vol. 2, pp. 943–959; Orders from A. A. G. Townsend to General Wadsworth, O.R., Series 2, 4, pp. 50, 32, 160.

34. Orders from A. A. G. Townsend to General Wadsworth, O.R., Series 2, 4, pp. 28, 275, 368, 375–376, 413.

35. Memo of understanding and instructions to Wadsworth from A. A. G. Townsend, ibid., pp. 944–945, 431, 501, 108; Record Group 393, Part II, Entries 3685/3691, January 10, 1863.

36. Abstract of Return of District of Washington, O.R. 12, Part 3, p. 448; Leech, *Reveille in Washington*, p. 177; letter from James S. Wadsworth, July 5, 1862, WFP. The daughter is identified only as "Kinsman."

37. Special Orders No. 310, July 17, 1862, issued by Assistant Adjutant General Townsend, WFP; Basler, *The Collected Works of Abraham Lincoln*, Vol. 5, pp. 320, 262–263. It appears that during this leave Wadsworth amended his will, which is dated July 8, 1862; Wills, Book 7, p. 3, Livingston County Surrogate Court.

38. Warner, *Generals in Blue*, pp. 195–196.

39. Telegrams, M504, Roll 101, June 14 and May 17, 1862; Adjutant General's Office, M711, Roll 35, June 23, 1862. Craig had also worked behind the scenes to obtain a field command for Wadsworth's Inspector General John Kress.

40. Basler, *The Collected Works of Abraham Lincoln*, Vol. 5, p. 287. Lincoln had long tired of trying to prod, in fact, direct, Fremont to action against Jackson in the Valley; ibid., pp. 269, 270–271, 273–274. William Swinton, *Campaigns of the Army of the Potomac* (New York: Charles Scribner's Sons, 1882), pp. 167–170.

41. Stanton's orders to Wadsworth, O.R., Series 3, 2, pp. 350–351, August 10, 1862, and repeated August 18, 1862, by A. A. G. Vincent, ibid., p. 402; Pearson, *James S. Wadsworth of Geneseo*, pp. 145–147. By most accounts (and repeated in the *Livingston Republican*, November 15, 1899) Charles Frederick turned down safer and more prestigious staff assignments for actual service. Phisterer, *New York in the War of the Rebellion*, Vol. 4, p. 3370, lists Charles Frederick as mustering as First Lieutenant, Company D, on September 3, 1862, with rank of Captain, Company A, May 19, 1863, and obtaining his discharge August 18, 1863. He was subsequently breveted Major for his role at Port Hudson under General Banks.

42. Swinton, *Campaigns of the Army of the Potomac*, pp. 171–174.

43. Secretary Welles's order to the Navy Yard commandant, Andrew A. Harewood, Navy O.R., Series 1, 5, pp. 62, 63, 64; Secretary Halleck dispatch to Major General John Parke, O.R. 12, Part 3, p. 594.

44. Basler, *The Collected Works of Abraham Lincoln*, Vol. 5, pp. 398–402; Tyler Dennett, *Lincoln and the Civil War in the Diaries and Letters of John Hay* (Westport, Conn.: Negro Universities Press, 1972), p. 46 (reprint).

45. Ibid.; Mark M. Boatner III, *Civil War Dictionary* (New York: David McKay Co., 1987), rev. ed., pp. 101–105; Bruce Catton, *Mr. Lincoln's Army* (New York: Fairfax Press), 1984, p. 11; Leech, *Reveille in Washington*, p. 192; telegram from General Wadsworth to I. R. Lawrence, Elmira, New York, indicating that he had "all the surgeons and nurses we require," Record Group 94, Microfilm 504, Roll 101, National Archives, no date.

46. Leech, *Reveille in Washington*, p. 192; Special Orders 218 from A. A. G. Townsend to Wadsworth, O.R. 12, Part 3, p. 807.

47. Editor's note, quoting Williams in McClellan, *McClellan's Own Story*, pp. 540, 541. It is revealing that McClellan's countersign was "Malvern."

48. Sears, *The Civil War Papers of George B. McClellan*, p. 371; McClellan, *McClellan's Own Story*, pp. 538, 546, 547.

49. Salmon P. Chase (David Donald, ed.), *Inside Lincoln's Cabinet: The Civil War Diaries of Salmon P. Chase* (New York: Longmans, Green & Co., 1954), pp. 123–125.

50. Letters from Stephen Shinn, an Alexandria Unionist, to Wadsworth and Secretary of the Navy Welles, Navy O.R., Series 1, 5, p. 86; reports by Commodore Harwood to Secretary Welles, ibid., pp. 101–102, 135.

51. Ibid., pp. 110–111.

52. Ibid., p. 104.
53. The orders were issued by General Banks to Wadsworth and Slouth, O.R. 19, Part 2, pp. 302–303.
54. Ibid., p. 336.
55. Fox, *Regimental Losses in the American Civil War*, p. 540; Boatner, *Civil War Dictionary*, p. 21; Leech, *Reveille in Washington*, p. 205. When the war began, Washington had only one hospital, Washington Infirmary, a three-story brick building constructed in 1804 as a jail, which in early 1861 was under the charge of Columbian College. By the end of the war there were twenty-five hospitals in the District of Columbia and vicinity, containing 21,426 beds, 13,865 of which were still occupied by wounded and sick soldiers on November 17, 1865; John W. Bulkley, "The War Hospitals," in Marcus Benjamin (ed.), *Washington During War Time* (Washington, D.C.: The National Tribune Co., 1902), p. 139.
56. General Dix's letter to General Halleck, September 29, 1862, O.R. 18, p. 409.
57. Pearson, *James S. Wadsworth of Geneseo*, p. 148.
58. Gurowski, *Diary from March 4, 1861 to November 12, 1862*, Vol. 1, pp. 273–274; Leech, *Reveille in Washington*, pp. 58, 177, 303. Leech even claims, p. 303, that Gurowski was one of the few men Lincoln feared.

CHAPTER 11

1. Pearson, *James S. Wadsworth of Geneseo*, pp. 148, 151; Weed, *Autobiography*, Vol. 2, pp. 424, 413.
2. Pearson, *James S. Wadsworth of Geneseo*, p. 151.
3. Doster, *Lincoln and Episodes of the Civil War*, pp. 52, 53, offers tantalizing glimpses of Wadsworth's role in Washington, but never fully reveals it.
4. Pearson, *James S. Wadsworth of Geneseo*, p. 153.
5. Letter from James S. Wadsworth to David Dudley Field, Horace Greeley, L. Robinson, George Opdyke, and Thomas B. Carver, September 14, 1862, WFP.
6. Ibid.
7. Seymour's position was well known as early as March 1861; Mitchell, *Horatio Seymour of New York*, pp. 227, 243, 244.
8. Ibid., p. 245; Weed, *Autobiography*, Vol. 2, pp. 424, 425; Francis Brown, *Raymond of the Times* (Westport, Conn.: Greenport Press, 1951), p. 237.
9. Chase, *Inside Lincoln's Cabinet*, p. 153.
10. Ibid. Chase claimed Wadsworth was nominated on the first ballot, ibid., p. 158. There may well have been only one ballot and a subsequent motion to make the nomination unanimous. Pearson, *James S. Wadsworth of Geneseo*, p. 155, also claims that there was only one vote. Transcribed copy of letter from Henry J. Raymond to James S. Wadsworth, dated September 29, 1862, Genesee Valley Collection, Milne Library, SUNY–Geneseo.
11. Letter from Alfred Wilkinson to James S. Wadsworth, September 25, 1862, WFP.
12. Transcribed copy of Wadsworth's Letter of Acceptance, dated October 2, 1862, Genesee Valley Collection, Milne Library, SUNY–Geneseo.
13. Henry J. Raymond letter to James S. Wadsworth, October 4, 1862, WFP.
14. Transcribed copy of "Speech of James S. Wadsworth, At Washington, Friday Evening, Sept. 26, 1862," Genesee Valley Collection, Milne Library, SUNY–Geneseo.
15. *Albany Atlas & Argus*, November 7, 1862, p. 2; *New York Times*, November 5, 1862, p. 4; ibid., November 4, 1862, p. 4; Weed, *Autobiography*, Vol. 2, p. 425; *Ontario Repository & Messenger*, October 22, 1862.
16. Handwritten, undated letter to James S. Wadsworth, WFP. The Kings were quite active politically, beginning with father Rufus, a member of the Continental Congress and Federal and Massachusetts constitutional conventions, a U.S. senator, minister to Great Britain, and a presidential candidate; letter from General Rufus King to Charles Henry Webb, October 31, 1862, Charles Webb Papers, Vol. 1, Library of Congress.
17. Howard K. Beale (ed.), *Diary of Gideon Welles* (New York: W. W. Norton, 1960), Vol. 1, p. 154, entry for September 27, 1862; Nevins and Thomas, *The Diary of George Templeton Strong*, Vol. 3, pp. 263, 264, entry for Wednesday, October 8, 1862.

18. Brown, *Raymond of the Times*, p. 238; *Speeches of William Curtis Noyes, Daniel S. Dickinson, and Lyman Tremain at the Great Union War Ratification Meeting Held at the Cooper Institute, in the City of New York*, October 8th, 1862 (New York: New York Tribune Co., no date).

19. Letter of Captain Henry A. Wiley, October 9, 1862, courtesy of Theodore Capron.

20. Mitchell, *Horatio Seymour of New York*, pp. 244, 247, 248; *Ontario Repository & Messenger*, October 15, 1862; *Ontario County Republican Times*, October 22, 1862, quoting the *Rochester Union and Advertiser*.

21. Pearson, *James S. Wadsworth of Geneseo*, pp. 156–158; letter from George B. McClellan to Samuel L. M. Barlow, October 17, 1862, in Sears, *The Civil War Papers of George B. McClellan*, p. 501.

22. Navy Secretary Welles refused to intercede unless convinced that the particular case demonstrated "active, offensive partisanship," thus, neglect of business. Welles did agree that he disliked politicians "taking advantage of an excited election to thrust miserable partisans in places which they are often indifferently qualified to fill" and, not surprisingly, found Wadsworth assenting "fully to my views." On the other hand, Wadsworth had achieved one of his goals, to get Welles to remove at least one partisan, "Fairion, master machinist"; Beale, *Diary of Gideon Welles*, Vol. 1, p. 178.

The second matter occurred when Ben Field, secretary of the Union State Central Committee, had requested the presence of General Franz Sigel to visit the state and address meetings on behalf of Wadsworth sometime during the last week of October. But Lincoln had denied the request; Basler, *The Collected Works of Abraham Lincoln*, Vol. 5, p. 472. Lincoln's rather curt denial suggests his exasperation at the political maneuvering. A subsequent letter left no doubt about his feelings. Immediately after the election Lincoln had been asked by Secretary of the Treasury Chase to revoke a political appointment to a Mr. Masten and award it instead to Eli D. Terwilliger. Lincoln easily saw through the maneuvering, presuming that Mr. Masten had supported Seymour against Wadsworth and that Chase was not about to allow a Democratic governor to enjoy the political spoils; ibid., pp. 490, 491.

23. Campaign poster by Union State Central Committee, October 24, 1862, Genesee Valley Collection, Milne Library, SUNY–Geneseo.

24. Mitchell, *Horatio Seymour of New York*, p. 249; letter from R. Campbell of Bath, New York, to S. F. Hazt(?), October 27, 1862, private collection; Mitchell, *Horatio Seymour of New York*, p. 259; Wayne Mahood (ed.), *Charlie Mosher's Civil War: From Fair Oaks to Andersonville with the Plymouth Pilgrims* (Hightstown, N.J.: Longstreet House, 1989), p. 83, entry for November 4, 1862.

25. Mitchell, *Horatio Seymour of New York*, p. 122. Seymour argued that the two of them, who had voted for Breckenridge in 1860 and now were abolitionists, were the real traitors, not himself. Their meddling had resulted in Union battle reverses. They were as guilty as Lincoln for violating the Constitution by supporting emancipation and remaining silent when the right of habeas corpus was suspended,

26. Pearson, *James S. Wadsworth of Geneseo*, p. 157; Weed, *Autobiography*, Vol. 2, p. 425; Mitchell, *Horatio Seymour of New York*, p. 252.

27. Wadsworth's entire Cooper Union Speech is reproduced in *James S. Wadsworth of Geneseo*, pp. 158–163.

28. Ibid.

29. Ibid., p. 163, quoting Alexander's *Political History of the State of New York*, Vol. 3, pp. 50, 51.

30. Letter from Martin F. Cogswell to "My Dear Old Friend," November 1, 1862, WFP; letter from Samuel A. Ruggles to James S. Wadsworth, November 5, 1862, WFP.

31. John Lothrop Motley (ed.), *The Correspondence of John Lothrop Motley* (New York: Society of English and French Literature, 1900), Vol. 2, pp. 301, 302.

32. Blake McElvey (ed.), *Rochester in the Civil War* (Rochester, N.Y.: Rochester Historical Society, 1944), Vol. 22, p. 109. Ironically, Breck would come to serve under Wadsworth and be exposed to considerable danger when his battery was placed in a precarious position at Gettysburg.

33. Mitchell, *Horatio Seymour of New York*, p. 254.

34. Nevins and Thomas, *The Diary of George Templeton Strong*, Vol. 3, p. 270.

35. Doster, *Lincoln and Episodes of the Civil War*, p. 51; *Ontario Repository & Messenger*, November 5, 1862. The 104th New York's Captain Henry Wiley indignantly wrote home three days after the election that the soldiers had "just heard that General Wadsworth has been defeated for Governor by the Pro-Slavery, Antiwar, Jeff Davis, Sympathizer, Demague [sic], Seymour." He considered it a "disgrace for New York"; letter from Captain Henry A. Wiley to his family in Springwater (Livingston County), New York, November 7, 1862.

36. Beale, *Diary of Gideon Welles*, Vol. 2, p. 27; letter from Edwards Pierrepont to James S. Wadsworth, November 5, 1862, WFP.

37. Motley, *The Correspondence of John Lothrop Motley*, Vol. 2, p. 302; *Albany Atlas & Argus*, November 7, 1862, p. 2; *New York Times*, November 5, 1862, p. 4.

38. Weed, *Autobiography*, Vol. 2, p. 431; Nevins and Thomas, *The Diary of George Templeton Strong*, Vol. 3, p. 271.

39. Pearson, *James S. Wadsworth of Geneseo*, p. 166.

CHAPTER 12

1. Doster, *Lincoln and Episodes of the Civil War*, p. 51; Welcher, *The Union Army, 1861–1865*, Vol. 1, pp. 546–550.

2. Doster, *Lincoln and Episodes of the Civil War*, p. 51.

3. Ira Berlin et al. (eds.), *The Wartime Genesis of Free Labor: The Upper South*, Series I, Vol. 2 of *Freedom: A Documentary History of Emancipation, 1861–1867* (Cambridge, UK: Cambridge University Press, 1993), pp. 243, 484, 245, 246, 267; telegram from General Wadsworth to Colonel George Biddle, Record Group 94, M504, Roll 101.

4. Berlin et al., *The Wartime Genesis of Free Labor: The Upper South*, pp. 245, 246.

5. Ibid., pp. 1, 12, 19; O.R., Series 3, 2, p. 397.

6. Basler, *The Collected Works of Abraham Lincoln*, Vol. 5, p. 496; Berlin et al., *The Wartime Genesis of Free Labor: The Upper South*, p. 250.

7. Berlin et al., *The Wartime Genesis of Free Labor: The Upper South*, pp. 275–276.

8. Ibid., pp. 249, 294. However, Wadsworth was credited with helping obtain pay for some freedmen who had been hired by the month, but fired without pay before the end of the month, p. 293.

9. Ibid., pp. 2, 23, 25, 10.

10. Ibid., p. 251; letter from General James S. Wadsworth to Secretary of War Edwin Stanton, September 25, 1862, in ibid., pp. 269–271.

11. A freed Black who had worked as a blacksmith for the government at $30 per month claimed that he left his employer because he could not support himself even on the $30, let alone the $25 remaining after the $5 deduction; ibid., pp. 274, 294.

12. Ibid., p. 247.

13. Dispatches from General McClellan to General Halleck, General Heintzelman to Wadsworth, Wadsworth to A. A. G. John Sherburne, Colonel Swain's report to Wadsworth, and reports from Lieutenant G. W. Smith and Captain W. B. Reyburn to General Wadsworth, O.R. 19, Part 2, pp. 537, 538, 539, 556.

14. Leech, *Reveille in Washington*, p. 221; Basler, *The Collected Works of Abraham Lincoln*, Vol. 5, p. 460.

15. Lincoln had hinted at relieving McClellan earlier in October, Richard B. Irwin, "Washington Under Banks," in Robert Underwood Johnson and Clarence Clough Buel (eds.), *Battles and Leaders of the Civil War* (New York: Century Co., 1884, 1887, 1888), Vol. 2, p. 544; Basler, *The Collected Works of Abraham Lincoln*, Vol. 5, p. 485; Leech, *Reveille in Washington*, p. 220; Kent Masterson Brown, *Cushing of Gettysburg: The Story of a Union Artillery Commander* (Lexington: University of Kentucky Press, 1993), p. 137.

16. O.R. 21, p. 777; Pearson, *James S. Wadsworth of Geneseo*, p. 166. An illustration of Wadsworth's influence was obtaining a leave for his oldest son, Charles F., who had telegraphed him: "Send leave by telegraph from Secretary of War. No one else can give it," Record Group 94, M504, Roll 101; telegrams from Craig W. Wadsworth to General Reynolds, October 6, 1862, and from General James S. Wadsworth to Reynolds, undated, Record Group 94, M504, Roll 101; letter from James Samuel Wadsworth to Governor Edwin Morgan, Morgan Papers, New York State Library; Phisterer, *New York in the War of the Rebellion*, Vol. 3, p. 2181.

17. Letter from Seth Wells, a quartermaster sergeant, to his brother, December 19, 1862, courtesy of Katherine Cooper.

18. Kress, *Memoirs*, pp. 4–5. Kress was subsequently (March 17, 1925) awarded a Silver Star for his gallantry at Fredericksburg, December 13, 1862, based on a War Department review of a petition by officers of the 94th who had recommended Kress for a Medal of Honor, February 1896, ibid., pp. 5, 6.

19. O.R. 21, pp. 777, 860, 876. Doubleday, who had replaced the wounded Brigadier General John P. Hatch, would become 3rd Division commander, January 18, 1863, O.R. 51, Part 1, p. 974.

20. General Orders No. 110, December 27, 1862, O.R. 51, Part 1, p. 965, per Special Orders No. 82, December 12, 1862. Wadsworth also requested Private John Fiedler, Company A, 4th Pennsylvania Cavalry, a "trustworthy and reliable soldier," detailed to him as orderly at headquarters. Whether this request was met cannot be determined. Two of Wadsworth's aides, Captains Henry Todd and Henry Lockwood, remained with General Martindale in Washington; Record Group 94, Office of the Adjutant General, Commission Branch, File No. W 17 CB 1863, National Archives.

  The relationship between Kress and Wadsworth apparently was a close one. Kress's recommendation of Colonel Adrian Root to command the 94th New York was seconded by Wadsworth's son Craig, a Root acquaintance, and was ultimately passed on by Wadsworth; letter from Root to his mother, December 8, 1862, courtesy of Benedict R. Maryniak.

21. Nolan, *The Iron Brigade*, p. 196; Rufus R. Dawes, *Service with the Sixth Wisconsin Volunteers* (Dayton, Ohio: Morningside, 1991), p. 115. Dawes's only exception was General Doubleday.

22. Nevins, *A Diary of Battle*, pp. 149, xiii–xiv. Editor Nevins, with an objectivity that often accompanies hindsight, was much more complimentary, recalling that Wadsworth did "indeed" possess "great natural abilities," performed "excellent service," and demonstrated "gallantry [that] . . . attracted national attention"; ibid., p. 149.

23. Circulars, January 7, 8, 9, 10, 14, 15, 17, 1863, Record Group 393, Part 2, Entries 3685/3691, National Archives.

24. Ibid., January 27, February 2, January 21, 26, 30. Description of Flanagan from O. B. Curtis, *History of the Twenty-Fourth Michigan of the Iron Brigade* (Detroit: Winn & Hammond, 1891), p. 41.

25. Circulars, February 6, 14, 16, 1863, Record Group 393, Part 2, Entries 3685/3691, National Archives.

26. Curtis, *History of the Twenty-Fourth Michigan*, p. 107; Circular, February 17, 1863, Record Group 393, Part 2, Entries 3685/3691, National Archives; Craig L. Dunn, *Iron Men, Iron Will: The Nineteenth Indiana Regiment of the Iron Brigade* (Indianapolis: Guild Press of Indiana, 1995), p. 165.

27. Bruce Catton, *Glory Road* (New York: Fairfax Press, 1984), p. 266 (reprint).

28. Orville Thompson, *From Philippi to Appomattox: Seventh Indiana Infantry in the War for the Union* (Baltimore: Butternut & Blue, 1993), pp. 147–148 (reprint); Alan D. Gaff, *On Many a Bloody Field: Four Years in the Iron Brigade* (Bloomington: University of Indiana Press, 1996), p. 218.

29. Henry W. Raymond (ed.), "Extracts From the Journal of Henry J. Raymond," *Scribner's Monthly*, Vol. 19, No. 3 (January 1880), pp. 419–420.

30. Ibid., p. 420.

31. Leech, *Reveille in Washington*, p. 227. Lincoln refused to allow Burnside to resign from the army and later would assign him to command the IX Corps.

32. Warner, *Generals in Blue*, pp. 233–234.

33. Leech, *Reveille in Washington*, p. 229; Nevins, *A Diary of Battle*, p. 163; O.R. 25, Part 2, p. 152. Some of the more famous corps patches, or badges, were the trefoil (cloverleaf) of the II Corps, the lozenge (or diamond) of the late Kearny's III Corps, the V's distinctive Maltese Cross, the VI's Greek cross, and the XI Corps' crescent; Francis Lord, *They Fought for the Union* (New York: Bonanza Books, 1960), pp. 183–187. Major General Daniel Butterfield designed the patches, which were worn on the left shirt front or, frequently, on the soldiers' caps; Patricia L. Faust (ed.), *Historical Times Illustrated Encyclopedia of the Civil War* (New York: Harper Perennial, 1986), p. 184.

34. The confusion that surrounds the designation of the 84th New York stems from the various names it carried, including 14th Militia, Brooklyn Phalanx, Brooklyn Chasseurs, and Chasseurs-á-Píed; Phisterer, *New York in the War of the Rebellion*, Vol. 4, pp. 2929–2943.

35. In 1847 it was reorganized and consolidated into the 14th Regiment, New York State Militia, under Colonel Philip S. Crook. It was first quartered in the old New York City Hall, then was moved to Poplar Hall in 1858. The ranks of the 14th Brooklyn were filled almost immediately after Lincoln's call for volunteers, and the recruits reported for duty on April 18, 1861, in their distinctive *Chasseur-á-Pied* uniforms, which the city of Brooklyn had supplied. The best account of the 14th Brooklyn is Tevis and Marquis, *The History of the Fighting Fourteenth*; James L. McLean, Jr., *Cutler's Brigade at Gettysburg* (Baltimore: Butternut & Blue, 1994), pp. 13–14, 15; Lord, *They Fought for the Union*, p. 175, called theirs a "half-fledged" Zouave uniform, borrowed from the French light infantry. A more complete description of their distinc-

tive uniform is in Frederick W. Hawthorne, *Gettysburg: Stories of Men and Monuments as Told by Battlefield Guides* (Gettysburg, Penn.: Association of Licensed Battlefield Guides, 1988), p. 22, to wit: "The kepi was red with the unit's numerical '14' on the front. The Chasseur coat was blue, trimmed in red, with three rows of brass buttons. The outer rows, on the blue material, were designed to give the appearance of this one garment being two, an open blue coat worn over a buttoned shirt. Red trefoil epaulettes were worn on the shoulders by all ranks. Their trousers were also made of red material and the uniform was completed by white, canvas gaiters which buttoned up on the side"; Tevis and Marquis, *The History of the Fighting Fourteenth*, p. 116.

36. Curtis, *History of the Twenty-Fourth Michigan*, p. 452.
37. The way Gibbon tells it, he was "shocked" by the "untidy negligent appearance" of men ordered to the brigade's guard-mounting and was initially at a loss. Then Gibbon chanced upon "a tall fine looking" soldier whose boots were polished, equipment neat, and "gun in good order." Singling out this recruit, he offered him a day free from duty to pick blackberries. A second recruit and third recruit were similarly treated. The rest of his brigade got the message; Gibbon, *Personal Recollections of the Civil War*, pp. 37, 38; Nolan, *The Iron Brigade*, p. 51.
38. Ibid., pp. 54, 165, 166.
39. Curtis, *History of the Twenty-Fourth Michigan*, p. 469, offers a humorous anecdote to explain its nickname. Apparently its first uniforms were so shoddy that the regiment's pants allowed "for their 'flags of truce' always to be kept in their rear. . . . Once on a review they were drawn up for inspection in their usual ragged pants, and the General's carriage with his little daughter therein stood directly behind them. Presently, she said, 'Pa, wouldn't it be just as well if our carriage stood *in front of this regiment?*"; ibid., pp. 453, 454.
40. Curtis, *History of the Twenty-Fourth Michigan*, p. 457. Cutler was instructed to report to General Wadsworth for assignment on March 25, 1863, by Special Orders No. 77, O.R. 51, Part 1, p. 995; Frank L. Byrne and Andrew T. Weaver (eds.), *Haskell of Gettysburg: His Life and Civil War Papers* (Kent, Ohio: Kent State University Press, 1989), p. 1 (reprint).
41. Lance J. Herdegen and William J. K. Beaudot, *In the Bloody Railroad Cut at Gettysburg* (Dayton, Ohio: Morningside, 1990), p. 38.
42. Dawes, *Service With the Sixth Wisconsin Volunteers*, p. 25; Faust, *Historical Times Illustrated Encyclopedia of the Civil War*, p. 488; Dunn, *Iron Men, Iron Will*, pp. 4–14, 161–163.
43. Curtis, *History of the Twenty-Fourth Michigan*, pp. 41, 65. The brigade ducked shell and canister during the battle of Fredericksburg, but was spared the bloodletting that others suffered; Dawes, *Service With the Sixth Wisconsin Volunteers*, pp. 108–114. Dawes's opinion of the 24th Michigan appears on p. 112.
44. Organization of the Army of the Potomac, O.R. 25, Part 2, p. 23.

CHAPTER 13

1. Abstract from consolidated morning report of the Army of the Potomac, February 28, 1863, O.R. 25, Part 2, p. 111. The command structure and placement of the Army of the Potomac is obtained from Welcher, *The Union Army, 1861–1865*, Vol. 1, pp. 261, 262. The IX Corps was transferred to the Department of the Army in mid-February 1863.
2. Undoubtedly Butterfield's greatest claim to fame was contributing the now familiar "Taps" to army bugle calls; Catton, *Glory Road*, p. 311. Catton's characterization of Sickles appears on p. 312.
3. Dawes, *Service With the Sixth Wisconsin Volunteers*, p. 129; Gaff, *On Many a Bloody Field*, p. 247.
4. Curtis, *History of the Twenty-Fourth Michigan*, pp. 113, 114.
5. Nevins, *A Diary of Battle*, p. 166.
6. O.R. 25, Part 1, pp. 16, 17, 18; Circular, April 2, 1863, Record Group 393, Part 2, Entries 3685/3691, National Archives.
7. O.R. 51, Part 1, p. 991; letters to Major General Henry Halleck and Major General John Reynolds, Record Group 94, Office of the Adjutant General, Commission Branch, File No. W 17 CB 1863, National Archives.
8. Order from General Wadsworth, March 9, 1863, Record Group 393, Part 2, Entries 3685/3691, National Archives; Pearson, *James S. Wadsworth of Geneseo*, pp. 173–174.

9. Nevins, *A Diary of Battle*, pp. 171–172. However, the haughty Colonel Wainwright found the event less than successful. He blamed part of it on the leaky roof, a downdraft in the chimney, and the cold air seeping in. More important "the company was not so pleasant." Chef Sanderson had "drawn out a list of toasts with quotations from Shakespeare to each; but our party were neither wits, nor much accustomed to public dinners, so that this part of the affair fell very flat."

10. Ibid., p. 172.

11. Circulars, March 12, 21, 1863, Record Group 393, Part 2, Entries 3685/3691, National Archives.

12. Dawes, *Service With the Sixth Wisconsin Volunteers*, p. 129; O.R. 51, Part 1, p. 995; Otis, *The Second Wisconsin Infantry*, p. 76; Letters Received, Record Group 393, U.S. Army Continental Command, 1861–1865, National Archives.

13. Benedict R. Maryniak, "Cutey in Kersey," *Buffalo Civil War Round Table Newsletter*, undated, unpaginated.

14. E. F. Conklin, "Elmina Keeler Spencer: Matron, 147th New York," *Gettysburg Magazine*, No. 8 (January 1, 1993), p. 122. There were other women in the Army of the Potomac as well. In the III Corps "were two women, MARY and ANN, MARY on horseback, having been appointed Sergeant by General KEARNY, and ANN in an ambulance. They are in Zouave dress; said to be very brave and present on all the battlefields. It is said that in the middle of Fredericksburg they were in the front," Arabella Willson, *Disaster, Struggle, Triumph: The Adventures of 1000 "Boys in Blue"* (Albany: The Argus Company, 1870), p. 151; A. P. Smith, *History of the Seventy-Sixth Regiment New York Volunteers* (Gaithersburg, Md.: Ron R. Van Sickle Military Books, 1988), p. 224 (reprint).

15. Telegram to Major General John F. Reynolds, March 22, 1863, Office of Adjutant General, M504, Roll 213, Record Group 94, National Archives; Dawes, *Service With the Sixth Wisconsin Volunteers*, p. 130; Special Orders No. 77, O.R. 51, Part 1, p. 995.

16. Dawes, *Service With the Sixth Wisconsin Volunteers*, p. 129; Curtis, *History of the Twenty-Fourth Michigan*, p. 119.

17. Dawes, *Service With the Sixth Wisconsin Volunteers*, p. 132.

18. Williams, *Lincoln and His Generals*, p. 234.

19. Orders by General Wadsworth, April 14, 18, 19, 1863, Record Group 393, Part 2, Entries 3685/3691, National Archives.

20. Orders by General Wadsworth, April 19, 1863, Record Group 393, Part 2, Entries 3685/3691, National Archives.

21. McLean, *Cutler's Brigade at Gettysburg*, p. 25, fn. 11, relying on a number of accounts. Lord, *They Fought for the Union*, p. 147, claims the lower amount. Pearson, *James S. Wadsworth of Geneseo*, p. 175, offers more extensive sources for estimates.

22. Smith, *History of the Seventy-Sixth Regiment New York Volunteers*, p. 255.

23. Dawes, *Service With the Sixth Wisconsin Volunteers*, p. 133.

24. Ernest B. Furgurson, *Chancellorsville 1863* (New York: Alfred A. Knopf, 1992), p. 66.

25. Abner Doubleday, *Chancellorsville and Gettysburg*, Vol. 3, *Campaigns of the Civil War* (New York: Thomas Yoseloff, 1963) p. 5 (reprint), Curtis, *History of the Twenty-Fourth Michigan*, pp. 121–122; Colonel Henry A. Morrow's report, O.R. 25, Part 1, pp. 1112–1115.

26. This account is from Kress, *Memoirs*, pp. 14–15, but Kress recalled that it occurred earlier in February. Unfortunately, Kress does not always approach his memoirs chronologically.

27. Dawes, *Service With the Sixth Wisconsin Volunteers*, p. 135.

28. Furgurson, *Chancellorsville 1863*, p. 66; Theodore Dodge, "The Battle of Chancellorsville," *Southern Historical Society Papers* (Richmond: Rev. J. Wm. Jones, 1886), Vol. 14, p. 278; Curtis, *History of the Twenty-Fourth Michigan*, p. 125; Dunn, *Iron Men, Iron Will*, p. 167; Pearson, *James S. Wadsworth of Geneseo*, p. 177.

29. Kress, *Memoirs*, p. 8; General Benham's report, O.R. 25, Part 1, p. 205. There is even disagreement about how many boats were to be employed. Reynolds, ibid., p. 253, recalled seventy-five men per boat and forty-four boats. Wadsworth recalled twenty, while General Henry Benham believed it was forty. Equally unclear is the degree of discretion allowed Wadsworth to decide; ibid., pp. 208–209. Colonel Phelps characterized the task of carrying the boats as "impracticable"; ibid., p. 262.

30. Benham's report, April 29, 1863, O.R. 25, Part 2, p. 206. Benham may have been trying to absolve his own responsibility, for Colonel Charles Wainwright claimed that "Old General Benham, who had charge of laying the bridges . . . had been up all night and had taken so much whiskey to keep himself awake that he was tight as a brick; had fallen off his horse once and scratched his face badly"; Nevins, *A Diary of Battle*, p. 186; General Reynolds's dispatch to General Sedgwick, O.R. 25, Part 2, p. 288.

31. Dawes, *Service With the Sixth Wisconsin Volunteers*, p. 135; General Reynolds to General Butterfield, O.R. 25, Part 2, p. 287; Wainwright commanded twenty light rifles above the mill, fourteen light rifles below the mill, plus six light 12-pounders, which were added later in the morning, O.R. 25, Part 1, p. 247; letter of James Samuel Wadsworth to eldest daughter Cornelia, May 9, 1863, WFP.

32. Kress, *Memoirs*, p. 9, recalled the meeting at roughly 8 A.M., but Curtis, *History of the Twenty-Fourth Michigan*, p. 125, wrote that it was 5 A.M. Given some other discrepancies in Kress's *Memoirs* and given other reports, Curtis is probably correct; Nevins, *A Diary of Battle*, p. 186; Chief of Staff Butterfield to General Sedgwick, O.R. 25, Part 2, p. 292.

33. Kress, *Memoirs*, p. 11; Dawes, *Service With the Sixth Wisconsin Volunteers*, p. 137; Pearson, *James S. Wadsworth of Geneseo*, p. 181.

34. Letter of Captain Henry A. Wiley, April 30, 1863, courtesy of descendant Theodore Capron; Furgurson, *Chancellorsville 1863*, p. 99; Curtis, *History of the Twenty-Fourth Michigan*, p. 126.

35. Pearson, *James S. Wadsworth of Geneseo*, p. 182; Kress, *Memoirs*, p. 11; Otis, *The Second Wisconsin Infantry*, p. 78; Dunn, *Iron Men, Iron Will*, p. 169; Letter of James Samuel Wadsworth to daughter Cornelia, May 9, 1863, WFP.

36. Reports of Colonels Kress and Phelps and General Cutler, O.R. 25, Part 1, pp. 262–263, 264; Dunn, *Iron Men, Iron Will*, p. 169.

37. General Reynolds's report, O.R. 25, Part 1, p. 557; Sedgwick reporting to Reynolds, ibid., Part 2, p. 311. Oddly, Colonel Adrian Root's 1st Brigade of Robinson's 2nd Division, across the river, was formed in a square about 4:00 P.M. to perform a religious observance by President Lincoln's proclamation; O.R. 25, Part 1, p. 282; Furgurson, *Chancellorsville 1863*, p. 111.

38. Furgurson, *Chancellorsville 1863*, p. 111.

39. Swinton, *Campaigns of the Army of the Potomac*, pp. 276, 277; Dodge, "The Battle of Chancellorsville," p. 278.

40. Wadsworth testimony, *Report of the Joint Committee on the Conduct of the War*, 38th Congress, 2nd Session, Part 1, p. 72; letter of James Samuel Wadsworth to daughter Cornelia, May 9, 1863, WFP; O.R. 25, Part 2, pp. 335, 342, 343, 328; Furgurson, *Chancellorsville 1863*, p. 128.

41. Letter of James Samuel Wadsworth to daughter Cornelia, May 9, 1863, WFP; Dunn, *Iron Men, Iron Will*, p. 171; Dawes, *Service With the Sixth Wisconsin Volunteers*, pp. 137, 138; Wadsworth testimony, *Report of the Joint Committee on the Conduct of the War*, 38th Congress, 2nd Session, Part 2, p. 72.

42. Cutler's, Paul's, and Meredith's reports, O.R. 25, Part. 1, pp. 264, 265.

43. Pearson, *James S. Wadsworth of Geneseo*, p. 190.

44. Colonel Phelps's report, O.R. 25, Part 1, p. 263.

45. Letter of James Samuel Wadsworth to daughter Cornelia, May 9, 1863, WFP.

46. Circular from General Wadsworth, May 4, 1863, Record Group 393, Part 2, Entries 3685/3691, National Archives; Dunn, *Iron Men, Iron Will*, p. 172; Dawes, *Service With the Sixth Wisconsin Volunteers*, pp. 138, 139.

47. Wadsworth testimony, *Report of the Joint Committee on the Conduct of the War*, 38th Congress, 2nd Session, Part 1, p. 72; Letter of James Samuel Wadsworth to daughter Cornelia, May 9, 1863, WFP.

48. Swinton, *Campaigns of the Army of the Potomac*, p. 307; Furgurson, *Chancellorsville 1863*, p. 339.

49. The difficult crossing is described in detail in Kress, *Memoirs*, pp. 13–14; letter of James Samuel Wadsworth to daughter Cornelia, May 9, 1863, WFP.

50. Reynolds's report, O.R. 25, Part 1, pp. 255–256. The I Corps lost 5 officers and 29 men killed, 15 officers and 189 men wounded, while 2 officers and 52 men were missing; ibid., pp. 173–175.

51. Curtis, *History of the 24th Michigan*, p. 136.

52. Letter of James Samuel Wadsworth to his daughter Cornelia, May 9, 1863, WFP.

53. Circulars May 9, 12, 1863, and letter, May 16, 1863, Record Group 393, Part 2, Entries 3685/3691, National Archives.

54. Letter from James Samuel Wadsworth to his daughter Cornelia, May 9, 1863, WFP; Record Group 94, Box 57, National Archives.

55. Ibid.

56. Williams, *Lincoln and His Generals*, pp. 243–247.

57. Dawes, *Service With the Sixth Wisconsin*, pp. 142, 143; cf. Dunn, *Iron Men, Iron Will*, p. 173.

58. Telegraph from Captain Craig W. Wadsworth to General James S. Wadsworth, May 21, 1863, Office of the Adjutant General, Microfilm 504, Roll 312, National Archives; Dunn, *Iron Men, Iron Will*, p. 175.

59. Nolan, *The Iron Brigade*, p. 323; Curtis, *History of the 24th Michigan*, p. 142; Welcher, *The Union Army, 1861–1865*, Vol. 1, pp. 304, 305. Many of the division would become members of the Invalid, later Veteran Reserve, Corps, established April 28, 1863, and composed of officers and men discharged for disability, but willing to reenlist to perform light armed duty, including guarding supply depots or prisoners; Nevins, *A Diary of Battle*, p. 270.

60. Dawes, *Service With the Sixth Wisconsin Volunteers*, pp. 146, 147, 149; Curtis, *History of the 24th Michigan*, pp. 142, 143; Circular, June 5, 1863, Record Group 393, Part 2, Entries 3685/3691, National Archives.

61. Welcher, *The Union Army, 1861–1865*, Vol. 1, p. 401; Circular, June 11, 1863, Record Group 393, Part 2, Entries 3685/3691, National Archives.

62. Dawes, *Service With the Sixth Wisconsin Volunteers*, pp. 150, 151; Herdegen and Beaudot, *In the Bloody Railroad Cut at Gettysburg*, p. 141.

63. While there are many accounts of this execution, the most extensive is in Herdegen and Beaudot, *In the Bloody Railroad Cut at Gettysburg*, pp. 141–143.

64. Thompson, *From Philippi to Appomattox*, p. 160.

65. Dawes, *Service With the Sixth Wisconsin Volunteers*, p. 149.

CHAPTER 14

1. Dispatches from General Pleasonton to General Hooker and General Hooker to General Tyler, O.R. 27, Part 3, pp. 101, 261; Swinton, *Campaigns of the Army of the Potomac*, p. 310; Edwin B. Coddington, *The Gettysburg Campaign: A Study in Command* (New York: Charles Scribner's Sons, 1968), pp. 8, 9, 49.

2. Basler, *The Collected Works of Abraham Lincoln*, Vol. 6, p. 257.

3. The description of the march to Gettysburg is taken from a number of accounts, including Curtis, *History of the 24th Michigan*, primarily pp. 147–152; Thompson, *From Philippi to Appomattox*; Pearson, *James S. Wadsworth of Geneseo*; Nolan, *The Iron Brigade*; Herdegen and Beaudot, *In the Bloody Railroad Cut at Gettysburg*. The quote is from Dawes, *Service With the Sixth Wisconsin Volunteers*, p. 152. Reference to the clothing inspection is from Circular, June 16, 1863, Record Group 393, Part 2, Entries 3685/3691, National Archives.

4. Smith, *History of the Seventy-Sixth Regiment New York Volunteers*, p. 226; McClean, *Cutler's Brigade at Gettysburg*, p. 22; Curtis, *History of the 24th Michigan*, pp. 147, 149.

5. Dawes, *Service With the Sixth Wisconsin*, p. 153.

6. Curtis, *History of the 24th Michigan*, p. 149; Dawes, *Service With the Sixth Wisconsin Volunteers*, p. 153.

7. McLean, *Cutler's Brigade at Gettysburg*, p. 23; Circular, June 26, 1863, Record Group 393, Part 2, Entries 3685/3691, National Archives; O.R. 27, Part 3, p. 256.

8. Report of Major General Julius Stahel to Major General John F. Reynolds that "the whole rebel army is marching toward Harrisburg"; June 26, 1863, U.S. Army Continental Command, Record Group 393, Part 2, Entries 3685/3691, National Archives. On June 24, General Halleck had learned from Brigadier General Daniel Tyler on Maryland Heights, overlooking Harpers Ferry, that McLaws's division of Longstreet's corps had crossed the Potomac; O.R. 27, Part 3, p. 294. Also Major General Couch at Harrisburg, Pennsylvania, had confirmed seeing Confederate cavalry east of Chambersburg; ibid., p. 295. Orders to Reynolds are in ibid., pp. 305–306, 312, 313, 415.

9. Dawes, *Service With the Sixth Wisconsin Volunteers*, pp. 156–157.

10. O.R. 27, Part 3, p. 375; Order of General James S. Wadsworth, June 28, 1863, and to Wadsworth from General Doubleday, June 29, 1863, U.S. Army Continental Command, Record Group 393, Part 2, Entries 3685/3691, National Archives; ibid., June 29, 1863.

11. Thompson, *From Philippi to Appomattox*, p. 167, claims that "those in the line of battle" did not learn of the change in command until after the conclusion of the battle, July 4. The command change was announced in O.R. 27, Part 3, pp. 373, 374, and was described by Charles F. Benjamin, "Hooker's Appointment and Removal," in Johnson and Buel, *Battles and Leaders*, Vol. 3, pp. 239–243. A fuller explanation is offered by Coddington, *The Gettysburg Campaign*, pp. 92–102, 128–133.

12. An example of the reaction of the 76th New York to the change in command is found in Smith, *History of the Seventy-Sixth Regiment New York Volunteers*, p. 231. See also Walker, *Second Corps*, pp. 254, 261. Meade's announcement is in O.R. 27, Part 3, p. 374. For Meade's reaction to his late-night appointment, see Benjamin, "Hooker's Appointment and Removal," pp. 239–243.

13. David G. Martin, *Gettysburg July 1* (Conshohocken, Penn.: Combined Books, 1995), p. 38; O.R. 27, Part 1, p. 67.

14. Russell F. Weigley, *Quartermaster General of the Union Army* (New York: Columbia University Press, 1959), p. 254; O.R. 27, Part 3, p. 378.

15. Generals Reynolds's and Meade's orders to division commanders, O.R. 51, Part 1, p. 1064; O.R. 27, Part 3, p. 375. The Wadsworth quotes are in Kress, *Memoirs*, p. 16, and in "George Breck's Civil War Letters from the 'Reynolds Battery,'" in Blake McKelvey (ed.), *Rochester in the Civil War* (Rochester, N.Y.: Rochester Historical Society, 1944), Vol. 22, p. 135.

16. Kress, *Memoirs*, p. 16.

17. Smith, *History of the Seventy-Sixth Regiment New York Volunteers*, p. 229; Pearson, *James S. Wadsworth of Geneseo*, p. 199; McLean, *Cutler's Brigade at Gettysburg*, p. 24. It is estimated that Wadsworth personally paid $250 for the straw, which in current dollars would be more than $4,000.

18. Smith, *History of the Seventy-Sixth Regiment New York Volunteers*, p. 233; Thompson, *From Philippi to Appomattox*, p. 161; Curtis, *History of the 24th Michigan*, p. 152.

19. General Meade's orders to General Reynolds, O.R. 27, Part 3, pp. 414–415, 416–417; Reynolds's circular, O.R. 51, Part 1, p. 1065.

20. General Meade's circular to corps commanders, O.R. 27, Part 3, p. 402; General Reynolds's report to General Butterfied, ibid., pp. 417–418. Meade had subsequently indicated to Reynolds that the latter could exercise his judgment and fall back to Emmitsburg; ibid., pp. 420. The bill for forage and wood is in Circular, June 30, 1863, U.S. Army Continental Command, Record Group 393, Part 2, Entries 3685/3691, National Archives.

21. Circulars from Meade to corps commanders, O.R. 27, Part 3, p. 415, juxtaposed as they are, are an unintended irony.

22. Dawes, *Service With the Sixth Wisconsin Volunteers*, pp. 157–158.

23. O.R. 27, Part 3, pp. 418, 419–420, 458; "Battle of the First Day of July, 1863," transcribed copy of anonymous, undated, unpaginated report, likely from General Doubleday's Adjutant General Eminel P. Halstead, courtesy of D. Scott Hartwig, Chief Park Historian, Gettysburg National Military Park Library. While helpful for some details, the report is quite biased toward General Doubleday and against many other participants, particularly Generals Meade and Wadsworth.

24. McLean, *Cutler's Brigade at Gettysburg*, p. 52; O.R. 51, Part 1, p. 1066; Doubleday, *Chancellorsville and Gettysburg*, p. 125.

25. J. Volnay Pierce, "Address by Capt. J. V. Pierce," *New York at Gettysburg*, Vol. 3, p. 990; Herdegen and Beaudot, *In the Bloody Railroad Cut at Gettysburg*, pp. 160–161; Curtis, *History of the 24th Michigan*, p. 187. The 7th Indiana of Cutler's brigade was detached to guard the corps wagon train, so was not engaged July 1; Thompson, *From Philippi to Appomattox*, p. iv; Smith, *History of the Seventy-Sixth Regiment New York Volunteers*, p. 236; Kress, *Memoirs*, p. 16. Times hereafter are from postbattle recollections and have to be considered only approximations.

26. Wadsworth's testimony, *Report of the Joint Committee on the Conduct of the War*, 38th Congress, 2nd Session, Vol. 1, p. 413; Halstead, "Battle of the First Day."

27. John W. Busey and David G. Martin, *Regimental Strengths and Losses at Gettysburg* (Hightstown, N.J.: Longstreet House, 1986), pp. 129, 16. Compare George Gordon Meade, *The Battle of Gettysburg* (Ambler, Penn.: George Gordon Meade, 1924), p. 11, where Meade claimed his total force was 95,659. Meade also claims that from "the meagre information obtainable . . . chiefly through the public press," he was under the impression that Lee's forces were in excess of 100,000; ibid., p. 12.

28. McLean, *Cutler's Brigade at Gettysburg*, pp. 32–34, with the excellent maps throughout by Blake Magner, is very helpful to understand the general terrain.

29. William Faulkner, *Intruder in the Dust* (New York: Signet New American Library edition, 1948), pp. 148–149, quoted at length by James M. McPherson, *Drawn with the Sword: Reflections on the American Civil War* (New York: Oxford University Press, 1996), p. 138. I'm indebted to Major Scott Price for calling this to my attention.

30. Heth had approximately 7,972 officers and men, of which 7,461 were actually engaged; Busey and Martin, *Regimental Strengths and Losses at Gettysburg*, p. 173. Buford had 4,880 officers and men with 4,073 engaged; ibid., p. 99. For a more detailed account, see Heth's and Davis's reports, O.R. 27, Part 2, pp. 637–639, 648–649. See also Martin, *Gettysburg July 1*, pp. 59–63, 82, which analyzes irregularities and anomalies about Heth's advance.

31. Wadsworth's staff at this time consisted of Lieutenant Colonel Kress; Major Clinton H. Meneely, aide-de-camp; Captain Clayton E. Rogers, provost marshal; Lieutenant Earl M. Rogers, aide-de-camp, Clayton's brother, both from the 6th Wisconsin; Lieutenant Edward Carrington, aide-de-camp; Captain Charles H. Ford, a six-footer of "soldierly bearing," another member of the 6th Wisconsin, who was acting aide-de-camp; Captain Timothy E. Ellsworth, aide-de-camp; and Captain Charles McClure, commissary of subsistence; O.R. 27, Part 1, p. 256; Dawes, *Service With the Sixth Wisconsin Volunteers*, p. 143. Dawes claims that "Wadsworth would have none but efficient men around him"; ibid., p. 144; Nevins, *A Diary of Battle*, p. 232; Loyd G. Harris, "With the Iron Brigade Guard at Gettysburg," *Gettysburg Magazine*, No. 1 (July 1, 1989), p. 31.

32. Richard S. Shue, *Morning at Willoughby Run* (Gettysburg, Penn.: Thomas Publications, 1995), p. 92.

33. Wadsworth's report, O.R. 27, Part 1, p. 265; D. Scott Hartwig, "Guts and Good Leadership: The Action at the Railroad Cut, July 1, 1863," *Gettysburg Magazine*, No. 1 (July 1, 1989), pp. 5–14, is particularly helpful for describing the movement of Wadsworth's division and its ensuing battle at the railroad cut, which involved the 6th Wisconsin, the 14th Brooklyn, and the 95th New York.

34. Martin, *Gettysburg July 1*, p. 102; "Report of Lt. Col. William W. Dudley," in David L. Ladd and Audrey J. Ladd, *The Bachelder Papers: Gettysburg in Their Own Words* (Dayton, Ohio: Morningside, 1994), Vol. 2, p. 940; "Newspaper Account" from surgeon Algernon S. Coe, ibid., Vol. 3, p. 1567.

35. Kress, *Memoirs*, p. 11.

36. Ibid.

CHAPTER 15

1. Wadsworth's testimony, *Report of the Joint Committee on the Conduct of the War*, 38th Congress, 2nd Session, Vol. 1, p. 413. A controversy arose over not only the quality of leadership but also the time frame. For example, the 56th Pennsylvania's Hofmann criticized the leadership of both Reynolds and Wadsworth, based on what he considered the tardiness or unreadiness of the 1st Brigade to march on July 1, but was countered by others; Lance J. Herdegen, "Old Soldiers and War Talk," *Gettysburg Magazine*, No. 2 (January 1, 1990), pp. 15–24. There was even disagreement over which regiment was first engaged, the 2nd Wisconsin or the 56th Pennsylvania; ibid., p. 22. However, this may be nothing more than "Old Soldiers and War Talk."

2. Wadsworth's testimony, *Report of the Joint Committee on the Conduct of the War*, 38th Congress, 2nd Session, Vol. 1, p. 413. Halstead, "Battle of the First Day," claims that Reynolds "intended to make a final stand" on Cemetery Ridge, not McPherson, and would concentrate Howard's XI Corps there. The significance of the disparity between the opposing forces is underscored by Abner Doubleday, *Chancellorsville and Gettysburg*, Vol. 3, *Campaigns of the Civil War*, p. 125. Doubleday wrote: "It must be remembered that the enemy had but *three* corps, while the Union army had *seven*. Each of their corps represented a *third*, and each of ours a *seventh*, of our total force. The same ratio extended to divisions and brigades." The quote about Wadsworth is from Howard, *Autobiography*, Vol. 1, p. 407.

3. Halstead, "Battle of the First Day."

4. Wadsworth's postbattle report, O.R. 27, Part 1, p. 265; Captain James Hall, "Letter of Captain James A. Hall," in Ladd and Ladd, *The Bachelder Papers*, Vol. 1, pp. 306, 307. In a subsequent letter, ibid., p. 386, Hall claimed he did not realize Davis's Brigade was "so near, till they rose up on my *front and right*, at a distance of not more than *fifty* yards." But this had to be later. Reports of the opening of the infantry battle are by Davis, who claimed he did not form until 10:30 (O.R. 27, Part 2, p. 649), whereas Wadsworth recalled it was a half hour earlier (O.R. 27, Part 1, p. 266). Recall Schaff's caveat about times and events in Chapter 1 where Gettysburg historian John Bachelder realized "that it would take a day of at least twenty hours instead of thirteen at Gettysburg to satisfy their accounts."

5. McLean, *Cutler's Brigade at Gettysburg*, pp. 58, 59.

6. Tevis and Marquis, *The History of the Fighting Fourteenth*, p. 132.

7. "Lieutenant J. Volnay Pierce to John Bachelder," in Ladd and Ladd, *The Bachelder Papers*, Vol. 2, p. 911; letter of surgeon Algernon S. Coe to John Bachelder, ibid., Vol. 3, p. 1564; Henry H. Lyman, "Historical Sketch," in *New York State Monuments Commission, Final Report on the Battlefield of Gettysburg* (Albany: J. B. Lyon Co., 1900), Vol. 3, p. 1004 (hereafter *New York at Gettysburg*).

8. "Letter of surgeon Algernon S. Coe to John Bachelder," in Ladd and Ladd, *The Bachelder Papers*, Vol. 3, pp. 1564–1565, 1567; Halstead, "Battle of the First Day." While some of Wadsworth's decisions that first day at Gettysburg deserve criticism, Halstead's obvious favoritism toward Doubleday, his superior, undercuts the credibility of his criticisms.

9. Ibid.

10. Ibid. Halstead's map shows Wadsworth and Cutler just north of the railroad cut and just west of the woods in front of Seminary Ridge; McLean, *Cutler's Brigade*, p. 68.

11. Ibid., p. 69.

12. "Newspaper Account Enclosed by Coe," in Ladd and Ladd, *The Bachelder Papers*, Vol. 3, p. 1568; Martin, *Gettysburg July 1*, p. 109, who, on p. 120, estimates the fighting lasted close to forty-five minutes; Busey and Martin, *Regimental Strengths and Losses at Gettysburg*, p. 239. For all intents and purposes these regiments were out of combat. By today's standards, the loss of 20–30 percent of an outfit's men would render it "combat ineffective" or "neutralized," indeed, annihilated, per phone interview with Richard "Scott" Price, Community Relations Officer, Department of the Army, Headquarters, Fort Riley, Kansas, July 31, 1996. Major Price is an army veteran and military historian.

13. Reports of Generals Doubleday and Cutler, O.R. 27, Part 1, pp. 245, 282.

14. Busey and Martin, *Regimental Strengths and Losses at Gettysburg*, p. 177; Marc Storch and Beth Storch, "What a Deadly Trap We Were In," *Gettysburg Magazine*, No. 6 (January 1, 1992), pp. 20, 21.

15. This description relies heavily on Martin, *Gettysburg July 1*, pp. 140–149; reports of Colonel Henry Morrow of the 24th Michigan, the 2nd Wisconsin's Major John Mansfield, Colonel William Robinson of the 7th Wisconsin, O.R. 27, Part 1, pp. 267–273, 273–275, 278–281; Storch and Storch, "What a Deadly Trap We Were In," pp. 13–27.

16. Kress, *Memoirs*, p. 18. Kress's account is helpful in many respects, but occasionally he is inaccurate in his recall. This particular part cannot be confirmed or denied. The other version is Coddington, *The Gettysburg Campaign*, p. 269.

17. Kress, *Memoirs*, p. 18.

18. A somewhat different version is offered by Lieutenant Colonel John Callis in correspondence with John Bachelder, in Ladd and Ladd, *The Bachelder Papers*, Vol. 1, p. 140. Callis claims that the 7th Wisconsin was hit while awaiting its deployment and he ordered his regiment to load and to charge, but was ordered to stop by Captain Craig Wadsworth. Callis tried to halt him men, but "our rushing charge seemed to be irresistible." Accounts differ over exactly who halted the 6th Wisconsin (and for how long), Herdegen and Beaudot, *In the Bloody Railroad Cut*, pp. 176–178.

19. Martin, *Gettysburg July 1*, pp. 142–143; Gates, *The "Ulster Guards,"* p. 429.

20. Doubleday's disdain for, if not acrimony toward, Wadsworth may well be illustrated by his staff officer Halstead's unpaginated, undated postbattle report, "Battle of the First Day." Lieutenant George Breck considered the loss of General Reynolds the key to the battle on July 1 and attributed the day's "disasters" to his death; Breck, "George Breck's Civil War Letters," p. 129; Wadsworth's testimony, *Report of the Joint Committee on the Conduct of the War*, 38th Congress, 2nd Session, Vol. 1, p. 413.

21. Rufus Dawes, "With the Sixth Wisconsin at Gettysburg," in Dawes, *Service With the Sixth Wisconsin Volunteers*, p. 345.

22. "Newspaper Account Enclosed by Coe," in Ladd and Ladd, *The Bachelder Papers*, Vol. 3, p. 1567; O.R. 27, Part 1, p. 266; ibid., Part 2, p. 649; Wadsworth's testimony, *Report of the Joint Committee on the Conduct of the War*, 38th Congress, 2nd Session, Vol. 1, p. 413.

23. "Letter of James A. Hall to John Bachelder," in Ladd and Ladd, *The Bachelder Papers*, Vol. 1, p. 386; Robert G. Scott, *Into the Wilderness with the Army of the Potomac* (Bloomington: Indiana University Press, 1985), p. 116; Hall to Bachelder, in Ladd and Ladd, *The Bachelder Papers*, Vol. 1, pp. 306, 386; and "Surgeon Coe letter to John Bachelder," Vol. 3, pp. 1565.

24. Hall's letter to Bachelder, in Ladd and Ladd, *The Bachelder Papers*, Vol. 1, p. 387. In the evening after things were quieter Hall and Wadsworth met again. Hall sarcastically noted that Wadsworth "supposed that he was looking out for me!!!"; ibid., p. 307. Neither Wadsworth's nor Hall's reports offer details regarding their confrontation; O.R. 27, Part 1, pp. 265–267, 359–360. See also Hall's letter to John Bachelder, in Ladd and Ladd, *The Bachelder Papers*, Vol. 1, p. 388.

25. Coddington, *The Gettysburg Campaign*, p. 270.

26. Phisterer, *New York in the War of the Rebellion*, Vol. 5, pp. 3705, 3711, 3715–3716. Davis's men were disorganized and shifting toward the 147th New York not only due to the success they had, but also due to the fire they were beginning to receive from Fowler's command, the 14th Brooklyn, and the 95th New York, on the south side of Chambersburg Pike. These regiments were no longer threatened, if ever, by Archer's charge and had shifted 90 degrees around to the north; Martin, *Gettysburg July 1*, p. 120.

27. McLean, *Cutler's Brigade*, pp. 81, 82. "We were nearly surrounded and the fight was very hot—," wrote Lieutenant J. Volnay Pierce. "We stubbornly held that line. No order to fall back had been received"; "Letter of Lieutenant Volnay Pierce to Bachelder," in Ladd and Ladd, *The Bachelder Papers*, Vol. 2, pp. 911, 912; "Letter from Timothy E. Ellsworth to Henry H. Lyman," in *New York at Gettysburg*, Vol. 3, p. 1005; Henry H. Lyman, "Historical Sketch," ibid., Vol. 3, p. 1002; Hartwig, "Guts and Good Leadership," pp. 10, 11; McLean, *Cutler's Brigade*, pp. 90, 92.

28. Dawes, *Service With the Sixth Wisconsin Volunteers*, p. 347; Tevis and Marquis, *The History of the Fighting Fourteenth*, p. 133. Doubleday's staff officer Eminel P. Halstead states that Colonel Fowler with his 14th Brooklyn and the 95th New York "had been left to shift for himself without orders"; Halstead, "Battle of the First Day."

29. Attributed to James P. "Mickey" Sullivan of the 6th Wisconsin; Herdegen and Beaudot, *In the Bloody Railroad Cut*, p. 139.

30. Dawes's report, O.R. 27, Part 1, p. 276; Fowler's report, ibid., pp. 286–287; Pye's report, ibid., p. 287.

31. Dawes, "With the Sixth Wisconsin at Gettysburg," in Dawes, *Service With the Sixth Wisconsin Volunteers*, p. 349. In the interest of accuracy, the charging Confederates, which had started with the 55th Mississippi on the left of Davis's Brigade, the 2nd Mississippi in the center, and the 42nd Mississippi on the Confederate right, had already been cut up by the Union firing, were "jumbled together without regard to regiment or company," and were being reorganized by Major Blair when they were "flanked and captured"; "Letter from Col. J. A. Blair to Henry H. Lyman," in *New York at Gettysburg*, Vol. 3, pp. 1005, 1006.

32. Herdegen and Beaudot, *In The Bloody Railroad Cut*, p. 206. Halstead, "Battle of the First Day," gets in one more dig at Wadsworth, claiming that "Gen'l Wadsworth, it seems, was ignorant that Gen'l Doubleday was out the ground [*sic*] and attributed all the movements to the spontaneous action of the Regiments themselves." On the other hand, Halstead labels this as a "brilliant affair" by Doubleday.

33. A field hospital was temporarily established in the Lutheran Seminary, "Letter of Surgeon in Chief George New to John Bachelder," in Ladd and Ladd, *The Bachelder Papers*, Vol. 1, p. 197; "Newspaper Account by Surgeon Coe to John Bachelder," in Ladd and Ladd, *The Bachelder Papers*, Vol. 3, pp. 1568, 1572; Hartwig, "Guts and Good Leadership," p. 11. In an after-battle speech Captain J. Volnay Pierce of the 147th said he was "ignorant" of Doubleday's report that the 147th was surrounded or "*rescued*"; "Dedication of Monument. 147th Regiment Infantry, July 1, 1888," in *New York at Gettysburg*, Vol. 3, p. 994.

34. Henry J. Hunt, "The First Day at Gettysburg," in Johnson and Buel, *Battles and Leaders*, Vol. 3, p. 277 ; Dawes, "With the Sixth Wisconsin at Gettysburg," in Dawes, *Service With the Sixth Wisconsin Volunteers*, p. 352.

CHAPTER 16

1. Howard, *Autobiography*, Vol. 1, p. 415; McLean, *Cutler's Brigade*, p. 126; Martin, *Gettysburg July 1*, p. 140. At best, these are estimates and may reflect the entire day's losses, according to Gettysburg Park Historian D. Scott Hartwig, notes to author, December 7, 1996.

2. See D. Scott Hartwig, "The Defense of McPherson's Ridge," *Gettysburg Magazine*, No. 1 (July 1, 1989), p. 15. In his inimitable style Wainwright called Doubleday "a weak reed to lean upon"; Nevins, *A Diary of Battle*, p. 233; Warner, *Generals in Blue*, p. 131. At Gettysburg criticisms of Doubleday would color judgments, quite possibly unfairly, of his conduct of the battle and lead to his recall by Meade and subsequent replacement by Major General John Newton; Doubleday, *Chancellorsville and Gettysburg*, p. 134, claimed "I had but four weak infantry brigades at this time against eight large brigades"; Nevins, *A Diary of Battle*, p. 233.

3. Wadsworth to Doubleday or Howard, O.R. 27, Part 3, p. 463. A conflicting account claims that Wadsworth, "the headstrong New Yorker," had ordered a withdrawal to Cemetery Hill, but Doubleday had countermanded him; Hartwig, "The Defense of McPherson's Ridge," p. 16.

4. Wadsworth testimony, *Report of the Joint Committee on the Conduct of the War*, 38th Congress, 2nd Session, Part 1, p. 413; Dunn, *Iron Men, Iron Will*, p. 189.

5. Martin, *Gettysburg July 1*, pp. 189, 190, 191; Nevins, *A Diary of Battle*, p. 234n; Wadsworth's report, O.R. 27, Part I, p. 265. Compare Wainwright, *A Diary of Battle*, p. 235.

6. "Letter of Capt. John A. Hall to John Bachelder," in Ladd and Ladd, *The Bachelder Papers*, Vol. 1, p. 388. Hall mentioned being ordered to position himself "to the right of [a clump of woods] on a knoll." Hartwig is under the impression that this meant returning Hall's guns to their earlier position; notes to author, December 7, 1996. Hall describes his countermarch to John Bachelder in Ladd and Ladd, *The Bachelder Papers*, Vol. 1, p. 388; Nevins, *A Diary of Battle*, p. 234n; Wainwright's report, O.R. 27, Part 1, p. 355; Hall's report, ibid., pp. 359–360. Wainwright considered the advanced position where Wadsworth wanted to post Hall as being too exposed and approachable by ravines that protected attackers; Nevins, *A Diary of Battle*, p. 234.

7. Martin, *Gettysburg July 1*, p. 191; Calef's report, O.R. 27, Part 1, p. 1031. Doubleday, *Chancellorsville and Gettysburg*, p. 140, recalled that Wadsworth simply "borrowed" Calef's battery; Calef's and Wadsworth's reports, O.R. 27, Part 1, pp. 1031, 266; Martin, *Gettysburg July 1*, p. 192; reports of General Doubleday, Colonel Wainwright, and Captain Hall, O.R. 27, Part 1, pp. 246, 356, 359–360. Scott Hartwig is particularly critical of Wadsworth; Hartwig, "The Defense of McPherson's Ridge," p. 16.

8. Nevins, *A Diary of Battle*, p. 233; McLean, *Cutler's Brigade*, pp. 126–131.

9. Heth's report, O.R. 27, Part 2, p. 638.

10. Hartwig, "The Defense of McPherson's Ridge," p. 16.

11. Howard, *Autobiography*, Vol. 1, p. 414; Wadsworth testimony, *Report of the Joint Committee on the Conduct of the War*, 38th Congress, 2nd Session, Part 1, p. 413; Wadsworth's report, O.R. 27, Part 1, p. 266; Kress, *Memoirs*, p. 19.

12. Hartwig, "The 11th Army Corps on July 1, 1863," *Gettysburg Magazine*, No. 2 (July 1, 1990), p. 33. Howard also claims that Doubleday had given him the same message; O.R. 27, Part 1, p. 702.

13. Kress, *Memoirs*, p. 20. Wadsworth's 1st Division had 3,857 officers and men engaged; Busey and Martin, *Regimental Strengths and Losses at Gettysburg*, pp. 20, 21. Robinson added another 2,997, while Rowley's division included 4,701. The Confederate strength is calculated in ibid., pp. 173, 179, 150. To be more accurate, Ewell would have on the field about 25,720, when Johnson's division, some 6,433, arrived. Doubleday, *Chancellorsville and Gettysburg*, p. 137. Doubleday claimed the head of the XI Corps column did not reach the field until 12:45, and the rear did not catch up until an hour later; ibid., p. 138.

14. Additionally Meade directed Major General John Newton, a VI Corps division commander, to replace Doubleday, though this would not occur until later, after the day's battle had been decided; Special Orders No. 178, O.R. 51, Part 1, p. 1066; Doubleday, *Chancellorsville and Gettysburg*, pp. 150, 154. Howard also requested Slocum to advance his XII Corps from Two Taverns, but the latter refused to do so without orders from Meade; Howard's report, O.R. 27, Part 1, p. 704.

15. Hartwig, "The Defense of McPherson's Ridge," p. 16; Lieutenant Calef's report, O.R. 27, Part 1, p. 1032. Likely, this was someone from Rodes's Artillery on Oak Hill, though it could have been Captain T. A. Brander's Letcher (Virginia) Artillery.

16. Wainwright's report, O.R. 27, Part 1, p. 356; Martin, *Gettysburg July 1*, p. 193, quoting Wainwright's unabridged, unedited journal. Reynolds's battery was hit almost immediately prior by enfilading fire, which cost Captain Reynolds an eye and drove off his battery.

17. Doubleday's report in O.R. 27, Part 1, p. 248; Martin, *Gettysburg July 1*, p. 209; Nevins, *A Diary of Battle*, p. 234. There is some doubt as to who ordered Biddle's brigade forward, allowing it to become so dangerously exposed. It appears to have been Wadsworth, who likely feared an attack against Meredith's left flank.

18. Hartwig, "The Defense of McPherson's Ridge," p. 17; Captain John D. S. Cook, "Personal Reminiscences of Gettysburg," in James L. McLean, Jr., and Judy W. McLean (comp.), *Gettysburg Sources* (Baltimore: Butternut and Blue, 1987), Vol. 2, p. 127; report of Col. Theodore Gates, O.R. 27, Part 1, p. 320; *New York at Gettysburg*, Vol. 1, p. 433. However, Gates recalled this operation as having begun before noon.

19. Martin, *Gettysburg July 1*, p. 181; Doubleday's report, O.R. 27, Part 1, p. 247.

20. General Wadsworth's report, O.R. 27, Part 1, p. 266; Hartwig, "The Defense of McPherson's Ridge," p. 23; Curtis, *History of the 24th Michigan*, p. 162.

21. Howard, *Autobiography*, Vol. 1, p. 417; Howard's report, O.R. 27, Part 1, p. 703; Curtis, *History of the 24th Michigan*, p. 168.

22. Scales's Brigade is estimated to have lost 77 percent of its men over the three days, primarily on that first day of July; Martin, *Gettysburg July 1*, p. 403.

23. Nevins, *A Diary of Battle*, p. 233. This stand of trees was known as the Wills–McPherson Woods.

24. Dawes, *Service With the Sixth Wisconsin Volunteers*, pp. 174–175; Doubleday, *Chancellorsville and Gettysburg*, p. 141. General Howard, according to Doubleday, had not "*echeloned* in the rear of the right of the First Corps." Instead, he had positioned his corps in advance.

25. "Letter of Colonel John A. Kellogg," in Ladd and Ladd, *The Bachelder Papers*, Vol. 1, pp. 205–206.

26. Wadsworth's report on Gettysburg to the corps' assistant adjutant general, July 4, 1863, O.R. 27, Part 1, p. 266; Tevis and Marquis, *The History of the Fighting Fourteenth*, p. 135.

27. Wadsworth testimony, *Report of the Joint Committee on the Conduct of the War*, 38th Congress, 2nd Session, Part 1, p. 413; Howard's report, O.R. 27, Part 1, p. 704.

28. Pearson, *James S. Wadsworth of Geneseo*, p. 221; Halstead, "Battle of the First Day." There is an unsubstantiated report by Halstead of another incident involving General Wadsworth about this time, wherein Wadsworth is supposed to have ordered Colonel Roy Stone's brigade to undertake a suicidal assault against guns supporting Scales's Brigade, but Stone dissuaded Wadsworth. No mention is made in any official or unofficial reports by officers or men in Stone's brigade.

29. Kress, *Memoirs*, p. 21; Dawes, *Service With the Sixth Wisconsin Volunteers*, p. 176; Wadsworth's report, O.R. 27, Part 1, p. 266; Wadsworth's testimony, *Report of the Joint Committee on the Conduct of the War*, 38th Congress, 2nd Session, Part 1, p. 413.

30. Dawes, "Service With the Sixth Wisconsin Volunteers," p. 176; Nevins, *A Diary of Battle*, p. 237; Martin, *Gettysburg July 1*, p. 451. Sergeant J. A. Leach of the 1st South Carolina claims that at least his regiment was in town, but pulled back to round up prisoners; "Letter of Sgt. J. A. Leach," in Ladd and Ladd, *The Bachelder Papers*, Vol. 2, p. 1047.

31. Estimates of arrival times differ. Kress, *Memoirs*, p. 21, did not believe the retreat started before 4:30, whereas Martin, *Gettysburg July 1*, p. 472, claims that Schurz's XI Corps had arrived before 4:30. Estimates of losses are by Martin, *Gettysburg July 1*, p. 463, and Fox, *Regimental Losses in the American Civil War*, p. 237. The latter lists 76 killed/mortally wounded, 146 wounded, and 79 missing, 301 total for the 147th New York. Losses for the 2nd Wisconsin are from O.R. 27, Part 1, p. 274. Fox, *Regimental Losses*, p. 393, reports a total loss (killed or mortally wounded) for the three days as only 46, although by the war's end the 2nd Wisconsin had "sustained the greatest percentage loss of any in the entire Union Army." Dawes's report is in O.R. 27, Part 2, p. 277. Fox, *Regimental Losses*, p. 396, reports 41 killed or mortally wounded for the 6th Wisconsin's three days at Gettysburg.

32. Martin, *Gettysburg July 1*, pp. 465–466.

33. The final altercation between the two occurred when Colonel Wainwright, who recalled Howard's "order to hold Seminary Hill to the last," protested Wadsworth's ordering of Stevens's battery to withdraw. However, when Wainwright realized that Wadsworth's and Robinson's divisions were starting to file through the railroad cut, he headed for town with his guns; Nevins, *A Diary of Battle*, p. 236.

34. Doubleday's and Howard's reports, O.R. 27, Part 1, pp. 253, 703; Coddington, *The Gettysburg Campaign*, pp. 274, 275, 307.

CHAPTER 17

1. Wadsworth's report, O.R. 27, Part 1, p. 266; Coddington, *The Gettysburg Campaign*, pp. 307–308; "Report of Lt. Col. Charles H. Morgan," in Ladd and Ladd, *The Bachelder Papers*, Vol. 3, p. 1351; Francis A. Walker, "Meade at Gettysburg," in Johnson and Buel, *Battles and Leaders*, Vol. 3, p. 409; Herdegen and Beaudot, *In the Bloody Railroad Cut*, p. 226; Dawes, *Service With the Sixth Wisconsin*, p. 178. Dawes recalled the colors as being the 73rd Ohio of the XI Corps.

2. Wadsworth testimony, *Report of the Joint Committee on the Conduct of the War*, 38th Congress, 2nd Session, Part 1, Army of the Potomac, p. 414; Meade, *The Battle of Gettysburg*, p. 57. This is the account compiled by the grandson from *The Life and Letters of George Gordon Meade* (New York: Charles Scribner's Sons, 1913).

3. "Address By Capt. J. V. Pierce," in *New York at Gettysburg*, Vol. 3, p. 993; Martin, *Gettysburg July 1*, pp. 470, 472; Wadsworth testimony, *Report of the Joint Committee on the Conduct of the War*, 38th Congress, 2nd Session, Part 1, pp. 413, 414.

4. Nevins, *A Diary of Battle*, p. 238.

5. Martin, *Gettysburg July 1*, p. 477, quoting the XI Corps artillery commander Major Thomas Osborn. Though Meade had authority from Washington to disregard seniority in certain extreme circumstances, there ensued a minor skirmish over rank and authority. The issue has been discussed too many times over the years to go into detail here. See Martin, ibid., pp. 478–488, for an extended discussion, including a version attributable to General Wadsworth; Doubleday, *Chancellorsville and Gettysburg*, Vol. 3, pp. 150–151; and Francis A. Walker, *History of the Second Army Corps* (New York: Charles Scribner's Sons, 1887), pp. 264–265; notes from D. Scott Hartwig, December 7, 1996.

6. "Report of Lt. Col. Charles H. Morgan," in Ladd and Ladd, *The Bachelder Papers*, Vol. 3, p. 1351–1352; Nevins, *A Diary of Battle*, p. 242.

7. Kevin E. O'Brien, "'A Perfect Road of Musketry,' Candy's Brigade in the Fight for Culp's Hill," *Gettysburg Magazine*, No. 9 (July 1, 1993), p. 84; George G. Meade, "A Letter From General Meade," in Johnson and Buel, *Battles and Leaders*, Vol. 3, p. 413. Reportedly General Jubal Early, one of Ewell's division commanders, was of the same opinion, arguing that "If you [Ewell] do not go up there tonight, it will cost you ten thousand men to get there tomorrow"; Martin, *Gettysburg July 1*, p. 555. General Isaac Trimble claimed that he strenuously agreed; "Letter of Maj. Gen. Isaac R. Trimble [to John Bachelder]," in Ladd and Ladd, *The Bachelder Papers*, Vol. 2, pp. 930–931.

8. Martin, *Gettysburg July 1*, p. 489; Thompson, *From Philippi to Appomattox*, pp. 162–163.

9. Ibid., p. 163.

10. Kress, *Memoirs*, p. 22. Kress recalled that Hancock was there also, but Meade, *The Battle of Gettysburg*, pp. 43, 61, remembered talking with Hancock earlier, before leaving for Gettysburg. Nor did Meade identify Wadsworth by name.

11. Thompson, *From Philippi to Appomattox*, pp. 164, 165; Dawes, *Service With the Sixth Wisconsin Volunteers*, p. 180; Report of Colonel Ira Grover, O.R. 27, Part 1, pp. 284–285; Martin, *Gettysburg July 1*, pp. 557–558.

12. Harry F. Pfanz, *Gettysburg–Culp's Hill and Cemetery Hill* (Chapel Hill: University of North Carolina Press, 1993), p. 81; Coddington, *The Gettysburg Campaign*, p. 367.

13. Henry J. Hunt, "The Second Day at Gettysburg," in Johnson and Buel, *Battles and Leaders*, Vol. 3, p. 283; Busey and Martin, *Regimental Strengths and Losses at Gettysburg*, p. 150.

14. General Slocum's orders to General Williams, O.R. 27, Part 3, p. 484; Jesse H. Jones, "The Breastworks at Culp's Hill," in Johnson and Buel, *Battles and Leaders*, Vol. 3, p. 316; Wadsworth testimony, *Report of the Joint Committee on the Conduct of the War*, 38th Congress, 2nd Session, Part 1, p. 414.

15. George W. New, "Letter of Dr. George New," in Ladd and Ladd, *The Bachelder Papers*, Vol. 1, p. 199.

16. Dawes, *Service With the Sixth Wisconsin Volunteers*, p. 180.

17. Pfanz, *Gettysburg*, pp. 120–122. There are any number of accounts about the Confederate failure to bring about a successful attack, including that of the biased Fitzhugh Lee; "A Review of the First Two Days' Operations at Gettysburg and a Reply to General Longstreet by General Fitzhugh Lee," in *Southern Historical Society Papers* (New York: Kraus Reprint, 1977), Vol. 5, pp. 162–194; Doubleday, *Chancellorsville and Gettysburg*, pp. 158–159.

18. Dawes, *Service With the Sixth Wisconsin Volunteers*, p. 181; Nevins, *A Diary of Battle*, pp. 244–245, 247.

19. Wainwright could be equally critical of others, as he was of officers of the XI Corps, most of whom he believed to be "adventurers, political refugees, and the like"; Nevins, ibid., p. 246. The references could have been to any number of XI Corps' officers, including Major General Carl Schurz, an ex-Prussian army officer and political appointee, or Brigadier General Adolph Wilhelm August Friedrich Baron von Steinwehr.

20. Dawes, *Service With the Sixth Wisconsin Volunteers*, p. 181.

21. Wayne Motts, "To Gain a Second Star: The Forgotten George S. Greene," *Gettysburg Magazine,* July 1, 1990, No. 3, pp. 71–72; George S. Greene, "The Breastworks at Culp's Hill," in Johnson and Buel, *Battles and Leaders*, Vol. 3, p. 317; report on Gettysburg by Brevet Major General George S. Greene, O.R. 27, Part 1, p. 855. Even with the additional 735 officers and men, Greene was trying to defend his position with less than 2,200 troops; Busey and Martin, *Regimental Strengths and Losses at Gettysburg*, pp. 150, 96, figuring 1,424 men engaged in Greene's brigade.

22. Lyman, "Historical Sketch," p. 1003.

23. J. N. Hubbard, "Wadsworth's Division on Culp's Hill," in Richard Sauers (ed.), *Fighting Them Over: How the Veterans Remembered Gettysburg in the Pages of The National Tribune* (Baltimore: Butternut and Blue, 1998), p. 360; Kress, *Memoirs*, pp. 22–23.

24. Ibid., p. 11.

25. Wadsworth's terse report on Gettysburg, O.R. 27, Part 1, p. 267; Wadsworth Testimony, *Report of the Joint Committee on the Conduct of the Civil War*, 38th Congress, 2nd Session, Part 1, p. 414. Other accounts are "Letter of Lt. Col. Rufus R. Dawes," in Ladd and Ladd, *The Bachelder Papers*, Vol. 1, pp. 325–326; McLean, *Cutler's Brigade*, p. 153, quoting the 56th Pennsylvania's Colonel John Hofmann and O.R. 27, Part 1, pp. 288–289; Dawes, *Service With the Sixth Wisconsin Volunteers*, pp. 181–182. General Greene, however, recalled that he directed the 6th Wisconsin, 14th Brooklyn, and 147th New York to occupy breastworks to the right and behind his own brigade, "sufficiently in the rear to support any part of the line"; Greene, "The Breastworks at Culp's Hill," p. 317. See also Lyman, "Historical Sketch," p. 1002.

26. Colonel Fowler's report, O.R. 27, Part 1, p. 287. Henry H. Lyman, the 147th New York's adjutant, claimed that the three regiments remained with the XII Corps "all the next day" (the 3rd); Lyman, "Historical Sketch," p. 1002.

27. There are any number of accounts of this council of war, including Meade, *The Battle of Gettysburg*, pp. 83–84. One of the more descriptive, especially of the officers present, is Byrne and Weaver, *Haskell of Gettysburg*, pp. 131–135.

28. Kress, *Memoirs*, p. 23; Motts, "To Gain a Star," pp. 71, 72.

29. Lyman, "Historical Sketch," pp. 1002, 1003. Lyman took umbrage at what he felt was the failure to "officially recognize" the 147th's role. He claimed that "The prompt reinforcement of Greene's weak and attenuated lines by the One hundred and forty-seventh New York and Fourteenth Brooklyn . . . undoubtedly frustrated Lee's plan of breaking through from Rock Creek to the Baltimore Pike."

30. Byrne and Weaver, *Haskell of Gettysburg*, p. 138.

31. Kress, *Memoirs*, pp. 23–24.

32. Gary Gallagher (ed.), *Fighting for the Confederacy: The Personal Recollections of Edward Porter Alexander* (Chapel Hill: University of North Carolina Press, 1989), p. 257.

33. Kress, *Memoirs*, p. 24.

34. "Letters of Lt. Henry H. Lyman," in Ladd and Ladd, *The Bachelder Papers*, Vol. 1, p. 330; Wadsworth testimony, *Report of the Joint Committee on the Conduct of the War*, 38th Congress, 2nd Session, Part 1, p. 414.

35. Nevins, *A Diary of Battle*, p. 249.

CHAPTER 18

1. Thompson, *From Philippi to Appomattox*, p. 167; report of Colonel Ira G. Grover, O.R. 27, Part 1, p. 285; Pfanz, *Gettysburg*, p. 368.

2. Pfanz, *Gettysburg*, p. 369; Nevins, *A Diary of Battle*, p. 254; Henry Morrow, "Notes regarding the 24th Michigan Vols. and its commander Col. Henry A. Morrow," in Ladd and Ladd, *The Bachelder Papers*, Vol. 1, p. 334.

3. Nevins, *A Diary of Battle*, p. 254; letter from Philetus Ruliffson regarding his uncle Seth Wells, July 27, 1863 (unknown source); Robert L. Bloom, *"We Never Expected a Battle": The Civilians at Gettysburg, 1863* (Gettysburg, Penn.: Adams County Historical Society, no date), p. 181, reprint in *Pennsylvania History*, Vol. 55 (October 1988).

4. Stephen Ambrose, *Band of Brothers* (New York: Simon & Schuster, 1992), p. 111, quoting Sergeant Carwood Lipton.

5. Record Group 393, U.S. Army Continental Command, Part 2, Entries 3685/3691; Return of Casualties, O.R. 27, Part 1, p. 187; Busey and Martin, *Regimental Strengths and Losses at Gettysburg*, pp. 270–276. Compare Nolan, *The Iron Brigade*, p. 399.

6. Report of Lieutenant Joseph G. Rosengarten, Army of the Potomac Ordnance Officer, O.R. 27, Part 1, p. 265; Busey and Martin, *Regimental Strengths and Losses at Gettysburg*, pp. 280, 290–291, 288–289.

7. Wadsworth testimony, *Report of the Joint Committee on the Conduct of the War*, 38th Congress, 2nd Session, Part 1, Army of the Potomac, pp. 414–415; Harry F. Pfanz, "The Gettysburg Campaign After Pickett's Charge," *Gettysburg Magazine*, No. 1 (July 1, 1989), pp. 118, 119; Byrne and Weaver, *Haskell of Gettysburg*, p. 180.

8. "Letter of Maj. Gen. Winfield S. Hancock," in Ladd and Ladd, *The Bachelder Papers*, Vol. 1, p. 227; Doster, *Lincoln and Episodes of the Civil War*, p. 51.

9. Thompson, *From Philippi to Appomattox*, p. 167; Record Group 393, U.S. Army Continental Command, Part 2, Entries 3685/3691; Thompson, *From Philippi to Appomattox*, p. 172.

10. The route is derived from Curtis, *History of the 24th Michigan*, p. 195, and Dunn, *Iron Men, Iron Will*, pp. 209–212.

11. Breck, "Rochester in the Civil War," p. 134.

12. Nevins, *A Diary of Battle*, p. 260.

13. Williams, *Lincoln and His Generals*, pp. 267–268; Byrne and Weaver, *Haskell of Gettysburg*, p. 180.

14. Meade, *The Life and Letters of George Gordon Meade*, Vol. 2, p. 363.

15. Ibid.; Howard, *Autobiography*, Vol. 1, p. 445, recalled nine commanders, which likely included General Warren, who was "present as chief of staff" and favored fighting according to Colonel Wainwright; Nevins, *A Diary of Battle*, p. 260. In that position, Warren probably would not have voted. Meade recalled that only Wadsworth and Howard favored an attack; Meade, *The Life and Letters of George Gordon Meade*, Vol. 2, p. 363; Byrne and Weaver, *Haskell at Gettysburg*, p. 181; Wadsworth testimony, *Report of the Joint Committee on the Conduct of the War*, 38th Congress, 2nd Session, Part 1, p. 415. Wadsworth recalled that Warren made "a strong and able argument" for attacking; ibid.

16. Nevins, *A Diary of Battle*, p. 260; Pearson, *James S. Wadsworth of Geneseo*, pp. 234, 237; Nevins, *A Diary of Battle*, p. 260.

17. Wadsworth testimony, *Report of the Joint Committee on the Conduct of the War*, 38th Congress, 2nd Session, Part 1, p. 415.

18. Coddington, *The Gettysburg Campaign*, pp. 570, 571.

19. Wadsworth testimony, *Report of the Joint Committee on the Conduct of the War*, 38th Congress, 2nd Session, Part 1, pp. 415, 416.

20. Ibid., p. 417.

21. Meade, *The Life and Letters of George Gordon Meade*, Vol. 2, p. 363; Nevins, *A Diary of Battle*, p. 260.

22. Dennett, *Lincoln and the Civil War*, pp. 67–68.

23. Beale, *Diary of Gideon Welles*, Vol. 1, pp. 374, 375.

24. Record Group 94, Office of the Adjutant General, Commission Branch, File No. W17 CB 1863, National Archives.

25. Ibid.

26. Smith, *History of the Seventy-Sixth Regiment New York Volunteers*, pp. 254, 255.

27. Doster, *Lincoln and Episodes of the Civil War*, pp. 51, 52; Nolan, *The Iron Brigade*, p. 266; Craig W. Wadsworth Military Service Papers, National Archives.

28. James McCague, *The Second Rebellion: The Story of the New York City Draft Riots of 1863* (New York: Dial Press, 1968), p. 144. For more on the New York City draft riots, see McPherson, *Battle Cry of Freedom*, pp. 600–611.

CHAPTER 19

1. McPherson, *Battle Cry of Freedom*, pp. 664, 665.

2. Kress, *Memoirs*, p. 29.

3. Record Group 94, Generals Papers and Books, National Archives; O.R., Series 3, Vol. 3, pp. 872–873.

4. Letter from Lincoln to Grant, August 9, 1863, in Basler, *The Collected Works of Abraham Lincoln*, Vol. 6, pp. 374–375.

5. Berlin et al., *The Wartime Genesis of Free Labor: The Lower South*, pp. 1, 9, 15.

6. *Statutes at Large*, Vol. 12, pp. 597–600; Berlin et al., *The Wartime Genesis of Free Labor: The Lower South*, p. 23.

7. Ibid., pp. 53, 54, 55. An example of the depredations by guerrillas is Ira Berlin et al., *Free at Last: A Documentary History of Slavery, Freedom, and the Civil War* (New York: New Press, 1992), pp. 255–257.

8. O.R., Series 3, Vol. 3, pp. 872–873.

9. *Livingston Republican*, June 30, 1864, quoting a correspondent of the *New York Tribune*. This caused a minor problem for the Quartermaster's Department, which was not about to reimburse him for his return

trip to Washington unless "his station" was identified; undated file in WFP. The notation of nonreimbursement appears on a brief, handwritten note by Wadsworth regarding his inspection trip, WFP.

10. Letter from James W. Wadsworth to Mary Craig Wadsworth, October 18, 1863, WFP.

11. Ibid.; dispatch from A. A. G. Thomas to Stanton, O.R., Series 3, Vol. 3, p. 873; letter from James S. Wadsworth to Salmon P. Chase, December 16, 1863, in Berlin et al., *The Wartime Genesis of Free Labor: The Lower South*, p. 757.

12. Letter from James W. Wadsworth to Cornelia ["Nellie"] Wadsworth Ritchie, October 29, 1863, WFP.

13. Ibid.

14. O.R., Series 3, Vol. 3, p. 1044; letter from James S. Wadsworth to Salmon P. Chase, December 16, 1863, in Berlin et al., *The Wartime Genesis of Free Labor: The Lower South*, p. 757.

15. James S. Wadsworth's report to the adjutant general was dated December 16, 1863, a copy of which was forwarded to Secretary of the Treasury Salmon P. Chase; Berlin et al., *The Wartime Genesis of Free Labor: The Lower South*, pp. 757–762. To help summarize his report, comments made at his "Testimony of a War Department Special Inspector before the American Freedmen's Inquiry Commission," ibid., pp. 492–510, are also interspersed here. The specific quotes here are from pp. 494, 495, 758.

16. Ibid., pp. 496, 760–761.

17. Ibid., pp. 500, 501, 762.

18. "Testimony of a War Department Special Inspector before the American Freedmen's Inquiry Commission," in ibid., p. 492, likely given in January 1864 in New York City.

19. Ibid., pp. 492, 494, 495.

20. Undated contract apparently prepared by James S. Wadsworth in New Orleans, 1863, WFP.

21. "Testimony of a War Department Special Inspector before the American Freedmen's Inquiry Commission," in Berlin et al., *The Wartime Genesis of Free Labor: The Lower South*, pp. 496, 509–510.

22. Ibid., pp. 508, 510n, 494–495.

23. Ibid., pp. 506, 503.

24. Ibid., p. 499.

25. I'm indebted to my good friend and twentieth-century historian Martin Fausold, who related this story to me, May 8, 1996, and identifies the scholar as Rice University professor Harold Hyman; "Testimony of a War Department Special Inspector before the American Freedmen's Inquiry Commission," in ibid., p. 498.

26. George E. Otott, Jr., thoughtfully raised this point in notes to the author, July 22, 1997.

27. Basler, *The Collected Works of Abraham Lincoln*, Vol. 7, pp. 101, 102. The most thorough analysis, which concludes that the letter is spurious, is Ludwell Johnson, "Lincoln and Equal Rights: The Authenticity of the Wadsworth Letter," *Journal of Southern History*, Vol. 32 (1966), pp. 83–87. David H. Donald, *Lincoln* (New York: Simon & Schuster, 1995), p. 683n, offers the most recent pronouncement on the letter's authenticity, siding with Johnson, who "convincingly demonstrates that this letter is spurious." Nothing has been located in the Wadsworth Family Papers in the Library of Congress or the Wadsworth Collection, Milne Library, SUNY–Geneseo, Geneseo, N.Y., to offer anything further.

28. Craig W. Wadsworth to James S. Wadsworth and reply by James S. Wadsworth, December 4, 1863, M504, Roll 213, Record Group 393, U.S. Army Continental Command, National Archives. In a September 3, 1864, letter to Mary Craig Wadsworth, Humphreys addresses the general's wife as "Cousin," WFP.

29. Special Orders 562, December 19, 1863, Record Group 94, Generals Papers and Books, Adjutant Generals Office, National Archives; Craig W. Wadsworth leave extension, January 5, 1864, Letters Received, M711, Adjutant Generals Office, National Archives; Nevins, *A Diary of Battle*, p. 309.

30. One possibility for General Wadsworth during this period was as military governor of Florida in line with an earlier, unsuccessful, federal law, which would have appointed a military governor and three judges over captured Confederate states. However, there was no appointment for a variety of reasons, the most significant of which was the Union defeat at the battle of Olustee, Florida, on February 20, 1864; Pearson, *James S. Wadsworth of Geneseo*, pp. 245n, in which he cites a letter from Wadsworth's aide, Colonel Meneely, for this assertion. Wadsworth's New York City address, 18 East 16th Street, is from his handwritten letter to the adjutant general from Louisville, Kentucky, February 23, 1864; Adjutant General's Office, W 17, CB 1863, Record Group 94, National Archives. The weather description is from Joseph W. Stahl, "A Cold Spell in Virginia," *Manuscripts*, Vol. 48, No. 1 (Winter 1996), pp. 47–49. In fact, it was so cold that Ma-

jor General John Sedgwick, who was acting Army of the Potomac commander, requested from the provost marshal a number of items, stressing "the stove I especially want."

31. Record of the Proceedings of the Court of Inquiry, O.R. 30, Part 1, p. 930.
32. Ibid., pp. 961, 1000, 1004, 1043.
33. Pearson, *James S. Wadsworth of Geneseo*, pp. 245–246.

CHAPTER 20

1. Martin T. McMahon, "From Gettysburg to the Coming of Grant," in Johnson and Buel, *Battles and Leaders*, Vol. 4, pp. 91, 93.
2. Special Orders No. 9, January 9, 1864.
3. Humphreys, *The Virginia Campaign of '64 and '65*, Vol. 6, p. 1.
4. Ibid., p. 2; Longstreet was wintering in Tennessee, having been detached from the Army of Northern Virginia the previous September when he fought with the Army of Tennessee under General Bragg at Chickamauga and then in the Knoxville campaign in November.
5. Walker, *History of the Second Army Corps*, p. 394; O.R. 33, pp. 502, 506–507, 515–516, 1148, 142–143; Walker, *History of the Second Army Corps*, p. 396. Later this decision by Warren would come to haunt him, for he was viewed as timid and unwilling to carry out orders.
6. Second Army Corps circular, March 9, 1864, in D. H. Baird CW Coll. No. 11, Box 1, Shelf A12, Geneva [New York] Historical Society. One individual pleased to see the change in command was Brigadier General Alexander Hays, an old friend of Grant's. "The science of war has been played out and we want a man, who, under the guidance of common sense, will give us hard knocks, for we can beat them at that if we cannot at strategy"; George Fleming (ed.), *The Life and Letters of Alexander Hays* (Pittsburgh: Gilbert Adams Hays, 1919), p. 477.
7. Nevins and Thomas *The Diary of George Templeton Strong*, Vol. 3, p. 405. Strong spares no words to condemn Gurowski ("Count Goggle-owski"), claiming he had "no original thoughts" and a "temper and taste" that is "vile." Eventually Gurowski would offend Secretary of State Seward, who then dismissed him from the minor post he held.
8. Ibid., p. 411.
9. Letter from Henry Bellows to Mary Craig Wadsworth, March 9, 1865, WFP.
10. O.R., Series 2, Vol. 6, pp. 852–853, Clothing Issued to Federal Prisoners of War at Richmond By A Committee of Officers, November 10, 1863–January 18, 1864; ibid., 8, p. 343, Testimony of Lt. Col. James M. Sanderson to the Joint Select Committee Appointed to Investigate the Conditions and Treatment of Prisoners of War; letter from Sanderson and Major William Russell, Jr., December 13, 1863, to Fitzhugh & Jenkins, private collection.
11. *Livingston Republican*, March 10, 1864.
12. Special Orders No. 118 from the Adjutant General's Office, O.R. 51, Part 1, p. 1151; telegram from James S. Wadsworth to Colonel Kingsbury, March 20, 1864, National Archives Microfilm Publication M504, Roll 322, Adjutant General's Office, Record Group 94, National Archives; Special Orders No. 76, March 25, 1864, O.R. 51, Part 1, p. 1153. General Wadsworth had also requested the return of Major Clinton Meneely and Captain Timothy Ellsworth, but there is no record that they joined him; Adjutant Generals Orders, Vol. 41, item 30, March 23, 1864, National Archives. His staff included Major Edward E. Baird, Assistant Adjutant General; Lieutenant Colonel George B. Osborn, 56th Pennsylvania, Acting Assistant Adjutant General; plus aides-de-camp F. H. Cowdry, 95th New York, and G. W. Gill, 14th Brooklyn, along with his son, Captain Craig Wadsworth, as Acting Aide-de-Camp, March 25, 1864, Circular No. 20, War Department Adjutant General's Office, U.S. Army Continental Command, Record Group 393, Part 2, Entries 3685, 3691, National Archives; General Orders No. 21 from James S. Wadsworth, March 25, 1864, Generals' Papers and Books, Adjutant General's Office, Record Group 94, National Archives.
13. O.R. 33, pp. 737–738; circular, March 23, 1864, Adjutant General's Office, Vol. 41, Entry 269, p. 1422, National Archives; Walker, *History of the Second Corps*, p. 398.
14. William H. Powell, *The Fifth Army Corps (Army of the Potomac): A Record of Operations During the Civil War in the United States of America, 1861–1865* (Dayton, Ohio: Morningside, 1984), pp. 591, 592.

15. O.R., 33, p. 738; Humphreys, *The Virginia Campaign of '64 and '65*, p. 3; Smith, *History of the 76th New York Regiment Volunteers*, p. 281; Welcher, *The Union Army, 1861–1865*, Vol. 1, p. 310.

16. Smith, *History of the 76th New York Regiment Volunteers*, pp. 280, 281; Warner, *Generals in Blue*, p. 533.

17. Circular from James S. Wadsworth to brigade commanders, March 28, 1864, U.S. Army Continental Command, Record Group 393, Part 2, Entries 3685, 3691; Smith, *History of the 76th New York Regiment Volunteers*, p. 282.

18. Schaff, *The Battle of the Wilderness*, p. 47; Theodore Lyman (George R. Agassiz, ed.), *With Grant and Meade in the Wilderness to Appomattox* (Lincoln: University of Nebraska Press, 1994), p. 81 (reprint).

19. General Orders No. 20, April 4, 1864; circulars from James S. Wadsworth to brigade commanders, April 4, 7, 8, 1864, U.S. Army Continental Command, Record Group 393, Part 2, Entries 3685, 3691, and Record Group. There is nothing to confirm that Craig became an aide to his father. His military service papers simply read "in the field."

20. Telegram from James S. Wadsworth, March 7, 1864, Generals' Books and Papers, National Archives Microfilm Publication M504, Roll 322, Adjutant General's Office, Record Group 94, National Archives; telegrams from Craig W. Wadsworth to James S. Wadsworth, April 5, 1864, and from James S. Wadsworth to Mary Craig Wadsworth, April 7, 1864, Generals' Books and Papers, National Archives Microfilm Publication M504, Roll 322, Adjutant General's Office, Record Group 94, National Archives. It may be revealing that the general's note was written on the reverse of a circular from Major General George McClellan, January 1, 1861; letter from James S. Wadsworth to Mary Craig Wadsworth, April 1, 1864, WFP.

21. Pearson, *James S. Wadsworth of Geneseo*, pp. 246–247. Charles and Jessie were married September 29, 1864, at the Burden country residence, "Woodside"; typed copy of the *Livingston Democrat*, November 15, 1899, courtesy of Charles Van Ry. Charles Frederick, who died November 13, 1899, was survived by his wife and their only child, Mary Wadsworth Chandler. Jessie, who died April 18, 1917, is buried next to her husband in the Wadsworth family plot at Temple Hill Cemetery, Geneseo.

22. Dawes, *Service With the Sixth Wisconsin Volunteers*, p. 242.

23. Ibid., pp. 245, 246.

24. Circulars from James S. Wadsworth to brigade commanders, April 16, 20, 1864, U.S. Army Continental Command, Record Group 393, Part 2, Entries 3685, 3691; Thomas Chamberlin, *History of the One Hundred and Fiftieth Regiment Pennsylvania Volunteers (Second Regiment, Bucktail Brigade)* (Philadelphia: J. B. Lippincott, 1895), p. 183.

25. Circulars from James S. Wadsworth to brigade commanders, April 16, 20, 22, 26, 1864, U.S. Army Continental Command, Record Group 393, Part 2, Entries 3685, 3691.

26. Ambrose, *Band of Brothers*, p. 20, quoting J. Glenn Gray, *The Warriors: Reflections on Men in Battle* (New York: Harper & Row, 1959), pp. 43, 45, 46.

27. Smith, *History of the Seventy-Sixth Regiment New York Volunteers*, p. 282.

28. Schaff, *The Battle of the Wilderness*, pp. 42, 43; Ulysses S. Grant, *Personal Memoirs of U.S. Grant*, Vol. 2 (New York: Charles L. Webster & Co., 1886), p. 216. Warren's biographer recognized that "Warren had made a few enemies [because] impetuous, always intolerant of incapacity, passionately addressed to the welfare of the troops, he was like to repeat in public what he had written his brother in strict confidence"; Emerson Gifford Taylor, *Gouverneur Kemble Warren, the Life and Letters of an American Soldier, 1820–1882* (Boston: Houghton Mifflin, 1932), pp. 149, 167, quoting from Grant's *Memoirs*.

29. Warner, *Generals in Blue*, pp. 191, 407, 408, 99.

30. Circular from James S. Wadsworth to brigade commanders, May 2, 1864, U.S. Army Continental Command, Record Group 393, Part 2, Entries 3685, 3691, National Archives.

31. O.R. 33, pp. 1284–1285, 1278, 1279, 1303, 1307, 1308; Wayne Mahood, *The Plymouth Pilgrims* (Hightstown, N.J.: Longstreet House, 1989), pp. 165–188; Weymouth T. Jordan, Jr., and Gerald W. Thomas, "Massacre at Plymouth: April 20, 1864," *The North Carolina Historical Review*, Vol. 72, No. 2 (April 1995), pp. 125–193.

32. Dawes, *Service With the Sixth Wisconsin Volunteers*, pp. 240, 242.

33. Letter from Eugene Holton, March 13, 1864, Holton Letters, Interlaken [New York] Historical Society.

34. Letter from Capt. Morris Brown, Jr., to Major Ira Smith Brown, May 1, 1864, Brown Scrapbook, Archives, Hamilton College, Clinton, New York.

35. Humphreys, *The Virginia Campaign of '64 and '65*, p. 2; reports of Major General Richard Ewell, Lieutenant General James Longstreet, and Brigadier General Joseph Kershaw, O.R. 36, Part 1, pp. 1070, 1054, 1061.
36. Humphreys, *The Virginia Campaign of '64 and '65*, p. 6.
37. Ibid., pp. 9, 10, 3, 12. The total for the Army of the Potomac, including the Provost Guard, Engineers, Reserve Artillery, and Cavalry Corps, was 99,438 men; O.R. 33, p. 1036. Burnside's IX Corps added another 19,331 soldiers.
38. Humphreys, *The Virginia Campaign of '64 and '65*, p. 18 and Appendix D, p. 421.
39. Dawes, *Service With the Sixth Wisconsin Volunteers*, p. 249. Dawes added that Wadsworth's leniency paid off, for the two "never left the skirmish line until both were shot and severely wounded" and were subsequently pardoned by Lincoln upon Dawes's plea later.
40. Letter from James S. Wadsworth to N. James, May 3, 1864, WFP; letter from James S. Wadsworth to his wife, Mary Craig Wadsworth, May 3, 1864. Seven years later, on July 16, 1871, Mary Craig scribbled "My dear husbands [*sic*] last letter to me."
41. Nolan, *The Iron Brigade*, p. 273.

CHAPTER 21

1. Nevins, *A Diary of Battle*, p. 347; circular from General Wadsworth, May 3, 1864, U.S. Army Continental Command, Record Group 393, Part 2, Entries 3685, 3691, National Archives.
2. Ibid.
3. Nevins, *A Diary of Battle*, p. 347.
4. Schaff, *The Battle of the Wilderness*, p. 75.
5. Nevins, *A Diary of Battle*, p. 347; instructions from Major General Gouverneur K. Warren to division commanders, O.R. 36, Part 2, pp. 358–359.
6. Humphreys, *The Virginia Campaign of '64 and '65*, Appendix D.
7. Nevins, *A Diary of Battle*, p. 348.
8. Letter from James Samuel Wadsworth to daughter Cornelia, May 9, 1863, WFP.
9. Curtis, *History of the 24th Michigan*, p. 229; Nevins, *A Diary of Battle*, p. 348; William W. Swan, "Battle of the Wilderness," in *Papers of the Military History Society of Massachusetts* (Wilmington, N.C.: Broadfoot Publishing Co., 1989), Vol. 4, p. 119 (hereafter *PMHSM*); Captain Nelson Penfield of the 125th New York, O.R. 36, Part 1, p. 403.
10. Porter Farley, "Porter Farley's Reminiscences of the 140th Regiment New York Volunteers," in *Rochester in the Civil War* (Rochester, N.Y.: Rochester Historical Society, 1944), Vol. 22, p. 237.
11. "On Historic Sites," *Southern Historical Society Papers*, Vol. 36, p. 203, taken from the *Richmond (Virginia) Dispatch*, July 23, 1899.
12. General Grant's report, O.R. 36, Part 1, p. 18.
13. Schaff, *The Battle of the Wilderness*, pp. 57–58.
14. Ibid., pp. 90, 96–97. The times of arrival, dispatching of pickets, and location are from General Warren's report; O.R. 36, Part 2, p. 378.
15. Schaff, *The Battle of the Wilderness*, p. 98; General Warren's report, O.R. 36, Part 2, pp. 378, 379; circular from General Wadsworth, May 4, 1864, U.S. Army Continental Command, Record Group 393, Part 2, Entries 3685, 3691, National Archives.
16. McHenry Howard, "Note on the Opening of the Wilderness Campaign of 1864," *Massachusetts Historical Society Papers,* p. 95.
17. Humphreys, *The Virginia Campaign in '64 and '65*, p. 22; John B. Jones, *A Rebel War Clerk's Diary at the Confederate States Capital* (New York: Time-Life Books, 1982), p. 198 (reprint).
18. Nevins, *A Diary of Battle*, p. 349; dispatches from V Corps Assistant Adjutant General Frederick T. Locke, O.R. 36, Part 2, pp. 416, 420.
19. Paul Fussell, *Wartime: Understanding and Behavior in the Second World War* (New York: Oxford University Press, 1989), p. 282.
20. Report of General Meade, O.R. 36, Part 2, p. 403; Schaff, *The Battle of the Wilderness*, p. 129.

21. Ibid., pp. 132, 133, 151. Schaff, p. 138, recalled that the order to General Griffin to advance was not given by General Meade until 11:30 A.M.

22. Dispatches from A. A. G. Locke, O.R. 36, Part 2, pp. 416, 417; Nevins, *A Diary of Battle*, p. 350. Swan, "Battle of the Wilderness," p. 130, recalled that Wadsworth's division was mostly in an open field to the right of Chewning's farm with his left on Wilderness Run.

23. Dispatch from General Wadsworth to General Griffin, O.R. 36, Part 2, p. 420; Dawes, *Service With the Sixth Wisconsin Volunteers*, p. 259.

24. Bruce Catton, *A Stillness at Appomattox* (New York: Fairfax Press, 1984), p. 500 (reprint); Dawes, *Service With the Sixth Wisconsin Volunteers*, p. 259; dispatch from A. A. G. Locke, O.R. 36, Part 2, p. 420.

25. Gordon C. Rhea, *The Battle of the Wilderness, May 5–6, 1864* (Baton Rouge: Louisiana University Press, 1994).

26. Swan, "Battle of the Wilderness," p. 131; Dawes, *Service With the Sixth Wisconsin Volunteers*, p. 260.

27. General Cutler's Report, O.R. 36, Part 1, p. 610; Dawes, *Service With the Sixth Wisconsin Volunteers*, pp. 259–261.

28. Dunn, *Iron Men, Iron Will*, p. 243; Robert Monteith, "Battle of the Wilderness, and Death of General Wadsworth," *War Papers Read Before the Commandery of the State of Wisconsin, Military Order of the Loyal Legion of the United States*, Vol. 1 (Milwaukee: Burdick, Armitage & Allen, 1891), p. 411; Thomas L. Livermore, "Grant's Campaign Against Lee," in *PMHSM*, Vol. 4, p. 422.

29. Rhea, *The Battle of the Wilderness*, p. 161.

30. Smith, *History of the Seventy-Sixth Regiment New York Volunteers*, pp. 284–288; Powell, *The Fifth Army Corps*, p. 612; General Humphreys to General Hancock, O.R. 36, Part 2, p. 409.

31. Scott, *Into the Wilderness*, p. 60.

32. Swan, "Battle of the Wilderness," p. 131.

33. Edward Steere, *The Wilderness Campaign* (Harrisburg, Penn.: Stackpole, 1960), pp. 155–156.

34. Dispatches between Generals Warren and Crawford, O.R. 36, Part 2, pp. 418, 419; Rhea, *The Battle of the Wilderness*, pp. 172, 173.

35. Otis, *The Second Wisconsin Infantry*, p. 98; Lieutenant Colonel George Harney's and Major Merit C. Welsh's reports, O.R. 36, Part 1, pp. 633, 617.

36. Schaff, *The Battle of the Wilderness*, pp. 157, 159; Dawes, *Service With the Sixth Wisconsin Volunteers*, p. 261.

37. Reliance for this description is placed on Rhea, *The Battle of the Wilderness*, pp. 175–184.

38. General Hancock's report, O.R. 36, Part 1, pp. 318, 319, 350, 320.

39. Schaff, *The Battle of the Wilderness*, pp. 188, 189; Swan, "Battle of the Wilderness," p. 143.

40. Humphreys, *The Virginia Campaign of '64 and '65*, p. 34; handwritten notes without regular pagination by "Miss Graham" for the National Park Service, recorded sometime before March 1939, copy of Memorandum from Acting Supervisor of Historic Sites, Francis S. Ronalds, National Park Service, March 13, 1939, courtesy of Benedict R. Maryniak. Smith, *History of the Seventy-Sixth Regiment New York Volunteers*, p. 290, recalled that General Rice's brigade was positioned a quarter mile from and facing the Plank Road sometime later. Whether this was the same location is uncertain.

41. Aide-de-Camp Emmor B. Cope to General Warren, O.R. 36, Part 2, p. 421; Schaff, *The Battle of the Wilderness*, p. 198; Assistant Adjutant General Frank H. Cowdrey's report, O.R. 36, Part 1, pp. 615; and General Cutler's report, O.R. 36, Part 1, p. 611.

42. Captain Richard Price, "Into the Breach," *Military Police* (Spring 1987), pp. 18–19; Cowdrey's report, O.R. 36, Part 1, p. 615.

43. Catton, *A Stillness at Appomattox*, p. 508; Rhea, *The Battle of the Wilderness*, p. 240; Isaac Hall, *History of the Ninety-Seventh Regiment New York Volunteers ("Conkling Rifles") in the War for the Union* (Utica, N.Y.: L. C. Childs & Son, 1890), p. 179.

44. Humphreys, *The Virginia Campaign of '64 and '65*, p. 33; Price, "Into the Breach," p. 19.

45. Hall, *History of the Ninety-Seventh Regiment New York Volunteers*, p. 179; "Miss Graham's Notes" on the Union positions night of May 5, 1864; Dawes, *Service With the Sixth Wisconsin Volunteers*, p. 261; General Meade's dispatch to General Grant, O.R. 36, Part 2, p. 404; Humphreys, *The Virginia Campaign of '64 and '65*, p. 37.

46. Orders from General Meade to General Hancock, O.R. 36, Part 2, p. 412. Horace Porter, *Campaigning With Grant* (New York: Century Co., 1907), p. 54, recalled that two of Burnside's divisions would be placed between Wadsworth's division and Griffin's or Robinson's.

47. Exchange of dispatches between General Meade and General Grant, O.R. 36, Part 2, pp. 404, 405; Schaff, *The Battle of the Wilderness*, pp. 189, 190.

48. Dispatch from General Warren to General Wadsworth, O.R. 36, Part 2, p. 458; Monteith, "Battle of the Wilderness," p. 413.

CHAPTER 22

1. Letter of 126th New York Volunteers Captain Morris Brown, Jr., May 20, 1864, Hamilton College Archives, courtesy of curator, Frank K. Lorenz. The date, some two weeks after the battle, reflects the on-going campaign, including Spotsylvania and Cold Harbor, during which there was virtually no rest for officers or men.

2. Schaff, *The Battle of the Wilderness*, pp. 239.

3. General Hancock's report, O.R. 36, Part 1, pp. 320–321.

4. Ibid., p. 321. Gibbon commanded the II Corps' left wing forces, his own (excluding Brigadier General Alexander Webb's brigade in reserve), General Barlow's division, and the artillery.

5. Schaff, *The Battle of the Wilderness*, p. 239; the distance General Wadsworth's troops advanced before and during the attack is in dispute. Historian Edward Steere's typed, 1936 notes for the National Park Service, which led to his authoritative, but dry, account, *The Wilderness Campaign*, offer a particularly critical analysis. Steere's notes, pp. 10–19, relying heavily on the reports of Captain Emmor Cope and Frank Cowdrey in O.R. 36, Part 2, p. 42, and O.R. 36, Part 1, p. 615, are courtesy of Benedict R. Maryniak.

6. Rhea, *The Battle of the Wilderness*, pp. 276–279.

7. Reports of Generals Getty and Wheaton, O.R. 36, Part 1, pp. 677, 682.

8. Hazard Stevens, "The Sixth Corps in the Wilderness," in *PMHSM*, Vol. 4, p. 199; Walker, *History of the Second Army Corps*, Vol. 4, pp. 421, 422.

9. Lyman, *With Grant and Meade*, p. 94; Schaff, *The Battle of the Wilderness*, p. 241. Hancock's own, postbattle report is more subdued, though he claimed that Hill's lines were broken "after a desperate contest, in which our troops conducted themselves in the most intrepid manner"; O.R. 36, Part 1, p. 321.

10. Schaff, *The Battle of the Wilderness*, p. 245. The report on the "masked" guns is from General Getty, O.R. 36, Part 1, p. 677.

11. Walker, *History of the Second Army Corps*, p. 422.

12. Ibid.

13. Hall, *History of the Ninety-Seventh New York Regiment*, p. 180.

14. General Cutler's report, O.R. 36, Part 1, p. 611; Scott, *Into the Wilderness*, pp. 115–116; Swan, "Battle of the Wilderness," p. 154.

15. General Henry Hunt's report, O.R. 36, Part 1, p. 287. General Warren estimated the number at 2,400; O.R. 36, Part 1, p. 540.

16. General Hancock's report, O.R. 36, Part 1, p. 322. The strength of General Longstreet's Corps was considered to be "A liberal estimate"; Longstreet, *From Manassas to Appomattox*, p. 553; Jeffrey D. Stocker (ed.), *From Huntsville to Appomattox: R. T. Coles's History of the 4th Regiment, Alabama Volunteer Infantry, C.S.A., Army of Northern Virginia* (Knoxville: University of Tennessee Press, 1996), p. 160.

17. This section relies heavily on Rhea, *The Battle of the Wilderness*, pp. 302–308; and Donald C. Pfanz, a staff member at the Fredericksburg and Spotsylvania National Military Park, who pointed out Wadsworth's realignment and consequences. Also Colonel Richard Coulter's report, O.R. 36, Part 1, p. 596.

18. Rhea, *The Battle of the Wilderness*, p. 306; Captain Cope's report to General Warren, O.R. 36, Part 2, p. 458. The 4th Alabama's historian claimed the Federals fell "back slowly and doggedly firing as they retired," Stocker, *From Huntsville to Appomattox*, p. 161.

19. Major Platt's report to General Humphreys, O.R. 36, Part 2, p. 451; General Cutler's report to Colonel Locke, O.R. 36, Part 2, p. 506; Rhea, *The Battle of the Wilderness*, p. 306; Schaff, *The Battle of the Wilderness*, p. 236.

20. Chamberlin, *History of the One Hundred and Fiftieth Regiment Pennsylvania Volunteers*, pp. 187; Account of Sergeant Frey, ibid., pp. 215, 216; Captain Cope's report to General Warren, O.R. 36, Part 2, p. 458; Stocker, *From Huntsville to Appomattox*, p. 161.

21. General Meade's orders to General Hancock were received at approximately 8:00 A.M.; O.R. 36, Part 2, p. 441. At this time Meade was under the impression that Wadsworth was commanding 5,000 men, as was Hancock; O.R. 36, Part 1, p. 321. This impression was corrected at 8:40 A.M. by Meade's aide, Colonel Theodore Lyman; O.R. 36, Part 2, p. 442; report of Captain Frank H. Cowdrey, 4th Division A.A.G., O.R. 36, Part 1, p. 615.

22. General John Rawlins dispatch to Major General Burnside, O.R. 36, Part 2, p. 461.

23. William F. Perry, "Reminiscences of the Campaign of 1864 in Virginia," in *Southern Historical Society Papers* (New York: Kraus Reprint, 1977), Vol. 7, p. 59; Monteith, "Battle of the Wilderness," p. 414.

24. Unidentified, undated account, which appears to have been part of the New York State Agricultural Society memorial to General Wadsworth, which, in turn, relied on Major Craig Wadsworth's recall, WFP.

25. Schaff, *The Battle of the Wilderness*, p. 83; letter from Mary Craig Wadsworth to James W. Wadsworth, May 6, 1864, WFP.

26. Report of Lieutenant Colonel Charles Merrill, 17th Maine, O.R. 51, Part 1, p. 234; letter from General Humphreys to Mary Craig Wadsworth ("Dear Cousin"), September 3, 1864, WFP. Note that the letter was written after General Wadsworth's death.

27. Kress, *Memoirs*, p. 31; letter from John Lothrop Motley to Mary Craig Wadsworth, June 26, 1864, WFP.

28. Colonel C. H. Banes in a footnote to Webb, "Through the Wilderness," p. 160.

29. Pearson, *James S. Wadsworth of Geneseo*, p. 283, citing "Colonel [Oliver] Edwards's Recollections, MS." Italics added.

30. John E. Laughton, "The Sharpshooters of Mahone's Brigade," in *Southern Historical Society Papers*, Vol. 22, p. 101; Longstreet, *From Manassas to Appomattox*, pp. 562, 563.

31. Colonel J. William Hofmann's report, O.R. 36, Part 1, p. 624; Monteith, "The Battle of the Wilderness," p. 414, which recalled that General Wadsworth's "last words to me were: 'I will throw these two regiments on their flank,' meaning the 56th Pennsylvania and 76th New York, 'and you hurry forward the 1st Brigade.'"

32. General Grant's dispatch to General Burnside, O.R. 36, Part 2, p. 461; Perry, "Reminiscences of the Campaign of 1864," p. 57.

33. General Webb's report, O.R. 36, Part 1, p. 437; Perry, "Reminiscences of the Campaign of 1864," p. 54.

34. Stocker, *From Huntsville to Appomattox*, p. 162; John Anderson, *The Fifty-Seventh Regiment of Massachusetts Volunteers in the War of the Rebellion* (Boston: E. B. Stillings, 1896), p. 41; letter from Dr. Frances A. Bock, September 18, 1996, describing Karpeles, an ancestor of Dr. Bock's husband.

35. Anderson, *The Fifty-Seventh Regiment of Massachusetts Volunteers*, p. 40; Benedict R. Maryniak, address at the Genesee Country Museum, Mumford, New York, July 21, 1996.

36. Anderson, *The Fifty-Seventh Regiment of Massachusetts Volunteers*, pp. 41, 38.

37. Ibid., p. 41.

38. Webb, "Through the Wilderness," pp. 159–160; O.R. 36, Part 1, pp. 437, 438.

39. Rhea, *The Battle of the Wilderness*, p. 364; Webb, "Through the Wilderness," p. 160; O.R. 36, Part 1, pp. 437, 438; Stocker, *From Huntsville to Appomattox*, p. 162.

40. Charles A. Stevens, *Berdan's United States Sharpshooters in the Army of the Potomac, 1861–1865* (Dayton, Ohio: Morningside, 1984), p. 404.

41. Dawes, *Service With the Sixth Wisconsin Volunteers*, p. 262; Rhea, *The Battle of the Wilderness*, p. 364. Compare Clifford Dowdey, *Lee's Last Campaign* (New York: Bonanza Books, 1960), p. 158 (reprint), who claimed that "Wadsworth evidently broke under the strain." Wadsworth's impetuousness is a better explanation.

42. Swan, "Battle of the Wilderness," p. 151; Edward Steere's typewritten 1936 notes, Vol. 3, p. 19, prepared for the National Park Service, which indicates Wadsworth was hit near what is now referred to as "Hill–Ewell Drive," courtesy of Benedict R. Maryniak; Schaff, *The Battle of the Wilderness*, p. 271; Pearson, *James S. Wadsworth of Geneseo*, pp. 283–284; George A. Bruce, *The Twentieth Regiment of Massachusetts Volunteer Infantry* (Cambridge: Harvard University Press, 1906), p. 353.

43. Schaaf, *The Battle of the Wilderness*, p. 271. Captain Robert Monteith is also credited with being the aide who was at Wadsworth's side and reported his mortal wounding.

44. "Chapters of Unwritten History by P. D. Bowles," in Stocker, *From Huntsville to Appomattox*, p. 219.

45. "William T. Lowry," South Carolina Division UDC, *Recollections and Reminiscences, 1861–1865* (n.p., 1994), Vol. 5, p. 497; note from Robert K. Krick to the author.

46. "Rogers' Bloody 6th Regiment: How General Wadsworth Died at the Battle of the Wilderness," *The Norfolk (Virginia) Ledger Dispatch*, April 16, 1935, courtesy of Benedict R. Maryniak. The account is by Arthur Jakeman's daughter, who recalled her father telling the story "one evening at the supper table."

47. Account of Private David Holt in Thomas D. Cockrell and Michael B. Ballard (eds.), *A Mississippi Rebel in the Army of Northern Virginia: The Civil War Memoirs of Private David Holt* (Baton Rouge: Louisiana University Press, 1995), p. 241. In its entirety, Holt is quoted as having written:

   "As we rushed forward, the line came up to General Wadsworth. He was between [Private J. F.] Williams and [Private John] Chapman [of Company K] and they were both covering him with loaded muskets and shouting to him to surrender. Instead of surrendering he was foolish enough to draw a silver-plated, pearl-handled Colt pistol of .38 calibre. While it might be an effective weapon elsewhere, it was a pretty toy in such a place as that. I could have knocked it out of his hand with the muzzle of my gun, but Williams put his gun to the right side of the general and fired. The general threw his arms around a small oak and sank to the earth."

   The 16th Mississippi was part of Anderson's Division, just behind Perrin's Brigade, so it would, indeed, have been possible for General Wadsworth and the 20th Massachusetts to run into the 16th Mississippi, especially if the general had advanced so far as to become isolated, which most accounts claim. However, it sounds apocryphal.

48. Adams, "In the Wilderness," p. 389.

49. Chamberlin, *History of the One Hundred and Fiftieth Regiment Pennsylvania Volunteers*, p. 211; Samuel P. Bates, *History of the Pennsylvania Volunteers, 1861–1865* (Harrisburg, Penn.: 1869–1871), Vol. 4, p. 615.

50. *New York Times*, May 19, 1864.

51. G. Moxley Sorrel, "The Battle of the Wilderness," in *Southern Historical Society Papers*, Vol. 20, p. 73. George S. Bernard, ibid., pp. 77–78, claims General Wadsworth's body was in a small, cleared space near the road "over which the left of the brigade [Mahone's] charged." This is also confirmed by the account of Joseph E. Rockwell, late sergeant of Company. A, 12th Virginia, who recalled that Dr. James W. Claiborne, Mahone's brigade surgeon, attended General Wadsworth; John R. Turner, "The Battle of the Wilderness," in *Southern Historical Society Papers*, Vol. 20, p. 84; account by Colonel V. D. Groner in Turner, "The Battle of the Wilderness," pp. 92–93.

CHAPTER 23

1. General Cutler's reports to Colonel Frederick T. Locke, O.R. 36, Part 2, pp. 458, 459. The aide probably was Lieutenant Earl Rogers, though Captain Robert Monteith is sometimes credited with being the bearer of the bad news; Nevins, *A Diary of Battle*, p. 353; *New York Tribune*, May 9, 1864. Later Grant issued a more characteristic and blunt statement deploring the loss of Wadsworth and Brigadier General Alexander Hays; O.R. 36, Part 1, p. 2.

2. Major Platt's dispatch to Major General Andrew Humphreys, likely referring to Lieutenant Rogers, O.R. 36, Part 2, p. 452; letter from Major General Gouverneur K. Warren to Major General Henry Heth, "The Heth Papers," in *Southern Historical Society Papers*, Vol. 46, p. 233; General Humphreys's dispatch to General Warren, O.R. 36, Part 2, pp. 453–454; General James Wilson's dispatch to General Philip Sheridan, May 8, 1864, O.R. 36, Part 2, p. 554; Captain Charles E. Cady to Captain King, May 15, 1864, O.R. 36, Part 2, p. 792, which reported that the prisoner may have been "a colored man by the name of Solomon Baker," who claimed to be the servant of a 1st South Carolina officer, and stated that a "major-general of our [Union] army" died in a Confederate hospital. The interrogator judged from Baker's account "that it must have been General Wadsworth, . . . [whose] body was taken to Orange Court-House."

3. General Butler to Secretary of War Edwin M. Stanton, May 8, 1864, O.R. 36, Part 2, p. 561; telegram to Montgomery Ritchie, WFP; General Lee to James Seddon, O.R. 36, Part 1, p. 1028; General Mahone's report, O.R. 36, Part 1, p. 1091.

4. Webb, "Through the Wilderness," p. 160.

5. One who persisted in trying to obtain details for at least another dozen years was Major General Gouverneur K. Warren, "The Heth Papers," in *Southern Historical Society Papers*, Vol. 46, p. 233. Warren asked General Harry Heth for "a full account" of who repulsed Wadsworth's attack. How far from Parker's Store

did he fall? Did the advance proceed beyond the spot where he fell? "What became of the papers on his person?" Whether he ever received answers is unknown. Haskell's recollections are in Gilbert E. Govan and James W. Livingood (eds.), *The Haskell Memoirs: John Cheves Haskell* (New York: G. P. Putnam, 1960), p. 64.

6. The *Enquirer* report appears in "Miss Graham's Notes," National Park Service, courtesy of Benedict R. Maryniak. The account of finding Wadsworth and the note appears in A. R. H. Ranson, "Reminiscences of the Civil War by a Confederate Staff: The Battle of the Wilderness and the Race for Richmond," *The Sewanee Review Quarterly*, Vol. 22, No. 4 (October 1914), pp. 446–447. Little is known about Ambrose Robert Hite Ranson, who was an adjutant to Lieutenant Colonel John Pegram, attained the rank of major, and signed the parole at Appomattox, O.R. 2, pp. 73, 268; ibid., Series II, Vol. 3, p. 43; ibid., Vol. 4, p. 448; Frederick M. Colston, "Recollections of the Last Months of the Army of Northern Virginia," in *Southern Historical Society Papers*, Vol. 38, p. 14; "Paroles of the Army of Northern Virginia at Appomattox," in *Southern Historical Society Papers*, Vol. 15, p. 3.

7. Letter from John Lee Carroll to Mary Craig Wadsworth, November 29, 1865, WFP. According to Carroll, Colonel Charles Marshall found Carroll's narrative "reliable in every respect." In the almost illegible handwriting that characterizes the Wadsworths by birth or marriage, Mary Craig ["MCWW"] wrote that she believed the letter was, in fact, "written by Mr. Marshall at the request of Mr. Carroll for me." From a cryptic, illegible note on the letter by Mrs. Wadsworth, it appears that the letter was a response to a letter she had written to General Lee himself. Pearson, *James S. Wadsworth of Geneseo*, p. 285, also attributes the letter to Marshall.

8. Letter from John Lee Carroll to Mary Craig Wadsworth, November 29, 1865, WFP; E. Porter Alexander (Gary Gallagher, ed.), *Fighting for the Confederacy* (Chapel Hill: University of North Carolina Press, 1989), p. 364; *New York Daily Tribune*, May 14, 1864, quoting Captain Philip Schuyler of General Patrick's staff and adding its own conclusion.

9. Letter from John Lee Carroll to Mary Craig Wadsworth, November 29, 1865, WFP; Sergeant Joseph Rockwell's account in Turner, "The Battle of the Wilderness," p. 84, the accuracy of which, particularly as to the surgeon and even more the time, cannot be verified, and it is at odds with Captain Adams's account in Adams, "In the Wilderness," pp. 373–399.

10. Ranson, "Reminiscences of the Civil War by a Confederate Staff," "Paroles of the Army of Northern Virginia at Appomattox," in *Southern Historical Society Papers*, Vol. 15, p. 3.

11. Unidentified account in "Miss Graham's Notes," dated May 10, 1864, National Park Service, courtesy of Benedict R. Maryniak (italics added); Adams, "In the Wilderness," pp. 373–399. Adams writes that his was "not an amusing tale, neither does it pretend to be the history of the battle. It is a narrative of actual occurrences and is substantiated by notes made on the spot" (p. 373). The description of General Wadsworth is found on pp. 389–394, with Adams's prefatory remarks on pp. 389–392.

12. Ibid., pp. 389, 390; but compare the observation by Dr. Arie B. Snell, a surgeon with Company K, 16th Mississippi, who recalled that the General was unable to speak, "but his eyes followed the [Confederate] doctor around with seeming consciousness as though [Wadsworth] had some[thing] to communicate," Cockrell and Ballard, *A Mississippi Rebel in the Army of Northern Virginia*, p. 251; Adams, "In the Wilderness," p. 389. An explanation for the variance in the accounts *could be* the time difference, namely, when Adams first began to observe Wadsworth.

13. Adams, "In the Wilderness," pp. 390–391.

14. Ibid., p. 391.

15. Ibid., p. 396; Carroll letter to Mary Craig Wadsworth, November 29, 1865, WFP.

16. D. Augustus Dickert, *History of Kershaw's Brigade* (Wilmington, N.C.: Broadfoot Publishing Co., 1990), p. 252 (reprint).

17. Carroll letter to Mary Craig Wadsworth, November 29, 1865, WFP; letter from Patrick McCracken to Mary Craig Wadsworth, May 9, 1864, WFP, which appears to have been included in a memorial by the New York State Agricultural Society, no date, pp. 52, 53. Compare a quite inaccurate account that has Wadsworth's body "carried into the Union lines" on Sunday, May 8, letter from John Midgeley, Company B, 57th Massachusetts Volunteers, *Civil War News*, June 1994, p. 47.

18. Letter from Patrick McCracken to Mary Craig Wadsworth, May 9, 1864, WFP; *Livingston Republican*, May 26, 1864, reprinting a report from the *Washington National Republican*, May 13, 1864. The *New York Times*, May 17, 1864, claimed that the coffin was "made by breaking up a door." The Wadsworths

would repay their benefactor, who would live only another eight years, with "the means [unspecified] for the McCrackens to improve their fortune by opening a farm implements store in Fredericksburg"; "Civil War Compassion Lives On," unidentified, undated newspaper release by the Associated Press, courtesy of Benedict R. Maryniak. Captain Adams, following the romantic custom of the time, cut a lock of the dead general's hair and presented it to Mary Craig Wadsworth in Boston; Adams, "In the Wilderness," p. 397. A Wadsworth descendant still has the lock in the general's field desk.

19. Letter from Major General George G. Meade to Mary Craig Wadsworth, July 2, 1864, WFP. However, it appears that by July 1, 1864, Captain Craig Wadsworth had left the army; Military Service Record, National Archives, and General Alfred T. A. Torbert's July 4 report on the campaign from the Rapidan to the James, O.R. 36, Part 1, p. 810; Francis B. Heitman, *Historical Register and Dictionary of the United States Army* (Washington, D.C.: Government Printing Office, 1903), p. 991, lists Craig as resigning July 16, 1864.

20. Telegram from Secretary Stanton to General Meade, O.R. 36, Part 2, p. 654; account of Dr. Benjamin T. Kneeland in a July 1, 1899, letter to James H. Bowen and reprinted in Bowen, *History of the First New York Dragoons* (Nunda, N.Y.: Author, 1900), pp. 306, 307.

21. Dispatch from Meade to General Lee, O.R. 36, Part 2, p. 783; handwritten dispatch from Lee to Meade, May 16, 1864, WFP; handwritten note from Major General Wade Hampton to Meade, May 16, 1864, WFP; Meade response to Lee's letter, O.R. 36, Part 2, p. 841; Bernard Baruch, *Baruch: My Own Story* (New York: Henry Holt & Co., 1957), Vol. 1, p. 7. Baruch asserted that this "instance of battlefield chivalry made so deep an impression that [Baruch's father] recalled it on his deathbed in 1921." This reference is courtesy of Stuart Symington, Jr., General Wadsworth's great-great-grandson, who brought this anecdote to my attention. Dr. Kneeland's account of recovering the body is in Bowen, *History of the First New York Dragoons*, p. 307.

22. G. Moxley Sorrel, *Recollections of a Confederate Staff Officer* (New York: Smithmark, 1994), p. 243; Cockrell and Ballard, *A Mississippi Rebel in the Army of Northern Virginia*, p. 251; Westwood A. Todd, *Reminiscences of the War Between the States From April, 1861 to June, 1865* (manuscript, Southern Historical Collection, University of North Carolina at Chapel Hill), Vol. 2, pp. 193–194; Todd claims that Bolote later returned the watch and received from Mary Craig Wadsworth "a very handsome acknowledgement of it," Fausold, *James W. Wadsworth Jr.*, p. 9; Cockrell and Ballard, *A Mississippi Rebel in the Army of Northern Virginia*, p. 251; Sorrel, *Recollections of a Confederate Staff Officer*, p. 247.

23. Dispatch from Major General George Meade to Lieutenant General U.S. Grant, July 1, 1864, O.R. 40, Part 2, p. 561; letter from General Robert E. Lee to General U.S. Grant, July 10, 1864, O.R. 40, Part 3, p. 125; letter from Major General George G. Meade to Mary Craig Wadsworth, July 2, 1864, WFP.

24. Letter from General Robert E. Lee to Mary Craig Wadsworth, May 19, 1865, WFP.

25. Beale, *Diary of Gideon Welles*, Vol. 2, p. 27.

26. Dennett, *Lincoln and the Civil War*, p. 182, entry for May 14, 1864. Edward Baker, killed at Ball's Bluff, was a long-time personal friend of Lincoln and the namesake of one of Lincoln's sons.

27. Walker, *History of the Second Corps*, p. 429; O.R. 36, Part 1, p. 133; Thomas Livermore, *Numbers and Losses in the Civil War in America, 1861–65* (Dayton, Ohio: Morningside, 1986), pp. 110, 111.

28. Announcement of funeral arrangements in an unidentified source dated May 10, 1864, WFP.

29. *Livingston Republican*, May 12 and May 19, 1864; *Geneva (New York) Gazette*, May 13, 1864.

30. General Orders 197, War Department, Adjutant General's Office, May 12, 1864; *South Dakota Department of History Collections*, Vol. 8 (1916), p. 263, and Vol. 31 (1962), p. 81; "Fort Wadsworth," ibid., Vol. 31 (1962), p. 81, courtesy of Dean North, Aberdeen, South Dakota, who brought this to my attention and supplied helpful background as well. The post, actually built about sixty miles east of Aberdeen, was renamed Fort Sisseton on August 29, 1876, and decommissioned June 1, 1889, when it was discovered that another fort bore the New Yorker's name; letter from Dean North to the author, May 28, 1996. The recommendation of the Staten Island fort is in the handwritten letter from Major General John A. Dix to Secretary of War Edwin Stanton, May 19, 1864, WFP. Major General Irvin McDowell approved the idea in a note to Dix the same day; Morgan Dix (comp.), *Memoirs of John A. Dix* (New York: Harper & Brothers, 1883), Vol. 2, p. 367.

31. *Livingston Republican*, May 19, 1864.

32. *Geneva (New York) Gazette*, May 13, 1864; *New York Times*, May 17, 1864. The coffin was reported to be "a good coffin, painted black"; ibid., May 19, 1864.

33. Ibid.; *Livingston Republican*, May 26, 1864; *New York Times*, May 19, 1864. The paper also inconsistently reported that it was a plain, rough coffin that bore Wadsworth's remains from Washington to New York City, May 20, 1864.

34. Ibid., May 20, 1864. It reported that the congressional committee consisted of soon-to-be governor Reuben E. Fenton (Chatauqua district), Moses F. Odell (New York City), Daniel Morris (Geneseo's district), John Ganson (Erie district), Augustus Frank (Wyoming County district), and Charles H. Winfield, while the *Livingston Republican*, May 26, 1864, substitutes Ambrose Clark (Monroe County district) for Winfield. The latter seems more correct.

35. *New York Tribune*, May 21, 1864, WFP. Virtually nothing further is known about this composition, published by Wm. A. Pond & Co., 547 Broadway, New York City, according to SUNY–Geneseo professor and musicologist James Kimball.

36. A copy of the proceedings, undated and untitled, was sent to Mrs. Wadsworth, in WFP.

37. For an interesting, brief account of the 21st New York, see Benedict R. Maryniak, "Flag Story: 21st New York Volunteers," *Civil War Courier*, July 1996, pp. 58–60.

38. *Livingston Republican*, May 26, 1864. While this particular article does not list Cornelia Wadsworth Ritchie's husband, Captain Montgomery Ritchie, as accompanying the general's body, it would seem quite likely that he did so. A special train was run from Avon at 11:35 for "parties" who wanted to attend the service, ibid.

39. Ibid. The service is variously listed as being held at 1:00 and 1:30. Also there are different versions about why the brothers Wadsworth changed churches and gave land to the Episcopal church, the most humorous of which is told by Alden Hatch, *The Wadsworths of the Genesee* (New York: Coward-McCann, Inc., 1959), p. 58. The quote from the Rev. Irish is from John D. Wells, "The Aristocracy of Citizenship," *New Yorker*, June 1931, p. 18, wherein Wells takes some liberties with the facts.

40. *Livingston Republican*, May 26, 1864. See Appendix A for the procession program. The cemetery is described by Doty, *History of Livingston County*, p. 528.

CHAPTER 24

1. Record Group 94, Commission Branch, Adjutant General's Office, File H, W 17 CB 1863, National Archives. Heitman, *Historical Register and Dictionary of the United States Army*, Vol. 1, p. 992, claims the brevet was awarded May 6, 1864, two days before General Wadsworth's death; Boatner, *Civil War Dictionary*, p. 84. Craig also was honored by successive brevets to Colonel of Volunteers, March 13, 1865. Heitman, *Historical Register and Dictionary of the United States Army*, Vol. 1, p. 991.

2. *Richmond (Virginia) Examiner*, June 10, 1864.

3. Letter from Major General George G. Meade to Mary Craig Wadsworth, July 2, 1864, WFP; Hancock's quote is in Pearson, *James S. Wadsworth of Geneseo*, p. 289, which cites the *New York Evening Post*, September 29, 1864. Pearson claims the letter was written June 25, 1864, but it has not been found in the WFP.

4. Letter from Major General Gouverneur K. Warren to Mary Craig Wadsworth, December 31, 1864, WFP. Warren reiterated this in a postwar letter to Confederate General Henry Heth, "The Heth Papers," *Southern Historical Society Papers*, Vol. 46 (1923), p. 233, wherein he wrote "that I felt his [Wadsworth's] loss more keenly than anyone I know of." On January 16, 1865, Warren also offered the general's youngest son, 18-year-old James W., an appointment to Warren's personal staff as captain and aide-de-camp, if Mary Craig approved; letter from Warren to Mary Craig Wadsworth, January 16, 1865; letter from Major General Andrew A. Humphreys to Mary Craig Wadsworth, September 3, 1864.

5. Tevis and Marquis, *The History of the Fighting Fourteenth*, p. 116; Gates, *The "Ulster Guards,"* p. 223; Dawes, *Service With the Sixth Wisconsin Volunteers*, p. 153; Thompson, *From Philippi to Appomattox*, pp. 182, 183; "Letter of Lt. J. Volnay Pierce," Ladd and Ladd, *The Bachelder Papers*, Vol. 2, p. 913.

6. Letter from John Lothrop Motley to Mary Craig Wadsworth, June 26, 1864, WFP.

7. Chittenden, *A Report of the Debates and Proceedings in the Secret Sessions of the Conference Convention*, p. 8; "Union Defense Committee of the Citizens of New York," May 21, 1864, WFP.

8. "General James S. Wadsworth: *Non nobis sed pro patria*," *United States Service Magazine*, Vol. 4 (July 1865), pp. 18, 20, 21, 27.

9. Hoppin and Cozzens, *Proceedings of the Century Association,* pp. 15, 17, 23, 28. The *Dictionary of American Biography,* Vol. 1, p. 201 (1928 edition), lists Allen (1800–1890) as a Buffalo stock breeder and farm writer, who claimed as intimates Daniel Webster, General Winfield Scott, and Henry Clay, and who, as president of the New York State Agricultural Society, knew Wadsworth.

10. Memorials by the Buffalo Historical Society and the Union Bank of Rochester, June 18, 1864, and July 14, 1864, WFP; *Livingston Republican,* May 26, 1864.

11. Letter from L. H. York to Mary Craig Wadsworth, August 1, 1871, WFP. G.A.R. Post #417 in Nunda, southwest of Geneseo, was named for "Capt. Craig Wharton Wadsworth" after his untimely death in 1872 at age 31, just prior to the birth of his second son and namesake; *New York Department, Union Veterans of the Civil War, 125th Anniversary Salute* (no author, date, or pagination), listing G.A.R. Posts in 1886.

12. Undated clipping in the Wadsworth file, Livingston County Historical Society. This was provided for by an $8,000 bequest "to erect a Library and Museum on the Atheneum Library lot," if he did not do so in his life time; Wills, Book 7, p. 1, Livingston County Surrogate Court.

13. John Rorbach, "History of the Geneseo State Normal School, Address Delivered at the Occasion of the Twenty-fifth Anniversary of its Establishment," in *Proceedings of Twenty-first Annual Meeting of the Livingston County Historical Society* (Nunda, N.Y.: C. K. Sanders, 1897), pp. 43, 38, 45; Grantor Deeds, Books 85, 86, pp. 15, 7, Livingston County Court House, Geneseo, New York. The price of the land, $300 per acre, clearly indicates the value at the time. This included part of the "Home Farm" and part of the village pasture adjoining the farm on the east

14. "In Memoriam: James Samuel Wadsworth, 1807–1864," in *Major-General James Samuel Wadsworth at Gettysburg and Other Fields* (Albany: J. B. Lyon Co., 1916), pp. 12, 14, 15, 22; *New York State Monuments Commission, the New York Auxiliary Monument on the Battlefield of Gettysburg* (Albany: J. B. Lyon Co., 1926), p. 3. The first monument, erected in 1888, honored General Warren. The second, in 1902, recognized Major General Henry Slocum, and the third, memorializing Brigadier General George S. Greene, was erected in 1907. The fifth monument honored Brigadier General Alexander Webb. These were paid for by private donations. In addition to paying for Wadsworth's monument, public moneys also funded the monuments to Major General Abner Doubleday (1917) and to Major General John Robinson, ex-lieutenant governor of New York, while in 1925 the Auxiliary dedicated a monument to forty-one other New York State commanders, including Generals Sickles, Butterfield, Merritt, and Ward, and Colonel George L. Willard; ibid., p. 15.

15. Ibid., p. 22; New York State Monuments Commission, "In Memoriam: James Samuel Wadsworth, 1807–1864," pp. 64–65, 66–67.

16. Donald C. Pfanz, "History Through the Eyes of Stone, a Survey of the Monuments in Fredericksburg National Military Park" (Fredericksburg, Va.: Fredericksburg and Spotsylvania National Military Park, 1983), pp. 160, 161, courtesy of Civil War historian and reenactor Benedict R. Maryniak. For a more detailed account, see Appendix D.

17. Letter from James R. Zinck to James Wadsworth Symington, September 26, 1985, National Park Service, and letter from James W. Symington to Benedict R. Maryniak, April 26, 1989, courtesy of Maryniak. The story of the uniting of the Wadsworth and McCracken families is told in "Genealogy, New York to Virginia," *New York Times,* May 24, 1986, and reprinted, with slight additions, in the *Rochester (New York) Democrat & Chronicle,* May 24, 1986.

EPILOGUE

1. Doster, *Lincoln and Episodes of the Civil War,* p. 50.
2. Ibid., p. 54.

APPENDICES

1. According to Alexander Webb, *The Peninsula,* Vol. 2, Part 1 of *Campaigns of the Civil War* (New York: Thomas Yoseloff, 1963, reprint), p. 197, the above units were in General Wadsworth's command.
2. *Livingston Republican,* May 26, 1864.

3. Letter from Robert K. Krick, Chief Historian, Fredericksburg and Spotsylvania National Military Park, to James Wadsworth Symington, August 23, 1985, National Park Service, courtesy of Civil War historian and reenactor Benedict R. Maryniak. On the other hand, there is a recent publication claiming that around 1917 the glasses were burned in the house of William T. Lowry, Company D, 8th South Carolina Regiment, Kershaw's Brigade; South Carolina Division UDC, "William T. Lowry," in *Recollections and Reminiscences, 1861–1865* (Author, 1994), Vol. 5, p. 497. The story even goes so far as to claim that Lowry fired the shot that killed General Wadsworth. I'm indebted to Robert K. Krick for locating this.

4. Letters from James W. Symington to Park Historian Robert K. Krick, August 27, 1985, and from Krick to Symington, September 22, 1986, National Park Service, courtesy of Benedict R. Maryniak. In reference to the errors in the article, Krick caustically noted that "Newspapers in 1864 weren't much more reliable than they are today." The article was included with the letter from Krick to Symington, August 26, 1986. Unfortunately, Krick wrote, "There was no Major McMullen of line," general or personal staff, "anywhere in the Confederacy."

5. Ibid., March 15, 1988.

6. Memorandum from Greg Mertz to Robert K. Krick, March 27, 1988, National Park Service, courtesy of Benedict R. Maryniak.

7. Pfanz, "History Through the Eyes of Stone," pp. 160, 161.

8. Ibid., p. 162.

9. Letter from Robert K. Krick to James Wadsworth Symington, August 23, 1985, National Park Service, courtesy of Benedict R. Maryniak. It was clear from the Park Superintendent's memorandum asking for approval to do the cleaning that he was aware of Mr. Symington, whom he labeled as "an influential Washington lawyer who is very active in the National Trust"; memorandum from Fredericksburg and Spotsylvania NMP to the Superintendent of the George Washington Memorial Parkway, October 9, 1985.

10. Ibid., September 11, 1985. The cleaning process, involving a project coordinator, the work of an experienced bronze preserver, 200 pounds of ground walnut hulls, an air compressor, and restoring the patina on the tablet, is interesting in itself; letter from James R. Zinck to James Wadsworth Symington, December 16, 1985, National Park Service, courtesy of Benedict R. Maryniak.

BIBLIOGRAPHY

MANUSCRIPTS AND CORRESPONDENCE

Campbell, R. Letter to S. F. Hazt, October 27, 1862. Private Collection.

Frothingham, Richard. "Documents showing the untrustworthiness of Gen. Wadsworth's Testimony to the President and before the War Committee," Massachusetts Historical Society, Boston, item 21.2.1d 108, 1862, p. 3.

Sears, Stephen. Correspondence, January 4, 1996.

Steere, Edward. Typewritten notes on the battle of the Wilderness, 1936, Part 3, p. 19 (prepared for the National Park Service).

Symington, James W. Correspondence, August 8, 1994; December 15, 1995; April 24, 1998; June 12, 1998.

Symington, Stuart, Jr. Correspondence, August 15, 1994; December 5, 1995; January 22, 1998; March 3, 1998; April 30, 1998; June 12, 1998.

Wadsworth Family Papers, Washington, D.C.: Library of Congress.

Wadsworth, James S. Letterbook 61. Geneseo, N.Y.: Wadsworth Collection, Milne Library, SUNY–Geneseo. Shelf 27.

Wadsworth, James S. Letterbook 1. Geneseo, N.Y.: Wadsworth Collection, Milne Library, SUNY–Geneseo. Shelf 27.

PRIMARY SOURCES

"The Abolition Candidate for Governor," *Ontario Repository & Messenger*, October 22, 1862; November 5, 1862.

Adams, Z. Boylston. "In the Wilderness," in *Civil War Papers, Commandery of the State of Massachusetts, M.O.L.L.U.S.*, pp. 373–399. Boston: The Commandery, 1900.

Alexander, E. Porter (Gary Gallagher, ed.). *Fighting for the Confederacy*. Chapel Hill: University of North Carolina Press, 1989.

Allen, Thomas S. "The Second Wisconsin at the First Battle of Bull Run," in George H. Otis (Alan D. Gaff, ed.), *The Second Wisconsin Infantry*. Dayton, Ohio: Morningside, 1984.

Basler, Roy P. (ed.) *The Collected Works of Abraham Lincoln*. 8 vols. New Brunswick, N.J.: Rutgers University Press, 1953.

Beale, Howard K. (ed.) *Diary of Gideon Welles*. New York: W. W. Norton, 1960.

Beauregard, G. T. "The First Battle of Bull Run," in Robert Underwood Johnson and Clarence Clough Buel, eds., *Battles and Leaders of the Civil War*, Vol. 1, pp. 196–227. New York: Century Co., 1884, 1887, 1888.

Bingham, Robert W. (ed.) *Reports of Joseph Ellicott*. 2 vols. Buffalo: Buffalo Historical Society, 1937.

Breck, George. "George Breck's Civil War Letters from the 'Reynolds Battery,'" in Blake McKelvey, ed., *Rochester in the Civil War*, Vol. 22, pp. 91–149. Rochester, N.Y.: Rochester Historical Society, 1944.

Buffalo Evening News, November 9, 1963.

Byrne, Frank L., and Andrew T. Weaver (eds.). *Haskell of Gettysburg: His Life and Civil War Papers*, 2nd ed. Kent, Ohio: Kent State University Press, 1989.

Chase, Salmon P. (David Donald, ed.) *Inside Lincoln's Cabinet: The Civil War Diaries of Salmon P. Chase.* New York: Longmans, Green & Co., 1954.

Chittenden, L. E. *A Report of the Debates and Proceedings in the Secret Sessions of the Conference Convention.* New York: D. Appleton & Co., 1864.

Christian Observer of London. "To the Editor of the Christian Observer: State of the Seneca Indians," *Christian Observer of London*, Vol. 20 (July 1821), pp. 423–427.

Cockrell, Thomas D., and Michael B. Ballard (eds.). *A Mississippi Rebel in the Army of Northern Virginia: The Civil War Memoirs of Private David Holt.* Baton Rouge: Louisiana University Press, 1995.

Cole, R. T. (Jeffrey D. Stocker, ed.) *From Huntsville to Appomattox: R. T. Cole's History of the 4th Regiment, 4th Alabama Volunteer Infantry, C.S.A., Army of Northern Virginia.* Knoxville: University of Tennessee Press, 1996.

Colston, Frederick M. "Recollections of the Last Months of the Army of Northern Virginia," in *Southern Historical Society Papers*, Vol. 38, p. 14. New York: Kraus Reprint, 1977.

Cook, John D. S. "Personal Reminiscences of Gettysburg," in James L. McLean, Jr., and Judy W. McLean, comp., *Gettysburg Sources*, Vol. 2, pp. 122–144. Baltimore: Butternut and Blue, 1987.

Croffut, W. A. (ed.) *Fifty Years in Camp and Field: Diary of Major-General Ethan Allen Hitchcock.* New York: G. P. Putnam's Sons, 1909.

Curtis, William George (ed.). *Correspondence of John Lothrop Motley.* 2 vols. New York: Harper & Bros., 1889.

Dana, Charles A. *Recollections of the Civil War.* Lincoln: University of Nebraska Press, 1996. Reprint.

Dawes, Rufus R. *Service With the Sixth Wisconsin Volunteers.* Dayton, Ohio: Morningside, 1991. Reprint.

Dennett, Tyler (ed.). *Lincoln and the Civil War in the Diaries and Letters of John Hay.* Westport, Conn.: Negro Universities Press, 1972. Reprint.

Dictionary of American Biography. Vols. 1, 6, 12. New York: Charles Scribner's Sons, 1928.

Dodge, Theodore. "The Battle of Chancellorsville," in *Southern Historical Society Papers*, Vol. 14, pp. 276–292. New York: Kraus Reprint, 1977.

Donald, David (ed.). *Inside Lincoln's Cabinet: The Civil War Diaries of Salmon P. Chase.* New York: Longmans, Green & Co., 1954.

Doster, William E. *Lincoln and Episodes of the Civil War.* New York: G. P. Putnam's Sons, 1915.

Dyer, Frederick. *A Compendium of the War of the Rebellion.* Dayton, Ohio: Morningside, 1978. Reprint.

Early, Jubal. "Letter to Henry Heth," in *Southern Historical Society Papers*, Vol. 44, pp. 236–239. New York: Kraus Reprint, 1977.

Farley, Porter. "Porter Farley's Reminiscences of the 140th Regiment New York Volunteers," in *Rochester in the Civil War*, Vol. 22, pp. 199–252. Rochester, N.Y.: Rochester Historical Society.

Fisher, Sidney George (Nicholas B. Wainwright, ed.). *A Philadelphia Perspective: The Diary of Sidney George Fisher Covering the Years 1834–1871.* Philadelphia: Historical Society of Philadelphia, 1967.

"Fort Wadsworth," *South Dakota Department of History Collections*, Vol. 31 (1962), p. 81.

Fox, William F. *Regimental Losses in the American Civil War, 1861–1865.* Albany: Albany Printing Co., 1889.

Friedlaender, Marc, et al. (eds.) *Diary of Charles Francis Adams.* 7 vols. Cambridge: Belknap Press, 1986.

Fry, James B. "McDowell's Advance to Bull Run," in Robert Underwood Johnson and Clarence Clough Buel, eds., *Battles and Leaders of the Civil War*, Vol. 1, pp. 167–193. New York: Century Co., 1884, 1887, 1888.

Geneva (New York) Gazette, May 13, 1864.

Gibbon, John. *Personal Recollections of the Civil War.* Dayton, Ohio: Morningside, 1978. Reprint.

Govan, Gilbert E., and James W. Livingood (eds.). *The Haskell Memoirs: John Cheves Haskell.* New York: Putnam, 1960. Reprint.

Grant, Ulysses S. *Personal Memoirs of U.S. Grant*, Vol. 2. New York: Charles L. Webster & Co., 1886.

Greene, George S. "The Breastworks at Culp's Hill," in Robert Underwood Johnson and Clarence Clough Buel, eds., *Battles and Leaders of the Civil War*, Vol. 3, p. 317. New York: Century Co., 1884, 1887, 1888.

Gurowski, (Count) Adam. *Diary from March 4, 1861 to November 12, 1862.* Boston: Lee and Shepard, 1862.

Halstead, Elminel P. Unpublished account of "The First day of July, 1863." Wadsworth Family Papers.

————. "Incidents of the First Day at Gettysburg," in Robert Underwood Johnson and Clarence Clough Buel, eds., *Battles and Leaders of the Civil War*, Vol. 3, pp. 284–285. New York: Century Co., 1884, 1887, 1888.

Hancock, Winfield Scott. "Letter to Mrs. James S. Wadsworth," *New York Evening Post*, September 25, 1864.

Harris, Loyd G. (Lance J. Herdegen and William J. K. Beaudot, eds.) "With the Iron Brigade Guard at Gettysburg," *Gettysburg Magazine*, No. 1 (July 1, 1989), pp. 29–34.

Heitman, Francis B. *Historical Register and Dictionary of the United States Army.* 2 vols. Washington, D.C.: Government Printing Office, 1903.

Heth, Henry. "The Heth Papers," in *Southern Historical Society Papers*, Vol. 46, pp. 232–240. New York: Kraus Reprint, 1977.

Holland, Frederick W. "A Freshman Hazing," in William Bentinck-Smith, ed., *The Harvard Book*, pp. 162–163. Cambridge: Harvard University Press, 1982.

Hotchkiss, Jed (Major). *Virginia, Confederate Military History*, Vol. 3. Atlanta: Confederate Publishing Co., 1899.

Howard, McHenry. "Notes on the Opening of the Wilderness Campaign," in *Papers of the Military History Society of Massachusetts*, Vol. 4, pp. 81–116. Wilmington, N.C.: Broadfoot Publishing Co., 1989. Reprint.

Howard, Oliver O. "From General Howard's Official Report," in Robert Underwood Johnson and Clarence Clough Buel, eds., *Battles and Leaders of the Civil War*, Vol. 3, pp. 287–289. New York: Century Co., 1884, 1887, 1888.

———. *Autobiography of Oliver Otis Howard*. 2 vols. New York: Baker & Taylor, 1907.

Hubbard, J. N. "Wadsworth's Division at Culp's Hill," in Richard Sauers, ed., *Fighting Them Over: How the Veterans Remembered Gettysburg in the Pages of The National Tribune*, pp. 359–360. Baltimore: Butternut and Blue, 1998.

Humphreys, Andrew A. *The Virginia Campaign of '64 and '65*. New York: Thomas Yoseloff, 1963. Reprint.

Hunt, Henry J. "The First Day at Gettysburg," in Robert Underwood Johnson and Clarence Clough Buel, eds., *Battles and Leaders of the Civil War*, Vol. 3, pp. 255–284. New York: Century Co., 1884, 1887, 1888.

———. "The Second Day at Gettysburg," in Robert Underwood Johnson and Clarence Clough Buel, eds., *Battles and Leaders of the Civil War*, Vol. 3, pp. 290–313. New York: Century Co., 1884, 1887, 1888.

Imboden, John D. "Stonewall Jackson in the Shenandoah," in Robert Underwood Johnson and Clarence Clough Buel, eds., *Battles and Leaders of the Civil War*, Vol. 2, pp. 282–298. New York: Century Co., 1884, 1887, 1888.

Irwin, Richard B. "Washington Under Banks," in Robert Underwood Johnson and Clarence Clough Buel, eds., *Battles and Leaders of the Civil War*, Vol. 2, pp. 541–544. New York: Century Co., 1884, 1887, 1888.

Jones, Jesse H. "The Breastworks at Culp's Hill," in Robert Underwood Johnson and Clarence Clough Buel, eds., *Battles and Leaders of the Civil War*, Vol. 3, p. 316. New York: Century Co., 1884, 1887, 1888.

Kellogg, John A. "Letter of Colonel John A. Kellogg," in David Ladd and Audrey J. Ladd, *The Bachelder Papers*, Vol. 1, pp. 205–206. Dayton, Ohio: Morningside.

Killip, W. W. "Reminiscences," in *Thirty-fifth Annual Meeting of the Livingston County Historical Society, 1911*, pp. 10–11. Nunda, N.Y.: Sanders Printers, 1911.

Kress, John A. *Memoirs of Brigadier General John Alexander Kress*. Philadelphia: Author, 1925.

Laughton, John E. "The Sharpshooters of Mahone's Brigade," in *Southern Historical Society Papers*, Vol. 22, pp. 98–105. New York: Kraus Reprint, 1977.

Lee, Fitzhugh. "A Review of the First Two Days' Operations at Gettysburg and a Reply to General Longstreet by General Fitzhugh Lee," in *Southern Historical Society Papers*, Vol. 5, pp. 162–194. New York: Kraus Reprint, 1977.

Livermore, Thomas. *Numbers and Losses in the Civil War in America, 1861–65*. Dayton, Ohio: Morningside, 1986.

Livingston Register. "Announcement of Public Auction to Sell Indian Reservation Lands," November 6, 1827.

———. 1830–1840.

Livingston Republican. 1846–1847; January 21, 1864; May 12, 1864; May 26, 1864; June 30, 1864; January 4, 1972.

———. "The Home of the Wadsworths," November 29, 1864.

———. "E. R. Hammatt," August 28, 1884.

Longstreet, James. *From Manassas to Appomattox*. New York: Mallard Press, 1991. Reprint.

Lucid, Robert E. (ed.) *The Journal of Richard Henry Dana, Jr.*, Vol. 1. Cambridge: Belknap Press, 1968.

Lyman, Henry H. "Historical Sketch," in *New York State Monuments Commission, Final Report on the Battlefield of Gettysburg*, Vol. 3, pp. 997–1010. Albany: J. B. Lyon Co., 1900.

Lyman, Theodore. "Addenda to the Paper By Lt. Col. Swan on the Battle of the Wilderness," in *Papers of the Military History Society of Massachusetts*, Vol. 4, pp. 165–174. Wilmington, N.C.: Broadfoot Publishing Co., 1989. Reprint.

———. *With Grant and Meade in the Wilderness to Appomattox* (George R. Agassiz, ed.). Lincoln: University of Nebraska Press, 1994. Reprint.

Mahone, William. "Report of William Mahone," in *Southern Historical Society Papers*, Vol. 6, pp. 84–85. New York: Kraus Reprint, 1977.

McClellan, George B. *McClellan's Own Story*. New York: Charles E. Webster & Co., 1887.

Meade, George G. "A Letter From General Meade [to G. G. Benedict]," in Robert Underwood Johnson and Clarence Clough Buel, eds., *Battles and Leaders of the Civil War*, Vol. 3, pp. 413–414. New York: Century Co., 1884, 1887, 1888.

————. *The Battle of Gettysburg*. Ambler, Penn.: George Gordon Meade, 1924.

Meade, George G., and George G. Meade, Jr. *The Life and Letters of George Gordon Meade*. New York: Charles Scribner's Sons, 1913.

Monteith, Robert. "Battle of the Wilderness, and Death of General Wadsworth," in *War Papers Read Before the Commandery of the State of Wisconsin, Military Order of the Loyal Legion of the United States*, Vol. 1, pp. 410–415. Milwaukee: Burdick, Armitage & Allen, 1891.

Morgan, Charles H. "Report of Lt. Col. Charles H. Morgan," in David Ladd and Audrey J. Ladd, *The Bachelder Papers*, Vol. 3, pp. 1345–1369. Dayton, Ohio: Morningside, 1994.

Motley, John Lothrop (ed.). *The Correspondence of John Lothrop Motley*, Vol. 2, pp. 301, 302. New York: Society of English and French Literature, 1900.

Motte, Jacob Rhett. "A Southern Sport at Harvard," in William Bentinck-Smith, ed., *The Harvard Book*, pp. 188–190. Cambridge: Harvard University Press, 1982.

Nevins, Allan (ed.). *A Diary of Battle: The Personal Journals of Colonel Charles S. Wainright, 1861–1865*. Gettysburg, Penn.: Stan Clark Military Books, 1993. Reprint.

Nevins, Allan, and Milton H. Thomas (eds.). *The Diary of George Templeton Strong: The Civil War, 1860–1865*, Vol. 3. New York: Macmillan Co., 1952.

New-York Daily Tribune, October 24, 1862.

New York State. *Report of the Special Committee to Investigate the Indian Problem of the State of New York*. Albany, 1889. Assembly Document No. 51.

New York State Agricultural Society Transactions for 1858, Vol. 28, pp. 299–300. Albany: Van Benthuysen, 1859.

New York State Monuments Commission. *Final Report on the Battlefield of Gettysburg*. 3 vols. Albany: J. B. Lyon Co., 1900.

Official Records of the Union and Confederate Navies in the War of the Rebellion. 31 vols. Washington, D.C.: Government Printing Office, 1894–1927.

"On Historic Sites," in *Southern Historical Society Papers*, Vol. 36, pp. 197–209. New York: Kraus Reprint, 1977.

Ontario County Republican Times, October 22, 1862.

Otis, George H. (Alan D. Gaff, ed.) *The Second Wisconsin Infantry*. Dayton, Ohio: Morningside, 1984.

"Paroles of the Army of Northern Virginia at Appomattox," in *Southern Historical Society Papers*, Vol. 15, p. 3. New York: Kraus Reprint, 1977.

Perry, William F. "Reminiscences of the Campaign of 1864 in Virginia," in *Southern Historical Society Papers*, Vol. 7, pp. 49–64. New York: Kraus Reprint, 1977.

Porter, Horace. *Campaigning With Grant*. New York: Century Co., 1906.

Ranson, A. R. H. "Reminiscences of the Civil War by a Confederate Staff: The Battle of the Wilderness and the Race for Richmond," *The Sewanee Review Quarterly*, Vol. 22, No. 4 (October 1914), pp. 444–457.

Raymond, Henry W. (ed.) "Extracts From the Journal of Henry J. Raymond," *Scribner's Monthly*, Vol. 19, No. 3 (January 1880), pp. 419–424.

Report of the Joint Committee on the Conduct of the War, Part I. Washington, D.C.: Government Printing Office, 1865.

Report of the Joint Committee on the Conduct of the War, Part II. Washington, D.C.: Government Printing Office, 1863.

Rochester Democrat & Chronicle. "Act of Kindness in Bloody War Links 2 Families," *Rochester Democrat & Chronicle*, May 24, 1986.

"Roger's Bloody 6th Regiment: How General Wadsworth Died at the Battle of the Wilderness," *The Norfolk Ledger Dispatch*, April 16, 1935.

Schaff, Morris. *The Battle of the Wilderness*. Boston: Houghton Mifflin, 1910.

Sears, Stephen W. (ed.) *The Civil War Papers of George B. McClellan*. New York: Ticknor & Fields, 1989.

Shirreff, Patrick. "A Tour Through North America," in Roger Haydon, ed., *Upstate Travels: British Views of Nineteenth Century New York*, pp. 201–206. Syracuse, N.Y.: Syracuse University Press, 1982.

Sorrel, G. Moxley. "The Battle of the Wilderness," in *Southern Historical Society Papers*, Vol. 20, pp. 73–84. New York: Kraus Reprint, 1977.

"Speeches of William Curtis Noyes, Daniel Dickinson, and Lyman Tremaine at the Great Union War Ratification Meeting Held at the Cooper Institute, in the City of New York, October 8th, 1862, Also the Speech and Letter of Acceptance of General James S. Wadsworth." New York: *New York Tribune*, 1862.

Stevens, Hazard. "The Sixth Corps in the Wilderness," in *Papers of the Military History Society of Massachusetts*, Vol. 4, pp. 175–204. Wilmington, N.C.: Broadfoot Publishing Co., 1989. Reprint.

Swan, William W. "Battle of the Wilderness," in *Papers of the Military History Society of Massachusetts*, Vol. 4, pp. 117–164. Wilmington, N.C.: Broadfoot Publishing Co., 1989. Reprint.

Todd, Westwood A. *Reminiscences of the War Between the States From April, 1861 to June, 1865*. Manuscript, Southern Historical Collection, University of North Carolina at Chapel Hill.

Trimble, Isaac R. "Letter of Maj. Gen. Isaac R. Trimble [to John Bachelder]," in David L. Ladd and Audrey J. Ladd, *The Bachelder Papers*, Vol. 2, pp. 921–934. Dayton, Ohio: Morningside, 1995.

Turner, John R. "The Battle of the Wilderness," in *Southern Historical Society Papers*, Vol. 20, pp. 68–95. New York: Kraus Reprint, 1977.

U.S. Bureau of Indian Affairs. "Seneca Indians Who Will Be Affected By The Kinzua Dam Reservoir," Report #175. Washington, D.C.: Department of the Interior, 1963.

U.S. Bureau of the Census. *Historical Statistics of the United States*. Washington, D.C.: Department of Commerce, 1970.

Wadsworth, James J. *The Silver Spoon: An Autobiography*. Geneva, New York: W. F. Humphrey Press, 1980.

Wadsworth, James S. "Speech at Washington, September 26, 1862." Geneseo, N.Y.: Genesee Valley Collection, Milne Library, SUNY–Geneseo.

_____. Letter. *New York Times*, May 19, 1863.

Walker, Francis A. "Meade at Gettysburg," in Robert Underwood Johnson and Clarence Clough Buel, eds., *Battles and Leaders of the Civil War*, Vol. 3, pp. 406–412. New York: Century Co., 1884, 1887, 1888.

The War of the Rebellion: A Compilation of the Official Records of the Union and Confederate Armies. 128 vols. Washington, D.C.: Government Printing Office, 1880–1891.

Webb, Alexander S. "Through the Wilderness," in Robert Underwood Johnson and Clarence Clough Buel, eds., *Battles and Leaders of the Civil War*, Vol. 4, pp. 152–169. New York: Century Co., 1884, 1887, 1888.

Weed, Thurlow (Harriet A. Weed, ed.). *The Autobiography of Thurlow Weed*. 2 vols. Boston: Houghton Mifflin, 1884.

OTHER SOURCES

Alexander, DeAlva S. *A Political History of the State of New York*, Vol. 3, p. 43. Port Washington, N.Y.: Ira J. Friedman, 1969.

Ambrose, Stephen. *Halleck: Lincoln's Chief of Staff*. Baton Rouge: Louisiana State University Press, 1990.

_____. *Band of Brothers*. New York: Simon & Schuster, 1992.

Anderson, John. *The Fifty-Seventh Regiment of Massachusetts Volunteers in the War of the Rebellion*. Boston: E. B. Stillings, 1896.

Bailyn, Bernard. "Why Kirkland Failed," in Bernard Bailyn et al., eds., *Glimpses of the Harvard Past*. Cambridge: Harvard University Press, 1986.

Barber, John W., and Henry Howe. *Historical Sketches of the State of New York*. Port Washington, N.Y.: Kennikat Press, 1970. Reprint.

Bates, Samuel P. *History of the Pennsylvania Volunteers, 1861–1865*, Vol. 4, pp. 611–648. Harrisburg, Penn.: 1869–1871. 5 vols.

Benjamin, Marcus (ed.). *Washington During War Time*. Washington, D.C.: The National Tribune Co, 1902.

Bennett, Brian. *Sons of Old Monroe: A Regimental History of Patrick O'Rorke's 140th New York Volunteer Infantry*. Dayton, Ohio: Morningside, 1992.

Berlin, Ira, et al. (eds.) *The Wartime Genesis of Free Labor: The Upper South*, Series I, Vol. 2 of *Freedom: A Documentary History of Emancipation, 1861–1867*. Cambridge, UK: Cambridge University Press, 1993.

_____. *The Wartime Genesis of Free Labor: The Lower South*, Series I, Vol. 3 of *Freedom: A Documentary History of Emancipation, 1861–1867*. Cambridge, UK: Cambridge University Press, 1991.

Billings, Elden E. "Military Activities in Washington in 1861," in *Records of the Columbia Historical Society, 1960–1962*, pp. 123–133. Washington, D.C.: Columbia Historical Society, 1989.

Boatner, Mark M., III. *Civil War Dictionary*, revised edition. New York: David McKay Co., 1987.

Brooks, Van Wyck. *The Flowering of New England, 1815–1865*. New York: E. P. Dutton, 1936.

Brown, Francis. *Raymond of the Times*. Westport, Conn.: Greenwood Press, 1951.

Bruce, George A. *The Twentieth Regiment of Massachusetts Volunteer Infantry*. Cambridge: Harvard University Press, 1906.

Bulkley, John W. "The War Hospitals," in Marcus Benjamin, ed., *Washington in War Time*, pp. 138–153. Washington, D.C.: The National Tribune Co., 1902.

Burton, William L. *Melting Pot Soldiers*. Ames: Iowa State University Press, 1988.

Busey, John W., and David G. Martin. *Regimental Strengths and Losses at Gettysburg*. Hightstown, N.J.: Longstreet House, 1986.

Chamberlin, Thomas. *History of the One Hundred and Fiftieth Regiment Pennsylvania Volunteers (Second Regiment, Bucktail Brigade)*. Philadelphia: J. B. Lippincott, 1895, 1905.

Coddington, Edwin B. *The Gettysburg Campaign: A Study in Command*. New York: Charles Scribner's Sons, 1968.

Cooling, Benjamin F. "Defending Washington During the Civil War," in *Records of the Columbia Historical Society, 1971–1972*, pp. 314–337. Washington, D.C.: Columbia Historical Society, 1989.

Curtis, O. B. *History of the Twenty-Fourth Michigan of the Iron Brigade*. Detroit: Winn & Hammond, 1891.

Davis, William C. *Battle at Bull Run: A History of the First Major Campaign of the Civil War*. Garden City, N.Y.: Doubleday, 1977.

Dickert, D. Augustus. *History of Kershaw's Brigade*. Wilmington, N.C.: Broadfoot Publishing Co., 1990. Reprint.

Doty, Lockwood L. *History of Livingston County*. Geneseo, N.Y.: Edward A. Doty, 1876.

Dowdey, Clifford. *Lee's Last Campaign: The Story of Lee and His Men Against Grant, 1864*. Boston: Little, Brown and Co., 1960.

_____. *The Seven Days: The Emergence of Lee*. Lincoln: University of Nebraska Press, 1993. Reprint.

Dunn, Craig L. *Iron Men, Iron Will: The Nineteenth Indiana Regiment of the Iron Brigade*. Indianapolis: Guild Press of Indiana, 1995.

Eliot, Samuel A. *Memoir of Martin Brimmer*. Reprint from Massachusetts Historical Society (April 1896). Geneseo, N.Y.: Wadsworth Collection, Milne Library, SUNY–Geneseo.

Evans, Paul D. *The Holland Land Company*. Buffalo: Buffalo Historical Society, 1924.

Fausold, Martin L. *James W. Wadsworth, Jr.: The Gentleman from New York*. Syracuse, N.Y.: Syracuse University Press, 1975.

Faust, Patricia L. (ed.) *Historical Times Illustrated Encyclopedia of the Civil War*. New York: Harper Perennial, 1986.

Fishel, Edwin C. "Pinkerton and McClellan: Who Deceived Whom?" *Civil War History*, Vol. 34, No. 2 (June 1988), pp. 115–142.

_____. *The Secret War for the Union: The Untold Story of Military Intelligence in the Civil War*. New York: Houghton Mifflin, 1996.

Furgurson, Ernest B. *Chancellorsville 1863*. New York: Alfred A. Knopf, 1993.

Fussell, Paul. *Wartime: Understanding and Behavior in the Second World War*. New York: Oxford University Press, 1989.

Gaff, Alan. D. *On Many a Bloody Field: Four Years in the Iron Brigade*. Bloomington: Indiana University Press, 1996.

Gates, Theodore B. *The "Ulster Guards" (20th New York State Militia) and the War of the Rebellion*. New York: B. H. Tyrrel, 1879.

"General James S. Wadsworth," *United States Service Magazine*, Vol. 4 (July 1865), pp. 18–27.

Gorham, George C. *Life and Public Services of Edwin M. Stanton*. Boston: Houghton Mifflin, 1899.

Gunderson, Robert G. *Old Gentlemen's Convention: The Washington Peace Conference of 1861*. Madison: University of Wisconsin Press, 1961.

Gunther, Gerald. "Governmental Power and New York Indian Lands—A Reassessment of a Persistent Problem of Federal–State Relations," *Buffalo Law Review*, Vol. 8 (Fall 1958), pp. 101–122.

Hall, Isaac. *History of the Ninety-Seventh Regiment New York Volunteers ("Conkling Rifles") in the War for the Union*. Utica, N.Y.: L. C. Childs & Son, 1890.

Hartwig, D. Scott. "The Defense of McPherson's Ridge," *Gettysburg Magazine*, No. 1 (July 1, 1989), pp.15–24.

_____. "Guts and Good Leadership: The Action at the Railroad Cut, July 1, 1863," *Gettysburg Magazine*, No. 1 (July 1, 1989), pp. 5–14.

Hauptman, Laurence M. "The Historical Background to the Present-day Seneca Nation—Salamanca Lease Controversy," in Christopher Vecsey and William Starna, *Iroquois Land Claims*, pp. 101–122. Syracuse, N.Y.: Syracuse University Press, 1988.

Hawthorne, Frederick W. *Gettysburg: Stories of Men and Monuments as Told by Battlefield Guides*. Gettysburg, Penn.: Association of Licensed Battlefield Guides, 1988.

Haydon, Roger (ed.). *Upstate Travels: British Views of Nineteenth Century New York*. Syracuse, N.Y.: Syracuse University Press, 1982.

Hedrick, Ulysses Prentiss. *A History of Agriculture in New York State*, p. 254. New York: Hill and Wang, 1966. Reprint.

Herdegen, Lance J., and William J. K. Beaudot. *In the Bloody Railroad Cut at Gettysburg*. Dayton, Ohio: Morningside, 1990.

Hoppin, William J., and Frederic S. Cozzens. *Proceedings of the Century Association in Honor of the Memory of Brig.-Gen. James S. Wadsworth and Colonel Peter A. Porter; With the Eulogies Read by William J. Hoppin and Frederic S. Cozzens, December 3, 1884*. New York: D. Van Nostrand, 1865.

Hunt, Roger, and Jack R. Brown. *Brevet Brigadier Generals in Blue*. Gaithersburg, Md.: Olde Soldier Books, 1990.

Hyman, Harold M. "Lincoln and Equal Rights for Negroes: The Irrelevancy of the Wadsworth Letter," *Civil War History*, Vol. 12, No. 4 (1966), pp. 258–266.

Jackson, Kenneth (ed.). *The Encyclopedia of New York City*. New Haven: Yale University Press, 1995.

Johnson, Ludwell. "Lincoln and Equal Rights: The Authenticity of the Wadsworth Letter," *Journal of Southern History*, Vol. 32 (1966), pp. 83–87.

Jones, Mary Alice. *Wealth of a Nation To Be*. New York: Columbia University Press, 1980.

Keegan, John. *The Face of Battle*. New York: Penguin Books, 1976.

Kittredge, Josiah E. "Historical Sermon," in *The Centennial Celebration of the Geneseo Village Presbyterian Church, 1810–1910*, pp. 52–73. Geneseo, N.Y.: Geneseo Presbyterian Church, 1910.

Leech, Margaret. *Reveille in Washington*. New York: Harper & Brothers, 1941.

Lord, Francis. *They Fought for the Union*. New York: Bonanza Books, 1960.

Lossing, Benson J. *The Empire State*, 2 vols. Hartford, Conn.: American Publishing Co., 1888.

Lynch, Denis T. "Party Struggles, 1828–1850," in Alexander C. Flick, ed., *History of the State of New York*, Vol. 6, Chap. 3, pp. 63–85. 10 vols. Port Washington, N.Y.: Ira J. Friedman, 1962.

Martin, David G. *Gettysburg July 1*. Conshohocken, Penn.: Combined Books, 1995.

Maryniak, Benedict R. "Patroon, Soldier and Hero: Brigadier General James Samuel Wadsworth of Geneseo, New York," "The Famous Long Ago," *The Courier*, Vol. 4, Issue 6 (November/December 1989), pp. 23–25.

Mather, Frederick. "Historic Homes: The Wadsworth House at Geneseo," *Magazine of American History*, Vol. 14, No. 5 (1885), pp. 425–437.

May, Arthur J. *A History of the University of Rochester, 1850–1962*. Rochester, N.Y.: University of Rochester, 1977.

McCusker, John J. "How Much Is That in Real Money? A Historical Price Index for Use as a Deflator of Money Values in the Economy of the United States," *Proceedings of the American Antiquarian Society*, Vol. 101 (1992), pp. 297–373.

McLean, James L. *Cutler's Brigade at Gettysburg*, revised edition. Baltimore: Butternut and Blue, 1994.

McNall, Neil A. *The First Half Century of Wadsworth Tenancy*. Rochester, New York: University of Rochester, 1977.

Meigs, M. C. "The Relations of President Lincoln and Secretary Stanton to the Military Conduct of the Civil War," *American Historical Review*, Vol. 26 (1920–1921), pp. 285–303.

Military Historical Society of Massachusetts (comp.). *The Wilderness Campaign: May–June, 1864*. Boston, 1905.

Mitchell, Stewart. *Horatio Seymour of New York*. Cambridge: Harvard University Press, 1938.

Naparsteck, Martin. "The Morgan Affair," *Genesee Country*, Vol. 2, No. 1 (April/May 1994), pp. 46–51.

New York State Monuments Commission. "In Memoriam: James Samuel Wadsworth, 1807–1864," in *Major-General James S. Wadsworth at Gettysburg and Other Fields*. Albany: J. B. Lyon Co., 1916.

Nolan, Alan T. *The Iron Brigade: A Military History*. Berrien Springs, Mich.: Hardscrabble Books, 1983. Reprint.

————. "Three Flags at Gettysburg," *Gettysburg Magazine*, No. 1 (July 1, 1989), pp. 25–28.

O'Brien, Kevin E. "A Perfect Road of Musketry, Candy's Brigade in the Fight for Culp's Hill," *Gettysburg Magazine*, No. 9 (July 1, 1993), pp. 81–97.

Parish, David W. "Elizabeth Wadsworth: Lily of the Valley," *Genesee Country*, Vol. 1, No. 3 (August/ September 1993), pp. 29–31.

Parker, Arthur C. *The History of the Seneca Indians*. Port Washington, N.Y.: Ira S. Friedman, 1967. Reprint.

Pearson, Henry G. *James S. Wadsworth of Geneseo: Brevet Major General, U.S.V.* New York: Charles Scribner's Sons, 1913.

Pfanz, Donald C. "History Through the Eyes of Stone, a Survey of the Monuments in Fredericksburg National Military Park." Fredericksburg, Va.: Fredericksburg and Spotsylvania National Military Park, 1983.

Pfanz, Harry F. *Gettysburg—Culp's Hill and Cemetery Hill*. Chapel Hill: University of North Carolina Press, 1993.

Powell, William H. *The Fifth Army Corps (Army of the Potomac): A Record of Operations During the Civil War in the United States of America, 1861–1865*. Dayton, Ohio: Morningside, 1984. Reprint.

Price, Captain Richard. "Into the Breach," *Military Police* (Spring 1987), pp. 18–19.

Renwick, James. "Life of James Wadsworth," *Monthly Journal of Agriculture*, Vol. 2, No. 4 (October 1846), pp. 145–156.

Rhea, Gordon. *The Battle of the Wilderness, May 5–6, 1864*. Baton Rouge: Louisiana State University Press, 1994.

Rosenberger, Jesse Leonard. *Rochester, The Making of a University*. Rochester, N.Y.: University of Rochester, 1927.

Rowland, Thomas J. "'Heaven Save a Country Governed by Such Counsels!' The Safety of Washington and the Peninsula Campaign," *Civil War History*, Vol. 42, No.1 (1996), pp. 5–17.

Scott, Robert G. *Into the Wilderness with the Army of the Potomac*. Bloomington: Indiana University Press, 1985.

Shue, Richard S. *Morning at Willoughby Run*. Gettysburg, Penn.: Thomas Publications, 1995.

Sifakis, Stewart. *Who Was Who in the Civil War*. New York: Facts on File Publications, 1988.

Silsby, Robert. *The Holland Land Company in Western New York*, Vol. 8. Buffalo: Buffalo and Erie County Historical Society, 1961.

Smith, A. P. *History of the Seventy-Sixth Regiment New York Volunteers*. Gaithersburg, Md.: Ron R. Van Sickle Military Books, 1988. Reprint.

Smith, James H. *The History of Livingston County*. Syracuse, N.Y.: Mason Publ., 1881.

Sobel, Robert, and John Raimo. *Biographical Dictionary of the Governors of the United States*. 4 vols. Westport, Conn.: Greenwood Press, 1978.

South Carolina Division of the United Daughters of the Confederacy (UDC). "William T. Lowry," in *Recollections and Reminiscences, 1861–1865*, Vol. 5. Author, 1994.

Stahl, Joseph W. "A Cold Spell in Virginia," *Manuscripts*, Vol. 48, No. 1 (Winter 1996), pp. 47–49.

Starr, Louis M. *Bohemian Brigade: Civil War Newsmen in Action*. New York: Alfred A. Knopf, 1954.

Stocker, Jeffrey D. (ed.) *From Huntsville to Appomattox: R. T. Coles's History of the 4th Regiment, Alabama Volunteer Infantry, C.S.A., Army of Northern Virginia*. Knoxville: University of Tennessee Press, 1996.

Strong, Alice Wadsworth. *Hartford House, 1835–1985*. Geneseo, N.Y.: Private printing, 1985.

Swinton, William. *Campaigns of the Army of the Potomac*. New York: Charles Scribner's Sons, 1882.

Tap, Bruce. *Over Lincoln's Shoulder: The Committee on the Conduct of the War*. Lawrence: University of Kansas Press, 1998.

Taylor, Emerson Gifford. *Gouverneur Kemble Warren, the Life and Letters of an American Soldier, 1820–1882*. Boston: Houghton Mifflin, 1932.

Tevis, C. V., and D. R. Marquis. *The History of the Fighting Fourteenth*. New York: Brooklyn Eagle Press, 1911.

Thompson, Orville. *From Philippi to Appomattox: Narrative of the Service of the Seventh Indiana Infantry in the War for the Union*. Baltimore: Butternut & Blue, 1993. Reprint.

Trefousse, H. L. *Benjamin Franklin Wade: Radical Republican from Ohio*. New York: Twayne Publishers, 1963.

Turner, Orsamus. *History of the Pioneer Settlement of Phelps and Gorham's Purchase, and Morris' Reserve*. Geneseo, N.Y.: James Brunner, 1976. Reprint.

Vecsey, Christopher, and William A. Starna (eds.). *Iroquois Land Claims*. Syracuse, N.Y.: Syracuse University Press, 1988.

Wadsworth, Horace A. *Two Hundred Fifty Years of the Wadsworth Family in America*. Lawrence, Mass.: Eagle Stream Job Printing, 1883.

Warner, Ezra J. *Generals in Gray*. Baton Rouge: Louisiana State University Press, 1959.

_____. *Generals in Blue*. Baton Rouge: Louisiana State University Press, 1964.

Weigley, Russell F. *Quartermaster General of the Union Army*. New York: Columbia University Press, 1959.

Welcher, Frank J. *The Union Army, 1861–1865: Organization and Operations*, Vol. 1, *The Eastern Theater*. Bloomington: Indiana University Press, 1989.

Wharton, Anne H. *Genealogy of the Wharton Family of Philadelphia 1664–1880*. Philadelphia: Author, 1880.

Whyte, James. "Divided Loyalties in Washington During the Civil War," in *Records of the Columbia Historical Society, 1960–1962*, pp. 103–122. Washington, D.C.: Columbia Historical Society, 1989.

Williams, T. Harry. *Lincoln and His Generals*. New York: Alfred A. Knopf, 1952.

_____. *Lincoln and the Radicals*. Madison: University of Wisconsin Press, 1969.

Winsor, Justin (ed.). *The Memorial History of Boston, 1630–1880*. 3 vols. Boston: James R. Osgood & Co., 1881.

Wood, Sally. *Family History of William Perkins Wadsworth and Martha Doty Scofield*. Geneseo, N.Y.: Private printing, 1994.

INDEX